7—

Frommer's 96

FRUGAL TRAVELER'S GUIDES

India

FROM $45 A DAY

by Jan Aaron

Macmillan • USA

About the Author

Jan Aaron has seen this Frommer guide to India through all its incarnations over the years; she has written about India for major magazines and newspapers. Her latest book is *101 Great Choices: Washington, D.C.; 101 Great Choices: New York* is in the works. She has traveled around the world on writing assignments.

MACMILLAN TRAVEL

A Simon & Schuster Macmillan Company
1633 Broadway
New York, NY 10019

Find us online at **http://www.mgr.com/travel**
or on America Online at Keyword: **Frommer's.**

ISBN 0-02861123-3
ISSN 1051-6816

Editor: Douglas Stallings
Production Editor: Phil Kitchel
Design by Michele Laseau
Digital Cartography by Devorah Wilkenfeld and John Decamillis

Special Sales

Bulk purchases (10+ copies) of Frommer's travel guides are available to corporations at special discounts. The Special Sales Department can produce custom editions to be used as premiums and/or for sales promotion to suit individual needs. Existing editions can be produced with custom cover imprints such as corporate logos. For more information write to: Special Sales, Simon & Schuster, 1633 Broadway, New York, NY 10019.

Manufactured in the United States of America

Contents

9 Calcutta: The Eastern Gateway 234

10 The Andaman Adventure 254

11 The Route to the South 260

12 Madras: Where the South Begins 285

13 Southern India: Pondicherry & Tamil Nadu 311

List of Maps

ACKNOWLEDGMENTS

I gratefully acknowledge the patient planning assistance and much-needed research backup provided by the staff of the Government of India Tourist Office in New York City. Other thank yous for guidance and assistance go to Air India, India's Department of Tourism, the India Tourist Offices, and the state departments of tourism in India, and those helpful individuals who work in and manage them; to airline, bus, and railway personnel for giving me updated information and getting me everywhere; to guides who never tired and provided updates to round out my data; and to the many other individuals at hotels, restaurants, museums, monuments, and shops who allowed me to look around and who supplied more answers to questions. Thanks also to the readers who wrote me helpful letters. Finally, thanks also to Lettergraph, Inc., of New York City for supplying much of the historical chronology and the Hindi phrases and to *Hello Madras* for the Tamil phrases.

AN INVITATION TO THE READER

In researching this book, I discovered many wonderful places—hotels, restaurants, shops, and more. We're sure you'll find others. Please tell me about them, so I can share the information with your fellow travelers in upcoming editions. If you were disappointed with a recommendation, I'd love to know that, too. Please write to:

Jan Aaron
Frommer's India from $45 a Day, 9th Edition
Macmillan Travel
1633 Broadway
New York, NY 10019

AN ADDITIONAL NOTE

Please be advised that travel information is subject to change at any time—and this is especially true of prices. We therefore suggest that you write or call ahead for confirmation when making your travel plans. The authors, editors, and publisher cannot be held responsible for the experiences of readers while traveling. Your safety is important to us, however, so we encourage you to stay alert and be aware of your surroundings. Keep a close eye on cameras, purses, and wallets, all favorite targets of thieves and pickpockets.

RESTRICTIONS

Some parts of India are politically sensitive and/or designated as protected areas and certain restrictions apply to traveling to them. Currently, a number of these areas are in eastern India—Manipur, Mizoram, Sikkim, and West Sikkim—and also some areas of Himachal Pradesh, Jammu and Kashmir, as well as Arunchal Pradesh and Nagaland. Special permits are also needed for the Andaman and Nicobar Islands in the distant Bay of Bengal and Lakshadweep off the coast of Kerala in the southwest.

Furthermore, we especially caution against travel to Kashmir due to continuing violence and unrest, especially in the Kashmir Valley and around Srinagar; Ladakh, in an isolated region in the Himalayas, is generally considered safe.

1 Getting to Know India

My friends seemed divided in their reactions when I first informed them that I was going to India. A substantial minority managed to look vaguely mystical, placed their hands together in a prayerful salute, and rolled their eyes reverentially as if they were already in the presence of holiness.

Then there were the others who sneered—"Ugh, you'll hate it; full of snakes and beggars, and so *poor,* and besides that, it's filthy."

These words were written a number of years ago for the first edition of this guide. Considering all the progress India has made since then, they seem pitifully out of date. Yet they are almost exactly the same words people say to me now when I set off for India to update new editions. Well, they don't mention the snakes much anymore.

And each time I'm back in New York, with India fully researched and documented, my suitcase full of knickknacks and my head a montage of overlapping images, it's easy to understand the differing reviews. India undeniably has beggars (so does New York, for that matter)—they are there, but so are many other things.

As for snakes, I've never seen one, except for the sluggish specimens displayed in the baskets of professional snake charmers or the occasional exotic breed to be found in a zoo. The average Indian's familiarity with snakes is about equal to an American suburbanite's encounters with foxes.

Holiness, though, is more pervasive: India is full of reverence. There are scores of religions (with Hinduism overwhelmingly predominate), and apart from sporadically bitter factionalism, they have made much the same accommodations toward each other as those in other countries. But somehow, in India, religion is more than that: It has endured as a reverence for life itself—a tolerance for and protection of every living thing. There are people who won't swat a fly, and millions more who won't touch meat, much less allow a cow to be harmed. If a man wants to abandon the day-to-day cares of this mundane life and return to nature by becoming an itinerant ascetic in search of higher truths, there are few who would not pay respect to the humble sadhu's robes he dons. If a woman decides to dedicate her life to similar pursuits, the path is hers to follow.

For above all else—despite independence as a modern nation since 1947, and a century and half before that of colonial rule; despite foreign aid, five-year plans, increasing industrialization, a nuclear blast, and space experimentation—India is still very close to nature.

In the countryside—and more than half of the nearly 900 million population lives in rural areas—families share their work, food, and sometimes the roof above their heads with their animals. And sometimes, when they move to the city, little is changed. True, there is no longer the plowing to be done, and there are cars to dodge, modern buildings and broad avenues to contend with; but amazingly, the beloved animals are still there—meandering without fear in this society that pleasantly accommodates all animal life.

Caught in a metropolitan traffic jam, cows and goats wander, oblivious to taxis, cars, buses, bikes, rickshas, and horse-drawn tongas. Occasionally, elephants, monkeys, donkeys, camels, and performing bears and parakeets are there too.

There is no such thing as a dull Indian street. A typical panorama seems an endless extravaganza of faces and physical types in saris, flowing dhotis (skirt-type male garments), impeccably tailored business suits, jeans, shorts, even loincloths. The range of activities, even on the smallest street, can include cycle rickshas waiting for customers, balloon sellers, squatting peanut vendors roasting their wares, fortune tellers, a man being shaved, another carving chair legs, fruit stalls, boys squirting each other at the water pump, a string of burros laden with newly baked bricks, women spreading their colored wash to dry on the sidewalk, a group of customers gathered at the tailor's hookah (water pipe), a bullock cart slantwise across the road blocking a half dozen trucks, bike riders, buses, and the pan wallahs sellers wrapping spices into betel leaves for the favorite after-meal snack. All of the above were hastily noted as my taxi wove slowly through a village street. Invariably, Indian streets offer more than a passerby can possibly absorb at one time.

One's memories of India become a shifting kaleidoscope of fragmentary images—from the happy faces of the children at the Tibetan self-help (refugee) center in Darjeeling to the morose expressions of the water buffalo hauling timber at the Auroville settlement; from the flight over the snowcapped Himalayas and descent into the Shangri-La of Ladakh, to the tropical lagoons of Cochin, lined with coconut palms, to the Chinese fishing nets gracefully rising and dipping into the tranquil waters.

For India is not one but many countries, a fusion of many races, traditions, and influences. To sit in a garden in Darjeeling sipping tea and nibbling cheese toast is to return to the leisurely days of the British Raj; to view the outlines of Mughal palaces against the skyline at dusk or to attend the centuries-old rites of cleansing and worship on the banks of the Ganges at Varanasi is to plunge back into an even older era.

And there's the India of today: the gigantic steel and electrical plants at Jamshedpur and Bhakra Nangal, the skyscrapers lining Bombay's waterfront, the discotheques of New Delhi, the sleek modern architecture of Chandigarh.

And there is the India of tomorrow—seen in glimpses today in the modern health services, electricity, improved water supplies, schools, and transportation systems that are constantly being expanded to improve villagers' lives.

The '80s saw the launch of India's space program, and the future holds more experimentation along these lines. Indeed, scientific and technical workers in India are said to number 2.3 million. And the India of the '90s is a story of powerful economic reforms that are helping the country make gains like never before. One thing has never changed, though: Through the years, India has remained one of the safest and most welcoming places for travelers. It remains thus with the exception of Kashmir.

Yet despite all these impressive gains, India still has much to do and is still a developing nation.

For those fortunate enough to go to India today, a ringside seat awaits at a simultaneous extravaganza of the past, present, and future.

1 India: Past & Present

Who the early peoples of India were is not known for certain. Possibly the original Dravidians became partially submerged by waves of Aryans who, as far back as 2000 B.C., poured into the country from the northwest.

The Aryans were pastoral. Their lives depended on the elements, so they worshipped the sun, moon, and rivers. Their mystics and philosophers composed songs in praise of nature, two of which, the lyrical poems the *Ramayana* and *Mahabharata,* influence the people to this day. These epics were not just the work of one poet but were the creations of generations who embellished the basic legends over thousands of years. The Aryans also laid the cornerstone of Hinduism, the principal religion of present-day India.

The early peoples of India blended with the Aryans and organized themselves into states. Led by the Aryans, they were not content with just farming: They contributed two basic mathematical concepts to the world, the decimal system and the zero, and the stories with which they amused their youngsters are those that entertain children now—*Aesop's Fables.*

As civilization spread, religious unrest grew and found expression in the *Upanishads* (Forest Books), written between approximately 1000 and 500 B.C. by philosophers who retired to the hills to contemplate. As doubt increased, many religious leaders arose, each claiming to have the answer. One of these was to change the lives of millions. He was Gautama, the future Buddha, who led a revolt against the established order in the 6th century B.C. Buddha urged people to lead ethical lives, thereby eliminating sorrow. He spoke in plain language and without regard for caste or creed. About the same time, Mahavira, the Jain prophet, laid the foundation for the creed of nonviolence—still an influence on current Indian thinking.

The West made contact with India, and Alexander the Great invaded the country in 326 B.C. This Greek invasion enriched Indian art and mythology, and the West in turn extended its knowledge of science and mathematics.

Dateline

- **326 B.C.** Alexander the Great invades India.
- **323** Alexander dies in Babylon.
- **322** Accessions of Chandragupta Maurya.
- **273–232** Emperor Ashoka rules most of India.
- **185** The last Maurya king is killed.
- **A.D. 320** Chandragupta I rules; beginning of Gupta era.
- **330** Samudragupta's reign begins.
- **380** Chandragupta II's reign begins.
- **405–11** Travels of Fa-hien in the Gupta empire.
- **415** Kumaragupta I's reign begins.
- **455** Skandagupta's reign begins.
- **476** Aryabhata the astronomer born.
- **480–90** Breakup of the Gupta empire.
- **505** Varahamihira the astronomer born.
- **606** Harsha-Vardhana's reign begins
- **622** Flight of Mohammed to Medina.
- **629–45** Travels of Hiuen Tsang.
- **647** Death of Harsha.
- **740** Defeat of Pallavs by Chalukyas.
- **973** Taila founds second Chalukya Dynasty of Kalyani.
- **1175–1290** Rise of Muslim power in India and establishment of the Sultanate of Delhi.

continues

India

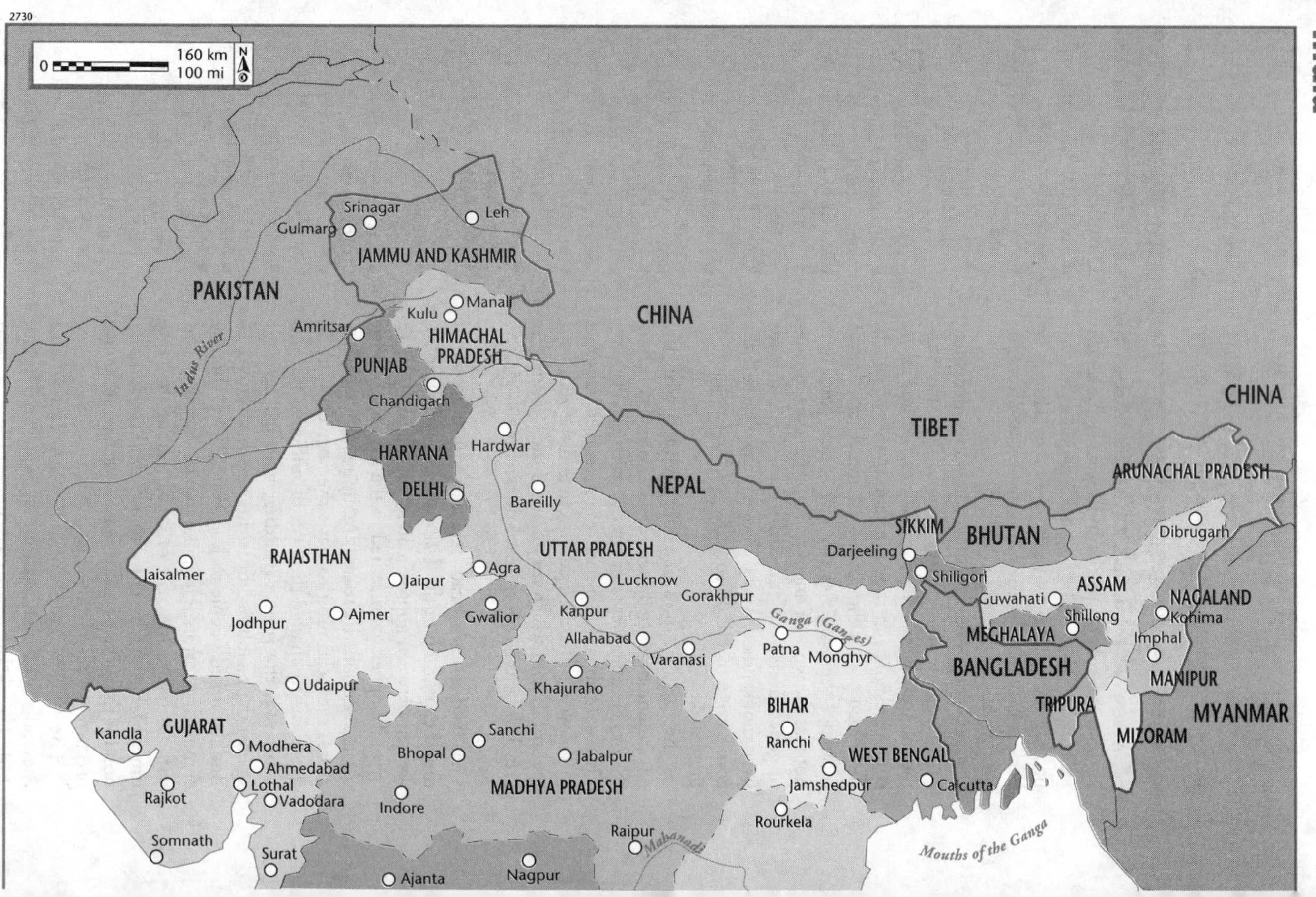

2730
0
160 km
100 mi
N
PAKISTAN
Indus River
Srinagar
Gulmarg
Leh
JAMMU AND KASHMIR
Manali
Kulu
Amritsar
HIMACHAL PRADESH
PUNJAB
Chandigarh
CHINA
HARYANA
Hardwar
DELHI
Bareilly
TIBET
CHINA
NEPAL
ARUNACHAL PRADESH
SIKKIM
BHUTAN
Darjeeling
Dibrugarh
RAJASTHAN
Jaisalmer
Jaipur
Agra
UTTAR PRADESH
Lucknow
Gorakhpur
Shiligori
Guwahati
ASSAM
NAGALAND
Kohima
Jodhpur
Ajmer
Gwalior
Kanpur
Allahabad
Varanasi
Ganga (Ganges)
Patna
Monghyr
Shillong
MEGHALAYA
Imphal
BANGLADESH
MANIPUR
Udaipur
Khajuraho
BIHAR
TRIPURA
MYANMAR
Kandla
GUJARAT
Sanchi
Ranchi
MIZORAM
Modhera
Bhopal
Jabalpur
WEST BENGAL
Ahmedabad
Lothal
Rajkot
Vadodara
Indore
MADHYA PRADESH
Jamshedpur
Calcutta
Rourkela
Somnath
Raipur
Mahanadi
Mouths of the Ganga
Surat
Ajanta
Nagpur

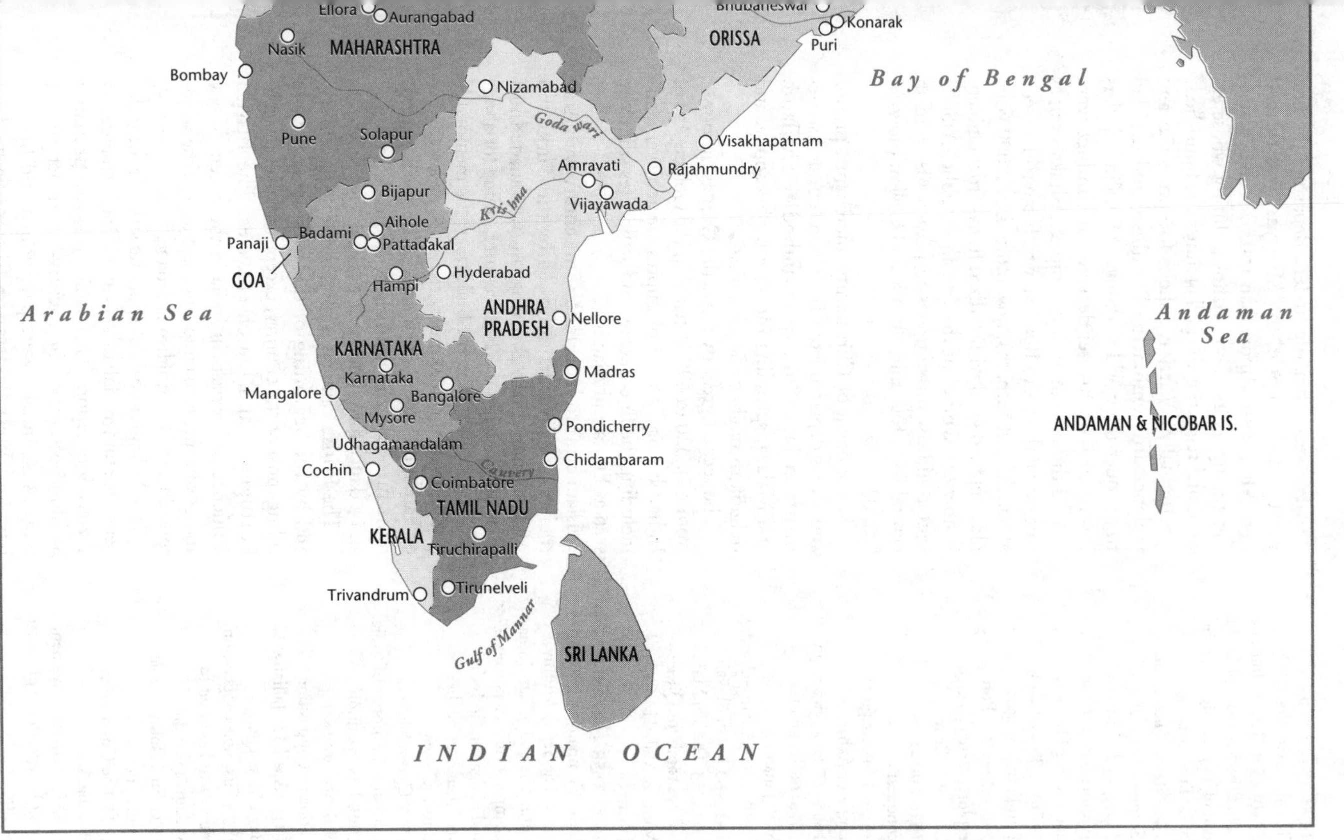

Ellora
Aurangabad
Nasik
MAHARASHTRA
Bombay
Nizamabad
ORISSA
Konarak
Puri
Bay of Bengal
Goda wari
Pune
Solapur
Visakhapatnam
Amravati
Rajahmundry
Bijapur
Kris hna
Vijayawada
Aihole
Badami
Panaji
Pattadakal
GOA
Hampi
Hyderabad
Arabian Sea
ANDHRA PRADESH
Nellore
Andaman Sea
KARNATAKA
Madras
Karnataka
Mangalore
Bangalore
Mysore
Pondicherry
ANDAMAN & NICOBAR IS.
Udhagamandalam
Cochin
Chidambaram
Cauvery
Coimbatore
TAMIL NADU
KERALA
Tiruchirapalli
Trivandrum
Tirunelveli
Gulf of Mannar
SRI LANKA
INDIAN OCEAN

- **1290–1340** Khilji and Tughlak dynasties rule.
- **1340–1526** The decline and fall of the Sultanate of Delhi; end of Tughlak dynasty; end of Lodhi dynasty.
- **1336–1646** The Hindu Empire of Vijayanagar.
- **1526–56** The Mogul Empire: Babur, Humayun, and the Sur Dynasty.
- **1600–1708** The Early European Voyagers.
- **1498 (May 20)** Portuguese explorer Vasco da Gama lands at Calicut.
- **1510** Portuguese conquest of Goa.
- **1555–1605** Reign of Emperor Akbar.
- **1605–27** Jehangir's reign.
- **1628–66** Reign of Shah Jahan.
- **1659–1707** Aurangzeb rules.
- **1627–80** Era of Shivaji.
- **1632–53** The Taj Mahal built as tomb for Queen Mumtaz Mahal by Shah Jahan.
- **1600–1858** The East India Company.
- **1857** The Sepoy Mutiny.
- **1858** The end of East India Company rule; its powers and obligations in India are taken over by the British Crown.
- **1877** Queen Victoria proclaimed Empress of India.
- **1905** First partition of Bengal arouses nationalist opposition.
- **1919 (April 13)** Jallianwala Bagh Massacre.
- **1920** First non-cooperation movement launched by Mahatma Gandhi.
- **1931** First Round Table Conference.
- **1935** The Government of India Act.
- **1942** Quit India Movement.
- **1947** Independence of India; partition of the country into India and Pakistan.

continues

A few years after Alexander's departure the first great Indian empire, the Mauryas, was formed in 323 B.C., lasting more than 150 years and producing among its monarchs Ashoka, during whose exceptional reign the arts and architecture flourished.

Originally a warrior, Ashoka foreswore war and violence after embracing Buddhism and decided to conquer the world with love. Monolithic pillars inscribed with his gentle rules of conduct were erected throughout his huge empire. Ashoka's stupas (memorial shrines to Buddha, which can still be seen at Sanchi and Sarnath), now more than 2,000 years old, were crowned with stylized lions—that emblem is now the symbol of the Indian republic. Ashoka sent Buddhist missionaries to preach his word in central Asia, Kashmir, Burma, and Ceylon (now Sri Lanka).

At the dawn of Christianity, merchants, priests, and artists departed from India and founded settlements in Java, Sumatra, Cambodia, Thailand, and Malaya, spreading India's art, philosophy, and religion throughout Southeast Asia.

The second great dynasty, the Guptas, in power from A.D. 320 to 495, ushered in the Golden Age of Indian history, a time of impressive achievements, including the fine frescoes and sculptures still to be seen at Ellora and Ajanta.

Islam came to India in the 8th century with Arab traders and invaders, followed by the Turks and Afghans, and finally the Mughals, who made India their homeland in the 16th century, ruling for about 250 years. They were the builders of the memorable Taj Mahal, the Red Fort, the now deserted city of Fatehpur Sikri, and more. During this period, miniature painting flourished, as did court music and a dance form known as Kathak.

The British came as traders in the 18th century, and by the beginning of the 19th century were ruling most of the country, except for small French, Portuguese, and Dutch enclaves. The British influence still persists in India in the system of law and government, in education, and also in the widespread use of the English language.

In 1947, after years of sporadic struggle for independence under Mahatma Gandhi, India emerged as a sovereign nation. That same year, two primarily Muslim portions of the country—East Bengal and Northwest India—were partitioned and became East and West Pakistan. Kashmir, claimed by both, remains part of India. East Pakistan is now Bangladesh, following the war in 1971.

India became a republic in 1950 under Prime Minister Jawaharlal Nehru, who, with the All-India Congress, governed until his death in 1964. The prime minister from 1964 to 1966 was Lal Bahadur Shastri.

From 1966 to 1977 Indira Gandhi (no relation to Mahatma Gandhi, but Nehru's daughter) was prime minister. She was voted out of office in favor of the Janata party, and Morarji Desai became prime minister, followed briefly by Charan Singh. Gandhi and the Congress party returned in 1979, and she was prime minister until her assassination on October 31, 1984. Her son Rajiv Gandhi became India's next prime minister.

In December 1989, Rajiv Gandhi and the Congress Party were voted out. The next prime minister was Vishwanath Pratap Singh, leader of the Janata Dal Party and the National Front, a coalition of centrist and leftist groups and regional parties. He served until November 1990. Then, until June 1991, Prime Minister Chandra Shekhar, head of the Janata Dal Socialists, led a caretaker government. In May 1991, while campaigning for reelection, Gandhi was assassinated by Sri Lankan terrorists. Following his death, the Congress Party was voted back in.

In 1996 they were again defeated; India's newest prime minister is Atal Bihari Vajpayee of the Baharatiya Janata Party, the Hindu Nationalist Party.

- **1948 (January 30)** Assassination of Mahatma Gandhi.
- **1950 (January 26)** Inauguration of the Republic of India; Rajendra Prasad is the first president of India.
- **1947** All-India Congress rules the country under Prime Minister Jawaharlal Nehru.
- **1964** Lal Bahadur Shastri becomes prime minister and continues Congress Party rule until 1966.
- **1966** Indira Gandhi becomes prime minister; Congress Party remains in power until 1977.
- **1977** Janata Party in power under Prime Minister Morarji Desai until 1979.
- **1979** Janata Party rule continues under Prime Minister Charan Singh.
- **1979** Congress Party regains power under Prime Minister Indira Gandhi.
- **1984 (October 31)** Assassination of Indira Gandhi.
- **1984** Congress Party government under Prime Minister Rajiv Gandhi, who rules until 1989.
- **1989 (December)** Janata Dal Party and the National Front form government under Prime Minister Vishwanath Pratap Singh; they rule until November 1990.
- **1990 (December)** Caretaker government formed under Prime Minister Chandra Shekhar, head of Janata Dal Socialists.
- **1991 (May 21)** Rajiv Gandhi is assassinated.
- **June 1991** Congress rules under P. V. Narasimha Rao.
- **1996** Atal Bihari Vajpayee becomes prime minister.

2 Geography

Few places evoke a more tropical image than does India. Yet India's most significant geographic feature is the massive Himalaya mountains to the north, as well as some of the country's most beautiful resorts in Kulu and Kashmir. The great Himalayan peaks rise to average heights of 17,000 feet, with 40 higher than 24,000 feet. The mountains that form the border between Burma and Bangladesh are slightly lower, but snow falls and the wind blows.

As to vital statistics: India is almost half the size of the United States, or about the same size as Europe, less the former Soviet Union. The seventh-largest country in the world, India is commonly referred to as a subcontinent because of its size and geographic separation from Asia. India stretches 1,930 miles from the northern Himalayas to the southern lagoons of Kerala, and 1,760 miles from the Arabian seacoast in the west to the Bay of Bengal in the east, with half of the country lying on either side of the Tropic of Cancer.

South of the Himalayas, India's heavily populated, flat, fertile Indo-Gangetic plain (150 to 200 miles across) is formed of the rich alluvium of the rivers Indus, Ganges, and Brahmaputra. In this region is the capital, Delhi with its layers of civilizations; to the northwest, the prosperous Punjab and the monument that virtually symbolizes India to many Westerners, the Taj Mahal, and the lesser-known Khajuraho; and to the east, fascinating Calcutta.

Then, south of the plains is the triangular peninsula, with its heartland, the Deccan plateau. In this area the sights are richly varied from the glamorous city of Bombay to the ancient Buddhist shrine at Sanchi and the soaring temples of the south. Finally, at India's southwesternmost state, Kerala, are some of the country's most splendid tropics.

With 900 million people, India is the second most populous country in the world. Such talk of overpopulation gives the prospective tourist the impression that overcrowding is everywhere in India. Nothing could be further from the truth. As in the West, much of the population is concentrated in big cities; in the vast stretches of lonely countryside and the mountainous regions, it's often hard to believe that India is so populous.

3 Religion

Always remember to remove your shoes at temples, mosques, and other holy shrines. You also remove your belt (if it's leather) at some Hindu temples. Cover your head when visiting any Sikh temple. Dress decorously at holy places—no shorts, please. (Would you wear shorts to church?)

HINDUISM

About 83% of India's total population is Hindu. Although Hinduism teaches belief in one supreme being, the religion's vast mythology includes numerous gods, goddesses, and avatars (incarnations). To understand, even superficially, you should know that when the Aryans arrived in India, the Dravidians had already established some religious beliefs and gods. The Aryans were smart enough to realize that if they were to make any headway, they had to adopt some of these gods—and so the synthesis began and continued through the ages. When gods were not assimilated or combined, they were welcomed as relatives of major gods' families or made into incarnations. Indian gods, unlike their fickle Greek "brothers," tend to be monogamous, and some of the most impressive powers were assigned to their female consorts, centuries before women's lib. There are, without exaggeration, millions of gods dealing with all forms of life and nature. Listed here are only the major deities to be encountered on tours to temples.

Brahma (The Creator): Once the mightiest of the Hindu gods because he set the world in motion. He lost importance with the emergence of Shiva and Vishnu. Brahma has four heads, each one looking over one quarter of the universe. From his quartet of heads sprang the Vedas (the four ancient Hindu scriptures). He carries these along with a scepter and other symbols. He wears white robes, rides a goose, and is considered the god of wisdom.

Saraswati: Brahma's consort. She rides a white swan and is the goddess of learning.

Shiva (The Destroyer): One of the two greatest gods of Hinduism, he represents power in its many aspects—war, famine, and death, for example, are under his control. He frequently wears a tiger skin and carries an ax, a trident, and a bowl made of a skull, itself sometimes adorned with snakes. He is worshipped as a lingam (a phallic symbol) and is also seen, in South Indian bronzes, as Nataraj, the God of Dance.

Parvati (also Mahadevi): Shiva's wife, she is often seen with him in statues and paintings looking like the model of the loving consort. In her incarnations she is **Durga,** 10-armed goddess of battle; or **Kali,** who wears snakes and desires blood; or **Uma,** the Beautiful, who sometimes acts as a moderator between Brahma and the other gods. Her transport is the tiger.

Nandi (The Bull): Shiva's sacred mount and his musician. Shiva wears Nandi's insignia, a crescent moon, on his brow.

Ganesh (Ganesha): The chubby, elephant-headed son of Shiva and Parvati, a very popular god and worshipped before new ventures to ensure success. He rides on a mouse.

Vishnu (The Preserver): The other great god, Vishnu usually holds four symbols: discus, conch, mace, and lotus. He appears in incarnation whenever mankind needs kind assistance. He is believed to have had nine avatars, and the tenth is yet to come. Two of his most popular incarnations are **Krishna** and **Rama,** the latter representing the ideal husband, wise ruler, and of greatest importance, a valiant crusader against evil. He inspired the *Ramayana* by killing the demon Ravana, a deed that is celebrated each year with the Dussehra festivities of the fall.

Krishna: The other important incarnation of Vishnu; plays the flute, is usually blue in color, and is the god of love. He is prominent in the *Bhagavad Gita.* Tales of his childhood pranks, his adolescent adoration by the *gopis* (milkmaids), and his heroic deeds have inspired a great many works of art.

Yet another incarnation of Vishnu is **Buddha**—a choice example of how Hinduism assimilates beliefs of other religions. In Hinduism, Buddha represents compassion toward animals.

Lakshmi: The wife of Vishnu, often shown seated on a lotus. She represents wealth and prosperity. Her attendants are white elephants. She is also worshipped as Sita, the incarnation of the perfect wife.

Garuda: Vishnu's mount, Garuda is a huge bird with the head and wings of an eagle and the body and limbs of a man. He carries his god on his gleaming golden back.

ISLAM

About 11% of India's population are Muslims. The holy Koran is their sacred book, and their greatest prophet is Mohammed.

CHRISTIANITY

About 2.43% of the population are Christians. St. Thomas (the Doubter) was said to have been martyred at Madras in A.D. 78. St. Francis Xavier was an early missionary in Goa in the 16th century; the Franciscans preceded him.

SIKHISM

About 1.96% are Sikhs. Founded in the 15th century as a branch of Hinduism and as a bridge between that religion and Islam, the Sikh religion gathered its greatest strength in the 17th century. Sikhs are not permitted to cut their hair, which is usually neatly tucked up into a turban.

BUDDHISM

About 0.71% are Buddhists. Born in Nepal, probably around 567B.C., Buddha preached his first sermon at Sarnath in India. Basic to his doctrine is that worldly desire is at the root of all that is bad. The ultimate goal is Nirvana, attained by following a four-fold path to awaken and free the heart and mind.

JAINISM

About 0.48% of the population practices Jainism. Nonviolence in deed and thought, plus complete tolerance for other religions, are basic concepts.

ZOROASTRIANISM

About 0.3% of the population are Zoroastrians. In the 7th century the Parsis fled Persia because of religious persecution and since earliest days have remained in and about Bombay. Their holy book is the *Zend Avesta;* they follow the Path of Asha—good thoughts, words, and deeds. Fire worship is part of the religion.

SADHUS

It is estimated that about six million orange-robed sadhus (holy men) live in India. They lead solitary lives as hermits or beggars near shrines and will take anyone into their fold. The sincere ones are searching for very deep truths indeed.

4 The Caste System

This serious subject is so complex that I offer only an elementary explanation here. The intricacies of the caste system, going back two millennia or more, involve literally thousands of communities divided by taboos about foods, occupations, intermarriage, and all manner of social interaction. Originally, there were four main castes: priests (Brahmans), warriors and administrators (Kshatriyas), businessmen, farmers, traders, and shopkeepers (Vaishyas), and craftsmen and hired help (Sudras)—each allegedly born from a part of Brahma. The four major castes were further divided into countless subcastes. Under all were the Untouchables (Gandhi's" Children of God") who did the most disagreeable tasks.

In the early villages this was a practical arrangement—ensuring a steady labor supply in various occupations to satisfy all needs. It did not encourage change or upward mobility by moving away. Punishment for leaving home was to become an outcast.

Obviously, this kind of system—inhibiting progress, splitting rather than uniting—would not work in building a democracy. Thanks to the untir-ing efforts of Mahatma Gandhi and others, discrimination is forbidden by law. This is especially encouraging to the lower castes. But the passing of a law doesn'tmean the immediate dissolution of worn-out practices and deep-ly ingrained beliefs. (We can all cite examples of this in Western societies.) Traces of the caste system still remain, but they are changing—in cities, all kindsof people are working together in new businesses and industries; in villages, people are moving away from home motivated by new opportunities and are being absorbed into the mainstream; there are intercaste marriages, and even the army plays a part by encouraging men to mingle and moving themabout.

Bigger changes have occurred in India in the past half century than in all past millennia. To Westerners accustomed to rapid and extreme change, these may not seem like much, but to Indians they are huge and irreversible. Each future generation of Indians will live less and less like the one before: Rigidity is being replaced by a more accepting way of life.

5 Language

There are 15 officially recognized languages in India, and you might hear about 700 minor language and dialects if you traveled widely enough around the country. Luckily, English, owing to the influence of the English, is also still spoken widely.

Of the major 15 Indian languages, the most important and widely spoken is **Hindi,** which falls into the Indic group of languages. This is the official language of the government (though not of the judiciary, where English is still recognized). Nevertheless, only about 20% of Indians, mostly in the north-central portions of India (Bihar, Madhya Pradesh, Rajasthan, and Uttar Pradesh), speak this language natively. In the southern states, the Dravidian group of languages predominate, of which **Tamil** is most widely spoken.

The other 13 languages you may encounter are **Assamese** (the state language of Assam); **Bengali** (the state language of West Bengal); **Gujarati** (the state language of Gujarat; **Kannada** (the state language of Karnataka; **Kashmiri** (spoken natively by more than half the population of Jammu and Kashmir); **Malayalam** (spoken in Kerala); **Marathi** (the state language of Maharashtra); **Oriya** (the state language of Orissa and widely spoken there); **Punjabi** (the state language of Punjab, but based on the same script as Hindi); **Sanskrit** (the language of classical India); **Sindhi** (though spoken mostly in Pakistan); **Telugu** (the state language of Andhra Pradesh); and **Urdu** (the state language of Jammu and Kashmir, influenced by Persian and traditionally embraced Indian Muslims).

6 Indian Customs

First, a couple of hand moves. Shaking hands is not a common habit in India. For the Indian greeting, "namaste," hands are pressed together as in prayer and lifted to the chin level (higher if the person is of great importance, but never mind the tiny formalities). There is some handshaking mainly among men when greeting foreigners. By all means, try to master the art of eating with your fingers—but right hand only, please—at the table.

India is a modest country, so public displays of affection are not considered good manners. (Smooching is even taboo on the silver screen.) Modesty is always in style: Indian women cover their legs and arms. Foreigners who wish to avoid unwanted stares and unwelcome attention do the same. Buy a salwar kamiz (tunics and trousers)—they're smart, comfortable, and modest. Indians are very hospitable. They are also very curious about people they meet and ask in great detail about your life. It's not an inquisition, just their way of getting to know you.

Shoes are removed at religious sites (you can wear your socks, but clean, cool marble floors are a feet treat). Rangoli are good luck designs on thresholds to homes and occasionally public buildings. Step over them or around them, not on them. If invited to a traditional Hindu home, do not go into the kitchen. Finally, don't worry too much about a gaffe or two. Indians are supremely tolerant. They'll laugh it off and so can you.

7 Eating in India

There are restaurants all over India where you can get good food at budget prices. Some of these restaurants specialize in Western and Continental fare, others in Chinese cuisine. In some top hotels, you'll find expensive French, Italian, Japanese, and Thai restaurants in appropriately evocative settings. Once in a while you'll find Middle Eastern and Mexican cuisine.

But the reason to go to India is to sample the tremendously varied Indian fare. These days a number of top hoteliers and restaurateurs have gone regional, digging deep into India's rich culinary history to find authentic dishes to serve in stylish surroundings. It's worth a splurge or two ($20 to $60 for two) to try some of the rarely prepared recipes. They might be cuisines of the old newabs cooked in casseroles and crowned by crusts, or unusual fish or vegetarian preparations in delicious sauces fragrant with subtle herbs and spices.

Among the simplest of all Indian eateries is the dhaba, meaning roadside village cafe, somewhat akin to the U.S. truck stop cafe. And while the old legend is not necessarily true that in America truckers know the best wayside places to eat, in India they insist it is positively so—"For authentic North Indian food, go to a dhaba," visitors are often told. But there are dhabas and then there are dhabas; the authentic, whether as truck stops or in city lanes, are hardly hygienic. But now in some major cities dhaba-visiting is much easier; they've brought the dhabas to people like you and me in the guise of restaurants that strive to create authentic truck stop atmosphere and typical foods safely prepared, and I've mentioned them in the chapters that follow.

In most restaurants, you will be served by gracious waiters (bearers) at tables with plates and gleaming flatware. In traditional restaurants, you will get the same efficient service, but instead of plates there will be a banana leaf or a thali (a brass, stainless-steel, or bell-metal platter) to hold all your foods. Porcelain plates, which contain bone ash, are not acceptable to orthodox Hindus. Banana leaves are further washed with water at the table—a step you may wish to forgo if you are concerned about the water—before foods are placed on it.

On thalis, little metal bowls called katoris hold portions of each of your foods—vegetable mixtures, or meat, fish, or chicken curry, dal (lentils), raita (yogurt with chopped vegetables), achar (pickles), and papads (cracker bread) will be placed around the outer rim, while the center is crowned with a snowy mound of rice or wheat puris or both. Traditionally, there were rules about the placement of dishes, but these have been relaxed over the years. Water, however, is placed to the left, not the right, and is the traditional drink with an Indian meal. Order it bottled or boiled, if in doubt. Beer and wine are not served with these Indian meals, but in sophisticated restaurants you can order them.

After washing your hands at the tap, you eat the food with the fingers of your right hand only, which is quite an art in itself. The best technique is to take a little of the dry food such as rice or bread and use it to scoop up the less solid foods like curry or dal. You might also pour some dal on your rice to make a workable combination. In the north of India, only the tips of the fingers are used; in the south, more of the hand is employed, including the palm. In the western region, wheat is eaten before the rice is served, although it's hardly necessary for you to worry about regional techniques. Your main concern will be to eat as neatly as possible without getting your meal all over yourself.

INDIAN CUISINE

If curry is the limit of your knowledge about Indian food, then you have a lot to learn about one of the most exotic and varied cuisines in the world. Curry dishes spiced just enough to be interesting can consist of meat, fish, eggs, or vegetables. They are served with rice or one of India's tasty breads and will taste very different from the curry you've had in the Western world. The spices that go into them will be freshly ground, and no two cooks will make exactly the same mixture of seasonings.

There's terrific variety, too, in the way the same dishes are spelled on restaurant menus. But even the most far-out spellings you'll encounter will match up to the dishes described below and elsewhere in this book.

SOUP *Mulligatawny,* a soup with a curry base, is world famous.

BREADS *Chapatis, parathas,* and *puris* are Indian breads made of whole-wheat flour, shaped into flat cakes, and grilled, roasted, or sautéed. Another popular bread is *naan,* made from white flour and long in shape. *Pappadums* are crispy, crackerlike concoctions, seasoned with peppers and anise seed and very tasty with any food. *Dosas,* thin pancakes made with a rice base and popular in the south, are often stuffed with vegetables, turnover style. *Idlis* are steamed rice and lentil cakes and are served with chutney and ground spices—a popular breakfast dish in South India.

MAIN COURSES *Vindaloo* is a marinated meat dish popular in Goa.

Biryani, a dish for special occasions, is made of chicken or lamb with fragrant whole spices and rice, and is garnished with raisins, cashews, almonds, and a sprinkling of rose water.

Tandoori defines a method of cooking, something like our barbecue except in a clay oven. Chicken tandoori is very popular, and sometimes lamb and fish are cooked this way.

Dum Pukht, popular with the old Nawabs, is succulent steamed cooking and is something like the Western casserole.

Seekh kebabs are skewered pieces of meat broiled over an open fire. Kebabs are minced pieces of meat, patty shaped, and are filled with chopped onion, green pepper, and fresh ginger.

Patrani machli is fish stuffed with chutney and baked in banana leaves—popular in Bombay.

ACCOMPANIMENTS *Dal, chutney,* and *raita* are side dishes. Dal will look like soup or gravy to you. It is made of lentils or dried peas and other ingredients and is served with the main course as a bland partner to other more highly seasoned foods. Chutneys are made with fruits or vegetables in a sweet-and-sour sauce. Mint and mango chutneys are especially good. Green coriander (Chinese parsley, perhaps better known as cilantro) makes another delicate chutney.

Pickles are also popular and can be made out of fruits or vegetables.

Raita is a yogurt preparation with vegetables or fruit. *Dahi* is yogurt and is used to tone down more spicy foods; it is also used in salads and as a marinade for vegetables.

VEGETABLES Cooked vegetables include *brinjals* (eggplant), *bhindi* (okra), and *mattar* (peas). Vegetarian dishes are especially good in India, prepared with unusual sauces, combined with cheese, and delicately spiced. Rice is also excellent in India and is served many ways, with vegetables, nuts, fruits, and spices.

DESSERTS & SWEETS *Firni* is pudding made with rice; *barfi* is a sweet similar to fudge; *jalebi* are pretzel-shaped pastries in sweet syrup; *sandesh* is a dessert made with milk; and *rasgullas* is a light dessert made with yogurt.

Carrots are disguised at dessert time and come to the table as *halwa.* India's ice cream is rich and creamy and often filled with chunks of fresh fruit. Any dessert may appear looking very dressy with a coat of thin, edible silver or gold, which is not only pretty but practical, as it is supposed to aid digestion.

FRUITS To top off any feast, there are a variety of fruits, some familiar (bananas, apples, incredibly tasty mangoes) and some exotic, such as *chikoos* (a cross between the fig and the russet apple) or the custard apple, which looks like an artichoke but is not.

DRINKS Indian-grown tea is excellent; coffee, also locally grown, is very good. Be sure to specify if you want your coffee black—the Indian way is to mix it with steaming milk before serving it. Local beer is very good and a fine partner to Indian foods. There is a large selection of fruit drinks, of which apple is excellent (but relatively expensive), so too fresh lime and soda. Drink bottled or boiled water to stay on the safe side. You can get bottled water in most restaurants and in many markets.

PAN After a big meal, try *pan,* an Indian digestive sold by vendors near restaurants. This is made of betel nuts and sweet and aromatic spices, all wrapped in crisp betel leaf. Ask for it not too hot. Pan leaves the mouth refreshed, as if you had just brushed your teeth.

8 Shopping in India

In a vast country with people of highly diverse backgrounds and talents, crafts are varied and plentiful. Indeed, artisans work the same way as they did centuries ago, with secrets handed down through generations. For instance, an artisan might take one whole day to weave an inch of elaborately patterned silk. Such a silk might cost as much as Rs 1,800 ($60) per yard; but it is also possible to buy six yards of a simpler fabric for Rs 180 ($6) and a cotton sari for half that or less.

Here is what to look for, in general, as you go to some of the popular places in this book:

Agra: Inspired by the Taj Mahal, local craftsmen make use of inlays of petal-thin strips of carnelian, lapis lazuli, and mother-of-pearl to create stunning boxes, coasters, plates, and even table tops.

Ahmedabad: Stunning embroidery studded with mirrors, suitable for dramatic wall hangings, pillow covers, or a dressy vest or skirt.

Amritsar: Embroidery work, shawls, and metalware; sheer kurtas (billowing embroidered shirts) from nearby Lucknow.

Bhopal: Chanderi, a sheer fabric often shot with gold and silver, and zari, a combination of silver and gold threads on black velvet, are local items.

Bhubaneshwar: A silver filigree made into lovely bracelets, pins, necklaces, and small ornamental items. Paintings in primary colors from nearby Puri can make interesting accents in any home.

Bombay: Boutiques for ready-made or tailor-made dresses. Men's clothes also can be made up quickly. Ceramic tiles are a modern specialty. Some antique stores are filled with items left behind by the British Raj and others.

Calcutta: Unusual toys in pottery and wood.

Cochin: Intricate wood carvings, cotton textiles, and coir (coconut fiber) mats, are inexpensive, durable buys.

Darjeeling: Rugs, shawls, jewelry, furs.

Delhi: Crafts from everywhere in India. Local specialties are ivories, carved so fine that you need a magnifying glass to see each perfect figure; pottery in blue and black, painted in bright designs; gold-embroidered handbags; copper made into lamps and other useful items.

Hyderabad: Bangles, more than anywhere else; Bidriware, an unusual mixture of stones and wires, inlaid in black or white alloy, comes in all shapes and sizes and types of useful items—from pins to pitchers. Amusing toys are cheap; pearls, expensive.

Kashmir: Thick, hand-loomed rugs rich with flowers; papier-mâchÉ objects coated with gold leaf and decorated with vines, flowers, and unusual figures; fine paisley shawls, caftans, and silver and turquoise jewelry. These items are sold by Kashmiri stores throughout India.

Jaipur: Headquarters for jewelry. Gems are set into enameled brooches, necklaces, and bracelets similar to those worn in the 18th century. Stones are carved into flowers and fanciful beasts. Another specialty is colorful enamelwork on brass, made into carafes, ashtrays, and other items. Pretty embroidered slippers, with turned-up toes, are another good buy, as are tie-dyed silks.

Madras: Fabrics, especially the famous cotton. Silks from the nearby temple city of Kanchipuram are very beautiful. Alligator cigar and cigarette cases and wallets are other specialties. Bronzes, old and new, and elaborate woodcarvings can also be found locally.

Mysore City: Fragrant sandalwood used for carvings and as the base of exotically scented soaps and oils.

Varanasi: Silks richly woven with silver and gold; also cutwork and embroidery on cotton, in saris or to make up into dresses.

THE ART OF BARGAINING

Bargaining goes on almost everywhere except in such government-run stores as Central Cottage Industries Emporium, and it's a way of life in bazaars like Chandni Chowk. In posh shops, merchants who claim they don't probably will bargain if you tactfully suggest that their prices are out of line.

Patience is rewarded when it comes to driving a good bargain. For example, you find the perfect woodcarving for your collection at home. When the merchant asks Rs 500 ($28.50) for the item, look at him passively and say, "For this? It's not that I don't like it. But who would pay more than Rs 150 ($8.55) for this?" Pick up the carving and look at it carefully and remark on its "flaws." "It's damaged, and the workmanship is not really good." Then quickly offer Rs 200 ($11.40) for the carving, put it down, and start to walk off. Don't worry. As soon as you've set foot in the direction of the door, you'll get another offer and finally settle on Rs 250 ($14.25 Rs 300 ($17.10).

If you think in terms of dollar equivalents, you'll be doomed when bargaining. Start equating rupees with dollars—Rs 1 to $1—and see how your perspective changes about how much you are willing to pay even for the piece of your dreams.

Always shop without your guide or driver, and shun shops they suggest since the merchants probably give commissions to those who steer buyers their way—commissions that are tacked onto bills in the form of higher prices.

Remember, too, that there are restrictions on exporting antiquities (items more than 100 years old). If you buy a fabulous antique or think you have, be sure that you get the proper permits through the merchant, or consult the **Director of Antiquities,** Archaeological Survey of India, Janpath, New Delhi 110001, or the equivalent authority in Madras, Bombay, or Calcutta, about getting it out of the country.

9 Nightlife & Entertainment in India

This is not India's strong point. There are **discotheques** in some top hotels in the major cities, and most of these hotels also have **supper clubs** with dance bands and singers. Some hotels have Indian folk and classical dance performances in the evenings. While less-than-authentic versions, they're pleasant diversions at dinner. **Pubs and cafes** are growing in popularity as meeting places.

Some sleazy **cabarets** with half-nude dancers are found in a few cities, but these are diminishing. At these performances, dancers wiggle around in something more covered up than we wear at the beach, but get a big round of applause nonetheless from male audiences. The statues on some of the celebrated temples are far more revealing.

Where more **movies** are made than anywhere else in the world, there are always movies to see. About 900 feature films are produced annually in India, mainly of the boy-meets-girl, morality- and/or mythological-themed type, although splat-and-gore action films are produced as well. Almost all movies have elaborate musical scores and singers. As a matter of fact, people go to the films to hear the dubbed-in voices of their favorite singers as much as they do to see the stars. When these favorite singers go on tour, they attract crowds larger than those who flock in the United States to see Madonna or Bruce Springsteen. No overt lovemaking is permitted on screen. Indeed, so extraordinary was India's first on-screen kiss—itself hardly more than a peck—that it merited coverage by *Life* magazine. Most often, however, the would-be passionate scene shifts to something symbolic of tenderness, while dancers dance and singers sing. English-language films also play in major cities, often after they have been censored to nonsense. The best films are always on a reserved-seat basis, so you have to call or drop by the box office early in the day to book.

The **son-et-lumière** (sound and light) performances at such attractions as Delhi's Red Fort, Madurai's palace, Ahmedabad's Sabarmati Ashram, and Calcutta's Victoria Memorial commence around sunset, offering poetical and colorful presentations of various aspects of Indian history. The top price is around a dollar. Performances are in English as well as local languages.

There are dance and music **recitals** where you can see authentic bharata natyam, for example, one of the graceful classical dances of India, or hear the sitar, sarod, or other instruments and singers. Check the newspapers' events listings for places and times of performances. These opportunities should not be overlooked.

10 Suggested Reading

The Wonder That Was India (Grove Press, 1959), by A. L. Basham, is an indispensable survey of the culture of the Indian subcontinent before the Muslims.

You'll learn about India's best-known contemporary leader in *Indira Gandhi: Letters to a Friend* (Weidenfeld and Nicholson, 1986), a collection of her correspondence with Dorothy Norman.

A Million Mutinies Now (Viking, 1991), by V. S. Naipaul, is an optimistic, sympathetic look at India as it is today from a writer who once saw little hope for the country.

R. K. Narayan's *Gods, Demons and Others* (Viking, 1964) is an enjoyable retelling of India's myths and legends by a contemporary writer.

The famous filmmaker Satyajit Ray shows his skill at story writing in the several exotic tales in *The Unicorn Expedition and Other Fantastic Tales of India* (E. P. Dutton, 1987).

Historic India (Time-Life Books, 1968), by Lucille Schulberg, is a broad survey of Indian history and culture from the third millennium B.C. to the 17th century A.D.

Two histories published by Oxford University Press are also indispensable: *The Oxford History of India* (1958), edited by Percival Spear, and Stanley Wolpert's *A New History of India* (1982).

Planning a Trip to India

2

After deciding where to go, most people have two fundamental questions: What will it cost and how do I get there? This chapter not only answers those questions but also addresses such important issues as when to go, whether or not to take a tour, what pretrip health precautions should be taken, what insurance coverage to investigate, where to obtain additional information, and more.

1 From $45 a Day—What It Means

The title of this book refers to a self-imposed allowance beginning at $45 a day ($90 for two) and goes up from there for basic living costs in India—that is, for a room and three meals. Before breaking this down, let me say that you can get by for less in India, but it would be a spartan life. For those who wish to try it, look for my lowest budget recommendations throughout this book. On the other hand, $45 a day stretches far in India in comparison with the West.

What brings the average cost into the $45 and over range in India are luxury and food taxes that affect most travelers. These taxes vary from place to place, but have been factored into the overall cost of living during your stay. Taxes, surcharges, and gratuities can add 17% to 20% to the average bill for room and board.

Now here is what you get for your money. Hotel rooms in India are usually a good two-thirds of your budget. This means $30 to $35 a day for your room, $2 to $3 for breakfast, $3 to $4 for lunch, and $5 to $6 for dinner. This will cover a comfortable stay even in the most popular, and therefore most expensive, cities; in off-the-beaten-path places, this budget will permit a surprisingly high standard for the money.

Many travelers choose to modify the above budget. For instance, there are those who prefer to stay at more modestly priced hotels and eat in higher priced restaurants, or vice versa. More frequently, travelers do a bit of both, which is the best way to travel in India. Stay spartan, stay in luxury, stay in a forest bungalow or a religious retreat. Try them all. This is, of course, a matter of personal preference. Nearly all travelers put something aside for a few splurges in accommodations and meals during their India tour.

The costs of transportation to and within India, of sightseeing, and of entertainment are generally not included in the $45 figure. But in some cases—especially where two people traveling together have

$90—you will find that this amount stretches to include a splurge or two, coach tours, and a number of other tourist essentials. In addition, every effort has been made to locate bargains in tours and transportation to help budget tourists keep expenditures in line.

This book is not a guide to mere subsistence living, but provides information about clean and comfortable accommodations that can be used safely by people of all ages and both sexes.

2 50 Tips for Saving Money in India

AIR TRAVEL

- Use Air-India's Pex (promotional) airfares.
- Fly nonpeak.
- Go with four friends for a GV4 tour fare.
- Plan carefully so that you can avoid fee penalties for changes.
- Shop the consolidators.

GETTING AROUND INDIA

- Take advantage of Indian Airlines special fares.
- Travel light; avoid overweight charges on planes.
- Report to and board planes on time (if you don't check in on time in India, you forfeit your fare).
- Take coaches or prepaid taxis from airports to cities.
- Buy an Indrail Pass if you plan multiple train trips.
- Go AC Chair and AC two-tier Sleeper on short train trips.
- If you have the time, travel by train: AC First trains costs less than planes for long trips.
- Overnight trains save on hotel bills.
- Train travelers can use low-priced Railway Retiring rooms.
- Plan carefully avoid train cancellation charges.
- When you travel on express trains, like the *Shatabdi Express,* take AC Chair. Executive is almost double the price. On other trains, AC Chair can be even more of a bargain: On *Rajdhani Express* trains, AC First is almost four times higher.
- Luxury and Express buses offer savings over trains.
- Strap on a backpack and trek the hills and valleys.

Note: Negotiate unmetered taxi/ricksha rates **before** your ride.

GETTING AROUND WITHIN CITIES

- Auto rickshas or cycle rickshas cost less than taxis.
- You do not need to tip cab drivers; Indians don't.
- In Calcutta, use the Metrorail.
- In Bombay, take the suburban trains.
- In Kerala and Goa, travel by public ferry.
- Use fixed-fare Vikram/Tempos.
- Use share taxis where avaiiable.
- Always make sure the taxi driver flags the meter, and ask to see taxi rate charts when you are unsure whether the fare is fair.
- Taxi drivers try to charge foreigners more if they pick them up from five-star hotels.
- Avoid taxis that are not yellow-topped; they're unmetered tourist taxis.

ACCOMMODATIONS

- Observe check-out times to avoid extra night's charges.
- Remember that room service usually carries a surcharge.
- Stay in simple, Indian-style hotels, especially in the south.
- Try to get by without air-conditioning; non–air-conditioned room rates are almost always cheaper.
- If your hotel room has a telephone, remember that phoning from it is expensive.
- Avoid peak seasons and festivals—often from October through April.
- Inquire about off-season discounts.
- Stay in a dorm, youth hostel, or government accommodation; many of these rates are very cheap indeed.
- Ashrams are low priced and spiritually uplifting.
- Dharmashalas (pilgrim housing) are usually free, requiring only a small donation.
- Be a paying house guest; you'll find lists at the tourist offices almost anywhere you go.
- Stay in a low-priced forest bungalow for wildlife-seeing.

DINING

- Eat vegetarian food; it is usually cheaper.
- If you are not traveling alone, share enormous portions. Your waistline and budget will both be slimmer.
- Take one of your meals at a sumptuous buffet.
- Eat thali meals, which give you several items for one low price—often with free refills.
- Eat fixed-price plate meals.
- Imports are expensive; order local beer, wine, and food.
- If you want to eat in posh places, choose the fixed-price meals, which usually are substantially cheaper than eating à la carte.
- Snack and sip in Indian coffee houses.
- Buy fruits in the market for snacks (be sure to wash and peel them).
- In South India, have a tiffin (snacks) with tea (instead of a full lunch).

SIGHTSEEING

- Get free maps, pamphlets, and advice from tourist offices.
- Take economical coach sightseeing tours; most local and state tourist bureaus have several money-saving tours that will enable you to see more for less.
- Remember that travel off the beaten path is both economical and interesting.
- Use government-approved guides at archaeological sites, and hire them at approved rates.
- Entry fees are often waived Fridays.

SHOPPING

- Bargain everywhere that isn't price fixed.
- Haggle in the bazaars.
- Buy local (for example, tie-dyes in Rajasthan, wool shawls in the hills).
- *Never* shop with a guide; they get commissions and will direct you only to the stores that pay them, not necessarily the ones that will give you the best buy.
- Don't buy gems or gold from anyone but recognized merchants.
- Buy bottled water in the bazaar, not the hotels.

IN GENERAL

- Stay cool when confronted by the insistent. Don't overtip (no matter how desperate the plea).
- Never believe anyone who says, "Whatever you wish," when you ask the price. Be firm. Set the price.
- Be fearless: Bargain for almost anything, anywhere.
- Relax, make new friends, share expenses.
- Above all, always think in rupees, not dollars. (If you don't, you're doomed as a budget traveler.)

3 Visitor Information, Entry Requirements & Money

GOVERNMENT OF INDIA TOURIST OFFICES

OUTSIDE OF INDIA

In Australia Level 1, 17, Castlereagh Street, Sydney, New South Wales 2000 (☎ 0061-2-232-1600/17961 or 0061-2-233-7579; fax (02) 2233003).

In Canada 60 Bloor Street (West), Suite 1003, Toronto, Ontario M4W 3B8 (☎ 416/962-3787 or 416/962-3788; fax 416/962-6279).

In the United Kingdom 7 Cork St., London WIX 2AB (☎ 01-437-3677/8; direct line: 01-434-6613; fax 01-494-1048).

In the United States **New York:** 30 Rockefeller Plaza, Suite 15, North Mezzanine, New York, NY 10112 (☎ 212/586-4901, 212/586-4902, or 212/586-4903; fax 212/582-3274). **Los Angeles:** 3550 Wilshire Blvd., Room 204, Los Angeles, CA 90010 (☎ 213/380-8855 or 213/477-38245; fax 213/380-6111).

IN INDIA

Agra 191, The Mall, Agra-282 001, Uttar Pradesh (☎ 363377 or 363959).

Aurangabad Krishna Vilas, Station Road, Aurangabad-431 005, Maharashtra (☎ 31217).

Bangalore K.F.C. Building, 48 Church St., Bangalore-560 001, Karnataka (☎ 5585417).

Bhubaneshwar B-20, Kalpana Area, Bhubaneswar-751 014, Orissa (☎ 54203).

Bombay 123 Maharishi Karve Rd., opposite Churchgate, Bombay-400 020, Maharashtra (☎ 2032932, 2033144, 2033145, 2036054; fax 91-22-2014496).

Calcutta "Embassy," 4 Shakespeare Sarani, Calcutta-700 071, West Bengal (☎ 2421402, 2421475, 2425813; fax 91-33-2423521).

Guwahati B.K. Kakati Road, Ulubari, Gawahati-781 007, Assam (☎ 547407).

Hyderabad 3-6-369/A-30, Sandozi Building, 2nd Floor, 26 Himayat Nagar, Hyderabad-500 029, Andhra Pradesh (☎ 660037).

Imphal Old Lambulane, Jail Road, Imphal-795 001, Manipur (☎ 21131).

Jaipur State Hotel, Khasa Kothi, Jaipur 302 001, Rajasthan (☎ 372200).

Khajuraho Near Western Group of Temples, Khajuraho-471 606, Madhya Pradesh (☎ 2047 or 2048).

Kochi (Cochin) Willingdon Island, Kochi-682 009, Kerala (☎ 6684521 or 666218).

Madras 154, Anna Salai, Madras-600 002, Tamil Nadu (☎ 8269685 or 8269695).

Naharlagun Sector "C," Naharlagun-791 110, Arunchal Pradesh (☎ 328).

New Delhi 88, Janpath, New Delhi-110 001 (☎ **3320008,** 3320005, 3320342, 3320109, or 3320266).

Panaji (Goa) Communidade Building, Church Square, Panaji-403 001, Goa. (☎ 43412).

Patna Sudama Palace, Kakarbagh Road, Patna-800 020 (☎ 800020).

Port Blair VIP Road, Junglighat, P.O. Port Blair-744 103, Andaman and Nicobar Islands (☎ 21006).

Shillong Tirot Singh Syiem Road, Police Bazar, Shillong-793 001, Meghalaya (☎ 225632).

Thiruvananthapuram (Trivandrum) Airport, Thiruvananthapuram, Kerala (☎ 451498).

Varanasi 15B, The Mall, Varanasi-221 002, Uttar Pradesh (☎ 43744).

ENTRY REQUIREMENTS

DOCUMENTS

U.S. Citizens A **passport** is required, and all tourists from the United States must have a **visa.** (U.S. residents used to be able to stay in India for 30 days without a visa, but this is no longer the case.) A three-month tourist visa ($40) is valid from the date of issue and permits single, double, or triple entry. You must make entry into India within one month of the issue date. The following visas are valid from date of entry into India and also permit multiple entries, which simplifies visiting neighboring countries such as Nepal: the six-month tourist visa ($60); the one-year visa ($70); and the one-year student or business visa ($70). Your fee must be accompanied by a completed application, your original passport, and two passport-size photos.

Visa forms are available through the Indian Embassy or Indian Consulates in the United States: **Embassy of India (Consular Section),** 2107 Massachusetts Ave. NW, Washington, DC 20008 (☎ 202/939-7000); **Consul-General India,** 3 East 64th St., New York, NY 10021-7097 (☎ 212/897-7800); or 540 Arguello Blvd., San Francisco, CA 94118 (☎ 415/668-0662); or 150 N. Michigan Ave., Suite 1100, Chicago, IL 60601 (☎ 312/781-6280). If you want it mailed, send the form along with a bank draft, money order, or certified check plus mailing fees, and a self-addressed envelope.

Tourist visas are issued within 24 to 48 hours if you apply in person, but take up to two weeks by mail. Fees for mailing visas are $3 per passport by certified mail and $10 per passport by express mail.

If you arrive in India without a visa, *you won't get in.* After 72 hours in the airport, or until a flight leaves for your home, you'll be sent out of the country. There are no visitors' permits.

For the latest requirements before you leave, check with the visa-issuing authorities—the Indian Embassy in Washington, D.C., or the consulates in New York, San Francisco, and Chicago.

Australian Citizens In addition to a passport, Australian citizens need a visa. Visa information, including exact prices and applications, can be obtained from the **Embassy of India,** 3–5 Moonah Place, Yarralumia, Canberera, ACT 2600 (☎ 06/273-3999); the **Consul-General of India,** at 2153 Walker St., 11th Floor, North Sydney, NSW 2060 (☎ 02/955-7055); or 13 Munro St., Coburg, Vic 3058 (☎ 03/384-0141).

Canadian Citizens In addition to a passport, Canadian citizens also need a visa. Visa information, including exact prices and applications, can be obtained from the **Indian High Commission,** 10 Springfield Rd., Ottawa, ON K1M 1C9 (☎ 613/744-3751); the **Consul-General of India,** 2 Bloor St. W., no. 500, Toronto, ON M4W 3E2 (☎ 416/960-0751); or 325 Howe St., 2nd Floor, Vancouver, BC V6C 1Z7 (☎ 604/662-8811).

U.K. Citizens In addition to a passport, U.K. citizens also need a visa. Visa information, including exact prices and applications can be obtained from the **Embassy of India,** India House, Aldwych, London WC28 4NA (☎ 0171/836-8484); or the **Consul-General of India,** 82 New St., Birmingham, B2 4BA (☎ 0121/643-0366).

Transit Visas

There are also transit visas issued for stays of three days ($4 single entry; $9 multiple). To get a transit visa you must fill out an application form and produce a ticket showing your ongoing destination.

Special Permits

For travel into restricted or protected areas foreigners require special permits. Currently, a number of these areas are in eastern India—Manipur, Mizoram, Sikkim, and West Sikkim—also some areas of Himachal Pradesh, Jammu, and Kashmir, as well as Arunchal Pradesh and Nagaland.

Special permits are also needed for the Andaman and Nicobar Islands in the distant Bay of Bengal and Lakshadweep off the coast of Kerala in the southwest.

The best advice about permits is to check **in advance** with your nearest India Tourist Office or diplomatic mission in the early planning stages of your trip to find out who can go where and how long it takes to get a permit to do it. The permit situation often changes so quickly that even state authorities in India are unaware that central authorities have changed the rules. Many a time, conflicting information about travel restrictions has led to a frustrating experience.

Other Useful Documents

International Student Identity Card You qualify if you're a full-time student or on the faculty at a secondary, college, university, or vocational school and you are at least 12 years of age, enrolled in a program of study leading to a diploma or a degree at an accredited secondary or postsecondary educational institution during the current academic year. The card costs $18 for students ($19 for faculty) and can be obtained from the Council on International Educational Exchange, 205 E. 42nd St., New York, NY 10017 (☎ 212/661-1450).

It entitles you to travel assistance by the **Student Travel Office** in New Delhi, which can save you a bundle when you're looking for a bargain fare home. The card also entitles you to automatic accident/sickness insurance anywhere outside the United States. If you're already in India and it occurs to you how useful a card can be, you can still get it—at the **Student Travel Information Center,** Imperial Hotel, Janpath, New Delhi 110001. This is also the place to get your card renewed. Proof may be required for cards issued in New Delhi: You may have to show a letter from your educational institution or similar identification vouching for your student status. Verification may also be required from the U.S. Embassy in New Delhi, which is usually quite helpful.

International Youth Hostel Membership Card You don't have to have one to use the youth hostels in India, nor do you have to be young to be a hosteler. But in some hostels preference is given card-holders, and most hostels grant members discounts on already cheap dorm accommodations (about 35¢ for members; 60¢ for nonmembers). For details on Youth Hostel membership, write: National Headquarters, **American Youth Hostels,** National Office, Box 37613, Dept. 804, Washington, DC 20013-7613 (☎ 202/783-6161).

CUSTOMS

There is virtually no restriction on the importation of personal effects—personal jewelry, one camera with five rolls of film (you may want to bring more), one pair of binoculars, one video camera, and other items are permitted without special declaration. You're also allowed one liter of liquor. If, however, you've got a lot of high-priced photographic equipment, transistor radios, tape recorders, and the like, you'll have to fill out a re-export form. It requires the serial numbers of your items; make a list in advance to save time. Keep this form; you will be asked for it when you leave India.

All items brought into India are to be re-exported when you leave. You can also take out souvenirs of Indian silk, wool, art wares, and other items without limit. As long as you're not a resident of India, you can take out gold jewelry up to Rs 2,000 ($66.66); a Rs 10,000 ($333.33) limit is applied to items set with precious stones. Banned entirely from export are articles made of animal or snake skin. Also, one is no longer permitted to buy or sell Indian ivory in India; should you buy something made of ivory for re-export, make sure you have the proper certificate to prove it was made before this ban went into effect. There are restrictions on the exportation of antiquities (more than 100 years old). To check on whether your purchases are considered antiquities, consult the director of antiquities, Archaeological Survey of India, Janpath, New Delhi 110001, or the local superintending archaeologist at three offices around the country: **Eastern Circle,** Archaeological Survey of India, Narayani Building, Brabourne Road, Calcutta 700013; **Southern Circle,** Archaeological Survey of India, Fort St. George, Madras 600001; **Frontier Circle,** Archaeological Survey of India, Minto Bridge, Srinagar 190001.

4 Money

CURRENCY At the time of this writing, approximately 33 Indian **rupees** were worth $1 U.S., but the value fluctuates from day to day. All dollar equivalents for Indian currency were calculated on the basis of $1 U.S. to Rs 30, the rate when the research for this book was conducted. Barring any significant alteration in the rate of exchange, these dollar equivalents will give you a fairly good idea of what you'll be spending. If you wish, check with your bank before you leave home to determine the latest official rate of exchange. Or pick up a copy of *The New York Times* or the *Wall Street Journal,* which lists daily values of world currencies in its "Foreign Exchange" column.

There are 100 **paise** to each rupee. You are not permitted to take rupees in or out of India. You can bring any amount of foreign currency or traveler's checks into India. You have to make an oral declaration of currency and, in some instances, fill out a special currency form. Whatever you do, don't discard the form: You have to show it again when you leave the country, along with receipts for changing traveler's checks and dollars. Changing your money in India only at authorized places is advised. On the black market, your seemingly fantastic deal may turn out to be counterfeit, or your dealer may well disappear with your hard-earned dollars without giving you a rupee. When there's a favorable rate of exchange, the few paise gained is hardly worth the risk.

Authorized money-exchanging facilities are available at the cashiers of major hotels, some guest houses, most banks, and in some shops as well. Its faster to change your money at hotel banks, and you get the official rate of exchange. International airports also have banks to change currency.

Be warned: when you change money, stock up on a plentiful supply of small change. It's an annoying fact (or fiction) that there isn't a curio or soft-drink seller or ricksha wallah in India with small change. You also need plenty of small change for tips. Further, check all notes for holes and tears. Indians won't accept damaged currency. You have to take it back to the bank to redeem it or keep it as a souvenir. It's especially unfortunate to have some vendor reject your damaged currency when you've found a special treasure in an out-of-the-way bazaar miles from the nearest money changer. At times like these, you might barter by offering the merchant something of your own in exchange for the coveted merchandise.

Traveler's checks are the best and safest way to carry your money. Major credit cards are widely accepted in India. At all but the smallest, low-budget hotels, **you're required to pay your bills in foreign currency,** which includes credit-card transactions.

5 When to Go

WEATHER

The best overall time to visit India is from mid-September to April. April, May, and June can be extremely hot in the plains, very humid in coastal regions, but comfortable in some of the hill resorts. (Ladahk, high in the Himalayas, for example, is best from May to October; Darjeeling, in the eastern Himalayas, from April to November; Kulu and Manali, in the lower northern Himalayas, mid-September to mid-November and from April to the end of June.) Outside of Kashmir and a few other hill stations, the monsoon usually begins in mid-June and sweeps across the country, generally to mid-September. This essential natural phenomenon seems to have a mind of its own; it can arrive late or tarry longer than expected. During the monsoon, there can be downpours that alternate with bright, dry, sunny weather. Sometimes, usually in the main tourist centers, the show goes on pretty much as scheduled. There is more information about the weather of specific areas in India in the individual chapters.

FESTIVALS

India shines at festival times. The following includes only major celebrations. Be sure to check with local tourist offices to see if any festivals are going on while you're around. As for dates, with the exception of **Republic Day,** they vary slightly from year to year. Again, check local tourist offices for details. Local and regional festivals are discussed in conjunction with each destination throughout the book.

INDIA CALENDAR OF EVENTS

January

- **Republic Day.** Always on the 26th and, in New Delhi, lasting for four days. This is the most spectacular of the festivals. It starts with a big parade down the majestic Rajpath. There are decorated elephants, camels, girls with flowers in their hair, floats from every region, and a shower of rose petals from above. The nation's leaders are in the grandstands. The parade is followed by folk-dance exhibitions and a military display, on Victory Square, facing the main government buildings and Presidential Palace.

- **Pongal.** In Madurai, Thanjavur, and Tiruchirapalli. There are special foods, and in some places you can see an extraordinary bullfight where money is tied to the horns of the animals and young boys pull it off.

March

- **Holi.** Very spirited. Mainly celebrated in the north. It's the time when everyone throws colored water and powder on each other and everything in sight. It symbolizes tarnishing the old and beginning the new—wear your oldest clothes.

June

- **Cart Festival.** When the gods go on their summer holiday, thousands go to Puri to see them off down "Main Street."

August

- **Onam.** Kerala's harvest festival; includes a great "snake" boat race through the lagoons.

October/November

- **Dussehra.** In the fall (October or November), commemorates the killing of the demon King Ravana by Rama and symbolizes the destruction of evil by good. It differs from place to place. For example, in Delhi the evil king literally gets blown up: Giant effigies are stuffed with firecrackers and set off. In Calcutta it's called Durga Puja, and pandals (displays) of traditional scenes bring out the best in the bustling city. In Kulu, gods are paraded on special palanquins with musical accompaniment.
- **Diwali.** Very pretty. Every house, village, and public building is lit with tiny flickering oil lamps (although the public buildings sometimes use electricity). The goddess of prosperity, Lakshmi, reputedly comes to call on lighted homes and scorns those that are not. Gifts are exchanged; mountains of sweets, mostly silver-wrapped, appear in the bazaars.
- **Pushkar.** A fair in Rajasthan, in November, where there is camel racing and spirited folk dancing.

December

- **Vaikunta/Ekadasi.** Procession of beautifully adorned gods from Srirangam's Temple in Tiruchirapalli.
- **Christmas.** Gift-giving goes on almost everywhere, even among non-Christians. In Goa and Kerala, where there are large numbers of Christians, the celebration is carried out traditionally.

6 Adventure Travel

Travel itineraries for the adventurous are becoming more popular. Geographically, India has an abundance of possibilities to offer every traveler who'd rather scale a peak or snorkel the deep than sit in a tour bus (or do a bit of both). Where altitudes vary from 9,000 feet to 14,500 feet, skiing and climbing both are extraordinary. Where great natural beauty often blends with man-made masterpieces, trekking can offer a dazzling panorama of wilderness, art, and architecture. White-water rafting on Himalayan rivers, fishing in trout streams, windsurfing, snorkeling, scuba diving: There are activities for every season. How's this for an exotic adventures? The state of Rajasthan offers camel safaris from one to many days into the Thar desert to sightsee among the villages (see Chapter 5, "Rajasthan," for more details).

To plan your own adventure, get more information from the **India Tourist Offices** before you take off or while in India.

WILDLIFE

About one-fifth of India's land is covered with a wide variety of wildlife. Rare species such as the Asian lion, one-horned rhinoceros, black buck, Kashmiri stag, and white tiger (seen today mainly in zoos) are protected animals. India's 20 national parks, 191 wildlife sanctuaries, and 9 bird sanctuaries make it possible to see rare animals and beautiful birds in various striking settings somewhere during your journey. Be sure to check with the tourist office on the best seasons to visit before you take off. Some preserves are inaccessible during the monsoon, and others have limited populations at some seasons. You'll read about a few of India's major sanctuaries in the following chapters. These, and some others equally worthwhile, include:

- **Bandipur** (Karnataka): elephants, bison, panthers, tigers, and spotted deer.
- **Corbett National Park** (Uttar Pradesh): tigers, sambhar, and chital.
- **Kaziranga National Park** (Northeast Frontier): one-horned rhinoceros and bison.
- **Palamau National Park** (Bihar): tigers and panthers.
- **Periyar Wildlife Sanctuary** (Kerala): elephants and wild boars.
- **Gir Lion Sanctuary** (Gujarat): Asian lions.
- **Jaldpara Wildlife Sanctuary** (West Bengal): rhinoceros, kakar, and peafowl.
- **Sariska Wildlife Sanctuary** (Rajasthan): tigers, nilgai, and deer.
- **Dandeli Wildlife Sanctuary** (Karnataka): tigers, elephants, sloth bear, gaur, chowsingha, and wild dogs.
- **Nagarhole** (Karnataka): tigers, elephants, sambar, and wild boar.
- **Bharatpur Bird Sanctuary** (Rajasthan): rare birds come from as far away as Siberia in winter.
- **Chilka Bird Sanctuary** (Orissa): waterbirds.
- **Ranganathittu Bird Sanctuary** (Karnataka): stork, ibis, white heron, Indian darter, and others.

Three **lion safari parks** have also been developed: at Hyderabad, at Borivili near Bombay, and at Nandankanan in Orissa.

7 Organized Tours & Packages

If you're short on time, you might seriously consider a package tour. Currently more than 60 tour operators have packages to India, and some schools, cultural institutions, and foundations also organize package tours.

Package tours run the gamut, from cover-the-top-sights tours to special-interest tours. A tour oriented around handicrafts is offered through **Journeyworld,** 119 W. 57th St., NY, NY 10019 (☎ 212/447-6091). Active adventure tours are offered by **Mountain Travel+Sobek,** 6420 Fairmount Ave., El Centro, CA 94530 (☎ 800/227-2384). Wildlife, jungle tours, and others are available through **Cox and Kings,** 511 Lexington Ave., Suite 335, New York, NY 10017 (☎ 212/935-3935). Even the highly specialized tours usually include some traditional sightseeing attractions while zeroing in on their themes.

Your travel agent should be able to give you more information on packages and special-interest tours.

8 Finding an Affordable Place to Stay

Throughout India there are **Western-style hotels** with every amenity, classified by the government according to the star system, from five-star deluxe to one star. They include some fabulous palaces turned into hotels, houseboats, and hunting lodges, as well as sleek, modern, international-style structures. There are also many well-run (and starred) **Indian-style hotels,** especially in the south. They are usually clean, functional, and comfortable places, with few frills, whitewashed walls, and stone floors. But newer Indian-style hotels are adding more of the interior decoration associated with Western-style places, racking up high star ratings and hiking room rates as well. Plain or fancy, the main difference between these hotels and their Western counterparts is the food—Indian-style hotels are strictly vegetarian.

Everywhere, **budget hotels** offer lower rates for non–air-conditioned rooms. Virtually all rooms have swirling ceiling fans to stir the breezes, and many have windows or balconies opening onto gardens. So to conserve funds, you might try to get by without air-conditioning. In cooler seasons, you won't need it; then hoteliers will charge you for a heater.

At all but the lowest-priced accommodations, foreigners settle their bills in foreign currency *only:* with cash, traveler's checks, or by credit card. Some top hotels now quote rates only in U.S. dollars.

Be sure to pay attention to check-out times to avoid being charged for a full day by missing your deadline. And if you're traveling in the off-season, ask about discounts that may be in effect but are not well publicized. No matter your budget, if you make a reservation, be sure and indicate an arrival time so your room will be waiting if you get in at some offbeat hour. If you're going to be delayed, get through to the hotel about it, or you may find your star accommodations are those you sleep under outdoors. Avoid peak seasons at resorts when rates are highest.

Additionally, there are no-star, low-priced hotels that are great finds. The lowest-priced hotels, usually clustered around bus and railway stations, often offer nothing more than cells with cots. **Guest houses** are other possibilities in major cities. They range greatly, from a notch or several above or below the three-, two-, and one-star hotels. The major difference between a guest house and a small hotel is limited meal service. Guest houses don't have restaurants, but will send food to your room.

Then there are **paying-guest accommodations,** where families take **paying guests** into their home. You'll find some mentioned on the following pages in the accommodation sections. For others, the government of India or state tourist offices have lists.

Out of the mainstream, where sights are plentiful but tourists are not, **government-run lodges, bungalows,** and **forest rest houses** offer comfortable places to stay. **PWD Inspection Bungalows,** also usually off the beaten path, are intended for government officials, but if no inspector is expected, tourists can move in for a modest fee.

Inns run by charitable organizations, temples, or towns, known as dharamshalas, will put you up for a few rupees. These truly humble places, meant primarily to house traveling pilgrims, have strict rules for all guests: They are purely vegetarian and do not permit alcohol or tobacco. In dharamshalas there are no cots or restaurants, and few or no toilets.

About Indian-Style Toilets

Sooner or later you'll learn to deal with Indian-style toilets, which are as hygienic as Western styles, but take some getting used to. Indian toilets are sunk in the floor, with little foot pedals to either side. You squat, not sit, on them and supply your own toilet paper. Indians use water to cleanse themselves, which explains the bowls and faucets near the toilets. The left hand is for cleansing. The right hand is for eating.

The best way to experience India is to vary your accommodations. No one would want to pass up the opportunity to spend a night or two in a fabulous marble palace turned into a luxury hotel. It's also enjoyable to stay in some of the fancy hotels, where there's every conceivable service and other foreigners. But be sure to stay in some of the Indian-style hotels and mix with Indian travelers, too. This can lead to wonderful new experiences—perhaps an invitation to visit new Indian friends when they are at home or the unexpected treat of going to a wedding (which is why they may be away from home).

9 Health & Insurance

STAYING HEALTHY

Water is said to be potable in many large Indian cities, but I recommend drinking it bottled or boiled—or stick to hot tea instead. Many hoteliers and restaurateurs offer safe-to-drink water; but if not, don't be shy—ask for it. You'll probably worry about the water if you don't, and worry in itself can cause upsets. Also, remember that ice is made of water. Take it easy on exploring new foods until you are adjusted to India. A spicy curry after a long and tiring international flight is hard to digest if you're not used to it, and any sudden change in diet can cause your stomach to play tricks in revenge. Use good sense when buying fresh foods, as you would anywhere. When in doubt, don't. Peeling your fruit is advised; buying from street stalls is not. Washing your hands before eating is good hygiene anywhere—and a cultural must in India, whether you eat with silverware or your right hand.

India is exciting, different, stimulating. There will be a tendency to overdo, which also can invite temporary upsets. It's a good idea to pack an over-the-counter medication for gastrointestinal upsets. If you do get a "bug," there are good doctors, drugstores, and hospitals in all towns and cities. In some places, the doctors have studied abroad. Your hotel reception desk can recommend a good doctor or point out the nearest pharmacy. And if they can't, check with your embassy or consulate.

INOCULATIONS

If you're coming from an infected area, you'll need proof of **yellow fever** inoculations. A **cholera** inoculation is not necessary, but some tourists take it anyway. Make sure any inoculation you have is entered on your World Health Organization card. Cholera inoculations are given in two doses if you've never had them before (make sure you allow enough time), and must be renewed every six months so keep them up to date if you plan an extended stay in India. For some areas malaria medication is advised. The lowest-budget travelers might consider a more extensive series of inoculations, including tetanus, typhoid, typhus, and bubonic plague. Some people take a gamma globulin inoculation right before leaving. Requirements change from time to time, so you'll want to check on the latest as you prepare for your India trip. For up-to-the-minute requirements, call the U.S. Public Health Service's Quarantine Department, or the equivalent department in Canada, the United Kingdom, and Commonwealth countries. The World Health Organization also has a special line for this information.

INSURANCE

HEALTH/ACCIDENT/LOSS

Even the most careful of us can experience the Murphy's Law of travel—you discover you've lost your wallet, your passport, your airline ticket, or your tourist permit.

Always keep a photocopy of these documents in your luggage; it makes replacing them easier. To be reimbursed for insured items once you return, you'll need to report the loss to the Indian police and get a written report. If you don't speak the local or regional language, make sure you have a translator for this process, although most officials in India will be able to speak English. If you lose official documents, you'll need to contact both Indian and U.S. officials in India before you leave the country.

Health Care Abroad, 107 W. Federal St. (P.O. Box 480), Middleburg, VA 22117 (☎ 703/687-3166 or 800/237-6615) and **Access America,** 6600 W. Broad St., Richmond, VA 23230 (☎ 804/285-3300 or 800/628-4908), offer medical and accident insurance as well as coverage for luggage loss and trip cancellation. Always read the fine print on the policy to be sure you get the coverage you want.

10 What to Pack

Here are some guidelines on what you need to get by in India. First, you should know that it's not a dressy country, and casual clothes will do for just about every occasion except a big event (and if something big comes up, you can buy something locally). Nor is India always hot. If you're going to be in northern India mid-November to mid-February, you'll need woolens, and the farther north you go during those months, the heavier the woolens. After mid-February, summer clothes will do everywhere, except Kashmir, Ladakh, and other mountain regions, where you'll need a sweater; and you should dress in layers so you can strip down during the warmth of the day. Summertime, you'll need summer clothes everywhere, though in the mountains you may need a light wrap at night.

Jeans or something comparable are acceptable almost everywhere (except, again, at a big occasion), and they're positively essential in outlying areas. Shorts are not worn in city streets, except by Westerners who don't take Indian sensitivities into consideration. Generally, women's shoulders and legs are covered in India. You need shoes that are easy to get in and out of at temples and other shrines. Plus, you'll need beachwear for beach resorts and trekking gear for trekking. Take sunblock, sunglasses, and insect repellent, the latter for jungly places. An umbrella and raincoat are necessary for visiting during the monsoon.

Imported cosmetics are expensive, as is imported film, so take a plentiful supply of both. (The domestically made products are not as good, but also check on restrictions as to the amount of film you can bring into India without paying a duty.) Also, if you take any medication, bring it along, as well as a prescription for a refill. An extra pair of glasses or a prescription for a new pair is a good idea in case you lose or break yours.

In the "other items" area, take a fits-it-all sink stopper. Some budget hotels don't have them (and it's impossible to make one). Take a small padlock—some of the lowest-budget hotels expect guests to bring their own. Take a flashlight—power failures occur. And remember your Swiss army knife for peeling fruits and dozens of other uses. (When flying, do not carry any kind of sharp implement—knife, scissors—in your carry-on luggage; it will be confiscated and you will have to take the time to retrieve it at the airport of your destination.) Take toilet paper, tissues, and soap (some cheap hotels don't provide any frills.) A small sewing kit is not a bad idea.

The best advice of all is to travel light: There are dhobis (clothes washers) all over India who can wash and press clothes in hours—and while at times I've found the job less than perfect, I've never had anything totally ruined. This is not the case with dry cleaners, which are not always top-notch.

11 Getting to India

BY PLANE

India is a far throw from the Western world when it comes to culture—and a far throw in terms of distance, too. That and the cost of fuel these days are the main factors in determining how much your plane ticket to this exotic land will cost. And before I even tell you about the options, let's say that all fares in this chapter, while accurate at press time, are subject to change.

FINDING THE BEST AIRFARE

The following section discusses options on **Air India,** the national carrier, which has the only 747-400 daily direct flight from New York or India via London. Keep in mind that airfares are in a constant state of flux; even travel agents find it hard to track.

APEX—THE MOST FREQUENTLY USED BUDGET FARE This round-trip fare gives you 14 days to four months to savor the temples, marble palaces, Mughal archways, and other exotic sights. Try to take off weekdays and in the least popular season to avoid paying a peak-time premium. The fares discussed are to Delhi and Bombay, the most popular ports of arrival; Madras and Calcutta fares are slightly higher, and fares vary to India's other international airports. The **peak fare** from June 1 to September 30 and December 1 to January 15 is $2,273 on weekends and $2,213 weekdays.

The **shoulder fare,** from May 16 to May 31 and October 1 to November 30, is $2,113 on weekends, $2,053 weekdays.

The **low-season fare** from January 16 to May 15 is $1,991 weekends and $1,931 weekdays. This is a fare worth serious consideration; with it you can get one stopover in London, Bombay, or Delhi in each direction. There is a 21-day advance purchase, and confirmed reservations are required; also, a cancellation penalty of $175 applies.

OTHER FARES Most important for budget travelers, Air India alone offers promotional fares (PEX in airline lingo)—recently $1,294 to Delhi or Bombay. These fares permit stays of seven days to six months; for an additional $125 open return is permitted. No advance purchase is required, but you must have a confirmed reservation. There is a $100 fee if you change your reservation before your date of travel, and $200 if you cancel. Be sure and inquire about any other penalties!

Another possibility—somewhat more complicated—is to round up a group of four friends and travel together on a GV4 fare of $1,665 peak and $1,297 basic to Bombay and Delhi. There's one major hitch to this fare: You also have to buy a seven-day land package in addition and make your purchase at least seven days in advance. The fare is good for a minimum of seven days and a maximum of 45 days. It permits one stopover in each direction at an additional $75 a stop.

ADDITIONAL CITIES AT NO EXTRA FARE While the additional-cities offers have changed over the years, it's still worth pointing out again that both the APEX and PEX round-trip fares give you one stopover in each direction. This means that your airfare for India may not be as costly as it appears since it can also transport you to two other points of interest.

Even big spenders occasionally get a special fare break on Air India's special fares for first and executive classes, such as companion fares (buy one, get one free for a companion); and first- and executive-class sale fares. For example, a recent round-trip, first-class sale fare was $3,499 (compared to $8,356), and executive class was $2,199 (compared to $5,202). It pays to ask.

THE MAJOR AIRLINES

Despite deregulation, all airlines flying to India charge almost the same and fly almost the same equipment. That said, I'll point out that my favorite airline is Air India and for good reason: Not only is it the only airline to offer the daily direct 646-400 flights I mentioned above, it also offers some dandy promotional fares to India from time to time in addition to the fairs most other airlines offer. An Air India flight is also a most pleasurable preview of the country you're about to visit. More likely than not, your flight attendant will be wearing a shimmering sari, or a raw-silk, high-necked serving jacket en route. He or she will be attentive, gliding up and down the aisles, offering curries and international cuisine, tending to you with true Indian hospitality. Should want to get further in the mood, your headset can be plugged into classical sitar or Indian film tunes. For reservations or information for **Air India** (☎ **800/223-2250**).

Other airlines that fly to India include the following: **Aeroflot** (☎ 800/995-9934); **Air Canada** (☎ 800/776-3000); **Air France** (☎ 800/237-2747); **British Airways** (☎ 800/247-9297); **Cathay Pacific Airways** (☎ 800/233-2742); **Egyptair** (☎ 800/334-6787); **KLM** (☎ 800/334-6787); and **Lufthansa** (☎ 800/645-3880), among others.

GATEWAYS TO INDIA

From virtually anywhere in the world, there will be a major international carrier to carry you to one of India's international airports: Delhi, Bombay, Calcutta, Madras, Ahmedabad, Amritsar, Bangalore, Goa, and Trivandrum. From North America, New York and Toronto are important gateway cities on the East Coast; from the West Coast, San Francisco and Los Angeles are popular. London, Paris, Frankfurt, Rome, Geneva, and Zurich are important gateways in Europe, but you can fly to India from most any European capital. In the Middle East, Bahrain is an important gateway. In Australia, Sydney is important. And from Asia, Tokyo, Hong Kong, and Singapore are major gateways to India.

OVERLAND TO INDIA

There are overland tours by coach that go through Europe, the Near and Middle East, and across India to Kathmandu. There are tours by train and variations on these themes. To get there from here isn't possible without going partway there—to London. **Hinterland Travel** (formerly Hann Overland), 2 Ivy Mill Lane, Godstone, Surrey RH9 8NH (☎ 01883-743574; fax 743912) specializes in inexpensive adventure holidays. "Asia Overland" goes from London to Kathmandu in either 75 or 97 days, starting in London and covering 1,200 miles through Europe, Western Turkey, the Middle East, Iran, Pakistan, India, and Nepal, aboard a 19-seat Mercedes bus carrying only 17 adventurers and driven by a Hinterland Travel driver/tour leader.

All camping equipment is provided except for sleeping bags and mats, but hotels (when they are used) and meals are not included in the tour price. Typical prices run from $2,475 for the 97-day tour leaving in March to $1,650 for the for the 75-day tour leaving in June. Prices include excursions to Lebanon (recently reinstated), Sinai,

Cairo, and Jerusalem. And it's possible to join this tour en route, taking a sector instead of the entire journey.

Hinterland's "Moghul Express"—London to Delhi by Train—takes 50 days, boarding in London and traveling via Munich or Vienna, Bulgaria, Istanbul, Damascus, Tabriz, Tehran, Lahore, Amritsar, and Delhi (and stops in between). The train tour costs $1,095 to $1,200. The same tour goes from Delhi back to London. Groups are limited to 25 to 30 people who are prepared to "go with the flow." Many sectors cannot be prebooked, so there can be delays and changes en route.

Another tour, the "Baku-Madras Express," is a 60-day escorted tour, starting in London and going to Moscow, Baku, Delhi, and Madras for $1,425 to $1,500. Again, this journey requires the ultimate in flexibility.

Hinterlands also offers some interesting bus tours with more conventional itineraries to various regions of India.

Considering the current political situation in a number of countries en route India, before embarking on an overland trip from London to Kathmandu or vice versa, American travelers should check with the U.S. State Department's **Citizen's Emergency Center (CEC),** 2201 C St. NW, Room 4811, Washington, DC 20520 (☎ 202/647-4000), for up-to-the-minute situation reports.

USING A TRAVEL AGENT

India is too mammoth to start making arrangements once you are there. The **Government of India Tourist Offices** (see the listings earlier in this chapter) can help; but while they can supply advice and information, they are not in the travel business and do not make bookings.

Good travel agents can assist you in untangling the mass of complexities. Using a travel agent doesn't necessarily increase your costs: If the agent just books your passage or purchases a package tour, it should cost you nothing (the agent's commission is paid by the airline and tour packager). But should an agent prepare a detailed itinerary from scratch and make all the arrangements, a small fee will be tacked on.

You can use one of the big agencies that sends tours to the four corners of the earth or a specialist in India travel. A personal favorite is **Cox and Kings,** 511 Lexington Ave., Suite 335, New York, NY 10017 (☎ 212/935-3935), the U.S. branch of a British tour company specializing in India for British travelers since 1758. They also have offices in Bombay, Delhi, Madras, and Bangalore, and Goa and offer all kinds of assistance in India, even if you're not a client. For instance, if you have to buy train tickets in India, it can be time-consuming because of the lines. But it needn't cut into your sightseeing. Call on a Cox and Kings Outbound Tour department, where for a percentage of the ticket, they'll buy your ticket while you go sightseeing.

12 Getting Around India

BY AIR

Indian Airlines (IC) is the second-largest domestic IATA carrier outside of the United States, operating to 54 Indian cities and 15 cities in the 8 nearby countries including Bangladesh, Maldives, Nepal, Pakistan, Singapore, Sri Lanka, and Thailand. The airline flies Airbus 300s and 320s, Boeing 707s, 737s, 747s, and DC-10s. Indian Airlines spans the country from Leh in the north to Trivandrum in the south, and from Calcutta in the east to Bombay in the west, and connects many places of touristic interest in between.

Private Airlines

Passengers also have a choice of private airlines that fly to several important destinations in India. They are **East West, Damania, Jet Airways, ModiLuft, Sahara, Archana Airways, NEPC,** and **Jagson Airlines.**

Foreigners traveling on any of these airlines must pay for their seats in U.S. dollars. Flights within India can be booked in most major cities. See the "Orientation" section of Chapter 3 for telephone numbers in Delphi.

PROMOTIONAL FARES

Indian Airlines offers a selection of special fares. Of greatest interest are these:

- **Discover India.** For $400 you have unlimited travel in India for 21 days with certain routing restrictions on domestic sectors.
- **India Wonderfares.** For $200 you get seven days of unlimited economy class travel within north, south, east, or west India. For an additional $100 they'll throw in Port Blair in either the eastern or the southern fares.
- **South India Excursion**. Gives you a 30% discount on the U.S. dollar fare on specified South India sectors.
- **Youth Fare.** Gives you a 25% discount on the U.S. dollar fare for tourists between the ages of 12 and 30.

There are no cancellation fees for fares paid in U.S. dollars. But fares are subject to change without notice. If an increase occurs, you pay it upon embarkation at the airport.

Reservations for Indian Airlines (and some private airlines) can be made when you purchase your international airline ticket; and it's a good idea to book them in advance, especially if you don't have all the time in the world. Planes in some sectors in India are heavily booked with business travelers who must travel long distances in the shortest time to keep their appointments, and who therefore go by plane rather than train. In the last few years, the domestic airlines have installed computerized reservations, so booking errors are fewer than in pretechnology days, when flights listed as booked were often half full and those listed as available were overbooked, and other variations on the seat theme.

Always remember to reconfirm your domestic flights if you have a break of 72 hours or more, or you may be canceled. Keep in mind that you should get to the airport one hour ahead of time for domestic flights, and 1½ hours ahead for international flights. It takes a while in India to check in at ticket counters, and security checks are very thorough.

It is standard procedure to go through the electronic devices, then a personal hands-on check, in addition to an open-baggage inspection. You will be asked to identify your luggage on the field before it is placed on the aircraft. Any luggage not identified is left behind.

If you have a Swiss army knife or other items that are remotely sharp, don't attempt to carry them aboard; nor are batteries permitted in hand baggage. They will be taken from you during the security check and given to the pilot to carry for you. You get them back once you reach your destination, but it can take time, so pack according to the rules.

When going through electronic security, don't leave exposed film in the pockets of your carry-on bag. The X-ray can ruin the film. There are special containers you can buy to carry film safely through checkpoints.

BY BUS

Indian buses are always crowded but convenient for getting to some places, and the fares are dirt cheap. In many cases the only discernible difference between "Ordinary," "Deluxe," and "Luxury" buses—aside from the ticket prices—is that the higher-priced buses hold fewer people, have leatherette seats, and at the very top, have push-back seats. An innovation in recent years is the video bus—taking a cue from the airlines, films are shown (but the Indian movies are played at a blast-you-out-of-your-mind sound level).

One highly recommended bus journey is the mountainous trip between Manali and Leh described fully in Chapters 7 and 8.

In some cases the bus is preferable because it's faster or more direct if your only alternative is a narrow-gauge train. This is not true for Darjeeling's "Toy Train" or Ooty's mountain railway, which are delightful rides at a creeping pace.

BY CAR

Self-drive car rentals are just getting underway in India and are not cheap—typically, Rs 620 ($20.66) for 24 hours/150 kilometers, and Rs 1860 ($62) for three days unlimited mileage in a small *Maruti 800* to Rs 15,810 ($527) for a month in the same type of automobile. Self-drive can be unnerving to foreigners. You might get stuck in an exotic traffic jam consisting of camel carts, rickshas, oxen, holy cows, and holy men, or have a nervous breakdown dealing with the volume of traffic in major cities.

You can hire a car and driver for a splurge, one that might seem affordable if you team up with a few friends. The prices are many times lower than for a chauffeur-driven car in the United States. For instance, a 16-hour round trip between Delhi and Agra (440km) runs about Rs 2280 ($76), inclusive of taxes, in a non–air-conditioned *Ambassador*; the cost would be Rs 2970 ($99) with air-conditioning.

BY TRAIN

Indian Railways, the second-largest railway system in the world, moves about 11 million people over routes covering 62,300 kilometers every day and offers two classes of accommodation: first and second. But there are other variations: AC First Class, AC Sleepers, AC Executive, AC Chair, First Class Sleeper; and Second Class for sitting (or sleeping); almost all Mail/Express trains involving night journeys have sleeper-class accommodations.

Not all classes are offered on all trains: AC is found mainly on the top express trains. There are also some special express trains like the *Rajdhani Express,* which have only AC First and AC Second. They cut down the time considerably between Bombay and Delhi, Delhi and Calcutta, and elsewhere, lopping off five hours on the Delhi–Calcutta run and seven from the Delhi–Bombay run, making them each 18 hours.

The superfast AC *Shatabdi Express* is the speedy way to many places of touristic interest throughout India. There are surcharges for traveling on both the *Rajdhani* and *Shatabdi* trains, from Rs 5 (17¢) in second class to Rs 25 (83¢) on AC First tickets.

A good deal for foreign tourists can be the **Indrail Pass** for anywhere from one to 90 days. The ticket can be purchased only with U.S. dollars or pounds sterling and can be an excellent value for the traveler making an extended trip. The cost of the pass depends upon the class in which you wish to travel (AC First, Second, etc.) and how long you wish to be able to travel without limit. Prices range from a one-day, second-class pass, which costs $15, all the way to a 90-day, AC First pass, which costs $960.

A tourist traveling on an Indrail Pass can travel on all trains at all times throughout India and is exempted from paying reservation fees, sleeper charges, supplementary charges for traveling on superfast trains, and for meals provided on *Rajdhani* and *Shatabdi Express* trains.

You can buy this pass in India through railway offices in New Delhi, Bombay, Calcutta, Madras, Agra Cantt., Ahmedabad, Aurangabad, Bangalore, Chandigarh, Gorakpur, Secunderabad/Hyderabad, Vijayawada, Jaipur, Rameswaram, Vasco-da-Gama, Trivandrum Central, Vadodara, Varanasi, Puttaparthi Town Booking Agency and Amritsar, and also from certain recognized travel agencies in metropolitan cities.

In addition, these passes are sold through certain recognized travel agents in Bombay, Delhi, Calcutta, and Madras.

Indrail passes should be handled with care: They are neither refundable nor replaceable if lost, stolen, or mutilated. Nor are the passes transferable, and the tourist must be prepared to show his or her passport whenever asked. Refunds are rendered at the office of issue before commencement of the first rail journey, provided that no advance reservation has been made. Otherwise, the Indrail Pass is subject to the same deductions as the regular refund rules, mentioned below.

To help you map out your tour, Indian Railways publishes *Trains at a Glance,* costing Rs 15 (50¢), which lists key trains, timings, and fares. To help you make reservations or purchase your Indrail Pass, there are Tourist Guides at the Bombay, Calcutta, and New Delhi railway stations. If you have trouble finding your train, ask for the station superintendent and you'll get assistance.

RULES OF THE RAILS

Generally, when traveling by train, reservations should be made as far in advance as possible to make sure you get what you want. You're expected to get to your train 10 minutes before departure, or your reserved seat will be assigned to someone else—but the earlier the better. There's lots going on (to say the least!) at the stations.

Cancellation Charges Best bet is to make sure of your plans before you purchase your tickets. You can lose up to 50% in some instances, on top of assorted minimum charges levied according to the type of ticket.

Reservation Fees If you're not on the Indrail Pass, you will be expected to pay a reservation fee, from Rs 25 (83¢) for AC First; Rs 15 (50¢) for AC two-tier sleeper or AC three-tier sleeper; Rs 10 (33¢) for first class and AC Chair; Rs 5 (16¢) for sleeper class and Second.

Travel Bag Service Requested three hours in advance, bags are supplied to the passengers in First and AC two-tier coaches. They contain two bed sheets, one towel, one blanket, one pillow, and a pillow cover; the cost is Rs 10 (33¢) per bag.

Dining on the Rails There are pantry cars for serving meals at passenger's seats on important trains; even if there are no pantry cars, arrangements are made to serve your meals from the stations en route. One of the best omelets I've had came to me wrapped in a banana leaf from a railway station, as I traveled through the south. The meals can be delivered, as mine was, to the train, or served in railway station's restaurant should you have a layover between trains.

Vendors also board with snacks—best avoided because they are probably not hygienically prepared; the coffee or tea are okay. They come in clay cups to be used and thrown away.

Luggage Indrail allows, free of charge, the following quantity of luggage from the starting station when you buy an adult ticket and half this quantity for a child:

70 kilograms (154 lbs.) in AC First; 50 kilograms (110 lbs.), first class AC sleeper; 40 kilograms (88 lbs.) in AC Chair and sleeper class; and 35 kilograms (77 lbs.) in Second. Luggage is placed in your compartment with you; if it exceeds the acceptable weight, it travels by luggage van attached to the train.

Railway Retiring Rooms Simple retiring rooms are available for a modest fee at all principal railway stations. Tourists can reserve these rooms for a period not exceeding 72 hours from time of occupation. To reserve a room, apply to the station master at your stopover station.

Royal Orient

Take *The Royal Orient Express,* Indian Railways' unique train expedition, between September and April. The fully air-conditioned train journeys for seven days to some cities and sights considered among India's royal experiences, including mighty Chittaugarh Fort; Udaipur, city of lakes; Palitana, a great Jain shrine; Somnath, famous Hindi shore temple; Diu, for a dip in the sea; Sasan-Gir Lion Sanctuary; Junagadh, third-century B.C. Ashoka edict; Ahmedabad, city of mosques and minarets; and Jaipur, princely and pink. Crowning the royal experience are cultural programs at various stops.

The itinerary changes from time to time. The price is $350 per person, per night single occupancy; $200 per night, per person, double sharing; $175 per person per night triple sharing. Accommodation is mainly in coupés with attached toilets, each with a common lounge and bar. For booking and inquiries contact the **Tourism Corporation of Gujarat Ltd.** at one of these addresses: A-6 State Emporia Building, Baba Kharak Singh Marg, **New Delhi** 110001 (☎ 3734015; fax 011-3732482); Nigam Bhavan Sector-16, **Gandhi Nagar** 382016 (☎ 22029; fax 027-1222029); H.K. House, opposite Bata Showroom, Ashram Road, **Ahmedabad** 380009 (☎ 449172; fax 079-428183).

FAST FACTS: India

Alcoholic Beverages There is total prohibition of alcohol only in Gujarat (at this writing). In other states the laws range from certain dry days to no prohibition at all, to other rules restricting drinking—and all these laws change from time to time. None of these need faze you if you have an **All-India Liquor Permit** (issued free at India tourist offices) to produce when you purchase drinks or bottles. You show your permit whenever you purchase a drink or bottle, and your name is recorded in a large Dickensian ledger, along with your permit number and other details. Waiting around for this paperwork, W. C. Fields might have switched to soda. However, there is no problem in buying alcohol from stores in the major cities of India.

Begging Make a contribution at a temple, mosque, or charity if you wish, but the government asks that you not give to beggars who hang around the hotels, restaurants, and shops, and creep up when your car is caught in traffic. You may find it hard to resist some of these pathetic types, but please do. According to my Indian friends, these are professionals who are often more well off than you.

Climate See "When to Go," earlier in this chapter.

Currency See "Visitor Information," earlier in this chapter.

Drug Laws It comes as no surprise to anyone from here to Kathmandu that ganja (marijuana) is readily available in India, where it not only grows but is sold.

What you may not know is that, contrary to popular mythology, the attitude in India is not "anything goes toward smokers," no matter what you've heard. It's not legal to smoke the weed in India unless you're a sadhu or an addict. Discretion is advised: Don't smoke in public, and keep it out of sight wherever you're staying. Searches are conducted from time to time in suspect areas: Paharganj in Delhi, Stuart Lane in Calcutta, and some borders leading to Nepal and Sri Lanka. "Hippie" looks are often associated with soft- and hard-drug problems in the eyes of some Indian authorities. You might want to dress extra-conservatively on days you're apt to cross paths with officialdom.

Electricity Electricity in India is at 220 volts A.C., 50 cycles. You'll need to take a transformer and special plugs for American gadgets; they are not easily available in India. Some of the high-priced hotels have dual current for Western travelers.

Embassies & Consulates The Embassy of the **United States** is in New Delhi, Shanti Path, Chanakyapuri 110021 (☎ **600651**). There are U.S. Consulates General in Bombay at Lincoln House, 78 Bhulabhai Desai Road, Bombay 400026 (☎ 3633611); in Calcutta at 5/1 Ho Chi Minh Sarani, Calcutta 700071 (☎ 223611); and in Madras at 200 Anna Salai (formerly Mount Road), Madras 600006 (☎ 8273040).

Diplomatic missions for other English-speaking countries are also located in New Delhi. For **Australia**: 5/50-F, Shantipath, Chanakyapuri, New Delhi (☎ 603331); for **Canada:** 7/8 Shantipath, Chanakyapuri, New Delhi (☎ 6876500); for **New Zealand:** 50 Nyaya Marg, Chanakyapuri (☎ 462254); for the **United Kingdom:** 50 Shantipath, Chanakyapuri, New Delhi (☎ 600651).

Guides English-speaking guides are available through the India tourist offices throughout the country. For local sightseeing for a group of four or fewer, the fee is Rs 250 ($8.33)for a half-day, Rs 350 ($11.66) for a full day. Guides who speak languages other than English are available in some larger cities and cost Rs 100 ($3.33) extra.

Transportation charges for the guide going out of town are not included in the above fees, nor are entrance charges to museums, monuments, etc. If the guide has to spend the night, the cost of board and lodging is paid by the tourist or group. Government-approved guides are also stationed at some of the country's leading monuments, and nonapproved guides also hang around. If in doubt, ask the guide to produce his certificate issued by the Department of Tourism.

Newspapers/Magazines Most newspapers are privately owned, and of the 25,536 newspapers published in a plethora of languages and dialects, 4,458 are in English. Two major wire services, Press Trust of India and United News of India, relay national news in English. The *International Herald Tribune* and *Wall Street Journal*'s Asian edition are sold in India. There are news, business news, economic, feature, and movie magazines in English throughout the country. In addition, you can buy the Asian editions of *Time* and *Newsweek,* though the prices are high.

Television & Radio Television stations are government run, and programs are sometimes in English. Color television is a fairly recent innovation. Most locally produced programs are on in the evenings; on weekends there are some daytime shows. The top hotels have television sets that are equipped for closed-circuit transmission of a range of videotapes, viewable without extra charge.

The more than 100 stations are in the government-run All India radio network, which reaches 94.96% of the population spread over 83.78% of the country. News is broadcast in English frequently throughout the day.

Time There is a $10^1/_2$-hour time difference between New York and India. In other words it's $5^1/_2$ hours ahead of Greenwich Mean Time.

Tipping Some hotels and restaurants add a service charge to your bill. You might tip over and above this service charge in hotels or bungalows where you have a bearer (personal servant) to see to your every need—a rare occurrence nowadays. Two to five rupees a night would be adequate. In a restaurant where there's a service charge and the service has been exceptionally good, leave some small change as well, perhaps to round out the total.

At hotels and restaurants without service charges, tip 10% to 12.5% for services rendered, unless the bill is moderate, and then probably 5% would do. Tip porters Rs 5 per bag. Tip coat room attendants Rs 5 when you retrieve your coat. Doormen do not get tipped. Give some small change to washroom attendants.

About Rs 50 ($1.66) per day should be given to a driver if he has done an excellent job. This can apply to individual travelers but does not increase when the party is made up of a carload. You might increase the driver's tip to Rs 100 ($3.33) for an especially demanding city assignment, challenging mountainous trip, or complicated multiple-day road journeys. Cab drivers don't get tipped, unless they've performed some special service for you, such as locating a hard-to-find address or watching your packages while you go off to admire the view. There are, however, official luggage charges. Little boys who appear from nowhere to carry packages deserve a rupee or two for their help. Guides receive tips; Rs 50 (1.66) per day is the norm. Sometimes a guide won't accept a tip, but a small gift such as a box of sweets is well received.

Porters at railway stations and airports are supposed to be tipped according to the fixed rate shown on a sign, but they'll hang around trying to get more from foreigners. Where there's no fixed fee, Rs 5 per bag will do.

Don't tip the help who crawl out of the woodwork at some hotels and hover when you leave unless they've actually done something for you.

Finally, a tip for you: Don't overdo when tipping in India. Service in India is far less expensive than it is at home. Five rupees go a long way and are considered a generous tip.

3

Delhi: Where the Tour Begins

From a traveler's point of view, New Delhi is both the best and the worst place to start one's itinerary in India. It's the best because making the transition from a Western environment to an Indian one is easier in a city that is relatively clean and uncluttered (New Delhi is similar in style to Washington, D.C.). It's the worst because in some respects New Delhi is both the least exotic and the least Indian town in India.

Because it's on most international air routes, however, it's where most visitors to India start spending a few pleasant days easing themselves into the leisurely Indian life. Delhi is a major stop for most airlines serving Asia and can be reached with ease from either the East or West Coast of the U.S., Western or Eastern Europe, the U.K., the Middle East, Australia and the Pacific Rim, and East Africa. You can reach Delhi by plane from Nepal, Sri Lanka, Pakistan, Bangladesh, and Afghanistan. Some tourist musts are within one day's trip from the capital, so it makes a suitable base for visiting such spots as Agra (Taj Mahal), Khajuraho (erotic sculptures), and Chandigarh (a Punjab city modernistically designed).

1 Orientation

ARRIVING & DEPARTING

BY PLANE International flights arrive at **Indira Gandhi International Airport**, which is about 20 kilometers southwest of the city center. If you are taking a domestic flight, **Palam** is the domestic terminal, about 4½ kilometers from IGIA. Palam has two terminals; the one just for larger jets is 15 kilometers from the city center.

E.A.T.S. (Ex-Servicemen's Airlink Transport) will transfer you to and from the city/airports by coach. The fare is Rs 20 (60¢) from the domestic terminal (15 kilometers from the center) and Rs 20 (60¢) from the international terminal. There's no extra charge for luggage. The city departures from F-Block, Malhotra Building, Janpath, start at 4am and continue every 30 minutes until 11pm. From the airport, they go to the city from 8:45am to 10:40pm.

There is prepaid taxi service from IGI Airport to city hotels. Tickets are purchased at the **Pre-Paid Taxi Booth.** The charges vary with your destination, but average Rs 120 ($4)—Rs 200 ($6.66) nights—from the international airport and Rs 75 ($2.50) from the domestic terminal to the center of town. Hold on to the receipt, as the driver will need it when you reach your destination.

Depending on your choice of transportation, traveling time from IGIA is between 35 and 70 minutes.

Domestic Airline Numbers The government run **Indian Airlines** has offices on Asaf Ali Road (☎ 3274609); Kanchenjunga Building, 18 Barakhamba Rd. (☎ 3313732); PTI Building, Sansad Marg (☎ 3719168); Malhotra Building, Janpath (☎ 3310517; closed Sundays); Ashok Hotel (☎ 606559); Indira Gandhi International (IGI) Airport, domestic departures (☎ 3295121; open 24 hours); Safdarjang Airport (☎ 4631335; open 24 hours). For prerecorded information, 24 hours a day, call 141 (general); 142 (arrivals); 143 (departures).

Private airlines telephone numbers include: **Archana** (city office, 6829323; airport, 329516; **Damania** (city office, 6888951/6888955; airport, 3295482); **East West** (city office, 3721510; airport, 3295126); **Jagson** (city office, 3721593; airport, 329126); **Jet Airways** (city office, 3724728; airport, 3295402): **Modiluft** (city office, 6430689/5481351; airport, 3295482); **Sahara India Airlines** (city office, 3326851; airport, 3295126)

Sample Domestic Fares Within India, flying nonstop to or from **Bombay** takes under two hours and costs $115; to or from **Calcutta** takes about two hours and costs $132; to or from **Madras** takes 2½ hours and costs $162.

BY TRAIN There are two main stations in Delhi: Old Delhi Station and New Delhi Station. Bus service connects the two. New Delhi Station is in Paharganj, a 25-minute walk from Connaught Circle. It links Delhi to all major destinations in India.

Good Train Choices The best trains include the speedy *Rajdhani Expresses,* which cover the distance in about 18 hours five times a week between New Delhi and **Calcutta** or New Delhi and **Bombay.** The 1,441-kilometer (895-mile) trip between New Delhi and Calcutta's Howrah Station costs Rs 2,400 ($80) in AC First, Rs 705 ($23.50) in AC Chair, and Rs 1,400 ($47) in AC two-tier. Between New Delhi and Bombay Central the distance is 1,542 kilometers (958 miles) and the cost is Rs 2,027 ($67.56) in AC First, Rs 483 ($16) in AC Chair, and Rs 1,104 ($36.80) in AC two-tier.

Among the less expensive (and slower) trains, the *Howrah-Delhi-Kalka Mail* to Calcutta takes 22 hours and costs Rs 1,445 ($48.16) in AC First, Rs 264 ($8.80) in second; from Bombay Central, the *Frontier Mail* takes 24 hours and costs Rs 1,542 ($51.40) in AC First, Rs 264 ($8.80) in second.

From Madras, the *Tamil Nadu Express* covers the 2,195 kilometers (1,363 miles) in 30 hours and costs about Rs 2,564 ($85.46) in AC First, Rs 308 ($10.26) in second.

For reservations in Calcutta, call 263583; in Bombay 291952, 292042, or 375986; and in Madras 132.

The best train ride from New Delhi to **Agra** is the speedy, air-conditioned *Shatabdi Express,* departing daily at 6:15am and arriving at 8:10am, then leaving Agra at 8:21pm and arriving New Delhi at 10pm, for Rs 250 ($8.33) Chair car; Rs 500 ($16.66) Executive one way. Breakfast is included. While the ride is fine, the food is not. Bring a snack.

Penny-wise tip for* Shatabdi *trips: Take the Chair car and save; the extra space and slightly larger meal in Executive class is not worth the extra rupees.

An old standby, the *Taj Express* to Agra, leaves Delhi daily at 7:15am and arrives at Agra at 9:45am, then returns from Agra at 6:45pm, arriving in New Delhi at

New Delhi

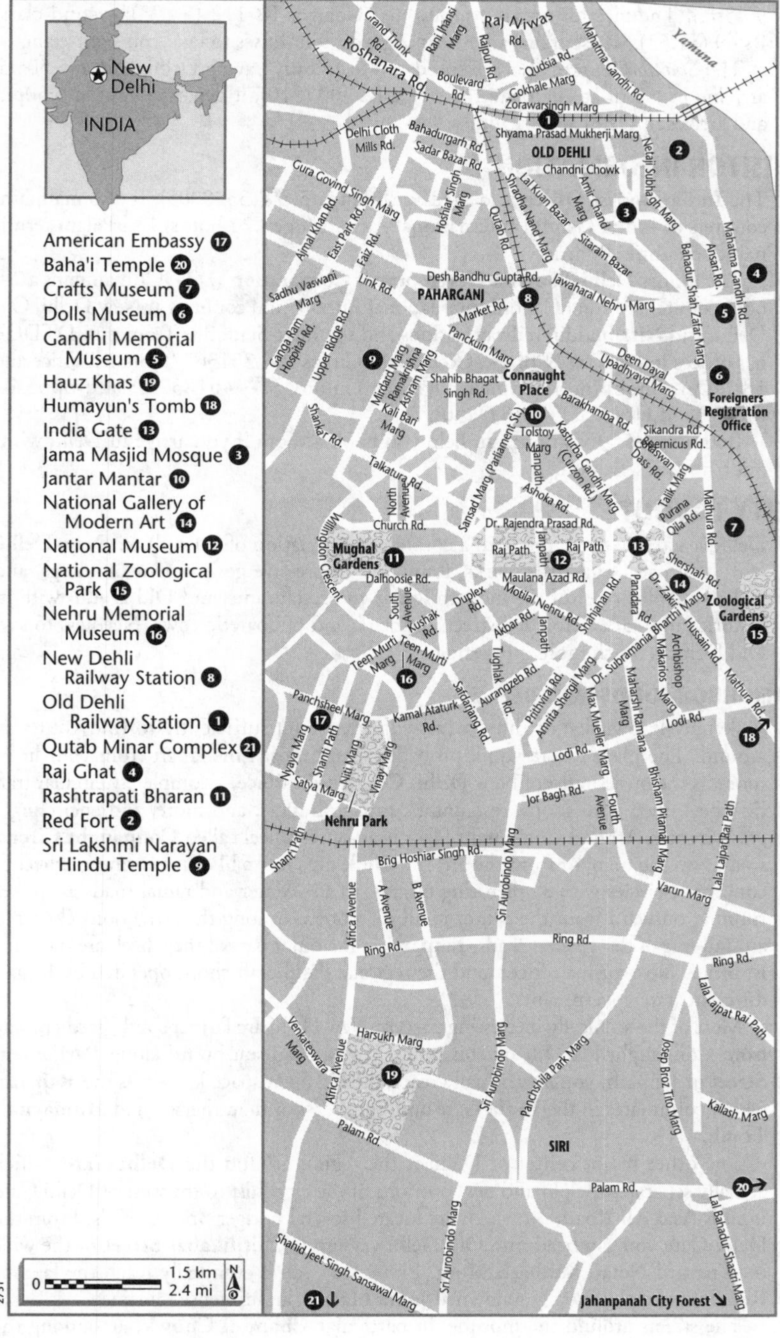

New Delhi
INDIA
American Embassy 17
Baha'i Temple 20
Crafts Museum 7
Dolls Museum 6
Gandhi Memorial Museum 5
Hauz Khas 19
Humayun's Tomb 18
India Gate 13
Jama Masjid Mosque 3
Jantar Mantar 10
National Gallery of Modern Art 14
National Museum 12
National Zoological Park 15
Nehru Memorial Museum 16
New Dehli Railway Station 8
Old Dehli Railway Station 1
Qutab Minar Complex 21
Raj Ghat 4
Rashtrapati Bharan 11
Red Fort 2
Sri Lakshmi Narayan Hindu Temple 9
Yamuna
Grand Trunk Rd.
Rani Jhansi Marg
Raj Niwas Rd.
Rajpur Rd.
Mahatma Gandhi Rd.
Roshanara Rd.
Boulevard Rd.
Qudsia Rd.
Gokhale Marg
Zorawarsingh Marg
Shyama Prasad Mukherji Marg
Delhi Cloth Mills Rd.
Bahadurgarh Rd.
Sadar Bazar Rd.
OLD DEHLI
Netaji Subhagh Marg
Chandni Chowk
Gura Govind Singh Marg
Hoshiar Singh Marg
Lal Kuan Bazar
Shradha Nand Marg
Amir Chand Marg
Qutab Rd.
Ajmal Khan Rd.
East Park Rd.
Faiz Rd.
Sitaram Bazar
Ansari Rd.
Bahadur Shah Zafar Marg
Mahatma Gandhi Rd.
Desh Bandhu Gupta Rd.
Link Rd.
Sadhu Vaswani Marg
PAHARGANJ
Jawaharal Nehru Marg
Market Rd.
Ganga Ram Hospital Rd.
Upper Ridge Rd.
Panckuin Marg
Mirdard Marg
Ramakrishna Ashram Marg
Shahib Bhagat Singh Rd.
Connaught Place
Deen Dayal Upadhyayd Marg
Foreigners Registration Office
Kali Bari Marg
Barakhamba Rd.
Shankar Rd.
Tolstoy Marg
Sansad Marg (Parliament St.)
Janpath
Kasturba Gandhi Marg (Curzon Rd.)
Sikandra Rd.
Copernicus Rd.
Bhagwan Dass Rd.
Talkatura Rd.
Ashoka Rd.
Talik Marg
North Avenue
Willingdon Crescent
Church Rd.
Dr. Rajendra Prasad Rd.
Purana Qila Rd.
Mathura Rd.
Mughal Gardens
Raj Path
Dalhoosie Rd.
Maulana Azad Rd.
Shershah Rd.
Dr. Zakir Hussain Rd.
Zoological Gardens
Duplex Rd.
Motilal Nehru Rd.
Shahjahan Rd.
Panadara Rd.
South Avenue
Kushak Rd.
Akbar Rd.
Dr. Subramania Bharthi Marg
Archbishop Makarios Marg
Teen Murti Marg
Tughlak Rd.
Aurangzeb Rd.
Prithviraj Rd.
Amrita Shergil Marg
Maharshi Ramana Marg
Safdarjang Rd.
Max Mueller Marg
Panchsheel Marg
Kamal Ataturk Rd.
Lodi Rd.
Nyaya Marg
Shanti Path
Niti Marg
Vinay Marg
Satya Marg
Bhisham Pitamah Marg
Jor Bagh Rd.
Fourth Avenue
Nehru Park
Lala Lajpat Rai Path
Shanti Path
Brig Hoshiar Singh Rd.
Sri Aurobindo Marg
Varun Marg
Africa Avenue
A Avenue
B Avenue
Ring Rd.
Venkateswara Marg
Harsukh Marg
Panchshila Park Marg
Josep Broz Tito Marg
Kailash Marg
Palam Rd.
SIRI
Lal Bahadur Shastri Marg
Shahid Jeet Singh Sansawal Marg
Jahanpanah City Forest
0
1.5 km
2.4 mi
N
2731

9:45pm. The fare for an air-conditioned Chair is Rs 112 ($3.73); second-class, Rs 49 ($1.63). These trains are met in Agra by tour buses to take you sightseeing.

The *Shatabdi Express* also will speed you to **Jaipur,** leaving Delhi daily at 5:50am, arriving in Jaipur at 10:20am; the fare is Rs 300 ($10); it departs Jaipur at 5:50pm and arrives in Delhi at 10:15pm.

VISITOR INFORMATION

The **India Tourist Office** is located at 88 Janpath (☎ 3320005). It also maintains counters at Indira Gandhi International Airport (open 24 hours) and Palam terminal (open until 10pm).

The tourist **Delhi Tourism Development Corporation (DTDC)** maintains a 24-hour counter at Indira Gandhi International Airport, and counters at New Delhi, Old Delhi, and Nizamuddin railway stations and the Inter-State Bus Terminus. DTDC's has offices in Delhi at N Block, Connaught Circus (☎ 3313637); branch office and 18 DDA, Shopping Complex, Defence Colony (☎ 4618374); and opposite Moolchand Hospital (☎ 4697250).

Both these organizations can help you book a room if you arrive in Delhi without a hotel reservation.

CITY LAYOUT

Delhi is actually two cities with a combined population of 9.1 million: **New Delhi,** with its broad boulevards, parks, fountains, impressive government buildings, and embassies, plus most of the modern hotels and restaurants; and **Old Delhi,** with its historic landmarks, crowded streets, bazaars, and peripatetic cows. Needless to say, Old Delhi is much more interesting.

NEIGHBORHOODS IN BRIEF

A sketchy knowledge of three areas will orient you sufficiently to find your way around. The place where you'll probably spend most time, apart from your hotel room, is the busiest area of New Delhi, **Connaught Place,** a completely circular traffic wheel lined with shops, restaurants, movie theaters, and more, and encircling a grassy center. Around Connaught Place is an outer wheel called **Connaught Circus,** so that on the map, or from the air, the whole area looks like an enormous wheel of concentric circles with a green ring of grass in the center and radial roads as spokes running outward from the center in all directions. Among the attractions clustered around one of these radial roads, **Janpath,** at the outer part of the wheel, are the tourist office, most airline offices, and the regional handicraft shops operated by India's different state governments.

Most of the scenically interesting parts of New Delhi are farther south (farther away from Connaught Place) from this point. If you head southward along **Parliament Street** or Janpath, you'll eventually reach the big open space known as the **Rajpath,** which culminates in the **India Gate** and, southeast of that, the zoo and **Humayun's Tomb.**

The other major center of Delhi is the region around the **Delhi Gate,** which actually separates the old and new portions of the city. Just to the west of Delhi Gate itself is **Asaf Ali Road,** on which are located several budget-priced hotels. From the Delhi Gate you can head into Old Delhi via either **Chitilikabar Street** or the wide road named **Netaji Subhash Marg.** Either way you'll eventually reach the famous **Red Fort** and the equally renowned **Jama Masjid,** an immense mosque.

The streets around the mosque, in particular **Chandni Chowk,** are among the most interesting of any to be found throughout India. Scores of narrow alleyways run off in all directions and an exploration of any of them is fascinating. Don't worry about getting lost; if you keep going long enough on any street you'll always hit a bigger (wider) one along which you can find a taxi or a motorized ricksha—or something.

Most first-time visitors to Delhi make the mistake of being overly cautious. They allocate one day to taking a sightseeing tour and a visit to Chandni Chowk for shopping, completely forgetting that the Golden Rule for this country is: There's no such thing as a dull Indian street—the less-traveled (by tourists) the street, the more interesting it is.

2 Getting Around

BY BUS **DTC buses,** invariably overcrowded, connect all points in the city via 300 routes; fares are Rs 1 (3¢) to a maximum of Rs 10 (33¢) depending on destination; **matador vans** and **deluxe buses** charge a flat fare with a maximum of around Rs 10 (33¢). There are information desks at all major stops. Or ask conductors or other passengers for help in mapping your route. The latter can end up in a committee discussion, so make sure you get the right route. Buses are usually packed to overflowing, so you will probably seek other transportation.

BY TAXI AND RICKSHA Both four-seater yellow-top **taxis** and three-wheel, two-seater, semienclosed scooter **rickshas** are metered. It's always a good idea to make sure the driver flags down the meter before you take off. Officially, the taxi meter should start at Rs 7 (23¢) and the scooter ricksha at Rs 4.40 (15¢). Meters have not been calibrated for a long time; their starting fares will be Rs 5 (16¢) and Rs 3 (1¢), respectively, and your final fare will come to about 50% over the meter. For both taxis and scooters, additional charges at night are 25% between llpm and 5am; for luggage, 50 paise for packages weighing over 20 kilograms (44 lbs.); waiting charges are 10 paise for every three minutes or part thereof. The first 15 minutes are free. When in doubt about your fare, ask to see the driver's rate card for verification. If you think you have been overcharged or have any other complaints about taxi or scooter ricksha drivers, call 3319334 (24 hours). Neither taxi nor motorized ricksha drivers are tipped. But so many tourists have been tipping them, some drivers seem to expect it from foreigners. Be firm.

Six-seater scooter rickshas, found around Connaught Place and near popular neighborhood shopping centers, take off when they get a load of passengers going the same way. Supposedly, they charge by the sector. For example, from Connaught Place to Red Fort, about Rs 5 (16¢) to Rs 10 (33¢). But to be on the safe side, set the fare before you get in.

Tongas and **cycle rickshas** operate in Old Delhi; bargain for a fair fare.

Always make sure your driver understands where you're going before you get in. And if you take one of the share vehicles, know where it's heading before you take off. You can usually find someone to interpret if the driver does not understand English. And, if not, a little pantomime goes a long way toward international understanding everywhere in India.

BY HIRED CAR A small, non–air-conditioned car with driver will cost Rs 480 ($16) for eight hours and 80 kilometers; Rs 350 ($11.66) for four hours, 40 kilometers. Extra kilometers cost Rs 4.30 ($1.43) per kilometer; and Rs 25 (83¢) per hour. These prices were quoted by ITDC's Ashok Travel and Tours at the Ashok Hotel. Before you hire a car and driver, consult the India Tourist Office, 88 Janpath (☎ 3320005), for a list of approved operators.

DRIVING YOURSELF Most tourists feel more comfortable navigating the exotic traffic jams with a driver, but should you wish to be behind the wheel, **Budget Rent-A-Car** (☎ 3318600); **Hertz** (☎ 3318695); and **Europcar** (☎ 603400) will put you in the driver's seat. Check the listings in the yellow pages for locations.

BY BICYCLE Several bicycle rental shops are near Minto Bridge, off Connaught Place, and on Mohan Singh Place (near Rivoli Cinema), and in Paharganj. Rentals cost from Rs 5 (16¢) per hour to Rs 30 ($1) a day, plus a refundable deposit.

FAST FACTS: Delhi

Alcohol Alcoholic beverages are available without a permit at bottle shops. They are also served in bars and restaurants of major hotels. A few restaurants outside of hotels serve liquor; a substantial number serve beer, however, which complements spicy foods. Dry days are the first and seventh of every month and three national holidays, when bottle shops are closed and consumption of alcohol is prohibited in public places.

American Express A central American Express office is located in A Block, Connaught Place (☎ 3327617).

Drugstores (Chemists Shops) The Super Bazar Medical Store, Connaught Circus (☎ 3314176); AIIMS, Ansar Nagar (☎ 661123); and Spring Meadows Chemists, F-44 East of Kailash (☎ 6410347) are open 24 hours a day.

Currency Exchange Major hotels will change money for guests 24 hours a day. The Central Bank of India branch at the Ashok Hotel (☎ 675469) and State Bank of India at IGI Airport are both open 24 hours a day. Otherwise banks are open 10am to 2pm Monday through Friday, and 10am to noon on Saturdays. They can be very busy, so you may have to wait a long time to exchange your money. Whenever you change your currency into rupees be sure to get receipts. You will be asked for them when you leave India and want to convert your rupees into dollars or other foreign currency. You also have to show your exchange receipts if you pay your hotel bills in Indian rupees in high-priced hotels. For overall rates and rules about rupees, see Chapter 1, "Getting to Know India."

Dentist Embassies and consulates have lists of dentists and can help you locate one in an emergency.

Doctor Embassies and consulates have lists of doctors; most hotels (except the lowest budget choices) have doctors on call.

Health Clubs Not in budget hotels, but for a fee you might use clubs in the posh hotels. Some hotels permit guests and members only to use facilities; you'll have to inquire directly. They are, like many U.S. hotel facilities, limited to a few machines, Jacuzzis and steamrooms/sauna; here yoga and massage are also on their agendas. Some clubs do not allow men and women to work out together; most attract men only. In India, the sight of a woman working out is still rare.

Magazines *Illustrated Weekly of India* is a news feature magazine with some interesting articles. *India Today* is the most popular of the local news magazines. Business news is covered by *Business India.* However, if you've been traveling a lot, you might be interested in the periodicals at the American Library, 24 Kasturba Gandhi Marg (☎ 3316841, open Monday to Saturday, 9:30am to 6pm). The Asian editions of *Time, Newsweek, International Herald Tribune,* and a few other Western periodicals can be found in the bookstalls at many larger hotels as well as many bookshops.

Mail Can be received at Post Restante, GPO (care of Postmaster), Baba Kharak Singh Marg, New Delhi 110001 (be sure to specify *New* Delhi), 8am to 7pm; at the Tourist Office, 88 Janpath, New Delhi 110001; and at American Express, Wenger House, A-Block, Connaught Place, New Delhi 110001.

Newspapers Every city and large town has at least one and often two or three English-language papers. The nationally circulated ones are *Hindustan Times* (Delhi), *Times of India* (Delhi and Bombay), *Statesman* (Delhi and Calcutta), *Indian Express* (Madras and Bombay), and *The Hindu* (Madras). *The Asian Age,* published daily in London, Delhi, Bombay, and Calcutta, is a sophisticated cross cultural mix of arts, entertainment features, hard news, and editorials.

Postage and Fax Services Foreign airmail letter rate is Rs 11 (36¢); Pakistan, Rs 6 (20¢); an Aerogramme is Rs 6.50 (21¢). Airmail post cards are Rs 6 (20¢). It takes about 10 to 14 days for airmail from India to arrive in the United States. Stamps can be purchased at most hotels. (Either make sure you see the stamp is to affixed to your mail and put in the hotel post box or personally affix the stamp and mail the item.) Purchasing stamps at the post office involves waiting in a long line and hanging around while the clerk prepares a detailed receipt even for the smallest one-stamp purchase. Less crowded are the post office hotel branch at the Ashok, Ashok Yatri Niwas, Kanishka, and Lodhi—very handy if you purchase something super-sized in the bazaar and would rather ship it than schlepp it home.

Speed Post, available at 22 centers, delivers mail to 39 countries within 24 to 72 hours from time of booking. There is a money-back guarantee in case of late deliveries. There is also same-day service within Delhi. This service is available at several Delhi locations; call 3295499 for information.

Fax facilities are available at the main telegraph offices and in some top hotels.

Radio News in English is broadcast periodically throughout the day, from 8am to 9pm. Special bulletins are broadcast in English when something extra newsworthy occurs.

Republic Day Tickets in the seating enclosures for the big event, on January 26, cost Rs 10 (33¢) to Rs 200 ($6.66). Tickets for the "Beating of the Retreat," which closes the festivities, are Rs 10 (33¢) to Rs 20 (55¢). Children under 12 are admitted to both at no charge. Consult the India Tourist Office, 88 Janpath, for details and reservations.

Shoeshine Indians usually spend Rs 5. If you're a tourist, shoe shiners will pretend it isn't enough.

Stand-in Rail Reservations Waiting in line to make train reservations is a fact of life in India, and a real drag. Cox and Kings travel agents, Indra Palace, H-Block, Connaught Circus (☎ 3320067), will send a stand-in to wait while you go out and admire the sights. Ask for the Outbound Tour Department and you will be charged a percentage of the ticket.

Student Information Center Located in the Students Travel Centre, Hotel Imperial, Janpath (☎ 3327528), is the place to go to renew or apply for international student identity cards.

Swimming Most budget hotels don't have swimming pools, but budget travelers can still be in the swim by paying a daily rate at some posh hotels; Maurya Sheraton (solar heated), Imperial, Claridges, Ashok, and Samrat charge a daily fee from around Rs 100 ($3.33) to Rs 250 ($8.50). To find out about swimming at other hotels check with them directly. Changing rooms and towels are available at the hotels. Most hotels drain their pools during the winter months.

Telephones Pay phones take a Rs 1 coin, and are found in shops, shopping centers, and airports—but they are in short supply. If there's no pay phone around, shopkeepers charge Rs 3 to Rs 5 (2¢) for a call, and the receptionist or person in charge of guest relations at any good hotel will let you use a phone for a small fee, or free of charge for a quick local call. You can dial most cities in India directly now (service has steadily improved over the years); also Japan, the United States, and many European and some southeast Asian countries. However, direct dialing overseas is one thing; getting through is quite another. Circuits are often busy.

Television There are a host of channels developing on cable TV with programs from the wee hours to 11:30pm. You'll find news and feature programming, and live telecasts of important events. Hotels in medium to upper price ranges have installed televisions in guest rooms; in some lowest price places, there are television rooms. Closed-circuit television is also being used in midrange to pricey hotels to show Indian films in which songs and dances stand in for hugs and kisses. Western films and reruns of TV programs such as *L.A. Law* also are channeled into hotel rooms as are news and features from the BBC and CNN. Television takes over lives during cricket season when sets are on everywhere all day long.

Temperatures In the summer, the temperature in Delhi ranges from 70°F to 100°F; in winter, from 45°F to 90°F.

Tipping In Delhi, a service charge is added to bills at some hotels and restaurants, and any tip above that is at your own discretion. Otherwise tip around 10%. Private car drivers who've done an excellent job get Rs 50 ($1.66) to Rs 100 ($3.33) a day, depending on the difficulty of the assignment. (For instance, mountainous driving merits Rs 100 to Rs 150.) Don't ask your guide's advice about tipping your driver, as you may end up paying a sum large enough to be split between the two of them. Some guides prefer small gifts of something they may need or admire, instead of a rupee tip. For overall tipping advice, see Essential Information in Chapter 1.

Tourist Guides Book guides through the India Tourist Office, 88 Janpath (☎ 3320005); the fees for one to four persons for one-half day is Rs 250 ($8.33), Rs 350 ($11.66) for a full day. This includes a lunch allowance. Foreign language fee is an additional Rs 100 ($3.33).

Weather Delhi's top season is from mid-October through March. April, May, and June are very hot. The rainy season is roughly June through September. November through January is pleasant, with clear skies and cool to chilly temperatures. February is lovely and springlike.

Yoga Classes in yoga are free of charge at Vishwayatan Yoga Ashram, Ashok Road (☎ 3718866), opposite Gurdwara Rakabganj. Hours are from 6 to 9am and 4 to 6pm every day, except Saturday evenings and Sunday.

3 Where to Stay

Even with business travelers from here to Timbuktu who have been filling all the hotels at every price year-round since India liberalized its economic policies, bargains are still here in lodging and meals (see "Where to Eat," below, for restaurant suggestions), and with a little planning you can find comfort, convenience and, at times, charm in some of the most affordable places. Such hotels are much appreciated by visitors, so you have to make reservations. The most central areas for budget-conscious rooms are in and about Connaught Circus or the New Delhi Railway Station.

Should you arrive without reservations, visit the India Tourist Office and DTDC representatives at the airports, and DTDC representatives at the railway stations in Old and New Delhi and at the Interstate Bus Station. They'll telephone around to help you find a place to stay. But it takes time and don't be surprised if you have to overpay for an underrated room.

In town, the **India Tourist Office,** 88 Janpath (☎ 3320005), will try to help as well with hotels and all kinds of touristic information.

A number of Delhi families welcome paying guests to their homes. Should you be interested, the **Government of India Tourist Office,** 88 Janpath, New Delhi (☎ 3320005) has a complete list.

Finally, hotel taxes take a bite of your budget: There's a 10% luxury tax; to which big spenders can add a 10% expenditure tax on room rates over Rs 1,200 per night; some hoteliers also levy a l0% service charge. (See Chapter 2, "Planning a Trip to India," for more general information on hotels.) If you go over budget on your room, there are good, cheap places to eat in Delhi to you keep costs in line.

When you look through these hotel suggestions, keep one thing in mind. For most of you, Delhi will be your first stop in India after a long and tiring international flight. You might especially want to think of comfort before budget. As throughout this book, the cheapest accommodations are presented first, but these are not always the most charming or comfortable: Finding a hotel room for two for around $50 will still allow you to meet a $45 a day budget quite easily—and you will have some more pleasant choices.

IN & AROUND CONNAUGHT PLACE

DOUBLES FOR LESS THAN $20

If you want to save money, then these clean, neat, and/or cheap accommodations are located in and about Connaught Place. However, attached bathrooms are no longer de rigueur at the following, and neither are hot and cold running water, room telephones, television, currency-exchange permits, restaurants, or bars.

At the 558-room **Ashok Yatri Niwas,** 19 Ashok Road, New Delhi 110001 (☎ 3324511; fax 3324253) about 1¹/₂ miles from the New Delhi Railway Station and half a mile from Connaught Place, management apparently feels that less is more when it comes to lighting, service, and maintenance. Still, beautiful views from the rooms on the upper floors and low rates almost obscure the negatives, and here you do get an attached bath as well as hot and cold running water. Singles are Rs 375 ($12.50); doubles, Rs 400 ($13.33). You need reservations. Other pluses are 24-hour money changing, post office, shopping arcade, and two bargain restaurants: a no-frills cafeteria and the more interesting Coconut Grove's regional cuisines (see "Where to Eat," below).

The budget crowd makes a beeline up one flight to the 18-room **Hotel Palace Heights,** D Block, Connaught Circus, New Delhi 110001 (☎ 3321369 or 3321419), which is accessible by elevator. Breakfast can be sent in for a modest charge, but meals are not served here (although there are numerous inexpensive restaurants nearby). Rates for singles are Rs 190 ($6.33) to Rs 225 ($7.50), for doubles Rs 310 ($10.33) to Rs 510 ($17). Higher prices are for a bigger room or attached bathroom. There is no service charge; air cooling is free, as is hot water, which is provided in buckets; there is a small charge for a heater (needed in winter).

DOUBLES FOR $50 OR LESS

You can still get quite a bang for your 50 bucks (often less)—such amenities as attached bathrooms with hot and cold running water, telephones, air-conditioning, television, multichannel music, room and laundry service, sometimes mini-refrigerators; most hotels in this price range accept major international and local credit cards and have restaurants and bars. A few offer tennis courts and swimming pools. Reservations are a must.

Where else but in India can two can stay in four-star digs for Rs 1,450 ($48) at **Nirula's Hotel,** L-Block, Connaught Circus, Delhi 100 001 (☎ 3322419; fax 324669). Tidy rooms have every modern amenity but evoke the Raj era of the building's origins in dark woods and printed chintz. Portraits of sugary sweet-looking Victorian ladies decorate one of the main corridors, and Victorian scenes are elsewhere. Single rooms are Rs 1,000 ($33.33); deluxe doubles Rs 1,600 ($53.33). Reservations are a must. The hotel's **Potpourri** restaurant is a popular meeting place; Nirula's also is famous for its ice cream parlor, pastry shop, and quick-service snack bar that ring its base (see "Where to Eat," below).

Nudging farther up the budgetary scale, **Hotel Marina,** G-59 Connaught Circus, New Delhi 110001 (☎ 3324658; fax 3328609), with antique French tapestries hung in marble halls and a sweeping marble staircase, attracts a sophisticated European clientele to its clean, well-appointed rooms. Rs 1,190 ($39.66) to Rs 1,320 ($44) single; Rs 1,600 ($53.33) to Rs 1,800 ($60) double. Conference room.

Hotel Alka, 16/90 Connaught Circus, New Delhi 110001 (☎ 344328; fax 3732796), is centrally air-conditioned and has carpeting, modern furnishings, and an overall cozy feeling. There are 22 rooms, 5 singles, 14 doubles, and 3 deluxe (meaning rooms face outside and have velvet draperies). Rates range from Rs 950 ($21.66) to Rs 1,450 ($48.33). The **Vega** restaurant serves excellent North Indian vegetarian dishes (see "Where to Eat," below).

The unkempt, ill-lit hallway leading to the **Hotel Asian International,** Janpath Lane, New Delhi 110001 (☎ 3321636; fax 3323077), gives no clue to the neat, tidy rooms that make this one of the nicest budget places in the city. Singles are Rs 600 ($20); doubles Rs 900 ($30). The Bhagat family, owners of the hotel, personally see that guests are happy and comfortable. The hotel's **Bamboo Hut** restaurant serves hotel guests only.

York Hotel, K Block, Connaught Circus, New Delhi 110001 (☎ 3323769; fax 3352419), with an upstairs location, is off the bustling street. Renovations have improved the reception area; silk wall panels have been added as a backdrop and the rooms, which have modern furniture, have been painted and the bathrooms updated. Rates are Rs 800 ($27) for singles, Rs 1,200 ($40) for doubles.

Hotel Fifty-Five, H-55 Connaught Circus, New Delhi 110001 (☎ 3321244; fax 3320769), has a pleasant terrace off the second floor, and 15 fairly clean, vest pocket–size rooms. Rates are $16 single and $22 double. There is 24-hour meal and drink service. No credit cards.

Host Inn, F-33 Connaught Place, New Delhi 110001 (☎ 3310704), above the **Host** restaurant, has 10 rooms with simple modern furnishings, but the corridors need better maintenance. Singles run Rs 750 ($25) to $800 ($27); doubles Rs 850 ($28.33) to Rs 950 ($32).

In the same price range is the 40-room **Hotel Jukaso Inn Downtown,** L-I Connaught Circus, New Delhi 110001 (☎ 3324451; fax 3324448). Management has added potted plants in the public rooms, but they should also paint the hall walls on the second-floor terrace. The decor pleasantly blends period and modern pieces and textiles hung like pictures. Rooms have every comfort, from attached bathrooms to Video Vision on their TVs. Singles are Rs 850 ($28.33) to Rs 950 ($32); doubles Rs 1,100 ($37) to Rs 1,200 ($42); the suite Rs 1,500 ($50). A tiny dining area adjoins the small lounge.

A three-minute walk from Connaught Place, **Centre Point,** 13 Kasturba Gandhi Marg, New Delhi, 110001 (☎ 3324895; fax 3320138) is in $45 a day territory for two sharing a standard double, Rs 1,400 ($46.66). Some of the 32 rooms are windowless, as are the duplexes. There's a lot of decor everywhere: platform beds with satin spreads; heavy period reproduction furniture, velvets, and silks; crewel wall coverings in the duplexes. Superior singles are Rs 1,100 ($36.66) to Rs 1,300 ($43.33); superior doubles Rs 1,800 ($60); duplexes Rs 2,200. ($73.33); all these rates include continental breakfast. Conference room.

Guest Houses

Guest houses behind the Government of India Tourist Office are headquarters for young backpackers and other penny-pinchers. Here, you can get by for $20 a day. While they won't do for the overly fastidious (look at a couple of rooms before checking in), they're fine if you're not fussy or concerned with ambience, and perfect if you want to connect with other young Westerners. In any of these, it is a good idea to come equipped with your own soap, towel, and lock for your room (they may not be provided).

While the hotel's card described the rooms as beautifully furnished, the **Janpath Guest House,** 82 Janpath, New Delhi 110011 (☎ 3321935), has simple, clean rooms and rates to match: Tariffs range from singles for Rs 275 ($9.16) to a double deluxe at Rs 650 ($22). The higher rates are for air-conditioned rooms. Of the 25 rooms, 23 have attached bathrooms. Hot water is solar-heated; there are steamy buckets full on cloudy days.

Among the most long-lived and popular guest houses are these three in Scindia House on Kasturba Gandhi Marg, all with 110001 pin postal codes. **Ringo,** no. 17 (☎ 3310605), has a pleasant outdoor courtyard. Cubicle rooms are Rs 210 ($7) to Rs 260 ($8.70) with attached baths; Rs 160 ($5.33) to Rs 180 ($6) with shared bath; dorm (extremely close quarters) Rs 60 ($2); on rooftop, Rs 50 ($1.67). Be sure to observe the checkout time. While looking around, I saw an ugly scene between the manager and a Western guest. She had slightly overstayed the deadline and he was insisting on a full day's tariff for her few minutes' infraction. **Sunny Guest House,** No. 152 (☎ 3312909), has rates a few rupees lower than Ringo's.

Similar spartan but tidier conditions prevail at **Asia Guest House,** no. 14 (☎ 3313393), where pluses are attached bathrooms with hot water and attentive management.

The clean, austere rooms of **Gandhi Guest House,** 80 Tolstoy Marg, New Delhi 110001 (☎ 332113), are located in a building more than 100 years old. The seven doubles and two singles have no private bathrooms, and hot water is on tap in winter only.

The 10-room **Prem Sagar Guest House,** Block P-11, First Floor, Connaught Circus, New Delhi 100001 (☎ 345263; fax 345263), offers higher-priced comforts such as wall-to-wall carpeting at no-frills rates: Rs 600 ($20) single and Rs 800 ($27) double. Manager-owner Shirpa Singh keeps everything tidy. A roof terrace is another plus. Room service for meals. No credit cards.

YMCAs near Connaught Place

The resortlike **YMCA,** Jai Singh Road, New Delhi 110001 (☎ 311915; fax 3746032), a 10-minute stroll from Connaught Place, with gardens, a swimming pool, tennis courts, and a shopping arcade, is open to adults and families and one of the best buys around, even if many of the rooms need fresh paint. Single occupancy runs Rs 295 ($9.83) to Rs 400 (13.33); double occupancy Rs 500 ($17) to Rs 880

($29.33). Lower-priced rooms don't have air-conditioning or private bathrooms and could benefit from paint jobs. Rates include continental breakfast. There's a Rs 10 (33¢) transient membership fee, service charge of 5% on room tariff, and 7% sales tax on meals. Book in advance. Major credit cards.

At the **YWCA International Guest House,** Sansad Marg (formerly Parliament Street), New Delhi 110001 (☎ 311561 or 311662), the rooms could use a coat of paint, but are clean and bargains to boot when you consider they include air-conditioning, little verandahs, telephones, and private bathrooms; all for Rs 300 ($10) single, Rs 500 ($17) double. The 24-room complex caters to both genders and families. Service charge is 10%, and breakfast costs Rs 45 ($1.50). No credit cards.

NEAR THE NEW DELHI RAILWAY STATION

DOUBLES FOR LESS THAN $20

Unless otherwise indicated, hotels have attached bathrooms, telephones, and televisions; some have gift shops and barber shops and accept credit cards. Hotels in this area are about a 20-minute walk from Connaught Place.

Hotel Tourist, Ram Nagar, New Delhi 110055 (☎ 7510334), is set off the street by a driveway and a strip of garden, and plants decorate the first-floor hall. The hotel tends to be noisy and it could do with a paint job, but the price is right, especially when you know that all rooms have such amenities as attached bathrooms and television: Rs 275 ($9.16) to Rs 500 ($16.66) single; Rs 375 ($12.50) to Rs 600 ($20) double; higher rates for rooms with air-conditioning—Rs 375 ($12.50) to Rs 600 ($20). There's a vegetarian restaurant on the premises.

Next door, the similarly named **Hotel Tourist Deluxe** (☎ 770985), is newer, and both slightly more expensive and better maintained. However, the gleam stops in the white marble lobby; the hotel is not for the overly fastidious.

The Nest, Corner House, 11 Qutab Rd., Ram Nagar, New Delhi, 110055 (☎ 7512575; fax 5732664), has 18 rooms with baths attached and 24-hour hot and cold water. Nine rooms are air-conditioned, at Rs 650 ($21.66) single, and Rs 750 ($25) double; without air-conditioning, Rs 450 ($15) and Rs 550 ($18) for single or double, respectively. In-house bank and travel desk; 15% discount May to July.

The four-story, 58-room **Hotel Ajanta,** 36 Arakashan Rd. (behind Shiela Cinema), Ram Nagar, New Delhi 110055 (☎ 7520925), has simple rooms with prices similar to the others near the New Delhi Railway Station. It's nicely situated across from a municipal park. In case this hotel is full, the owners' relatives run other guest houses in the area.

THE PAHARGANJ AREA

DOUBLES FOR LESS THAN $15

About a mile west of the New Delhi Railway Station and a 25-minute walk from Connaught Place is the *Paharganj* area, a main shopping center, with row upon row of fruit and food stalls and a number of moderate- to low-priced hotels where rooms run about Rs 150 ($5) to Rs 200 ($6.66) single, and Rs 200 ($6.66) to Rs 400 ($13.33) double (lower if you bargain). There are lower-priced rooms as well, with even more minimal comforts and cleanliness. Still, some of the most casual travelers don't mind putting up with primitive conditions. You must eat out. The best strategy is to look at a room or two before checking in so you can see what you're getting. I offer two of the better selections.

Worn around the edges, with faded wallpaper and in need of a paint job—but given high marks for warmth and friendliness—is **Hotel Natraj,** Chitra Gupta Road,

Paharganj, New Delhi 110055 (☎ 522699). The compact rooms have seen better days but are fairly clean. Service charge is 10%. It's centrally air-conditioned.

The 50-room **Vivek Hotel,** 1550 Main Bazaar, Paharganj, New Delhi 110055 (☎ 523015 or 7777062; fax 7522410), has a fancy lobby off a dismal entryway. Rooms are small and basic, but a bit better maintained than others in this area, and all but five have bathrooms attached. You get hot water on tap only in the deluxe rooms; otherwise it comes in buckets upon request. There is 24-hour room service.

ELSEWHERE IN NEW DELHI

DOUBLES FOR LESS THAN $30

Behind the bustling Main Market, **Lexus Holiday Inn,** E-25 South Extension Part 1, New Delhi, 110049 (☎ 4631765; fax 5437247), has the friendly S. K. Maker, whose title is "managing worker" at the helm. Rooms have the basics, plus attached bathrooms and frills not always found at modestly priced places, such as refrigerators, air-conditioning, telephones, and color TVs. Rates are Rs 595 ($19.83) single, Rs 695 ($23.16) double; add about Rs 100 ($10) more for deluxe rooms. Light snacks and thali meals (Indian foods arrayed on a platter)—Rs 60 ($2) vegetarian, Rs 80 ($40) non-vegetarian—are served in rooms, and there are a number of inexpensive restaurants nearby. Add Rs 50 ($1.66) to Rs 60 ($2) for motorized ricksha runs to Connaught Place.

DOUBLES FOR $50 OR LESS

Attached baths, air-conditioning, and televisions—the alphabet of tourist comforts—are available throughout these hotels, as well as telephones, channel music, currency exchange, and room service; some offer room refrigerators, swimming pools, gardens, restaurants, and bars. Most accept major international and local credit cards.

It's hard to find a room for around $40 in surroundings as atmospheric as **The Oberoi Maidens,** 7 Sham Nath Marg (formerly Alipur Road), New Delhi 110054 (☎ 2525464; fax 2929800), bordering on Old Delhi, a 12-minute, motorized, metered ricksha ride from Connaught Place—Rs 50 ($1.66). Set in well-tended gardens, with a swimming pool and tennis courts, this historic hotel is in superb condition. Its spacious rooms are well appointed with dark wood furniture, and some have dressing rooms and windows into hallways for additional light and ventilation. Singles $38; doubles $75. Photos in the Curzon Room restaurant evoke the Raj era of this hotel's earliest heyday.

The Ambassador Hotel, Sujan Singh Park, New Delhi 110003 (☎ 4632600; fax 4632254), in the Taj Group, is on the edge of cool and green Sujan Singh Park and the Delhi Zoo. This old hotel is being updated and renovated in stages. Currently, the rooms are more spacious than some newer hotels and contain some nice old pieces of furniture. They have all amenities and comfortable rates: $39 single, $59 double. There's a 10% service charge. The renowned South Indian restaurant Dasaprakash, has a branch here and well worth trying (see "Where to Eat," below). There is a conference/banquet room.

The pleasant **Tourist Holiday Home,** at 7 Link Rd., Jangpura, New Delhi 110014 (☎ 4625750; fax 3030170), has 18 simply furnished, air-conditioned rooms, 16 with private attached bathrooms, all with attractive price tags: Rs 280 ($9.33) single, Rs 300 ($10) to Rs 800 ($27) double. There is a 10% service charge.

Where Old and New Delhi meet, the ITDC's **Hotel Ranjit,** Maharaja Ranjit Singh Road, New Delhi 110002 (☎ 3311256; fax 3713165), was about to undergo a much-needed makeover and may be all spruced up by now. Check it out. Its location is superb, just a short metered, motorized ricksha drive from the Red Fort and Chandni Chowk, the old bazaar with lanes bursting with silver, ivory, and brocades. From many of individual covered balconies off the 186 rooms—Rs 500 ($16.67) to Rs 600 ($20) single, Rs 700 ($23.33) to Rs 900 ($30) double— you can see the immense Jama Masjid, India's largest mosque. The hotel restaurants were also being renovated and reconceptualized. To the Connaught area, a ricksha should cost around Rs 50 ($1.67), or it's a 10-minute walk.

ITDC's **Lodhi Hotel,** Lala Lajpat Rai Marg, New Delhi 110003 (☎ 362422), is named for the nearby Lodi Tombs and lovely gardens (see its description under "Gardens," below). It has 207 rather undistinguished modern rooms, but a nice garden with a swimming pool, and is about 7 kilometers from the center. Rates are Rs 850 ($28.33) single, Rs 1,100 ($36.66) to Rs 1,300 ($43.33) double. The **Sagar Ratna** restaurant has delicious South Indian food (see "Where to Eat," below).

The pleasant but simple **Sartaj,** A-3 Green Park, New Delhi 110016 (☎ 667759; fax 686240), has a tiled mural on the outside and a small coffee shop adjacent to the lounge, set off by artificial flowers. Near the All-India Medical Institute and on the road to the famous Qutb Minar tower, the hotel is about a Rs 55 ($1.83) taxi ride from Connaught Place. The rates are Rs 590 ($19.67) single, Rs 750 ($25) double, and up to Rs 1,050 ($35) for a deluxe (larger) double room. Ask about off-season discounts from May to June.

Guest Houses

Guest houses usually do not have restaurants or spacious lobbies or lounges, which is why they are classified as guest houses and not hotels. Snacks, beverages, and light meals are generally available through room service. They have many comforts and amenities such as attached bathrooms, air-conditioning, telephones, and televisions.

Amid the mansions in elegant Sunder Nagar are a number of guest houses (three of the best below) as well as the posh and pricey Sunder Nagar Market (see "Shopping," below).

Maharani, 3 Sunder Nagar, New Delhi 110003 (☎ 4693128), has a rooftop terrace and tidy rooms, some with white-painted carved furniture; rates are Rs 800 ($26.66) single, Rs 1,000 ($33.33) double, Rs 1,100 ($36.66) double deluxe.

Not quite as spiffy, **Shervani Fort View,** 11 Sunder Nagar, New Delhi 110003 (☎ 4611771; fax 4694228), is a pleasant place with 16 doubles and suites—all in need of a fresh coat of paint—and rates from Rs 775 ($25.83) single to Rs 1,400 ($46.66) for a deluxe suite. There is an old fort to view.

At **Jukaso Inn,** 50 Sunder Nagar, New Delhi 110003 (☎ 4692137), the approach to the rooms is through an interior courtyard with trailing vines; the inn needs better maintenance and a friendlier receptionist. All rooms are doubles: single occupancy Rs 800 ($26.66), double occupancy Rs 1,250 ($41.66), up to Rs 1,740 ($58) for a suite. Near the inn, **Sweet Corners** has a tempting array of caloric treats. There is a **Jukaso Inn Downtown** as well and in better shape.

HOTELS IN OLD DELHI

Doubles for Less Than $50

New Delhi postal zones aside, these are Old Delhi hotels. Two of the three accept popular international and local credit cards. All offer attached bathrooms, air-conditioning, telephones, TV, and music channels. And remember that in all but the lowest-budget hotels, foreigners pay in U.S. dollars, even if the room is charged to a credit card.

Straddling both Old and New Delhi—and halfway around the world from New York—the nice, neat, clean budget **Hotel Broadway,** Asaf Ali Road, New Delhi

110002 (☎ 3273821; fax 3269966), has a New York accent. The corridors are decorated with three sheets of stage plays and photos of movie stars such as Marilyn Monroe and Cary Grant, whose films played at Broadway theaters. Rooms at the back face Old Delhi and have fabulous views of the Red Fort and Jama Masjid; the front faces New Delhi. Furnished in quiet, functional good taste, they cost Rs 595 ($19.83) single, Rs 725 ($24.16) single occupancy in a double, Rs 925 ($30.83) double; credit cards accepted. The Chor Bizarre restaurant rates a visit (see "Where to Eat," below). There is a conference room, and currency exchange is available.

Up a flight of stairs off the busy street, **Flora,** Dayanand Marg, Daryaganj, New Delhi 110002 (☎ 3273634; fax 3280887), is a modest place with friendly management and clean, small, simply furnished rooms. They are air-conditioned, and there is hot and cold running water in the attached bathrooms, some with Western-style toilets. The rates are Rs 300 to Rs 320 ($10 to $10.66) single, Rs 610 to Rs 630 ($21.10 to $22.20) double. No credit cards.

CHEAP ALTERNATIVES—CAMPING & A YOUTH HOSTEL

New Delhi Tourist Camping, at J. Nehru Marg, opposite JP Narayan Hospital, New Delhi 110002 (☎ 3272898), has neat, clean rooms with basic furniture in little huts dotting the lawns and gardens. Singles are Rs 90 ($3); doubles, Rs 130 ($4.33). Your own tent will run Rs 25 (83¢). There is a restaurant serving budget-priced meals in Indian, Chinese, and Continental styles; hot showers and money-changing facilities, too. The camp's travel agency runs city sightseeing tours as well as excursions to popular destinations away from Delhi. The EATS buses to the airports stop here 16 times a day; the fare is Rs 25 to Rs 35 (83¢ to $1.16), the higher rate to the international terminal.

Another Tourist Camping Park at Qudsia Gardens, opposite the Interstate Bus Terminal, is cheaper, but not as nice. **Vishwa Yuwak Kendra (International Youth Center),** Circular Road, New Delhi 110021 (☎ 3013631), has 37 rooms, some with bath attached, for travelers of any age for Rs 281 ($9.36) single, Rs 331 ($11.03) double; dorm beds run Rs 50 ($16.66) per head. Breakfast is included. For reservations, write the manager. From here, bus 620 goes to the Connaught area.

Nearby is the **Youth Hostel,** 5 Nyaya Marg, Chanakyapuri, New Delhi 100021 (☎ 3016285), offering dorm beds for Rs 22 (73¢) per head, and full breakfast for a small additional fee. The hostel needs sprucing up, but would do in a pinch. Members of the International Youth Hostel Association are given preference.

WORTH A SPLURGE

Hotels in this price range have everything the tourist needs and some have conveniences for business travelers. Several of these hotels are still possible on our $45 a day budget if two people are traveling together.

IN & AROUND CONNAUGHT PLACE

Steps from Connaught Circus, **The Connaught,** 37 S. Bhagat Singh Marg, New Delhi 110001 (☎ 344225; fax 310757), has a mirrored elevator to take guests up to 80 rooms. Neat and clean, they are adequately but unimaginatively done up. Several offer an unusual bonus: The hotel is adjacent to Shivaji Stadium, and from some rooms—#604, for one—you can see the sports events as clearly as if you were in the bleachers. The rates include buffet breakfast: Rs 1,600 ($53.33) single, Rs 2,000 ($66.66) double, Rs 2,200 ($73.33) to Rs 2,400 ($80) deluxe.

Hotel Janpath, Janpath, New Delhi 110001 (☎ 3320070; fax 3327083), part of the ITDC's Ashok Group, is right off the entrance to Connaught Place. This old hotel has been modernized and, in the process, lost much of its personality. Rooms are spare, bare, and in need of TLC. Indeed, readers have complained about cleanliness. The manager told me renovation was in the about-to-take-place stage, so everything might be all right now. Rates are Rs 1,195 ($39.83) single and Rs 1,700 ($56.66) double.

At **Park Hotel,** 15 Parliament St. (now Sansad Marg), New Delhi 110001 (☎ 352477; fax 3732025), the lobby tinkles with the sounds of fiberglass stalactites hung above the shiny granite floor. Perhaps no longer, however. The hotel was about to start massive renovations when I stopped in, and by now they should be completed. In the planning stages were a disco, Some Place Else, off the lobby, and a new look for the restaurant and coffee shop. Some rooms overlook the 18th-century Jantar Mantar observatory. Rates are $110 single, $120 double, $130 deluxe. There is a minuscule swimming pool.

There are stunning views from the rooms at **Hans Plaza,** 15 Barakhamaba Road, New Delhi 110001 (☎ 3316868; fax 3314830), which starts on the 16th floor of a modern, white, balcony-trimmed, 20-story office building. (Reader Jessie P. Krodel, of Torrance, California, is concerned about the lack of a fire exit on the 20th floor.) All rooms are twin-bedded with the same modern furniture, but there's a variety of color schemes, including sophisticated black and white with coordinating patchwork bed spreads. Rates are $62 single occupancy and $78 double. The rooftop restaurant is a plus.

An oasis in the heart of town, the **Imperial Hotel,** Janpath, New Delhi 110001 (☎ 3325332; fax 3324542), is set in a spacious palm-shaded garden. Opened in 1930, it was the city's premier hotel when travelers arrived with steamer trunks and servants to look after them. The hotel combines its old-world ways with modern amenities. The big, well-maintained bedrooms are furnished in dark wood period pieces, with larger than average attached tiled bathrooms. Room rates are $91 single, $97 double; suites go up to $260. There's lawn service in fair weather, but one big drawback: The hotel is usually booked months in advance by tour groups.

ITDC's **Kanishka,** 19 Ashok Road, New Delhi 100001 (☎ 3324422; fax 3324242), is about 1 kilometer from the center. The rooms have no distinctive personalities, but the views are fine from upper floors, Rs 1,600 ($53.33) single, Rs 2,200 ($73.33) double. The attractive split-level lobby has cushioned marble-backed banquettes and coordinating chairs under well-known contemporary painter M. F. Husain's 16-panel ceiling mural, showing the first century A.D. reign of the great Kushan Emperor Kanishka, as well as contemporary scenes. There is a rooftop restaurant.

Beyond Connaught Place

The Claridges, 12 Aurangzeb Rd., New Delhi 110011 (☎ 3010211; fax 3010625), prides itself on personalized service, and readers' letters agree. But there's been one complaint about improper room ventilation (avoid rooms above kitchen) and sloppy arrangements made through the travel desk. The dark wood decor gives the rooms an earlier-era feeling. The sparkling marble lobby with a sweeping staircase makes good first impressions, and everyone agrees that two of Delhi's best restaurants are in this hotel (see "Where to Eat," below). Rates are $115 to $135 single and double—higher, of course, for suites. You're 4 kilometers from the Connaught Place.

It's a 25-minute, Rs 90 ($4) taxi ride to Connaught Place from ITDC's **Qutab Hotel,** off Sri Aurobindo Marg, New Delhi 110016 (☎ 660060; fax 660861), the former U.S. AID headquarters. Rooms have a functional, international-modern decor. There's a swimming pool, tennis courts, and bowling alley (the only one in India, as far as I know), and Rs 1,195 ($39.83) single and Rs 1,700 ($56.66) double.

The pentagon-shaped **Samrat,** Chanakyapuri, New Delhi 100021 (☎ 603030; fax 6887074), also owned by ITDC and next to the Ashok, needs a facelift and a zippier attitude. A passageway connects with the Ashok, described below in the most expensive category; the two hotels have a total of six restaurants and two coffee shops. Rates are Rs 1,600 ($53.33) single; Rs 2,200 ($73.33) double. This is a favorite choice, as is the Ashok, of Russians who fly in to buy India-made merchandise to sell at home.

Delhi's Highest-Priced Hotels

These hotels offer all amenities for tourists and business travelers found at the finest international hotels worldwide, and service that rivals the best and, at times, outdoes the West. Most have lovely gardens, swimming pools, and health clubs (modest by western standards), and business centers with fax and other facilities; conference halls are widely available. Rates range from around $200 to $250 for singles and $300 to $400 for doubles, up to $700 for suites. Some of Delhi's best restaurants are in these hotels and are covered in "Where to Eat." Below are a few distinguishing characteristics of the top hotels.

ITDC's **Ashok Hotel,** 50-B Chanakyapuri, New Delhi 110021 (☎ 600121; fax 6873216), has a huge, comfortable lounge and is often home to visiting diplomats, large international conferences, and Russian merchants buying Delhi bargains to sell at home. The rooms don't overwhelm with personality, but are functional and comfortable. (For restaurants, see "Where to Eat," below).

In the heart of town, at the 25-floor, 450-room **Holiday Inn Crowne Plaza New Delhi,** Bharakhamba Avenue, Connaught Place, New Delhi 110001 (☎ 3320101; fax 3325335), the oddly proportioned lobby takes its inspiration from the better-looking Hyatt Regency's. A glass elevator ascends to the rooms, said to be the biggest in Delhi, but not the best maintained. High floors have smashing views; some nonsmoking rooms. (Some time after my inspection, I learned the hotel was to be taken over by the Hilton chain and renovated).

There is a hint of the Raj at the **Hyatt Regency Delhi,** Bhikaiji Cama Place, Ring Road, New Delhi 110066 (☎ 609911), whose lobby has stately marble pillars and a waterfall; chairs and chaises—both antique and made-to-look-antique—in conversation groups make this grand space seem intimate. This hotel is one of the few in Delhi to frequently update its decor and redo restaurants to stay abreast of latest trends. It is popular with business travelers.

Steps from the center of town, the sophisticated steel-and-glass **Le Meridien,** Windsor Place, New Delhi 110001 (☎ 3710101; fax 3714545), has a sexy, dimly lit plant- and pool-filled lobby where glass elevators trimmed with tiny lights rise like jeweled boxes to the 358 rooms—done in earth tones—around the atrium, as well as the elegant rooftop Le Belvedere restaurant 20 floors above. There's a circular swimming pool and a row of chic shops.

At **The Oberoi,** Dr. Zakir Hussain Marg, New Delhi 110003 (☎ 4363030; fax 4360484), the new-look lobby combines an eclectic mixture of Raj period pieces and reproductions with modern art, and carries this theme to the refurbished rooms. The hotel's swimming pool is an unusual design: The water is at ground level instead of the usual step or two down. This hotel is known for excellent service.

Lavish gardens make **The Taj Mahal Hotel,** 1 Mansingh Rd., New Delhi 110001 (☎ 3016162; fax 3017299), seem much farther than a few miles from bustling Connaught Place. Brightly painted concave canopies turn the lobby's ceiling and wall panels into oversized replicas of zari, the intricate local embroidery. Striped banquettes pick up this color scheme and make good vantage points for watching the smart international crowd. Rooms are handsomely appointed; some on the higher floors offer views of parliamentary buildings, while others have lovely garden views.

Under the same management is the **Taj Palace Inter-Continental,** 2 Sardar Patel Marg, Diplomatic Enclave, New Delhi 110021 (☎ 3010404; fax 3011252). This hotel was built for tour groups, conventions, and business travelers, the latter finding luxury and privacy on special floors. The lobby looks to the Mughal era—all marble with tents topping cushioned sofas. Ten kilometers from the center, it is handy to the airports. The **Orient Express Restaurant** is popular.

The 504-room **Welcomgroup's Maurya Sheraton Hotel and Towers,** Diplomatic Enclave, New Delhi 110021 (☎ 3010101; fax 3010908), is lavishly appointed, an amalgam of modern and ancient styles. The soaring lobby recalls the ancient Mauryas with its soaring chaitya-shaped (Buddhist prayer hall) lobby ceiling embellished with a mural by modern artists M. F. Husain and Krishen Khanna; the Towers offer luxuries and the latest technologies for today's movers and shakers on business missions. There's a solar-heated swimming pool, disco, jazz bar, and delicious Lucknawi cuisine in the **Dum Pukht** restaurant. (See "Where to Eat," below, for this and other restaurants located here.)

AT OR NEAR THE AIRPORTS

International flights often leave at the wee hours or early in the morning from Delhi's Indira Gandhi International Airport, so it's less of a struggle to be on time if you stay nearby. This is also a good place to stay if you're spending the night between one domestic flight and another with a crack-of-dawn departure.

Within 1 kilometer of the international airport (5 kilometers to domestic) is the 376-room **Centaur Hotel,** Gurgaon Road, New Delhi 110037 (☎ 5452223; fax 5452256), with singles Rs 1,900 ($63.33), doubles Rs 2,200 ($73.33). There's a 10% service charge. Modern, functional rooms open onto an atrium lounge. There are floodlit tennis courts and a putting green. Bus service is offered to the airports every 30 minutes, and seven times a day to and from Connaught Place.

4 Where to Eat

The authentic dishes of India's capital, such as tandooris (delicately spiced and baked in a special clay oven), kebabs (food on a skewer), and biryani (meat or chicken on a rice base garnished with nuts, pomegranate seeds, and other tasty tidbits), had their origins in Mughal days and once graced the table of Emperor Shah Jahan. This is also the origin of such Northern curries as korma, made with meat that has been tenderized in yogurt, and rogan josh, an elaborate curry that is indebted to saffron for its color and taste. Pulau, also typical of the north, is a less elaborate version of biryani; sweet pulau—very tasty—combines rice, spices, vegetables, fruit, and nuts. North India's bread is the chapati, which may remind some of the tortilla. Of course, you can get dishes from the other regions of India too—and from the Far East and West—because Delhi, like other cosmopolitan cities of the world, has a large population of foreigners and visitors, whose tastes are catered to by many restaurants.

A 7% tax is added to the prices in Delhi's restaurants. Only a few restaurants outside of hotels serve alcohol; I've made special notations on them below.

BOUNTIFUL INTERNATIONAL BUFFETS

A good transition from West to East and an excellent way to sample some Delhi specialties are the eat-as-much-as-you-like buffets featuring foods from both sides of the globe. Served at many of Delhi's finest hotels at lunchtime—sometimes at dinner—the meals start with a soup served at table before you head to the buffet table, where bearers assist you in the selection of outstanding arrays of Indian and Western foods at the buffet table: Sliced cold meats and pâtés studded with amber aspic jewels; veg- and non-veg curries; hills of pearly rice; piles of chapatis; strips of raw vegetables; shredded, chopped, and tossed salads. A roast perhaps, or a little chicken? Try the chutney, pickle, and raita (curds). Return again if one abundantly full plate was not enough. Or toss your calorie counter out and head for the desserts—sweets topped with mounds of whipped cream, cheese, and fruits. Sample one or sample them all, then settle back over coffee or tea, usually an extra charge. With their popularity, it's not surprising that some hotels now also offer breakfast buffets with East/West menus.

Prices for buffets have risen over the years, and indeed some are now splurges. A 7% food and beverage tax, 10% expenditure tax in the high-priced hotels, and gratuities add to their costs. If some stretch your budget a bit thin, they offer good value for the money. Since you can eat as much as you want of many different foods, you can make this your main meal of the day; your other meals can be lighter and less expensive. Or figure this way: After eating inexpensively for days, don't you deserve a splurge?

Generally, the buffets operate in-season seven days a week, although a few are Monday-through-Saturday affairs; some schedules change during the off-season summer months. Here are some of the best buffets and their prices; unless otherwise noted, they do not include taxes or gratuities.

Both lunch—1 to 3pm, Rs 150 ($5)—and dinner—8pm to midnight, Rs 175 ($5.83)—are tasty buffets at the **Orbit Room,** in the **Janpath Hotel,** Janpath (☎ 3320070).

Similarly priced and a tradition with many Delhites is the grand array of rich North Indian dishes at lunch—12:30 to 3:45pm—and dinner—8 to 11:30pm—each Rs 250 ($8.33), in the Mughlai-domed **Durbar,** at the **Ashok Hotel,** 50-B Chanakyapuri (☎ 600121).

At **Hotel Kanishka,** 19 Ashok Road (☎ 3324422), in the **Dilkusha** (meaning heart pleasing), lunch—12 to 3pm—or dinner—8 to 11pm—can be had for Rs 150 ($5). Next door, the budget hotel Ashok Yatri Niwas (☎ 3324511) has a buffet for Sunday brunch in the **Coconut Grove** restaurant, Rs 140 ($4.66)

The **Park Hotel,** 15 Parliament St. (☎ 3732025), had suspended its buffets but planned to start again when renovations were completed. Check it out.

Monday through Saturday, **Le Meridien,** Windsor Place (☎ 383960), serves a lunch buffet in **Windsor Hall**—12:30 to 3pm—for Rs 300 ($10), and a dinner spread in **La Brasserie**—7:30 to 11pm.

In the **Holiday Inn Crowne Plaza** (soon to be Hilton), Barakhambha Avenue (☎ 3320101), a buffet breakfast costs Rs 150 ($5), lunch and dinner each Rs 350 ($11.66) in the **Rendezvous.** Nearby, Hans Plaza, 1 Barakhamba Road (☎ 3316861), serves buffets with a 21st-floor view: breakfast Rs 117 ($3), lunch Rs 170 ($5.66).

The **Hyatt Regency,** Bhikaiji Cama Place, Ring Road (☎ 609991), has many buffets: A regional Indian buffet lunch amid a folk-art motif in **Aangan** (meaning courtyard)—12 to 2:30pm, Rs 350 ($11.66). The palm-accented **Cafe Promenade** is buffet headquarters for lunch—12 to 3pm—and dinner—7 to 11pm. Each is Rs 325 ($10.83) and features Continental foods. You can also have a salad bar buffet lunch—Rs 200 ($6.66), desserts only buffet—Rs 85 ($2.83); or a buffet breakfast of hot and cold dishes—Rs 200 ($6.66), Rs 175 ($5.83) if you choose only cold dishes. On Sundays, in the **Piazza** there's an Italian brunch—12 to 3pm, Rs 350 ($11.66).

Eating Italian and feasting your eyes on a Renaissance-themed decor are lunch attractions in the **Casa Medici** in **The Taj Mahal Hotel,** No. 1 Mansingh Rd. (☎ 3016162). Lunch goes from 1 to 2:45pm, Rs 425 ($14.16); the hotel's breakfast buffet in the **Machan** (Lookout) costs Rs 150 ($5).

At the **Taj Palace Inter-Continental,** 2 Sardar Patel Marg (☎ 3010404), there are two buffets in the Persian-inspired **Isfahan:** breakfast for Rs 165 ($5.50), and lunch—12:30 to 3pm, Rs 300 ($10). Similarly priced, in the hotel's rustic-looking **Handi,** 12 delicious selections—six vegetarian and six nonvegetarian from Northern and Western India—are served from clay pots called handis, from 12:30 to 3pm.

At the **Welcomgroup Maurya Sheraton Hotel and Towers,** Diplomatic Enclave (☎ 3010101), the **Pavilion** has two tasty buffets featuring round-the-world cuisine, salad bar, and 25 desserts: Lunch—12 to 3pm, and dinner—7:30 to 11:30pm, Rs175 ($5.83) for either one. On Fridays, Saturdays, and Sundays, the buffet brunch switches gears to feature an outstanding array of South Indian foods, including 10 main dishes, various rice dishes, a chef making delicious dosas (thin rice pancakes) to order, and to polish off, South Indian coffee (steamed with milk). Catch this brunch! (Reservations necessary.)

The Oberoi, Dr. Zakir Hussain Marg (☎ 4363030), offers a buffet breakfast for Rs 140 ($4.66), and salad bar, for Rs 95 ($3.16), in **The Palms;** Indian and Continental buffet at lunch—1 to 3:30pm, Rs 375 ($12.50), in **La Rochelle;** and a Thai-food express lunch in **Baan Thai,** for Rs 350 ($11.66).

Back in the center of town, the **Hotel Imperial,** Janpath (☎ 3325332), offers lunch—12:30 to 2:30, Rs 250 ($8.33)—and dinner—7:30pm onwards—Rs 293 ($9.76); both are seven days a week.

Bordering on Old Delhi, **The Oberoi Maidens,** 7 Sham Nath Marg (☎ 3316868), sets its Indian and Continental lunch buffet—1 to 3pm, Rs 250 ($8.33)—every day but Sunday in Raj-evocative **Curzon Room,** with such specialties as Shepherds pie from those old *Jewel in the Crown* days.

In Old Delhi at dinner time? Head to the **Hotel Broadway,** 4/15A Asaf Ali Road (☎ 3273821), and **Chor Bizarre** for an all-you-can-eat buffet dinner, Rs 130 ($4.33).

For a lunch buffet in a swanky restaurant, it's **aab-o-dana,** 12A Connaught Place (☎ 3713780), featuring regional Indian dishes, Rs 135 ($4.50), 12:30 to 3pm.

Take your taste buds touring at **El Arab,** 13 Regal Building, Connaught Place (☎ 311444), where the buffet consists of Middle Eastern and Mediterranean cuisine. Delectable roast lamb with delicately seasoned rice and grilled fish are standouts among a spread of 16 delicious dishes, Monday to Saturday, 12:30 to 3:30pm and 6:30 to 10:30pm, for Rs 118 ($3.93).

THALIS

Here are some of the tastiest thali meals in Delhi. Prices do not include the 7% food or 10% liquor tax or tip. (For an explanation of thalis and traditions, see "Essential Information," in Chapter 1.)

At the **Sagar Ratna** in the **Lodhi Hotel,** Lala Lajpat Marg (☎ 362422), overlooking a lovely garden, the top-of-the-line veg thali costs Rs 70 ($2.33) at lunch or dinner; it starts with an appetite-arousing soup before an array of several South Indian vegetable dishes, such as eggplant and okra, in unusual sauces and green beans sautéed with fresh coconut. Sides and seasonings include dal (lentil gravy), pickles, dahi (curds) to cool down spicy dishes, mango and tamarind chutneys, chapatis, and steaming rice. A rich Indian-style dessert such for gulab jamun, Rs 25 (83¢) (cheese ball in rosewater syrup), doesn't necessarily end your meal; you might still have pan, a traditional digestive made from a betel leaf, enclosing betel nuts, sweet lime paste, mild spices, and sometimes tobacco (omitted upon request), topped with shredded coconut. Pan isn't on the menu, but can be ordered. It's extra, as are soft drinks, tea, or coffee. The additions should set you back another Rs 50 ($1.67).

If you're not in the mood for such a hearty meal, try some snacks: The masala dosa (paper-thin rice-and-lentil pancake), stuffed with curried potatoes and cashew nuts, or idly (steamed rice and lentil-flour cake) is served with sambar (souplike and spicy) and chutney, Rs 30 ($1) to Rs 40 ($1.33). Sagar Ratna is open every day from 8am to 10:30pm: Lunch is served from 11am to 3pm; dinner from 7 to 11pm. Come early for lunch or dinner, and reserve in advance or wait in a long line.

Famous in South India, **Dasaprakash** has a branch in **the Ambassador Hotel,** Sujan Singh Park (☎ 674966). Tables and banquettes surround a temple flagpost, and here and there gods and goddess peak out from niches. A hearty South Indian vegetarian thali of several curries and rice with rasam (a fiery broth) and the usual curds, pickles, chutneys, and sweets, followed by South Indian coffee, costs Rs 110 ($3.66) at lunch and dinner. A less abundant thali costs Rs 50 ($1.67). A wide range of snacks such as idly (steamed rice pancakes) and ravi dosa (rice pancake with onions) cost Rs 50 ($1.67) to Rs 60 ($2). The black grape juice here is said to be unavailable elsewhere in Delhi. Ice creams and Indian sweets, such as badami halwa (almond sweet), start around Rs 45 ($1.50) to Rs 50 ($1.66) and go up. Lunch is noon to 3pm, dinner 7:30 to 11pm.

For some Delhi's least expensive thalis, try the **Caravan** cafeteria at the **Ashok Yatri Niwas,** 19 Ashok Rd. (☎ 3713052); nonvegetarian thali, with chicken or lamb curry, costs Rs 60 ($2); Rs 50 ($1.66) for vegetarian. Open 24-hours a day.

Then there are North Indian thali meals at tiny **Vega,** in the **Hotel Alka,** 16/90 Connaught Circus (☎ 344328), where according to a Jain belief banning consumption of odorous foods, no onion or garlic is used. The dishes change daily, but usually include some kind of vegetable dish with paneer (cheese), curries, lentils, dahi, pulao, puris (puffed wheat bread), chapati, salad, fresh fruits, Indian sweets, pappad, chutneys, and espresso. The cost is Rs 110 ($3.66); an Rs 90 ($3) version features smaller portions and excludes the espresso. Hours are daily 12:30 to 3:30pm, 7 to 10pm.

SALAD BARS

Salad bars in India? Their popularity surprised me since many travelers shun fresh salads while here. The impeccably clean salad bars below offer varied selections from leafy greens to marinated beans and pastas, as well as dressings, toppings, and breads—a refreshing change from traditional Indian fare. The salad bar trend is growing rapidly, and by this time there are undoubtedly many more. To the prices below you have to add taxes and/or gratuities.

Chor Bizarre, in the **Hotel Broadway,** 4/15A Asaf Ali Rd. (☎ 3278321), is named for its eclectic collection of bazaar memorabilia. Its "Salad and Chaatmobile"—a cleverly redesigned 1927 Fiat convertible—displays 15 to 16 salads as well as soups, breads, and sweets, for Rs 85 ($2.83). Open 12 to 3pm and 8pm to midnight; from 3:30 to 7:30pm, chaat (snacks) come aboard.

Nirula's Potpourri, L-Block, Connaught Circus (☎ 3322419), invites you choose the greens and other things to create a salad that "will complement both your mood and palate today." For Rs 72 ($2.40) this is an excellent value in a cheerful setting.

The Palms, in **The Oberoi,** Dr. Zakir Hussain Marg (☎ 363030), offers two soups, about 10 salads, and rolls, for Rs 95 ($3.16), in a spic-and-span palm-studded coffee shop with a rare nonsmoking section.

Cafe Promenade, in the Hyatt Regency Delhi, Bihkaiji Cama Place, Ring Road (☎ 609911), features salads beside a refreshing 90-foot indoor waterfall; the cost is Rs 95 ($3.16).

El Arab, 13 Regal Building (☎ 311444). A satisfying salad platter gives you a chance to sample a number of Middle Eastern specialties, such as hummus, baba ghanoush, tabouleh, and pita bread, for Rs 50 ($2.85).

REGIONAL INDIAN, CHINESE & INTERNATIONAL CUISINE

Many of Delhi's restaurants are dotted around the Connaught area. For the most part, they are places where culinary time seems to stand still, so little have their menus changed over the years. Many also feature Indian, Chinese, and Continental dishes in such a similar array that you feel you could take the menu from one restaurant to another with no difficulty. Still, chefs have their specialties and decor differs. Here are a few of the places where chefs carry on traditions, and some where they are innovators. Unless otherwise indicated, they are air-conditioned and accept major international credit cards. Figure on Rs 200 to Rs 300 ($6.66 to $10) for a three-course meal for two people, without drinks or gratuities, unless noted.

Possibly the best traditional Indian, Chinese, Continental restaurant in this area is the newcomer **Amber,** N-19, Connaught Circus (☎ 3312092), a branch of a famous Calcutta eatery. Bilevel, its decor incorporates bejeweled elephant tapestries, tiny lights in artificial trees, and red canopies over the banquettes. While most people choose Amber's non-veg tandooris, my hungry friends and I shared a half a dozen generous dishes from the menu's bagiche-se ("from the garden") section, including channa masala (chick peas), aloo tandoori kasa (potatoes tandoor-style), pudina parantha (mint wheat bread), and a rich dal (gravy) for about Rs 153 ($3) each, split among all of us; those who had ice cream and drinks rang up an additional Rs 150 ($3). Hours are 11am to 11pm.

Wander into **aab-o-dana,** 12-A Connaught Place (☎ 3713780), and you see difference (in light beige silk walls and blond woods rather than the dark decor of many Connaught area restaurants) and taste newness in a menu straying beyond Delhi and the North into the other regional cuisines of India. The chef has a way with the famous Hyderabad biryani (rice dish). Other specialties from the Northwest Frontier, Lahore, Delhi, U. P., Lucknow, and Punjab come off well. Entrées peak at around Rs 100 ($3.33). Hours are 12:30 to 3pm, 7:30 to 11:45pm.

Stepping upstairs, aab-o-dana's management also runs **Rodeo** (☎ 3713780), which, as far as I know, is Delhi's only Tex-Mex restaurant. Its wood paneling and saddle-seat bar stools give it the look of a ranch tack room. Try the chicken burritos or lamb tacos with a beer—Rs 65 ($2.16)—or wine—Rs 150 ($5) for a small glass. Prices for the Saloon Special (a Bloody Mary) and other high-voltage drinks are Rs 85 ($2.83). Non alcoholic "Mocktails" are around Rs 50 ($1.66). Open 11am to 11pm.

A new Chinese spot, **Zen,** B-25 Connaught Place (☎ 3310077), stylishly combines light furniture, black quilted silk walls, and thick black carpeting with a pattern of tiny white bow ties. The menu is a blend of innovative and traditional Chinese and a few Japanese dishes. Though unusual dishes, such as "Duck with Precious Stuffing" (mushrooms and shrimp) at Rs 225 ($7.50), will run up your tab, there are plenty of cheaper options. "Zen Special Vegetables" (in hot garlic sauce) are Rs 65 ($2.16), but other veg dishes are less. Such standards as chicken with almonds or cashews are Rs 85 ($2.83). Try honey apples or the date pancake for dessert. Open 11 am to llpm. Plan on Rs 300 ($10) to 500 ($16.66) for two.

At 11-D Connaught Place, **The Embassy Restaurant** (☎ 3320480), is a fancy-looking place with rust and brown decor on the upper level and mirror-spangled pink walls, beaded curtains, and orange tabletops reflected in a mirrored ceiling. Among the specialties are chicken tandoori, the Indian dish akin to barbecue; murg masalam (spiced chicken); and Embassy mixed vegetables. Some people order backward here to make sure they save room for the Embassy special pudding, a cake and brandied concoction. Hours are 10am to 11:30pm. Whisky, wine, and beer are available.

Gaylord, 14 Regal Building (☎ 310717), is one of the oldest of Delhi's restaurants. Creamy white walls form a neutral backdrop for red banquettes and glass dividers, and planters make the large room seem more intimate. It has endured by offering the usual array of Indian, Chinese, and Continental dishes reasonably well prepared at decent prices. Open daily 10:30am to 11pm. There is a bar.

Kwality, 7 Regal Building (☎ 334156), is attractive with wood paneling and earth-tone glazed tile decor. They claim they were first years ago to make ice cream in Delhi, and even now people make sure to save room for ice cream desserts here. One of the restaurant's most famous dishes is chana buatura (chick peas on a special whole wheat disc bread). Continental dishes are well prepared and decently priced at Kwality, acting as a magnet to foreign tourists. Open (except Sunday) 12:30 to 3:30pm, 6:30 to 11pm. There is a bar, where you can get whisky, wine, and beer.

At 13 Regal Building, there are three restaurants all under the same management. Tops among them is the one on the top floor: **El Arab** (☎ 311444) has hearty à la carte Middle Eastern dishes, and has explanations for each of them. Popular choices a include samak iskanderani (whole herbed fish, grilled over charcoal) and kebabs (skewered chicken cubes or lamb with eggplant, onions, and tomatoes). For dessert, try fritters doused with orange syrup and rosewater; follow with mint tea. Open Monday through Saturday 12:30 to 3:30pm, 7 to 10:30pm.

You won't find any blini or borscht on the menu of **Volga,** 19-B Connaught Place (☎ 3322960), but there is a hint of Russian in the dishes on the menu and the stylized balalaikas used in the murals. Chicken Petrograd à la Kiev is breast of chicken with butter inside, as it should be; a non-Russian but delicious poulet à la Volga (chicken with mushrooms, peas, and carrots in rich sauce) is a house specialty. The chef also prepares vegetables à la Kiev. There are Indian, Chinese, and Italian dishes on the menu. It is open daily 10am to midnight.

The small, intimate **Ginza,** K-Block, Connaught Circus (☎ 3323481), named for the famous Tokyo district, is meant to be a port for Japanese visitors. The decor is pleasant, with brocade banquettes and wood-paneled walls adorned by Japanese prints. But only a few Japanese foods, including ebi tempura and sukiyaki, are on the menu. Prominent are the Chinese dishes, including an array of satisfying noodle dishes under Rs 70 ($2.33) and some unusual wonton. Open daily noon to 3pm, 7 to 11pm.

Yorks, K-Block, Connaught Circus (☎ 3323769), is under the same management as Ginza but serves everything from milkshakes to midnight snacks. The tandoori kebabs are specialties here. Try fish tikka as a tasty change from the usual chicken tandoori. On the Continental side, a chicken sizzler (on a piping hot platter) is another good choice. Open daily 9am to 11pm.

Popular for a power lunch, **The Host Inn Restaurant,** F-33 Connaught Place (☎ 3316576), in The Host hotel, has a vaulted ceiling, mirrors, stone walls, brocade upholstery, and well-prepared Indian dishes. The menu temptations include rich murg Mumtaz (chicken tandoori with cream) and mutton rogan josh, which are among the highest priced dishes on the menu—around Rs 150 ($5). You can go

Continental with fish Portuguese (made with tomatoes), or Western with fried chicken. Hot fudge sundaes star as desserts. Whisky, wine, and beer are available. Open daily 10am to 11:30pm.

At the entrance to Connaught Place, the pricey, silk-paneled, lantern-lit **Mandarin Restaurant,** Hotel Janpath, Janpath (☎ 3320070), is a comfortable place and a staple among Cantonese Chinese restaurants in town. Figure on Rs 300 ($10) to Rs 450 ($15) for a three-course meal for two consisting of such standard Cantonese items as hearty sweet-corn soup, ginger chicken or prawns, chicken with black mushrooms or almonds, a shared single portion of fried rice, and ice cream for dessert. A vegetarian meal for two would cost about half this. Open daily 1 to 2:30pm, 7 to 11pm.

Also in the Hotel Janpath is **Gulnar Restaurant** (☎ 3320070). Under a dark mirrored ceiling and near a splashing waterfall, enjoy Mughali dishes said to be fit for royalty. Certainly their price is princely. You pay as much as Rs 400 ($13.33) to Rs 500 ($16.66) for a three-course meal for two. This might include any number of Mughali specialties, such as chingri (shrimp) malai curry, murgh (chicken) tikka masala, or a fancy biryani, dai (yogurt), and dal (gravy) Vegetarian choices cost less, as always. Open 1 to 2:30pm and 8 to 11:30pm. Ghazals—Indian love songs—are performed here in the evenings.

A short distance from Connaught area, in a narrow, untidy lane leading to an old mosque, the modest **Dastar Khawne Karim,** Hazrat Nizamuddin West (☎ 4698300), is renowned for kathi kebabs (kebab wrapped in roomali roti, a paper-thin bread). The menu offers other tandoori and Mughali dishes. Figure on Rs 200 ($6.66) to Rs 300 ($10) for two. Karim also has a stall near the Jama Masjid.

FAST FOOD—DELHI STYLE

Fast-food restaurants, reminiscent of those in the West, are springing up around Connaught Place and throughout Delhi. Their plate meals usually cost around Rs 50 ($1.66), but are somewhat higher, of course, if you order a full chicken tandoori. Here are a few fast-food places in the center of town:

Wimpy's, N-5 Janpath, Connaught Place (☎ 3313101), is modeled after a British chain and looks somewhat like a McDonald's, with order-takers calling out selections from behind a counter and realistic pictures of foods near the billboard-style menus. However, this Wimpy's is in a grand old building with regal marble stairs and huge mirrors, and the burgers are vegetarian or mutton. There is also a chicken-in-a-bun with fries and a cola. It is open Monday through Saturday 10am to 11pm, Sunday 11am to 11pm, and very popular.

Old standbys when it comes to light meals and snacks are Nirula's **Snack Bar/Hot Shoppes** at the base of hotel of the same name, L-Block Connaught Circus (☎ 332491). Hours vary slightly from shop to shop: The pastry shop is open from 9am to 8pm; hours are 10am to midnight at **21 Ice Creams** (21 flavors), where you'll pay Rs 25 (83¢) to Rs 37 ($1.23) to create your own banana split. Other Nirula shops selling dosas, burgers, pizza, franks, cold drinks, espresso, and thalis open from 9:30 to 10:30am and close at 10:30pm. Nirula's branches around Delhi also can be counted on for quality and cleanliness.

When I saw a sign saying this new place, **Croissants** (9 Scindia House, Connaught Place), sells bagels for Rs 18 (6¢), I was irresistibly drawn inside; however, there were no bagels when I stopped in. Lots of buns for sandwiches, something that looked like croissants, and pastries, though. The music was loud, the place tidy and friendly.

Also new is **Minute Chef,** 120 New Delhi House, 27 Barakhamba Road (☎ 3315688), with burgers, pizzas, and other fast foods. It's open from 9:30am to 7pm.

A similar array of foods is offered at spotlessly clean, cheerful **Cafe 100,** B-20 Connaught Circus (☎ 332663), open l0am to 11pm.

TANDOORI, MUGHLAI & KASHMIRI DELICACIES IN OLD DELHI

The unpretentious but famous **Moti Mahal** (meaning Pearl Palace), Netaji Subhash Marg, Daryaganj (☎ 3273011), has opened under new management with its chefs preparing the tandooris with their old panache but in a modernized kitchen. During the tandoori process chefs turn and baste their chickens or kebabs sputtering on iron spikes above the red-hot coals in clay ovens. Two notable breads also come out of these ovens—kulcha (round and flat) and naan (teardrop shaped). The chicken runs Rs 55 ($1.83) for one-half and Rs 100 ($3.33) for a whole. The breads cost Rs 12 (4¢) for naan and Rs 35 ($1.16) for keema naan (stuffed with meat). If you wish to eat tandoori vegetarian, the paneer shashlik (cheese, onion, peppers cooked on a skewer) is quite tasty. You can split a generous order of any of the rice dishes, such as plain rice, Rs 25 (83¢), or the slightly more expensive peas pulao (peas, rice, herbs); one order of dal (lentils) and raita (curds) also serves two. Kulfi falooda is Indian ice cream with dry fruits and sweet vermicelli, and costs Rs 30 ($1). Eat outdoors under the colorful tent (heated in winter) rather than the uninspired indoor section. After dinner, ask for anise seeds to refresh your palate. Open daily noon to midnight. Indian songs are played at night, except Tuesdays.

Almost next door is **Peshawari,** 3707 Subhash Marg, Daryaganj (☎ 3282938), a tiny restaurant with tiled walls and a clean kitchen. The chef makes delicious butter chicken, which, at Rs 120 ($4) for a full chicken, is about the highest-priced item on the menu; a full tandoori chicken costs Rs 70 ($2.33), and a range of kebabs are Rs 25 (85¢) each; naan is Rs 5 (16¢). Vegetarian choices run Rs 8 to Rs 15 (45¢ to 85¢). Open daily except Tuesday from noon to 4pm, 7 to midnight.

The **Tandoor** in the President Hotel, Asaf Ali Road (☎ 3273000), has modern Indian murals and traditional Mughal decor and a glassed-in kitchen so you can watch chefs work—nothing unusual these days. It's the delicious bargain-priced fixed tandoori dinners—offering a choice of chicken or lamb dishes, breads and salad for Rs 180 ($6) to Rs 210 ($7)—that make it worth a visit. Beer runs Rs 65 for 650 ml. Desserts include the kulfi and numerous ice creams. Open daily 12:30 to 3:30pm, 7pm to midnight.

Highly regarded by Delhites are the Mughlai dishes at **Flora** (☎ 3264593), opposite the Jama Masjid. You can eat in the cozy dining hall where tiny lights outline Mughal-style archways inset with scenic murals, or dine Indian-style, seated on floor cushions around a low table. A well-prepared meal shared by two with one-half chicken tandoori, a rich Mughlai mutton curry, a vegetable, and Indian bread should cost about Rs 200 ($6.66). Hours are 9am to 12:30am daily. There is a little gift shop in front of the restaurant.

The kebabs at **Karim's** near the Jama Masjid are always among Delhi's best, but now they are even more appealing to foreigners. Going from a cramped stall to a full-fledged restaurant, Karim's seems also to be more hygienic. Figure on Rs 25 (83¢) to Rs 50 ($1.66) for a kebab and another Rs 5 (16¢) or Rs 10 (33¢) for bread. There is another Karim's at Hazrat Nizzamudin West (see above).

A charmingly eclectic mix of antiques from several chor bazaars ("thieve's markets") decorate the **Chor Bizarre** in the Hotel Broadway, 4/15A Asaf Ali Rd. (☎ 3273821). (See also "Salad Bars," above.) The restaurant is famous for delicious Kashmiri cooking. Look for goshtaba, a blend of mutton and cardamom in a yogurt marinade, then slow-simmered, traditional at Kashmir wedding feasts; Kashmiri kebab, skewered mutton, onions, tomatoes, and chilies; rajmah (red beans) with Kashmiri spices, and a host of others. Figure on spending about Rs 200 ($6.66) to Rs 300 ($10) for two. The antiques are occasionally auctioned off to make room for new acquisitions. Open from 12:30 to 3:30pm, 7:30 to 11:30pm.

WORTH A SPLURGE

Delhi's splurge restaurants are located in the top hotels. Only part of the lure is dining in glamorous, evocative settings. The real reason to splurge is to try some of India's highly varied, well-prepared regional fare, or historic dishes enjoying a revival, or to eat international cuisine if you hunger for a change from Indian cuisine. Hotel restaurants serve alcoholic drinks and accept major credit cards.

Figure on Rs 600 ($20) and up for a meal for two. Prices that do not include taxes, gratuities, or drinks. If the drinks are alcoholic, be prepared to part with plenty of rupees. For instance, a bottle of innocuous French wine can run somewhere around Rs 1,000 ($33.33) to Rs 3,000 ($100). Indian wines are less; the most palatable, Marquis de Pompadour, a sparkling white wine costs about Rs 750 ($25). Beer can run from Rs 45 ($1.50) to Rs 125 ($4.16), depending on where you're dining.

A bit of advice: These restaurants are very popular. Make reservations and check timings while you're at it. Most hotel restaurants open for lunch from 12:30 or 1 to 2:30 or 3pm, and for dinner from 7:30 or 8 to 11:30pm or midnight. Some are open evenings only.

Westerners, accustomed to dining between 7 and 9pm, are often surprised to find themselves almost alone in restaurants. Indians tend to dine later, around 10 or 10:30pm, often in large parties made up of people of all ages, from babes in arms to seniors.

Live Indian music is played nearly everywhere Indian foods are served, at times to accompany Indian classical or folk dancers. The Continental-style restaurants have dance bands, often featuring tunes long ago retired to Tin Pan Alley heaven.

Two innovative restaurants are **Dhaba** and **Corbett's,** both **at Claridges Hotel,** 12 Aurangzeb Rd. (☎ 3010211). *Dhaba* means truck stop cafe, and the restaurant's designer has replicated off the lobby a brightly painted Indian truck in front of a roadside eatery. Corbett's (inspired by Jim Corbett National Park) turns part of the hotel's garden into a fantasy jungle. Settle into a machan (lookout) and sip and eat to the chirping of birds, the roaring of game, and the chattering of monkeys (all on tape). Your waiter wears a forest ranger outfit. Both restaurants are for upscale expeditioners. Figure on Rs 400 ($13.33) to Rs 600 ($20) for dinner for two without drinks. Have a seat on a rustic bench and loosen your belt for hearty portions that can serve two. Tandooris, handis (casseroles), curries, and grills are on both menus as well as a number of Indian breads and desserts. Both restaurants are immensely popular. Reservations are essential; for weekends, book five days in advance. Open 12 to 3pm, 7:30 to 11:30pm.

In the **Welcomgroup Maurya Sheraton Hotel and Towers,** Diplomatic Enclave (☎ 3010101), **Dum Pukht** offers the rare epicurean delights of the old Newabs of Awadh (Lucknow) who perfected the art of slow cooking in small casseroles. Today Chef Imriaz, whose ancestors' culinary skills delighted the old rulers, dips into their treasury of recipes for today's royal treats. **Bukhara,** in the same hotel, offers some of the city's best Northwest Frontier dishes, hot from the tandoori or sizzling on skewers.

Northwest Frontier foods are less expensive at **Khyber** in **Hotel Siddarth,** 3 Rajendra Place (☎ 57222501), where the outdoorsy decor is completed with an artificial tree, a single red kite tangled in one of its leafy branches. Consider also exploring Northwest Frontier foods at the **Frontier** at the Ashok, 50B Chanakyapuri

(☎ 6-0121); **Baluchi** at Holiday Inn Crowne Plaza Barakhamba Avenue, Connaught Place (☎ 3320101), almost a copy of the decor at Bukhara at the Welcomgroup Maurya Sheraton and Towers (but this is soon to be a Hilton, so the restaurants in the hotel may also change); and the pricey **Kandahar** in The Oberoi, Dr. Zakir Hassin Marg (☎ 4360484).

For a selection of northern regional dishes, go to **Haveli,** in **The Taj Mahal,** 1 Mansingh Rd. (☎ 3016262), and try dhaba murg, a complicated chicken creation simmered in a double-decker pot. Like the famous painted havelis (decorated houses) of Rajasthan, the restaurant's walls are covered with delicate murals. They form a lovely setting for diners as well as for the folk dancers who perform in the evenings.

Your taste buds discover historic Delhi dishes at **Aangan** (meaning courtyard) at **Hyatt Regency Delhi,** Bhikaiji Cama Place (☎ 609911), a comfortable room with gleaming granite floors and plush wall hangings and wood carvings.

The top hotels also have specialty restaurants for non-Indian cuisines in swank settings. Many are devoted to Chinese cuisine. At **House of Ming,** in **The Taj Mahal Hotel,** 1 Mansingh Rd. (☎ 3016162), a chef from mainland China prepares peppery-hot Szechwan foods, served on traditional blue-and-white China. The **Teahouse of the August Moon,** in the **Taj Palace Inter-Continental** (☎ 3010404), with bridge, pond, and bamboo grove, was the first in Delhi to serve dim sum (dumplings and other small dishes) and undoubtedly first in the world to offer this typical Chinese lunch in a setting inspired by a play based in Okinawa. **Jewel of The East,** in the **Ashok Hotel,** 50-B Chanakyapuri (☎ 600121), is decorated in black and navy with etched glass panels; for something different order the Mongolian Steamboat, a do-it-yourself dish. Finally, you might try **Golden Phoenix,** at Le Meridien, Windsor Place (☎ 3710101).

In a Thai mood? Go to **Baan Thai,** in **The Oberoi,** Dr. Zakir Hussain Marg (☎ 4360484).

TK's (short for Teppanyaki), is described in the hotel's literature as an Oriental grill in the **Hyatt Regency Delhi,** Bhikaiji Cama Place (☎ 609911). The attractive, modern restaurant borrows the seating arrangement Benihana introduced to the states some years ago. Diners are seated around counters surrounding a grill where they can watch the chef preparing their foods to order. TK's menu offers both Eastern and Western foods; try one of the one of the four multicourse east-meets-west fixed-price meals, from Rs 390 ($13) to Rs 690 ($23). A meal like this certainly calls for exercise afterward, so get up and walk to the dessert table. There is **La Piazza,** with stylish tile flooring and a wealth of pricey Italian dishes cooked in an open kitchen; a wood oven pizza "Margherita" (tomato, basil, cheese toppings) runs Rs 195 ($6.50).

For French and continental dishes try the hushed and elegant **La Rochelle, in The Oberoi,** Zakir Hussain Marg (☎ 3603030).

With stained-glass windows, elegant Regency inlaid chairs, and walls hung with copies of priceless Raj period photographs, the **Curzon,** in the **Oberoi Maidens,** 7 Sham Nath Marg (☎ 2525464), a lovely intimate room, was about to open with a new menu. The setting seemed ideal for a quiet special meal.

Finally, for the setting of settings in Delhi, it's **The Orient Express,** in the **Taj Palace Inter-Continental** (☎ 3010404), a replica of the dining car of the famous belle epoque train of the same name, with gaslights and leather chairs. The menu is inspired by the cuisines of cities through which the real, renovated train still passes—Paris, Lausanne, Milan, and Verona among them. The four-course, fixed-price meal costs Rs 800 ($26.66) per traveler; add Rs 600 ($20) or more for a bottle of imported wine. Call four to five days in advance if you hope to hop aboard.

Snacking in Delhi

There are countless snack stalls in Delhi, but for the some of the best, head to Bengali Market—a Rs 25 (83¢) scooter ricksha ride from Connaught Place—and **Bhim Sain's Sweet House,** where a great array of sweets and savory dishes are displayed like jewels in glass cases. Settle into a booth and enjoy desserts such as halwa (made of fruit, nuts, or vegetables) and gulab jamun (cheese balls in rosewater syrup) for Rs 45 ($1.50) per generous helping, and slightly less expensive snacks such as chaat (lentils and grains seasoned with tamarind) and samosas (turnovers filled with vegetables or meat) and puffy puris. During Diwali when giving sweets is a tradition, customers queue up for hours so prized are gifts from this shop. Open daily 7:30am to 10:30pm.

Another famous and equally good sweet shop, **Nathus,** is directly across from Bhim Sain's.

If you've got a couple dollars and you're in the mood for a little nibble, grab a motorized ricksha in Connaught area for a 3-kilometer ride—Rs 20 (66¢) or Rs 25 (83¢)—to the **Anjlika Pastry Shop** in Ajamul Khan Market, Karol Bagh, among the best known of the many confectioners here for a piping hot puri or an outrageously rich sweet.

Feeling like a nosh in the center of town? Go to **Shah Jahan Road,** not far from The Taj Mahal and The Claridges Hotels, and stop at the chaat walla's (snack seller's) cart near the Union Service Commission. Most people nearby know it, and many people make a point to stop here whenever they're in the neighborhood. For about Rs 20 to Rs 30 (60¢ to $1) you can get a lot chaat (grains, lentils with spices) and probably a chat with the other customers.

The most popular snack sellers stalls **outside the Indian Oil Building** features Bombay's favorite snack, bhel-puri (puffed rice, spiced grains, chutney), served in little individual throwaway bowls made of banana leaves. (Do not eat them

For an à la carte three-course lunch or dinner for two, figure Rs 500 ($16.66) to Rs 1,500 ($50) exclusive of taxes, gratuities (check to see if service is on the bill), and drinks. Most of these places have music at night.

French-accented foods are served at chic **Le Belvedere,** in **Le Meridien,** 1 Windsor Place (☎ 3710101). Besides the smashing view, the room is elegant, softly lit, and romantic—quite intriguing at night. Open only for dinner, 8pm to midnight.

Casa Medici, in **The Taj Mahal,** 1 Mansingh Rd. (☎ 301612) (also see "Buffets," above), has graceful archways framing its city view. While there's nothing Renaissance about the food, the chef's contemporary creations include fresh pastas, risottos, veal, and seafood. Open 1 to 2:45pm, 7:30 to 11pm.

At the **Hotel Kanishka's Panorama Restaurant,** 19 Ashok Road (☎ 3324422), an understated earth-toned color scheme plays up the lovely view. Relax and enjoy some unusual Indian dishes, such as tangri kebab (chicken with nut sauce) at prices slightly under the others in this section. Open 1 to 2:45pm, 8pm to midnight.

The silver-accented **Sanpam,** on the rooftop of **Surya Best Western,** New Friends Colony (☎ 6835070), serves Chinese food with views of the Yamuna River, Baha'i Temple, and the city beyond, from 8:30pm to 1:30am. More Chinese foods are dished up with a view at **Bali Hi,** atop Welcomgroup Maurya Sheraton Hotel and Towers, Diplomatic Enclave (☎ 3010101), from 8pm to midnight.

from plates, which are not thoroughly washed.) For a few paise you can have a real spicy treat.

After a bargaining session at Chandni Chowk, or any time you're in Old Delhi, stop for refreshment at Delhi's only tea-tasting tea parlor, **Aap Ki Pasand** (meaning "as you like it"), opposite Golcha Cinema, 15 Netaji Subhash Marg (☎ 3260376), where owner Sanjay Kapur is Delhi's only tea taster. Choose from 20 different kinds of tea. Is it from Assam, Darjeeling, the Nilgiri Hills? You'd have to check the label to make sure, but Kapur, with years of experience in tea tasting, can sip and tell. Your own taste buds will tell you you're onto something deliciously different with badam Kashmiri kahwa (almond-and-spice flavored tea), or when you sample the fragrant Darjeeling clonal leaves and buds that go into an Iced Tea Holiday. You can get a cup of tea or a neatly done-up drawstring packet of tea for sipping or gifting later on. Teas can run up to $10 per 100 grams for the finest. Many herbal teas, such as chamomile and mint, are available as well. Open Monday through Saturday 10am to 2pm, 2:30 to 6pm; tea service, 10:30am to 1:45pm, 2:30 to 5:45pm. Teas carrying the Sancha label are packaged by this shop and sold at Cottage Industries Emporium (Janpath) and ITDC's duty-free airport shop.

For Western pastries or finger sandwiches, try **Wenger's,** A-16 Connaught Place (☎ 3324373), where an entire chocolate truffle cake costs Rs 220 ($7.33), and a strawberry tart is or a dainty cheese sandwich costs Rs 20 (66¢).

For pleasant refreshment in the center of town, it's hard to beat tea or coffee with assorted sandwiches and cakes on the **Tea Terrace** in the cool and leafy garden at the Imperial Hotel, Janpath (☎ 3325332). It's pricey, though, around Rs 50 (1.66) to 150 ($3) depending on what you order.

Szechwan specialties at top-of-the-line prices can be had at **Taipan,** atop The Oberoi, Dr. Zakir Hussain Marg (☎ 4363030).

5 Seeing the City

CENTRAL NEW DELHI

Government Buildings Go through the **India Gate** and you'll be on **Rajpath,** the scene, each January 26, of the spectacular Republic Day parade, and the site of the main governmental buildings. India's **Parliament** is the circular structure where members of the two houses (Peoples and States) come from every region—Bombay to Assam, Kashmir to Kerala. Also on the Rajpath, and very impressive, is **Rashtrapati Bhavan,** the Presidential Palace, with 340 rooms and 330 surrounding acres of Mughal-style gardens (open to the public in February and March, see "Gardens," below). This was the imperial abode of the viceroy when India was the brightest jewel in England's crown of colonies.

Connaught Circus Built in the Colonial style with colonnaded verandas, Connaught's architecture commemorates the visit of its namesake the Duke of Connaught in l931. While much has changed since all this went up, Connaught Place is still central to the lives of residents and tourists alike who come here for shopping and entertainment. Its galleries and cinema houses display modern creations, its shops sell old, new, and new-made-to-look-old, and its restaurants feature foods for all tastes and pocketbooks. And when all this gets to be a bit much, you can do as Delhites do: Take a breather in the park at the center. When it's time to move on, the roads fan out to important avenues that lead to the key sights and cultural centers.

Jantar Mantar The Maharaja of Jaipur, a noted astronomer and mathematician of his time, built a series of observatories during his reign 250 years ago, and you can still see the remains of some of them today. Just off Parliament Street (walk over from the Air India office and turn left) is one of these, the Jantar Mantar, a series of redstone structures built for astronomical purposes in 1719 and still impressive today. The centerpiece is an enormous stone sundial—fully 40 feet high—around which are various structures with carved dials to ascertain longitudes and latitudes around the world. Two circular buildings at the far end of this little park measure, respectively, the sun's and moon's rays, to determine via astrology the auspicious times for action. There's a narrow slit in one wall through which the sun shines only twice a year, on March 23 and September 21.

Sri Lakshmi Narayan Hindu Temple West of Connaught Place, the Sri Lakshmi Narayan Hindu Temple houses a colorful collection of carved and decorated marble, plus turrets and towers of red and yellow sandstone. It was built in 1938 but appears to be a classic collection of all the facets of the Hindu faith. It is always thronged with white-robed pilgrims, some of whom will invariably be squatting before the full-color statue of Lord Krishna in the main hall. The marble walls are etched everywhere with drawings and admonitory texts such as this one: "Just as the bird loses its freedom when enchained, so are those doomed to bondage who are enslaved to desire." Behind the temple is a small, pleasantly informal garden, and at the front is a small room where visitors can leave their shoes while walking around the temple itself.

Raj Ghat The place where Mahatma Gandhi was cremated in 1948 (he was shot by a Hindu fanatic at a meeting on January 30 of that year) is maintained as a tranquil open-air shrine open to all every day from 5:30am to 7pm. It is just off Ring Road, the popular old name for Mahatma Gandhi Road, not far from the Red Fort and can be reached by taxi from the latter for about Rs 10 (55¢) to Rs 12 (70¢), about half that by scooter ricksha.

After a walk through a grassy park, you come to the **Gandhi Shrine** proper, a stone-enclosed garden in the center of which is a black marble slab inscribed with Gandhi's last words, "Oh God," in Hindi.

A **museum** with books, photographs, and personal mementos of Gandhi is opposite the park and is open Tuesday through Saturday from 9:30am to 5:30pm. Films on Gandhi's life are shown on Sunday from 4 to 5:30pm. The museum itself attracts about 1,000 visitors a day. Admission to the museum and the films is free.

OLD DELHI

The Red Fort For just over 300 years much of India's history has ebbed and flowed around its magnificent Red Fort, an immense, heavily guarded palace built of red sandstone by the Mughal emperors, the symbol of the oligarchy that ruled into this century. Magnificent as it is, with its inner gardens, marble buildings, and tricky architectural perspectives, it was once even more so.

Until the 18th century its pride and joy was the world-famous Peacock Throne, situated in a room whose ceiling was solid gold and whose walls were studded with valuable gems. "If paradise be on the face of the earth, it is here, it is here, it is here," reads a couplet still engraved on the portico. Then came the reign of a merry monarch, the legend goes, who failed to safeguard this trust. The Persians invaded and looted almost everything of value.

There have been continuing attempts to restore the ornate decorations on the marble pillars, but it is slow and costly work. At one time water flowed through the palace, but today the marble channels are dry and the **Pearl Mosque** no longer gleams as it did when copper covered its dome. Aurangzeb, son of Shah Jahan, built this mosque in 1659 for Rs 160,000.

The entrance to the fort (open from sunrise to sunset daily; modest entrance fee, free on Friday) is lined with small stores that don't have any particular bargains to offer but are fun to look at anyway, especially the old print stall. Centuries ago it was at this point that all visitors had to dismount and proceed on foot with heads bowed.

Probably the least painful history lesson you'll ever have is that presented by the **son et lumière** (sound and light) at Delhi's Red Fort at sunset each night—except during heavy rains (July to September) or some chilly evenings in January. In fact, *lesson* is the wrong word because, although you'll learn quite a lot of Indian history, the sound-and-light experience through which it comes to you is pleasantly aesthetic. Unlike some of its kind, this particular son et lumière is extraordinarily interesting and presented with a great deal of imagination. On the face of it you wouldn't think that the simple ingredients—static buildings, lights, and noises—could be combined into anything very attention-getting, but the people responsible for this show have many surprises up their sleeves. They'll gently lull you into a sort of reverie as you watch the light patterns play on the palaces of the inner courtyard and listen to the commentary, and then, suddenly, your attention will be cunningly diverted by the sound of horsemen rapidly approaching from behind. A measure of how well the trick works is that most people instantly turn around, only to see that the lights have shifted to another area. Attend the son et lumière early in your Indian trip and then again just before you leave the country. You'll be amazed at how much you've learned between visits.

The cost for the son et lumière is Rs 10 (33¢) to Rs 20 (66¢)—this may well increase by the time you visit. An English performance is usually at 8:30 to 9:30pm, depending on the time of sunset. There are Hindi performances from 7 to 8pm. You almost always need a wrap from October to February. Reservations can be made by telephone (☎ 600121, ext. 2295 for the English show; 3274580 for the Hindi show). Tickets are also available at the Naubat Khana in the Red Fort. Currently, you can also purchase tickets at the gate 15 minutes before show time.

Jama Masjid There's something indefinably intriguing about Asian religions, and that something manifests itself in the buildings connected with them. The Jama Masjid Mosque, begun in 1644 and completed in 1658, is an impressive elevated sandstone edifice almost opposite the Red Fort. Its two 130-foot-high minarets striped with white marble dwarf the hundreds of jam-packed stalls nearby. However, interesting as the huge 120-by-201-foot mosque is, it is overshadowed by the variety of life in the adjoining streets. The mosque is open 7am to noon, 2 to 5pm each day. The entry fee for the minarets is 50 paise (3¢), free on Friday (but Friday is not recommended, as it's a prayer day for Muslims).

SOUTH DELHI

Humayun's Tomb It isn't any startling new idea for people to erect dramatic monuments to their dead—witness the Egyptian pyramids—but the enormous sandstone and marble mausoleum of Emperor Humayun began a new style in monuments of this kind. It was built by the emperor's widow, Haji Begum, in the 16th century and may have been the inspiration for the later Taj Mahal at Agra. Many similar architectural wonders were constructed by other Mughal rulers of this era. Today it is considered the best preserved tomb in Delhi.

The tomb holds not only the body of Humayun, but also that of his widow and later members of the dynasty, as is the custom with family mausoleums of today. Set in attractive gardens, it's an impressive sight, topped with a symmetrical dome and lined on the bottom with what appear to be guest rooms (but which, of course, are different vaults for other members of the royal line, many of whom met violent deaths).

There is an entry fee, which is waived Fridays. Use of a video camera will cost you Rs 25 (83¢); open from sunrise to sunset. The best strategy for Humayun's Tomb is to make a sunrise visit before the group tours start. It's a quarter mile from Connaught Circus in Nizamuddin, a medieval village tucked into the residential area Nizamuddin West.

And while you're in the vicinity, see the grave of the famous Urdu poet, Mirza Gahib; it's one of many tombs that grew up dargarh (shrine) Sheik Nizamuddin. Then it's off to the Lodi gardens (see "Gardens," below).

Qutb Minar & Vicinity It seems an obvious idea, but very few builders have constructed towers that are noticeably wider at the bottom than at the top.

The fluted tower of Qutb Minar, built of hard, red sandstone nearly 800 years ago, once seen is never forgotten. Imposingly fat at the bottom, it tapers to a narrow platform at the top, 230 feet above. Its interior spiral stairway is as sound today as when it was first built. It has survived earthquakes, wind, and rain—and the recent experiments of a Delhi professor who tried to disprove the law of gravity by projecting stones from an intricate bamboo and string contrivance halfway up.

First begun in 1199 by Qutb-ud-Din, Delhi's first Muslim sultan, it was subsequently added to and for years has been a favorite picnic spot.

The beautiful tower (modest entry fee) stands in the attractive gardens of India's first mosque, whose intricately carved pillars belong to an earlier structure and were plastered over when the mosque was first built. The covering has since been worn away, revealing the attractive carvings. In the ruins of the mosque stands a 24-foot shaft of iron, worn shiny about a fifth of the way up by the arms of countless people who believe the legend that it brings good luck to join their hands behind their back around the pole.

The column, which has remained free of rust—much to scientists' amazement—ever since it was built in the 5th century, is a monument to the divine Vishnu, according to a legend in Sanskrit translated in extravagantly flowery terms nearby (". . . he, by the breezes of whose prowess the southern ocean is even still perfume . . .").

Two hundred yards from the ruins, past the keekar trees whose branches are used as toothbrushes, is the never-completed **Alai Minar,** a much wider tower that was meant to loom over its fluted neighbor. After two years of building, it was abandoned when its designer died.

The tower and the grassy lawns at its base are open from sunrise to sunset daily. It is a tranquil place, populated by tiny squirrels and wild green parrots, which flutter among the ruins. Qutb Minar can be reached by city bus, motor-scooter taxi for Rs 60 ($2), or a regular taxi from downtown Delhi, costing about Rs 80 ($1.33).

Tughlaqabad Only 8 kilometers from Qutb Minar is Tughlaqabad, the ruins and tomb of Delhi's third city, built by Ghiyas-ud-din Tughlak, the first Tulhlak king. Talk about speedy construction: Tughlak took only two years to build this entire city, which had hundreds of residences, palaces, a mosque, and more behind its seven-mile perimeter of battlements and walls— but it stood only seven years. Tughlak hoped for a longer run, but then it suddenly was curtains (literally) for him. The story is that the king's son rigged an awning to fall on his father at a victory celebration. (Another story claims the city was cursed by a Sufi saint.) In any case, the king was killed, and the prince soon moved his capital to the Deccan.

Only the bastioned walls, enormous ramparts, and massive gates remain, but they still manage to convey the powerful personality of its builder. Almost equally memorable is the panoramic view from the highest part of the fort.

Across the road, connected by a causeway, is the small, marble-domed **tomb of Ghiyas-ud-din Tughlak** on an elevated platform. Once, all this was in the middle of a lake, accessible only via the causeway. The most notable aspect of this tomb is the sloping walls, the earliest example of such a design in India. Eerily enough, the tomb also contains the remains of the son who murdered him.

A few miles south of Tughlaqabad is **Surajkund** (Pool of the Sun), built by a 10th-century king. It is believed that a sun temple stood here long ago—one of the few in India—and these steps led to its sacred tank.

Baha'i Temple North of Tughlaqahad, not far from the Best Western Surya, is the Baha'i House of Worship, Kalkaji (☎ 6444049). The latest of world's seven major monuments to the Baha'i faith, Delhi's white marble structure was inspired by the lotus blossom, a Baha'i symbol, which is invariably associated with religions in India. Gardens and reflecting pools offer the visitor a quiet respite. The Baha'i faith, founded in the mid-19th century by Baha'u'llah, a privileged Persian who gave up his life of comfort and ease to spread his beliefs, has been part of India's rich religious tapestry since its beginnings. The Baha'i House of Worship is open to visitors April through September from 9am to 7pm, October through March from 9:30am to 5:30pm. The staff is helpful and will show you around; English-language audio visual shows also provide background at 11am, noon, 2, and 3pm.

Diplomatic Enclave If you've had enough of historic monuments, grab a scooter ricksha up to the far southern end of town and take a look at the broad and leafy park-and-pool-studded Diplomatic Enclave (Chanakyapuri), where missions from all over the world form a permanent modern architectural exhibition. Why Chanakyapuri? The area is name for a minister under Chandragupta's reign (300 B.C.) who wrote the first treatises on goverment and diplomacy.

Among the easiest missions to identify is the **American Embassy,** designed by architect Edward Durrell Stone and opened in 1959. It's a graceful building, cool, spacious, dignified, and yet welcoming. Influenced by Mughal styles, the building front is a mosaic grillwork of white stone enhanced by a fountain-filled reflecting pool. You can stroll the area looking for styles of architecture from many parts of the world.

While in this area visit the **Rail Transport Museum** behind the Bhutan Embassy (see "Museums," below).

PARKS & GARDENS

Delhi's gardens, each with its own special beauty, can be restorative places; here are only a few:

The **National Zoological Park** (open 9am to 5pm winters; 8am to 4pm summers; closed Fridays; admission 50 paise [2¢]), a 214-acre park in which many of the animals roam under keekar trees and beside pools. It's a lovely place to wander around, so big that it could easily provide a full day's outing. Be sure to buy some peanuts from one of the sellers; you'll find plenty of birds to give them to. (Don't feed the other animals, though.) And don't miss the rare white tigers or the harmonica-playing elephant.

The zoo is located in the shadow of the **Purana Qila,** a 15th-century fort, at the far end of Rajpath. Buses from here go to the zoo (check the tourist office or your hotel for numbers); a scooter ricksha should cost Rs 35 ($1.16) from Connaught Place. Though little more than a shell now, the fort is nonetheless worth a visit; the main entrance is through the north gate eerily named, "Forbidden Gate" (Talaqi Darwaza). Floodlighting at night makes this site especially dramatic.

Buddha Jayanti Park, on Upper Ridge Road, commemorates the 2,500th anniversary of Lord Buddha's parinirvana (freedom from the cycle of life after death). A sapling of the original bodhi tree, which was taken to Sri Lanka, was planted here and thrives today. Woods, streams, bridges, rockeries, and pebble paths leading to secluded glades make this public parkseem a private meditative place.

Lodi Gardens is located on the Lodi Estate, which is about 4 kilometers south of Connaught Circus. When the Raj reigned, this was Lady Willingdon Park; by any name, it's one of Delhi's gems. Landscaped with flowering trees, streams, fountains, and flower gardens, the garden also houses the tombs and mosque of the Lodi Kings. It's a popular spot for a brisk constitutional, yoga, and meditation or just a restorative break after day's work.

Mughal Gardens in Rashtrapati Bhavan (☎ 301-5321) are open to the public in February and March, when flowers bloom. You might get a special entry permit; inquire at the India Tourist Office, 88 Janpath.

National Rose Gardens on Shanti Path, Hauz Khaz, are opposite Safardarjang's Tomb.

Nehru Park, Chanakyapuri (adjacent to the Ashok Hotel), pays tribute to the late prime minister, Jawaharlal Nehru; some of his famous sayings are inscribed on the rocks in the 85-acre park. There is a swimming pool and snack stall.

Qudsia Bagh, located north of Kashmiri Gate. These Mughal gardens were laid out along the Yamuna river in 1748 by Empress Qudsia Begum, who was a slave at birth. During the uprising of 1857 the British fired from here on the Water Gate and Kashmiri Gate. The striking gateway remains from its heyday as do the pavilions.

Talkatora Gardens, Willingdon Crescent. Japanese style, the gardens have a lake (tank or "tal") and fountains.

MUSEUMS

Museums are usually on the visitor's obligatory stops in any city. In Delhi, they are generally closed on Monday and public holidays, unless otherwise noted; a few interesting museums follow, with three of the most worthwhile in the lead:

About 1½ kilometers from Parliament is the **Nehru Memorial Museum and Library,** in Teen Murti House, Teen Murti Marg, where the late Prime Minister Jawaharlal Nehru lived for 16 years. The interior has been preserved just as he left it. It is open daily except Monday from 10am to 5pm. You can see a compelling **son et lumière** (sound and light) show here every evening after sunset, except during the rainy season (roughly mid-July to mid-September). It tells the story of the movement that brought to an end the days of the British Empire in India, and the life of the late prime minister during the country's first two decades of independence. An effective, often poetic show, it's well worth seeing. Performances are in Hindi (at 7pm) and English (at 8:30pm); each lasts one hour. For details, telephone 3016734, or inquire at the Delhi Tourist Office, 88 Janpath, or at the reception or travel desk in your hotel. There is a modest admission charge.

Up the road from Teen Murti House, the white bungalow at 1 Safardjang Rd. (☎ 3010094) was the residence of the late Prime Minister **Indira Gandhi.** Now it, too, is a museum, and the story of her life and times is told through a collection of her personal effects and a photographic mural. In the well-tended garden, Mrs. Gandhi can be heard via tapes addressing the public on various subjects, her voice blending with the rustling trees. A highly polished black granite slab with rough-hewn edges, guarded by soldiers, marks the place she was standing when assassinated on October 31, 1984. The bright flowers always near the stone are brought by the many visitors to the memorial. The museum is open Tuesday through Saturday from 10am to 5pm.

North of the National Gallery of Modern Art is the **Crafts Museum,** Pragati Maidan, Bhairon Marg (☎ 3317641), not far from the Supreme Court. This is not only a display of 20,000 folk and tribal arts and crafts, it's also a living museum showcasing craftsmen weaving or engaged in other handicraft artistry from different parts of India. There are beautiful items for sale, film showings on Sunday, occasional lectures, and a library. The museum is open from 10am to 5pm; entry is free. Closed on the second Saturday, and the fourth Saturday and Sunday of every month.

Also at Pragati Maidan is the **National Science Centre Museum,** near Gate 1 (☎ 3328193), highlighting India's modern achievements. It is open from 11:30am to 7pm.

The **National Gallery of Modern Art,** Jaipur House, just off Rajpath, near India Gate (☎ 382835), showcases Indian art from the middle of the last century on, and is an object lesson in the sensitivity of artists to foreign influence. Since 1930 the major star has been the half-Indian, half-Hungarian painter Amrita Shergil (1913–1941). The museum owns almost 100 examples of his work, including a self-portrait. Another gallery is devoted entirely to the drape-covered paintings and etchings of Rabindranath Tagore, India's Nobel Prize–winning poet, who started "doodling" after his reputation as a poet was well established (and who eventually, in the opinion of some art critics, deserved equal praise for his art). Since 1952 Indian contemporary art has almost equaled that of New York or any other international art center in scope and quality. Some fascinating works on the first floor permit you to see India through the eyes of Westerners, such as British artist Thomas Daniell, whose paintings record Westerners' visits to India; and you can trace the decreasing use of Western styles as the Nationalist movement grew in the 19th century. The gallery, formerly the Delhi home of the Maharajah of Jaipur, is open from 10am to 5pm. If there's a special exhibition, hours are extended to 8pm.

A bit further north is **Shankar's International Doll Museum,** B. Shah Zafar Marg (☎ 3316970), of interest especially for collectors or those with youngsters. A well-known journalist, Shankar founded this museum starring 6,000 dolls, including a children's library with a play corner. Open from 10am to 6pm; admission for adults Rs 1 (3¢), children 25 paise.

Commissioning art and encouraging artists has always been a high priority for India's rulers through the centuries, so it is not surprising that the **National Museum,** about 2 miles farther out of town from the Janpath Hotel, on Janpath (☎ 3019538), should possess a rich collection of art covering 5,000 years. Archaeology rooms, with intricately carved stone groups and 3,000-year-old stone beads that could have been strung together only yesterday, are on the ground floor. The upper rooms are devoted to Indian textiles, silver tables and trays, robes and costumes, and cotton temple hangings embellished with the story of Krishna—all full of toylike elephants, voluptuous dancing girls, and paunchy little men with curved swords on horseback.

Indian and Persian miniatures (the Persian influence is manifest in more detailed backgrounds) bear study for the delicately presented everyday scenes they unfold. Reproductions of frescoes from the Ajanta Caves (near Aurangabad) are more interesting in light of the fact that they are the earliest known Indian paintings, dating from some 2,300 years ago. One section of the second floor is devoted to charts—different facial structures illustrating the human family tree and the different physical types to be found in India's heterogeneous population; the symbolic meaning of illustrations on early coins; and the development of different letters in Indian script. Reproductions of some of the more interesting pieces can be obtained cheaply at the shop on the ground floor. The museum, which has no admission charge, is open Tuesday through Sunday from 10am to 5pm. There are free film shows at 2:30pm daily and free guided tours every day at 10:30, 11:30am, Noon, and 2pm.

Centrally located, the **National Museum of Natural History,** FICCI Building, Barakhamba Road (☎ 3314849), is a small treasury of exhibits tracing India's natural heritage. Children will especially enjoy the Discovery Room where natural specimens can be touched and where they can create models for display at home. Films are at 11:30am and 3:30pm. Lecture programs and exchange exhibitions with like museums are often sponsored. Open from 10am to 5pm.

In Chanakyapuri, in South Delhi behind the Bhutan Embassy, is one of Delhi's most famous museums, the **Rail Transport Museum,** Chanakyapuri (☎ 601816). On exhibit are the oldest working steam locomotive in the world, the *Faerie Queen,* and many other unusual locomotives and classy coaches that in their heyday chugged around India with their maharajah owners. Open 9:30am to 5:30pm. Entry fee is Rs 1 (3¢) for adults, 50 paise (2¢). for children.

GUIDED TOURS

Budget-priced tours of New Delhi are conducted daily from 8am to 1pm, and of Old Delhi from 2:15 to 5pm by ITDC and DTDC. ITDC's tours cost Rs 80 ($2.66) for New Delhi, and Rs 70 ($2.33) for Old Delhi. If New and Old Delhi tours are combined, the total price is Rs 140 ($4.66). Reservations and information are available at **Ashok Travels and Tours** counters at L-1 Connaught Circus (☎ 3322336); India Tourist Office, 88 Janpath (☎ 3320005); and the following hotels: Ashok (☎ 600121, ext. 2156); Janpath (☎ 3320070,); Lodhi (☎ 4362422, ext. 207); Kanishka (☎ 3324422); Samrat (☎ 603030, ext. 2119); Ashok Yatri Niwas (☎ 3324511 or 3324515); and both of the IGI Airports (☎ 3925825 domestic, ☎ 3294410 international).

These ITDC tours cover the following sights in New Delhi: Jantar Mantar, Laxmi Naryan Temple; India Gate, Humayun's Tomb; Lotus Temple (except Mondays), Qutb Minar, Rashtrapati Bhavan, and Parliament Street. The pick-up points are Ashok Travel and Tours, L-Block Office, Connaught Circus (☎ 3322336), and Ashok Yatri Niwas.

The following sights are covered in the ITDC Old Delhi tour: Red Fort, Jama Masjid (seen from Fort), Shanti Van, Raj Ghat, Firozeseh Kotla (drive-through only). The Old Delhi pick-up point is Ashok Yatri Niwas; both tours end at Ashok Yatri Niwas.

Covering similar routes, are the **DTDC's tours** of New Delhi (9am to 2pm) and Old Delhi (2:15 to 5:15pm). The DTDC also has an **evening tour,** which includes Lakshmi Naryan Temple, the floodlit monuments, the son et lumière at the Red Fort; dinner of Indian cuisine at a restaurant is part of this package deal lasting 6 to 10pm. For information and reservations call 3313637. **DTDC's museum tour** operates on Sunday. All tours depart from DTDC, N-Block, Bombay Life Building, Connaught Place (☎ 3313637).

A number of private tour operators conduct similar city tours. One such operator is **Travelite,** 34 Janpath, New Delhi (☎ 3327243), which offers tours of both Old and New Delhi. For the names of other private operators, inquire at your hotel.

You might also choose to do it yourself. Six hours of sightseeing, covering 60 kilometers in a non–air-conditioned car with a driver, costs about Rs 350 ($11.66). Finding a couple of tourists to share with you brings it in line with most budgets and gives you the flexibility to see what you want at your own pace.

EASY EXCURSIONS FROM DELHI

ITDC and DTDC are among those offering same-day coach tours to **Agra** from 6:30am to 10pm. Covered on the ITDC's tour are Sikandra, the Taj Mahal, and Agra Fort. ITDC charges Rs 400 ($13.33), Rs 350 ($19.95) for ages three to 12; ITDC's tour includes breakfast, entrance fees at monuments, and a guide. Reservations and pickup points are L-1 Connaught Circus; Janpath Hotel, Ashok Yatri Niwas, Ashok and Lodhi Hotels.

Tours depart from the Delhi Tourism Office, N-36 Bombay Life Building, Connaught Place (Middle Circle), New Delhi (☎ 3314229), which is open from 7am to 9pm.

DTDC charges slightly less for a similar tour that also includes the ghost city of Fatehpur Sikri. DTDC's tour includes guide and entry fees. By non-air-conditioned car with driver to Agra and Fatehpur Sikri and return to Delhi the same evening costs around Rs 2,280 ($76).

The Delhi-Jaipur-Delhi same-day coach tour by ITDC, from 6:30am to 11:30pm, costs Rs 350 ($11.66) and Rs 300 ($10), including lunch in Jaipur, entrance fees, and guide. The package includes transportation, guide, entrance fees, and a Jeep ride at Amber Fort.

6 Delhi After Dark

Entertainment for foreigners centers around the top hotels, where there are bars, supper clubs, and discos. Drinks are expensive everywhere. At top hotels expect to pay something like Rs 75 ($2.50) for beer; Rs 200 ($6.66) to Rs 600 ($20) for 60 milliliters of imported whisky (about the equivalent of a double shot); about Rs 70 ($2.33) for local gin, vodka, or rum; Rs 150 ($5) to Rs 200 ($6.66) for a glass of wine; Rs 700 ($23.33) for a bottle of local sparkling wine, such as Marquise de Pompadour; and Rs 100 ($3.33) for a small sherry. Fruit juices cost about Rs 40 ($1.33) to 70 ($2.33). Taxes of 10% on soft drinks and 12% on liquor are not included in these prices. Snacks in bars cost around Rs 100 ($3.33) for seekh kebab and Rs 80 ($2.66) for cashews, to give some typical examples, plus 7% tax.

BARS, DANCING, MUSIC

Most of the top hotels have dance bands and, as they say in India, crooners in their swanky Continental restaurants. Some bars offer refreshment and music, here are some of the best.

Connaught Bar, on The Oberoi's rooftop, has a splendid view, a live band, and dancing; **Jazz Bar,** decorated in striking black and white, at the Welcomgroup Maurya Sheraton Hotel and Towers appropriately offers live jazz; the **Polo Lounge** at the Hyatt Regency Delhi features a Phillipine band. Other bars, with their own charms, are **Aloha,** with a polynesian theme, at Le Meridien; also **Captain's Cabin** at The Taj Mahal; **The Quiet Place** at Taj Palace; and **Thugs** at Hotel Broadway.

DISCOTHEQUES

Located in high-priced hotels, discotheques operate like private clubs. Hotel residents are permitted to bring one guest. Those not staying at the hotel must pay a temporary membership fee. East meets West when it comes to the music, but the local dancers are always a step or two behind the times.

Ghungroo, in the Maurya Sheraton, was inspired by Juliana's in London and has a glass-brick dance floor. Other discotheques include the following: **Annabelles,** at the Holiday Inn Crowne Plaza; **My Kind of Place,** Taj Palace Inter-Continental; **CJ's,** in Le Meridien;, and **Oasis,** in the Hyatt Regency. **Some Place Else** was to open soon at the Park Hotel. Generally, things get underway around 10pm and wind up around 3am.

MOVIES

Most of the movie programs are listed daily in the newspapers. Showings are usually at 3, 6, 9, and 11pm (but you'd better double-check). You can call in advance at the box office to book your seat. Though buying a ticket when you get there is cheaper, you probably won't get in because of the crowds. This problem is starting to disappear as many people have started staying home to watch videos. Some movie theaters show English-language films, usually censored for their sexy parts.

OTHER ENTERTAINMENT

Outside the hotels, an evening entertainment is **Dances of India.** This combination of classical, folk, and tribal dances takes place daily at 6:45pm for 70 minutes at the Parsi Anjuman Hall, Bahadurshah Zafar Marg, opposite Ambedkar Football Stadium, Delhi Gate (☎ 3275978, 3317831, or 3320968). Reservations are available through hotel receptionists, travel agents, or Tourist Aid Bureau, 3rd Floor, Delite Cinema, Asaf Ali Road.

As in major cities the world over, Delhi's special events and entertainment possibilities change rapidly. To keep up-to-date, watch the daily papers or buy a copy of ***Delhi Diary***—Rs 6 (2¢)—or ***Genesis, The City Guide***—Rs 12 (4¢)—at any newsstand.

7 Shopping

Remember that bargaining goes on just about everywhere, except in government emporia. For how to bargain and other overall shopping tips, see Chapter 1, "Getting to Know India."

SHOPPING HOURS

In the government Central Cottage Industries Emporium, Jawahar Vyapar Bhawan, off Janpath (☎ 3326790), and state government emporia on Baba Kharak Singh Marg off Connaught Place, hours are 10am to 6pm, with a lunch break from 1:30 to 2:30pm. Other stores are open from 9:30am to 7:30pm, with a one-hour lunch break sometime between 1 and 3pm.

Shops are closed as follows:

- **Sunday:** Centrally located shops in Connaught Place, Janpath, Baba Kharak, Singh Marg, Jor Bagh, Khan Market, Malcha Marg, Nehru Place, Sunder Nagar, Yashwant Place, Chandni Chowk, Sadar Bazar.
- **Monday:** Bhogal, Defence Colony, I.N.A., Janpura, Karol Bagh, Kotla Lajpat Nagar, Nizamuddin, Sarojini Nagar, South Extension.
- **Tuesday:** Greater Kailash, Green Park, Hauz Khas, Safdarjung Enclave, Vasant Vihar, Shahdara, Yusuf Sarai.

- **Wednesday:** West Delhi, Paschim Vihar, Rajouri Garden, Shalimar Bagh, Tilak Nagar.

Hotel shops are open Monday through Saturday, and some stay open Sunday as well (and well into the evening for late shoppers).

SHOPPING STRATEGY

First, visit the government-run stores—to survey the merchandise, if not to buy. It gives you a clue to the standard of goods and prices before you venture into the privately owned shops and bazaars.

If you've only got time to make one shopping stop, go to the **Central Cottage Industries Emporium,** Jawahan Vyapar Bhawan, Janpath (☎ 3326790), the government-run department store of arts and crafts from all over India. From the Delhi area are embroidered slippers with turned-up toes and zari (gold embroidery aglow on dark velvet bags), costing Rs 100 to Rs 2,000 ($3.33 to $66.66) or more, depending on the amount of work or metal; copper lampshades, shaped and shined with tiny floral cutouts to cast a soft glow are Rs 300 ($10) for a large shade; pottery from nearby kilns, in blue or black, with bright designs, made into pitchers, vases, plates, and pencil jars, with prices ranging from Rs 100 ($3.33) to Rs 200 ($6.66) for a pottery pencil jar.

The Emporium has an excellent collection of ready-made salwar-kamiz (shirts and trousers) starting around Rs 650 ($21.66) and going up, and lovely duppatas (scarves) to coordinate with them from Rs 120 ($4) and up. The store stocks silk dresses, dresses, wool and cotton robes, and flowing embroidery-trimmed cotton caftans. For those who prefer to make their own, there are inexpensive cotton fabrics and lustrous silks that go up to the thousands of rupees. Easy to pack are men's ties and women's silk clutch bags. Papier-mâché boxes from Kashmir, decorated with magical gardens and mythical beasts are colorful gifts. In the precious-jewelry section, find glittering diamond ear studs as well as those made of semiprecious stones. The antique department has a variety of decorative and wearable items, which you may be assured are the real things.

OTHER PLACES TO SHOP

BABA KHARAK SINGH MARG Stroll off Connaught Place to the three-block stretch of state- and territorial-run shops on Baba Kharak Singh Marg for some unusual wares from all over India, including remote and rarely visited places. One of the best selections can be found at **Gujari** (Gujarat), A-6, where you'll find attractive ankle-length salwar (tunics), embroidered and accented in tiny mirrors; matching kamiz (trousers that tie at the waist) and coordinating scarves, the cost depending on whether the fabric is cotton or silk. Decorative mirrored wall hangings and tie-dyed scarves, both moderately priced, make nice gifts; costing a bit more are nubby or smooth-textured hand-loomed woolen shawls.

At **Trimourti** (Maharastra), A-8, cotton saris, to wear as is or to whip up into a skirt or dress, cost less than you think, as do printed cotton salwar-kamiz. **Zoon** (Kashmir), A-7, features rugs, patterned papier-mâché boxes and bowls, wool and silk caftans and robes, and elegant carpets at wide-ranging prices, depending on the intricacy or pattern, number of knots, and whether the carpet is silk or wool. Other **Kashmir emporia** are at 5 Prithviraj Rd. and at the Hotel Ashok.

For arts and crafts from little-traveled regions, visit **Ambapali** (Bihar), A-5, which has striking paintings of gods and goddesses done by villagers, priced according to size and intricacy of design. Or go to **Utkalika** (Orissa), B-4, for delightful primary-colored paintings showing Krishna cavorting with the gopis (milkmaids), dancers, and fanciful animals, as well as bright appliqued hand-held fans and garden umbrellas. From distant **Nagaland,** C-2, handlooms with traditional spear patterns are made into shawls, shoulder bags, and skirts. From **Assam** at B-1, come gleaming heavy-textured silks by the meter at various prices, or you can have them made into quilted bedspreads; and from **Himachal Pradesh,** C-3, are embroidery-edged woolen caps and woolen shawls, dyed jute slippers for about $1, and bargain-priced papier-mâché dolls.

Black Partridge (Haryana), C-8, displays goods from one of Delhi's neighboring states, including necklaces of polished semiprecious stones and boxes inlaid with stone fragments (priced according to box size and the number of inlaid stones used in the designs).

Phulkari (Punjab), C-6, is the name of not only the shop, but also of the renowned intricate Punjabi silk-embroidered cotton fabric, a traditional gift to North Indian brides. Useful for pillow covers, upholstery, and spreads, it is priced up or down depending on the ornateness and size of the piece. About the same price structure covers another textile specialty, khes, which is cleverly embroidered for use on both sides. It's also ideal for draperies or covering pillows, but could be used for an interesting jacket or vest. At **Gangotri** (Uttar Pradesh), B-5, also representing the northern region, look for kurtas, the long flared shirts popular since Mughal days. Prices depend on the fabric and intricacy of embroidery trimming; they now make attractive beach cover-ups, cool summer shirts, or nighties.

Lepakshi (Andhra Pradesh), B-6, has Bidriware—stones and wires embedded in black or white alloy—made into dozens of items including buttons, boxes, and bangles, prices depending on the size of the piece and the intricacy of the work; decorative scrolls, woodcarvings, perfumes, and gleaming glass bangles are available at modest prices.

Mrignayani (Madhya Pradesh), B-8, is the place to find hand-loomed fabrics so sheer that the 17th-century diarist, Bernier, said they'd wear out in a day. For a modest amount of money you can get enough of this gossamer material to make a pretty and cool summer dress—which will wash easily and wear about as well as any other, despite the diarist's dire prediction.

At **Poompuhar** (Tamil Nadu), C-1, there are lustrous Kanchipuram silks for a sari; famous Madras plaids to make a dress, skirt, or a couple of tailored shirts; and gaudy but nice, ornate and gilded Tanjore paintings of deities. **Kairali** (Kerala), B-7, has ivory carvings (supposedly African tusks to conserve India's) of various subjects, some so intricate they look like fine lace, and placemats and doormats of palm-leaf fiber and rugs made of coir (coconut husk fiber), both durable and cheap. Be aware, though, that international law now forbids the import and export of most authentic ivory, no matter where it comes from. At **Kaveri** (Karnataka), no. C-4 (☎ 343202), you'll find ivory-inlaid ebony walking sticks, bangles, boxes; rosewood and sandalwood carvings of deities and elephants; and jasmine and sandalwood soaps.

On Baba Kharak Singh Marg are also shops with merchandise from **West Bengal,** A-2; **Tripura,** B-3; and **Manipur,** C-7; and Delhi's own emporium at no. A-3/4, with a varied selection of the cut-out copper shades, pottery, and zari (embroidered) bags, slippers, and belts.

JANPATH SHOPS Don't limit yourself to the government-run stores. Check out the many stalls on Janpath selling surplus and export-quality ready-to-wear clothing at low prices, which become not only lower, but fair after bargaining. On Janpath also the **Tibetan Bazaar** sells a variety of wares, including jewelry and copper pots just waiting for a bargainer. For a wider variety of objects, try **Palika Bazaar,**

Connaught Place, an underground market with 300 stalls selling everything imaginable from brassware and jewelry to ready-to-wear including bags, saris, and shoes.

IN AND ABOUT CONNAUGHT PLACE Here you'll find abundant shops offering bargain-hunting opportunities. **The Shop,** 10 Regal Building (☎ 3310972), reinterprets traditional Indian styles for contemporary fashions for Western women; you'll find such items as skirts, apron-style dresses, cotton dresses, and tote bags. For something fashion-forward in a sari or salwar kamiz, try **Kalpana,** F-5 Connaught Place (☎ 3315368), where there are modern prints and colors.

For traditionalists, shimmering silks, mainly from Benares, Bhawalpur, and Bangalore, are staples at **Banaras House Ltd.,** N Block, Connaught Place (☎ 3314751). The store's selection includes heavy gold brocades which are priced per meter, according to the amount of gold in the material. Less expensive are scarves and shirts.

At **Ivory Mart** 22-F Connaught Place (☎ 3310197), the range includes intricate ivory carvings (permits needed to export), jewelry, paintings, embroidered items, sandalwood carvings and figures, silks, boxes, and other craft items. Ivory Mart has a branch in old Delhi the Northern Gate of the Jama Masjid.

Tribhovandas, 2 Scindia House, Janpath (☎ 3313336), a famous name in jewelry, is a huge emporium filled with precious gems and gold, a splurge for most of us. Some smaller items, such as pave diamond earrings or studs, will cost only a few hundred rupees. For more extravagantly set pieces, you'll need to win big in the lottery back home, yet the price will be somewhat less than you pay in the states for similar quality—the gold is 18 karat and up. For contemporary art, the aptly named **Art Today,** A-I Hamilton House, Connaught Place, is worth checking out. **Giggles,** E-24, Connaught Place (☎ 3328139), has T-shirts and other small gift items.

OLD DELHI One of the most famous Old Delhi shops is **Ivory Palace,** Northern Gate, Jama Masjid. Craftsmen at the entrance show how they make some of the items sold inside. Among these are zari (gold-and silver-embroidered) clutch bags, with some garnets added to the design. The store has on display an uncomfortable-looking, elaborately carved ivory drawing room suite, which took two craftsmen 25 years to complete—it's not on sale. It's priceless.

MARKETS, BAZAARS & SPECIALTY SHOPS

BEYOND CENTRAL DELHI

SUNDER NAGAR MARKET Easily one of the most enjoyable places to shop is Sunder Nagar Market, a group of well-appointed stores not far from the bustling center, but in comparison an island of serenity. This is where serious collectors from all over the world hunt for antiques—miniatures and bronzes, jewelry, woodcarvings, and unusual household objects. Prices for the extremely valuable items may seem high until you compare them with prices for similar objects in the West—providing you could find them at home. In some of these shops, subtly suggesting that the price might be out of line could get you a slight markdown. There are some inexpensive wares also. If you have more time than money to spend, then you can browse to your heart's content.

The following listing will give you some highlights:

Bharany's 14 Sunder Nagar Market, is run by Chhote Bharany, a world-famous collector-merchant-author, who has exhibited his heirlooms in museums and sold them abroad at such well-known department stores as Bloomingdale's in New York. Bharany inherited some of his valuable artifacts and purchased others from maharajas in distress. If the jewelry set with emeralds and 24-karat gold is too rich for you, the shop has pretty garnet necklaces, enamel earrings, and strands of seed pearls. Bharany also has antique textiles, some as costly as his gems.

Ellora 9 Sunder Nagar Market, has stunning antique silver jewelry, including belts and bangles. No matter how delicately worked or elaborate, silver and gold jewelry is weighed and sold by the gram. Since there are only 25 grams to an ounce, several ounces of silver belt can easily run up a fat bill. Here also are unset stones and miniature paintings, some exceedingly rare.

Indian Arts Corner 30 Sunder Nagar Market, carries old silver belts that harem charmers once swiveled around their hips, and ankle bangles—now bracelets (sold by the gram)—and semiprecious and precious stones, set and unset.

Kumar Art Gallery 11 Sunder Nagar Market, specializes in rare antique rugs and equally rare Tantric art (symbolic, occult, diagrammatic stuff), both of which cost thousands of rupees depending on the age, size, and intricacy of the piece.

Ladakh Art Gallery 10 Sunder Nagar, offers Indian and Tibetan art objects and old jewelry.

Lall's 8 Sunder Nagar Market, has antique and new jewelry and interesting jewelry boxes to keep it in, as well as metal chests for safekeeping other precious possessions.

La Boutique 20 Sunder Nagar Market, sells antique silver, paintings, and old ivory carvings (remember the restrictions; you will probably need a special permit to leave the country with purchases).

Maharaja's Carpets 13 Sunder Nagar, as the name implies, carpets to please royalty and princely prices to match.

Mascot's Book Shop 6 Sunder Nagar Market, carries a large selection of art books.

Mittal Stores 12 Sunder Nagar. Sells quality tea.

HAUZ KHAS & BEYOND En route the Qutb Minar, Hauz Khas Village, a group of shops in a village setting with high-priced Indian designer wares in furniture, jewelry, and ready-to-wear, offers prime territory browsing and buying. For styles chic enough to cause a few fashion tremors in the West, check out **Fusion,** A-18 Hauz Khas Village; **Glitterati,** 29 Hauz Khas Village; and **The Studio Apparelli,** 1 Hauz Khas Village. Another well-stocked shop, **Shiraz Gallery,** 12 Hauz Khas Village, has carpets as well as shawls in amazingly soft pashmina and shahtoosh (check on export rules).

If you want to take a break in one of the narrow lanes, **Khas Bagh,** 12 Hauz Khaz Village (☎ 663905), colorfully decorated with murals showing crowded buses and eager bicyclers, claims to serve the city's most authentic kebabs and tandoori dishes—from Rs 85 ($2.83) to Rs 250 ($8.33). The highest price covers tandoori prawns in cream sauce. Open 12:30 to 3:30pm, 7:30 to 12pm. Two other villagelike restaurants, also at no. 12 with the same management and pricing, are **Mohalla,** which features Indian cuisine at the same hours as Khas Bagh, and **Al Capone,** which offers Italian and Continental cuisines, some of the latter with their calorie counts listed on the menu. It is open 10am to midnight. You might want to schedule a dinner out here, when folk dancers entertain, rather than lunch when there's no entertainment. The price for the show is Rs 100 ($3.33), which is at 6:45pm.

Near the Qutb Minar, Mehrauli Road has shops from which to unearth treasures: At H-5/6 Mehrauli Road, across from the Qutb Minar, **Once Upon a Time** specializes in wearable art in evening wear, jewelry, and accessories for men and women. **Indian Handicrafts Emporium,** 5 Main Mehrauli Road, has a wide range of craft items, and at the **Indo Kashmir Carpet Factory,** C-225, Lado Sarai, Main Mehrauli Road, you can buy carpets and see weavers at work. Everywhere in India there are increasing numbers of Kashmir shops run by merchants who have reclocated because of the unrest in their Himalayan state.

SANTUSHTI SHOPPING COMPLEX Easily Delhi's most serene place to shop is **Santusthi** (opposite the Samrat Hotel), an enchanting complex of about 30 shops in bungalows dotted among lovely gardens. The property belongs to the Indian Air Force, and the tenants donate a percentage of their rents to assist the Airport Wives Association's charitable works. Among the most interesting of the shops are **Anokhi** (for updated classical Rajasthani prints) and **Amaya** (both known for fashionable Indian wear with a Western flair).

While browsing and buying you can have tea a **Flury's,** a branch of Calcutta's most famous patisserie, or get a bite to eat at **Basil and Thyme** (and use their clean restrooms).

CRAFTS MUSEUM, PRAGATI MAIDAN See craftsmen at work and buy what they make at the Crafts Museum, Mathura Road; among the bargains are shawls and pottery.

BARGAINS IN BANGLES Every Tuesday at **Hanuman Mandir** (Temple), dozens of vendors display a dazzling array of bangles from near and far. You'll get an education in the diversity of the simple circle—there are bangles in every color; bangles embedded with chips of other colors, with metal, mirrors, and fake gems; candy-striped bangles, faceted bangles, flowered bangles—and that hardly covers the assortments at this bazaar. With a little bargaining, for Rs 30 to Rs 130 ($1 to $4.33) you buy enough to dress up your wrists and still take some bangles home for gifts.

Hanuman Mandir Bazaar is also a little mela (fair) where you can get your palm read by a strolling fortune teller or get your palm "red" by having an artist paint it with henna designs. These days Indian women have their palms painted for good looks or good luck. In earlier times henna painting was a ritual for new brides only, and it's still a bridal tradition. It takes a week of more for the henna designs to wear off, so one sure way to pick out a new bride in a crowd is to look for the young woman with designs painted on her hands and feet.

THE BIG BAZAAR If you don't mind being hassled and hustled, bustling **Chandni Chowk,** famous for bargaining since the 18th century, can be a lot of fun. My favorite is **Dariba Kalan,** the fascinating lane of silversmiths, where you'll find rings for your fingers, toes, ears, and nose; bangles for your arms and ankles; and necklaces and combs. In other winding lanes are perfume oils, sparkling garlands, baskets, brocades, and copper pots, all for prices you can almost name yourself—but you have to bargain. While you look for bargains, be sure to keep an eye on your handbag and wallet.

4 Excursions from the Capital

The speedy *Shatabdi Express* makes it easy and pleasant to take off from Delhi and visit a number of interesting places spanning widely disparate miles and centuries: Agra (16th and 17th centuries); Khajuraho (temples from 950 to 1050); newly popular Jhansi and Orrcha (16th and 17th centuries); and Bhopal (18th and 19th centuries) and Sanchi (3rd century B.C.). These destinations can all be reached on a round trip from Delhi, or you can take other routes from any of them. And if you don't feel like taking a train, read on for other ways to see these places.

1 Agra & the Taj Mahal

128 miles (207 kilometers) southeast of Delhi

The sleepy little town of Agra began its career in the 16th-century era of the Mughal emperors. Today its population numbers about 1.5 million, and it is one of Uttar Pradesh's biggest cities. Yet it hints of its village past, especially in the main part of town on the right side of the Yamuna, where tiny lanes are lined with silk sellers. Even the so-called modern buildings in the Cantonment area are a century old. What is new—including some of the newest hotels—has already begun to look old (more about that later.)

Most tourists who visit Agra today see little of the narrow crowded lanes and colorful shops—perhaps an occasional glimpse through the windows of the deluxe coaches that take them from the train station to the Taj Mahal and back again. For the famous marble tomb is what everyone comes to see, and rarely do they stay longer than one night. A pity.

Agra was the capital of the Mughals in the 16th and 17th centuries and, in addition to the Taj, it is a repository of many of their most famous monuments. The city has long astonished visitors: Elizabethans picked up their quills to pen messages back to England, describing it as more opulent than London. Some places of interest are connected to the Afghans, who predate the Mughals.

The city thrives on tourism, hence the abundance of hotels, shops, restaurants, and, alas, pesky souvenir sellers. Rarely, if ever, does a visitor depart without a trinket made of marble inlay to take home. You might also consider a side trip to the ghost city of Fatehpur Sikri, which is described at the end of this section.

ESSENTIALS

GETTING THERE

BY AIR The daily Delhi to Agra flight takes about 30 minutes and costs $23. You must be there an hour ahead for check-in and security check, and there can be delays. (With regard to time, it's better to take the train). Between Agra and Jaipur the flying time and costs are about the same as the Delhi to Agra run.

BY TRAIN Your best bet is the speedy, air-conditioned *Shatabdi Express,* which departs Delhi Monday through Friday at 6:15am and arrives Agra at 8:10am. Fares are Rs 235 ($7.83) AC Chair, Rs 470 ($15.66) Executive. Remember this penny-wise tip: Take the *Shatabdi* chair and save. The *Taj Express* is a pleasant train excursion from Delhi, departing at 7:15am and arriving Agra at 9:45am. Fares are Rs 112 ($3.73) AC Chair, Rs 49 ($1.63) Second.

BY BUS Agra is well connected by bus services to Delhi and a number of other cities. For information on **express bus service** between Delhi and Agra, call Delhi's Interstate Bus Terminus (IBST) (☎ 2529083); or UP Road Transport Corporation's Interstate Bus Terminus (IBST) in Delhi (☎ 2518709).

A Note on Bus Tours: Bus sightseeing trips from Delhi (described in Chapter 3, "Delhi: Where the Tour Begins") compress the famous sights in a one-day blur and are recommended only for those truly pressed for time.

BY HIRED CAR The trip from Delhi in a small, non–air-conditioned car with driver to Agra and Fatehpur Sikri, returning to Delhi via Bharatpur bird sanctuary, costs approximately Rs 2,780 (about $100), perhaps more by publication time. It is cheaper to take the train from Delhi to Bharatpur (see Chapter 5, "Rajasthan: Golden Deserts and Great Palaces").

VISITOR INFORMATION

The **Tourist Information counters** at the airport or Agra Cantonment Railway Station, or the **India Tourist Office,** 191 The Mall (☎ 72377), can help with hotel reservations and information. Government-approved guides congregate at two offices: **Take-A-Guide** and **Guide Office,** both open from 6am to noon and located in the Karim Shah Complex (across from Mansingh Hotel and on either side of Rajasthan Emporium).

GETTING AROUND

Tourist Taxis can be hired through a reputable travel agency, such as the **Travel Bureau,** near Hotel Taj View, Fatehabad Road (☎ 360118); one-half day (six hours, 60 kilometers) sightseeing by non–air-conditioned taxi should run about Rs 350 ($10.16). There are no fixed rates for **auto rickshas,** so set the price before you get in. They usually run tourists to the Taj from the Agra Cantonment Railway Station or any hotel for Rs 25 (83¢), Rs 75 ($2.50) to 100 ($3.33) for a full day of sightseeing. Bargain also with **tempo rickshas** (larger than auto rickshas); they usually get Rs 20 (66¢) for a one-way trip Fatehpur Sikri. Finally, bargain with **cycle rickshas** and **tongas** for a fair fare. **Bus fare** within the city rarely runs higher than Rs 1.

FAST FACTS: AGRA

Film The photography shops Taj Photo, Taj Complex, Mercury Photo Studio, all on Taj Road, Sardar Bazaar, are among the shops in town that sell and develop film.

Newspapers Book Depot on Taj Road next to the Jaiwal Hotel has Asian editions of Western news magazines, best-sellers, and loads of postcards (many candidates for the worst photography awards).

Swimming The swimming pools at the hotels Clark's Shiraz, Welcomgroup Mughal Sheraton, Taj View, Agra Ashok, and Lauries are open to nonguests for a fee.

Special Event

Taj Mahotsav, annually in February, is a huge 10-day festival with something for everyone—music, dance, food, and especially great displays of irresistible handicrafts; bring your wallet stuffed with rupees.

WHAT TO SEE & DO

Taj Mahal

The famous marble tomb was built between 1631 and 1653 (with features added until 1657). It took 20,000 laborers, masons, stone cutters, and jewelers to complete the task. Marble was brought from one part of India, sandstone from another, semiprecious stones from all over Asia, Russia, Egypt, Baghdad, and other places. The final product is a masterpiece of symmetry: a landmark so famous that every visitor's first reaction is to exclaim how much smaller it is than they had believed.

The size is an illusion, as you discover when walking toward it. It actually seems to float in the air (an impression that is much heightened at sunrise), and somehow it is so delicately balanced that it fosters countless optical illusions. The main illusion is experienced if you face the Taj from the entrance gate, walking forward a few steps and then back: The whole building appears to move toward you. Atop this gate, incidentally, are 22 small domes, ostensibly recording the number of years the mausoleum took to build.

And it was constructed as a monument to love. Mumtaz Mahal was 20 when she was married to Shah Jahan, fourth in the illustrious line of Mughal rulers that began with Babur. The lovely Mumtaz was Shah Jahan's second wife—his favorite—and she bore him 14 children before dying in childbirth in 1631. Hearing of her death while away at battle, he vowed to build her the most extravagant monument the world had ever seen. That monument became the Taj Mahal, universally acknowledged for centuries to be one of the world's most perfect pieces of architecture.

A fountain-filled reflecting pool leads up from the entrance gate; the mausoleum itself is flanked by four gentle minarets (which lean slightly outward, so that they'd fall without damage to the main structure in case of an accident). A red sandstone mosque to the left is matched by an identical building to the right, purely for the sake of architectural harmony. Around the 90-foot-high entrance portico are quotations from the Koran in Arabic script. Inside the Taj itself, an intricately carved marble screen shields the tombs of Mumtaz and her husband. These tombs are fakes placed directly over the real tombs, which are in the chamber underneath. The marble walls are exquisitely decorated with pietra dura inlay, the method of setting semiprecious and precious stones into marble tile. Some of the decorative flowers are composed of as many as 64 separate inlays, so skillfully placed in a one-inch square that even your fingers cannot detect the joints. The ceiling of this inner dome is 80 feet high, and the guard delights in demonstrating the 15-second echo. (Do not tip.)

Behind the mausoleum, an open terrace looks across the river to a crumbling red stone wall that is generally believed to have been the site for a replica of the Taj in black marble for Shah Jahan. Upon its completion, the two were to be linked by a black and white marble bridge. Before this could be built, Shah Jahan was deposed and arrested by his son, Aurangzeb. When he died in 1666, he was buried beside his beloved wife.

During the 1971 war between India and Pakistan, the Taj Mahal was closed to the public for the first and only time in more than 300 years. The renowned monument also was covered over with straw matting, wildflowers, vines, and grass. This camouflage kept Pakistani bombers from using the reflection cast by the Taj under moonlight to lead them to important Agra targets.

For years, tourists made special trips to see the unforgettable sight of the Taj on full-moon nights. Many of these visitors would spend the entire night gazing at the Taj until the sunrise made the dome seem to be tinted pink. Now, however, it is not possible to see this sight—the Taj is closed on full-moon nights, as it is on all others.

As Agra develops economically there's been widespread concern over the effects on the Taj of industrial pollution. Now as a safeguard, nearby foundries are being shut down and relocated away from the Taj, where they can do it no harm. To continue to check air quality as well, pollution-monitoring devices have been concealed in the garden and under the Taj dome.

The Taj Mahal is open daily from October 1 through March 31, 8am to 4pm; from April 1 through September 30, 7:30am to 5pm. Admission is Rs 100 ($3.33) before 8am and after 7pm (preferable because it's less crowded); Rs 2 (6¢) other times; free on Friday. Because of terrorists threats, the main entrance is off limits for tourists; they go to the side of the monument, where there's a security check. The museum in the Taj compound is open from 10am to 5pm, and the entry fee is included in the Taj ticket. It's easy to find the Taj Mahal from almost anywhere in Agra: Many signposts around town bear its silhouette and an arrow.

Other Major Sights in Agra

Although the Taj Mahal is the major attraction in Agra, it is by no means the only one. There's the Fort, an incredible forerunner to the Taj, and a number of less significant sites.

Agra's Red Fort Agra's famous fort, sprawling along the river in the center of today's city, predates the Red Fort in Delhi by more than 75 years, having been built from 1565 to 1573. Although designed by Akbar, the third Mughal emperor, it was added to and improved by three of his successors and has changed little since the 17th century—still an impressive combination of military fortress and delightful palace.

It is massive in size and strategically located—the outer wall is almost 2 miles long and 70 feet high—adjoining the broad Yamuna River. A moat and another wall are supplemented by a semitropical jungle area so wide that the fort's guardians would gather on the palace roof high above to watch staged fights between tigers and elephants. Monkeys play among the trees there today.

Adjoining the palace within the walls is another richly decorated palace, the octagonal **Mussamman Burj,** of richly inlaid marble, where Shah Jahan spent his final years (after being imprisoned by his son, Aurangzeb) gazing up the river at his beloved Taj Mahal.

The most romantic and least military part of the fort is undoubtedly the area around the **Anguri Bagh,** or grape garden, where the women of the harem lived and played. Here the walkways were covered with rich Persian carpets, silken drapes hung over the doorways, and green parrots fluttered around the rosewater swimming pool, which had seats for the harem women between the two-score fountain jets. Nearby is the **Palace of Mirrors,** thousands of tiny, concave reflecting glasses inset into its walls, in which were the hot- and cold-water baths and a stairway leading down to the moat, for those athletic women who wished to swim in the open.

Under the grape garden, subterranean chambers offered a welcome cool respite from the summer heat. Here, too, dungeons were located, a couple of marble grills allowing unfortunate prisoners to see their friends still at play in the garden.

The women had their own little mosque too, but a bigger one; the **Moti Masjid** (Pearl Mosque), is the largest of its kind in the world and took Shah Jahan seven years to build. Another inner courtyard of the fort, **Machchi Bhawan,** is a neat garden today, but once it was filled with water and stocked with colored fish that the various emperors delighted in catching as they sat languidly on a throne above.

The Red Fort is open daily from sunrise (around 6am) to sunset (usually about 6pm). Admission is Rs 2 (6¢), free on Friday.

Itimad-ud-Daula Building just seemed to come naturally to those old Mughals. Fourteen years before Shah Jahan started on the Taj Mahal, during the reign of his predecessor Jahangir—between 1622 and 1628—the magnificent tomb of Itimad-ud-Daula was built. This was the work of Jahangir's wife, Nur Jahan, who constructed it in memory of her parents. It is chiefly notable for being the first example of pietra dura inlay—precious stones intricately recessed in marble tile. The whole place is covered in it. Like the Taj, it has the real tombs downstairs and the replicas above. This was common practice so that visitors would not walk across the real graves. The woman's tomb, incidentally, is usually identifiable by the replica of a slate on its surface—the implication being that the woman's heart is as clear as a slate, and her husband should write on it what he will. Two of the tombs look exactly like wood, but they are actually made of yellow marble. The bodies are buried seven feet below, in accordance with Muslim custom.

The engraved walls bear some inspection. A recurring theme is a wine flask with snakes for handles, supposedly a sly reference by Nur Jahan to her husband's poisonous drinking habits. Atop the marble arches in some places are delicate carvings copied from Nur Jahan's real-life embroidery. The mosaic marble floor of the tomb is designed like a Persian carpet.

Itimad-ud-Daula is just beyond the Yamuna bridge on the east side of the river. It is the least visited of the Mughal landmarks and, thus, the most serene. Admission is Rs 2 (6¢). Give the shoe watcher Rs 1 (3¢)—he'll ask for Rs 50($1.66). Open sunrise to sunset.

Jami Masjid Near the railway station, the Jami Masjid was built in 1648 by Shah Jahan in honor of his daughter, Jahanara—the same who looked after him in his dying days. It doesn't hold a candle to the Delhi mosque near the Red Fort, but as long as you're here, you might as well visit.

Sights Nearby

Chini-ka-Rauza (China Tomb) The burial place of Afzal Khan (a Persian poet, he was Shah Jahan's prime minister) and his wife, this tomb has a Persian feel to its glazed tile exterior and is about 1 1/2 miles north of Itimad-ud-Daula.

Rambagh Said to be India's first Mughal garden, Rambagh was created by Babur (1526–30), the founder of the Mughal dynasty as one of his first acts in Agra. The garden, designed along Persian lines as a pleasure place, was originally "Arambagh," meaning "resting garden." Babur, a ferocious warrior, also was a highly cultivated man who wrote poetry, encouraged the arts, loved fine food and more than just a little wine. His tomb was here until it was moved to Kabul. Excavations have unearthed animals and floral frescoes, and work continues to clean and restore Rambagh's former beauty. Rambagh is north of Chini-ka-Rauza.

Sikandra This tomb is 6 miles north of Agra and well worth seeing. Several years before Akbar died in 1605, he began work on his own mausoleum, as was the custom; his son, Jahangir, took until 1613 to finish it. It stands today at Sikandra, an ornate tomb in 150 acres of lovely gardens filled with deer, black buck, and monkeys. Its four minarets are situated in such a manner that only three can be seen from the minarets of the Taj Mahal, and vice versa. They were stylistic forerunners to those at the Taj.

The real tomb of Akbar is in a chamber below and illuminated by a single ray of light from a high window. Inscriptions in the catacomb describe the attributes of Allah. A priest demonstrates the echo effect for a few paise.

The gateway to Akbar's tomb, with its distinctive mosaic designs, is more impressive than the tomb itself, the latter having been ransacked by vandals late in the 17th century.

Entry fee Re. 2 (6¢). Black-faced monkeys lining the walkway expect peanuts; those with hearts of stone can ignore their pleas. Packets of peanuts are on sale here for Rs 25 (83¢), but you can buy two packets for Rs 5 (16¢) if you bargain. Better, buy your peanuts in town (where they are cheaper), since the stalls here are often sold out. Very peaceful in the early morning.

GUIDED TOURS

The **U.P. State Tourism Development Corporation (UPSTDC)** conducts a guided coach tour (from 10am to 6pm) of the Taj Mahal, Agra Red Fort, and Fatehpur Sikri. The cost is Rs 100 ($3.33). Pick-up points, starting at 7:45am, are Taj Khema, U.P. Tourist Bureau office, and Agra Cantonment Railway Station (to meet *Taj Express* at 9:15am). There are also guided half-day tours to Sikandra and Fathepur for about Rs 70 ($2.33). For reservations, contact **UPSTDC,** Taj Khema (☎ 360140).

U.P. Roadways guided coach tour—Rs 90 ($3)—starts and ends at the Agra Cantonment Railway Station, its beginning timed to coincide with the arrival of the *Taj Express,* and includes Fathepur Sikri, a lunch stop at the Hotel Mayur, the Taj Mahal, and Agra's Red Fort. Shop, stop, and return to the station; check details with U.P. Roadways, 96 Gwalior Rd. (☎ 72206). If you zipped down on the Shatbadi Express, you'll have about an hour's wait for either tour. All tours include guide and entry fees.

For travelers on a tight schedule these tours cover the sights in kaleidoscopic brevity; local hotels and travel agents also conduct similarly paced guided tours. It's far better to negotiate a fair fare with a taxi and sightsee at your own pace.

SHOPPING

From the days of the Mughals, Agra's artisans have excelled in marble inlay work. Today craftsmen—some claiming to be direct descendants of the early artists—still lay petal-thin strips of mother-of-pearl and semiprecious stones in translucent marble that tourists take home. Other popular crafts sold in Agra include brass ware, carpets, ivory and wood carvings, textiles, and leather goods. Silk items, such as ties for men and scarves for women, are also popular. Merchants in Agra are generally less inclined to bargain than those where sales are harder to make, but some will give in to attractive offers. They are accommodating about shipping your large purchases; make sure to shop in a reputable place so your merchandise will be shipped and insured properly. Most stores are open from 10am to 7pm. Here are just a few shopping opportunities in Agra.

At **Krafts Palace,** 506 The Mall (☎ 364103), artisans at the entrance show how the exacting inlay work is done. The shop sells inlaid plates, boxes, trays, and paperweights, all easy to take home as souvenirs; prices run from Rs 100 ($3.33) to many times higher, depending on the intricacy of the inlay design. The store also has a full range of other gift items, such as costume jewelry with dangling stones plus ivory, brass, sandalwood, and silks.

Kohinoor Jewellers, 41 Mahatma Gandhi Rd. (☎ 364156), have been precious stone merchants for five generations. Among the unusual gems are rare emeralds, which cost up to Rs 10,000 ($334) per carat. Much less rare, and therefore cheaper, are the smoky topaz for $1 a carat. You might pick up some blue sapphire stud earrings for about Rs 550 ($18) and up. Silver bangles run Rs 200 ($6.66) and up. On display is an elephant inlaid with 5,000 jewels; made for the 1970 World's Fair in Japan, it is now among the Kohinoor's priceless treasures.

Oswal Emporium, 30 Munro Rd., Agra Cantonment (☎ 363240), open daily from 10am to 7pm, has some of the highest-priced and most handsome inlay in town: Elaborate inlaid tabletops cost from Rs 5,000 ($167) to Rs 60,000 ($2,000), depending on size and workmanship. Marble boxes start at around Rs 450 ($15); trays and plates up to Rs 15,000 ($500). Silk scarves at Oswals, hand-stitched in gold designs, cost Rs 1,000 and up. The store's eight-minute sound and light show (in English and French) covers Agra's treasures as well as their own.

Cottage Industry, 18 Munro Rd. (☎ 363103), deals in hand-knotted carpets and durries, which are lavish and expensive; a rug measuring 120 by 180 centimeters (47 bt 70 inches) takes more than four months to make and costs around Rs 10,000 ($333). Shoppers are shown a variety of rugs and can get explanations of how they are woven and why they are so dear.

More beautiful floor decor is available at **Bansal Carpets,** Naulakha Market. Figure on a four-by-six-foot Persian-style silk carpet from Kashmir for $1,000 to $3,000. Smaller woolen rugs, measuring two by three feet, are $50 to $75. Something in between runs around $200 to $300. Prices depend on quality and workmanship.

Akbar International, 289 Fatehabad Rd. (☎ 360076), open daily from 10am to 7pm, is opposite the Taj View Hotel. See the craftsmen making marble inlaid objects by hand and watch how they carefully embed slivers of semiprecious stone in patterns. Step inside and experience sticker shock: How about a five-inch box inlaid with coral, turquoise, lapis lazuli, and malachite for $2,900? A table top for $12,000? Cheese platter for $140?

On the same road, **Cottage Industries Exposition Ltd.,** 30 Fatehabad Rd. (☎ 360323), also has an amazing array of marble inlay and carpets.

Subhash Emporium, 18/1 Gwalior Rd. (☎ 363867), has a similar inventory; here, boxes begin at around Rs 400 ($13.33) and go up.

Berry Shoes and Leather Crafts, Sadar Bazar (☎ 364646), open from 11am to 8pm except Tuesdays, sells leather shoes for women and men; among these is a selection of chappals (sandals) for women for around Rs 200 ($4.66). The store also stocks leather handbags starting at Rs 385 ($12.83).

WHERE TO STAY

When calculating your budget, remember that there's a 3% to 7% room tax and 6.5% sales tax on food; 32.5% tax on imported liquor.

Unless otherwise indicated, rooms in the following hotels have air-conditioning, attached bathrooms, telephones, and televisions; the hotels have restaurants; and most accept major credit cards.

You'll probably take a scooter ricksha or taxi from the train station to your hotel. If you don't specify where you want to go, you will be taken to an establishment that offers a commission to the driver.

Doubles for Less Than Rs 300 ($10)

Unless indicated otherwise, these low-budget rooms still have attached baths and are occasionally air-conditioned; otherwise, fans stir the breezes. Expect few other amenities.

A private home during the Raj period, the green-accented pink **Agra Hotel,** General Cariappa Road, Agra 282001 (☎ 363331), is said to be the oldest hotel in Agra; established in 1926, it hints at its glory days. Some of the 18 rooms (four with air-conditioning) have old British tables, chairs, cupboards, dressing tables, and overhead fans. Rates are Rs 125 ($4.16) for a non-AC single, Rs 200 ($6.66) for a non-AC double, Rs 300 ($10) for a non-AC suite, Rs 500 ($16.66) for an AC suite. The hotel has an old-fashioned, high-ceilinged dining room where you can get Western, Chinese, Mughlai, and other Indian cuisines. The lawns have a view of the Taj.

"Every year, we change everything, paint everything," says the manager at **Hotel Safari,** Shaeed Nagar Shamsabad Road, Agra 282001 (☎ 360013). Perhaps I saw the hotel before one of these annual makeovers. Friendly, helpful management—not decor—makes the Safari very popular with budget tourists, and I have fan letters to prove it. A splendid rooftop Taj view is an added attraction. The management does not give ricksha or taxi drivers commissions, so if you want to try this place, you have to insist on it or reserve in advance. The price is right: The highest rate is Rs 200 ($6.66) for one of the five air-conditioned doubles. There's food service and a garden.

The Taj Mahal is on full view from the hilltop at the UPTDC's **Hotel Taj Khema** ("Tents"), on prime property at the eastern gate of the Taj Mahal, Agra 282001 (☎ 360140), but that's where the superlatives stop. The hotel's six simple doubles and eight camping huts all need improvement. They are overpriced at Rs 400 ($13.33) with air-conditioning, Rs 125 ($4.16) without. The food is good, though. Come at sunset or even later on a full-moon night for tandoori and the ravishing view; stay somewhere else.

Tourists Rest House, Kutchery Road, Baluganj (☎ 363961), a friendly no-frills place, is a favorite of young backpackers. Rates are some of the lowest in town: From Rs 30 ($1) for a spartan single to Rs 70 ($2.33) for a double, with air cooler and running hot water in the bathroom. In lower-priced rooms, air coolers costs Rs 15 (5¢) per day and there's a common hot shower. The garden is a meeting place for guests. Amiable management confirms and makes train, bus, and plane reservations without charge, and supplies helpful advice on touring the area. Scooter-ricksha and taxi drivers do not get a commission for bringing guests here, and they try to steer tourists to similarly named but not as nice places.

Pleasant management and low rates make the **Jaggi Jaiwal Hotel,** 183 Taj Rd., Agra 282001 (☎ 364142), popular with young travelers. The 15 basic, high-ceilinged rooms have overhead fans and stone floors, attached bathrooms have cold water only; hot water is provided in buckets, upon request. Two bathrooms have geysers for hot water. All rates are under Rs 250 ($8.33). Campers with vans pay a small fee. In fair weather, dinner is served by candlelight in the hotel's open-air restaurant.

The **State Government Tourist Bungalow** is located opposite the Raja-ki-Mandi Railway Station (☎ 72123). It is clean, but inconveniently located. All rates are under Rs 250 ($8.33).

The **Youth Hostel,** Sanjay Place, M.G. Road (☎ 65812), charges Rs 20 (6¢) per head.

For other low-budget accommodations, follow Taj Road toward the Yamuna to Kinara Road behind and near the Taj South Gate; you'll find some low-priced hotels and guest houses. I found nothing appealing about them but their prices.

Doubles for Less Than Rs 600 ($20)

The following hotels have attached bathrooms and are non– or partially air-conditioned; rates range from Rs 200 ($6.67) for a single to Rs 600 ($20) for a double.

Lauries, Mahatma Gandhi Road, Agra 282001 (☎ 364536), has old-fashioned charm and 28 non–air-conditioned rooms opening onto a breezy, marble-floored, pillared verandah. All rooms have window seats, whirling fans, and appointments reminiscent of the days of British rule, including big old tubs in their bathrooms. Breakfast and snacks are served by the swimming pool or in the garden under the gulmohar and kachnaar trees shading the 24-acre property. This hotel is close to the railroad station. A 20% discount applies from April to September. Nonresidents pool fee is Rs 50 ($1.66) for a half day. Credit cards are accepted, and there is also camping.

Jaiwal Hotel, 3 Taj Rd. (next to the Kwality Restaurant), Agra 282001 (☎ 363716; fax 363757), has 17 fairly clean rooms in need of TLC opening onto balconies or the central courtyard; front-facing rooms are a bit nicer than the others. Either Continental or Indian breakfast costs Rs 32 ($1.06).

Under the same ownership as the Grand is the 29-room **Hotel Ranjit,** 263 Station Rd., Agra Cantonment, Agra 282001 (☎ 364446; fax 364271), which could use also some TLC. Still, the prices are a bit lower than the Grand's. The rooms are not air-conditioned, but have air coolers. All rooms have balconies.

The **Basera Hotel,** 19 Ajmer Rd., Baluganj, Agra 282001 (☎ 363641), is a two-story, 17-room hotel arranged around a garden courtyard on a noisy street in a residential area about half a mile from town and 1½ miles from the Taj. Management is nice, but maintenance needs much improvement.

Doubles for Less Than Rs 300 ($30)

For standard rooms in the next seven hotels expect to pay around Rs 450 ($15) to Rs 600 ($20) for a single, Rs 600 ($20) to Rs 850 ($28.33) for a double; for non–air-conditioned rooms, shave off Rs 50 ($1.66). All are walking distance from the Taj.

Lack of maintenance is a common problem with some of the hotels located in the Tourist Complex area and Hotel Lane. The first two hotels are tidy enough.

A tidy new find is **Hotel Sunrise,** Sector B-I, Vibhav Nagar, Agra 282001 (☎ 360616; fax 360126), with 20 air-conditioned rooms and a homey ambience. The standard rooms are neat and clean, with modern furniture and local crafts and artwork here and there. A deluxe room has a settee with bolsters. The ceiling is mirrored in the honeymoon suite. A monumental plus here is a roof-garden restaurant with flowering plants, a smashing view, and good food.

With the owner in the marble business, every hall has a marble lining at the neat and clean 11-room (planning to add 11 more) **Hotel Chakraview,** Vaibhav Nagar, Agra, 282001 (☎ 365609). Fancy walls extend to the rooms, some with patterned paper and others with wood paneling or paint (the honeymoon suite has a heart-shaped bed). The three roof terraces offer a smashing Taj view.

Of the new hotels in the Tourist Complex Area, the best and most professionally run is the 44-room **Hotel Atithi** ("Guest"), Tourist Complex Area, Agra 282001 (☎ 361474; fax 360077). The rooms are adequately (if not imaginatively) furnished, but recently the walls needed a coat of fresh paint. The oversized dining room downstairs is open to nonguests; placemats are shaped like the jumbo banana leaves that are used instead of plates for thalis in the south. Thali meals here cost Rs 80 ($2.66) non-veg, Rs 100 ($3.33) veg. Off-season discount from April 16 to July 16.

The other similarly priced hotels in the Tourist Complex Area advertise all kinds amenities, but unfortunately, as I said before, cleanliness and professional management are not among them. The best are listed below, but their rooms vary, so look at a few before checking in (postal code for all is 282001). **Hotel Neelkanth,** Hotel Lane, 5 Bansal Nagar, Fatehabad Road (☎ 362069); **Hotel President,** Fatehabad Road (☎ 360246); **Hotel Vandna,** Hotel Lane, 7 Bansal Nagar, Fatehabad Road (☎ 261232); and Hotel **Kim,** Hotel Lane, 8 Bansal Nagar, Fatehabad Road ☎ 369412).

In the same neighborhood but higher in price, the 68-room **Hotel Amar,** Tourist Complex Area, Fatehabad Road, Agra 282001 (☎ 360695; fax 366999), offers singles from Rs 700 ($23.33) to Rs 1,100 ($36.66); doubles from Rs 900 ($30) to Rs 1,300 ($43.33); the higher rates are for more spacious deluxe rooms, with patterned wallpaper, vivid bedspreads, and minirefrigerators. Cleanliness and maintenance could be a tad better. Swimming pool and health club; credit cards.

Mayur Tourist Complex, Fatehabad Road, Agra 282001 (☎ 360310), is composed of 30 cottage-style rooms and two suites—Rs 750 ($25) to 950 ($31.66)—set in a delightful garden with a swimming pool. The name *Mayur* means "peacock," but there's nothing that colorful here. However, if sales assistant Peter West's warmth and friendliness were decor, this place would be a peacock palace. As it is, the rooms could use much better maintenance, and travelers I met staying here confirmed my observation. Still if you are not too fastidious, you'll be happy here. Non–air-conditioned rooms are available.

Not really grand, but okay, the **Grand Hotel,** 137 Station Rd., Agra Cantonment, Agra 282001 (☎ 364014; fax 364271), is a two-story gray and white building resembling a U.S. motel set on pleasant grounds. The 58 rooms are fairly clean, but the halls could use a paint job. Singles are Rs 430 ($14.33) to Rs 630 ($21), doubles Rs 530 ($17.66) to Rs 720 ($24); lower rates are not air-conditioned. There's a small dining room and a glittering mirrored bar room. Credit cards are accepted.

Guest Houses

The top guest house in Agra is **New Bakshi House,** 5 Laxman Nagar, Agra 282001 (☎ 61292), an attractive and spotlessly clean place run by a hospitable couple, retired army Col. S. S. Bakshi and his wife. Rates run as low as Rs 40 ($1.33) up to Rs 700 ($31.35), with variations along the way. Higher rates include air coolers or air-conditioning. Rooms have private, attached bathrooms. Meals can be prepared on request; breakfast costs Rs 50 ($1.66) to Rs 75 ($2.50); lunch Rs 50 ($1.66) to Rs 60 ($2); and dinner Rs 125 ($4.16) to Rs 140 ($4.66). The Bakshis gladly help guests with ongoing travel itineraries and local sightseeing. Their guestbook has been filled with favorable comments from many Westerners, and so has my mailbox.

Recommended also is Agra's oldest guest house, **Major Bakshi's** (father of the colonel mentioned above) 33/83 Ajmer Rd., Agra 282001 (☎ 363829), the residence of the major's widow, and managed by the younger Bakshis. Here are 15 tidy rooms; singles are Rs 125 ($4.16), doubles, Rs 250 ($8.33). Light meals are prepared upon request. Guests are permitted to use the owner's huge collection of books, and management will make travel and sightseeing arrangements for you. A reader complained about the owner's inhospitable dog.

Worth a Splurge

In these choices, you'll find every amenity found in international hotels of the highest standard and then some. Some of these hotels are still possible on our $45 a day budget for two people traveling together.

ITDC's **Hotel Agra Ashok,** 6B The Mall, Agra 2822001 (☎ 361223; fax 361620), a white, 55-room, two-story hotel on spacious lawns, has comfortable rooms with modern furniture. There's an attractive lobby with a fountain and chandelier displaying crystal icicles; and Mughal style grillwork and marble inlays pay homage to the Taj. There are a bar, coffee shop, and two restaurants. The Shalimar serves both Indian and Western foods; the Mandarin menu is Chinese (see "Where to Eat," below). The hotel has a swimming pool, puppet shows, astrologer, and shopping arcade, as well as an ITDC travel and tour counter.

Hotel Clark's Shiraz, 54 Taj Rd., Agra 282001 (☎ 361421; fax 361428), set in a garden with well-manicured lawns and a mango-shaped swimming pool, welcomes many tour groups. There are 237 rooms furnished in modern, international style; some offer Taj views as does the **Mughal Room,** Agra's only rooftop restaurant (see "Where to Eat," below). Doubles run Rs 2,250 ($75). The hotel's giant dining hall offers both a Taj and an Agra Fort view. There's a health club, astrologer, beauty parlor, and business services. At the hotel gate is a snake charmer. As you go in or out, the music starts up, and so do the cobras.

The **Mansingh Agra,** 181/2 Fatehabad Rd., Agra 282001 (☎ 361711), was just completing renovations when I stopped. The 97 rooms have no special personality but are clean, comfortable, and modern. From the east rooms the decor is outside: a breathtaking Taj view. These rooms are also are more expensive; a Taj-facing double is Rs 1,850 ($61.66); a standard double is Rs 1,500 ($50), which is within our budget for two people traveling together. There's a restaurant, bar, and astrologer.

Novotel, Taj Nagri Scheme, Fatehabad Road Agra 282001 (☎ 368282; fax 368299), offers both quality and quiet good taste. Singles $38, doubles $75 (probably a bit higher by press time). The motif is modern with a nod to its Mughal ancestry in stylized stone work and garden courtyard. Cleanliness is the other main motif: Rooms in the 139-room hotel, a collaboration between the French Novotel and India's Oberoi chain, have modern furniture, tiled floors (easy to keep spotlessly clean), with a colorful kilim to one end; blankets for beds lie hermetically sealed on closet shelves. There is a nonsmoking section and rooms for the disabled (the first in India, I'm told), swimming pool, travel desk, and meeting room. Reserve *far* in advance.

If you're looking for luxury and smooth, seamless service, these final two hotels are your best choices. So are prices of over $100 for a double.

Taj View Hotel, Fatehabad Road, Taj Ganj, Agra 282001 (☎ 361171; fax 361179), a member of the Taj Group, is white with filigree concrete screens across its balconies. Whether your pleasantly furnished room overlooks the hotel's pool and/or Agra countryside or is one of the more elegant rooms with individualized decor and platforms for viewing the Taj, you'll find this an appealing and well-run hotel. Rates range from $110 for a standard double to $160 for a deluxe double. There's a restaurant with striped banquettes, grill work, and Mughal art (see "Where to Eat," below).

Tops for splurging in Agra is the **Welcomgroup Mughal Sheraton,** Taj Ganj, Agra 282001 (☎ 361701; fax 361730), an extravaganza of architecture, set in a 27-acre garden, for which in 1980 architect Ramesh Khosla won the first Aga Khan Prize for Architectural Excellence. From the white marble lobby, glass-enclosed marble bridges lead to spacious guest rooms in two styles—international, with comfortable, tasteful contemporary furniture, and Indian, with smooth marble floors, marble platform beds partly shaded by embroidered canopies, and simple stone bathrooms with showers only. All 300 rooms overlook the lovely garden and/or pool; a few have Taj views. Flowers, shrubs, and trees and discreet bird-watching signs line garden paths which lead to a puppy kennel and all manner of sports, from archery and minigolf to swimming and tennis. The main attractions for nonresidents include the lobby bar/lounge for drinks and prime people-watching; the tea lounge, with an enchanting Taj view and five different restaurants (see "Where to Eat," below), and the shopping arcade known for treasures. The hotel has a business center.

WHERE TO EAT

Agra's Mughal past is complemented by its Mughali cuisine, which is characterized by rich, creamy sauces and a variety of kebabs; look for burra kebabs (meat cubes) and a range of tandooris with their accompanying naan and parantha breads. Try also interesting "new wave" cooking.

BUFFETS

These eat-as-much-you-wish buffets generally offer wide arrays of Indian, Mughali, and Continental dishes. Open to nonresidents of the hotels, they are excellent values.

At **Hotel Clark's Shiraz,** 54 Taj Rd. (☎ 361421), there are three delicious, budget-stretching buffets daily: breakfast, 6 to 9:30am, $5; lunch, 12:30 to 2pm, $10; and dinner, 7:30 to 9:30pm, $10.

In the marble and red-brick restaurant, Taj Bano, at the posh **Welcomgroup Mughal Sheraton,** Taj Ganj (☎ 361701), three sumptuous buffets are offered: breakfast, 6 to 9:30am, $8; lunch, 12:30 to 3pm, $12; dinner, 7:30 to 10pm, $13. An interesting aspect of the hotel's decor is the open archways that permit diners in the Taj Bano or the Nauratna (Mughlai foods) and Bagh-e-Bahar (Continental) to see each other in these diverse settings. In the evenings, ghazals are sung in the Nauratna, and there's dance music in the Bagh-e-Bahar. Other Mughal Sheraton restaurants are the Mahjong Room (Chinese) and Roe's Retreat, in the garden (barbecue, cold cuts, and salads).

At the **Taj View Hotel,** Taj Ganj (☎ 64171), there are three buffets in an attractive restaurant with antiqued white furniture and striped banquettes: breakfast $5; lunch $9, dinner, $10. Chinese dishes are served as well as Mughali, other Indian dishes, and Continental. Hours are similar to the other hotels.

The **Novotel,** Taj Nagri Scheme, Fatehabad Road (☎ 368282), serves buffets in a sleek, neat, wood-trimmed brasserie: breakfast $6; lunch $10; and dinner $15. The food is well prepared; hours about the same as the other hotels.

REGIONAL INDIAN & CHINESE CUISINE

At **Kwality,** Taj Road (☎ 363624), a longtime favorite with tourists, a three-course soup-to-dessert lunch or dinner for two runs about Rs 200 ($6.66). Most popular dishes on the extensive menu are Cantonese Chinese, such as chicken with almonds or sweet-and-sour fish, vegetables, or pork, for about Rs 70 ($2.33) and the similarly priced Italian dishes with pasta. The usual Indian dishes, such as curries and tandooris, also stay within this range. Kwality bakes its own luscious pastries, which are worth a caloric splurge at Rs 6 (2¢) to Rs 8 (3¢) each. Open every day from 10am to 11pm.

When you enter **Zorba the Buddha,** E-13, Shopping Arcade, Sadar Bazar, you'll see stars—a star-studded ceiling and star-accented murals of mountains and stars. The spotlessly clean restaurant is a showcase for Ma Anand Usha's "new wave" nutritious and tasty vegetarian dishes. Entrées are around Rs 50 ($1.66); no smoking on the premises (a novelty in India); open noon to 3pm, 6 to 9pm.

Another restaurant in Sadar Bazar is the bright and cheerful **Hot Bite,** 7 Shopping Arcade, which has cream-colored walls, wood trim, and a multicuisine menu. Try the Hot Bite biryani (rice, chicken)—Rs 70 ($2.33)—or the similarly priced rich murgh (chicken) makhanwala—Rs 120. Open 10:30am to midnight.

Almost next door, **Brijwasi,** St. John's College Crossing, D-2 Shopping Arcade, Sadar Bazar (☎ 261622), has rich Indian sweets and crispy South Indian snacks.

Only Restaurant, 45 Taj Rd., Phool Sayad Crossing (☎ 364333), has a dark, air-conditioned indoor section. Far more pleasant are the umbrella-shaded tables in a garden with borders of poppies, roses, and marigolds; your best bet is a Hyderabadi thali, for Rs 125 ($4.16), a complete meal including desert. Otherwise, the menu features the usual Indian, Chinese, and Continental menu and is in the Rs 50 ($1.66) to 110 ($3.66) range (the highest price for a full tandoori chicken). Delightful for breakfast after an early morning Taj visit. Open 7am to 10pm.

Cantonese Chinese dishes are especially well prepared at **The Mandarin,** Hotel Agra Ashok, 6-B, The Mall (☎ 361223), with a with dramatic black and green color scheme, including an atrium garden. Figure on Rs 200 ($5) for a three-course meal—soup to dessert and a soft drink. It might consist of chicken coriander soup, sweet and sour vegetables on crispy noodles, and a fried stuffed apple (like a fritter); other selections include a range of noodle dishes and prawn recipes. Portions are generous and can serve two. Open for lunch and dinner; there is music at night.

Near the Agra Ashok and one flight off the street, **Dasaprakash,** 1 Gwalior Rd. (☎ 363368), brings its renowned South Indian dishes and ice creams to Agra in attractive, clean surroundings that combine faux Tiffany glass shades with Mughal-style grillwork. You can get a multidish thali for Rs 70 ($2.33) or a chef specialty, which changes every day, for this same price. There are masala dosas and idly as well as a few Italian and Chinese dishes in the Rs 50 ($1.66) to Rs 70 ($2.33) range.

The following two restaurants are convenient to the Taj Majal.

Taj Restaurant (☎ 76644), which is right outside the western gate of the Taj Mahal, consists of an air-conditioned section and bar, as well as a quick, self-service cafeteria. The restaurant is nothing to rave about, but it's convenient. Prices run Rs 35 ($1.16) to Rs 60 ($2) for entrées—the lower price is for veg dishes; at Rs 85 ($2.83), a tandoori butter chicken is a little more. Many inexpensive snacks. Beer ranges from Rs 70 ($2.33) to Rs 80 ($2.66). Hours are 8am to 10pm daily.

Taj Khema, near the eastern gate, specializes in tandoori barbecue (See "Where to Stay," above).

Worth a Splurge

Expect to spend around Rs 1,000 ($33.33) for a three-course meal for two, excluding beer, wine, and gratuity. Beer will add anywhere from Rs 70 ($2.33) to Rs 130 ($4.33), Indian wine around Rs 400 ($13.33).

Tucked into an intimate corner of the **Welcomgroup Mughal Sheraton,** Fatehabad Road, Taj Ganj (☎ 361701), is the sleek, dimly lit **Nauratna,** with bronze canopies studded with imitation gems, graceful grillwork, and cushy velvet chairs—a regal setting for fine Mughali cuisine. Try the murgh malai kabob as an appetizer while studying the menu, then follow up with murgh lajawaab (chicken with tomatoes), palak paneer (greens and cheese), dal makhani (rich gravy), and naan, but no matter what you decide, you won't go wrong. For those who want to taste a little of a lot of things, thalis are Rs 200 ($6.66). Reservations are essential. Open from 12:30 to 3pm, 7:30 to midnight. There is Indian music at night.

Agra's only rooftop restaurant, at the **Hotel Clark's Shiraz,** 54 Taj Rd. (☎ 361421), has a fabulous Taj and Agra Fort view and delicious Mughali cuisine. It's romantic at night. Open 12:30 to 3pm, 7:30 to midnight; reservations are essential. There is Indian music at night, also a rooftop bar for a stop before or after dinner or between.

AN EXCURSION TO FATEHPUR SIKRI

For 14 years the glorious city of Fatehpur Sikri, located 37 kilometers southwest of Agra, was the talk of the civilized world. Visitors from Shakespeare's England returned with wondrous stories of this fairy tale city of marble and sandstone. It grew out of nothing in the first place, and almost as suddenly it was abandoned. By the end of the 16th century it had been forgotten, a ghost town in the desert, and it has remained that way ever since. Today Sikri is maintained by the government, and Fatehpur is privately maintained by the Sunni Central Bakhav.

Only the tiny village of Sikri (current population 25,000), home of some stonecutters, existed at the site when the Mughal emperor Akbar first came this way in 1568 to seek out the blessings of a mystic named Salim Chishti. Akbar was childless and badly wanted a son. Anyway, whatever the holy man put into those blessings seemed to work, and when Akbar's wife became pregnant, the emperor was so overjoyed he decided to build a fabulous city overlooking the village.

Construction began in 1569 when an artificial lake was dug out (it has since been drained); a magnificent mosque, **Jami Masjid,** was built; and by 1575 Fatehpur Sikri was completed. Even today it's quite a place, and it's not hard to imagine what the court life must have been like in the days of its grandeur. There are marked tiles in the big courtyard where Akbar is said to have sat on a low stool and played Parcheesi—dozens of dancing girls in brightly colored dresses were the living pawns. In a three-room house known as **Ankh Michauli,** Akbar supposedly played blindman's bluff with members of his harem, although it is more likely that this was the treasure house and the narrow passage surrounding the rooms a walkway for the guards.

The recessed stone tank in the courtyard, now dependent on the rains, used to be regularly filled up with water—and with coins, which were distributed to the poor.

Most of the buildings are outstanding. **Maryam's House** (Maryam was Akbar's Christian wife) is a good example, with its gilded frescoes, brightly painted ceilings, and portrait of a lady riding a parrot. And the house of the Turkish sultan is said by some to be the most richly decorated building in the world: Every inch is ornamented with elaborate carvings. The effect is like having 3-D pictures chiseled onto your walls instead of hung on them. (The carvings of birds and animals were later mutilated by Akbar's great-grandson, Aurangzeb (1655–1706), a puritanical monarch who also happened to be a Muslim, a faith that prohibits the representation of living creatures.)

The most noticeable buildings at Fatehpur Sikri are the tapering **Panch Mahal,** so called because of its open, five-storied structure, each floor with half the pillars of the preceding one; and the red sandstone **Diwan-i-Khas,** or Hall of Special Audience, with its carved elephant-tusk props and enormous octagonal center pillar fed by four walkways from the upper balcony. The wise and tolerant Akbar used to sit on his throne on the top of the pillar while his Hindu, Muslim, Buddhist, and Christian viziers would toss ideas at him from each of the four walkways. (Later, he became interested in astrology and consulted an astrologer daily.)

There are many other buildings worthy of attention, most of them an amalgam of the Hindu and Muslim styles. The impressive mosque, with its vast courtyard, lit at night by flaming torches (and a perfect place for the staging of a colorful historical pageant today), is flanked by the rooms of what once was an Arabic university. The white marble mausoleum contains the tomb of the respected Salim Chishti, the holy man who first brought Akbar to this remote place. Delicate, lace-like, carved marble screens and a chamber of mother-of-pearl and sandalwood house the holy man's remains. Colored threads, tied by pilgrims (usually childless women) from all over India who hope a visit to the mausoleum will bring them luck flutter from the marble screen.

At the south end of the mosque, overlooking the village of Fatehpur, is the enormous **Buland Darwaza,** a lofty gate 134 feet high, built in 1602 to commemorate Akbar's victories in the south. Inscribed on one side, in Persian, are these words:

> He that standeth up to pray and his heart is not in his duty, does not draw nigh to God but remains far from Him. Your best possession is what you give in alms; your best trade is selling this world for the next. Said Jesus—on whom be peace—the world is a bridge, pass over it but build no houses on it. He who hopes for an hour may hope for eternity. The world is but for an hour; spend it in devotion. The rest is unseen.

In 1584, before Akbar was able to move with his Hindu wife, Jodh Bai, into the big palace built specially for them (to the southwest of Maryam's house), the whole court shifted from Fatehpur Sikri to Lahore, possibly because political unrest had broken out but more probably because the water supply at Sikri was running out. It was 15 years before Akbar disentangled himself from these troubles, and when he returned it was not to Sikri, but instead to Agra, where he remained until his death in 1605.

A thorough look at Fatehpur Sikri includes the seldom visited area to the northwest not far from the stables, where you follow a paved lane to the **Hathi Pol** (Elephant Gate), the ceremonial palace entrance in bygone days, its huge elephants now damaged. Here are other structures in the city's intricate design, such as the waterworks, including the stone well with cool chambers and a staircase; an inn for travelers; and a view of a tower with tusks, which legend says was a gravestone for Akbar's elephant—more likely it could have been a milestone.

These days, souvenir sellers are the new occupants of the entrance to the magnificent ruins. Be firm!

The entry fee for Fatehpur Sikri is Rs 10.50 (35¢); it's open from sunrise to sunset.

Every half hour buses leave from Agra's Idgah Bus Stand (☎ 366588) to the Fatehpur Sikri or vice versa for about Rs 10 (33¢) for an hour's trip, with two stops along the way. Buses are very crowded.

A huge mela takes place during Ramzam, which is also timed with the anniversary of Salim Chishti's death. At this time, Fathepur is turned into a colorful tent city full of stalls selling all kinds of religious and secular souvenirs.

Where to Stay & Eat

For those who would like the adventure of spending the night near a ghost town, there's the UPTDC's **Gulistan Tourist Complex** (☎ 2490), with 24 clean functional rooms for Rs 150 ($5) per person. The surrounding garden is a gathering place for peacocks and many other exotic birds. It is often their base before or after Bharatpur (see Chapter 5, "Rajasthan"), which is about 30 kilometers away. Continental breakfast costs Rs 50 ($1.66); lunch or dinner will run about Rs 150 ($5).

2 Khajuraho

400 miles (648 kilometers) southeast of Delhi

In one of the quietest villages in India sit some of the world's most celebrated statues. Khajuraho (pop. 5,000) is miles from anywhere. Inaccessible by train, barely reachable by road, and so isolated that the nearest movie house is 30 miles away, it is nonetheless an important outing in conjunction with the *Shatabdi Express* from

Delhi (400 miles away), Agra (via Jhansi), or Bhopal; it can also be stopover on the Delhi-Agra-Varnasi flight.

Tourists who come to Khajuraho dip briefly into a way of life that has remained virtually unchanged for 1,000 years, apart from the imposition of a handful of modern amenities—a jet strip in the midst of fields for the Boeing 737 flights, a photo supply shop with a very limited supply of film, souvenir and gem shops, and a few hotels that import—from hundreds of miles away—everything needed to make guests comfortable.

The magnets for tourists are a group of temples that were built during the Chandela's dynasty from 950 to 1050; little is known about them, although some sources say they claimed to be descended from the moon. Maybe space scientists will prove this one day. Meanwhile, we can see their miraculous architectural works here on earth.

ESSENTIALS

GETTING THERE

BY AIR The easiest way (not as interesting as the train, though) and more expensive is the daily flight that links Khajuraho to Delhi, Agra, and Varanasi. One-way fares from Delhi to Khajuraho are $53; from Agra $39, and Varanasi, $57.

BY RAIL Easier on the wallet, the air-conditioned, speedy *Shatabdi Express* links Delhi, Agra, Jhansi, and Bhopal. For Khajuraho-goers from Delhi or Agra, Jhansi is the most convenient station. Fares for an AC Chair seat: New Delhi to Jhansi, Rs 350 ($11.66); Agra to Jhansi, Rs 195 ($6.50). The state transport bus meets the train at 11:30am and reaches Khajuraho—176 kilometers away—around 4:30pm; the fare is around Rs 45 ($1.50).

Splurgers can arrange for a tourist taxi and driver to meet them at the station through MPSTDC in Khajuraho or before leaving Delhi. This cost about Rs 1,500 ($50). The price is high because you must pay the taxi's round-trip charges; sharing with other tourists shaves off the cost. If your plans also include Bhopal, take the *Shatabdi Express* from Delhi to Agra, where you'll want to stop over, and then onto Bhopal, returning to visit Khajuraho (via Jhansi). Then fly onto Varnasi or any other destination.

BY BUS From Varanasi, Khajuraho's railhead is Satna on the Bombay–Allahabad line; from here, the bus trip is 117 kilometers to Khajuraho.

From Agra, Bhopal, Indore, Jabalpur, Jhansi, Satna, and Harpalur, there's Madhya Pradesh State Road Transport Corporation (MPSRTC) bus service to Khajuraho.

VISITOR INFORMATION

The **Government of India Tourist Office,** near the Western Temples, Khajuraho 471690 (☎ 2047), is open from 9am to 5:30pm; this is where you can pick up pamphlets, get help with plans, and hire an approved guide (very helpful). The guide fee, as elsewhere in India, is Rs 250 ($8.33) for one-half day, Rs 350 ($11.66) for a full day for one to four persons. Guides also congregate at Raja's Restaurant or the Western Group's gates, but only those with special IDs are supposed to enter the temple grounds.

The **Madhya Pradesh State Tourism Development Corporation (MPSTDC),** Tourist Bungalow Complex A (☎ 2051), is another good source of information.

GETTING AROUND

A few tourist **taxis** are available for an exorbitant Rs 350 ($11.66) per day. You will not need a car unless you plan to tour the Panna National Park and Diamond Mines, or temples, forts, and waterfalls out of town. Tourist taxis charge around Rs 60 ($2) from the airport to anywhere in Khajuraho; after bargaining, you might get this ride for half price. **Cars** can be hired through tourist car operators (see the list at the tourist office). **Cycle rickshas** are available for short hauls in town—bargain for your ride.

WHEN TO GO

October to the end of March is best. Rains during July and August are heavy and constant, causing the closing until October of the Bandhavgarh National Park, a popular day trip during dry months. Very special times to visit are during Shiva Ratri (February or March), when people come from all around the area for a big bazaar and other merriment, and for the weeklong dance festival; sometime between March 1 and March 20, well-known dancers perform with the Western Group of Temples as their backdrop (it will be March 10 through 17 in 1997. (Reserve accommodations early.) Summer sizzles at around 100°F.

WHAT TO SEE & DO

For the four centuries from 900 to 1300, the region around Khajuraho—the name probably comes from *Khajurvahak,* meaning "date palms"—was ruled by the Chandela kings. They left a legacy of 85 temples, built mainly between 950 and 1100, of which only 22 remain.

Despite their international reputation as a sort of repository of sexual sculptures, these temples offer more than erotic tableaux. Still, the extraordinary explicitness of the statues makes them the outstanding feature, even though they comprise only 10% of the carvings to be seen.

The Khajuraho Temples were built before the Muslims put women in purdah (seclusion). The Chandelas were richly bejeweled, scantily clad followers of a Tantric form of Hinduism that saturated sexual pleasures with divine qualities. The kingdom ended in 1200 when Turkish powers won the holy war they had waged for 100 years.

Couples were shown in a variety of postures that have been reproduced too often for them to be worth describing, and there are occasional scenes of soldiers, cut off from their women by war, taking animal lovers. In light of today's sexual permissiveness in the West, it is hard to imagine anyone being shocked.

The main temples, called the **Western Group,** are clustered in a pleasant park. Like the others, these are built in a series of hills building up to a towering peak, symbolizing the Himalayas, where the gods were supposed to reside.

It's best not to approach any of them too academically, but just appreciate them for what they are—a jubilant paean to life, built by thousands of craftsmen working every daylight hour during the century or so that it took to build the temples.

The first temple, **Lakshmana,** is typical of the rest. The incredible plasticity of the carvings is one of the first things you'll notice: bodies twisted in all directions displaying supple limbs, as though permanently frozen in a graceful dance. Young maidens are a favorite subject (women were worshipped as the main force of creation), and the hairstyles and facial expressions on even the smallest figures are exquisitely portrayed.

The artists took the entire range of human activity as their subject but dwelled most lovingly on females at their daily chores—washing and applying henna to their hair, writing letters, looking in mirrors, playing with balls, singing, and strumming instruments. There are also delicate scenes of couples kissing and mothers with babies.

Around the Lakshmana Temple, about six feet off the ground, runs a long continuous frieze in which erotic scenes are more or less interlaced with military processions of horsemen, camels, elephants, and musicians. Wild boar and crocodiles underfoot denote the procession is through jungle and not on the road.

Originally, the Western Group of temples was set in an artificial lake, and people went from one temple to another by boat. Another batch of temples, the **Eastern Group,** half of these of the Jain faith, are within walking distance.

The three **Jain temples** occupy their isolated compound in a rather modern tableau: sheets hanging to dry on an outdoor line alongside the temple, an old man squatting quietly in the yard chanting to himself, children skipping about, the inevitable well on the temple grounds, and workmen standing ready with a bucket for the just-as-inevitable tourist camera.

Not as interesting as the Western Group, the Eastern temples display the 23 Jain teachers, including Mahavira, who came last and who is most revered as the religion's founder. To identify a Jain prophet is easy: They're always shown nude with a diamond shape on their chests. At the adjacent **outdoor museum** are more Jain sculptures and free pamphlets on Jainism. In the Eastern Group there are also three Hindu temples. Of these, **Vamana,** dedicated to Vishnu's dwarf incarnation, also carries the erotic motifs of the Western Group.

The **Southern Group** of temples, about 2 kilometers (1¼ miles) from the tourist office, is the least interesting; these are visited mainly for **Chaturbujha** temple, which has a huge well-carved image of Lord Vishnu. The sculpture has a special glow at sunset.

All temples are open sunrise to sunset. At the Western Group, the 50 paise (2¢) entry fee also permits you to visit the small archaeological museum (☎ 2023), with galleries of stone-cut art (open Saturday through Thursday from 10am to 5pm).

SHOPPING

If you wish to purchase alcohol, there's a **bottle shop** near Raja's Restaurant (open from 10am to 9pm, closed on national holidays).

Interesting crafts are for sale at the **Madhya Pradesh Emporium.** Buys in **silver and brass ware** are main attractions at the bazaar each Tuesday in **Rajnagar,** 5 kilometers away. Many souvenir stalls near the Western temples were built in the ruins of a maharaja's palace and are being moved to another area.

WHERE TO STAY

MPSTDC HOTELS

Madhya Pradesh State Tourist Development (MPSTDC) runs four decent, pleasant, clean, well-priced places to stay. Their amenities include attached private bathrooms, fans, partial air-conditioning, and restaurants. They are extremely popular and should be booked well in advance. The postal code for Khajuraho is 076861.

Hotel Jhankar, Airport Road (☎ 2063), has 19 rooms, five air-conditioned; the highest rate is Rs 490 ($16.33) for an air-conditioned double; Rs 440 ($14.66) for an air-conditioned single. The hotel has a bar and conference facilities. Credit cards are accepted.

Hotel Payal (☎ 2076), has 25 nicely done-up rooms, 14 air-conditioned, each with a little verandah and private bathroom. Doubles and singles, non–air-conditioned, are available with rates the same as Jhankar. The air-conditioned restaurant has coir (coconut fiber fabric) paneled walls and ebony finished chairs.

Hotel Rahil (☎ 2062), a cut below the two above, has 19 clean, cool, and breezy, though basic, rooms without air-conditioning. Rates are Rs 130 ($4.33) to Rs 150 ($5) there's a congested 72-bed dorm for Rs 30 ($1) per bed. The gardens are nice.

MPSTDC's Tourist Village Complex offers 13 attractive bungalows with carved doors and red tile roofs in attractive gardens. One has one double room, accommodating two people; the remainder have two double rooms, accommodating four people. Rates are Rs 110 ($3.66) to Rs 150 ($5). The restaurant is in a separate bungalow. This is a perfect hideaway if you crave privacy.

For reservations more than five days in advance contact: Central Reservations, Tours Division, M.P. State Tourism Corporation Ltd., 4th Floor, Gangotri, T.T. Nagar, Bhopal 462003 (☎ 0755-55434043; fax 0755-5522384). If you just drop into MPSTD's Khajuraho office in Tourist Bungalow Complex A (☎ 2051), they'll try to find you accommodations.

Other Budget Rooms

Hotel Sunset View, opposite Pahil Batika, near Beni Sagar Lake (☎ 2077), has 18 simple, clean accommodations, each with attached bath, fan, and/or air-cooler; one is air-conditioned. There's no restaurant, but room service is available for snacks, tea, and coffee.

Yogi Lodge (☎ 2158), offers bare-bones comfort in close proximity to the bazaar.

Hotel Temple (☎ 2049), has 11 double rooms in so-so condition with cold-water bathrooms, hot water supplied in buckets upon request. Indian vegetarian and nonvegetarian foods are available. The hotel is in the same building as Indian Airlines.

Hotel Surya, Jain Temple Road, set off and above the street across from Mediterraneo (see "Where to Eat," below), has velvet walls and wood carvings in the reception area. There are 20 fairly clean, spartan rooms, six with air-conditioning and six with air coolers; all have ceiling fans and hot running water in their bathrooms. From the rooftop there's a view of temples, and management plans a restaurant up there. Meanwhile, thali meals costing Rs 25 (90¢) and are sent to the rooms.

Worth a Splurge

The following hotels have all kinds of creature comforts, including attached bathrooms, air-conditioning, restaurants, bars, swimming pools, gardens, closed-circuit TV, and shopping. They accept major credit cards. Rates at these hotels run from about $38 for a single to $75 for a double, and up. Discounted rates apply from April to September, but you must ask for them.

The **Hotel Khajuraho Ashok** (☎ 74250; fax 74255), run by the India Tourism Development Corporation (ITDC), has 40 cheerful rooms with modern, functional furnishings. Second-floor rooms have terrific temple views. There's restaurant with floor-to-ceiling windows and white furniture.

Hotel Chandela, Khajuraho District, Chhatarpur, Madhya Pradesh 471606 (☎ 2054; fax 076861-2095), about 1 kilometer from the Western Group of temples, has sweeping marble halls, central air-conditioning, and 102 rooms furnished in modern international style. The post office here is a convenience. When the staff worships at the small garden in the temple, guest are welcome at the rituals—but they must be up by 5am.

Nearby and new to the scene is the **Holiday Inn,** Airport Road (☎ 2187), which has 56 temple-view rooms and suites in a huge garden that was all patches of brown and green when I saw it but should be in better shape now. Rooms are spacious but lack distinctive personality. There are conference and banquet facilities.

Hotel Clarks Bundela, Khajuraho (☎ 2360; fax 2359), is new; its lobby is a blend of styles—a large, round Victorian table is a focal point amid modern club chairs in conversational groupings; the furniture in the rooms is large and heavy. The waterfall plunging into the swimming pool gives it an edge over other hotel pools. When the garden grows, the setting will improve. Bhoj Bundela restaurant is definitely worth a visit.

An imposing red statue of beloved Ganesh (elephant-headed god of good luck) is prominent in the reception area at the 94-room **Jass Oberoi Hotel,** Bypass Road (☎ 2085; fax 2088), which has the intimate ambience of a private country estate. Beautiful miniature paintings and bronze statues (some valuable antiques among them) decorate all the public rooms. Works of art are used as well in bedrooms, which have old/new themes, restful neutral color schemes and graceful furniture. Rooms away from the reception are preferred for quiet. Well-prepared food is another plus here.

WHERE TO EAT

Raja, across from the Western Group of temples, is a Swiss-owned outdoor restaurant and long a great gathering place. "Everything here is fresh," it says on the menu, which runs the food gamut from a breakfast for Rs 65 ($2.16) to a complete dinner for Rs 50 ($1.66) to Rs 90 ($3), including many à la carte dishes. Inside there's a little book shop. At the cafe, imported items such as cosmetics, candies, and cassettes can be exchanged for new, white, temple-logo ashtrays—a status symbol for your home.

Bhuj Bundela, in the **Hotel Clarks Bundela** (☎ 2360), serves excellent Indian food. If you're undecided about what to order (though you can't go wrong here), chef A. K. Shukla will gladly assist you with your selections. For a top-notch three-course meal for two, figure on Rs 500 ($16.66) to Rs 700 ($23.33); portions are generous enough to share. Prices do not include beer or wine or a gratuity. Open for lunch and dinner.

When Patrizia Marapodi came to India from Italy on a holiday a few years ago, she got a souvenir she didn't expect: She fell in love with and married a Rajasthani. Now Khajuraho has her **Mediterraneo** restaurant, featuring the authentic Italian dishes she learned from her mother. Marapodi makes her own pastas, even turning out a passable pizza without mozzarella (not available here) and terrific cappuccino. Expect to spend around Rs 50 ($1.66) for an entree. Open from 7:30am (nice for a light breakfast) to 10pm. She and her husband are scouting locations in other cities. In the same building is the Modiluft airlines office, represented here by the Marapodis.

3 Jhansi & Orchha

Until recently, few thought of Jhansi except as a jumping-off point for visiting Khajuraho (it's the closest stop on the rail lines), but this city (pop. 370,000) and the much smaller Orchha, 16 miles southeast, having played interesting roles in Indian history, are relatively undiscovered treasuries of important artifacts.

Jhansi is renowned for both the Jhansi Fort, built by the powerful Bir Singh Deo of Orchha, who ruled this area from 1605 to 1627, and its brave queen-rebel Rani Laskshmi Bai, who led revolts against the British. Orchha's claim to fame are rulers who managed to stay on friendly terms with the Mughals and produce marvelous palaces and temples.

Jhansi was at its peak in 1803 when the British East India Company gradually took it over. It was about then that the Rajah of Jhansi died without a male heir and his wife, the Rani, who was only in her twenties, expected to ascend to the throne. But she was a queen without a kingdom. A new British law permitted them to take-over princely states in their domain when the ruler died without a son, so they pensioned off the Rani. Angered, she joined the rebels. In 1857, when the Mutiny erupted, she was a leader of the rebellion at Jhansi during which many British lost their lives; the following year, the rebels were still so disorganized that the British retook the fort. The Rani, however, went on to join the rebel forces in Gwalior. Disguised as a man, she rode out with the troops against the British. Holding her reigns between her teeth so she could wield her sword with both hands, she was killed in action with two other female liberators. Now revered as an independence hero, Rani Lakshmi Bai is also called a modern Joan of Arc.

Orchha's history starts with the Bundela Raja Rudra Pratap (1501–31), who established this site on a small island in the Betwa River as its capital. Orchha is seen today for its memorable palaces, unusual palace-temple and graceful chhatris.

Most of Orchha's sites are either from the days of Madhukar Shah (ca. 1537), who was distinguished by the fact that he was defeated by Akbar's army but nonetheless became friendly with the Mughal emperor, or Bir Singh Deo, the builder of the Jhansi Fort, a friend of Emperor Jahangir. Bir Singh Deo built the Jahangir Mahal to honor the Emperor's visit to Orchha. His first son, Jhujan, fell out of favor with Shah Jahan (he murdered a neighboring chieftain), and ultimately the Mughal army under Aurganzeb charged against him and ransacked Orchha. In 1783, the Bundela capital was reestablished at Tikamgarh, and Orchha was abandoned to the elements. Today Orchha is a relatively well-preserved page of history and a fascinating stop during a visit to Khajuraho or Bhopal.

ESSENTIALS

GETTING TO JHANSI & ORCHHA

BY AIR Currently, the nearest airport is Gwalior (120 kilometers away); an airport is to open at Jhansi for flights from major cities.

BY RAIL From Delhi or Agra, the quickest train is the *Shatabdi Express,* although others ply this route; from Bombay's Victoria Terminus, the *Punjab Mail* takes 21 hours; from Varnasi, the *Bundlekhand Express,* take 17½ hours. The *Shatabdi Express* departs daily at 7pm, for Agra, 2½ hours and Delhi, four hours. To or from Bhopal, the *Shatabdi Express* takes 3½ hours.

TRAVELING BETWEEN JHANSI & ORCHHA

Between Jhansi and Orchha and vice versa, take a **Tempo** (large auto-ricksha) from the bus stand in either city, for about Rs 20 (66¢) for the 45-minute one-way trip. Ordinary **auto-rickshas** are available in both Jhansi and Orchha. Bargain to set a price. From Orchha, take the bus or a Tempo to get the *Shatabdi Express* in Jhansi. Allow ample time; the 45-minute trip can take more than an hour, depending on traffic. If going to Khajuraho (see the previous section), take the UP or MP deluxe buses from Jhansi to Khajuraho, about four to five hours.

WHAT TO SEE & DO IN JHANSI

Jhansi Fort, built by Bir Singh Deo around 1613, was protected by formidable fortified walls and had a road to the top and around the ramparts. Much altered over the years, the fort's main attraction today is its panoramic views from the ramparts. The **Rani Mahal** is now a small museum with sculpture. In 1858 the British ceded Jhansi Fort to the Maharaja of Scindia and, in 1866, traded it for Gwalior.

WHAT TO SEE & DO IN ORCHHA

The approach to Orchha **palace-fort complex** is over a 17th-century granite bridge with graceful arches to three palaces in a spacious quadrangle (take your flashlight to see the murals). **Jahangir Mahal,** the most commanding of these structures, was built by Bir Singh Deo to honor the Emperor Jahangir's visit to his city. From the heyday of the Bundelas, it is magnificent example of medieval palace-fort architecture. Constructed around a large, square, central courtyard, the multitiered palace has chambers on each of three stories. Domes with chambers are interspersed with terraces and hanging balconies; eaves, arches, and trellis work add richness to the exterior and soften its strong lines, having the unusual effect of adding delicacy to the huge structure. Open from 10am to 5pm.

Raj Mahal, to the right of the quadrangle, was built by Mahdukar Shah, the deeply religious predecessor to Bir Singh Deo. This is my favorite of the three because its royal chambers have vibrant murals (ask the watchman to unlock the chambers for you) with a variety of religious themes, said to be the some of the finest examples of Bundela art. Bits of blue tile remain on the otherwise plain exterior. The structure exemplifies Bundela architectural style, typically built around an interior courtyard with floors rising in terraced tiers. The exterior walls are plain and topped with lovely chhatris.

Rai Praveen Mahal was built by Indramani (ruler from 1672 to 1676) for his musician-poet-lover, who once briefly sojourned with the powerful Akbar. Her two-story palace was designed to be no higher than the trees in the surrounding gardens.

The **Ram Raja Temple** is in the village. One day, the story goes, the pious Madhukar Shah had a vision of Rama. So he brought from Ayodhya (believed by some Hindus to be Rama's birthplace) an image of the god and placed it in his palace with plans to give it to a new temple. When he went to move it, the idol would not budge. Too late, the king remembered the warning that the deity must remain wherever it was first placed. So he turned his palace into a temple. To this day, it is the only such palace-temple structure in India where Rama is worshipped as a king.

Steep stairs lead to the **Chaturbhuj Temple,** which was meant to house the Rama image. The walls have been damaged with graffiti, but the view is very fine. A path through the village connects the **Lakshmnaryan Temple** with the Ram Raja temple, a blend fort and temple architecture. Colorful murals depicting a melange of religious and secular scenes in a remarkable state of preservation decorate the walls and ceilings of three chambers. (If locked, see Sheesh Mahal hotel reception for help.) There are good views from here of the chhatris along the riverside and landscape.

Shahid Samak is a memorial-museum-library honoring freedom fighter Chandrasekhar Azad.

WHERE TO STAY & EAT IN ORCHHA

Orchha's your best bet with two delightful locations, both run by MP tourism: **Sheesh Mahal** (☎ 224), an aerie outpost located between the Raj and Jahan Mahals, has only eight rooms, a few deluxe with air-conditioning and bath attached. Restaurant and panoramic views are other features. Rates for a tiny single are Rs 100 ($3.33) to Rs 600 ($20) for a deluxe with air-conditioning.

Betwa Cottages (☎ 218), along the riverbank, have murals on their exteriors and cleanliness inside. There are a total of 10 rooms and plans to add four more. Four rooms are air-conditioned; all have attached bathrooms. There is a restaurant (headwaiter Barelal Ven is quite a character) as well as lovely garden and river views. Rates are Rs 225 ($7.50) to Rs 450 ($15).

For either place, reserve early; if more than five days in advance, contact Central Reservations, M.P. State Tourism Development Corporation Ltd., 4th Floor, Gangotri, T. T. Nagar, Bhopal 462003 (☎ 554340; fax 552384); if less than five days, contact the manager at the accommodation itself.

4 Bhopal & Sanchi

Bhopal is 436 miles (704 kilometers) from Delhi
Sanchi is 42 miles (68 kilometers) north of Bhopal

Half hidden among the mountains of Madhya Pradesh is the beautiful town of Bhopal, with its two picturesque lakes providing a beautiful background for each and every sunset. Bhopal (pop. 1.5 million) was ruled mostly by Begums, enlightened women of the 19th and 20th centuries, one of whom, Shah Jahan Begum, could have been right at home with today's women's liberation movement so vast was her work for equal rights (albeit within the confines of her Muslim beliefs).

In true Mughal fashion, lakes and gardens are among Bhopal's attractions. The city also has beautiful mosques, one of which, **Taj-ul Masjid,** is billed as one of the largest mosques in Asia, and the handiwork of Shah Jahan Begum (1860–1901), with additional modern work in 1971. The others are **Jama Masjid,** which can be identified by its golden-spiked minarets and was built in 1837 by Kudsia Begum, and **Moti Masjid,** built by her daughter and similar architecturally to the Jama Masjid in Delhi.

Ironically, the world learned of Bhopal through the worst industrial accident in history on December 3 and 4, 1984, when clouds of toxic gases from the Union Carbide plant spread throughout this central Indian city, injuring and killing hundreds. A huge white statue of a woman and child has been erected at the site to commemorate the dreadful event, but all is safe now.

As always, the main reason for visiting Bhopal is as a gateway to Sanchi, 42 miles away, which is famous throughout the world as a 2,000-year-old center of Buddhist art.

ESSENTIALS

GETTING TO BHOPAL & SANCHI

BY AIR Daily flights connect Bhopal with Bombay for $70, with Delhi for $62, and with Gwalior for $39, to name the most popular routes. Taxis from the airport to town (15 kilometers to center of Bhopal) cost about Rs 250 ($8.33). For Indian Airlines' bus schedule to the airport call the city office at 550480.

BY RAIL Bhopal is served by the *Shatabdi Express,* which connects Delhi with Agra, Gwalior, and Jhansi (starting point for Khajuraho). The train departs Delhi at 6:15am, making the journey to Bhopal by 2pm. AC Chair fare is Rs 495 ($16.50) from Delhi to Bhopal; Jhansi to Bhopal is Rs 280 ($9.33).

Since Bhopal is on the major Delhi-to-Madras and Delhi-to-Bombay broad-gauge lines, many other trains also serve this city. For instance, from Bombay, it's about 837 kilometers (523 miles), a 16-hour journey, Rs 1,258 ($41.93) for AC First and Rs 150 ($5) Second, mail, or express.

Sanchi is on the Jhansi-to-Itarsi section of the Central Railways. First-class passengers on mail and express trains have to ask the guard or stationmaster in advance to stop at Sanchi, 68 kilometers (42 miles) north of Bhopal; the fare is about Rs 216 ($7.20) AC First; second-class passengers should check on train service when buying tickets. Better yet, just buy your ticket to Vidisha (10 kilometers away), the most convenient stop. You can take a taxi or auto-ricksha from there.

VISITOR INFORMATION & TOURS

For information and pamphlets, and to book tours, check with the **MP State Tourism Development Corporation Office,** Gangotri, 4th Floor, T.T. Nagar, Bhopal

(☎ 554340). There also are tourist information representatives at the airport and railway station.

Tours of Bhopal and Sanchi had been operating on Sunday, Tuesday, and Thursday, from 9am to 4pm, but check with MP Tourism. During my recent visit, there were no tours. MP Tourism runs a variety of tours to a variety of places within the state and beyond. For information, contact MP State Tourism Development Corporation, Gangotri, 4th Floor, T.T. Nagar (☎ 5544340).

Going Between Bhopal & Sanchi

By Bus Buses depart from Hamidia Road bus stand (3 kilometers from railway station) about seven times a day from 5:30am until 7:30pm between Bhopal and Sanchi; the fare is about Rs 7 (23¢), and the trip takes about 2½ hours, to Vidisha Rs 15 (5¢). Buses to Khajuraho cost Rs 120 ($4) and take 10-plus hours.

By Taxi Tourist Taxis (check with MP Tourism in Bhopal on reputable firms and approved rates) should run about Rs 600 ($20) round-trip, Rs 750 ($25) if going on the Udaygiri and Vidisha. If overnighting, there will be extra charges.

Getting Around Bhopal

Buses, tempos, taxis—all unmetered—are available; set the rate before you get in. Auto-rickshas are metered. Get approved fares for tourist taxis and jeeps from MP Tourism Development Corporation. The yellow booth at the Railroad Station houses police, who will gladly help you book a taxi and negotiate a rate.

What to See & Do in Bhopal

Bhopal's history dates from the 11th century, when the Raja Bhoj built the two impressive lakes around which the city is still clustered. The most outstanding is the **Great Lake,** 4½ miles long and nearly 2 miles wide, which is separated by a bridge from the 2-mile-long **Lower Lake.**

Apart from the three mosques, about which there is nothing special to note except possibly their size, Bhopal's major architectural attraction is a 12th-century **Shiva Temple** at **Bhojpur,** 24 miles from town. It was never completed, but even in its semifinished state it is an impressive pile of purple sandstone, its dome lying nearby on the grounds as if waiting for someone to get on with the job.

While moseying around town, be sure to note some of the schools, the Lady Landsdowne Hospital, and the waterworks, built by the Begums.

Bhopal has some worthwhile museums and art galleries. The **State Museum,** opposite Ravindra Bhawan on Banganga Road (open 10am to 5pm, except Mondays) ranges from the Stone Age to present; it houses a collection of sculptures from various parts of Madhya Pradesh, as well as opulent decorative arts that once belonged to former rulers.

On Shamla Hill above the Upper Lake, as well as at the top of the tourist's must-see list, are two museums. The **Bharat Bhawan** (☎ 73945) is a center for the creative and performing arts. The sleek, low-lying design by famous Indian architect Charles Correa harmonizes with the landscape. It is open from 3 to 8pm, except Mondays. Here also is the **Indira Gandhi Rashtriya Manav Sangrahalaya** (Museum of Man), an open-air exhibition of typical contemporary tribal habitats, cultural artifacts, and related special exhibitions. It is open from10am to 6pm, except Mondays.

The **Birla Museum,** open daily from 9am to 5pm, houses a rare sculpture collection. Also see **Van Vihar,** adjacent to Upper Lake, a man-made wildlife retreat for lions, tigers, leopards, and bears. **Boat clubs** at both the Upper and Lower Lakes will provide boats for lake explorations.

Shopping in Bhopal

Main shopping areas are the **Chowk,** in the old part of town, with narrow lanes crowded with little shops that bulge with such local specialties as embroidery, bead work, and silver jewelry, and **New Market.** Be sure to visit the **Women's Cooperative Zari Center,** at Peer Gate, where richly embroidered bags, made with gold and silver threads, and chiffon saris are the major attractions. Other stops on the shopping route might well be the **Mrignayani** (Madhya Pradesh State Emporium), 23 New Shopping Center, New Market (☎ 554162), and the **Avanti Handlooms,** State Emporium, GTB Complex, T.T. Nagar. Look for the local fabric called chanderi, a combination of silk and cotton so sheer that Emperor Aurangzeb insisted that his daughter wear seven layers of this transparent cloth—when he allowed her to wear it at all.

Where to Stay in Bhopal

Hotels on Shamla Hill

Unless otherwise noted, the following hotels have air-conditioning, attached bathrooms, TVs, restaurants, and bars; they all accept credit cards. Figure rates ranging from Rs 500 ($16.66) to Rs 1,200 ($40) for a standard single or double. (The STD code is 0755.)

Rated tops is the 60-room **Jehan Numa Palace,** 157 Shamla Hill, Bhopal 462013 (☎ 540100; fax 540720), a mélange of British, Colonial, Italian Renaissance, and Classical Greek styles, the hotel's rooms are surprisingly on the non-evocative side. But they're clean, and the garden is inviting. However, there's no lake view. There are a business center, fitness facilities, and swimming pool.

Also on Shamla Hill, **Lake View** (☎ 540452), in a weird modernistic style, has rather laissez-faire management (children use the stairs and halls as their playground); still, this is the place to be for stunning lake views. The restaurant, open to nonresidents, dishes up this view with tasty Indian specialties. Because of the romantic views, the hotel is a honeymoon favorite.

Another hotel with a historic past, the 34-room **Imperial Sabre,** Palace Grounds (☎ 540702), was a royal guest house but retains none of the regal trappings. The atmospheric location on the lake is plus, though. Get a room away from the lobby.

Hotels in Maharana Pratap

Well-located in the Maharana Pratap Area near the government buildings are three fairly new hotels. But on my latest visit, at least, one already looked run-down and all suffer to one degree or another from lack of maintenance; rates and amenities are similar to those in Shamla Hill hotels.

Tops among these, the 31-room **Hotel Amer Palace,** 209 Zone-I, Maharana Pratap Nagar (☎ 557127; fax 553309), furnishes its lobby in the more-is-more school of decorating: Heavy furniture with gleaming brocade upholstery has white, carved wooden legs and is surrounded by riotously patterned rugs; a huge Muhgal style glass mural forms the reception backdrop. Things are a bit calmer in the bedrooms. Each floor has its own minilobby. Jharokha ("balcony") restaurant, which incorporates a fluted balcony in its decor, offers the usual multicuisine menu; Jhankar discotheque has the latest lighting effects. There are conference and banquet facilities, and a business center.

The Residency, Zone-I, M.P. Nagar (☎ 556001; fax 557637), is almost on a par with its neighbor above; its lobby, however, is almost austere, with a minimum of furniture placed on granite floors. A typical twin-bedded room had a wine and cream color scheme. The low ceilings throughout are a drawback. The hotel has a swimming pool, health club, and in-house bakery; there's a coffee shop, multi-cuisine restaurant, and bar. Service charge is 10%.

Hotel Nisgara, Plot 211, Zone-I, M.P. Nagar (☎ 555701; fax 555702), has 41 rooms with walls in vivid aqua and rose sateen spreads with trapunta work designs; a nice feature is a separate luggage/dressing room. But more welcome would be cleaner carpeting and freshly painted walls. I was told they were going to renovate soon.

Holiday Inn's five-star deluxe hotel might be open now.

HOTELS ON HAMIDIA ROAD

So many hotels are located there that Hamidia Road might be named hotel road; a mere sampling follows. In case you want to write for a reservation, they all have the same postal code: 462001. Most are not for the fussy and have little to recommend them but price. Their rates range from singles at Rs 150 ($5) non–air-conditioned and Rs 275 ($9.16) air-conditioned, to doubles for Rs 200 ($6.66) non–air-conditioned to Rs 600 ($20) air-conditioned deluxe. All have attached bathrooms, room telephones, and TVs. Here are some of the better spots: **Jyoti,** 53 Hamidia Rd. (☎ 76838), clean, vegetarian hotel; no alcohol. **Rajdoot Delux,** No 7 Hamidia Rd. (☎ 75271) is deluxe in name only; it's so-so, but with 120 rooms, some of them air-conditioned, it's also larger than many. So if you don't have a reservation, you might get in here. **Shivalik Gold,** 40 Hamidia Rd. (☎ 74242) is a cut above okay.

Hotel Surya (☎ 536925), with 30 rooms, is one of Hamidia Road's better (and cheaper) places, although the lobby is run down and rooms vary when it comes to maintenance. Look at more than one; some air-conditioned rooms. Management is pleasant, and rates slightly lower than some others on Hamidia Road; 10% service charge. **Ranjit,** No 3 Hamidia Rd. (☎ 75211), has 29 rooms and is at the low end with regard to price and very popular.

Hotel Ramsons International, Hamidia Road (☎ 72299), has become seedy over the years and needs renovation. **Hotel Taj,** 52 Hamidia Rd. (☎ 74769), has 48 rooms and a rooftop restaurant with a fine view and good food.

HOTELS ON STATION ROAD

Station Road is the other place to find budget hotels, with rates ranging from Rs 150 ($5) to Rs 250 ($8.33) Among these hotels are the **Samrat** (☎ 77023) and **Sangam** (☎ 77161) with some air-conditioned rooms.

ELSEWHERE IN BHOPAL

The following hotels have slightly lower rates, ranging from Rs 300 ($10) for singles to Rs 650 ($21.66) for a double. Facilities include attached bathrooms, telephones, restaurants, and bars; some have air-conditioning and accept credit cards.

MP Tourism runs two pleasant places: **Hotel Panchanan,** New Market (☎ 551647; fax 552384), with air-conditioning and five rooms; and **Hotel Palash,** near 45 Bungalows (☎ 553006; fax 552384), with 33 doubles (also a single-occupancy rate), 12 of them air-conditioned. This hotel has conference facilities. Both hotels are popular; if booking more than five days in advance: M.P. State Tourism Development Corporation Ltd. 4th floor, Gangotri, T.T. Nagar, Bhopal 462003 (☎ 554340; fax 5522384). If less than five days, contact the managers of the hotels.

A commercial hotel, the **President International,** Berasia Road, Bhopal 462029 (☎ 77291), is fairly clean and attractive, with comfortable rates. Some rooms are air-conditioned.

Not as good on Berasia Road is **Hotel Mayur** (☎ 540826), with some air-conditioned rooms.

The **Youth Hostel,** T.T. Nagar (☎ 66671), offers the not-at-all-fastidious accommodations with absolutely no frills. About Rs 50 ($1.66) for doubles, Rs 20 (66¢) per head in 40-bed dorm. It's out of town.

WHERE TO EAT IN BHOPAL

Three places to try Bhopali cuisine are **Madina Hotel,** on Sultania Road, **Afgani Hotel,** on Pir Gate, and **Hakeems** in New Market and at Jummerati. All are modest, as are their prices. For cheap snacks and delicious coffee, there's the **Indian Coffee House** in New Market and also at Sivaj Nagar. The ever-reliable **Kwality** on Hamidia Road (also in New Market) is clean, comfortable, and popular, with a knack with Western dishes; for Chinese, try the **Nanking** in the Nisagara Hotel, Maharana Pratrap Nagar; for Mughali food with a view, it's the restaurant in the **Lake View,** Shamla Hill, or try the other higher-priced hotel restaurants with the usual repertoire of Indian, Chinese, and continental cuisines.

WHAT TO SEE & DO IN SANCHI

Everything about Sanchi is awesome. For more than 2,000 years it has been the site of what is now renowned as one of the major archaeological prizes in the world. Buddha never set foot here, but in the 3rd century B.C. Emperor Ashoka did, after he had adopted Buddhism. He chose this site for the construction of his monuments because his wife, Devi, who came from nearby Vidisha, had established a monastery here and because there was already an important religious center nearby.

The eight stupas, vast stone mounds, he erected at Sanchi were memorial shrines to house relics of Buddha and his disciples; three of them remain. As Buddhism went into a decline in India, these stupas lay neglected on their hilltop, camouflaged by sand and vines and undiscovered even by the Mughal emperor Aurangzeb, who mercilessly desecrated most Buddhist shrines that he came across.

Sanchi's stupas were rediscovered in 1811 by a British military officer, but were not cleared away by archaeologists until Sir Alexander Cunningham dug here in 1851. Sloppy archaeologists damaged some of the monuments later in that century, and they were not properly restored until about the time of World War I.

THE ARCHAEOLOGICAL SITE

The structures at the archeological site consist of stupas, pillars, shrines, and convents, and a 50 paise (2¢) charge admits you to all of them and the archaeological museum. The periods covered are from the 3rd century B.C. to the 10th century A.D.

The high spot, of course, is the **Great Stupa,** its shape representing the heavens embracing the earth. At the top is a square surrounded by a balustrade, symbolizing the heaven of the gods, with the umbrellas pointing upward like a spire, as if they were reaching for the heavens. A platform around the stupa was used by the pious, who would walk in the direction of the sun. It is guarded by a stone fence with four gateways, corresponding possibly to the seasons of the year, and the inscriptions on the balustrades represent the names of the people who contributed to its building.

The Great Stupa, 106 feet in diameter and 42 feet high, was built originally of brick by Ashoka and embellished into its present shape in the 1st or 2nd century A.D. The toranas, pale stone gateways, were originally inspired by crude bamboo village fences. They are made of two pillars surmounted by three horizontal bars and were constructed from stone quarried at nearby Udaygiri.

Only a profound student of Buddhism could possibly identify all the carvings and legends on the gateways, but it might be helpful to know that (1) *Birth* is signified by a lotus, either alone or in a bouquet; (2) *Enlightenment* is shown by the bo-tree;

(3) *The Great Sermon* is symbolized by the Wheel of Law; and (4) *Death* is represented by stupas. The Buddha, according to the religious custom of the time, was never depicted except in disguise. Other common symbols of the Buddha are footprints, umbrellas, deer (for the first sermon given, at Deer Park near Sarnath), ducks and geese (perhaps standing for Buddha's flock), and the peacock, symbol of Ashoka's empire.

One of the more interesting toranas is the **South Gateway,** the carvings atop which depict the birth of the Buddha: Maya, the mother, stands on an open lotus while elephants shower water on her and the dwarfs bestow garlands.

The **East Gateway** shows the Buddha renouncing wealth and leaving his father's house to begin his search for truth. On the left pillar you can see a miracle—the Buddha walking on water, one of the miraculous deeds he performed to dispel doubts among the incredulous.

On the **North Gateway,** he not only walks on water, he does so while flames issue from his feet and angels bang drums to draw everybody's attention.

Near the South Gateway are the remains of **Ashoka's Pillar,** once 42 feet high and weighing 40 tons. It is believed to have been brought from Chunar near Benares by waterways. The four lions that once adorned the pillar are now in the small museum and are, of course, the emblem of the Indian republic. Ashoka originally erected 30 pillars throughout India, 10 of which remain. Some pillars mark sites made holy by Buddha; others mark the route for pilgrims on their way to holy places. All bear inscriptions asking the people not to swerve from the path of truth. Also of note near the South Gateway is the 7th-century **Chaitya Hall,** with its classic columns.

In 1995, archaeologists were working on recently discovered Buddhist sites not far from Sanchi, a drivable road was to be in place by publication time. It's worth investigating.

NEAR SANCHI

Northeast of Sanchi, at **Udaygiri,** are 20 rock-cut caves, and at nearby **Vidisha** a pillar dating back 20 centuries, erected by the Greek ambassador to India of those days to glorify Vishnu and signify his conversion to the Hindu religion. Vidisha is on the main line from Bhopal, about Rs 35 ($1.16) first class; buses run regularly from Sanchi, about Rs 5 (16¢). A taxi from Bhopal to Sanchi and on to Udaygiri and Vidisha, will run about Rs 700 ($23.33) round-trip. Check with MP Tourism on approved rates or book yours in advance in Delhi or Agra.

WHERE TO STAY & EAT IN SANCHI

(*Note:* Bhopal offers more choices of accommodation; a taxi takes 1 1/2 hours each way.) The STD Code: 07592.

MP Tourism's **Traveller's Lodge,** Near Bus Stand, Sanchi 464661 (☎ 81223), is pleasant. Its veranda overlooks the ancient shrines. In fact, both the Great Stupa and railway station are within walking distance of the lodge. There is a long covered passage leading from the lounge to the eight rooms, all of which have attached baths, ceiling fans, and motel-modern furniture. None are air-conditioned. Rates are Rs 225 ($7.50) single, Rs 275 ($9.16) double. A banyan tree and mango grove shade the adjoining garden.

Near the museum, **MP Tourism's Cafeteria** (☎ 81243) has food, with no reservations required, as well as two rooms: Rs 175 ($5.83) single, Rs 225 ($7.50) double.

Reservations for either accommodation are advised. If booking more than five days in advance (advised), write to MP Tourism Development Corporation, 4th floor,

Gangotri, T. T. Nagar, Bhopal 46200, India. If not, write to the manager at the Traveller's Lodge.

If you want to mingle with monks in residence and pilgrims visiting the shrines, stay at the **Buddhist Guest House,** where there are 20 basic (not for the fussy) rooms. Rates are Rs 40 per person ($1.33), some with baths attached; dorms cost Rs 35 ($1.16) per head, with a common bathroom. To reserve in advance, write to Manager, Mahabodhi Center, Sanchi 464661, Madhya Pradesh. If you eat here—under $1 per meal—you must inform the cook in advance so he can stock up on food. Better yet, eat at the Tourist Cafeteria. Also, it is a nice gesture to leave a small donation for the society.

Another possibility is the **Railway Retiring Rooms**—two in all—cheap and clean. You can take your meals at the **Traveller's Lodge** with advance notice to the manager; MP Tourism's **Cafeteria;** or bring something with you for a picnic. Carrying some fruit for a snack is a good idea, as there is no place to buy it here.

Rajasthan: Golden Deserts & Great Palaces

Rajasthan often makes the news in India because of its comparative poverty, aggravated by the occasional droughts that come as an unwelcome reminder of how much of the state is desert.

But in some ways it's also one of the most attractive states, with numerous distinctive assets: the marble mines of **Makrana** (from whence came the stone for Agra's Taj Mahal); the forests of **Sawai Madhopur,** filled with wild animals; that otherwise rarely seen beast of burden, the aloof camel; and the artificial lakes that have made lovely cities bloom. There also is a fresh and fertile greenbelt in this state.

And then there are the people: women in swirling bright skirts, literally covered from head to toe in bangles, balancing brass jugs on their heads; men with rose-red and pink turbans like full-blown roses in a desert. (It takes 10 yards of silk to wind that headgear—amateurs need not even try.)

Rajasthan was home to the Rajput dynasties as far back as the 7th century, and they controlled much of North India through the 12th century. They were warriors who fought against each other and, at times, defended Hinduism from the Muslims, who eventually conquered them.

Remnants of earlier civilizations dating from as early as 2500 B.C. have been uncovered here by archaeologists. Ashoka once ruled part of this state, and his successors—Greeks from Bacteria (2nd century B.C.), followed by the Sythians (2nd to 4th centuries), the Guptas, and White Huns from Central Asia (4th to 6th centuries)—also made their home here. In fact, scholars believe the Rajputs probably were descendants of Central Asian tribes.

What is left of the Rajputs today are the legends of heroism and chivalry, and their many stone and turreted fortresses, palaces, temples, gardens, and lakes of their glory days.

1 Jaipur

Jaipur, with a population of 1.5 million, is the most renowned of Rajasthan's cities. It is often referred to as rose-pink because of the delicate flamingo color with which so many of the most arresting buildings are painted

Jai Singh, who was only 13 when he became ruler, was dubbed Sawai (prodigy) by the Mughal emperor Aurangzeb, who ruled in

Delhi at the time, and the title is still borne today by the princely house of Jaipur. Jai Singh, not content with city planning, went on to become one of the world's major astronomers, building observatories not only in Jaipur but also in Delhi and other cities.

The famous colorful outfits of Rajasthan are rarely seen in Jaipur anymore. But the city's residents are trying to preserve some of the traditional atmosphere by painting all of the buildings in the old part of town their original rosy pink shade and printing all their signs in the local language.

ESSENTIALS

GETTING THERE

BY AIR From Delhi, there are two daily flights to Jaipur, 35 air-minutes away, starting as early as 5:45am; the fare is $28. There are also daily flights from Jodhpur, at $34; from Udaipur, at $35; from Bombay Indian Airlines flies to Jaipur Tuesday through Thursday, Saturday, and Sunday; East-West Airlines flies there daily except Saturday (Monday Thursday for $98). The airport is about 15 kilometers from downtown, a drive of about 30 minutes. The trip from the airport to the city by auto ricksha costs Rs 80 ($2.66), by taxi Rs 150 ($5).

BY RAIL The speedy *Shatabdi Express* departs Delhi at 5:50am, arriving in Jaipur at 10:15am; the fare is Rs 320 ($10.66) for AC Chair, Rs 620 ($20.66) Executive. The train departs Jaipur 2 at 5:15pm, arriving in Delhi at 9:15pm. (***Penny-wise tip for Shatabdi travel:*** Buy the AC Chair; all your extra $10 buys in Executive is more space and a slightly bigger, but no better, meal.) The *Pink City Express* from Delhi takes about five hours and costs Rs 161 ($5.36) for AC Chair, Rs 72 ($2.40) in Second. Should you want to stop in Agra first, take the *Agra–Jaipur Express.*

BY BUS These are some of the most popular routes. From Delhi: 24 deluxe buses depart from 6am until 10:45pm, AC buses at 6:30am and 2pm; the deluxe fare is Rs 122 ($4.06); AC Express, Rs 61 ($2). From Agra: five deluxe coaches depart from 6:30am to 10pm, the trip takes five hours; the deluxe fare is Rs 74 ($2.46); express Rs 61 ($2.03). From Jodhpur: one departure at 4pm, arriving 9:50pm; deluxe fare is Rs 101 ($3.36), express Rs 78 ($2.60). The roads are good, and there are refreshment stops en route. Buses also connect from Bharatpur (see below).

VISITOR INFORMATION

The **Government of India Tourist Office,** Hotel Khasa Kothi (☎ 372200), hands out helpful information, pamphlets, and maps, and is the place for hiring approved guides. It is open daily from 9am to 6pm; there is also a counter at the airport, open at flight times (☎ 550222). The **Government of Rajasthan Tourist Office,** at the railway station (☎ 315714), and **Tourist Information Bureau,** Central Bus Stand, Sindhi Camp, open from 10am to 5pm, are other sources of information.

CITY LAYOUT

Mirza Ismail Road separates the new city from the old, but once you pass through the ancient **Sanganeri Gate,** you'll be surprised to find the centuries-old **Johari Bazar** as wide a street as in any modern city in the world. Truly, it is an example of farsighted planning: Sawai Jai Singh (1699–1743), who founded the city in 1727, determined that it should be the best-planned metropolis of its time.

The streets, 110 feet wide (to accommodate old-time elephant processions), were laid out to intersect at right angles in the now familiar grid system; eight gateways were built in the surrounding city wall, 20 feet high and eight feet thick.

Heritage Hotels

In 1947, when India became an independent, democratic country, rajas, the rulers in the state of Rajasthan, gave up their titles and privy purses (some came to many multithousands of dollars a year) but kept their personal treasures—private lands (most of them now national parks) and their palaces.

By the 1960s, the most astute and mighty princes started to promote their ornate, and hard to manage, palaces as hotels where tourists could pretend to lead the life of a maharaja or maharani amid opulence only steps from the desert. This romanticized image caught on, and today these palaces are well established luxury hotels and splurges in this book.

But grandiosity is a minor part of Rajasthan royal real estate story. Rajput rulers of hundreds of smaller principalities, clan-by-clan, had always built numerous palaces, forts, and forest lodges amid their local villages, as well as townhouses for city visits. They were the handiwork of all manner of royalty. Now the heirs of these former rulers are reclaiming their heritage. They are opening their ancestral properties, not to lure tourists with regal splendor, but to draw them closer to the traditional life of India's most colorful state.

Some of these near-ruins have been restored with family heirlooms; others look near the brink. Yet, even with patched chintz upholstery and worn carpeting, they are still palaces rooted deeply in the communities above which they loom.

In one palace, over tea with the owner, I learned that this now perfectly restored property had been closed for 100 years following a flood from which the entire village took refuge inside the building. At another palace, the owner showed me to a threadbare room with a degree of chivalry that made the room seem extraordinary. That night, in this same room, chanting from a nearby temple lulled me to sleep. Elsewhere, on a drive into the countryside to another palace, I was mesmerized by a family tending an ancient water wheel as it lifted tiny clay jugs of water, tipping them into the field to the accompaniment of the child's laughter whenever the water splashed him.

No matter the state of disrepair of some former royal lodgings or how off the beaten path, the rooms have private bathrooms, ceiling fans (some have air-conditioning), and windows to open for refreshing night breezes.

From Mandawa in the north to Mt. Abu, the highest point in the southern Aravalli range, you will find palace gates open to welcome guests. Right now you can catch many of these palaces, castles, and other enchanting dwellings (and their tiny hamlets) before they are discovered. They have surprisingly affordable rates. (How about Rs 800 ($6.66) to Rs 1,000 ($33.33) for a double?) The Heritage Hotels, as they are officially known, are scattered widely in Rajasthan, so almost everywhere you go you might find a royal night's resting place. (See "Where to Stay" sections for specific Heritage Hotels.)

Getting Around Jaipur

There are no yellow-top taxis in Jaipur, only private taxis; you'll also find three-wheeler taxis, tempos, bicycle rickshas, tongas, and buses.

Private taxis, found mainly at all the gates along M.I. Road, cost around Rs 275 ($9.16) to Rs 345 ($12.50) for four hours (or 40 kilometers), and Rs 400 ($13.33) to Rs 575 ($19.16) for eight hours (or 60 kilometers).

For **auto rickshas** (locally "three-wheelers") insist on paying what's on the meter (plus an additional charge Rs 1 per piece should you have luggage). When hiring a three-wheeler for a half or full day, negotiate—usually around Rs 35 ($1.16) to Rs 45 ($1.50) per hour (8 kilometers). **Bicycle rickshas** are unmetered and the drivers unprincipled when it comes to tourists. Be sure to set the rate before you get in. Within the city, expect to pay about Rs 5 (16¢) for 1 kilometer, Rs 7 (23¢) for 2 kilometers, and gradually increase to Rs 25 (83¢ to 28(93¢) for 8 kilometers. For a half day, a bicycle riksha costs about Rs 50 ($1.66) to Rs 75 ($2.50), for a full day Rs 75 ($2.50) to Rs 100 ($3.33); luggage charges are extra.

For car-with-driver rentals, contact **RTDC's Gangaur Tour and Transport Unit,** Tourist Hotel, M.I. Road Mirza (☎ 371648), or **ITDC's Transport Unit,** Hotel Khasa Kothi (☎ 368461), or a reliable travel agency such as **Aravalli Safari and Tours,** M.I. Road (☎ 373124).

FAST FACTS: JAIPUR

Bank The Bank of Rajasthan in Rambagh Palace is open from 7:30am to 8:30pm.

Swimming Nonresidents can use the swimming pools at the Hotel Khasi Khoti from 6:30am to 7pm (the fee is Rs 10) and at the Jaipur Ashok from 7am to 7pm (fee is Rs 15).

Telephone **STD, ISD,** and **PCO** signs around town mean national and international calls can be made from these locations (**Penny-wise tip:** half rates are from 6 to 8am and 7 to 10pm; quarter rates are from 10pm to 6am; service charge Rs 2.)

Transportation Information Indian Airlines, Nehru Place, Tonk Road, Jaipur (☎5145000); rail inquiries ☎ 131; Railway reservations ☎ 135; rail schedules, 8am to 8pm, until 6pm Sundays; Central Bus Station, Sindhi Camp; (☎ 375834); Narain Circle Bus Station (☎ 564016).

WHAT TO SEE & DO

THE PALACE & OBSERVATORY

In the center of the old town is the **City Palace,** built by Maharaja Sawait Jai Singh in 1728, with additional sections added by later rulers. The palace, half of which is still a private residence, is a treasure trove of royal acquisitions and is occasionally used as a setting for special events.

One of the latest additions to the palace is the **Mubarak Mahal,** built by Sawai Madho Singh II in 1900, and today housing the **Textiles and Costumes Museum**—worth some attention. The building itself looks as if it is made of marble lace, while some of the costumes inside are probably the best examples you'll see of the way Rajput women dressed in days gone by.

Another interesting collection is located in the **Pothikhana.** Originally this was the coronation hall of the palace—it's a huge room with an enormous venetian glass chandelier and extensive ceiling decorations painted 75 years ago; 17th-century carpets made in Pakistan(when it was part of India), Afghanistan, and Persia hang on the walls. Filled with interesting and beautiful artifacts, this museum is both a repository of the culture and a family album of the long line of maharajas who ruled this area for so many years. Among many lovely Rajput miniatures is one of the Shah Jahan and Mumtaz Mahal—the lovers of Taj Mahal fame. Another shows a battle with ying ships, and a third illustrates an Indian elopement (but instead of the perennial ladder, the suitor has brought his elephant upon which to whisk his love away). For the visitor with lots of time, there are about 2,000 of these fine miniatures, illustrating rulers, holy men, and the way of life of the people (usually the noble-type people).

Other cases display fascinating and rare manuscripts written in very fine and beautiful Persian, Arabic, and Sanskrit script. Sawai Jai Singh's works on mathematics and astronomy are here, too. Scattered among these are extremely delicate paperwork cutouts, including one done in 1743 by the second ruler of Jaipur, Ishwari Singh, when he was a young boy.

The doors throughout the palace are worth noting: Some are huge brass ones, others delicately carved ivory (real ivory, by the way—like wood—always has a grain). Passing through the gate flanked by two large marble elephants, you come to the **Sharbata,** a deep pink-colored court with white patterns. Here the marble-pillared **Diwani-i-Khas** (Hall of Private Audience) is located. Connected to its patio is the **Diwan-i-Am** (Hall of Public Audience). Festivals are still celebrated in its large courtyard in the months of March, April, and September. Flanking this yard is the screened latticework gallery from which the royal ladies would view the proceedings below. As you enter the **Ladies' Apartments,** you will see a large photograph, taken in 1926, of the late maharaja atop his elephant en route to his first marriage. The foreign community of that time can be seen in the left corner watching the procession. This is a tinted enlargement of the original photo.

Dominating the palace is the majestic **Chandra Mahal,** the towering yet delicate seven-story white building that was started in 1728 by Sawai Jai Singh, who built the ground-floor **Chandra Mandir** (Moon Palace), and was added to by later rulers. Gold leaf was used in the ceiling decorations, and again there are portraits of the Kachhawa monarchs dating from 958 when the court resided at Amber. On the wall, a large mural resembling the sun is made of alternating guns and arrows, with a warrior's shield at the center. One room is furnished the same way it was then: with a rug, canopy, backrest pillow, gadi (floor cushion), spittoon, and hookah.

Tucked into a lovely leaf-filled niche along the passageway to the Chandra Mahal are a number of 14th-century sandstone statues representing a group of musicians, each playing a different instrument. Found 70 miles from Jaipur, they're interesting because they are much less stylized and look much more alike than the statues usually seen in temples.

The **Silehkhana** (Armory) is famous for the finest collection of arms and armor in India; it contains 2,000 weapons dating from 1580 and later. (Maharaja Man Singh's sword weighs at least 10 pounds.) Entrance to the armory is Rs 20 (66¢); to use a camera Rs 10 (33¢). (Readers comment that guards expect tips if photographed.)

Easily one of Sawai Jai Singh's greatest feats was the construction of the adjoining **Jantar Mantar,** the still futuristic-looking observatory, which has been described as both the most surreal and the most logical landscape in stone. A passionate and knowledgeable student of astronomy, Jai Singh often spent hours among these massive yet precise structures, which are even more impressive when one remembers that they were built in the very early 1700s.

The sundial gives the actual local time in Jaipur, accurate to the minute.

The largest structure—90 feet high—gives time in units of two seconds. The high steps were used both to take the reading and to forecast the weather.

The structure that looks a bit like a tilted, twin-faced clock is really the equinox dials. Only one of the two circular surfaces is ever touched by the sun's rays at any one time: one side in winter, the other in summer; between March 21 and September 21 the sun passes from one side to the other.

Horoscopes have played—and still play—a large role in Indian life, so it is not at all surprising to find here a separate structure for each of the 12 signs of the Zodiac.

Someone skilled in taking the readings can ascertain from these structures the position of the dominant planet in relation to the earth and the sun, and if supplied with such information as the exact local time and the time of birth of the subject, the astrologer can chart a full-fledged horoscope. The scales are also devised to allow calculation of each person's most auspicious time of day.

Jai Singh built five observatories throughout India, but this one is the largest, and certainly—even without any knowledge of how to read or use the information these grand structures provide—the intrinsic beauty of construction is impressive.

The palace and observatory are both open daily, the palace from 9:30am to 4:45pm, the observatory from 9am to 4:30pm. The museum is closed on some holidays. The entry fee for the palace is Rs 30 ($1); to use a camera is an additional Rs 10 (33¢)—and small change for tips if you plan to photograph costumed guards. The entry fee for the observatory is Rs 4 (13¢), free on Monday.

Hawa Mahal

The best-known landmark in Jaipur, reproduced in innumerable pictures, is the **Hawa Mahal** (Palace of the Winds); while it is also in the palace compound, it is best seen from the front, on the main street called Sireh Deori Bazar. With five stories of small, semioctagonal overhanging windows covered with lattice screens, it's a distinctive example of architectural delicacy. Hawa Mahal was an architectural veil with air-conditioning; its multitude of little chambers allowed air to circulate, while the screens permitted ladies of the harem to view the city below through while remaining hidden from the public. The Hawa Mahal now houses a well-designed museum of historic artifacts and a display focusing on Jaipur's past and present. It is open from 10am to 4:30pm. Entrance is Rs 3 (1¢), free Mondays; the museum is closed Fridays (☎ 48862).

Other Attractions in Jaipur

Notable museums connected with Jaipur's two most famous landmarks are described above; here are a few others. The **Central Museum** (Albert Hall), Ram Niwas Garden, open from 9:30am to 4:30pm, entrance Rs 3 (10¢), free Mondays (☎ 560796), houses a fascinating mélange of arts and crafts in an striking 19th-century building blending Oriental and Victorian architectural styles. Ram Niwas Garden also houses the zoo. The **Museum of Indology,** Prachya Vidya Path, 24 Ganwall Park, open from 9 to 6pm, has a collection of folk art, tantric hangings, and textiles. Near Statue Circle are the newly constructed **Planetarium** and **B. M. Birla Science Centre.** Entrance to both is Rs 7 (23¢), students Rs 3.50 (12¢).

Nearby Attractions

Northwest of the old town, the roads lead to the fabulous **Palace of Amber (Amer),** 7 miles away. Originally, this was the ancient capital of Kachhawah rulers. Maharaja Man Singh, a contemporary of the Mughal emperor Akbar and one of his most successful generals, began to construct the Palace of Amber back in the early 17th century; subsequent rulers added bits and pieces. As it was never threatened, much less conquered, it almost remains today in its original pristine state and is proudly regarded, rightly or wrongly, as being one of the most glorious palaces of India.

Traditionally, tourists navigate the hill to the palace via elephant, sitting on a kind of padded box atop the gaily painted animal. The local joke is to convince unsuspecting tourists that they must allow the elephant to wrap his trunk around each customer and swing him up and over, into position—the only way to mount. Actually, the mounting is performed rather more prosaically by climbing stone steps to an ancient platform at the level of the patient creature's back.

The ride is not particularly comfortable, but where else can you ride an elephant to a palace? Why is the elephant ride so expensive? Because even lady elephants, like these, eat 200 pounds of fodder a day.

At the top of the hill is the palace, its marble pillars topped with elephant-head sculptures, each animal holding a lotus in its trunk. The **Ganesh Pol** (gate), covered with 300-year-old paintings, leads into an inner courtyard whose garden is patterned like a Persian rug. To the east of this inner court stands the **Jai Mandir,** literally a glass palace whose walls and ceilings are covered with mirrors and spangles. The concave ceiling in one room is shaped so that it would fit snugly over an elephant's back. The guides in the palace are wont to light candles, demonstrating thousands of overhead reflections, like shimmering stars in the sky.

The maharani's apartments are adjoining, all rooms and balconies connected by a ramp, up which the royal mistress was carried in a ricksha (one of the original rickshas, its wheels padded to eliminate unnecessary noise, can be seen behind a glass door in the courtyard below). From the upper vantage point of the maharani's quarters, one can peer discreetly through filigree marble windows into the public courtyard below, or gaze out at the brightly colored gardens laid out in pretty **Maota Lake.** Through the gorge at the foot of the hill—a narrow, well-defined pass—a winding road eventually leads to Delhi.

At the back of the palace, the servants' quarters are naturally much sparser. From here an underground tunnel once led to another fort on the hill to the rear, but this tunnel has now been filled in.

Back in the inner courtyard at the entrance to the palace, visitors can admire the inventive air-conditioning system of three centuries ago: water pouring down a ribbed marble channel, cooled by winds blowing through the perforated marble screen at each side.

Just outside—off the public courtyard where the elephants wait to begin their downward journey—is the small **Kali Temple,** in which a five-minute aarti ceremony takes place at 10am and 6pm each day. Priests invoke the goddess with brass lamps having many lights. The palace is open from 9am to 4:30pm; The entry fee is Rs 4 (13¢); still-camera photography is an additional Rs 50 ($1.66) for foreigners, Rs 20 (66¢) for Indians; the cost to use your video camera is Rs 100 ($3.33) for foreigners, Rs 50 ($1.66) for Indians. The elephant ride is Rs 250 ($8.33) for up to four persons. If the fare is too rich for your blood, you can walk up to the palace's main gate (Suraj Pol), and an elephant will give you a little ride around the palace square at the top for a smaller fee.

A winding road from Amber Palace and Fort leads to **Nahargarh Fort** (Tiger Fort), under construction from 1734 to 1836, once a royal retreat. It's open daily, and there's a cafeteria (10am to 10pm) with a splendid view. En route is **Jaigarh Fort,** said to be the site of the world's largest cannon on wheels, which was built by Jai Singh in 1720. It has a 20-foot-long barrel, and its wheels are 9 feet in diameter. It took 100 kg of gunpowder to fire a single shot. Jaigarh is also famous as the treasury of the former royal family. The views are great, especially from the tallest watchtower at an elevation of 3,000 feet.

Because this fort was never captured, you get a real feeling of its glory days. Explore the armory, gardens, a granary, reservoirs (one of them, 158 feet by 138 feet and 40 feet deep, held thousands of gallons of water) ancient temples, and dark hallways leading to once royal chambers.

Entrance to Nahargarh Fort is Rs 10 (33¢); it is open from 10am to 4:30pm. Entrance to Jaigarh fort is Rs 2 (6¢); it is open from 10am to 4:30pm. Camera fees are Rs 10 at each fort.

Getting to Amber & the Forts From Hawa Mahal, buses to Amber (Amer) depart every half hour for Rs 2.50 (8¢) for a scenic trip through flowering meadows to the Fort complex and it's lovely Dil-e-Aaram Garden. From the Jaipur railway station, buses to Amber depart regularly from 5:10am until 9:20pm; they return to the railway station from Amber from 6:15am to 10:30pm.

Alternatively, a taxi from Jaipur costs about Rs 40 ($1.33) to Amber, Rs 60 ($2) to Nahargarh; if you're up to a good hike, you can hoof it between Amber and Jaigarh. Leave the palace from the Suraj Pol, and follow the stone road up the steadily winding steep incline for about a 30 minutes. The road is shielded by a high wall all the way to the main fort gate. En route you can visit Nahargarh Fort and stop there at the cafe for refreshment, in either direction.

Walking & Shopping

Walking about Jaipur's bustling streets is a rewarding experience and, not surprisingly, it's popular with photographers. The flower sellers with their bright piles of marigolds in the bazaars, the delicately carved, tiny sandstone windows (to keep the women unseen in bygone days) in some of the old houses of the nobles, the occasional camel and oxcarts—all these are eye-catchers.

The town is rich in handicrafts—more than 200,000 locals are said to be so employed—and the best place to find them under one roof, price-fixed, is **Rasathali,** the Rajasthan Government Handicraft Emporium, at Ajmeri Gate, M.I. Road (☎ 367176), opposite the Ajmeri gate on Mirza Ismail Road. Look for tie-dyed and block-painted textiles, enameled household objects, filigree, bold folk paintings on cloth, but above all, jewelry. Jaipur sparkles here with gems faceted or carved into fanciful creatures or bright blossoms. Oft-times these are mounted into enameled settings painted so delicately that you can see each tiny bird, flower, leaf, and scroll quite plainly—even on the smallest of pieces. The markets are open from 10am to 1pm, 3 to 8pm; closed Sundays and holidays. Other government emporia are: **Handloom House** and **Khadi Ghar,** both on M.I. Road; and **Rajasthan Handloom Project Board,** Chomu House (☎ 313683).

Many of the town's leading jewelers and curio dealers are located on Mirza Ismail Road, among them the reliable **Rakyan's** (☎ 373115). They have been known to send out for a piece of jewelry tucked in some secret cache to make a sale. (Rakyan's does not pay commissions to guides, so they will not take you there.) The folks at Rakyan's will be glad to let you look at their beautiful jewelry and think it over at your hotel; then they will send someone over with your piece when and if you're ready to buy.

Also on M.I. Road, in the Tholia Building, check out **Amprapali** (☎ 377940), for silver and tribal jewelry, and **Tholia's Kuber** (☎ 367334) for interesting selections of old and new jewelry and art objects; **Maneeka,** H-10 Chameliwala, opposite the G.P.O. (☎ 375913), also has old tribal silver ornaments. **Marco Polo,** Shop 44, opposite the Palace of the Winds, is open seven days a week and has stoneware, crafts, and a host of gift items at prices they say are cheaper than at other stores—only after bargaining, that is.

No visitor to Rajasthan should leave without buying something made from the wonderful block-printed or tie-dye textiles or a piece to sew at home. Old and valuable textiles for wall hangings and other decorative uses can be found at **Rajasthan Fabric and Arts,** near the City Palace (☎ 41432), and **Saurashtra Oriental Arts,** Amer Road (☎ 42609); for a good selection of traditional textile patterns, used contemporary ready-made fashions and accessories, visit **Anokhi,** Tilak Marg, behind the Secretariat (☎ 381619).

At **Carpet Mahal and Textile Mahal,** outside Zorawar Singh Gate, Amber Road (☎ 541546), the name says it all— here you find beautiful hand-knotted wool and silk carpets, and block-printed textiles and silk fashions, including some easy-to-pack items for gifts, such as attractive pillow covers and men's ties.

Keep in mind when shopping that various areas have specialties and special days:

Johari Bazar (partially closed on both Tuesdays and Sundays) for tie-dyes, jewelry, and lacquer ware.

Mirza Ismail Road shops for jewelry and a hodgepodge of other souvenirs. Many M.I. shops accept major credit cards (they are closed Sundays).

Bapu Bazar (closed Sunday) and Nehru Bazar (closed Tuesdays) for textiles, local perfumes, and footwear (shoes made of camel skin!).

Chaura Rasta and Tripolia Bazar for textiles, ironware, and assorted trinkets (closed Sundays).

GUIDED TOURS

RTDC offers four daily tours; pick-up points for passengers are at the Railway Station, Hotel Gangaur, Hotel Teej, and the Tourist Hotel.

The **Half-day City Tour** (at 8am to 1pm, 11:30am to 4:40pm, and 1:30 to 6:30pm) covers Hawa Mahal, Amber Palace and Fort, Jai Mahal, and Gaitore Maharaja Cenotaphs (the bus drives by), City Palace and Museum, Jantar Mantar, Central Museum (closed Fridays), and Jawahar Kala Kendra (Art Gallery). The cost is Rs 50 ($1.66) per person). The **Full-day Tour** (from 9am to 6pm) covers the same city sights plus Nahargarh and Jaigarh Forts (with a lunch break), and the Dolls Museum. The cost is Rs 80 ($2.66) per person. The **Nahargarh Fort Tour** (from 6 to l0pm) includes points of interest en route and vegetarian dinner at the Fort's restaurant. The cost is Rs 85 ($2.83) per person. **The Chokhi Dhani** (from 6 to 10pm) takes tourists to a dinner and entertainment in a village atmosphere outside the city. The cost is Rs 100 ($3.33) per person. For information and bookings contact: Rajasthan Tourist Office, RTDC Tourist Hotel, M.I. Road (☎ 371648).

The **ITDC** offers a **Full-day Tour** of the city and environs (from 9:30am to 5:30pm. Check with the Hotel Jaipur Ashok (☎ 320091) or the ITDC in the Hotel Khasa Kothi (☎ 368461) for information and reservations. The cost is Rs 70 ($2.33) per person.

WHERE TO STAY

Jaipur is bursting at the seams with former palaces turned into hotels—grand palaces, small palaces, parts of palaces. While none possesses the ethereal fairy-tale beauty of Udaipur's Lake Palace Hotel (described under "Where to Stay in Udaipur," below) they, too, have historic grandeur, and even the very modest among them has great charm. Since that is part of the fun of Jaipur, I've deviated from the regular format and put those first, regardless of their price. At all price ranges, hotels have the amenities you need for a comfortable stay, and all except the most modestly priced accept local and international credit cards.

PALACES, HERITAGE & HISTORIC HOTELS

Narain Niwas Palace Hotel, Kanota Bagh, Narain Singh Road, Jaipur 302004 (☎ 563448), advertises itself as an Ancient Palace in a Shady Grove. Ancient might be stretching it, as the palace was started by Narain Singhji, chieftain of Kanota, in the 19th century as a garden house. But palatial it is, and in a grove it stands. The trappings are certainly regal—huge rooms, high ceilings, big fireplaces, attached bathrooms, Rajasthani portraits of the Singhjis going back through the years, guns, rugs, crystal chandeliers, and a swimming pool in the garden. Eighteen of the 22 rooms are air-conditioned, the other four are air-cooled (which, as you probably know, is not air-conditioning, but quite effective). In the winter months (the peak time for visiting Jaipur) it gets chilly here—the last thing you need is any kind of cooling. A sweater is nice, though. The most enchanting rooms are on the top-floor terrace. Singles Rs 650 ($21.66), doubles Rs 865 ($28.83), suites Rs 1150 ($38.33). Nonvegetarian meals and a full breakfast cost Rs 350 ($11.66) per person (but try to eat out in Jaipur).

While the approaching streets are thoroughly off-putting, the intimate 33-room **Bissau Palace,** outside Chand Pol Gate, Jaipur 302016 (☎ 310371; fax 371628), once the home to the Rawal (chief minister) of Bissau, has lots of charm in beautiful public rooms: a book-lined library, a small armory with valuable antique weapons, a family portrait gallery stretching back centuries, and a handsome dining room. You'll be happy in this little palace if you don't expect the bedrooms to live up to the public rooms—they need care—and will overlook slight sluggishness in the service. The rates, however, are right for the budget traveler: Rs 495 ($16.50) for a bed-and-breakfast single, Rs 780 ($26) for bed-and-breakfast double. Lunch and dinner will each run about Rs 180 ($6) per head. All rooms have individual air conditioners; there's a swimming pool, garden, and grand view of the Amber Palace.

When the Mandawa family left their palace-fort and visited Jaipur, they stayed in their ancestral city home, now **Hotel Mandawa House,** Sansar Chandra Road, Jaipur 302001 (☎ 365398; fax 371795). Converted into an intimate 17-room hotel and run by the family, it still has the feel of a private home. Gracious and spacious (but needing a paint job), the house was built in 1896, but the ancestral portraits in the elegant dining room date from the 14th to 20th centuries. The roof terrace is a perfect place to watch the sunset. Newer rooms have beds set on marble platforms; all rooms are comfortable and have modern bathrooms. Rates range from Rs 300 ($17.10) single to Rs 400 ($22.80) double. Meals cost about another Rs 200 ($11.40) a day per person. Mandawa House is near both the railway and the bus stations and within a few steps from Mirza Ismail Road with its shops and city center.

The enchanting **Samode Haveli,** Ganga Pol, Jaipur 302002 (☎ 42407; fax also 42407), has 19 rooms around a typical haveli courtyard. Blink and you can easily believe you are experiencing the haveli's 19th-century heyday, so atmospheric are the individually decorated rooms; the dining room murals are feasts for the eyes. Rates are a bit higher at Rs 1,000 ($33.33) for a single, Rs 1200 ($40) for a double. Air coolers and fans stir the breezes. Especially prized are sunrise or sunset views from the garden. There is talk is of adding five to six rooms and a second story. Reserve far in advance.

Newly renovated in impeccable old style, the **Alsisar Haveli**, Sansar Chandra Road, Jaipur 302001 (☎ 368290), a 102-year ancestral home, is now an 11-room hotel (with plans to add up to 25 rooms over the years) filled with antiques. Each room has unique decor, and all are air-conditioned. Rates are Rs 1,100 ($36.66) single, Rs 1,200 ($40) double. The attractive marble flooring comes from many different state quarries. Birds are at home in the flower- and tree-filled garden. While close to the bus stand and railroad station, the haveli exudes all manner of country charms. Alsisar Haveli organizes one-half day, jeep-camel-hike safaris to a village situated in a former royal hunting preserve. For reservations, contact Safari Tourism Finance Ltd., Bhandari Chambers, M.I. Road, Jaipur 302001 (☎ 370357; fax 3638330).

Off in the western part of town, **Hotel Khasa Kothi,** Mirza Ismail Road, Jaipur 302001 (☎ 375151; fax 74040), is government operated and shares a huge lawn-filled compound with the government of India Tourist Office and a local radio station. The once-attractive regal chambers are a bit threadbare; it's clean, however, and there are such nice features as verandas to sit out on, from which you can admire the shrubs, nice examples of the art of topiary, trained and cut into various shapes. Standard rooms are Rs 450 ($15) single, Rs 700 ($25) double. The rooms and restaurant are air-conditioned. There's a swimming pool too.

Next to the glamorous Rambagh Palace, **Laskhmi Vilas,** Sawai Ram Singh Road, Jaipur 302025 (☎ 521567), the late Maharaja's stables, have been turned into a modest hotel with 22 clean basic rooms and a generous swathe of lawn. Rates are Rs 450 ($15) single, Rs 500 ($16.66) double air-conditioned; less if non-AC. Should you wish to ride the royal horses, it costs about Rs 50 ($1.66) per hour.

Diggi Palace, Diggi House, Hospital Road, 302006 (☎ 374265), once was the palatial home of a thakur (landowner) although little of its glory days remains. Now bargain-priced, at Rs 100 ($3.33) to Rs 200 ($6.66) for a single, Rs 300 ($10) to Rs 500 ($16.66) for a double, it's a good place for frugal travelers. Some rooms are in cottages. There's a reasonably priced restaurant, or you can eat in the South Indian Woodlands restaurant in the nearby Meru Palace.

Palace Splurges

The following three palaces are in the Taj Group of Hotels:

The **Rambagh Palace,** Bhawani Singh Road, Jaipur 302005 (☎ 381919; fax 381098), in the southwest corner of town and formerly the home of the late maharaja, has 110 rooms and suites done up with works of art, freshly potted plants, lovely local decorative themes, and every conceivable comfort you can possibly imagine. The hotel's public rooms—the lounges and dining rooms and the attractive Polo Bar—are definitely in the palatial style: Fresh flowers everywhere complement the elegant furnishings and mirrored and marble halls. The extensive 25-acre parklike grounds, where peacocks strut and spread their tails, house a glass-enclosed swimming pool adjoining a nine-hole golf course. Rates for standard rooms are $135 single, $150 double; superior rooms $160 to $175; suites go up many times.

Nonresidents can sample some of the opulence at the Rambagh by having a meal in the **Suvarana Mahal** Restaurant (Golden Hall) that, appropriately enough, is done up in golden brocade. The food is definitely prepared for the most timid Western palate, with very little seasoning in either Eastern- or Western-style dishes. Snacks are served on the garden terrace if you want to drop in for tea and a quick look at the palace's public rooms. There's a shopping arcade, travel counter, and post office on the premises—and usually lots of tour groups too.

Another pretty palace, the **Jai Mahal Palace Hotel,** Jacob Road, Civil Lines, Jaipur 302006 (☎ 371616), is located near the main shopping center. This former palace has 102 rooms with every conceivable amenity, plus a charming quality. Beautiful lawns with live peacocks and a rooftop terrace for sitting out with drinks are nice attractions. There's a swimming pool, shopping arcade, jogging track, horseback riding facilities, and a giant chess board in the garden for your amusement. Standard rates run $120 to $130 for a single, $140 and $150 for large room, and up to $400-plus for a suite.

The Rajmahal Palace, Sardar Patel Marg, Jaipur 302001 (☎ 381757), has 11 attractive rooms and a lovely garden with a swimming pool. Founder of the city Jai Singh built this palace for his favorite maharani, Chandra Kumari Ranawatji, daughter of the maharana of Udaipur, in 1729. In 1821, it served as the residence for the agent general of Rajputana. The rates are $65 to $85 for single or double rooms. The ambience is still suffused with the British Raj.

HOTELS & GUEST HOUSES

DOUBLES FOR LESS THAN RS 300 ($10)

RTDC's **Swagatam Tourist Bungalow,** Station Road, near the railway and bus stations (☎ 310595), has 40 rooms and is a bit rundown, but it remains attractive because of its low rates: They range from singles from Rs 100 ($3.33) to doubles up to Rs 300 ($10).

At RTDC's 40-room **Tourist Hotel,** M.I. Road, opposite the G.P.0. (☎ 360238), singles start at Rs 100 ($3.33), doubles at Rs 150 ($5); dorm rates are Rs 30 ($1) per person.

Popular with low-budget travelers, the **Jaipur Inn,** Bani Park (☎ 316157), has low-priced rooms, pleasant management, and camping facilities.

Hotel Rose, B-6 Shopping Centre, Subhash Nagar (☎ 377442), run by Tanwar family, is a clean unassuming place to stay and eat made-to-order meals in an outdoor restaurant. Rooms have all the basics plus modern bathrooms. If you're truly a budget traveler, you'll like this place.

A nice feature of the otherwise rather plain 65-room **Hotel Mangal,** Sansar Chandra Road, Jaipur 302001 (☎ 361333), is the roof terrace where barbecues are held at night. There's also a vegetarian restaurant and bar. The higher priced rooms are clean, tidy, and air-conditioned. General manager Chakya Yarty said the rundown, lower-priced rooms—Rs 160 ($5.33) to Rs 275 ($9.16)—and careworn hall walls were about to be renovated.

DOUBLES FOR LESS THAN RS 500 ($16.66)

Hotel Arya Niwas, behind the Amber Cinema on Sansar Chandra Road, Jaipur 302001 (☎ 372456; fax 364376), once part of an old palace, has been much altered and added onto over the years. Now it's a spotlessly clean, friendly, 50-room hotel run by the hospitable M. K. Bansal and family, who will treat you royally. The rates range from 150 ($5) to Rs 450 ($15) depending on the size of the room and number of persons occupying it. There's no service charge or taxes, and tipping is not allowed. One of the delights of staying here is the vegetarian food (eggs are served), which is both delicious and hygienically prepared (see "Where to Eat," below).

RTDC **Hotel Gangaur,** Mirza Ismail Road, near the Pink City petrol pump (☎ 371641), is a bit dark but well-maintained. The 63-room hotel has restaurants, an around-the-clock coffee shop, and the Sakee Bar (serving chilled beer, among other things). Highest price is Rs 500 ($16.66) for a deluxe double. Slightly lower rates apply to RTDC's **Hotel Teej,** Collectorate Road, Bani Park (☎ 374206), 48 rooms, which is not as well maintained. It, too, has a restaurant and bar.

At the 17-room **Atithi Guest House,** 1 Park House Scheme (opposite All India Radio), Jaipur 302001 (☎ 378679), you'll enjoy cleanliness, friendliness, an upstairs "courtyard," small garden, and good vegetarian food. Rates range from Rs 350 ($11.66) to Rs 400 ($13.33) for a double. There's street noise in the front.

Next door, **Aagan Guest House** has 12 rooms, but not nearly as tidy as Atithi's. Rates are Rs 150 ($5) single, Rs 200 ($6.66) to Rs 350 ($11.66) double.

DOUBLES FOR LESS THAN RS 1500 ($50)

Not a palace, **Meru Palace,** 14/1-2 Sawai Ram Singh Rd., Jaipur 302004 (☎ 371111; fax 378882), is an extremely pleasant and friendly 48-room centrally air-conditioned hotel with marble-accented interiors—an excellent value. Rates are Rs 855 ($28.50) single, Rs 990 ($33) double. Each room has a balcony; those in the rear are preferred for the quiet. Tops in this price range. The hotel's restaurant,

Woodlands, is a branch of the famous vegetarian South Indian chain. There's another multicuisine restaurant, shopping arcade, and bar. Reserve far in advance.

Charging similar rates, the **Hotel Aditya,** 2 Bhawani Singh Rd., Jaipur 302005 (☎ 381720; fax 381730), has 24 functional rooms and a nice terrace garden and conference hall. Rates are Rs 750 ($25) single, Rs 1000 ($33.33) double.

Megh Niwas, C-9 Jai Singh Highway, Bani Park Jaipur, 302006 (☎ 321018; fax 321420), is a family home that has been enlarged into a modest 22-room hotel with swimming pool. The decor is nothing to rave about, but you will be comfortable and feel you're staying with friends. Some larger rooms have refrigerators and private verandas. Rates range from Rs 400 ($13.33) single to Rs 850 ($28.33) double. All are air-conditioned. Meals are prepared to order upon request. Lunch and dinner are Rs 110 to Rs 120 ($3.66 to $4), the higher price is for non-veg. There's a travel desk.

In the city's center, **LMB Hotel,** Johari Bazar, Jaipur 302003 (☎ 565844; fax 562176), instructs guests to keep their windows closed so the monkeys don't scamper in and make off with something. This is a nice, centrally air-conditioned vegetarian hotel with 33 attractive, if not imaginative, rooms. Rates range from Rs 625 ($20.83) single to Rs 825 ($27.50) double. One of them, however, is all done up in red—for honeymooners. The adjoining restaurant serves delicious vegetarian foods (see "Where to Eat," below).

Worth a Splurge

The hotels in this section will all set you back more than $50 a night for a double room. The costs go up to $200 a night.

Large, luxurious, smart and full of interesting works of art, the **Welcomgroup Rajputana Palace Sheraton,** Palace Road, Jaipur 302006 (☎ 36001; fax 367848), reinterprets the haveli look with a towering indoor courtyard. Eye-catching accouterments include a heavy silver door and a handmade crystal roof topping the Sheesh Mahal. The 202-room hotel's second courtyard is lined with interesting shops and filled with entertainers each night (see "Entertainment," below). Rooms are comfortable and pretty, with decorative local textiles and handicrafts. There's a swimming pool, well-prepared food (see "Where to Eat," below), and a garden with sports facilities—also a separate wing for the business traveler.

Looking much like a palace in red sandstone and marble is **Mansingh,** Sansar Chandra Road, Jaipur 302001 (☎ 378771; fax 377582), with marble interiors and spacious rooms. **Ripples,** the coffee shop, overlooks the lobby, and top-floor **Shivir** restaurant views the city. There's a garden, swimming pool, and shopping arcade. Convenient central location.

Holiday Inn Jaipur, Amer Road, Jaipur (☎ 609000), blends modern and traditional architecture with an interior courtyard decorated with bold murals and filed with musicians and dancers to entertain visitors. There are 72 modern rooms and a constantly cordial staff. Rates include a sumptuous buffet breakfast. The hotel is near the handicrafts hub of Jaipur.

The ITDC's comfortable, although not highly imaginative, 99-room **Hotel Jaipur Ashok,** Jai Singh Circle, Bani Park, Jaipur 302006 (☎ 320091; fax 313423), has adequate and pleasant singles and doubles with all the expected amenities and a swimming pool.

Nearby Heritage Hotels

These palace hotels may not have room telephones, TV, air-conditioning, or multichannel radios, but almost every room has a modern attached bathroom, ceiling fans, and usually ample windows to let in night breezes. And to get to these hotels, you'll have to hire a car and driver.

Figure on a basic rate of Rs 4.40 (15¢) per kilometer for a non-AC Ambassador car, plus night-halt charges of Rs 100 ($3.33); Rs 9 ($3) per kilometer for an imported air-conditioned car, plus night-halt charges of Rs 180 ($6). If you make your own arrangements, check with the India Tourist Office, Khasa Kothi Hotel (☎ 22200), for approved car agents or risk getting a raw deal. It's easier and advisable to negotiate a package rate through a travel agent such as **Aravalli Safari and Tours,** M.I. Road (☎ 373124). Others include **RTDC's Tours and Transport Unit,** Tourist Hotel, M.I. Road (☎ 371648), or **Ashok Travel and Tours,** Khasa Kothi (☎ 368461).

Only 15 kilometers (20 minutes by car) from Jaipur on the Jaipur-to-Agra Road is **Kanota Castle** (☎ 563448), a 200-year-old fort under the same management as Narain Niwas Palace Hotel in Jaipur. Here, you'll experience old grandeur in an armory, museum, and library with rare books, miniature paintings; bedrooms have atmospheric antique furniture; the palace has a garden and fruit orchard and affordable rates: Rs 650 ($21.66) single, Rs 895 ($30) double; meals run about Rs 400 ($13.33) per head. Contact the Narain Niwas Palace Hotel (see above) for reservations.

About 33 kilometers northeast of Jaipur (45 minutes by car), Ramgarh Lake has long been a popular getaway. In splendid gardens overlooking the lake, **Ramgarh Lodge,** a former royal hunting lodge is now an intimate, 11-room Taj Group hotel. Remaining from bygone days are hunting memorabilia, furniture, a small museum, and a library. Sightsee at the old Kachhawah Fort. You can fish, but essentially this is a pleasant, do-nothing place. Rooms vary according to season. Standard rooms October through Dec 22 and January through September 3 run $48 single, $65 double; superior lake-view rooms are $80. From December 23 to January 5, singles are $50, doubles $85, superior rooms $100, all modified American plan (MAP). Ask about the Monday through Thursday discount available in the off-season.

If you only have time for one of these old citadels make it **Hotel Samode Palace,** Samode District, Jaipur, 303806 (☎ 14234114; fax 014234123), one hour by car (40 kilometers) northwest of Jaipur toward Bikaner. The palace's lofty walls are richly painted with Rajasthani floral and scenic frescoes (à la Shekhawati). More than a century ago, this was the residence of the Rawal Sheo Singhji, a prime minister in the Jaipur court. Converted some years back into a 30-room hotel by one of his descendants, Samode retains a true feeling of the regal past and is worth a detour. Built around a courtyard, with traditional archways and latticed screens, the hotel has many old furnishings. Some of the deluxe rooms are quite spacious, with canopied beds, settees cushioned with colorful bolsters, and patterned rugs. The rich frescoes in the dining room are such a delight that people often drive out for a meal and a feast for their eyes. Double rooms cost Rs 1,800 ($60), singles Rs 1,195 ($39.83), and deluxe rooms Rs 2,200 ($73.33). Add another Rs 600 ($20) per person for breakfast, lunch, and dinner. Figure on a minimum of Rs 275 ($9.16) round-trip from Jaipur by tourist taxi if you drive out for a meal and look-see. Non-residents pay a Rs 50 ($1.66) entry fee.

Sightseeing note: Above Samode Palace, the old fort, accessible via 300 steep, stone stairs, offers superb views.

Three kilometers from Samode (on the Jaipur-to-Agra Road) is **Samode Bagh,** a lovely garden, where there are silk-lined tents with all the trappings and modern amenities to put you up in grand style. The garden is under restoration.

Bissau Palace runs the **Bissau Camp Retreat** as part of its heritage project. It is located 27 kilometers from Jaipur (45 minutes by car) on the Jaipur-to-Agra

Highway. Surrounded by the Aravalli Hills, the retreat features stone cottages with modern conveniences and a swimming pool set amid orange, lemon, and gooseberry plantations. The idea is to stay here and go sightseeing atop camels in nearby the villages. For rate information and reservations contact: Bissau Palace (☎ 310371; fax 371628).

Quite a bit farther (138 kilometers from Jaipur and 120 kilometers from Delhi, 2½ hours by car), **Neemrana Fort Palace,** Neemrana District, Alwar, Rajasthan 301705 (Jaipur, ☎ 6005; Delhi, ☎ 4616145; fax 4621112), is a majestic citadel on a horseshoe-shaped rocky outcropping. Each antique-filled room has its own decor and private veranda. A luxury tent on one of ramparts has typical old fold-and-carry campaign furniture. The cuisine is both Indian and French and in the grand dining room. Rates are Rs 3,000-plus ($100-plus). This is a worthwhile splurge. (*Note:* The fort, wishing to provide guests peace and privacy, discourages day trippers by charging a hefty entry fee.)

Sightseeing note: See the 18th-century stepwell and be sure to take treks in the hills.

WHERE TO EAT

INTERNATIONAL BUFFETS

The following Jaipur hotels serve all-you-can eat buffets for breakfast, 6 to l0am (about $5); lunch, 12:30 to 3pm (about $9); and dinner, 6 to 10pm (about $10)—serving hours and prices may vary slightly from place to place:

Mansingh, Jai Mahal and **Rambagh Palace, Welcomgroup Rajputana Palace Sheraton.** Also check out the **Jaipur Ashok** and **Clark's Amer** and the new **Holiday Inn.**

During the summer months, when there are fewer tourists, some buffets may be canceled.

REGIONAL INDIAN, CONTINENTAL & CHINESE RESTAURANTS

Mirrors, clay murals, and blond wood chairs with brocade upholstery make **Niro's,** Mirza Ismail Road (☎ 374493), attractive. But excellent food keeps Niro's a favorite among Jaipuris and Westerners who enjoy eating in either of the two air-conditioned dining rooms. For a tandoori (clay-oven) meal, try chicken tikka masala (boned chunks) accompanied by naan (bread from the clay oven), add soup as a starter, some rice and dal (one portion serves two), and finish with the special dessert of whipped egg whites mixed with fruits and nuts. Your tab will come to about Rs 150 ($5); eat a vegetarian meal and you'll shave about Rs 50 ($1.66) off the bill. Open daily 9:30am to 11pm; lunch noon to 4pm, dinner 6 to 11pm.

Also on Mirza Ismail Road, **Copper Chimney** (☎ 372275), formerly Kwality, has a mirror-studded ceiling, wood-paneled walls, and blue-green banquettes. The menu offers the usual mixture of Indian, Continental, and Chinese foods. The mutton lal maas (mildly spiced white mutton) with kurmi naan (cheese and garlic tandoori bread) steal the show. Prices are about the same as Niro's. Open daily 11am to 3:30pm, 6:30 to 11pm.

LMB, Johari Bazar (☎ 565844), in the hotel of the same name, has wonderful vegetarian foods. Spacious and dimly lit with room for 500 people, the restaurant has brocade chairs and playing-card murals, and (unfortunately) music turned up to top volume. The food is rich and intriguing: bahar-e-chamon blends such ingredients as cauliflower, potatoes, and green peas with fresh and dried fruits in a subtly seasoned tomato gravy. Another dish, dahi badi, is herbed lentil balls stuffed with dried fruits and served with yogurt gravy. Paratha (unleavened wheat-flour bread) is delicious

Eating in a Folkloric Village

In these three places on the outskirts Jaipur, you can eat Rajasthani vegetarian specialties in evocative village settings and be entertained by local singers, dancers, and puppeteers: **Choki Dhani,** 19 kilometers outside of town and on one of the RTDC package tours (see the tours section under "What to See and Do," below) also has a haat bazaar where you can watch craftspersons create items for sale; similar am bience and attractions can be found at **Apna Gaon,** on the Jaipur-Sikar Road, and in the **Village** near Sanganer Airport.

with almost any dish. Figure on Rs 100 ($3.33) to Rs 150 ($5) for a delectable three-course meal with a sweet. (Incidentally, no onions are served at LMB because of the Jain religious belief that anything picked from the ground with such a strong odor is not to be eaten.) Open daily 8am to 11:30pm.

The action almost never ends at **LMB's outdoor stalls** where such snacks as samosas (turnovers) and pakoras (fritters) and cups of tea are bought and downed on the spot by the hundreds each day. Another stall features LMB's famous kulfi (Indian ice cream) in 15 delicious flavors—some made with saffron and rare fruits. Prices range from Rs 20 (66¢) to Rs 30 ($1) for a single dip. Among the other sweets is rasmalai: a cheeselike patty cooked in milk, garnished with nuts and flavored with saffron, costing around Rs 20 (66¢) per plate.

Delicious vegetarian food and courteous, quick service are combined at **Chanakya,** M.I. Road (☎ 376161), the largest vegetarian restaurant in Rajasthan (it seats 1,250 people in five different halls); the royal dishes are a delicious and rich medley of vegetables, nuts, dried fruits, cream, and saffron. Figure on Rs 125 ($4.16) for a three-course vegetarian meal. Open daily 12 to 3pm; 6:30 to 11pm.

In the cheerful **Chitra** cafeteria at the **Hotel Arya Niwas,** Sansar Chandra Road (☎ 368524), behind the Amber Complex, a delicious vegetarian thali from a spotlessly clean kitchen costs Rs 40 ($1.33) at lunch or dinner and includes a variety of vegetable dishes, yogurt, dal, plain rice, four chapatis, and papad. An American-style breakfast with fresh fruit juice, an omelet, toast with butter and marmalade, and coffee or tea costs about Rs 37 (1.03¢). Non-residents are welcome. Open 6 to 10am, 12 to 3pm, and 6 to 10pm. No tipping is allowed.

The upscale **Chandravanshi Pavilion,** in the lobby of the elegant **Welcomgroup Rajputana Place Sheraton** (tel 360011), serves top-notch food 24 hours a day. Try the kathi kebabs (thin, soft paratha wrapped around a filling of chicken or cheese) with dipping sauces for Rs 125 ($4.16); generously sized and two to a serving, they make a memorable light meal or can be shared as an appetizer.

Garden Cafe, A-6 Mahaveer Marg, near Statue Circle, C Scheme, offers fast food for wallet watchers including 27 different types of dosas (South Indian rice-flour pancakes) as well as idlis (steamed rice cakes), chat (snacks), pizza, burgers, and ice cream. South Indian breakfast is served from 7:30am.

JAIPUR AFTER DARK

INDIAN-STYLE ENTERTAINMENT

World-renowned dancer Gulabi and her group move into the **Welcomgroup Rajputana Palace Sheraton's** courtyard daily from 7 to 9pm. The show features

Kalbelia dancers, whose twirling while balancing clay jugs atop their heads is amazing, and amusing puppeteers. Free. There's also an especially fine mehendi artist (henna designs) to turn your hand into a masterpiece that lasts for about a week. There is a fee for the handiwork.

Dancers and drummers appear at **Panghat,** an outdoor theater at the **Rambagh Palace Hotel**. Shows each evening at 7pm from October to April only. Admission—Rs 600 ($20)—includes dinner, entertainment, and taxes. For information, call reception at ☎ 383919. This is a worthwhile splurge.

BARS

The **Polo Bar** in the **Rambagh Palace Hotel** is also one of the most popular meeting places in town. There are bars in other major hotels.

2 Bharatpur

Bharatpur (pop. 157,000), an important fortified city in the 18th century, is now chiefly renowned as the location of the nearby **Keoladeo Ghana Bird Sanctuary**. It is an easy side trip from Jaipur (175 kilometers away), but could also be a direct excursion from Delhi or Agra, even Bombay. This is a sight no bird-watcher, or nature lover, will want to miss. A stopover here even for a few hours can be a restorative for any hectic-paced traveler.

GETTING THERE

BY AIR The nearest airports are Agra and Jaipur, so flying isn't a very good option if you're seeing the sanctuary as a side trip from Jaipur.

BY RAIL There's rail service to the town of Bharatpur from Delhi. The fare is Rs 182 ($6.06) first class, Rs 45 ($1.50) second. Trains also leave from Agra and Jaipur with fares slightly less than from Delhi to Bharatpur. Bombay is 4½ hours by train.

BY BUS Bharatpur is 184 kilometers (110 miles) from Delhi by road via Mathura (there are frequent buses). Buses from Jaipur take five hours; the fare is Rs 42.50 ($1.42).

BY CAR WITH DRIVER Bharatpur can also be reached by car in combination with Agra, Fatehpur Sikri, and Jaipur: Rs 4.30 to Rs 6 per kilometer, plus overnight charges.

THE BIRD SANCTUARY

This was once the royal hunting preserve of the maharajah of Bharatpur (1919–95). An especially avid duck hunter (royal visitors used to down thousands of ducks a day), he did an about-face after independence and helped to convert this prime duck-shoot area into India's most famous bird sanctuary.

Comprising 29 square kilometers (52 square miles) the preserve is one-third marshland where babul trees, however thorny, are the favorite nesting places for many different exotic birds. Indeed, the sanctuary is a nesting ground for around 150 species of birds; it is said to be one of the best places in the world to see nesting herons. Among the resident species, belonging to 56 families, are painted storks, egrets, pelicans, ibis, cranes, spoonbills, and purple moorhens. Birds from Siberia, the Arctic, central Asia, Afghanistan, and elsewhere can be sighted here.

The peak time for seeing feathered friends is October to February. Migratory birds flock here in July and August, and they breed in the preserve until October or

November. The thorny babul trees, their tops jutting out of the water, hold the nests of thousands of birds in this sanctuary.

In addition, you're almost certain to see more than birds—pythons, porcupines, nilgais, spotted deer, hyenas, sambars, and wild boars also make Bharatpur their home. Of course, sightings are not guaranteed. I remember one trip I took to the sanctuary. We stopped. "Python place," says the ricksha wallah, helping me down. We troop off through the brush on a python-sighting mission. So do a few other visitors, similarly following their ricksha guides. We search, we walk, we turn back. No luck. (Wear sturdy shoes, not open sandals.)

The sanctuary is open from sunrise to sunset throughout the year. Sunsets can be beautifully colorful, and prime time for bird-watching is at sunrise, from about 6 to 9am. Early winter mornings can be chilly, so take a wrap. Also take bottled water and wear sunscreen and a hat.

The entry fee to the sanctuary is Rs 25 (83¢) for foreigners (Indian nationals are charged a lower rate); use of a still camera is Rs 10 (33¢); use of video and movie cameras ranges from Rs 50 ($1.66) to Rs 1,500 ($50).

The best way to get around is by cycle ricksha—Rs 25 (83¢) per hour for two persons (fees for rickshas and boatmen are posted at gate, but inevitably you'll be asked for more). Not only are the ricksha wallahs knowledgeable about the terrain, the birds, and other inhabitants of the preserve, but some have binoculars, which they lend in exchange for a tip.

Tongas also are available for Rs 50 ($1.66) for three to four people, as are electrovans at Rs 10 (33¢) per person. You can rent a bicycle in town—or at RTDC's Saras Bungalow, or from your hotel—for about Rs 35 ($1.16) per day. Make arrangements the night before to avoid delays in early hours, and be prepared to leave a large deposit and your passport as collateral.

However you choose to travel, your destination is the lake. The best way to see the birds is by boat, punted through the rushes, although there are roads suitable for jeeps. Boatman are also excellent guides. They can be hired at the Rest House near the jetty, or check with the book shop in the preserve.

WHERE TO STAY

IN BHARATPUR PRESERVE

ITDC's Bharatpur Forest Lodge (☎ 22722 or 22760; fax 22864), is right at the entrance to the bird sanctuary. With 17 rooms, it seems more of a small hotel than a lodge. You couldn't ask for a handier location—armchair naturalists can see game wandering through the compound at night—but the place needs sprucing up. Ten rooms are air-conditioned; there is a restaurant and bar. Rates from October to April ranged from Rs 1,195 ($39.83) for a single to Rs 1,450 ($48.33) for a double; May to September rates are lower, with singles for Rs 900 ($30), doubles for Rs 1,050 ($35).

RTDC's **Saras Bungalow,** Fatehpur Sikri Road (☎ 23700), offers 25 modest rooms and rates to match. Singles range from Rs 200 ($6.66) to Rs 350 ($11.66), doubles from Rs 250 ($8.33) to Rs 550 ($18.33); higher rates are for air-conditioning. Dorms cost Rs 40 ($1.33) per head. There's a restaurant and bar.

IN BHARATPUR TOWN

Golbagh Palace, off Agra Road (☎ 3349), is an 18-room palace hotel with loads of old-fashioned charm. Rates are Rs 300 ($10) to Rs 650 ($21.66); some are air-conditioned.

3 Shekhawati

Probably the largest concentration of fresco art in the world is found on scores of turn-of-the century houses called havelis in the several sleepy little towns of Shekhawati, encompassing the districts of Jhunjhunu and Sikar. The area named for Rao Sheka (1433–88) was earlier a part of Jaipur state.

The heartland of Shekhawati lies in the desert sands about 125 miles from Delhi, from 90 to 120 miles from Jaipur. The towns of Jhunjhunu, Mandawa, Dundlod, Nawalgara, and Sikar are all within an hour by car from one another through a landscape of fragile-looking trees, dried bushes, and shifting golden sand dunes. Several other towns of interest, covered in this chapter, are also within easy reach from Jaipur.

Shekhawati was the homeland 200 years ago of Marwari merchants and their families, who moved to Bombay and Calcutta to trade in the great port cities. After becoming wealthy, they returned to their ancestral homes and built their fine havelis. As the finishing touch, they hired artists to paint them inside and outside with frescoes. Their chhatris (commemorative monuments), temples, wells, and sarais (caravan stops) also were embellished with murals.

Constructed around courtyards with overhanging top stories to form protective canopies for the paintings, the havelis were decorated with spectacular gusto using traditional and contemporary themes. Every inch of their walls inside and outside vibrates with imagery: British visitors in bright ultramarine waistcoats share space with ochre gods and goddesses; there are portraits of the owner's family in silks and jewels, and of peasants holding jugs on their heads; musicians play as processions wind endlessly in relief; and almost life-size camels and elephants plod past. Fine depictions of limousines and bicycles reflect the changes of the 20th century, as does a house with paintings of the Wright Brothers and Kitty Hawk. The result of all these images is somewhat like a charming comic strip in peeling paint.

Although the havelis are still owned by the original Marwari families, their descendants long ago departed for the big cities. (Today, 75% of India's wealthiest industrialists are Marwaris.) The havelis that were not deserted were looked after for a time by faithful retainers or poor relations. Today some are inhabited, at least two have been turned into schools, and all are in various states of repair.

Until a few years ago, no one understood the value of these paintings, and the little towns of Shekhawati were specks on the deserts sands of Rajasthan. But the profusion of murals has put them on the tourist route and prompted the Indian National Trust for Art and Cultural Interest (INTACH) to document and perhaps spur interest in saving them.

ESSENTIALS

GETTING THERE

BY TRAIN Among the trains serving the towns of Jhunjhunu and Sikar is the *Shekhawati Express,* which leaves Delhi at 11:25pm and arrives at Jhunjhunu at 7am, Sikar at 9am, and Jaipur at 11:10am. The fare to Jaipur is Rs 589 ($19.63) first-class, Rs72 ($2.40) second-class. The same train departs Jaipur at 5:15pm, arriving in Delhi at 4:15am.

BY BUS Buses ply the roads between Delhi and all the cities of Shekhawati. However, they are crowded, and it is difficult to make bus connections. If you travel through Shekhawati by bus, try to end your day in a place with overnight accommodations or be prepared to bunk with local families or under the stars.

Indian Fresco-Making

This ancient Indian art is hundreds of years old. There are various techniques, but the one used in Shekhawati is a perfection of this craft. The artisans were called chiteras, and they belonged to the caste of potters (chejaras). They also were masons, as they both built and decorated the structures. At first the Rajasthani chiteras used only natural vegetable pigments such as lime (white), indigo (blue), saffron (orange), red stone powder (red), and yellow clay (yellow), among others. Mixed with lime water and beaten to make plaster, the pigments were applied to buildings and were color-fast for the life of the structure. The artisans worked in the fresco-buono technique, plastering a part of the building and painting the designs while it was damp. Late in the 19th century, chemical pigments from Europe were added. They could be applied to dry plaster, which gave the chiteras more time to create intricate designs.

Early frescoes here were interpretations of the residents' lavish lifestyle; at the turn of the century, the British influence on India became part of the passing picture parade.

BY CAR WITH DRIVER From Delhi or Jaipur, a non–air-conditioned car with driver should cost about Rs 5 per kilometer. From Delhi, Jhunjhunu is 231 kilometers away; Mandawa is 259 kilometers away; and Sikar (with a stop in Jhunjhunu) 299 kilometers. The distances are slightly less from Jaipur. There are modest charges for the driver's overnight stays and meals.

Getting Around

Jeeps usually can be found at the railway stations at Jhunjhunu, Sikar, and Mukundgarh; tongas and bicycle rickshas are also available. Bargain for the best fare before getting in. Some hotels will send transport to meet your train.

At Mukandgarh Fort hotel, ornamented camel carts tour the visitors to area highlights; other hotels, such as the Desert Resort, Dera Danta Kila, and Dera Dundlod Kila organize varying transportation at the following average rates: Camel rides, Rs 175 ($5.83) an hour; horseback rides, Rs 200 ($6.66) per hour; jeep safaris, Rs 900 ($30) for one-half day, and Rs 1,200 ($40) for a full day, with a four-passenger minimum.

Buses (jammed to overflowing) run between the towns.

Tours in and around Shekhawati

Jeep & Horse Safaris One- to seven-day safaris visiting several of the Shekhawati towns are offered by the **Dera Heritage Hotels** at Dundlod and Danta; they cost from Rs 1,200 ($40) for one day by jeep for a minimum of four to somewhere around Rs 3,000 ($100) per head and a minimum of six for a seven-day horse safari; this fee includes transportation, accommodations, meals, and folk entertainment. (Guests at the two hotels get a discount.) For more information, contact: Sales Executive, Dera Chain of Hotels, Dundlod House, Civil Lines, Jaipur 302019 (☎ 0141-366276).

The **Rajasthan Tourist Development Corporation** (RTDC), Chandralok Building, New Delhi (☎ 3322323), occasionally runs tours to Shekhawati. Call or drop in for information.

Visitor Information

The **Government of India Tourist Offices** in Delhi, 88 Janpath, and in Jaipur, at the **State Hotel,** have colorful pamphlets devoted to Shekhawati. Other sources of information are the **Tourist Information Bureau,** Hotel Shiv Shekhawati, Jhunjhunu (☎ 2651), and the **Rajasthan Tourist Office,** with branches at the Railway Station, Jaipur (☎ 31574), and at the Central Bus Stand, Sindhi Camp, Station Road. A good book on the area is *Rajasthan: The Guide to Painted Towns of Shekhawati* by Ilay Cooper—Rs 35 ($1.16)—which has rudimentary street maps and considerable information. The book is available in Shekhawati markets and some havelis.

When to Visit

Like the rest of Rajasthan, October to March is the best time to tour Shekhawati. During the winter months you may need a shawl or sweater if you're up early for the sunrise.

JHUNJHUNU

Havelis are scattered throughout Jhunjhunu (pronounced "june-june-oo"), and there are also a few chhatris, wells, and temples. You'll need to hire a tonga or bicycle ricksha in the bazaar for your explorations. The bazaar alone is worth a stop; Jhunjhunu (pop. 72,000) is known for beautiful tie-dyes and screen-printing, and there are also brass wares and beautifully crafted household objects worth seeing, if not buying.

Among the outstanding havelis are **Tibrewala** (built in 1883), with frescoes of accountants settling bills with workers, carpenters at their trade, trains, soldiers, and a European with his dog. **Nurudin Farooqi's haveli** is rare for its lack of figurative paintings. As a Muslim, he had his haveli painted entirely with floral and decorative designs, because his religion does not permit depicting the human form. Also important is **Sri Bihariji Temple** (built in 1776), handsomely painted with scenes from the Ramayana. The **Khetri Mahal** (built in 1760), with its elegant pillars, is considered an architectural star of Shekhawati.

Where to Stay & Eat

Hotel Shiv Shekhawati, Muni Ashram, Jhunjhunu 333001, Rajasthan (☎ 32651), the absolute antithesis of the painted haveli, is simplicity itself: Clean, with the necessary amenities of attached bathrooms and hot and cold running water. Some rooms have shared baths. Vegetarian food is good. Rates will run around Rs 600 ($20) for an air-conditioned double, Rs 300 ($10) single occupancy. All non–air-conditioned rooms have desert coolers.

For a snack stop on the Delhi–Bikaner Highway: **Jamuna Midway** consists of four huts, a garden, and a snack pavilion with tables and chairs covered by thatch. Among the refreshments, fresh mosambi juice (similar to orange) costs about Rs 10 (33¢). There is a clean restroom.

MANDAWA

All 10 havelis in Mandawa are in town and easily seen on a walking tour, most comfortably done in the cool mornings or evenings before sunset. Looming over all is the 18th-century **fort**—now a hotel—with its own murals and a small museum. Among the most interesting havelis are **Saraf** (1870), with erotica, a woman giving birth, a train, and a well scene; **Sneh Ram Ladia** (1906), with a man being bathed for his wedding and another listening to a gramophone; and **Gulab Rai Ladia** (1870 building, 1890s paintings), perhaps the best for its paintings of elephants, camels, and erotica censored with blue paint. (Until the end of the 19th century, almost every house had an erotic scene on its exterior as well as an interior erotic fresco, but later puritanical types destroyed or defaced some scenes.) At **Nand Lal Murmuria** (1935), murals depict the owner's visit to Venice, as well as Gandhi, Nehru, and King George; and **Bansidar Newatia** (1910) features cars, an airplane, a bicycle, and a boy making a phone call.

In the desert, water was precious, and building a new well was cause for celebratory paintings such as those enhancing **Harlalka Well** (1850). Make your visit in the early morning or at evening, when the well is irrigating the surrounding fields. **Sonthlia Gate** (1930s), the western gate to Mandawahas, has a room above it with murals from the 1940s combining florid designs with portraits of town leaders. Other fresco feasts for the eyes are offered by a few **chhatris** (from the 1800s) and the **Thakurii Temple** (1870).

WHERE TO STAY

Reflecting its heritage as an 18th-century fort/palace **Mandawa Castle,** Mandawa 333704 (☎ 524; fax via Jaipur 0141-382214), now a 51-room hotel, has a wide range of frescoes and retains a great deal of the feeling of bygone days. About the only modern touches are the welcome additions of modern bathroom and air coolers for each room. Rooms—no two alike—are tucked between rooftop turrets and on terraces along airy passageways. A standard single runs Rs 1100 ($36.66), double Rs 1200 ($40); deluxe rates run Rs 1150 ($38.33) to Rs 1500 ($50). Meals will add approximately Rs 550 ($18.33) per head. Reserve far in advance. This is a heritage hotel.

Less than a kilometer away and run by Mandawa Castle is the 32-room **The Desert Resort,** Jhunjhunu District, Rajasthan 333704 (☎ 551; fax via Jaipur 0141-382214), an architectural tour de force by Delhi architects Revathi and Vasant Kamath, who re-created a mud-walled desert village with modern comforts. No two thatch-covered huts are exactly alike, and each takes its theme from village life—three potter's huts, five weaver's, and two farmer's, all with electricity and attached bathrooms. Each thatch, in a unique pattern, was the handiwork of villagers, as are the exterior paintings. There's a swimming pool; trees and a small garden add patches of color to the desert surroundings. Singles are Rs 1100 ($36.66), doubles Rs 1200 ($40); add about Rs 550 ($18.33) per person for three meals. Camels can be hired for desert explorations.

For reservations at either Mandawa Castle or Desert Camp, contact: 9 Sardar Patel Marg, Jaipur 30201, Rajasthan (☎ 0141-91-141-38906; fax 382214).

WHERE TO EAT

Mandawa Castle (☎ 324) serves buffet meals, in the old dining hall or in the garden. If there's a full house or a group in residence, there's a colorful dinner show with local entertainment—strutting torch bearers, singers, and musicians. Figure on Rs 400 ($13.33) for all three meals here; dinner only around Rs 250 ($8.33).

DUNDLOD

The best murals are in the kila (fort), built in 1750, now the **Dera Dundlod Kila,** a hotel. There are hints of murals on the building's exterior. The visitor enters through the Suraj Pol gateway to the fort and continues through a couple of gateways and courts to the Uttar Pol where there stairs lead to steps lead to the Diwan Khana. Exuding elegance after all these years, this grand Mughal-style hall has graceful pillars, period furniture, European-style portraits, and a library with rare books on Indian history. Upstairs is the private balcony where ladies in purdah watched ceremonies below without being seen. The reception will send someone to unlock the family's painted chhatris near the fort.

Around town, the group of **Goenka havelis**—one north of the main road and three others south of it on the square—have traces of murals, including erotica on the most southern of the group. Nearby, to the east of the town gate, is **Satyanarayan Temple,** with religious murals.

Where to Stay & Eat

Dundlod Dera Kila (a Dera Heritage hotel), Dundlod, India 302001 (☎ 2519), the dominant structure in this tiny desert town, has 25 attractive rooms, no two alike; some have four-poster beds, all have verandahs. Rates are Rs 550 ($18.33) single, Rs 750 ($25) double. Add another Rs 400 ($13.33) per head for three meals, sometimes served atop the fort. Take a swim, ride a camel, or walk around the ramparts. The nearest railway station is Mukundgarh. For reservations contact: Sales Executive, Dera Chain of Hotels, Dundlod House, Civil Lines, Jaipur 302019 (☎ 141-366276; fax 141-41763).

NAWALGARH

Frescoes in various stages of deterioration appear on many of the buildings around town; the best preserved is **Anandi Lal Paddar Haveli** (1920), now a school. In the forecourt are paintings that show, among other things, trains and cars, a Gangaur festival procession, and ancients playing checkers.

Where to Stay & Eat

Hotel Roop Niwas Palace, Nawalgarh, Dist. Jhunjhunu, Rajasthan 333707 (☎ 22008; or in Jaipur 368726), about a kilometer from the town, has 25 rooms with old-fashioned charm, as well as gardens and a swimming pool. Rates are around Rs 600 ($20) for a double.

MUKUNDGAH

The handicrafts bazaar known for textiles is an attraction here, as are the **Kanoria** and **Ganeriwala** havelis. The 300-year-old fort is now a heritage hotel.

Where to Stay & Eat

Mukundgarh Fort Heritage Hotel, PTC Travels, with 42 old-world rooms, all with modern attached bathrooms, is about 11 kilometers from Nawalgarh. Rates are Rs 1,100 ($36.66) single, Rs 1,800 ($60) double. There are both interesting interior and exterior frescoes. There's a restaurant, pool, shopping arcade, and open-air stage for puppet shows. For reservations, contact: Cross Country Hotels Limited, H-31 Green Park Extension, New Delhi 110016 (☎ 6850451).

SIKAR

Havelis take a back seat here to a number of painted temples, as well as a clock tower and a step well with handsome carvings. Many of the havelis were built by the Biyanis, a major merchant family. The most interesting of these is **Deen Dayal Biyani Haveli** (around 1900), decorated in blue and white. Another blue and white painting is at **Mahal** (1845), in the Chini (China) room, so named because its designs resemble Chinese porcelain.

Where to Stay & Eat

Danta Dera Kila (a Dera Heritage Hotel), P.O. Danta, 322707, Dist. Sikar, Rajasthan (☎ 89362), built in the 18th century in a combination Mughal and

Rajput styles, offers 12 rooms in the residential wing and spectacular views of the old fortresses looming above. Plenty of peacocks shrieking in the morning, strutting at sunset. Rates are Rs 550 ($18.33) single, Rs 750 ($25) double. Another Rs 400 ($13.33) will cover your three meals. The hotel offers pick-up transportation from any of a number of railway stations; inquire when making your reservation. For reservations, contact: Sales Executive, Dera Chain of Heritage Hotels, Dundlod House, Civil Lines Jaipur 302019 (☎ 141-366276; fax 141-41763).

Natraj on the main road in Sikar is a clean reasonably priced restaurant serving snacks and meals.

4 Ajmer

Founded in the 7th century by Raja Ajai Pal Chauhan, Ajmer (pop. 401,000) was annexed in 1556 by Akbar, who made it a royal residence and military headquarters. Akbar's huge fort-palace (open from 10am to 6pm; closed Fridays) is now a museum of sculptures and armor. Later, in 1616, Jahangir met with Sir Thomas Roe here, one of the earliest meetings between the Mughals and British, and it was in this city that the sons of Shah Jahan fought their war of succession, in which Aurangzeb emerged victorious. Later, the city was ruled by the Scindias, who handed it over to the British; thus, it became one of the few Rajasthani cities ruled by the Raj rather than part of a princely state.

The city is pleasantly situated on the banks of Ana Sagar, an artificial lake constructed in the 12th century by Raja Anaji (1135–50) with gardens and marble pavilions added later by the Mughal emperors.

ESSENTIALS

Getting There

BY AIR The nearest **airport** is in Jaipur, from which there is train and bus service.

BY RAIL The *Shatabdi Express* connects Jaipur and Ajmer, AC Chair is Rs 195 ($6.50); Executive Rs 375 ($12.50).

The following fares are for first class AC and second class. Train service is available from Delhi, Rs 797 ($26.56) or Rs 97 ($3.23); from Jaipur, Rs 320 ($10.66) or Rs 35 ($1.16); from either Abu Road or Udaipur, Rs 572 ($19.06) or Rs 66 ($2.20); from Jodhpur, Rs 225 ($7.50) or Rs 33 ($1.10); Ahmedabad, Rs 865 ($28.83)or Rs 101 ($3.36).

BY BUS Buses run every half hour between Jaipur and Ajmer, and cost around Rs 20 (66¢) one-way. The 138-kilometer trip takes about three hours. From Ajmer you can catch buses to Pushkar, other cities in Rajasthan, Agra, Delhi, and beyond.

Visitor Information

The tourist office in the **Khadim Tourist Bungalow** can provide information on sights, guides, and tourist taxis.

WHAT TO SEE & DO

To Muslims, especially, Ajmer is an important place. They come from everywhere in India to visit **Dargah,** the tomb of a great Sufi saint, Khwaja Muin-ud-Din Chisthi (1142–1246), who came to Ajmer in 1192. The shrine was completed by the Emperor Humayan, and the gates were gifts from the Nizam of Hyderabad. Akbar made annual visits to Dargah; it is said his prayer for a son was granted as a result of his pilgrimages. (For more about Akbar's desire for a son, see the listing for Fathepur Sikri, page 75.)

The approach to the brilliantly white tomb is crowded with people (no cars permitted) and lined with shops selling some interesting bangles and holy trinkets. But kids pestering for handouts take the fun out of browsing. Take a cycle ricksha to and from the site to avoid them. (Bargain for your fare.)

Kids also hang around the entrance where you remove your shoes, and at least one junior entrepreneur is sure to tag along as your guide. Two gargantuan caldrons on either side of the entrance are used during festivals to hold gifts of rice and delicacies to be given to those who tend the shrine. A mosque in an inner court, built by Shah Jahan, has 11 lyrical marble arches.

The centerpiece is the saint's tomb, set on a silver platform. My guide led me inside, where I was showered with rose petals and blessed in return for a few paise. In the cloisters where pilgrims rested, a group of musicians played songs of praise while birds chirped in leafy trees.

Beyond Dargah, on the fringes of town, is the **Adhai-din-ka-Jhonpra Mosque,** in a state of disrepair. Early British visitors went into raptures over its architectural details, and today one can still see striking reminders of its glory days in the pillars, each unique in design. The building was originally a college before its conversion to a mosque.

NASIYAN JAIN TEMPLE Don't leave Ajmer without seeing the amazing **Nasiyan Jain Temple** (Red Temple). Completed and opened with fanfare in 1895, it honors the first of 24 Jain Tirthankars (saviors/teachers), Lord Rishabedev. Upstairs, in the double-story **Avarna Nagari Hall,** miniatures in gold leaf interpret the five main events in the life of the first Lord Rishabdev in incredible detail.

Ajmer has long had a sizable Jain community (today about one-fourth of the population). Prominent among them, many years ago, was a diamond merchant, Raj Bahadur Seth Moolchand Nemichand Soni, the founder of this temple. Diamonds in fact are embedded behind a colored glass window to enhance lighting in the exhibit area. About 1,000 kilograms of gold leaf is said to have been used to cover the models on display. The ceiling and pillars are decorated in gold-embossed glass. Looking through clear glass windows placed above the display, visitors see the doll-sized Jain universe from various perspectives; there is explanatory text near the windows. Central to the display is the holy mountain, Sumeru. There is a richly detailed rendition of the revered golden city of Ayodhya, the Tirthankara's birthplace, with each cupola and balcony depicted perfectly. Eye catching, too, are many toy-sized temple replicas of Jain shrines throughout India. In airships of gold, suspended from strings of silver balls, the gods get the best view of all the elaborate proceedings. Celestial figures march in regal dress and decorated elephants do what elephants on parade do best—carry gods in golden howdahs to festivities—to mention only a few of the tiny actors in this dramatization of Jain beliefs.

Before you leave the temple, stop on the ground floor to see religious items that are taken on parade each November during the Jain festival.

The temple trust keeps the premises in mint condition. Hours are 8am to 5pm daily. The entry fee is Rs 2 (6¢). A helpful booklet on the temple costs Rs 7 (23¢). Tip the shoe-watcher.

SHOPPING

Ajmer is famous for tie-dyes, silver jewelry, and camel hide embroidered slippers. Scout the **Naya Bazar, Madar Gate, Bala Bazar,** and any individual shops you find.

WHERE TO STAY IN AJMER

Most Westerners stop and look around in Ajmer before going on to stay in Pushkar, 7 miles away. (Rates increase sharply during the Pushkar Fair each fall, a time when advance reservations are necessary.) Here are suggestions for those who wish to stay over in Ajmer itself.

RTDC's **Khadim Tourist Bungalow,** Savatri Girls College Road (☎ 52490), near the bus station, offers 50 modest bath-attached rooms from Rs 150 ($5) for an ordinary single to Rs 400 ($13.33) for a super deluxe double (with air-conditioning). Dorms cost Rs 40 ($1.33) per head with linens. There's a restaurant on the premises. This is a pleasant and popular place.

RTDC's **Hotel Khidmat** (☎ 52705) has 10 rooms, all with a bath attached, from Rs 150 ($5) to Rs 200 ($6.66); a dorm runs Rs 40 ($1.33) per head.

Tops in Ajmer, **Hotel Mansingh Palace,** Vaishali Nagar, Ajmer 305001 (☎ 50855), has a Rajasthani dance mural in the lobby and 60 rooms with many amenities including central air-conditioning. The compact rooms, pleasantly decorated in cool blue and white color schemes, are clean and comfortably furnished. Standard singles Rs 1,190 ($39.66) single, Rs 1,800 ($60) double. There is an occasional folk dance or puppet show. The **Sheesh Mahal** restaurant features tandoori and other dishes; entrée prices range from Rs 60 ($2) to Rs 150 ($5). Indian music is featured in the evenings.

A number of modest hotels are near the bus and railway station, with nothing more than cheap prices to recommend them.

WHERE TO EAT

The **Hotel Mansingh Palace** has multicuisine menus. **Honey Dew,** opposite the railway station, is set back from the road by a garden; dimly lit, it's popular with families and offers inexpensive, acceptable Indian dishes.

5 Pushkar

Pushkar (pop. 11,500) is a holy pilgrimage center during the fall festival of Kartik Poornima, when hundreds of devout Hindus come here to bathe in the holy lake at dawn, before going to the temples to worship. After a day of chanting and prayer, there is the aarti, a ritual in which tiny candles are placed on leaves and set afloat on the lake. Crowds gather on the ghats (steps) around the lake to watch. It is easily visited as a side trip from Ajmer.

ESSENTIALS

GETTING TO PUSHKAR

BY BUS Buses from Ajmer to Pushkar run regularly from outside the Ajmer Railway Station and are always packed. A minibus or taxi is better if you want to admire the view. The ride is very pretty through the curving and twisting Snake Hills, where darting squirrels play hide-and-seek among the willows and camels lumber along pulling carts or slumbering in the sun by the side of the road.

GETTING AROUND PUSHKAR & BEYOND

You can walk just about everywhere, but should you want to ride a camel to the temple from town, it costs Rs 5 (16¢) to 10 (33¢); a camel ride to explore the desert runs Rs 30 ($1) for an hour to Rs 100 ($3.33) for four hours, per person after bargaining.

WHAT TO SEE & WHEN TO GO

Some 52 buildings around the lake were formerly maharajas' summer palaces. The Brahma Temple is the most important of the estimated 1,000 or more temples surrounding the lake. Marked by a distinctive red spire and with a carving of a goose

(Brahma's vehicle), this is reportedly the only Brahma temple in India, a site the god chose for it. The view from the top is excellent.

According to ancient beliefs, Pushkar owes its existence to Brahma—the first of the Hindu Trinity—who let a lotus blossom slip from his fingers to the ground during a visit here. The lake was formed where the petals fell and called Pushkar, which means lotus, and the city grew up around it.

There is also a Vishnu Temple and temple to Saitri (consort of Brahma), among the many others.

To further honor Brahma, a huge cattle fair also is held during Kartik Poornima, during November, coinciding with the full moon. The fair lasts two weeks and has become an enormous tourist attraction, hyped by the Rajasthan tourism authorities. Hordes of Westerners come to Pushkar at this time of year to witness the colorful event. Since the exact dates of Kartik Poornima vary according to the full moon, check before taking off, and be sure to make reservations for accommodations.

The cattle fair attracts villagers from everywhere in North India, who come to buy and sell cattle, camels (it is estimated that 100,000 camels are traded during this event), handicrafts, textiles, and other wares. Even the cattle look festive with brightly painted horns, and there are camel and horse races. If you've never seen a camel race, it's something you're unlikely to forget when you do. The fair also includes musicians and dancers performing under stars; jugglers, acrobats, magicians, and tightrope walkers also perform. Fair-goers will find handicrafts and textiles in tempting array, but precious few bargains these days. Bargaining has gotten harder over the years as the fair has become more popular, and merchants know how foreigners cave in when it comes to prices.

Aside from the autumn festivities, Pushkar is an uneventful place, perfect for a peaceful break.

WHERE TO STAY IN PUSHKAR

Reminder: Reserve far in advance during Pushkar Fair and expect high rates.

A HERITAGE HOTEL

The former Maharaja Brajrajsingh of Kishangarh sold his summer palace to Jagat Singh Rathore, who converted it into the pleasant **Pushkar Palace Hotel,** Pushkar Lake, Pushkar 305022 (☎ 2001; fax 2226), with 44 clean rooms, each accented by antique furniture. The highest-priced rooms, on the top floor with superb views and big regal chairs in front of large windows to admire them from, have air-conditioning and heating for Rs 1,050 ($35) double, Rs $950 ($31.66) single. But you can get a comfortable room with lake view and attached bath for Rs 500 ($16.66). Single monastic, cell-like rooms with common bath are Rs 100 ($3.33). Guests enjoy relaxing in hotel's rose-filled, palm-shaded garden. This is strictly a vegetarian hotel. The buffet dinner costs Rs 60 ($2); breakfast costs Rs 55 ($1.83). No alcohol is permitted. Check with the travel desk about camel and horse safaris.

OTHER HOTELS & GUEST HOUSES

A former palace of the Maharaja of Jaipur is now the well-maintained RTDC's **Sarovar Tourist Bungalow,** Pushkar 305022 (☎ 2040), with a courtyard garden, on the banks of the lake opposite the Brahma Temple. There are 38 rooms in all, three superdeluxe rooms with extraordinary lake views and special air coolers are highest in price: Rs 285 ($9.50) to 370 ($12.33) for a double; lowest priced are seven rooms, Rs 170 ($5.66) for a double without a private bathroom. Dorm beds are Rs 40 ($1.33). There is a vegetarian restaurant. An Indian meal in the restaurant, starting with soup and ending with a sweet, is about Rs 40 ($1.33); Continental breakfast Rs 28 (93¢).

Peacock Holiday Resort, Pushkar 305022 (☎ 2093), has 42 rooms with essential amenities but without good maintenance. Rates run from Rs 300 ($10) for an ordinary single to Rs 750 ($25) for an air-cooled suite. There is a 10% service charge. Frills include a small swimming pool and Jacuzzi, horse and camel rides, and an excursion to the hotel's farm and garden. The hotel enjoys a central location.

Among the guest houses, the best are **Krishna** (☎ 2043), with simple rooms, a nice garden, and rooftop restaurant **Everest Guest House,** with basic, clean rooms and a dorm. Rates for each range from Rs 100 ($3.33) to Rs 200 ($6.66).

TENT CITY

During the fall fair, the government erects a **Tourist Tent City** housing 100,000 persons. Tents come with beds and linens, and some have running water and Indian-style toilets. Deluxe tents with meals are about Rs 700 ($23.33), but you can get into a dorm tent for as little as Rs 50 to 60 ($1.67 to $2) per person. You must reserve far in advance: Senior Manager, Rajasthan Tourism Development Corporation, Bikaner House, India Gate, New Delhi (☎ 383837; fax 382823).

Royal Camp, run by Maharaja Resorts, consists of 35 custom-made silk-lined tents fit for royalty with all amenities including private toilets and private verandahs. A tent for dining features Rajasthani cuisine, The reception area is the setting for campfire-lit entertainment nightly. For bookings and rates contact: Maharaja Resorts, Umaid Bhawan Palace, Jodhpur 3420006 (☎ 33316, ext. 231; fax 35373).

WHERE TO EAT

Either the Sarovar or Pushkar Palace are your best bets. Other places to eat are **RS** across from Brahma Temple. The proprietor, Rajguru, also offers camel rides. Near the Brahma Temple, **Sun 'n' Moon Garden Restaurant** has Indian dishes and a few Western standards.

6 Jodhpur

Jodhpur (pop. 648,000) has been a primary city of the Great Indian Desert since medieval days. Once the state of Marwar, meaning land of death, Jodhpur was actually founded in 1211. The city was built by Rao Jodha in 1459. His descendants, some among the residents today, ruled these parts for half a millennium, until Indian independence in 1947.

The city's walls are almost 6 miles in circumference. Through its seven huge gates—five are named for the towns to which the roads go that pass through the gate—passed some of Rajasthan's most valiant warriors. As with all Rajputs, they claimed that their history of heroic deeds went back as far as the epic poems, the *Ramayana* and *Mahabharata,* and they upheld their heritage with honor. The focal point here, the **Mehrangarh Fort,** is a truly awesome sight.

More than in Udaipur or Jaipur—and despite this Rajasthani city's abundant flowers, trees, vast artificial lakes, and lawns—in Jodhpur you sense that only a step away is a desert landscape, almost as barren as the moon. This makes the medieval fort seem more magical, a larger-than-life version of an idealized illustration in a child's book.

And talk about pink! Horseshoe-shaped Jodhpur blushes like a bride as it nestles into the ridge of rosy sandstone hills whose quarries gave birth to the stones for its major structures. Less majestic buildings in white or yellow are dazzling against a flawless blue sky.

You will also want to visit Mandor, only a few miles away, the earlier capital of Marwar.

By the way, many Westerners are familiar with jodhpurs, tight-fitting riding trousers that are flared at the hips. Their name came from the local style of men's attire.

ESSENTIALS

GETTING THERE

BY AIR There are daily flights from Delhi ($56); you can also fly daily (except Tuesday and Thursday) from Jaipur ($34) and Udaipur ($28); and daily from Bombay ($87). Indian Airlines flights usually link Jodhpur, Delhi, and Bombay; Jagson flies Delhi-Jodhpur-Jaisalmer; East-West connects Jodhpur with a daily flight to Bombay. For airport inquiries call 28600. Transfer charges by taxi from the airport are Rs 170 ($5.66) to Rs 200 ($6.66); by **auto ricksha**, the fare is only Rs 25 (83¢) to 30 ($1).

BY RAIL The *Inter-City Express* departs Jaipur at 5:30pm, arriving in Jodhpur at 10:30am; it departs Jodhpur at 5:30am, arriving in Jaipur at 10:30am. The fare is Rs 192 ($6.40) AC Chair Second; Rs 85 ($2.83) for non-AC Second.

From Delhi, the fastest train, the *Delhi–Mandor Express,* departs Delhi Sarai Rohillia at 6:10pm and arrives at 7:45am; the train departs Jodhpur at 8:30pm, arriving back in Delhi at 10am. Fare for AC First is Rs 1,256 ($41.86), AC Second Rs 148 ($4.93). If you want to depart from Agra, take the *Jodhpur-Marudhar Express,* departing Agra at 9:20pm, arriving Jodhpur at 10:15am. Other important train links are to Jaisalmer, Udaipur, and Ahmedabad. Taxis from the railroad station to hotels run abut Rs 65. For inquiries call 131 or 132; for reservations 20842.

Train journeys are lengthy because of the great distances between stops, nor are trains on this route known for their speed. Take some fruit, bottled water, and a snack, as there is little or no food at the stations en route. Take a wrap in winter.

On the plus side, Jodhpur's Western Railways' meter-gauge line offers transit passengers showers, toilets, and comfy chairs in its international waiting room; inquire at the Railway Tourist Bureau.

BY BUS Luxury and deluxe coach service operates between Jaipur (eight hours), Ajmer (4½ hours), Abu Road (seven hours), Udaipur (eight to 10 hours), Jaisalmer (six hours), Agra, and Delhi. The Bus Stand (☎ 44686 or 44989), is near the Raikabagh Railway Station.

GETTING AROUND

There are unmetered taxis and auto rickshas. Taxis have fixed rates for some destinations; recently, a half-day tour around Jodhpur cost Rs 175 ($5.83); for a full day expect to pay Rs 275 ($9.16). Auto rickshas cost Rs 25 (83¢) to Rs 30 ($1) for 6 to 7 kilometers. Bargain hard! Bicycle rentals are available at Sojati Gate for Rs 1.5 (5¢) per hour after bargaining.

SPECIAL EVENTS

Jodhpur's colorful past is recreated during the **Marwar Festival,** held annually in October, which revives graceful dances of the desert, Rajasthani folk songs and legends, and other traditions. If you missed the Pushkar Cattle Fair, you might try for one hereabouts; while not as large as Pushkar's, they take place throughout the year. Check with the Tourist Information Bureau, Hotel Ghoomar, High Court Road (☎ 44010).

WHAT TO SEE & DO

MANDOR Most people start in Mandor, which is a very wise thing to do. Now a pretty park, 5 miles north of the city, it was the early capital of Marwar. The park contains the shrine of 330 Million Gods, a series of gigantic painted figures, some covered by the pious over the years in layer upon layer of silver leaf and looking strangely like enormously oversize foil-wrapped sweets. Nearby, the Hall of Heroes was carved from a single rock wall. These brightly painted figures represent local heroes and more deities. (Sadly, some were damaged by flooding monsoon waters some years back, but they are still well worth seeing.)

The park's other main attraction are the cenotaphs of former rulers, handsomely constructed in a combination of Saivite and Buddhist styles with Jain details on the columns. These structures—pink sandstone again—stand on places where cremations took place. Above the cenotaphs, and a perfect vantage point to view it all, is a 2-mile reservoir overlooking some fairly new Mughal-style gardens. It's a pleasant place to sit and rest, when it's hot.

Before leaving Mandor, stop in at the small museum.

MEHRANGARH FORT Jodhpur's massive Victory Gate was erected by Ajit Singh to mark a military defeat of the Mughals in the 18th century. Above it, medieval Mehrangarh Fort looms almost 500 feet, is more than 500 years old, and dominates the entire landscape. Now your entry fee permits you to pierce its grim, once nearly impenetrable walls, which conceal extraordinary palaces, spanning five centuries of Rajput glory. A steep zigzag ascent goes to the summit where there are handprints of 15 maharajas' widows who committed suttee (death by immolation when husbands died in battle, happily no longer a custom) rather than suffer at the enemy's hands. An elevator was under construction for those unable to make the ascent on foot and may be finished by now.

Inside the fort, behind the lotus-patterned, lacework sandstone facade, are many palaces to be inspected. The earliest of the muraled and mirrored rooms date from the 15th century but were added to even into the 20th century. There are sumptuous brocades and marble-topped furnishings from the 18th century. The **Moti Mahal** ("Pearl Palace") is white, mirrored, and so sumptuous that some believe it could have been a Hall of Public Audience.

In the 300-year-old **Rose Palace,** the windowpanes are tinted pink in keeping with the theme. From the **Jhanki Mahal** ("Glance Palace") you can glance through perforated marble screens, as the ladies in these chambers did years ago, at a view of the courtyard, countryside, and town below—a view that probably summed up their universe. Here, too, are gold-encrusted cradles still waiting to rock royal infants.

The 200-year-old **Takhat Vilas Palace** (a royal bedroom) has splendid floor-to-ceiling murals showing—in minute detail—marchers, feasting, wars, games, weddings, religious rites, beautiful women, proud warriors, and even palace pets. From the ceiling hang large Belgian Christmas ball ornaments. Why? The light bouncing off of them fascinated royalty back then.

Throughout your tour, you get many great views of the city. Standing out among the buildings below are the blue structures that signify Bhramins' homes.

Room after room houses fantastic collections of folk instruments, miniature paintings, jewel-studded robes, jewels, howdahs (seats used on the back of elephants or camels), tents, and many other relics of the old regal life. On the outside the display continues with a collection of old canons.

The palace museums and old Fort Museum include many of these sights. From Singar Choki Chowk (the interior square, a short distance from main entrance), a guide takes you through the layer-upon-layer of palaces. Be sure to ask if the Music Room is open.

The fort is open from 8:30am to 5:30pm in summer, 9am to 5pm in winter. The entry fee, Rs 35 ($1.16) includes guide and musicians to play you in (who also expect a tip). Use of still cameras is Rs 35 ($1.16), Rs 50 ($1.67) if you use a flash, and the use of movie cameras or video recorders is Rs 100 ($3.33).

On the way down is **Jaswant Thada,** the 19th-century white marble memorial built by the widow Maharani of Maharaja Jaswant Singh II, which houses portraits of Jodhpur's rulers. The memorial is used as a crematorium for family members. Bits of colored thread, tied to the decorative marble, have been left by local women who consider the place a shrine. Hours are 8am to 4pm.

Museums & Gardens

Behind the building of the **Umaid Bhawan Palace** (now the Welcomgroup Umaid Bhawan Palace—see its entry under "Where to Stay," below) is an interesting story. The foundation was laid in November 1929 by the late Maharaja Sri Umaid Singhi, who commissioned the building to give jobs to thousands of his subjects during several years when a severe drought created a famine. Employing 3,000 workers over 13 years, the palace was completed in 1942. It took a few more years to put all the finishing touches on it so that the royal family could move in.

Today, part of the palace is a museum, which includes the Durbar Hall, armory, miniatures, clocks and watches, books and other royal artifacts. You may see tiny threads tied to grillwork in the palace; they have been placed there as talismans by local visitors. Hours are 9am to 5pm, and there is a modest entry fee.

The formal gardens of this palace hotel are open to the public from 9am to 5pm, and there is a modest entry fee.

The **Old Palace Museum** Displays royal palanquins and howdahs—starring one in silver, a gift of Shah Jahan to Jaswant Singh I, paintings, a golden throne, pearl-encrusted slippers, and other memorabilia. Hours are 8:30am to 5:30pm in the summer, 9am to 5pm in the winter.

Set in a park with a zoo known especially for its rare birds, the **Government Museum** (a relic itself) houses trophies from hunts, weapons, and sculptures from nearby sites.

Nearby Attractions

Five miles out of town is the 12th-century **Balsamand Lake** with a 20th-century palace, open from 8am to 7pm for an entry fee of Rs 6 (2¢), use of cameras Rs 5 (2¢), a pretty garden spot for picnics.

About 2 miles from town is **Mahamandir,** a small, old walled city, with a temple noted for 100 pillars.

Guided Tours

Daily tours depart from RTDC's **Hotel Ghoomar** (☎ 45083) at 9am and 2pm (but they are less frequent off-season, so check); they take in the Fort, Jaswant Memorial, Umaid Bhawan, and Mandor for Rs 50 ($1.67).

If public transport isn't adventurous enough for you, there are **camel safaris** into the desert. Cautionary note: Book only through a reputable resource, such as **Aravalli Safari and Tours,** 4, Kuchaman House Area, Airport Road (☎ 34146), or the **Ajit Bhawan** or **Umaid Bhawan** hotels. They'll also arrange private cars and guides for the conventional. Or consult with the RTDC about tour operators and cars before booking your yours.

SHOPPING & WALKING

Jodhpurs, those flared-at-the-hips trousers, are indeed sold in the bazaars, as are badlas, useful local thermos-type bottles, lined in zinc and covered with cloth; look also for tie-dyes, embroidered slippers, and items in metal; some antiques also.

The enormous **Sardar Market** for general merchandise is spread around the Old Clock Tower in the old city. Famous among these vendors is Mohan Gehani's spice shop, **Mohanlal Verhomal,** near the Clock Tower, open from 7 to 10pm, or see him and his wares at the Fort from 9am to 7pm. It's also interesting to wander in the lanes off the market. (One lane, not far from the Agra Sweet Home, is the red-light district.) Other markets are: **Sojati Gate** (gifts shops and emporia); **Station Road** (jewelry); **Tripolia** (handicrafts); **Mochi** (embroidered slippers); **Khanda Falsa** (tie-dyed saris; and **Lakhara Bazaar** (lacquer work and bangles).

Government-run emporia are **Rajasthan Khadi Sangathan,** on B.M. ka Bagh, and **Rajasthan Khadi Sangh,** on Station Road.

WHERE TO STAY

HERITAGE HOTELS

Formerly a small palace, **Ajit Bhawan,** Near Circuit House, Jodhpur 342006 (☎ 37410; fax 37774), is run by Maharaj Swaroop Singh, of the former maharaja's family. Many regal trappings remain in the main building where there are 10 well-appointed guest rooms. Better by far are the stone cottages dotting the spacious gardens, each done in a different motif and some accented with antiques. Singles run $36; doubles $48, without meals. There's a 10% off-season discount. Marwari food, among the richest of the Indian cooking styles, is served at meals, which cost another $15 dollars per person. Take a dip in the pool or play tennis. Singh himself takes guests on tours to give them an inside look at village life. Tours cost Rs 400 ($13.33) each for three to five people in a jeep, including lunch. Back at the Ajit Bhawan, there's a swimming pool and tennis courts.

Ajit Bhawan offers a few luxury tents. Lined with colorful Rajasthani textiles and furnished simply with beds and bucket chairs, they have attached bathrooms and are clean, comfortable, and different. They are also affordable at about Rs 650 ($25).

Hotel Karni Bhawan, Defence Laboratory Road, Ratanada, Jodhpur 342006 (☎ 32220; fax 33495), a former Rajput home, is now an intimate 25-room hotel with neat, clean rooms and a friendly, personalized attitude. What's special? Rooms furnished in various Rajathani festival themes; dinner on the roof with a view of the floodlit fort and folk dancers (for an extra charge); breakfast in the court; and lunch and dinner in dhanis (village huts) in the garden; there's a swimming pool. Rates are Rs 800 ($26.66) single, Rs 900 ($30) double. Meals charges are: Rs 85 ($2.83) breakfast, Rs 145 ($4.83) lunch, and Rs 165 ($5.50) dinner.

OTHER HOTELS

Private attached bathrooms, air-conditioning, telephones, and TVs in rooms are de rigueur unless otherwise mentioned. The top-priced places accept credit cards and cash travelers checks.

Doubles for Less Than $16.66

The fairly clean **Adarsh Niwas,** opposite the railway station, Jodhpur 342001 (☎ 26936), is a friendly place on a noisy street, with AC doubles for Rs 500 ($16.66); for Rs 600 ($20), you can get quite a nice suite here. The hotel's **Kalinga** restaurant is discussed separately (see "Where to Eat," below).

Madho Niwas, New Airport Road, Ratanada, Jodhpur (☎ 34486), is a simple, clean place with some nice murals and folk paintings in the courtyard. Rates are

Rs 300 ($10) to Rs 350 ($11.66). The hotel offers village tours for Rs 350 ($11.66) per head.

Modest and also good value for the money is **Hotel Akshey,** opposite Raikabagh Railway Station, Jodhpur 342006 (☎ 37327), with a nice garden. The highest priced rooms are Rs 400 ($13.33) for an air-conditioned double. Non-AC doubles are Rs 150 ($5). A bed in the dorm is Rs 30 ($1). Meals are served in the garden or your room.

Marudhar International Hotel, opposite K. N. Hall, Raikabagh, Jodhpur 342006 (☎ 23208), near both the railway station and the bus stand, has modest, modern rooms grouped around a garden. Rates range from Rs 300 ($10) to Rs 500 ($16.66). The higher rate is for air-conditioning. The hotel has declined over the years.

RTDC's Hotel Ghoomar, High Court Road (☎ 44010), has 60 rooms, all doubles, with bathrooms. Built in 1972, it is an unpretentious place with some very grand adornments, such as marble floors and a sweeping staircase. Birds often take shortcuts through the bungalow, though some stay on as guests, building their nests in the window grills. Offices of the Tourist Bureau and Indian Airlines are on the premises. The bungalow seems to have severe ups and downs when it comes to maintenance. Check it out for yourself. Rs 500 ($16.66) gets you a highest priced room—the superdeluxe double. Dorm beds with a common bathroom start at Rs 40 ($1.33). Inexpensive, Indian-style meals are served in the dining room. City tours start from here at 9am and 2pm.

Doubles for Less Than $33

Inspired by a former Maharaja's camp, **Raj Basera,** Residency Road, Jodhpur 3420003 (☎ 31973), has nine circular, rustic brick and thatch huts in a compound with palms, potted plants, and rattan chairs. The ceiling of each hut is covered in a different tie-dye pattern; twin beds with brightly painted headboards and a matching table between them more or less the sum of the rest of the decor. The maintenance could be a tad better. Rates (which may be higher now) are Rs 700 ($23.33) single, Rs 800 ($26.66) double. Breakfast is an additional Rs 75 ($2.50), lunch and dinner Rs 150 ($5) each. There is also a separate block of eight additional rooms.

A simple place with a fancy moniker **Rajputana Palace,** Panch Batti Circle, Airport Road, Jodhpur 342011 (☎ 3162; fax 38672), is a 24-room hotel with low ceilings, modern furniture, and is in need of better maintenance. The prices make it a prize, though: Doubles from Rs 600 ($20) air-cooled to Rs 825 ($27.50) air-conditioned. Breakfast is an additional Rs 65 ($2.16), lunch and dinner Rs 135 ($4.50) each.

Hotel City Palace, 32 Nai Sarak, Jodhpur 342001 (☎ 39033; fax same as telephone), is new and in good shape. The hotel is in the main market, and there is a street noise problem for guests. Positives are a swimming pool and health club, plus a view from the rooftop restaurant and a fresh juice bar in the Gossip coffee shop. Rooms have modern decor and such amenities as minirefrigerators. Rates are Rs 790 ($26.33) single, Rs 990 ($33) double.

Worth a Splurge

A splurge is the **Ratanada Polo Palace,** Residency Road (P.O. Box 63), Jodhpur 342001 (☎ 31910; fax 33118). Rooms are decorated in a blend of furniture with a Raj-period look; the vintage photos on the walls and trophies from the old days, here and there, are decorative motifs. Room rates are Rs 2,000 ($66.66) to Rs 2,500 ($83.33) for doubles. A swimming pool, restaurants, and bar are attractions.

Rajasthan means "land of kings," and so here again in Jodhpur we find another palace—one of the most imposing in all of India—**Welcomgroup Umaid Bhawan,**

Jodhpur 342006 (☎ 33316; fax 22366), turned into a hotel. If you've been traveling around Rajasthan, you may be getting blasé about palace hotels. Well, wait till you see this one. How do you begin to describe it? For openers, it's a sensational pink sandstone structure, reminiscent of New Delhi's Parliament House and Secretariat Building. One of the architects, H. U. Lancaster, had in fact worked with Sir Edwin Luytens, renowned planner of New Delhi. The immense structure, built at the twilight days of India's maharajas, lacks the lightness of the palaces at Udaipur.

A huge dome, 105 feet high, crowns the central marble hall, itself circled with ornate balconies spiraling higher and higher. Thirty feet underground is an immense swimming pool, surrounded by archways painted with fantasy fish and undersea plants. Private changing rooms adjoin the pool. In other rooms, gold ceilings and parquet floors seem to await elegant couples arriving for official receptions or social occasions, perhaps to preview a movie in the intimate screening room. At present, 94 bedrooms are open for guests, some in a new wing which blends with the original. Rates are definitely in the splurge range, as you might imagine for such a splendid chunk of history: $145 to $180 for standard singles; $160 to $200 for standard doubles. The restaurant serves buffet meals; there's a terrace for tea and snacks.

WHERE TO EAT

Buffets are served at the **Welcomgroup Umaid Bhawan** (☎ 33316); **Ratanada Polo Palace,** Residency Road (☎ 31910); and, near the Circuit House, **Ajit Bhawan** (☎ 37410), which must be booked six hours ahead. Prices range from around $9 for breakfast to $12 for lunch and dinner. (See "Where to Stay," above, for addresses of these hotels.)

The **Kalinga Restaurant** (☎ 23658), in the Ardash Niwas Hotel, dimly lit, has brass- and wood-accented walls, brocade chairs, red carpet, and top-notch tandoori specialties such as butter chicken, kebabs, nan, and a host of other well-prepared North Indian dishes. Prices range from Rs 150 ($5), for a three- to four-course vegetarian meal, to Rs 215 ($7.16), for a non-veg meal. Most portions can be shared. Hours are 10am to 10pm.

Rajasthali, Station Road, is a pocket-size restaurant on the first floor landing of midtown building. The interesting murals indoors were painted by the father of Jaideep Singh, the owner. There's an open-air section on the roof (preferred). Here's a rare chance to have a view while trying Rajasthani foods in a restaurant—these from "From the Heart of the Desert." I found them disappointing, but interesting and with potential. Try the special thali—Rs 75 ($2.50) for a sampling of a number of desert dishes, a sweet, and coffee. There's also a smaller, less expensive thali. If you don't go the thali route, try the bran dumplings or krer sangri (beans and nuts curry). Rajasthali's roof is most popular with tourists for breakfast or tea and snacks. Open from 8am to 11pm.

With clay murals and a mirrored, spangled textile ceiling, **Midtown,** Station Road, opposite the railway station, is attractive and clean, with an interesting well-designed menu, offering vegetarian foods—Rajasthani, Indian, and Western. A delicious North Indian thali is Rs 40 ($1.33); Rajasthani Rs 60 ($2), and about the highest priced item on the menu. There are a number of noodle dishes (no eggs in the noodles) and interesting pizzas. For dessert, try apple clincher, a little apple pie, hot or cold, crowned with vanilla ice cream. There's an array of lassis (a yogurt drink, a local specialty). Hours are 7am to 11pm.

SNACKS & SWEETS

The **Mehrangarh,** opposite the Fort Museum, offers a place to snack while sightseeing.

In the old city near Sojati Gate is the **Agra Sweet Home**—worth a special trip for the local specialty, makhania lassi (a creamy, saffron-cardamom–flavored yogurt drink). You may have to elbow your way in. It's a favorite and sells more than 1,000 glasses a day. You'll understand why when you taste it, at around Rs 10 (33¢) per serving.

During your stay you might also like to try another local specialty, mawa ki-kachori (cake filled with sweet syrup) at **Rawat Mishtan** near the Clock Tower or any one of the local sweet shops.

Softy 'n' Softy, Nai Sarak, Sojati Gate, offers its version of lassi (from a Diary Queen–like machine), but is better-known for ice cream. Prices are reasonable: Rs 8 (4¢) for 8 ounces of lassi; ice cream slightly higher. It is open from 9am to midnight.

South Indian coffee with a masala dosa or idly costs around Rs 12 (4¢) at the modest **Jodhpur Coffee House** at Sojati Gate.

EXCURSIONS FROM JODHPUR

KHIMSAR

This small town is 73 miles north of Jodhpur on the Jodhpur-Naugaur-Bikaner Highway. Aurangzeb is said to have ordered the invasion of Jodhpur from this once isolated desert outpost. It's recommended as a restorative getaway during a hectic journey.

Where to Stay

If you stop, you might also wish to spend the night at a Heritage Hotel. The **Royal Castle** (☎ 28), part of which dates from the 15th century, is now a Welcomgroup Hotel, with an atmospheric old wing. The palace is still home to the Thakur of Khimsar. Reservations are made through Maharaja Resorts, Umaid Bhawan Palace, Jodhpur 3424006 (☎ 0291-33316, ext. 231; fax 35373).

FORT POKARAN

This fort, 168 kilometers from Jodhpur, 110 kilometers from Jaisalmer, and 240 kilometers from Bikaner, is a fascinating place. The massive cream-colored 14th-century fort dwarfs a town (pop. 15,000) of little lanes bordered by shops and houses. Pokaran (formerly Balagarh) Fort once sheltered 16th-century Emperor Humayan (his tomb is one of Delhi's greatest landmarks) from the Afghans as he made his way to Persia.

Today, much of the huge fort is a museum of artifacts and objects in charming, if not professional, array. In one wing, there are displays of jeweled clothing, arms, medals, and miniature paintings. To celebrate gods in their shrine, a musician strums a stringed instrument nearby. Across the courtyard in another part of the fort, the exhibits are mainly devoted to royal household furnishings. Admission to the fort is Rs 5 (30¢). (Pokaran was the site of India's nuclear test explosion on March 18, 1974.)

Where to Stay

Part of the fort is now the atmospheric **Fort Pokaran Hotel,** Pokaran 345021 (☎ 2274), where 14 clean, bath-attached double rooms cost Rs 700 ($23.33) single and Rs 800 ($26.67) double. The hotel's restaurant is noted for desert cuisine. Lunch and dinner are Rs 150 ($5) each; breakfast is Rs 80 ($2.66). Reservations in advance are advised. While not officially a Heritage Hotel, it is colorful with a historic past. For reservations and information, contact: Manager, Fort Pokaran. P.O. Pokaran, 345021 (☎ 2274).

7 Jaisalmer

In every adventurous traveler's imagination is a city like Jaisalmer—a golden city rising from the wilderness waiting to be discovered. Jaisalmer (pop. 238,000), founded in 1156 by Rawal Jaisal, lies at the western end of Rajasthan, in the heart of the Great Indian Desert. When camel caravans carried precious cargoes to central Asia, Jaisalmer was in its glory days as a trading center and stop en route to Delhi. Traces of this former opulence are seen in lacelike buildings of luminous sandstone. New construction today must also be ochre-toned to blend with the old. Against this theatrical background are handsome Rajasthanis in bright turbans and vivid skirts and blouses.

As Bombay rose in importance as a seaport, Jaisalmer began to lose its luster. After the 1947 partition, the trade routes to Pakistan were closed, and Jaisalmer went further into decline. During the 1965 and 1971 wars with Pakistan, Jaisalmer, with its strategic border position, was reborn as an important military base. Today the army is Jaisalmer's main industry.

While a good paved road makes it a six-hour drive from Jodhpur—and Jagson flies in—Jaisalmer has remained off the main tourist route. This gives visitors a chance to truly savor the magic of this golden and glowing city rising in the desert wilderness.

ESSENTIALS

GETTING THERE

BY AIR Jagson Airlines flies to Jaisalmer from Jodhpur for $80. (Flights are usually cancelled during sand storms.) The airport counter opens one hour before flights.

BY RAIL There are day and night trains (they're grungy; take your sleeping bag) from Jodhpur (10 hours) Rs 572 ($19.06) in first class, Rs 66 ($2.20) in second. Reservations for train travel can be made at the railway station (☎ 52354), which is open from 8am to 11am, 2pm to 4pm.

BY BUS Rajasthan Tourism coach from Jodhpur, 287 kilometers (179 miles) away, takes five to six hours and costs about Rs 50 ($1.67). For reservations contact the Hotel Moomal (☎ 52392). There are Rajasthan Roadways buses from such towns as Ajmer, Barmer, Bikaner, Jaipur, Jodhpur, and Mt. Abu; for reservations and information, contact the Bus Stand in town (no phone) from 10am to 5pm. Private bus operators also ply these routes.

A note on traveling by car: If you're traveling by car, make a stop at **Fort Pokaran** (see page 145) to sightsee and at RTDC's **Midway**, where there are snacks, soft drinks, and a clean bathroom. Road travelers also should take a plentiful supply of bottled water with them. This dry desert area causes terrific thirst. Stalls along the roadside have tea, tepid soft drinks (no refrigeration), and an occasional bottle of warm mineral water.

The road trip through the desert—whether by day bus or car—from Jodhpur is an unforgettable journey through villages where camels doze and desert sands are occasionally relieved by patches of green.

GETTING AROUND JAISALMER

Auto rickshas and tourist taxis (the latter of which are in short supply), cycle rickshas, and tongas all have negotiable rates. Jeeps are available at the railway station, bus stand, and through travel agencies. Should you want to travel by camel for a day, it will cost about Rs 150 ($5) after bargaining for a few hours around the immediate area—higher if you want to go out to the villages (see "Camel Safaris," below, under "What to See and Do").

Special Events

Initiated in 1979, the **Desert Festival,** held annually in February, has grown into a spectacle of dancing, music, and shopping opportunities. Camels are featured in races, polo matches, and acrobatics. Prizes are presented to the best-decorated camel, as well for the most intricately tied turban.

Holi, the spring festival where people shower others with colored powder is especially lively in Jaisalmer.

WHAT TO SEE & DO

There are RTDC tours (see below) of Jaisalmer, but they are not necessary. Meandering through the town is the best way to experience it. Below the walled fort is the **main market,** where women in vibrant Rajashtani colors bargain for their wares. Another shopping area is near the **Amar Sagar Gate.** The bus stand is near this gate, as is the new palace and tourist office. Out this way also is **Mool Sagar,** a pretty garden and tank, which you'll need a taxi or tonga (horse-drawn cart) to reach. In this direction, 40 kilometers (25 miles) from town are Sam Sand Dunes. The railway station is at the end of town near the fort.

There are a number of shops selling antiques and made-to-look-like antiques as well as handicrafts near the fort, and some guides and ricksha wallahs around there. You'll find it interesting to look in the shops, although the prices are rather high. From the fort you can take a taxi, jeep, or tonga out south to Gadi Sagar and eventually north to Bada Bagh for the sunset. The taxis are unmetered. Be sure to bargain and set the price before you get in.

The Fort

From a distance, the fort, built in 1156 by Rawal Jaisal, looks like a rich fantasy of golden crenelated walls outlined against a sapphire blue sky. Nor does it disappoint on closer inspection. What makes this fort fascinating is that about a quarter of Jaisalmer's residents live inside its walls. Within the first gate of the fort is the Rawal's seven-story palace—open from 8am to 1pm, 3 to 5pm; Rs 6 (20¢)—with beautifully carved balconies and crowns of pagoda-shaped cupolas. The fort is situated on a hill 262 feet high and offers a magnificent view of the town and desert.

In the fort, and open only from 7am till noon, are a group of seven Jain temples (no leather permitted) dating from the 12th to the 15th centuries, richly sculpted with friezes showing the sensuous and the divine. There are 6,000 Jain images to see, some with jewel-studded eyes. Jain priests, with scarves across their mouths lest they inadvertently swallow an insect, minister to the deities and tend the temples. Of special interest is the emerald figure (viewing from 10 to 11am) in the Mahavir Temple.

The **Jain Bhandar,** the library (open from 10 to 11am) established in 1835, contains 3,000 manuscripts written on palm leaves and paper and composed between the 11th and 13th centuries. They cover religious as well as secular subjects. There are also Shiva and Ganesh temples in the fort.

Havelis

Off the main market, and remarkably preserved, are five handsome, lavishly carved golden sandstone mansions built by the wealthy, mainly in the 19th century, and known as havelis. Most extravagant of all is **Patwon ki Haveli,** a flamboyant fantasy of intricate designs. The building is closed off except for one narrow staircase, which leads to an old chamber decorated with murals.

Salim Singh ki Haveli was built by a former prime minister when Jaisalmer was in its heyday. His mansion is identified by the blue cupola. The extravaganza of sculpture on Singh's mansion virtually covers the entire house. Its most outstanding figures are the beautiful peacocks with fan-shaped tails melding into the designs on the richly carved support brackets.

Nathmalji ki Haveli, while also handsomely carved, is somewhat of a curiosity. The former prime minister who built this lace-like house hired two brothers to delicately sculpt the right and left sides; while similar, they are slightly different from each other.

Gadi Sagar

Slightly south of the city is **Gadi Sagar Tank,** once a reservoir for the city, now the site of some small temples. The striking stone gateway across the road leading to the tank was supposedly built by Telia, a favorite courtesan of one of the rawals. When the royal family found out who was responsible for the gate, they threatened to destroy it. But the clever courtesan topped it with a statue of Krishna and had the gate consecrated as a temple. Not even royalty would tear down a sanctified gate, although they never again used the tank.

Museums

Government Museum, near Hotel Moomal, is open from 10am to 5pm, closed Fridays. The **Folklore Museum,** in Gadar Sagar, is a well-edited private collection and worth seeing; the museum's founder, N. K. Sharma, is often there (open from 9am to noon, 3 to 8pm; modest entry fee).

Guided Tours

RTDC runs half-day tours daily—from 3:30 to 7:30pm; Rs 30 ($1)—to the fort, havelis, Gadisagar, and Sam Sand Dunes. For information and reservations, contact RTDC, Hotel Moomal, Amar Sangar Road (☎ 52392).

If you need help negotiating a tour rate by taxi or jeep, here are some agents in town to check for details about private touring: **Aravalli Safari and Tours** (☎ 52632); **Jaisal Tours** in the Narayan Niwas Palace (☎ 52397); RTDC's Moomal Hotel (☎ 52392); and **Rajasthan Tours** (☎52561), among others.

Camel Safaris

Camel safaris are very popular with visitors to Jaisalmer. You explore the desert while swaying through the dunes on a padded saddle atop a ship of the desert—and you get a close-up view of the harsh life in desert settlements. Trips range from day-long introductory tours for a few hundred rupees to long distance excursions lasting a week or more for thousands of rupees. Even in one day you can visit some villages and sense the desert way of life.

They can be rugged sleep-under-the-stars experiences, or luxurious excursions with tented camps and dancers and musicians for entertainment. The average trip includes a camel driver and a cook/bearer/guide. A spot check found camel-tour per-day fees ranging from around Rs 250 ($8.33) to Rs 300 ($10) for a day to Rs 700 ($23.33) to Rs 850 ($28.33) for two or three days; and Rs 1,500 ($50) for seven days with a luxury tent. You can do a combination tour—camel out to the desert and jeep back to town. Full-day desert village trips made by jeep cost around Rs 500 ($16.66) to Rs 700 ($23.33).

When I first wrote about these safaris, a cautionary note was not necessary. But since then, many people have entered the safari field, and not all are reliable. For the sake of safety and honesty, book your desert safari through one of the better hotels (you do not have to be a guest). **Jaisal Tours** (☎ 52397) at Narayan Niwas Hotel; **Fort View** (☎ 52241); and RTDC's **Moomal Hotel** (52392) are reliable choices. Recommended outside the hotels is **Aravalli Safari and Tours** (☎ 52632). For additional choices, check with the tourist office. Make sure your safari operator supplies food, utensils, and a two-way radio to stay in touch with Jaisalmer in case of emergency.

SHOPPING

The specialties are mirror-studded embroidery on apparel, small totes, coin purses, and decorative panels; camel's wool blankets, silver jewelry, and wooden boxes are other crafts. Prices are uniformly high. **Shri Bhawani Emporium,** 4th Gate, Fort, and **Arjun Makeshwari,** Chiriya Haveli, are two merchants among many. Locally made leather chappals (sandals) wear like iron and can be purchased at **BSC Ashok Boot House,** Bhatiya Market, and other shops for about Rs 60 ($2). For price-fixed shopping it's the **Rajasthan Emporium,** Rajasthali (closed Tuesdays), and **Rajasthan Handloom** (closed Sundays), both in Gandhi Chowk. Should you want a made-to-order shirt or salwar kamiz, visit the tailor in the fort.

WHERE TO STAY

Jaisalmer's better hotels cater to tour groups, so reserve far in advance if possible. If you arrive without a reservation, visit the tourist office at Moomal Bungalow or the railway station for help. Be sure to ask about off-season rates April 1 to July 31. Rates go up precipitously during the Christmas–New Year period.

HOTELS WITHIN & NEAR THE FORT

Other cities in Rajasthan have palaces, but Jaisalmer has a castle—**Jaisal Castle,** 168 Fort, Jaisalmer 345001 (☎ 52362), a unique place to stay right in the fort. It's modest for a castle—more a private-home atmosphere—with 10 pleasant rooms, all with bathrooms. But maintenance has fallen off over the years. From the roof, there's a wonderful view of the desert, which is especially beautiful at sunrise and sunset. This is the most professionally run of all the hotels within the fort. Rooms cost around Rs 600 ($20).

Within the fort are shops, service business, and houses, some of the latter turned into small hotels. The tiny, winding lanes in the fort do not have street names, and actual addresses are few and far between. Directional signs point the way to the hotels, which are also marked by signboards. Should you have difficulty in finding the hotel you seek, don't worry. There's always someone happy to show you the way (but they might also be hotel touts, so check out the hotel before checking in). When writing the hotels without addresses, use the name of the hotel, followed by "Fort, Jaisalmer, 345001," and hope for the best. These are casual places, without the formalities of the conventional hotels. You might want to look at more than one before settling in. Some of the budget hotels also require guests to book their camel or jeep tours; make sure you understand everything before checking in so you don't find yourself out on the street when you refuse to comply. When not in the fort or nearby, most hotels have street addresses and may be more apt to reply to requests for reservations.

The following hotels, typical of many in and about the fort, charge Rs 100 ($3.33) to Rs 250 ($8.33). Unless otherwise noted, rooms have attached bathrooms, but hot and cold running water is rare.

Hotel Suraj, Fort (no phone), high up behind the Jain Temples, has four sparse rooms with cots and smashing desert views from some windows. Navneet Vyas and the family who run hotel have many letters from Westerners singing its praises.

Deepak Guest House, Fort (☎ 52665), also high up, has a panoramic rooftop view and clean, spare rooms. Look at more than one room before settling in; the small ones are very cramped, but some have balconies with lovely views. The dining room (vegetarian food only) is a wooden bench. **Hotel Paradise,** Fort (☎ 52674), opposite the palace, has its own regal-looking archways and a lovely courtyard. Of the 18 rooms, nine have baths. One larger room has window seats; another has a balcony. The door is locked at 11:30pm. **Hotel Shri Nath Palace,** Fort, opposite the Jain Temples, has five simple rooms, some without private bathrooms.

At the base of the fort are many other reasonably priced, spartan guest houses and hotels.

One of the nicest basic places near the first gate of the fort is Vijoy Bhatia's eight-room **Rama Guest House.** Nearby, under the same management, is the more comfortable 20-room **Hotel Rama,** Salam Singh-ki-Haveli Margh, Dibba Para, Jaisalmer 345001 (☎ 52570). The hotel, built of typical golden sandstone, has fine views from the roof. The rooms have real beds and colorful bedspreads. Many Westerners have praised this place. Within a stone's throw of the fort, **Hotel Fort View,** Gopa Chowk (☎ 52214) has 20 rooms, some with balconies and private bathrooms, and a restaurant. Also near the fort, **Raj Palace** (☎ 53264) has clean simple rooms, serves snacks, and organizes jeep and camel safaris.

Similar rates and simplicity prevail at **Hotel Tourist,** opposite the State Bank of India, Ward 16, Dibba Para. (☎ 52484), where all rooms have attached bathrooms; **Hotel Swastika** (in India, a good luck sign) also opposite the State Bank of India (☎ 52483), is especially nice with eight clean rooms, a dorm, and food via room service; and there is also the five-room **Madhuvan** (☎ 52323), near the State Bank of Baroda, which is so-so.

Hotels Elsewhere in Jaisalmer

Unless otherwise indicated, rooms have private bathrooms and hot and cold running water.

Neeraj Hotel, Station Road (☎ 52442), opposite the State Bank of Bikaner, faces the fort and has 24 rooms on two floors; simple, basic, and fairly clean. Bathrooms have hot and cold running water.

The RTDC's **Hotel Moomal Palace,** Amar Sagar Road (☎ 52392), outside the city walls, has 40 rooms in a nice-looking building, and 20 basic huts. It's a more-than-adequate place to stay, with attractive rates; air-conditioned rooms are around Rs 600 ($20). Huts are Rs 200 ($6.66); dorm beds Rs 40 ($1.33) per head. There's a restaurant and bar. The tourist office is located in this hotel (open 8am to noon, 3 to 9pm). RTDC also has eight huts at Sam Sand Dunes.

Not far from Hotel Moomal, a beautiful old haveli in typical golden sandstone was once a royal guest house. It is now the **Hotel Jawahar Niwas Palace** (☎ 52208), with 15 down-at-the-heels spacious rooms and careworn antique furnishings, high ceilings, and big bathrooms in the main building. The annex has smaller modern rooms. There's a restaurant on the premises and garden. Its beauty is fading, and needs care.

Hotel Sona, Jaisalmer 3450001 (☎ 52732), built in golden sandstone, has 24 rooms with Rajasthani pictures on the walls as well as swords and shields. This is a family-run hotel and its restaurant features daily fixed-price menus of Rajasthani foods.

Worth a Splurge

The following hotels are often filled with group tours. They offer all creature comforts and such services as camel and jeep tours, and currency exchange; they accept international credit cards. Some are possible on our budget, if two are sharing.

Tops is **Gorbandh Palace Hotel,** Sam Road, Jaisalmer (reservations via City Palace, Udaipur; ☎ 0294-528016; fax 528006), which has 67 tasteful rooms built around a central courtyard and is centrally air-conditioned. It's about 2 kilometers from the heart of town. A swimming pool should ready by now. Rates are Rs 1,750 ($58.33) double.

Narayan Niwas Palace, Malka Road (☎ 52408; fax 52101), is a converted caravanserai (camel stop), which still has the camel mangers and other trappings of bygone days. Built into the old structure is a modern 43-room hotel with all modern conveniences. Rates range from Rs 1,175 ($39.16) for an AC single to Rs 1475 ($49.16) for an AC double. It is partially air-conditioned. Buffet meals run about Rs 500 ($16.67) per person. There is a swimming pool. The hotel offers a 20% off-season discount from May 1 to June 30.

Himmatgarh Palace, No. 1 Ramgarh Rd. (☎ 02992), about 3 kilometers from town, has a tower and rampart garden. The highest priced rooms—Rs 1,950 ($65) double—are in the air-conditioned burj (tower); other rooms are air-cooled. Meals adds about Rs 600 ($20) per person to your bill. There's a 40% discount from April to July.

Hotel Heritage Inn, P.O. Box 43, Sam Road, Jaisalmer 345001 (☎ 52769; fax 53038), has 42 air-conditioned rooms—rates for AC doubles from Rs 1,300 ($43.33)—and a view of the fort, a restaurant, and shopping arcade. Taking your meals here adds about Rs 400 ($13.33) per person. There's a 30% off-season discount from April 15 to July 15.

Hotel Dhola Maru, P.O. Box 49, Jaisalmer 345001 (☎ 52863; fax 52761), has a lot of going for it—golden sandstone exterior with a haveli feeling, 42 rooms with Rajasthani wood-carved furniture and local printed textiles, plus air-conditioning. Singles are Rs 1,100 ($36.66), doubles Rs 1,500 ($50). There's a restaurant and badminton and tennis courts, desert golf, and a shopping arcade. Meals will run about Rs 460 ($15.33) per person. There's a 30% discount from May 1 to July 31.

WHERE TO EAT

There are few restaurants to speak of except those in the Hotel Moomal Palace and the top-priced hotels. Outside the hotels, the top price for a hearty meal is about Rs 60 ($2). In this range, one of the best restaurants is the **Trio,** Gandhi Chowk, Amar Singh Pol, tented, with a pleasant terrace, and serving well-prepared Indian, Chinese, and Western cuisines with entertainment at night. Other restaurants in the same area with similar menus, but less expensive, are **Kalpana** and **Gay Time,** both in Gandhi Chowk. **Monika,** Asni Road, serves thali meals. **8th July,** opposite Main Gate inside the fort, a rooftop restaurant, is popular for breakfast and snacks. Try **Mohan Juice Centre** for lassi. There are many tea and soft-drink stalls, some of these nowadays sell bottled mineral water.

NEARBY EXCURSIONS

Thàr Desert National Park (36 kilometers southwest), the most distant of these excursions, also is the most fascinating. The park, covering 3,000 square miles, was created as a sanctuary to protect a number of dwindling species, including Indian bustard, desert fox, and desert cat, which manage to survive the harsh desert environment where temperatures range from 122°F to –10°F and rainfall is in the mini-millimeters. The Bishnois tribe inhabit this region, and their religion calls for them to protect these species and the environment. This park is a popular destination for camel and jeep safaris.

Wood Fossil Park (14 kilometers south, toward Barmer, a handicraft village) has a park with tree fossils 180 million years old.

Bada Bagh (6 kilometers northwest) is a garden oasis and old dam, where a great deal of the town's produce is grown. There are graceful cenotaphs overlooking the garden. This is the obligatory place for watching the fiery desert sunsets.

EN ROUTE TO UDAIPUR—THE PALACE/FORT ROUTE

Returning from Jaisalmer to Jodhpur, you head off on this new palace- and fort-studded route south to Udaipur, and desert sands become fertile lands as you go through Rajasthan's green belt. (You can, of course do this in the reverse, north from Udaipur to Jodhpur.) Buses and/or trains serve these tiny villages, but a car and driver gives you greater flexibility to look around.

FORT CHANWA

56 miles (35 kilometers) from Jodhpur (45-minute drive from Jodhpur)

Long ago during a flood, the entire village took refuge inside this 19th-century fort that overlooks tiny Luni. Closed for years—but authentically restored by Dalip Singh and his wife—this red sandstone citadel once again welcomes guests to evocative interiors and plant-dotted courtyards. The Singhs might even show you some secret passageways. Rooms evoke the past; bathrooms are updated. Rates are 700 ($23.33) single, Rs 800 ($26.66) double. Breakfast, lunch, and dinner cost around Rs 325 ($10.83); cuisine is Rajasthani. Stay for awhile, or stop for a meal between Jodhpur and Udaipur (or vice-versa). In any case, be sure to reserve whether staying or eating here. The address is: Luni, Dist. Jodhpur (☎ 0291-84216), or Dalip Bhawan, No. 1 House, PWD Road, Jodhpur 341001 (☎ 32460).

Activities include exploring the village for handicrafts, visiting the nearby black buck sanctuary; and touring the area by camel, horse, or jeep.

ROHET GARH

40 kilometers (one-hour drive from Jodhpur)

At this 350-year desert home of Siddarth Singh (descendent of an indestructible knight who, the story goes, didn't let his severed head stop him from fighting his way out of a battle in Jodhpur), there are colorful entrance murals, a surprisingly homey parlor full of family memorabilia, and pleasantly appointed rooms in a garden annex. Rates are Rs 900 ($30) single, Rs 1,100 ($36.66) double. For reservations, write to: Village P.O. Rohet Dist., Pali, Rajasthan, India (☎ 02932-66231), or Rohet House, P.W.D. Road, Jodhpur 342001, Rajasthan, India (☎ 0291-31161).

Activities include Siddarth Singh taking guests in a four-wheel drive on a village safari, where you might meet the Bishnois, a desert tribe whose religion is to preserve the natural environment.

RAWLA NARLAI

259 miles (160 kilometers) from Jodhpur, 226 miles (140 kilometers) from Udaipur

First a 17th-century fortress then a hunting lodge of Maharaj Ajit Singh, Rawla Narlai is now expertly restored as an enchanting, antique-filled, 15-room Heritage Hotel by his son Maharaj Sawroop Singh and family (see the entry for **Ajit Bhawan** in Jodhpur). Rates for bed and breakfast are Rs 1,090 ($36.33) single, Rs 1,390 ($46.33) double; a two-night package, which includes a room, three meals, sightseeing, snacks, and entertainment, is $100 per person. From the graceful archways, there's a view of the area's famous landmark: a mammoth 350-foot rock of solid granite, which houses caves and temples and is topped with a statue of a white elephant, guardian of the desert. For reservations write: Ajit Bhawan, Jodhpur 342006 (☎ 0291-37410; fax 3774).

Activities include visiting the temples in the great granite rock and climbing up to see the big white elephant; also strolling in the village. You can ride the owner's horses at his nearby farm and watch the old waterwheel irrigate the fields with little jugs full of water. Ranakpur's temples are within easy reach.

GHANERAO ROYAL CASTLE

283 miles (175 kilometers) from Jodhpur (4 1/2-hour drive from Jodhpur)

This imposing red sandstone and marble structure is the Norma Desmond of the forts along this route—a striking grande dame in its day, now badly in need of a restorative facelift to make it a star again. Founded in 1605 by Thakur Gopal Das Rathod, it has been in Sajan Singh's family since the early 17th century, and his warmth and knowledge is a good reason to overlook the careworn decor and stay for a night or just have a meal. You must make arrangements in advance. The rate for a double is Rs 1,140 ($38) with breakfast and dinner. Singh's properties also include **Ajit Bagh,** cottages in a grove near the castle available for longer stays, and **Bagh-Ka-Bagh,** a rustic, 10-room hunting lodge with no electricity, en route to Kumbhalgarh Sanctuary. Ranakpur's temples are 18 kilometers away. For reservations write: Ghanerao Royal Castle, Ghanerao 306704, Dist. Pali, Rajasthan, India (☎ 7335).

Activities include visiting the village to see havelis, wall paintings, handicrafts. You could also visit Mahavir Temple (5 kilometers), dating from the 10th century, or Kumbhalgarh Sanctuary (5 kilometers) where you might see panthers, sambars, wild boars, or bears as well as many exotic birds.

MAHARANI BAGH ORCHARD RETREAT

300 miles (185 kilometers) from Jodhpur (5 1/2-hour drive from Jodhpur)

Designed in the 19th century by the Maharani of Maharaja Takhat Singh, these lovely mango orchards now have rose-pink, thatch-top cottages amid the trees, a swimming pool, and thatch-top dining hut for buffet meals. Maharani Bagh can be a rest stop between Udaipur and Jodhpur or a base for visiting Ranakpur, 4 kilometers to the north. Doubles are Rs 975 ($32.50), singles Rs 675 ($22.50); buffet meals are Rs 200 ($6.66) each. For reservations write: c/o Umaid Bhawan Palace, Jodhpur (☎ 0291-20941), or 51/55 Sadri via Faina). Ranakpur is about 8 kilometers.

Nearby, **The Castle** is less opulent. Rooms are Rs 350 ($11.66), and a meal costs Rs 150 ($5). The birds do enjoy the trees.

8 Udaipur

The picturesque town of Udaipur (pop. 308,000) is a fertile oasis in the dry deserts of Rajasthan. Three large, artificial lakes built centuries ago for irrigation still form the heart of the city, which is enclosed on all sides by mountains.

Udaipur is a colorful place, with beautiful murals on the whitewashed walls of many of its homes—it's a local custom to paint a horse and an elephant on each side of the gateway when a marriage takes place. The women here prefer the royal colors of orange and red for their saris.

The city, originally capital of the State of Mewar, was founded in the 16th century by Udai Singh, its first maharana (meaning "prince among princes")—a title bestowed only upon this Rajput royal family for valorous deeds and its heroic resistance to the Muslim rulers in Delhi. They gave in to the Muslims in 1614, but the city remained until Indian independence under the rule of this same royal family, who built many gorgeous palaces over the years.

ESSENTIALS

GETTING TO UDAIPUR

BY AIR Daily flights connect Udaipur with Delhi ($58), Jaipur ($35), Jodhpur ($28), Bombay ($70), and Aurangabad ($63). Dabok Airport is 25 kilometers from the city; there is no bus service to and from there. Taxis charge about Rs 150 ($5) to the any where in town (about 30 to 45 minutes).

BY RAIL The *Pink City Express* from Delhi takes 22 hours and costs Rs 1,188 ($39.60) AC First; and Rs 137 ($4.56) Second. The *Pink City Express* also stops at Jaipur, Ajmer, and Chittaurgarh. The *Ahmedabad–Udaipur Express* costs Rs 290 ($9.66) A/C First, and Rs 33 ($1.10) Second. These are just two options; there are trains also from Jodhpur. The railway station is about 4 kilometers from the center (☎ 131).

BY BUS Private bus operators run luxury coaches (two abreast, push-back seating) between Udaipur and many other places, among them Bombay, taking 18 to 20 hours, for Rs 180 ($6); Jaipur, taking about nine hours, for Rs 80 ($2.66); Jodhpur, for Rs 65 ($2.16); Mount Abu, for Rs 75 ($2.50); Jaisalmer, for Rs 65 ($2.16); Ahemadabad, for Rs 70 ($2.33), and several other places. In Udaipur, check with travel agents along City Station Road and elsewhere about reservations. The Rajasthan, Gujarat, Uttar Pradesh, and Madyha Pradesh State Road Transport Corporations run buses to Udaipur from various cities. The State Transport Bus Stand is on City Station Road, NH8, Udaipol; for information and reservations ☎ 27191; reservations is open from 7am to 7pm.

VISITOR INFORMATION

For information or brochures, or to hire approved guides, stop at the **Tourist Information Bureau** in Hotel Kajri (☎ 29535); **Tourist Information Counter at the City Railway Station,** Platform 1 (☎ 25105); the **Tourist Information Bureau at Dabok Airport** (☎ 28011); or the **Information Center, Mohata Park,** Chetak Circle (☎ 24924).

CITY LAYOUT

The center of Udaipur could be regarded as **Chetak Circle,** up in the northeast section of town. Here are the **Jumma Mosque,** the offices of Indian Airlines, the **Chetak Cinema** (Indian movies), and the aforementioned **Kwality** and **Berry's Restaurant,** the former air-cooled. The narrow streets to the older part of town and bazaar lead off from here. Udaipur is renowned for its carved and painted wooden toys, and numerous shops up these little streets stock them in great quantity. Search, also, in the **City Bazaar** for bargains on silver, a local specialty.

GETTING AROUND

Bikes at **Mewar (M.K.) Cycle** and other stores near Hotel Kajri, cost Rs 25 (83¢) per day; auto rickshas are unmetered, and you must haggle, not just bargain, for your fare before you get in. Figure on a minimum fare of about Rs 30 ($1) per hour. Private taxis are found at Taxi Stand, Chetak Circle Tourist Taxi Service (☎ 25112), also on Lake Palace Road (☎ 24169) and Udai Pol. Cycle rickshas and tongas are also available. (Everyone complains that ever since the stars of *Octopussy* were here and literally threw their money around, drivers expect all foreigners to do more of the same.)

For three to four hours of city sightseeing by car, the fee is Rs 175 ($5.83) to 200 ($6.66); for excursions to Ranakpur and Kumbhalgarh via Gogunda (six hours), figure Rs 700 ($23.33); via Eklingji (eight hours) to Chittor (eight hours) Rs 800 ($26.66); to Jaisamand Sanctuary (four hours) Rs 300 ($10.80). Split between four in a car, these rates might even be managed on a moderate budget.

When to Go

Most people visit Udaipur and Rajasthan from September to March. But the dry and arid area is beautiful when fringed with green during the monsoon, July to September. Rainfall is light in this desert region. It's very hot from the end of March until the rains come.

Mewar Festival takes place each spring; **Gangaur** celebrates the marriage of Shiva and Parvati some days after Holi.

WHAT TO SEE & DO

The **City Palace** is now public property and can be visited. Its upper balconies are the highest point in town and offer a splendid view of Lake Pichola at one side and the city at the other—it's easy to visualize the royal guests sitting up here watching the elephants at play in the spacious courtyard below. Although the 20 elephant stables remain untouched, they are unoccupied today. The government of Rajasthan, which now administers the palace, has higher priorities for its funds than maintaining elephants.

The palace is an intricate warren of inner patios, courtyards, and balconies, connected by narrow passageways and flights of stairs. The Peacock Courtyard features beautiful glass peacocks, composed of thousands of tiny colored-glass slivers inset into the walls. Above is the maharana's private apartment, still occupied until 30 or so years ago; below that is a tiny room containing a golden sun, which could be illuminated on days the real sun was obscured by the monsoon. There are rooms with mirrored walls, ivory doors, colored-glass windows, and carved and inlaid marble balconies. The pièce de résistance must be the tiny room in which every inch of space, even the ceiling, is covered with brightly colored, painted miniatures of festivals, flowers, jungle scenes, and dancing girls. Adjoining are portraits of all the maharanas.

Attached is a small and somewhat indifferent museum containing textiles, armor, inscribed stone blocks, and row upon row of turbaned plaster heads.

City Palace is open from 9:30am to 4:30pm daily. The entry fee is Rs 15 (5¢), plus fees for still cameras and for movie cameras.

Until the death of the last maharana, the City Palace was the major one in use. On a distant hill can be seen the monsoon palace; the summer palace, Jag Niwas, is the one now the Lake Palace Hotel. The other island palace, **Jag Mandir,** was in use in the 17th century and has a lovely black marble pagoda with eight life-size stone elephants guarding its entrance.

Fateh Sagar is the more northern of the two lakes, and along its eastern bank (town side) twists a serpentine road dotted with pretty parks. A recent addition, **Sanjay Park,** is known for its beautiful floral displays. In the center of Lake Fateh Sagar on a lush island is **Nehru Park** with a restaurant; there's motorboat service out from the jetty. The fare is Rs 3 (10¢) round-trip; it is open from 9am to 7pm.

On the inland side is **Pratap Samak Memorial,** atop Moti Magri (Pearl Hill). The walk up goes through delightful gardens to the hilltop rock gardens dominated by a black bronze statue of the 16th-century Rajput patriot Maharana Pratap astride his steed, Chetak. It is open from 9am to 6pm; entry is Rs 3 (10¢); vehicle fees Rs 5 and Rs 7 (20¢).

To the north are the lovely gardens known as **Sahelion ki Bari,** whose pathways and courtyards feature fountains (turned on by attendants) in ingenious combinations. A square tank in the inner courtyard contains a white marble cupola in the center—whose roof turns into a waterfall—and black marble pavilions at each corner, on the roofs of which birds revolve in a circle of spray. In another part of the garden, four marble elephants spray water through their trunks as birds emit jets from their beaks.

The gardens themselves, which are lovely, date from the 18th century. The legend is they were used to amuse young ladies who had been sent as a peace gift from Delhi's ruler. (But local guides say they were designed by the Maharana back then for the Maharani and her friends.) The fountains were not added until later, in the last century. A sign at the entrance commands "Let thy voice be low." Open from 9am to 6pm, entry is Rs 2 (6¢); fountain fee Rs 3 (10¢).

Opposite the entrance in a former royal enclave is a small **Children's Museum** with a variety of small fry exhibits.

The maharanas were apparently great ones for entertainment. The **Gangor Ghat,** a stone gateway opening on to lakeside steps just north of the City Palace, is where dancing girls used to perform, watched from an elevated barge on the lake by all the nobility and their guests.

Just behind this gate is the **Jagdish Temple,** a richly carved structure dating back three centuries. Today it possesses such a valuable collection of treasures that an armed guard stands perpetually on duty.

Toward the south end of town, on the way to the railroad station, is **Nehru Children's Park** (within the Municipal Town Hall), public gardens with a pond, and boat and camel rides for the kids.

Museums, Crafts Village & Gallery

Just north of Chetak Circle on Panchvati is the nationally celebrated **Folk Art and Puppet Museum,** also known as **Bhartiya Lok Kala Mandal** (☎ 24296), which, since its founding in 1952, has been collecting, recording, filming, practicing, and performing folk art and dancing of the region. It's open from 9am to 6pm. A one-hour puppet show is at 6pm. Admission is Rs 10 ($1).

Shilpi Gram, about 3 kilometers from town, is a crafts and performing arts center and showcase for craftspeople from various localities who show their wares and a shopper's haven. On site are 26 huts built in styles and materials representative of the entire West Zone—Goa, Gujarat, Maharashtra, Rajasthan, Daman and Diu, and Dadra and Nagar Haveli. In addition to crafts, see shrines, a museum, and a folk art gallery here.

Inside Fateh Prakash Palace (see "Where to Stay," below) is what must be Udaipur's most unusual attraction, the **Crystal Gallery,** a testimony to a former maharana's obsession with crystal, and a monument to an earlier era of royal indulgence. This fantastic collection had been in storage for many years until recently, when it was assembled for this multiroom exhibit. See entire suites of crystal furniture, lighting fixtures, trays, mirror and picture frames, and indeed all manner of objects made from crystal. From the gallery, there's a fine view of Durbar Hall (former royal Hall of Public Audience, now rented out for banquets/receptions), with its gargantuan cascading crystal chandeliers, ancestral portraits and opulent furniture. Admission $10.

A Cruise

As a respite from sightseeing, cruise lovely Lake Pichola. Fares are Rs 110 ($3.66) for adults, Rs 75 ($2.50) for children. This cruise goes to Jag Mandir. One-half trip around Lake Pichola (excluding Jag Mandir) is Rs 45 ($1.50) adults, Rs 30 ($1) children. From April to September, cruises are at 11am, 3pm, and 6pm. From October to March, you can sail at 10am, noon, 2pm, 5pm. Purchase tickets at Bansi Ghat, at the base of the City Palace.

Guided Tours

From Hotel Kajri, you can catch the government's daily 8am to 1pm coach tour and cover the city's highlights for Rs 30 ($1). A tour in the afternoon from 2 to 7pm is Rs 70 ($2.33) and takes in the outskirts as well: **Eklingji,** a temple village; **Haldighati,** a former battle site; and **Nathdwara,** an 18th-century temple (which non-Hindus can't enter).

If you still have time on your hands, you can explore the city on your own. Stroll, take an auto ricksha, or rent a bike from one of the shops near the tourist information bureau in the Hotel Kajri and make your own tour at your own pace (rates vary, but bargaining keeps them moderate).

Shopping

Because Udaipur has become so touristy over the years, bargains are hard to find, and bargaining is necessary and expected to get a fair price at all but price-fixed stores. There are interesting crafts a-plenty, especially in folk toys, silver, hand-printed textiles, and cane furniture. Main shopping areas are Bapu Bazaar, Chetak Circle, City Market, Clock Tower, Hathi Pol, and Palace Road. At one shop near the clock tower, **Ashok Art,** 96 Patwa St., near Jagdish Temple, artisans are at work on miniatures. Some of these run as high as Rs 15,000 ($855), but you can get something small for Rs 300 ($17.10)—less if you bargain. For price-fixed merchandise, go to the Rajasthali Government Handicrafts Emporium in Chetak Circle. Shop hours are usually 10am to 7pm.

WHERE TO STAY

Unless otherwise indicated, these hotels are air-conditioned and offer all the services of internationally known hotels.

Penny-wise tip: Some of them advertise off-season discounts, from April 1 to September 30; in others, be sure to ask about discounts if visiting off-season.

Doubles for Less Than $13.33

At these prices, we're talking mostly six-, seven-, and eight-room hotels, usually no telephones or air-conditioning (air coolers also rare), and travelers dropping in without reservations. During peak season, you may have to make the rounds to find a vacancy, and when you do, it's best to check out the room before checking in.

"Best shower in India and if there's no hot water, you don't have to pay," said the manager at the **Hotel Mahendra Prakash,** Lake Palace Road, Udaipur 313001 (☎ 29370). Twelve big rooms, clean, spare and good buys: Doubles are Rs 300 ($10). There are courtyard and rooftop restaurants. This is one of the nicest hotels in this price range and has one of the nicest managers, too.

On Lake Palace Road are the low-priced **Haveli** (☎ 28294) and **Shambhu Vilas** (☎ 27338), with some air-cooled rooms.

A strip of land north of the city palace above Lake Pichola is Lal Ghat, the location of some of the best inexpensive accommodations: **Jagat Niwas,** 25 Lal Ghat, a refurbished old house, with a fine lake view; **Sai Niwas,** with a rooftop restaurant and good food to eat while admiring the view; **Lake Ghat,** 4/13 Lal Ghat, which the guests I met praised for its cleanliness, friendliness and view; two others, **Hotel Lal Ghat,** 33 Lal Ghat (☎ 25301), has a few bath-attached rooms, some windowless rooms, and a dorm, and **Evergreen,** next door to the Lal Ghat, are possibilities, but neither of these is for the overly fussy. Rooms vary, so check them out before checking in.

Raj Palace, Bhatiyani Chotta, occupies an atmospheric building behind the City Palace, with a garden, plus clean comfortable rooms; it is more professionally run than some others in this price range.

Low-budget travelers should also remember the Rs 40 ($1.33) dorm accommodations at the government's **Hotel Kajri** Shastri Circle (☎ 23509).

The Government of Rajasthan Tourist Bureau in the Kajri Hotel (☎ 29535) has a list of **paying guest accommodations,** from Rs 50 ($1.66) to Rs 250 ($8.33) per person.

Doubles for Less Than $23.33

The family-run **Rangniwas Palace Hotel,** Lake Palace Road, Udaipur 313001 (☎ 523891), is a pleasant, unpretentious, and very popular place (so book far in advance). Most of its 20 clean, simply furnished rooms face the garden, where you can sit out in the evenings with tea or a drink. Of the 12 rooms in the new block, the six upstairs are most expensive—Rs 700 ($23.33) for a double—but they are also the nicest, with air coolers and big tubs in their bathrooms. The eight rooms in the old building have their own charm. There's a 10% service charge. Breakfast is served on the rooftop of the restaurant. A swimming pool, in the planning stages, might be completed by now. Rajasthani folk dances are performed in the hotel's garden daily, except Sunday, at 7pm (nonresidents are welcome); tickets are Rs 30 ($1) and can be purchased at hotel's reception (perhaps not off-season).

RTDC's 53-room **Kajri Hotel,** Shastri Circle (☎ 29509), in the center of town, has a variety of simple rooms in various price ranges—the highest is Rs 500 ($16.66); the lowest is a dorm for Rs 40 ($1.33) per head. There's also a restaurant and bar. Not among RTDC's finest.

Saheli Palace Hotel, 222/17 Sahelion Ki Bara Marg, Udaipur 313001 (☎ 27814), in a 50-year-old palace-like structure, has 22 simply furnished rooms; there is a 10% service charge.

Doubles for Less Than $50

Almost adjoining the Laxmi Vilas (listed under "Worth a Splurge," below), and also on a hilltop with a spectacular view, is the 25-room **Anand Bhawan,** Fateh Sagar Road, Udaipur 313001 (☎ 523256; fax 523247), with wide balconies overlooking both the Lake Fateh Sagar and the Swaroop Sagar. It's a bit plainer than its neighbor but was, at one time, a royal guest house. Now run by the Rajasthan government, it's something of a bargain—AC doubles for Rs 800 ($26.66)—but you must reserve very far in advance. The spacious rooms have carpets, comfortable couches and chairs, dressing rooms, and high ceilings. There is a pleasant garden with huge tamarind and mango trees. Highest-priced rooms have lake views.

Also overlooking Lake Fateh Sagar is the modern **Hotel Hilltop Palace,** 5 Ambavgarh (☎ 28764; fax 525106), which over the years has grown from a modest 24-room budget place to sleek 65-room (48 lake view, 17 city view) hotel. Still, prices are not out of line for sleek modern rooms with small refrigerators, bathrooms, and balconies. Doubles are Rs 1,400 ($46.66). The dramatic interior design features a sweeping marble stairway, cut-glass windows, and a glass elevator, but the star attractions here are the stunning lake and city views. This is tour-group territory.

Nicely situated on a plot of land jutting into Lake Pichola is the **Lake Pichola Hotel,** outside Chand Pol, Udaipur 313001 (☎ 29387). Although recently built, this hotel has the domed look of traditional Udaipur architecture, and the interior decoration carries through these traditional motifs. Of the 23 rooms, the best have balconies hanging over lake. Doubles are Rs 800 ($26.66) and are air-conditioned. Forget the economy rooms at Rs 600 ($20) double; you can do better elsewhere. The hotel has two restaurants—one on the roof—if you decide to take your meals here. There's also a bar and a boat to take guests around the lake.

Hotel Rajdarshan, 18 Pannadhai Marg, Udaipur 313001 (☎ 526601; fax 525887), on the banks of Swaroop Sagar, built into the remains of the old city wall, has 52 centrally air-conditioned rooms, 32 with lake views. All rooms are furnished in the same modern, functional style, but the restful, earthy color schemes vary from floor-to-floor, and those with small balconies offer smashing panoramic city or lake views. There is a swimming pool. This is an excellent value, with doubles at Rs 1300 ($43.33). The food rates raves, too.

On the banks of Fateh Sagar Lake, the intimate **Hotel Rampratap Palace** (☎ 528700), has 17 rooms with balconies and/or verandahs. Air-conditioned rooms facing the lake—at Rs 850 ($28.33) for a double—are preferred, not only for the panoramic view, but to avoid the noisy road. A rooftop restaurant was in the planning stage and perhaps finished by now. There are 30% and 20% discounts from April 15 to September 30.

Chandralok Hotel, Saheli Marg, Udaipur 313001 (☎ 560011), has 14 clean rooms, all with twin beds and comfy chairs; two rooms have dressing rooms, but they are priced the same as the others at Rs 800 ($26.66) for a double.

Hotel Lakend, Alkapuri, Fateh Sagar, Daipur 313001 (☎ 23841; fax 523898), offers 78 rooms and a view of Lake Fateh Sagar. This is a modern, casually run hotel, which has declined over the years. Now it's seriously in need of better maintenance and is overpriced in this rundown state—an AC double is Rs 900 ($30). The restaurant serves vegetarian food. There's a swimming pool and garden. It's well positioned on the lake.

A former royal home is now **Hotel Gulab Niwas** (meaning "Rose Garden"), Khudala House, near Fateh Sagar Lake (☎ 523644), an unpretentious Heritage Hotel, with 16 neat, clean rooms, some with very high ceilings; five suites are air-conditioned and have fireplaces for winter—a buy at Rs 800 ($26.66)—the other rooms are air-cooled. Have breakfast in the lovely garden.

Worth a Splurge

The opportunity to sleep in one fabulous palace, let alone two of them, doesn't come often for most people, so if you can possibly manage to stretch your budget, you should try to spend at least one night in either of Udaipur's two marble palaces turned into hotels. The most famous of the two, **The Lake Palace,** Pichola Lake, Udaipur 313001 (☎ 527962; fax 525804), is perhaps the quintessential palace hotel of the world. Originally the summer residence of the maharana and supposedly converted into a hotel at the suggestion of Jacqueline Kennedy, its marble halls have since played host to kings and commoners. Enlarged artfully over the years (from 17 to 86 rooms), the Lake Palace plays host now to many tour groups. Architecturally, this palace of curved archways, domes, and cupolas appears to be floating on the lake. Throughout the interior there's a blending of furnishings with carved marble and mirror-studded murals. Some of the suites are truly splendid, with stained-glass windows, marvelous views across the lake, rooftop terraces, and cupolas that overlook courtyards and lotus-filled pools. For its opulence, the rates are not unreasonable: Standard doubles and singles are $165, a double with a sitting room is $190; a small suite is $220. The splendid multiroom suites run

$550. In the evenings, puppet shows and dance displays are often held for guests' entertainment.

Regular launch service connects the hotel with the mainland, and launches also take hotel guests around the lake on sunset tours. The 3-mile-square lake, built in the 14th century, is 30 feet deep.

Across the way on the mainland, at the south end of the imposing group of white buildings making up the City Palace, is now the exclusive and intimate **Shiv Niwas Palace,** Udaipur 313001 (☎ 528016; fax 528006), a former guest house of the maharana for entertaining such dignitaries as the queen of England and the king of Nepal. It's now a hotel, with only 17 sumptuous multiroom suites—furnished with the maharana's treasured antiques, blended with new custom-made furnishings, and 14 beautifully appointed smaller suites. There are crested towels and terry-cloth robes in the marble bathrooms. All the elegant suites ($150 to $350) have secluded terraces for sun- or moonbathing in the buff, and other terraces for partying. Taking your meals here adds around Rs 850 ($28.33) per person. Standard rooms ($55) in an annex are truly poor relations. The lowest-price suite is $150. Discounts from 20% down to 10% from April 1 to September 30.

A charming alternative to the large, glitzy, multiroom palaces is the intimate, antique-filled **Fateh Prakash Palace Hotel** (City Palace, Udaipur 313001 (☎ 528016-19; fax 528006), with six suites and three deluxe rooms, in a recently opened wing of the City Palace. Hidden away up a steep flight of stairs, these perfectly restored rooms have sensational views of Lake Pichola and the entire area, plus all the frills of the larger palace hotels with the additional bonus of personalized service. Wonderful for nongroup tour-goers. Rates are $100 to $150 for a double room and are discounted by 20% or 10% from April 1 to September 30. The hotel's glass-fronted Gallery Restaurant (open to nonresidents) overlooks Lake Pichola and offers tea (great sunset!) as well as delicious meals (see "Where to Eat," below). (Thanks for the suggestion to Karel de Wit and Juliette Wariels of Amsterdam.)

If the splurge palaces are too pricey for you, but you still want something in a class above, try the **ITDC's Laxmi Vilas Hotel,** Fateh Sagar Road, Udaipur 313001 (☎ 529711; fax 525536), once a guest house for VIPs visiting the maharana. There are 54 rooms—spacious in the main palace, smaller in the newer wing. A single runs Rs 1,500 ($50), a double Rs 2,300 (76.66), suites from Rs 2,700 ($90) to Rs 3,000 ($100). The view, which is very good, makes up for a certain lack of opulence in the furnishings—though there are still many beautiful rugs and other trappings of earlier, more regal days. There's a swimming pool and tennis court.

The Lake Palace, once known as Jag Niwas, Shiv Niwas, and Fateh Prakash all offer splendid views of Jag Mandir, a palace on a nearby island. A charming but probably apocryphal tale says that Emperor Shah Jahan hid out on this island after feuding with his father and got the inspiration for the Taj Mahal while here.

Out of Town

Pratap Country Inn, Airport Road, Titadhia Village (☎ 83138; fax 83058), is 6 kilometers from town (call for free transport from railway station). This old country estate, which has seen better days, has 33 rooms. The highest rate is Rs 500 ($16.66) with air-conditioning; there is a swimming pool, horses and camels to ride. The ambience is casual. Bus service to downtown Udaipur from Pratap is frequent, so you can go to and from without depending on taxis or auto rickshas—if you don't mind crowds.

Tops out of town, **Hotel Shikarbadi,** Goverdhan Vilas, Udaipur 313001 (☎ 83200-3; fax 28323), a former royal hunting lodge, is only 5 kilometers from the city in a lush jungle (somewhat isolated for lone travelers). Still owned by the

Maharaj Arvind Singhji Mewar, son of the Maharana of Mewar, the 25 well-maintained rooms have a charming rustic look with rocking chairs, attractive bird and animal prints on the stone walls, and modern bathrooms. Doubles are $45, singles $30; 9 deluxe, well-furnished tents are $30. The spacious grounds house a small stud farm for those who like to ride, an animal park for sightseeing, and swimming pool for a refreshing dip. A taxi to Udaipur is Rs 90 ($3); auto ricksha Rs 40 ($1.33).

WHERE TO EAT

A good choice for good food at a fair price is **Park View** (☎ 24098), opposite of Town Hall. It's dimly lit and restful, air-conditioned and spacious, and the menu features well-prepared Indian, Chinese, and Continental cuisines: vegetarian entrées, Rs 20 (66¢) to Rs 30 ($1); non-veg Rs 30 ($1) to Rs 50 ($1.66). Hours are 8:30am to 11pm. There are some restaurants in Chetak Circle: **Kwality** and **Berry's,** the latter the more attractive and popular of the two, both with the by-now-memorized Indian, Chinese, and so-called Continental menu. Entrées in the Rs 50 ($1.66) range; they are both open 8:30am to 10pm.

Some of the best Indian food in town is at the **Amantran**, Hotel Rajdarshan (☎ 526601), on the banks of Sawroop Sagar, where there's usually a buffet for Rs 150 ($5) at lunch, Rs 175 ($5.83) at dinner, so you can try a little bit of a lot of things.

For views with modestly priced food, **Shamiana** (the sign says "Hiltop") near the Nehru Jetty, overlooking Fateh Sagar, is a good snack and view stop. Snacking atop the **Roof Garden Cafe,** 1st Floor, Delwara House, opposite Lake Palace Main Gate, Lake Palace Road, offers a view the City Palace and Fort, but those stained tablecloths can be off-putting. Hours are 8:30am to 9:30pm. They do offer a 20% discount to students. Better view and maintenance, similar menu, prices, and hours can be found at the nearby **Rooftop Palace View,** Lake Palace Road. At the modest **Sai Niwas,** Lal Ghat, you get a lake view, cleanliness, and good food.

For a splurge and a delicious Continental meal, served with a marvelous view, go to the elegant **Gallery Restaurant,** Fateh Prakash Palace, City Palace (☎ 528016). The fixed-price lunch is Rs 400 ($13.33); dinner Rs 500 ($16.66); light and airy ravioli, grilled fish, and other dishes go perfectly with a bottle of India's best wine, Riviera white for Rs 750 ($25).

Nonresidents can soak up some of the glitz and glamour at the **Lake Palace Hotel** with the boat trip/buffet excursion for lunch or dinner, for around Rs 500 ($16.66). The food is a bit bland, but there's rich atmosphere. The lunch cruise is from 12:30 to 2:30pm; dinner from 7:30 to 8:30pm. This is a popular venue for tour groups, so reserve in advance (☎ 527962).

Shilpi (3 kilometers from the city, near Fateh Sagar) has thatch huts, a garden, swimming pool, a village atmosphere, and reasonable prices. Entrees are Rs 25 (83¢) to 30 ($1) vegetarian; up to Rs 60 ($2) nonvegetarian. Hours are 11:30am to 3pm, 7 to 11pm.

A BAR

Back in town, Udaipur's most atmospheric bar is located in Shiv Niwas Hotel, with massive mirrors, cascading crystal fixtures, cushy furniture, royal portraiture, and great lake view. Open from 11am to 11pm. Enjoy tea at sunset at the sumptuous Gallery in the Fateh Prakash Palace Hotel.

EXCURSIONS FROM UDAIPUR

Of the many side trips from Udaipur, these are most rewarding. Guided, same-day excursions from Udaipur depart at 8am and take in both Kumbhalgarh and Ranakpur (described below) for around Rs 900 ($30). Inquire at travel agencies or tourist bureau (see "Visitor Information" under "Essentials," in this section).

KUMBHALGARH FORT Kumbhalgarh Fort (84 kilometers, three-hour drive from Udaipur) is not yet overrun with tourists and is a most interesting experience. The second most important fort in the area (Chittaurgarh is first), Kumbhalgarh was constructed in the 15th century by Rana Khumba, a great hero, who built 32 of the 84 fortresses in Mewar and added on to it over the years. The fort has seven great gates, 33 kilometers of walls over 20 feet thick, and commands a hunk of what was the border of Udaipur (Mewar) and Jodhpur (Marwar). These formidably high and sleek walls could not be climbed, but were wide enough to accommodate chariots. They enclosed a palace, village, and some 365 temples and shrines.

A fairly steep half-hour climb from the parking area up a winding road leads to the entrance; once inside, you can usually find the watchman, who will take you—give him an Rs 10 (33¢) tip at the end of the tour—around the highlights, which helps you imagine some of the private and public life in those long-ago days. Here's a palace with its crumbling but still recognizable Maharani's quarters in yellow with glass windows, the dressing room in the zenana (women's quarters) with interesting elephant, crocodile, and camel frieze; and the adjacent bathroom, which is impressive given when it was built: a stone latrine whose ventilation was assured by a perforated stone screen. But the high point of any tour literally is the light and airy pastel-colored "Cloud Palace" at the summit (almost a mile high) above the grim ramparts of the fort. From here and elsewhere, admire the beautiful views. Returning to the parking area, walk on to see the temples at the base of the fort. There's also a stall with snacks and soft drinks.

Nearby is **Kumbhalgarh Wildlife Sanctuary** a breeding round for the wolf and haven for leopard, sloth, flying squirrel (native to Rajasthan only), and others. Best times to visit the sanctuary are from March to June and September to November for wildlife. Garacias and Bhils tribes inhabit this region.

Where to Stay near Kumbhalgarh Fort

Possibilities for accommodations nearby include the **Aodhi Hotel,** Kumbhalgarh, P.O. Kelwara, Dist. Raj Samand, Rajasthan, India. Book reservations at City Palace, Udaipur (☎ 0294-238230; fax 23823). It is located in a wooded grove, with spacious rooms with lovely bird prints on the walls and comfortable furnishings. There's a thatch-roof restaurant (open to nonresidents, but call for reservations).

Or stay at one of the Heritage Hotels (described in the section "En Route to Udaipur—The Palace/Fort Route," above).

RANAKPUR Rankapur (98 kilometers away from Udaipur) is a major pilgrimage center for Jains. The focal point of a visit is a large group of 15th-century temples that are said to be inspired by a prime minister's dream. Maharana Khumba took his prime minister's dream as a sign from the divine, and alotted funds for the temples, which took 50 years to build, from 1446 to 1496. The most important temple, **Chaturmukha,** has four main entrances and, near them, deities 6 feet tall. There are 24 cenotaphs in the shrine, 184 cellars, and 85 spires. But the main attraction is 1,444 intricately carved columns, with no two designs alike. The temple is open to non-Jains from noon to 5pm. A dharamasala and tourist bungalow offer modest accommodations and vegetarian meals. Many Heritage Hotels offer more comforts (see "En Route to Udaipur—The Palace/Fort Route," above).

CHITTAURGARH FORT A 2½-hour drive (98 kilometers east) from Udaipur is Chittaurgarh Fort. Located on a hill, the Fort occupies 700 acres; its foundations go back to the 7th century, and it remained the site of the ancient capital of Marwar state until 1567. Little is left of its former glory as a Rajput stronghold and capital of Marwar.

Highlights include the Fort's three pols (gates) associated with the three times the famous fort was sacked. The crowning glory of Chittaurgarh is the Tower of Victory built by Rana Kumbha in the 15th century to commemorate his victory over the Moslem rulers of Gujarat and Malwa. Within a few miles of the Rajasthan border, the fort is over 8 miles in circumference and encloses ruins of temples, tanks, and palaces that were built from the 9th to 17th centuries, and the Tower of Fame built by Jains in the 12th century.

WHERE TO STAY NEAR THE FORT

About the best of the modest accommodations in Chittaurgarh are **Hotel Padmini,** Chanderiya Road (☎ 41), which has 20 rooms priced at Rs 400 ($13.33) for a double; and RTDC's **Hotel Panna** (☎ 4123), which has 31 rooms, priced at Rs 450 ($15) for a double.

9 Mount Abu

The colorful city of Mount Abu (pop. 15,600), in southern Rajasthan, is both a charming hill resort and an important place of pilgrimage for the Jains, who come to visit the beautiful Dilwara Temples. Celebrated as a Jain religious site since the 11th century, Mount Abu was important even earlier to Shiva worshippers. Today the many centuries-old archeological treasures found here remain relatively unknown to Westerners, who rarely visit.

On a plateau 4,000 feet above sea level, the 25-square-mile resort has a terrific climate. When the plains sizzle, the local temperature rarely goes above 85°F; in winter temperatures reach highs of 75°F and lows of about 55°F. Even the rainy season, June to September, is relatively light. So it's not surprising that in summer whole families make their way to Mount Abu by train, bus, or car for a breath of cool air. The crush is on again during the 10-day fall Diwali holiday.

ESSENTIALS

GETTING TO MOUNT ABU

BY AIR The nearest airport is Udaipur, 185 kilometers away; see section 8, "Udaipur," above, for more information on available flights and prices.

BY RAIL go to Abu Road, the railhead, 27 kilometers (16½ miles) below Mount Abu, where you pick up a bus from 6am to 9pm, Rs 8 (26¢) for the 27-kilometer, one-hour trip to Mount Abu. You can also buy a taxi or jeep seat for about Rs 10 (33¢) per person. There's a Rs 5 (16¢) passenger tax.

The shortest train ride is from Ahmedabad, approximately five hours on the *Ahmedabad Mail.* From Jodhpur it's about six hours on the *Surya Nagri Express.* There's also train service from Jaipur (11 hours); Agra (25 hours); and Delhi (18½ hours).

BY BUS Most people travel by bus to Mount Abu from any of a number of cities in Rajasthan and Gujarat. Good roads in Gujarat make Ahmedabad a popular starting point for a seven-hour bus trip, at Rs 85 ($2.83) in a deluxe bus run by travel agents. Alternatively, there are four state roadways buses from Ahmedabad, at a lower price. From Udaipur, the seven-hour trip by deluxe coach costs about Rs 70 ($2.33); by state-run buses, the trip takes seven to 11 hours, depending on the route, and costs about half that amount.

BY HIRED CAR Car and driver from Ahmedabad is of course costlier, but the drive is especially interesting from Udaipur, which takes you through Pindwada, a tiny town famous for tailors who make colorful full skirts and short, midriff-baring tops worn by women in this region.

Visitor Information

The **Tourist Information Center** is opposite the Bus Stand (☎ 3151), open from 8 to 11am, and 4 to 8pm in season; 10am to 5pm off-season.

City Layout

When you arrive in Mount Abu you'll be on the main street in town. Here are the bus stand and, opposite it, the tourist bureau bazaar, travel agents, and many hotels.

Getting Around Mount Abu

Local taxis have fixed fares for sightseeing; small carts for carrying luggage sometimes also carry people. Jeep tours can be arranged through local travel agents. The RSRTC runs buses to Dilwara and Achalgarh. You can walk almost everywhere; for instance, it's about one hour to Dilwara, a half hour to Sunset and Honeymoon Points, or just a few minutes to Nakki Lake from the bus stand.

WHAT TO SEE & DO

Follow the main road from the bus stand for a pleasant walk of about three minutes through the bazaar, and you will be at **Nakki Lake,** one of the main centers of activity. The many photographers' stalls near the lake display velvet robes in royal blue and deep red trimmed with gold braid—costumes to rent for a picture to take home. Nakki Lake's landmark is **Toad Rock,** so named because it looks like a toad about to leap into the water. Locals are fond of pointing out other rocks that resemble Nandi and camels, but they are open to many interpretations.

You can rent a boat with or without a boatman to row you. Ponies with handlers can be hired to take you around the lake. It's a nice walk as well, with a stop to see **Raghunath Temple.** Or you can head away from the lake up Raj Bhavan Road to the **Art Museum and Gallery** (hours are 10am to 5pm, closed Friday; no admission charge) opposite the post office. In the small collection are some textiles and stone pieces from the 9th to 12th centuries.

Early morning is the best time go 3 kilometers (2 miles) from town to join the pious for the steep climb up 226 stone-cut steps to the old **Adhar Devi Temple** dedicated to Durga. The goddess's shrine is carved into a natural cleft in a huge rock. To enter, you bend down and slide in.

The five **Dilwara Temples,** 5 kilometers (3 miles) from town, welcoming non-Jain visitors from noon to 6pm, are the outstanding sight of Mount Abu. Before entering them, you must remove all leather, shoes, belts, handbags, and camera cases; there's a Rs 5 (17¢) camera fee, and photography of images is prohibited. Built and rebuilt over 11 centuries, the temples are kept in flawless condition through generous donations by believers.

Two of the temples are most important: **Adinatha** and **Luna Vasahi,** or **Neminatha Temple.** Their carvings are some of the more splendid in all of India. The five temples are in a compound enclosed by a high white wall. There are guides on the premises.

The oldest temple, **Adinatha,** was built in 1031 by Vimal, a minister under an early Gujarati ruler Bhim Deva. One of the earliest Jain temples in India, it is made of pure white marble, austere outside and extravagantly sculptured inside, with deities and dancing figures and fantastic lacelike designs. In a hall outside the temple, images of Vimal and his family ride marble elephants in a procession to the handsomely carved domed portico. Inside the temple, within his little shrine, the smooth bronze statue of Adinath sits cross-legged, adorned with jewels and gazing out at passing pilgrims. The elaborately carved dome is supported by richly carved pillars. More carved pillars—48 freestanding in all—lead to the temple courtyard enclosed by a wall with 52 little cells, each a house for a seated image of a Jain saint.

The **Luna Vasahi** or **Neminatha Temple**, to the north, was built about 200 years later by the brothers Tejapala and Vastupals, ministers to Raja Viradhawaler, a ruler of Gujarat. While this temple follows the same general plan as the first, it is even more richly ornamented, resembling a marble tapestry. Here, however, marble carving reaches its apogee in the partly opened lotus flower drooping like a pendant from the dome. The mason-laborers were surely a dedicated group of craftsmen. They were also encouraged to do carvings of the utmost delicacy with gifts of gold and silver coins equal to the weight of the marble shavings.

Lesser temples are **Chamukha,** the drab structure to the left of the entrance, an amalgam of 13th- and 15th-century styles. Inside there's a statue a Tirthankara Parsvanatha (a Jain teacher), and Ganesha is outside. **Risah Deo**, opposite the Luna Vasihi, was never completed. Construction began in the late 13th century, stopped during a war with Gujarat, and never resumed. It houses an enormous brass Tirthankara image made of gold, copper, brass, silver, and zinc. The fifth temple, **Digambara,** is severe in style.

Eleven kilometers (6½ miles) from town is the **Achalgarh Fort** housing the **Achaleswhar Temple.** Instead of a lingam in this temple, there's a deep pit, which is supposed to go to the netherworld. My guide told me that Shiva jumped in and made the pit, leaving behind his right toe, which is now worshipped here. Shiva's sacred bull, Nandi, is handsome here in bronze; the wounds on his back were made long ago by Muslims searching for riches they thought were inside. A path lined with souvenir stalls leads up to a notable group of Jain temples—there's a Rs 5 (16¢) camera charge and, again, no leather and no pictures of idols—not as minutely decorated as the Dilwara Temples, but eloquent on their own and on a higher plateau with fine views of the valley. Down in the parking area is an empty tank and some stone statues of buffaloes and a king taking aim at them with a bow and arrow. The grouping illustrates an old legend about the tank: It was once filled with ghee (clarified butter), which greedy demons disguised as buffaloes drank at night until the king put an end to their pleasure by piercing them with his arrows.

Fifteen kilometers from town is the end of the plateau and **Guru Shikhar,** at 1,722 meters (5,653 feet) the highest point in Rajasthan. Up some 300 steps is **Ari Rishi Temple,** nearly always full of tourists admiring the view.

Seven miles southeast, off the Mount Abu Road, a flight of 700 stone stairs gently descends through the lush valley to **Gaumukh Temple,** where a small stream flows through the mouth of a marble cow and gives this temple its name. According to ancient legend, the tank here, Agni Kund, marks the spot where the sage Vashista ignited the fire that created the four Rajput clans. On this site is a stone figure of Vashista, with Rama and Krishna on either side. Around the ashram are a number of interesting stone carvings excavated nearby. Before you climb up, monks will ask you to sign their guest book and give you a write-up to read.

There are many lovely viewpoints in Mount Abu. At least once during any visit every tourist joins the huge crowd on the rocks and steps at **Sunset Point** to see the surroundings at the end of day. **Honeymoon Point** is also popular in the flush of sunset. Other viewpoints are **The Crags** and **Robert's Spur**.

Guided Tours

The **RTDC** and **RSRTC** conduct two daily tours that include Dilwara Temples, Achalgarh, Guru Shikhar, Nakki Lake, Sunset Point Toad Rock, Adhar Devi, and Om Shanti Bhawan at 8:30am to 1:30pm, and 1:30 to 7pm, at Rs 30 ($1) per person. For information and reservations call 3151, 3129, or 3434, or drop in at the tourist information center for a booking (see "Visitor Information," above); check to make sure the guide speaks English. Tours are heavily booked in season, so advance reservations are advised.

Shopping

Some of the most popular shops are clustered around Nakki Lake; others are near the Bus Stand, and there are stalls near most of the monuments. Look for objects in local soft marble, sandalwood, and sandstone; lac bangles; and printed linen. Custom-tailored and ready-made salwar-kamiz are other good buys.

The **Rajasthan Government Emporium,** Raj Bhavan Road, features the local crafts, **Khadi Gramudyog** and **Saurashtrsa Emporium** have similar inventories.

Chacha Museum, one of the best-known stores in town, has some one-of-kind and unusual items in a special room. They may not be antiques, but they'll be treasures you won't find in other places. Hours are 9:30am to 10pm daily. Prices are fixed.

Roopali, near Nakki Lake, open from 9am to 9pm every day, has a fine selection of silver jewelry that is sold by weight. Locally, silver anklets are chic; hook two together, and they become a charming necklace.

Where to Stay

Most peak-season rates apply during **Diwali** (in October/November; see "Festivals" in Chapter 1, "Getting to Know India") and from May to June, although Mount Abu is officially in season from March to June and September to December. It's possible to find bargains even when the resort is in season, but not at its peak. Sales taxes add about 6% to 12% to your food. The following are only a few of the hotels found in Mount Abu. You will undoubtedly make your own discoveries, so let me hear about them if you do.

Most hotels feature rooms with private attached baths, some have air-conditioning (not essential up here), and several accept international credit cards.

Doubles for Less Than $10

At the **Hotel Saraswati,** opposite the taxi stand, Mount Abu 307601, the best rooms are in annex. The lower-priced rooms are off the courtyard and not as well maintained. Hot water is available on tap from 7 to 9am. The dining hall is open from 11am to 1:30pm, 6:30 to 8:30pm and serves vegetarian food.

Nearby is the better maintained **Tourist Guest House** (☎ 3160), which also has a pretty garden. There is no restaurant, but room service meals and snacks are available.

Near the bus stand, the **Sheratone** (☎ 3544) has no decor to speak of, but the maintenance is a cut above others in this low price range, and that's worth mentioning.

If none of these appeals to you, there are many other cheaper hotels in and about Mt. Abu in various states of repair. You might have to look at more than one before settling in. The **Youth Hostel,** a claustrophobic dorm near the bus stand, charges about Rs 30 ($1) per head.

DOUBLES FOR LESS THAN $23.33

Set back from the road by a small courtyard, bordered by potted plants, two hotels under the same management are **Hotel Navjivan** (☎ 3153) and the **Hotel Samrat International** (☎ 3177). They also share a glitzy reception area with a mirrored ceiling, crystal chandeliers, a sunken conversation pit surrounded by a marble rail, wood and metal molded doors, and pictures of Shiva, Ganesha, and Krishna on the walls.

Samrat International, the fancier of the two is also bit more expensive. Western-style bathrooms predominate. Punjabi vegetarian meals are available at the Samrat. Gujarat-style vegetarian food predominates at the Navjivan.

Near the bus stand, the **Hotel Madhuban,** Mount Abu 307501 (☎ 3121), has 10 nice, clean rooms and a convenient location.

Opposite the polo grounds, the **Hotel Abu International,** P.O. Box 29, Mount Abu 307501 (☎ 3177), has 43 simply furnished, clean rooms with granite floors. The hotel serves both Punjabi- and Gujarati-style vegetarian foods.

About half a mile from town is **Sunset Inn** (☎ 3194), which offers 40 pleasant, modern rooms with good ventilation, in a refreshing wooded setting.

RTDC's Hotel Shikhar (☎ 3129) has a beautiful view and rooms ranging from run-down (in the old block) to pretty good (in the newer cottages and annex). Better maintenance overall would help; yet the pretty view, pleasant management, and modest prices are attractive—the highest price is Rs 400 ($13.33) for a superdeluxe—and these rooms are usually fully booked.

Opposite the Tourist Bungalow, **Hotel Aravali** (☎ 3216), near the veterinary hospital, has 18 doubles, pleasantly furnished and well maintained, in little buildings around a pretty terraced garden with plants lining the walks and stairs.

DOUBLES FOR LESS THAN $50

If you've been staying in palace hotels in Rajasthan, you can also have a royal resting place here in one of the two Heritage hotels. The first is a Heritage Hotel, the stately **Palace Hotel** (Bikaner House), Dilwara Road, Mount Abu 307501 (☎ 3121, 3133, or 3673; fax 3672), about half a mile from town. This imposing granite and sandstone mansion, with acres of gardens and a lake, was the summer palace of the Maharaja of Bikaner from 1893 until 1961. The palace is loaded with atmosphere and antiques—overstuffed chairs, tiger heads, and faded photos of the tiger hunts at which they met their fates, and photos of the family and visiting friends. Rooms are regal sized, with bathrooms large enough to hold a polo team. In the grand old dining room, a latticed screen conceals the gallery that once permitted the harem ladies to see activities below without being seen. The food is good and the service superb, but the linens need attention. Having all your meals here will cost about Rs 400 ($13.33) per person; the food is good. There's a 10% service charge for both lodging and meals.

The cozier **Connaught House,** Rajendra Marg (☎ 3360 or 3439; fax in Jodhpur 0291-35373), formerly the summer residence of Jodhpur's Maharaja and still in his family, is also filled with memorabilia of bygone days. The six-room bungalow set in a pretty terraced garden and the uninspired eight-room motel-like block in back (quieter than the bungalow) are walking distance from town. The rooms are simply but creatively furnished with pieces that recall the past, as do the chintz-upholstered wicker furnishings in the lounge. Having all your meals here costs about Rs 400 ($13.33) per person. Tariff is similar to the Palace.

Sunrise Palace, Old Bharatpur Kothi (☎ 3214; in Ahmedabad ☎ 0121-443658; in Baroda ☎ 0265-54061); this charming, 16-room palace-turned-hotel atop a hill has a lot of charm and a lovely view. Cozier than some palaces, its ambience nonetheless speaks of a colorful past.

You might also try **Cama Rajputana Club Resort,** near the Circuit House, Mount Abu (☎ 3163), a Heritage Hotel with 42 rooms. It has all the comforts you only wish you had at home—swimming pool, squash and tennis courts, golf course, health club, and huge, landscaped gardens; multicuisine restaurant, and more.

Hotel Hillock, P.B. no. 40 (opposite the petrol pump), Mount Abu (☎ 3467), has pretty gardens and lawns and 31 rooms with no special decor to speak of. It's modern and clean, though, and friendly as well.

Centrally located near the Bus Stand, the three-star **Hilltone Hotel,** P.B. no. 18, Mount Abu 39751 (☎ 3112), has 46 rooms, in a main block and cottages, as well as a swimming pool surrounded by two acres of landscaped grounds. The airy, cheerful rooms are simply but adequately furnished. The privacy of the cottages makes them popular with honeymooners; their decor varies. One of them has a big round bed, drum tables with leather trim, rustic chairs, straw floor matting, and peaked thatch roof. The pleasant **Handi** restaurant is open for breakfast, lunch, and dinner, serving vegetarian and nonvegetarian dishes. Inquire about off-season discounts.

Set in a big garden, the **Chacha Inn Hotel**, Main Road, Mt. Abu (☎ 3347), has 22 up-to-date rooms and a restaurant featuring service under the stars. The hotel, a 10-minute stroll to the town center, is owned by Chacha Museum, one of the best known shops in town.

WHERE TO EAT

The Hilltone Hotel's **Handi** is decorated with clay pots (handis) and serves many dishes in metal handis. This is one of the places to head if you're tired of vegetarian food. A meal with soup, chicken main course, and sweet should cost Rs 200 ($6.66). The hours are 7 to 10am, noon to 3pm, and 7 to 11pm. The hotel's **Kalali Bar** is open from 10am to 11pm. Multicuisine restaurants can also be found in the **Hotel Savera Palace, Hotel Hillock,** and **Chacha Hotel** (which serves in the garden).

The no-frills **Angan Dining Hall** in the Hotel Navjivan serves an excellent, abundant Gujarati thali with wheat bread, rice, and four vegetable curries for about Rs 25 ($1.20); if you want curds and a sweet it's a bit more. Hours are 1 to 2:30pm, and 7 to 9pm. The restaurant is popular with Gujarati tour groups. Other places with good vegetarian thalis are **Hotel Maharajah International** and **Hotel Saraswati.** Both serve from 11am to 1:30pm, and 6:30 to 8:30pm.

The cheapest snacks and light meals are served in the small restaurants near the Taxi Stand; among them is **Veena,** with delicious South Indian specialties. More South Indian fare is available at the aptly named **Madras,** also nearby. Try **Nakki Lake Sarovar** for tasty budget-priced Indian and Rajasthani dishes.

Heading North

6

1 Haridwar & Rishikesh

Thousands of Hindus every year make their pilgrimage to the little town of Haridwar (pop. 190,000), whose major claim to fame is that it's about as near as most people can get to where the holy River Ganges emerges from the mountains and meets the plains.

It's an article of faith among many people who can afford it to carry to Haridwar the ashes of a dead relative and to carry away some sacred water from the river—the same river that is treated with equal devotion in the holy city of Varanasi, which nestles alongside its bank so many hundreds of miles to the south.

From Delhi (216 kilometers; 134 miles), visitors can make their own pilgrimages to Haridwar by either train or road, the road passing through countryside thick with sugarcane fields and clay pits, which are studded with primitive brick-making plants to mold the raw material.

Rishikesh, another town of spiritual significance, is easily visited as an excursion from Haridwar, which has more direct bus and train service, is discussed separately at the end of this section.

ESSENTIALS

GETTING TO HARIDWAR

BY PLANE Jolly Grant Airport is 35 kilometers away from Haridwar, but at present there are no flights.

BY TRAIN There are four trains a day from Delhi—Rs 600 ($20) AC First; Rs 400 ($13.33) two-tier sleeper; Rs 65 ($2.16) Second—but the trip takes more than seven hours on the fastest.

BY BUS There is regular bus service from Delhi to Haridwar (four hours). The fare in luxury class is Rs 50 ($1.66) to Rs 60 ($2). There is also service from Dehra Dun (1¼ hours)and other places within Uttar Pradesh and India.

BY HIRED CAR By car it's a leisurely drive of about four hours; **Cheetal,** about halfway between Delhi and Haridwar, with a flagstone terrace, garden, and immaculate toilets, is a pleasant stop for snack—tea and toast, Rs 27 (90¢)—or meal.

A four-passenger car and driver from Delhi for a two-day trip to Haridwar and Rishikesh runs about Rs 3,000 ($100), plus overnight charges for the driver.

Visitor Information

The **U.P. Government Regional Tourist Office,** opposite the Railway Station in Haridwar(☎ 427330), is open from 10am to 5pm; the **Tourist Information Centre,** Railway Station (☎ 427817), is open from 5am to 12pm; another office is located in Ganga Sabha, near Hari-ki-Pairi (☎ 427925).

Getting Around Haridwar

Vikrams ply fixed routes with fixed fares (Rs 1 [3¢] per stage, may be slightly higher now). Taxis can be hired at the Haridwar Road Bus Stand and Railway Station, at taxi stands for fixed rates (supposedly), or arranged through hotels. Bargain for cycle rickshas, auto rickshas, and tongas.

Sightseeing an entire day in Haridwar by scooter ricksha should cost Rs 70 ($2.33) to Rs 75 ($2.50) after bargaining to set the rate; by taxi you will pay Rs 150 ($5).

Share taxis run between Haridwar and Rishikesh; their rates are given under "Getting to Rishikesh," below.

When to Visit

Haridwar welcomes thousands of pilgrims each spring to celebrate the river's birth. Another key time is mid-April for Bishwawat Sankranti, a huge fair. But the fall, too, is very pleasant from September to November, and because this is a holy city, there can be festivals at any time. During the Kumbh Mela, every 12 years (the next is in 1998), millions throng to bathe in the Ganges. May to November is peak tourist season.

WHAT TO SEE & DO IN HARIDWAR

There are two main centers of attraction in Haridwar. First is the **Hari-ki-Pairi** ("Steps to God"), the main bathing ghat; this is also the name of the fascinating bazaar that leads off it.

The time to get to Hari-Ki-Pairi, the steps on which the priests perform their blessings called *Ganga Aarti,* is about 6pm. Then the whole area, including the area beside the clock tower across the water, as well as the Centenary Bridge that leads to it, is thronged with pilgrims.

Many of the faithful float lotus leaves made into incense-lit boats on the river. Each tiny boat filled with flower petals and camphor chips finally becomes a mere twinkle downstream. Conch horns sound, bells ring, holy chants fill the air. Saffron-robed sadhus and beggars compete for the good will of Hindus intent on immersing themselves in the holy waters that flow so fast that chains anchored to the steps are used for support by bathers.

All around are stalls from which visitors can buy every possible kind of container to carry home the holy water. It is said to be so pure that it will remain fresh for years. There are brass and copper bowls as well as cheap vessels converted from old ghee (clarified butter) or food tins sold for a few paise.

Walking along the river you see many bathing ghats (landings), holy men squatting under trees, and lanes leading off to the main bazaar. Five bridges span the river away from the hubbub.

The most interesting temple is **Mansi Devi,** crowning a hill of the Shivaliks and accessible by ropeway or foot, a five-minute journey—Rs 10 (33¢) round-trip, from 8am to noon, and 2 to 5pm. The temple is dedicated to the goddess who grants wishes, but you won't have to wish for a better view. The tank below the temple honors the Sun god, Surya Kund.

Guided Tours

U.P. Tourism in Haridwar offers four full-day tours from the Motel Rahi (☎ 427370), opposite the Railway Station in Haridwar. Tour no. 1 lasts from 8am to 7pm and covers major temples, aarti, and local market shopping. Tour no. 2 is from 8am to 6pm, visiting religious sights in Rishikesh, Lahksman Jhula, and Chilla Wildlife and Rajaji National Parks. The prices for both of these tours are Rs 100 ($3.33) for adults (with lunch), Rs 70 ($2.33) without lunch; prices for children are Rs 65 ($2.16) with lunch and Rs 50 ($1.66) without lunch. Tour no. 3, from 8am to 7pm, includes Haridwar, Rishikesh, and Rajaji National Park. Tour no. 4, to Dehra Dun, Mussoorie, and Kempty Falls, is from 8am to 8pm. Prices for the latter two tours are Rs 135 ($4.50) for adults with lunch, Rs 100 ($3.33) without lunch; for children, Rs 90 ($3) and Rs 65 ($2.16).

Shopping

Browse the **Moti Bazar** with its piles of colored powders and gleaming brassware and colorful saris. Woolens, wooden handicrafts, semiprecious stones, and, of course, Gamgaka (a bottle of Ganga water) are other local items.

WHERE TO STAY IN HARIDWAR

Because pilgrims come to Haridwar in such numbers in the warmer months, it's best to reserve a room. Be sure to check on out-of-season rates wherever you stay. Remember that in both Haridwar and Rishikesh all nonvegetarian foods (including eggs) and alcoholic drinks are prohibited at all times. Many visitors base in Rishikesh and sightsee in Haridwar. Following are some choices in Haridwar.

Doubles for Less Than Rs 750 ($25)

Mansarovar, Upper Road, Haridwar (☎ 426501), has 56 clean rooms, a few air-conditioned; this hotel also has a conference hall and shops. Rates range from a non-AC single for Rs 200 ($6.66) to an AC double for Rs 500 ($16.66). It's the best in this price range.

Hotel Midtown, Railway Road, Haridwar 249001 (☎ 426507; fax 426001), has 23 double rooms, all with modern furniture, 10 with air-conditioning. Rates are about the same as for the Mansarovar. Service charge is 10%.

The river view is a plus point at the otherwise undistinguished **Teerth,** Subhash Ghat, Hari-ki-Pairi (☎ 427111). There are 29 rooms, some air-conditioned at Rs 750 ($25) for a double; there are shops and a parking area.

The **Hotel Aarti,** Railway Road (☎ 427456), with 33 rooms, all air-cooled doubles, has clean, no-frills rooms; some air-conditioned. The rate for a double room is about Rs 350 ($11.66) to Rs 400 ($13.33). There is no restaurant, but you can get snacks.

The UP's **Tourist Bungalow** is at Belwala (☎ 426430), on the far side of the Ganga Canal, isolated by the wide canal from all the noise and crowds, yet near enough so you won't miss the action. There are 19 simple rooms and a dorm. At the bungalow the highest rate is Rs 500 ($16.66) for an air-conditioned double. The dorm is Rs 40 ($1.33) per person. There's also a pleasant riverside snack bar and indoor restaurant.

With 19 rooms, UP Tourism's **Motel Rahi,** opposite the Railway Station (☎ 426430), is another option in this price range. Prices start at Rs 200 ($6.66) for non–air-conditioned double and top off at Rs 500 ($16.66) for an air-conditioned double. A dorm bed is Rs 40 ($1.33). There is a restaurant.

Doubles for Less Than Rs 1,500 ($50)

Surprise, Delhi-Haridwar Road, Jwalapur, Haridwar 249001 (☎ 427780), is the swankiest. Located 1 1/2 kilometers out of town, it has 45 rooms, some with air-conditioning. Rates begin at Rs 325 ($10.83) or Rs 450 ($15) for an air-cooled single or double and go up to Rs 600 ($20) or 950 ($31.66) for an AC single or double. There is a nice lawn and two restaurants—rooftop for Indian food and a view, ground floor for nonvegetarian (since the hotel is outside the city), a swimming pool, and shops.

Suvidha, Sharavan Nath Nagar (☎ 427423), with 29 rooms, is well maintained, partially air-conditioned, and centrally located; restaurants are for residents only. Air-cooled doubles are Rs 500 ($16.66); AC doubles are Rs 700 ($23.33). Singles are about 20% less.

Indian-Style Hotels

There is a long row of simple Indian-style hotels on the opposite (main) bank of the canal. They are extensively used by pilgrims and some come equipped with kitchens. A number of hotels are near the railway station, and tariffs range from Rs 100 ($3.33) to Rs 300 ($10). Here are some choices in this price range that were a cut above the others.

Kailash Hotel, Shiv Murti (☎ 6789), near the railway station, has 70 air-cooled rooms, all with baths attached, half with Western-style toilets. The furnishings are modern, and the 24 deluxe rooms have such amenities as telephones, carpeting, TVs, and running hot water. The restaurant is open from 6am to 10pm. There are generous off-season reductions. Tops in this price range.

Gurdev, Railway Road (☎ 427101), has 30 rooms, seven air-conditioned, some with baths attached. Rooms with balconies are nicest.

Sahni, Niranjani, Akhara Road, SN Nagar (☎ 427906), has 22 rooms; some with baths attached are better than others. Hot water in buckets is available without charge.

Ashrams

Haridwar's ashrams and other religious sites predate those more well known at Rishikesh. One of the most important, **Saptrishi Ashram,** is dedicated to Seven Sages who trapped the Ganges and agreed to release it after King Bhagirath agreed to split the river into seven streams. For a list of other ashrams and holy sites, consult the Regional Tourist Office, opposite the railway station. Tourists can stay in ashrams for a nominal donation, and vegetarian meals are served. Tourists usually stay in the better known ashrams in Rishikesh.

Where to Eat in Haridwar

Since Haridwar attracts visitors from all over India, you can find a variety of Indian regional cuisines.

On Railway Station Road, **Chotiwala Restaurant,** across from the tourist office, **Ashiana,** and **Aahar** all have tasty vegetarian curries, as does **Hoshiapuri** on Upper Road. They're all open from 8am to 10pm. For South Indian foods, try **Bester,** on Jassa Ram Road, or **Hoshiapuri.** All are cheap by Western standards. Two blocks up the road is the **Brijwasi Mathura Wak Sweet Center,** with all kinds of Indian sweets in clean glass cases. One of these is chandralaka, at Rs 5 (16¢) per piece, a crisp pastry with syrup and nut filling.

An Excursion to Rishikesh

About 16 miles away from Haridwar (with regular, connecting buses) is Rishikesh (pop. 72,000), whose very name brings to mind religious sages. It's a small and not particularly fascinating town although there are some pretty views where the River Ganges first emerges from the Himalayan foothills. It is usually visited as an excursion from Haridwar.

Essentials

GETTING TO RISHIKESH Rishikesh is usually an excursion from Haridwar, which is a more convenient rail and bus stop. There is one train a day from Delhi to Rishikesh via Haridwar. If you did not engage a car and driver in Delhi, a share taxi from Haridwar to Rishikesh costs about Rs 25 (83¢) per person; a full taxi costs Rs 225 ($7.50) to Rs 250 ($8.33).

VISITOR INFORMATION There's a **UP Government Tourist Office** in Rishikesh on Railway Road, and during Yatra season another is open at Samyukt Yatra Bus Stand.

GETTING AROUND RISHIKESH Vikrams operate on fixed routes with fixed fares; auto rickshas are available for negotiated rates. Cycle rickshas and tongas are easily available; bargain for a fair fare. Taxis can be hired from the taxi stand on Haridwar Road or at other taxi stands around town, at the bus stands, or at the railway station. Ferry service crosses the river at Sivananda (Ram) Jhula; boatmen will take you for a ride on the Ganges from the Swargashram Ghat; negotiate the price.

What to See & Do in Rishikesh

The **Divine Life Society** is probably the best-known organization in a town positively filled with ashrams and other religious organizations. Started by Swami Sivananda in 1936, it maintains a lovely blue-domed temple on the hillside, always filled with adherents from many countries chanting prayers, consonant with the society's theme that all religions are one and have more to share than to fight about. Just in front of the temple, at river's edge, is the society's office with plenty of literature available, and if you wait patiently, a boat (free) will ferry you across the swift-flowing Ganges to some well-worth-visiting temples and ashrams on the opposite bank. Or you can walk over the river on Sivananda (Ram) Jhula, one of the two suspension bridges in town, the site of **Parmarth Niketan,** and immense ashram with 100 rooms.

A 1-mile walk on the far side will bring you to the ashram of **Maharishi Mahesh Yogi,** one-time guru to the Beatles and other well-known Westerners. It's relaxing to just stroll along the Ganges with no specific mission, stopping to admire views, meditate, or enjoy solitude.

Crossing Lakshman Jhula, the other suspension bridge upstream near the Lakshman Temple, offers picturesque views and the opportunity to look in at a number of religious centers. The **Nilkanth Mahadev Temple,** topping a 1,700-meter-high hill, ten kilometers from town, offers some other impressive vistas.

Aarti (prayers) are offered to the Ganga each evening at **Triveni Ghat.** To participate, buy a little leaf boat, and when the time comes, set it off to sail at sunset with all the others, their sticks of incense perfuming the air.

Outdoor Activities

Rishikesh is beginning to gain importance as a river-sports center for white-water rafting, canoeing, and kayaking, and also as a base camp for treks and hikes into Garhwal Himalayas (some very challenging peaks) and other destinations. The **Garhwal Mandal Vikas Nigam** (GMVN), Muni-ki-Reti organizes treks, hikes, and sports activities from Rishikesh. The GMVN office at Muni-ki-Reti can give information on these and other sports activities. You might try some of the local travel agents as well.

Shopping

You can browse and buy at bazaars in Dehra Dun Road, Haridwar Road, Ghat Road, and Railway Road. **The UP Handlooms,** Haridwar Road, and **Gandhi Ashram Khadi Bhandar,** Haridwar Road have especially good textile sections and lovely handlooms shawls. Local crafts include basket weaving.

Where to Stay in Rishikesh

Doubles for Less Than Rs 400 ($13.33)

Popular with trekkers is the **GMVN's Tourist Bungalow Complex Rishilok,** Muni-ki-Reti, Rishikesh 249201 (☎ 30373), consisting of 46 rooms in cottages, some with private bathrooms and some with shared baths. Non-AC doubles range from Rs 120 ($4) to Rs 400 ($$13.33); singles pay 75% of double rates. The restaurant serves Chinese and Indian foods.

Hotel Green, Swargashram Area, Rishikesh, is clean and quiet, with some air-conditioned rooms, and near the Parmarth Niketan ashram. To get to the hotel, take a taxi from Rishikesh to the Sivananda Jhula footbridge. Walk across the bridge, and follow the directional signs to the Parmarth Niketan Ashram and Ved Niketan Ashram, which are separated by a narrow passageway and turn left. Continue through to the end of the passageway for Hotel Green.

In the Lahksman Jhula area, **Shikar,** is simple, neat, and clean; hot water is supplied in buckets; the rooftop view and good food are pluses. Nice quiet ambience.

Reader Aziz Kommel of Etna, New York, suggests **Peasant's Cottage,** Tapovan, near Lahksman Jhula Bridge (☎ 31167). There are seven simple rooms, two with baths attached, and splendid Ganges views. A double is Rs 390 ($13) with meals.

A Double for Less Than Rs 600 ($20)

The centrally located **Inderlok Hotel,** Railway Road, Rishikesh 249201 (☎ 30555; fax 30556), has a plant-decked patio and roof garden with mountain views. The 52 wallpapered double rooms, some air-conditioned, are clean and functionally furnished, and management seems more professional than many others in town. The **Indrani** restaurant serves Indian and some Western dishes.

Doubles for Less Than Rs 1,250 ($41.16)

Most of these hotels offer yoga or can arrange yoga instruction for you.

Among the top spots, **Hotel Natraj,** Dehra Dun Road, Rishikesh 249201 (☎ 31099) has 38 air-conditioned rooms, an elaborate crystal chandelier above the reception counter, and lots of imitation marble and brocade throughout. The hotel needs sprucing up with a paint job and better maintenance. Frills include a swimming pool and health club. There's a 24-hour Indian vegetarian restaurant and a multicuisine vegetarian restaurant with open-terrace dining. A suite with a Jacuzzi runs Rs 1,250 ($41.16).

Vying for top honors is **Hotel Ganga Kinare,** 16 Virbhadara Rd., Rishikesh, 240201 (☎ 30566), with central air-conditioning and a riverside restaurant on a private ghat. Rooms are functional, but from some the river view more than makes up for the lack of decor. Rates range from Rs 1,100 ($36.66) to Rs 1,600 ($53.33) for a double. The hotel's management will send someone with you to the best place to see the sunrise on the river. The hotel holds its own Aarti ceremony during peak season.

Hotel Mandakini International, 63 Haridwar Rd., Rishikesh 240201 (☎ 30781) has 31 clean rooms, some air-conditioned, and very accommodating management. Traffic noise is a problem for front-facing rooms. Singles range in price from Rs 600 ($20) to Rs 800 ($26.66); doubles are Rs 700 ($23.33).

Hotel Baseraa, 1 Ghat Rd., Rishikesh 240201 (☎ 30720), is a clean and unpretentious place with 39 freshly painted rooms. When I looked in, the halls were in need of a paint job. Some rooms are air-conditioned. A non-AC single costs Rs 350 ($11.66), a non-AC double Rs 400 ($13.33); AC rates are Rs 450 ($15) and Rs 550 ($18.33) for a single or double, respectively. The pleasant rooftop terrace is a plus.

Ashrams

Many people who come to Rishikesh want to stay in one of the ashrams to experience the spirituality for which India is world-famous. Among the ashrams most welcoming to Westerners is **Sivanand Ashram** (Divine Life Society). To apply, you must write at least two months in advance to: General Secretary, Divine Life Society, Rishikesh (U.P.) 249201 (☎ 30040), and enclose a letter saying why you would like to stay at the ashram. The ashram offers lectures, meditation, and yoga.

Rishikesh is a major center for ashrams that offer accommodations to pilgrims. Other important ashrams accepting visitors to stay for meditation and study yoga include **Yoga Niketan, Omkaranand Ashram**, located above Yoga Niketan, which also conducts classes in Sanskrit, Hindi, music, classical dance, and English at the **Omkaran** and **Visvakul** at Muni-ki-Reti; **Swargashram** ashram; **Geeta Bhavan** (however, foreigners are not accepted at the ashram); **Parmnath Niketan,** a mammoth ashram with 600 beds (foreigners must apply in advance); and **Ved Niketan,** to name only a few Rishikesh ashrams. In checking, I found instances where cleanliness is not next to godliness. Facilities were dirty, and some rooms little more than windowless cells with cots. You are advised to look at the accommodation before you make a choice. Rates start at about Rs 50 ($1.66). The tourist information office on Railway Road in Rishikesh can give you information on ashrams as well as dharmashalas, simple accommodation for pilgrims.

WHERE TO EAT IN RISHIKESH

As in Haridwar, you can get vegetarian food only, and no alcohol. The local favorite is **Chotawala,** Sivananda Jhula; among the restaurants on Railway Road, try **Darpan.**

2 Chandigarh

The "ivory tower school of architecture" is the way iconoclasts describe Chandigarh (pop. 575,000), capital of Punjab and Haryana states. Supporters say it's the prototype of all Indian cities to come. Looking around is the best way to understand these widely disparate views. Chances are, if you're an architect, you'll like the city better than other travelers do.

Chandigarh, coordinated by Le Corbusier, was designed by a team of international architects, including the master's cousin, Pierre Jeanneret, England's E. Maxwell Fry and Jane Drew, and a number of Indians. It was planned, like Brasilia, solely as a capital.

Gaudily painted cycle rickshas are about the only visible links to the past here, outside of the saris, salwar-kamiz, and other traditional clothing, museum exhibits, an occasional camel looking as abstract and committee-constructed as some of the buildings, and numerous wandering and highly revered cows, which span all centuries. In Chandigarh there are no winding lanes, cozy bazaars, and rakish houses. It's a rigidly laid-out, 50-sector city that looks cubistic and cold. The designers made extensive use of readily available concrete in its natural state, and as a result Chandigarh looks like a cement prairie, relieved only by some pastel-painted buildings.

The modern structures look more harmonious together than they might if grafted onto an older city—which almost was the case. After the Partition of 1947, when Lahore, then the capital of Punjab, went to Pakistan, both Shimla and Jullundur were used as new seats of government. When it was decided to start from scratch, the site for Chandigarh, at the base of the Shivalik Hills, was selected for its good soil and water supply, accessibility, and beauty. Construction was carried out mainly between 1951 and 1965.

Chandigarh was named a double capital when Haryana state was created out of the eastern portion of Punjab in 1966. The state was further divided in that same year—the hilly areas are now part of Himachal Pradesh. Shimla, the hill station summer seat of government during British days, is now year-round capital of Himachal Pradesh.

ESSENTIALS

GETTING THERE

BY PLANE Flights from Delhi on Indian Airlines, Jagson, and Archana cost $36; Indian Airlines flies on to Leh.

The airport is 11 kilometers from downtown. There is no airport bus, so negotiate a fair taxi fare.

BY TRAIN The best train from Delhi is the twice-daily (once on Sunday) *Shatabdi Express,* at either 10:20am, arriving 1:10pm; or 5:15pm, arriving 8pm. The fare is Rs 250 ($8.33) AC Chair, Rs 500 ($16.66) Executive. Other trains from Delhi include the *Howrah-Kalka Mail* (six hours) and *Himalayan Queen* (about 4 1/2 hours), the latter going on to Calcutta for Rs 493 ($16.43) AC First, Rs 57 ($1.90) Second. The railway station is 8 kilometers from the downtown are; prepaid (set fare) auto rickshas are available; taxis are also available at negotiable rates. CTU buses running to and from the station coordinate with train times. For railroad station inquiries call 22105; for reservations 22260.

BY BUS Interstate buses from the Interstate Bus Stand, Sector 17, offer the most frequent service between Chandigarh and various northern cities, such as Haridwar and Rishikesh (about 276 kilometers), Amritsar (452 kilometers), Kulu (270 kilometers), Manali (286 kilometers) and many others extending to the southern tip of Kanya Kumari (3,195 kilometers).

Between Delhi, 248 kilometers to the southeast, and Chandigarh there are several air-conditioned buses daily. The trip takes about five hours. Deluxe buses run between Chandigarh and Delhi, Jaipur, Shimla, Amritsar, and Manali.

The Inter-State Bus Terminus is the center of all roadway travel. It houses a post office, the City Rail Reservation Service Office, and is open from 8am to 1:45pm and 2 to 8pm; Sunday from 8am to 2pm. There is also a waiting room, a retiring room, snack stands, tourist information stands, a main taxi stand (open 24 hours; ☎ 544621), and a prepaid auto ricksha service. Here are some other important telephone numbers: **Haryana Roadways** (☎ 544014) and **Punjab Roadways** (☎ 544023); both offices are open from 6am to 11:45am, and 1:15pm to 8pm.

Air-conditioned bus service to Amritsar is offered by **Maharajah Travels;** the bus leaves from the Aroma Hotel Complex, Sector 22-C (☎ 44434).

VISITOR INFORMATION

Chandigarh Tourism Information Centre, located in the Inter-State Bus Terminums, is open from 9am to 5pm (☎ 543839). Chandigarh Tourism also has a counter at the airport and should have a counter open at the railway station by this time. In the same location is the **Punjab Tourism Information Centre**, which is open from 9am to 5pm.

You can also visit the **Tourist Information Office,** Chandigarh Administration, First Floor, ISBT, Sector 17 (☎ 544614), open from 9am to 5pm; **Information Office, CITCO tourist office** (☎ 544356); tourist offices for **Himachal Tourism,** Sector 22 (☎ 43569); for **Uttar Pradesh,** Sector 22 (☎ 41649); for **Haryana,** Sector 17 (☎ 542955); for **Punjab,** Sector 22 (☎ 43570).

Getting Around

Auto ricksha fares must be negotiated before you get in. The same goes for hugely popular cycle rickshas. Buses, invariably crowded, run throughout the city. Tourist taxis are unmetered; stands are in Sectors 17, 22, and 35. Bargain for the best rates. Here, as elsewhere, Westerners, being less savvy bargainers, usually pay more than Indians.

When to Visit

October to March is the best time for Punjab and neighboring Haryana. April, however, is the time of the Baisakhi festival, when bhangra dancers perform with wild abandon—their movements include standing on their fellow dancers' shoulders to form a human tower.

WHAT TO SEE & DO

The focal point of Chandigarh is the **Government Complex** at the city's northern end. The Secretariat, an elongated structure, cost Rs 14,049,000 to build. Tours are given every half hour; ask at Main Reception. Usually 15 people go together, but if that number doesn't show, you can go with those on hand, or by yourself for that matter. The nicest part about this building is the roof garden. It provides a refreshing vantage point for surveying the other buildings and the bustling officials below.

Nearby, the multipillared **High Court,** with its strange stucco sun screen, stands in a reflecting pool. This is the most frequently photographed of the government buildings. Primary-color panels break up gray expanses. There is no organized tour, but you are permitted to look around on your own. This building cost Rs 6,465,000.

Atop the huge chamber room in the **Assembly,** there's a dome that can be removed to let in light. Here you also can see a mural by Le Corbusier, which was given to Chandigarh by the French government and symbolizes evolution. The cost of this building: nearly Rs 12 million. There are tours on the half hour from 10:30am to 12:30pm and again from 2:30 to 4:30pm, or you can go on your own. Ask at the public reception desk.

In this same sector is a huge **Open Hand,** to symbolize the unity of humanity. A Museum of Knowledge is to be built in the future.

The **Cultural Zone,** in the west part of town, houses a museum and an art gallery, well worth seeing. Exhibits, which include modern works, date from 5,000 years ago or more to the Indus Valley Civilization. Hours are 10am to 4:30pm; closed Monday.

Connected with the Cultural Zone is a park in which the colleges are situated. More colleges—engineering, architecture, medicine, and research—lie to the north.

In other sectors, each approximately a half mile wide and 3 miles long, are housing, medical, shopping, and educational facilities for the residents. The city, home to 575,000, was planned for 500,000 maximum. There are 14 ranks of housing for government employees, from multiroom mansions for chief ministers to two rooms for the lowest-paid employees. Each sector supplies all the family's basic needs, as did the old-style villages of India. Newly arrived villagers, seeking work, live outside of town.

BEYOND THE GOVERNMENT ENCLAVE—FANTASIES & FLOWERS

Three of the best sights in and about Chandigarh are striking gardens,two in the city and one about 10 miles from town.

Almost in the shadows of Le Corbusier's geometric buildings in Sector 1 is the extraordinary 12-acre (and still growing) **Garden of Nek Chand.** He was the talented, self-taught artist who has created an epic out of found objects. One of the most remarkable aspects of Chand's park is that he got hold of so many castoffs. In India, almost nothing is thrown away: What can't be used again may be sold for some other use.

Entering Chand's fantastic park you first encounter several hundred statues of courtesans made from bicycle frames. But this is no X-rated show; in fact, meandering on the curving paths may take you back to the imagined wonderlands of your childhood.

In this remarkable community are hundreds of glistening birds made from more than a million broken-glass bangles, thousands of dancers molded from motorcycle mudguards, and intricate mosaics created from 10,000 electrical outlets. There are block-long fences constructed from burnt-out fluorescent tubing and warriors fashioned from cloth scraps astride scrap cloth steeds.

To go from one delightful section to another, you have to bend through archways suitable for Lilliputians. Chand's reason for constructing the three-foot-high passageways was to make sure that visitors bowed to the many gods and goddesses making their kingdom in his garden.

About two hours is needed to savor the garden, pausing in shady nooks where terra-cotta tykes forever play soccer in pottery-shard shorts, cork musicians strum sitars, and airy castles are splashed with waterfalls. Be sure you see the lovely Japanese-style garden imagined by this Indian artist who has never been to the Orient or seen pictures of this kind of architecture.

Chand has been constructing his garden over the last 30 or so years. At first he worked secretly at night because he was afraid that if his creation were discovered it might be destroyed by officials as not in keeping with the carefully planned new city. In 1972, as his accomplishments became known and acknowledged by respected artists and intellectuals, a city official also recognized his genius and got the local government to back him. He plans eventually to cover 40 acres with castles, creatures, waterfalls, and other figments of his fertile imagination.

Chand is also becoming known outside India: He has exhibited his work at the Museum of Modern Art in Paris and was given a high French award. A book on his garden has also been published in France, and Australians have made a documentary about him. He has been honored with India's highest artistic award. Chand created a miniversion of this garden for the Children's Museum in Washington, D.C.

But he prefers to stay home and add to his garden and have everyone come to admire his work. In his huge guest ledger are comments from visitors the world over. You may ask for the book if you'd like to add your reactions.

In his youth Chand was a road laborer. Later, as a supervisor at a warehouse and storage yard that stood on his present site, he began scavenging the surrounding area for interesting discards from which his wonderful garden grew.

To see Nek Chand's Sculpture Garden (open every day from 10am to sunset) it costs 50 paise. Early morning or late afternoon are recommended times. There are plenty of benches so that you can relax while admiring the remarkable creations. Snacks and soft drinks are available in the garden at **The Chef.**

Since Chand works alongside his staff as many as 12 hours a day, he's often around and glad to answer visitors' questions about new sections or show them his workrooms. If he's busy, one of his assistants supplies the facts about the fantasies.

In Sector 16 is the handsomely landscaped **Zakir Rose Garden.** With 30 acres, it's supposed to be the largest rose garden in Asia. Featured in the immense tract are 2,400 varieties of roses. The peak time to see many of the roses in full bloom is February during the Rose Festival, when activities include naming a prince and princess of roses. Zakir Rose Garden is open year-round. From April 1 to September 30, the hours are 5am to 9pm, and from October 1 to March 31, 6am to 8pm. From 5 to 9pm throughout the year the ornamental fountain is turned on.

Travel 10 miles from Chandigarh, and you'll find yourself back in the 17th century at **Mughal Pinjore Gardens.** They're cool, green, and as carefully planned as Chandigarh, but delightfully frivolous compared with the severely designed city. The Pinjore Gardens, once the private preserve of the Maharaja of Patiala, are now a popular picnic spot. The gardens are open from 8am to 10pm daily. Special lighting effects on Saturday and Sunday evenings draw crowds. The best time for a visit is during the week, when fewer people go. Buses for the garden leave the Bus Terminus, Sector 17, about every half hour and cost about Rs 8 (27¢) one way. In a four-seater taxi, it's about Rs 150 ($5) round-trip, including a one-hour stay, but not including petrol, which is an extra charge.

Sports & Outdoor Activites

Swimming pools in Sector 14 and 23 are open to the public; Sukhana Lake, northern edge of the city, has water sports facilities; Roller skating is offered at the rink in Sector 10. Leisure Valley, the 8-kilometer narrow park that runs through Chandigarh, has a fitness trail.

WHERE TO STAY

A clean room and well-maintained hotel at almost any price is hard to find in Chandigarh. Unless otherwise indicated, hotels have private attached bathrooms with hot and cold running water and such amenities as room telephones. The top-priced hotels accept international credit cards and have currency exchanges.

At the lowest end are hotels in the Rs 100 ($3.33) to Rs 250 ($8.33) price range, and there are few to recommend. At this level, you can expect basic rooms and basic common bathrooms; low price is their main attraction. However, if you look carefully, some rooms are better than others. Two to check out are **Alankar,** Udyog Path, and **Vrindavan,** near the Bus Stand.

Doubles for Less Than Rs 750 ($25)

In Sector 22-A, the **Hotel Pankaj** (☎ 41906; fax 546222), is a cut above some others in this price range, with a red-carpeted stairway and small wood-paneled lobby. All 14 rooms are doubles and are better maintained than many others in town. The **Noor** restaurant, attached to the hotel, serves everything from snacks to full meals and is open from 7am to 11:30pm every day.

You can try the **Union Territory Guest House,** Sector 6, Chandigarh 160007 (☎ 540961-65). Primarily for government officials, it also takes other travelers in its 27 rooms, if vacancies permit. It's not overly tidy, but better than some hotels in town. Rooms are air-conditioned and have ceiling fans and attached private bathrooms. The seven acres of landscaped gardens surrounding the guest house are its outstanding feature. For reservations, write: Director of Hospitality and Tourism, Chandigarh Administration (U.T. State Guest House), Union Territory, Sector 6,

Chandigarh 160007. **Yatri Niwas** is another government accommodation accepting nonofficial guests.

Hotel Piccadilly, Himalaya Marg, Sector 22-B (☎ 43112; fax 40692), is supposed to be a four-star hotel, but it hardly lives up to this expectation. The public rooms are nice, but the bedrooms and halls upstairs need better maintenance. The highest-priced double is Rs 470 ($15.66), usually more in the two-star than four-star range.

Doubles for Less Than Rs 1350 ($45)

Chandigarh Mountview, Sector 10, Chandigarh 160010 (☎ 54773; fax 547120), government-run, has 71 air-conditioned rooms in a lovely old-fashioned garden; the rooms have modern furniture. There's a swimming pool, as well as tennis courts, a health club, a bar, and a restaurant. This is a two-star hotel, but it has higher rates than the four-star establishments.

Also government-run, **Hotel Shivalikview,** Sector 17 (☎ 544651; fax 32094), has 100 air-conditioned rooms, almost always filled with business travelers. A nice feature is the rooftop bar. There's also a barbecue and other restaurants, as well as the expected business conveniences such as conference rooms and secretarial services.

Also in sector 35-B, **Hotel Maya Palace** (☎ 600547; fax 600547), has 26 air-conditioned rooms. The highest double is about Rs 800 ($26.66). There's a bar and restaurant.

In a similar price range with about the same amenities are the 14-room **South End,** Sector 35-C (☎ 607935), and the 14-room **Hotel Heritage,** Sector 35-B (☎ 602479).

Sunbeam, Sector 22 (☎ 41335), has 57 rooms. Its highest double runs Rs 895 ($29.83); there is a restaurant and a bar.

The centrally air-conditioned **Hotel President,** Madya Marg, Sector 26 (☎ 40840; fax 43410), with 20 rooms, has a gleaming marble lobby and rooms for Rs 500 ($18.33) single, Rs 750 ($25) double, Rs 950 ($31.66) suite. There are print bedspreads, bird prints, and cushy carpeting in all the bedrooms, which also have attached modern bathrooms. There are two restaurants—Indian and Chinese—and a health club on the premises. From here it will cost about Rs 25 (83¢) by motorized scooter ricksha to Sector 17, the part of town for the most action.

WHERE TO EAT

Sector 17 (location of all the following places; except where indicated) is the main place to head for a snack or a meal. You'll have plenty of company; going out to eat is a favorite activity among the residents of Chandigarh. ***Penny-wise tips for restaurant-goers:*** Try a variety of tandoori breads and kebabs for a filling, bargain-priced meal. Portions are usually generous, so another way to save is to share.

For inexpensive snacks, it's the **Indian Coffee House,** open from 9am to 10:30pm in summer and 9am to 10pm in winter. South Indian coffee (with hot milk) and paper-thin dosas are specialties. **Hot Millions** is the popular choice for cheap fast food.

In the following restaurants figure on paying about Rs 150 ($5) for a three-course nonvegetarian meal, Rs 25 (83¢) to 50 ($1) less for vegetarian. Sweets and fast foods are less.

Kwality (☎ 543183) serves affordable full meals as well as snacks from 8am to 11pm. Also for meals and snacks are two nicely decorated, dimly lit restaurants with extensive Indian, Continental, and Chinese menus: **Mehfil** (☎ 543539), open from 9am to 11pm daily, and **Ghazal,** open from 8am to midnight. The former has comfortable banquettes and mirrored murals, the latter a fancy doorway, wooden grillwork, and mirrors.

In Sector 17 also is **Shangrila,** serving comfortably priced Chinese food, and **Sindhi Sweets** for Indian sweets; the Iranian food at **Pakhtoon,** Sector 17-C, offers a change of pace. In either Sector 22 or 17, **Chopsticks** is reliable for Chinese cuisine.

3 Amritsar & Its Golden Temple

Amritsar (pop. 709,000), the busiest city in Punjab, is famous for its Golden Temple (formerly known as Hari Mandir), which is of great religious importance to the Sikhs, who form the bulk of the population here. Amritsar (its name means Tank of Nectar) was founded in 1579, and the old city is still surrounded by a wall in which there are about 20 city gates.

In addition to the old sights, looking around Amritsar provides a prime glimpse at what may be India's most prosperous region. Modern farming methods are reaping success for the Punjabis and bringing some of the luxury goods that go with it to mingle with the old traditions. All around Amritsar (and elsewhere in Punjab) turbaned Sikhs drive their motor scooters and automobiles like fury, and numerous television antennas (Punjab is third after Delhi and Bombay when it comes to television sets) share the skyline with the resplendent gold-domed temple. Beyond these material possessions is undoubtedly a more important result of the new prosperity: All the villages in Punjab have electricity.

Modern history in Punjab since 1983 has seen hostility toward the central government increase as Sikhs press for greater autonomy.

ESSENTIALS

GETTING THERE

BY PLANE **Indian Airlines** and **Archana** operate flights from Delhi ($58); **Modiluft** connects from Bombay ($52) and Delhi; flights also operate from Srinagar ($45). There's a weekly flight from Birmingham (United Kingdom).

Raja Sansa Airport is about 12 kilometers from downtown. There is no coach service to town, but plenty of taxis (negotiate rates).

Indian Airlines has an office in the city (☎ 356); Modiluft and Archana's offices are in the Ritz.

BY TRAIN Trains connect Amritsar with Delhi, Calcutta, Bombay, and Puri. The best train from Delhi, the *Shatabdi Express,* takes six hours and 40 minutes, departing Delhi at 4:20pm and arriving Amritsar at 11pm. The fare is Rs 270 ($9) AC Chair, Rs 740 ($24.66) Executive, both including a meal. ***Shatabdi penny-wise tip:*** Take the chair car; the extra space and larger meal in Executive is not worth an additional $15.66. Among the trains from Delhi, the *New Delhi-Amritsar Express* (7½ hours) costs Rs 797 ($26.56) AC First, and Rs 94 ($3.13) Second. Calcutta, via Varanasi, takes 23 ½ hours; Bombay 34-plus hours. For reservations (☎ 66486).

If you are changing trains in Amritsar with a couple of hours to kill, hop into an auto ricksha or taxi and visit the Golden Temple, 15 minutes away from the railroad station.

BY BUS Bus service from Chandigarh takes five hours and costs around Rs 60 ($2) deluxe; direct bus service is also available from Delhi (10 hours) and Dharamshala (seven hours), and buses service Himachal Pradesh, Haryana, Jammu, Kashmir and other northern places. The Bus Stand Enquiry office is open from 9am to 5pm daily

(☎ 51734); Maharajah Travels runs air-conditioned services to Chandigarh from their office near Hall Gate (☎ 31417).

Visitor Information

The **Government of Punjab Tourist Bureau** is opposite the railway station (☎ 42164).

Getting Around

Auto rickshas and cycle rickshas are readily available; taxis are not. Find taxis at the airport, Mohan International Hotel, or have your hotel arrange one for you. Rates are negotiable for all of these conveyances.

WHAT TO SEE & DO

THE TEMPLE The Golden Temple, besides being the centerpiece of Sikh devotion—it is every Sikh's desire to visit it at least once—is one of the most interesting temples in the world. And I don't say this lightly. Contained within in an immense enclosed patio, the temple sits in the center of a vast pool, several feet deep, with a causeway connecting it to the marble-tiled courtyard.

At one end of the compound is the ornate Akal Takht (Immortal Throne) for the temple priests. Normally, the compound is a scene of fascinating activity. All around the pool, squatting cross-legged on the carved and decorated marble tiles, sit hundreds of men, women, and children—thinking, sleeping, talking, eating, and reading. Occasionally an elderly woman will step gingerly into the water and immerse herself. Followers of the militant Gobind Singh (10th and last guru, or teacher, of the Sikh religion, 1675–1708), in bright-blue robes, sheathed swords at their waist and steel-tipped pikes in their hands, stride proudly past. Flower-sellers dispense garlands of golden marigolds. Old ladies sit behind a stall filled with shiny brass saucers offering free drinks of water.

The panorama continues for 24 hours each day the temple is open. And when it is closed, many of the homeless visitors stay in a free hostel that adjoins the temple precincts. As many as 10,000 hungry will file through to sit on stone floors and be served a kind of gruel by volunteers passing back and forth with buckets and ladles. Even between meal times the kitchens are a beehive of activity, with volunteers preparing the chapatis. An old man sits beside a boiling tank of syrup making sugar candies, while another piles firewood in stacks to keep the ovens going. All this charity is a constant feature of Sikh temples; there is even a section to which private citizens are invited to bring their home-cooked food and give it away to the poor.

Before entering the temple precincts, visitors must empty their pockets of cigarettes (Sikhs are not supposed to smoke or drink); they must cover their heads and go barefoot or don special socks that have never been used before. At the entrance, feet must be dipped in a tank of water, a ceremonial cleansing.

Then, crossing the covered portico where whole families lie resting on straw mats under the spreading branches of the 400-year-old jamun tree, visitors make their way around the edge of the tank (pool), noting underfoot the occasional marble tile engraved with a donor's name. They pass the Akal Takht, a building that has been the administrative center of Sikhdom since it was built three centuries ago. Then they traverse the walkway into the center of the pool and the Golden Temple itself, so called because the dome and upper part are covered with fine filigree and enamel work in gold.

There is no admission charge to the temple, but it is customary to make a small donation in return for several hours of entertainment and enlightenment.

The temple was built in the 16th century by Guru Ram Das, the fourth of the 10 gurus who shaped and directed the Sikh religion over a period of two centuries. Many times the temple changed hands, the Sikhs were driven out, and the premises desecrated by different rulers. In 1740 the local Mughal commandant was using it as a dance hall when two valiant Sikhs disguised themselves to enter the precincts and assassinate him. On another famous occasion, in 1758, a Sikh named Baba Dip Singh led an avenging body through to the temple where, legend says, he finally let go of his already-severed head and went to the eternal abode of martyrs. A mausoleum named after him stands within the temple precincts. Nine years later the Sikhs reconquered Punjab and have remained in possession of the temple ever since.

In l984, an incident at the Golden Temple shook the world. A three-day battle took place between Sikh extremists seeking autonomy and the Indian Army with tanks and other weapons within the compound. The shrine had become an arsenal under Jarnail Singh Bhindranwale and his followers, who had moved into the site months earlier. After failing to persuade the occupiers to leave the temple, the siege ended when the army brought combat vehicles into the compound. Although the army had firm orders not to fire at the temple, the Akal Tahkt was badly damaged in the skirmish. Repairs are underway now, financed by fund-raising among the Sikhs. But it doesn't end here: Bhindranwale was killed in the temple, which was evacuated in June l984. As a result, Indira Ghandi was assassinated four months later. Her death and continued separatist strife are the consequences of this incident at the Golden Temple.

THE FLAME OF LIBERTY Amritsar's other major monument is the **Jallianwala Bagh** (Flame of Liberty), which is not far from the Ghee Mandi Gate in the crowded city center. The monument, an impressive red sandstone pillar, commemorates the miserable day in 1919 when British General Dyer ordered his soldiers to fire on a gathering of about 1,500 people who were meeting at this spot to demonstrate for Indian independence. Independence finally came, but not until 29 years later when the British left.

SHOPPING

Lively lanes are found at **Guru Vihar,** near the Golden Temple, among the assortment of wares, especially wonderful are woolen shawls, ranging from Rs 50 ($1.66) to Rs 2,500 ($83.33). There are blankets, duppattas (stolelike scarves) with traditional phulkari embroidery; handmade jootis (shoes), made of buffalo and goat hides, run no higher than Rs 250 ($8.33) and go much lower in price. Bargain everywhere! The old lanes also house tea and silver markets.

WHERE TO STAY

DOUBLES FOR LESS THAN RS 750 ($25)

Below this price range, accommodations have nothing to recommend them but price.

Airlines Hotel, Cooper Road, Amritsar 143001 (☎ 64848), is not too tidy, but it's nearest the Golden Temple and offers Aryuvedic treatments for scalp and hair, as well as partial air-conditioning, two restaurants, and a downtown location.

At **Hotel Astoria,** 1 Queens Rd., Amritsar 143001 (☎ 60646), 28 partially air-conditioned rooms have the essentials in the way of furnishings; there's a 10% service charge and restaurant. It's also located near the railway station.

Also on Queen's Road is **Grand Hotel,** Amritsar 143001 (☎ 62977), with similar amenities and convenient location. This hotel has a bar as well as a restaurant. Service charge is 10%.

Doubles for Less Than Rs 1,200 ($40)

The most pleasant place, just outside of town, is **Mrs. Bhandari's Guest House,** 10 Cantonment, Amritsar 143001 (☎ 264285). Her room tariff is within a lower price bracket, but taking meals here—which is advised because the food is fresh and well prepared and there is no other place to eat nearby—runs the price into the range above. For these rates, you get a nice, clean room in a well-maintained place with plenty of atmosphere that was once Mrs. Bhandari's private house. She grows her own fruits and vegetables. For an additional fee, Mrs. B. will arrange transfers to and from the airport and sightseeing.

Most of the rooms in the hotels below are cookie-cutter copies with minor variations, functional modern furniture, and very often walls and carpets that could do with TLC. All, except where mentioned, have attached bathrooms; top-priced hotels accept international credit cards, equip rooms with TVs, and sometimes have refrigerators.

At the top in terms of price is **Mohan International Hotel,** Albert Road, Amritsar 143001 (☎ 227801; fax 226520), with 39 functionally furnished rooms, central air-conditioning, and a swimming pool, but what it needs is careful attention to maintenance. There's a 10% service charge. The restaurants here are popular.

Ritz Hotel, 45 The Mall, Amritsar (☎ 226606), is fully air-conditioned, has 49 rooms, and is slightly lower in price than the one above but better maintained. A swimming pool and lovely landscaped gardens are added attractions.

Amritsar International Hotel, City Centre (☎ 31991), run by the Punjab Tourist Development Corporation, is an angular modern building, centrally air-conditioned, and conveniently located next to the bus stand. The 56 rooms are reasonably clean and have all the essential comforts. There's a 24-hour coffee shop.

WHERE TO EAT

The cooking in Amritsar is notably North Indian. ***Penny-wise tip:*** Portions are generous (share dishes, save dough) and prices are reasonable. You can easily find a vegetarian meal for under Rs 100 ($3.33). Nonvegetarian foods also are served, but the vegetarian are more outstanding. Look for sag (a spinachlike green vegetable); panir (cheese); and parathas (rich flat bread) filled with potatoes, cauliflower, and panir. The latter is a dish every visitor should taste.

Restaurants on and about Queens Road include **Crystal, Odeon** and **Napoli,** as well as **Kwality,** on The Mall; they serve the usual multicuisine mixture of Indian, Chinese and Continental dishes plus some tandoori preparations. Also on Queens Road, **Velveeta** (not the processed cheese!) is renowned for sweets; the **Novelty Complex** on Lawrence Road is a lively food/snack stop. Simple veg food is free in Golden Temple's "Langar."

Mohan International Hotel has a 24-hour coffee shop and two other restaurants with Chinese, Indian, and Continental food.

4 The Valley of the Gods—Kulu (Kullu) & Manali

Two enchanting mountain towns in the Valley of the Gods offer everything mortals need for heavenly holidays: Kulu (pop. 14,500; 4,000 feet), also spelled *Kullu,* and Manali (pop. 2,600; 6,000 feet). Perched above the thundering Beas (pronounced "Be-ahs") River in the lower Himalayas, these mountain hamlets are only half as far from Delhi as celebrated Kashmir, but they seem many times more remote—and are much less expensive. (At this writing, travel to Kashmir is not advised because of the persistent tense situation there. So these Kulu Valley towns are becoming more popular and losing their quaint, remote feeling.)

For centuries, missionaries, traders, and adventurers have traveled through here. Basically, the fertile valley, about 1 mile wide and about 50 miles long, is a major fruit-producing region. Everywhere en route in the fall are little apple juice bars for the traveler's refreshment. Spring turns the valley into a flower basket filled with bouquets of blossoming fruit trees against a background of giant red rhododendrons brightening the upper slopes. In summer, tiny buttercups spread an elusive mist from gold to red and spears of purple iris sway in the fields. The winter colors Kulu nutty brown with a cloak of green from the cedars and pines.

In any season, the sturdy people are among the valley's main delights. An aspect of their life foreigners find most interesting is their division of labor: Women tend the house and fields while men stay indoors and weave wool into warm shawls, blankets, and textiles for their homespun clothing. Not surprisingly, hand-woven shawls are among the items sold in the bazaar, as are the distinctive embroidered caps and heavy silver jewelry, imported and sold by the towns' Tibetan merchants.

In the late 1960s the valley where ganja (marijuana) grows wild was high on the list of hangouts for Western wanderers shuttling between Goa and Nepal. The permanent Western hippie residents in the surrounding villages shuttled here back then and never shuttled on. Enjoying another kind of high life are trekkers, especially in the spring and fall, and the Japanese who come to ski in winter.

Yet while the valley grows increasingly more popular, the only time during the year there's anything approaching a huge crowd is during the week-long Dussehra festival in October or November. This annual fall festival, hailing Rama's victory over the evil King Ravana, marked all over India, is so spectacularly celebrated in Kulu that it attracts visitors from all over the country, and since the 1960s many Westerners have been turning up for the event as well. The main festival attraction is a procession in Kulu of more than 100 gods from all the valley temples. Thus the name valley of the gods. There is also dancing and music and an extra-tempting array of wares on sale in the market.

Still, modern times are knocking on the valley's door. Video-equipped buses and jet planes are bringing more travelers in. The uncontrolled building of hotels, if not checked soon, will make Manali a mess.

Budgeting Your Valley Visit

The Himachal Pradesh government levies a luxury tax on rooms: As high as 10% on some rooms. You'll want to remember this when budgeting. You might get a break during the mid-November to mid-April off-season when some managers reduce their rates. Be sure to ask about these special rates during these times. Reductions may not be offered if you don't.

Basically, the season is April 15 to July 30 and again from September 1 to October 30, although some accommodations may be discounted during September as well. The fall Festival of Dussehra, usually in October, is especially colorful in Kulu and attracts many visitors; rates go up then. Be sure to make reservations if you hope to share in the excitement.

Most travelers stay in Manali, where accommodations are more plentiful and accommodating. However, since Kulu is more convenient to transportation, you can stop off here, either on the way to Manali or when moving on. Since only 49 kilometers separate the two, excursions to Kulu are another possibility.

ESSENTIALS

GETTING THERE

BY PLANE The nearest airport is Bhuntar, 9 kilometers from Kulu (49 kilometers from Manali); **Jagson Airlines** flies daily from Delhi via Chandigarh ($15); **Archana** flies nonstop daily from Delhi, $13. There is no coach service from the airport, and taxi prices are supposedly fixed to Kulu and Manali, but expect to bargain. Taxis to Kulu run from Rs 75 ($2.50) to Rs 85 ($2.83); to Manali, 50 kilometers further, Rs 400 ($13.33), including return fare for driver. Regular public buses also can be taken from the airport to Kulu.

Airline booking agent for both Jagson and Vayudoot in the Kulu Valley is **Ambassador Travels** (P), Ltd., The Mall, Manali (☎ 2110); and near the LIC office, Dhalpur, Kulu (☎ 2286); for **Archana Airways,** Shant Kumj, National Hwy. no. 21, Shamshi (☎ 01902-6230).

BY BUS AC and non-AC coaches run by HRTC and HPTDC and others in neighboring states, as well as private companies, serve both Kulu and Manali. National Highway 21 runs through the valley connecting it with Chandigarh and other places. HPTDC's AC coach from Delhi takes off at 6am for a 16-hour trip, with a fare of Rs 400 ($13.33): non–air-conditioned buses cost Rs 200 ($6.66); there have been complaints about safety on the low-priced trip. From Shimla, the coach departs at 9am for a nine-hour trip, for Rs 160 ($5.33).

BY TRAIN Chandigarh is the best railhead for people coming from Delhi or Bombay. The best train from Delhi to Chandigarh is the speedy, all-AC *Shatabdi Express,* Rs 250 ($8.33) for the chair car, Rs 500 ($16.66) Executive. Fares include meal service. The train leaves Delhi at 7:30am, arriving in Chandigarh at 3:30pm; you'll have to stay overnight before going on by road to Kulu or Manali. ***Penny-wise tip:*** Take the *Shatabdi* Chair and save; Executive is not worth the extra money). Shimla can also serve as a railhead for the Kulu Valley. The best part of going via Shimla is the change at Kalka-Shimla Railroad, one of India's delightful "toy trains" (narrow gauge). Completed in l903, the Kalka-Shimla line runs for 95 scenic kilometers; there are 103 tunnels and many bridges and curves on its circuitous course as the train rises to Shimla (7,000 feet). Buses from Shimla depart at 9am for a 9-plus hours trip, for Rs 160 ($5.33) one way. (The bus from Shimla to Manali departs at 8am.) Share taxis also connect Shimla with Kulu.

If you've chosen Chandigarh as your railhead, the Kulu Valley is a spectacularly scenic one-day, 173-mile curvaceous road trip where frequent rock slides make detours common. Cars with drivers are very pricey because the drive is in the hills: A round-trip from Chandigarh should cost in the area of Rs 3,000 ($100), plus detention charges and driver's overnight. It's best not to bargain with a cab driver for this trip but to take a government-approved car, at a fixed rate, fit for the difficult journey. See the box above for details about this trip by road.

HPTDC operates buses between Chandigarh and Kulu (12 hours, bypassing Shimla) and on to Manali (two more hours). From Delhi, the trip is 15 to 18 hours. Motion sensitive passengers take care shortly after Chandigarh as the trip is curvy as it climbs.

Rules of the Road

If you decide to go by road, by bus or private car, from Chandigarh take some bottled water, biscuits, and fruit (remember a knife to peel it)—a good idea on any long drive in India. On this particular mountainous drive, you can get stuck quite literally in the middle of nowhere, with no place to get food or hygienic water to drink, if there's a rockslide or road washout and you have to wait for help (which always turns up sooner or later in the form of a tractor or friendly hands). If you're splurging on a car and driver, from perhaps Chandigarh, getting an early start is another good idea. You'll want to travel the mountain roads before dark.

A few kilometers beyond the Shimla turnoff, is **Bilaspur,** where you can stop for a snack or meal or to use the tidy bathroom (patrons only) at the clean **Lake View Cafe.** Here, Continental breakfast is under $1. On the way back from Manali, the **Mandav at Mandi** is handy for a bite and a clean bathroom. Bus drivers also give passengers various rest stops. If you're driving from Delhi, the Haryana State Government runs small, clean rest-stop cafes and motels all named after local birds; look for signs with birds painted on them.

KULU

ESSENTIALS

Visitor Information Information is available at the **HPTDC's Tourist Office,** Dhalpur (☎ 2349), open from 9am to 7pm in season, and 10am to 5pm off-season. The HPTDC's counter at Bhuntar Airport is open only during flight times.

Getting Around Tourist taxis and auto rickshas can be found in the Akhara Bazar. Rates are supposed to be fixed, but have to be negotiated.

WHAT TO SEE & DO

First, stop in at the tourist office (☎ 2349), right off Dhalpur maidan (grassy center), anytime between 10am and 5pm. Buy an area map. If you fish and it's March to mid-April, arrange for your license, rent a rod and line. Go to **Aut** (pronounced "out"), 20 miles away, where trout are plentiful.

Shop in the **Akhara Bazar** for caps, shawls, quilts, baskets, and other crafts at the Himachal Emporium, HP Khadi, and Village Industries Emporium, Khadi Gram Udyog Bhavan, and the Bhutu Weavers Coop's retail store and various vendors.

Take in the temples in the vicinity. The most renowned temple is **Bijli Mahadevi,** 8 kilometers from Kulu at a height of 8,000 feet. You'll need to go by bus or jeep to Trampali, the midway point, and then trek 3 1/2 miles. Perched on a bluff, the stone-block temple, built without cement, is topped with a 65-foot-high flagpole that attracts lightning, which here is considered a blessing. When lightning strikes the rod, they say it shatters the Shiva image inside. Temple priests repair it and await the next bolt of lucky lightning. The less energetic can see the flagpole gleam from town.

Jaganathi Devi is 3 1/2 miles from Kulu at 5,000 feet. Take your time up the steep path, and pack a picnic lunch to eat while you admire the panoramic view from atop.

Raghunathji Temple is only about a half mile from Kulu and the abode of the chief deity of the valley; but the least interesting.

Visheswhar Mahadev Temple at Bajaura, 15 kilometers south of Kulu at an altitude of 3,600 feet, possibly dates from the mid-8th century. There are interesting stone sculptures and carvings.

Where to Stay & Eat

In Kulu choices are very limited, since most people prefer to stay in Manali. None of these hotels have air-conditioning, nor it is needed in the cool lower Himalayas; however, you might want a heater in winter and early spring. Rates fall between Rs 300 ($10) and Rs 800 ($26.66) for a double.

A good bet is the HPTDC's **Hotel Sarvari** (☎ 2471), located a short stroll from town on a big grassy lawn, which offers better-than-average accommodations and great big rooms. There are eight doubles—highest price Rs 800 ($26.66)—and four dorms with six beds each—Rs 45 ($1.50)—on big lawns at a slight elevation. Common toilets and showers are for dorm-users. There are modest fees for heaters. The dining hall food is very tasty

Even better is the HPTDC's **Hotel Silver Moon** (☎ 2488), about 2 kilometers from town. Perched on a hill near the entrance to town, it has six doubles with large windows and a pleasant ambience. All the rooms pass inspection, but those upstairs are brighter, sunnier, and quieter than those on the first floor. They top off at Rs 800 ($26.66) for a double.

The three-story **Hotel Rohtang,** Dhalpur (☎ 2303), has a good view from its 12 simply appointed rooms carpeted with coir (made from coconut fiber). The more expensive rooms have TVs that don't amount to much around here, so save your rupees. The restaurant, open from 9 to 11am, 1 to 3pm, and 7 to 10pm, serves Indian and Continental cuisine, with many main dishes a little more than $1.

You might also want to try the **Apple Valley Resort,** Village Mohal, on National Highway, Kulu 175126 (☎ 5470-75; fax 4116). Chalet-inspired architecture and splendid views of the Beas are among the attractions; the rooms are comfortable with every possible amenity. The resort offers a full range of adventure sports or just a place to relax. Meals are delicious. Double rates range from Rs 2,700 ($90) to Rs 3,000 ($100) and include all meals.

The lowest-price accommodations follow here, with doubles ranging from Rs 125 ($4.16) to Rs 250 ($8.47).

Bijleshwar Guest Hotel, Dhalpur (☎ 2677), has eight rooms, some with antique furniture and fireplaces, and some of the lowest rates around. Take your meals at the cafe (open from 7am to 10pm), where a thali costs about $1. In the same price league, but not as good otherwise, is **Shoba,** across Dhalpur Maiden (☎ 2800).

For more cheapies, check out the area around the Ahkara Bazaar.

AN EXCURSION TO MANIKARAN

You can trek through apple orchards for 45 kilometers or grab the bus to **Manikaran,** 5,700 feet high, site of what are purportedly the hottest springs in the world. The bus goes to Manikaran Bridge. A 200-meter steep walk goes down to the springs from there. The springs are believed to have curative powers and many people make special pilgrimages here for restorative dips. Here's the Hindu myth about why we have these springs today: One day, before stepping into the river to bathe with Mahadev (Shiva), Parvati placed her beautiful gold earrings on the riverbank for safekeeping. But they were taken by the Serpent God Naga, who stuffed them up his nostrils and fled to his underground den. Mahadev found out about the theft and confronted Naga. This made Naga so angry, he sneezed fiery steam, dislodging the earrings from their hiding place and piercing the ground with such force the earrings and clouds of steam formed these warm springs.

While you're here, you can stay at the government-run **Parvati Hotel,** which offers 12 simple rooms, a restaurant, and lovely views. Contact the HPTDC's Tourist Office, Dhalpur (☎ 2349) about reservations. More commonly, it's a day trip.

EN ROUTE TO MANALI

Of the two roads running the 26 miles to Manali, the old circuitous bumpy back road, which can take four hours, is full of fascinating sights and is therefore recommended over the direct route taking about two hours. Buses leave every two hours on the direct route and twice a day via the old road. If it's raining, you'll want to wait for dry weather or take the direct route (the old road becomes slippery when wet).

You'll also want to check bus timings so you can either stop at Naggar (about the halfway point) to see the famous **Naggar Castle** and continue later by bus, or plan far enough ahead to reserve one of the 14 rooms in the HPTDC **Hotel Castle Naggar,** on the Naggar Castle grounds; rates are Rs 125 ($4.16) to Rs 400 ($13.33) for a double room. For reservations, contact the Tourism Development Officer, Kulu (☎ 2349). The castle itself, built by Raja Sidh Singh more than 400 years ago, remarkably withstood the earthquake of 1905 when other buildings around here collapsed like cardboard cartons. If the castle's booked up, try the **Poonam Fruit Garden** in town.

On the castle grounds, **Jagti-Pat Temple** has a stone slab which is off-limits because it's supposed to hold all the deities. Legend has it that to test this, a foreigner once stepped on this forbidden territory and was swallowed up by a huge crack that mysteriously opened. Since then no one's ever slipped up by stepping on the slab.

For temple-trotters, there's a **Shiva temple,** perhaps 900 years old, on the approach to Naggar Castle, a **Vishnu temple** almost at the entrance, and **Devi** and **Krishna** temples above it.

Also a steep climb from behind the castle is the charming old stone cottage in which the Russian adventurer/artist Nicholas Roerich lived more than 50 years ago. It's now a small **museum** full of his paintings of the valley, some abstract and others realistic. All around the house, the foundations of the house, and in the garden are marvelous stone carvings, and of course, the view is quite a special sight.

WHERE TO STAY ROUTE

Only 10 miles from Kulu is a camping site at **Raison,** if you're trekking through, where there are also rooms in huts for Rs 150 per day.

At Katrain, 2 miles farther along, there's the well-located **HPTDC Hotel Apple Blossom** (☎ 8336). The spectacular view and cleanliness make up for the rather spartan furnishings. Nine rooms have bathrooms attached; some also have geysers to supply hot water, and in others you pay a few rupees for a bucket of hot water. Rates are Rs 200 ($6.66) to Rs 250 (8.33); no catering. For reservations at the Hotel Apple Blossom or in the camping ground huts, contact the Tourism Development Officer, Kulu (☎ 2349).

Also near Katrain is the romantic **Span Resorts,** Village Katrain, 27 kilometers from the airport, 15 kilometers from Manali (☎ 83138-40), offering comfortable, attractive accommodations in well-appointed stone cottages overlooking the Beas River. In the main building are a big well-stocked bar, restaurant, video room, and lounge. Even though meals are included, it's a splurge for us—a double runs Rs 3,950 ($131.66). (There's a 35% off-season discount.) However, you might stop for a special meal or snack between Kulu and Manali. Figure on Rs 150 ($5.70) for lunch or dinner. For reservations, contact: Span Motels Pvt., Ltd., "Vijaya," First Floor, 17 Barakhamba Road, New Delhi 110001 (☎ 3311434; fax 011-3312628); or Union Co-op Insurance Bldg., 23 Sir P. Mehta Road, Bombay 400001 (☎ 2873797; 240516).

MANALI

GETTING AROUND

Tourist taxis are the only mode of transportation; rates are fixed for the more popular sites and generally adhered to except in peak season when you can expect to bargain. Hire taxis from the **Taxi Operators Union Office,** near the tourist office, The Mall (☎ 2450). Rates for some key spots are as follows: tourist office to Log Huts, Club House, Aleo are all Rs 40 ($1.33); to Vashist Thermal baths or Quality Inn Rs 50 ($1.66); to Naggar, Rs 250 ($8.33); to Solang Nala for glacier-viewing one-way, Rs 200 ($6.66, includes 1 1/2-hour waiting time).

WHAT TO SEE & DO

Take a half-mile hike through the piney woods to the **Hadimba Devi Temple,** which is accessible via a footpath running near the Hotel Rohtang Manaslu (ask for directions at the Tourist Information Office). Hung with antlers, the temple has ornate carvings outside and footprint-shaped humps of rock inside, which are considered holy. When the bell isn't being used by fun-loving kids as a toy, it's rung to summon people to worship, around 8:45am and 5pm. A big celebration takes place at the temple on May 15 and 16. Local legend has it that the king who commissioned this temple had the architect's right hand chopped off to keep him from duplicating his masterpiece elsewhere. The craftsman was not to be stopped, however. He taught his left hand to take over and built an even better temple at Chamba. The people there did not want this temple duplicated either, and to prevent this, they dealt the artist a blow more effective than the king's: They cut off his head.

Another favorite tourist activity is a visit to **Vashisht Hot Springs** (6,200 feet), about 3.2 kilometers from the Manali Bus Stand, and a pleasant 40-minute hike from the tourist office. Like the springs at Manikaran, the waters here are said to be curative, and there are some communal springs. More appealing, for your restorative soak, try these waters piped into the modern **Hot Baths** (hours are 7am to 1pm, 2 to 5pm, and 6 to 10pm.), where a 30-minute private bath costs about Rs 30 ($1). There is a cafeteria for a snack and drinks, open from 7am to 10pm. Nearby is a temple dedicated to Vashishta Muni.

Guided Tours

Early in your visit, stop in at the **Tourist Information Office,** The Mall (☎ 25116), and sign up for a luxury coach tour to Rohtang Pass, about 32 mountainous miles away over an old Tibetan trade route and 13,500 feet high. The tour lasts from 9am to 4pm and costs Rs 65 ($2.16); for a five-passenger car and driver you'll pay Rs 600 ($20). En route see **Nehru Kund,** the beautiful **Rahla Falls** and **Marhi** (a wonderful viewpoint). Take a sweater—it can be cold at the top. The coach trip goes every day in season if there are 10 or more people, which is the magic number that activates the following tours as well. The trek to Rohtang is a popular all-day excursion. Check weather conditions before you start off.

Another luxury coach tour, which lasts from 9am to 4pm and costs Rs 35 ($1.16)—or Rs 250 ($8.33) for a five-passenger car—goes to Naggar and nearby sites. Coach tours also go to Manikaran, from 9am to 6pm at Rs 70 ($2.33) per person—Rs 300 ($10) for a five-passenger car. Manikaran is on the trekking route to Pulga and Pin Parbati Pass.

Outdoor Adventures

Manali is headquarters for the **Himachal Pradesh Institute of Mountaineering and Allied Sports,** which organizes courses in mountaineering, skiing, water sports, high-altitude trekking, and mountain rescue for foreigners and Indians. Their vast complex has a hostel, conference center, auditorium, and an equipment display.

The HPTDC has a pamphlet of suggested trekking routes, with rudimentary maps. You can get this pamphlet and more information from the Tourist Information Office in Manali. Treks can run anywhere from three to 23 days.

Manali can be your base for a range of exciting travel experiences—jeep safaris over the moonscape-like terrain through Lahaul and Spiti to Leh via the 18,000-foot-high Tanghlang-La Pass, one of the highest mountain roads in the world; camping with folk dancers and music as entertainment by the campfire; skiing, trout fishing, river rafting, and rock climbing—all with experienced guides and equipment hired locally. Of the local agents setting up customized treks and other adventures, one of the most experienced is **Himalayan Adventures Pvt. Ltd.,** The Mall, Manali, H.P. 175131 (☎ 2182); write or telephone for sample itineraries. Other reliable agents are **International Trekkers,** Sunnyside, Chadiyari (☎ 2372), and **Arohi Travels,** The Mall (☎ 2139).

Shopping

Check out the Main Market, Tibetan Bazar, Tibetan Carpet Centre and Government Emporium, The Mall. Look for woolen shawls, caps, handicrafts, and Tibetan carpets. Sometimes you can find beautiful antique handlooms.

Where to Stay

For a more extensive listing, inquire at the Tourist Office and the Private Hotels Information and Booking Office, both in The Mall. Keep in mind when planning your visit that in peak season, May through June and again from September to November—especially during the Dusshera—rooms must be reserved in advance, the earlier the better for government-run accommodations. There's a 10% tax on the upper-end accommodations. A few newer places offer air-conditioning, but it's not essential here. Central heating is available in a some of the newer places, and floor heaters are offered elsewhere to take the chill off in the winter and early spring. Unless otherwise indicated, the hotels below offer attached bathrooms with hot and cold running water. Some of the small guest houses and hotels convey the charm of Manali more than the large new hotels.

The **lowest-priced accommodations** are located right off the market in the inappropriately named "Model Town," where you'll find rows of them; two other places to bargain hunt are The Mall and School Road. The best way to get a suitable room in these lowest-priced places is to look at several before settling in. (If off-season, remember to ask for the off-season rates.) Better yet, try to get in one of HPTDC's lowest-priced places. Just remember, most of these places have little to recommend them but price.

Doubles for Less Than Rs 600 ($20)

The main recommendation for the HPTDC's **Hotel Beas** is the magnificent river view and the low tariff. Doubles range in price from Rs 200 ($6.66) to Rs 500 ($16.66).

There are 32 four-bedded rooms at the HPTDC's **Tourist Lodge.** Bring your own towel. These rooms are spartan but acceptable, and right on the bank of the River Beas. Rates are about the same as the Hotel Beas.

Hill Top, on School Road (☎ 2140), appropriately on a hill top, has nine modest rooms; those upstairs are preferred for the views and the quiet. The restaurant serves tandoori, Indian, and Chinese dishes. You'll pay Rs 500 (($16.66) for a double.

The Banon family were among the English settlers who came to the valley more than 100 years ago and planted the apple orchards; some Banon descendants now run some of the best guest houses and small hotels (which you'll find throughout this round-up) in these ancestral orchards. For simple, quiet accommodations, try the **Sunshine Guest House,** The Mall (☎ 2120), run by the Banon family. Its 10 rooms, with no decor to speak of, are divided between a gray stone building and white annex (best) and surrounded by a terraced garden and orchard. Rates are about the same as those for Hill Top. There is a restaurant.

Mountview (☎ 2465) has a rooftop terrace, 10 spacious rooms, and a family feeling. A double will cost about Rs 350 ($11.66).

Doubles for Less Than Rs 700 ($23.33)

The HPTDC runs two places in this price range. About 2 kilometers from the center, and looking not unlike an old-style U.S. motel, are the HPTDC's 12 pleasant **Honeymoon Cottages** (☎ 2334). Their decor is very simple, but with Himalayas outside your window, who's looking inside? If you did, however, you would see a double room, kitchen, and dining room—cozy, cheerful, and clean. Doubles are about Rs 700 ($23.33).

In the HPTDC's vine-covered **Hotel Rohtang Manaslu,** near the Circuit House, The Mall (☎ 2332), doubles are in the new section, four-bedded rooms in the old section. All have attached bathrooms (no showers) and the necessities you need, but are a bit overpriced for such a basic place. There's a modest per-day charge for heaters. Doubles range in price from Rs 300 ($10) to Rs 500 ($16.66). There's also a restaurant. Nice views.

The Banon-run **Hotel New Hope** (☎ 2178) has 14 twin-bedded bedrooms, some with pine-paneling and all with smashing Himalayan views, fireplaces, and connecting bathrooms. Doubles run about Rs 700 ($23.33). The hotel serves Chinese, Indian, and Continental foods.

Pinewood Hotel (☎ 2113), another Banon-owned place, has 10 rooms with working fireplaces. Upstairs rooms are best, with both garden and mountain views. Rates are about the same as those of Hotel New Hope. Meals are à la carte and taken in a Victorian dining room with a large fireplace. For reservations, write to the manager and enclose a 50% deposit.

Hotel Highland (☎ 2399), set in a garden filled with roses and marigolds, has 34 thickly carpeted bedrooms (20 in a new annex). In the old, white, wood-trimmed stone building, the bright and cheerful rooms in the rear have balconies; main floor rooms open onto the garden. Rates range from Rs 600 ($20) to Rs 700 ($23.33) for a double.

You can get a double for Rs 350 ($11.67) at the eight-room **Manu Deluxe,** Manali (☎ in Delhi: 332-9469; fax 332-9824; bookings 6 Hailey Rd., Delhi, 110001). Decor is simple. A 30% discount is offered from November through April.

Doubles for Less Than Rs 1500 ($50)

The glitzy **Ram Regency Honeymoon Inn,** Aleo, Manali (☎ 2233), has a bridal suite with a round bed and mirrored walls! With a glass-inlaid mural in the reception area, wood paneling, rough-hewn stone halls, and patterned wallpaper and cut-velvet spreads in the bedrooms, this hotel's decor is a bit much, but it's also comfortable and clean. Doubles range in price from Rs 900 ($30) to Rs 1,490 ($49.66). There's a fabulous view from the upstairs veranda as well as a discotheque.

Hotel Tragopan, P.O. Box 38, Log Huts, Manali, 175131 (☎ 2434/2439), has 20 rooms, an in-house travel agency, a downtown location, and a multicuisine restaurant. Doubles range from Rs 895 ($29.83) to Rs 1,545 ($51.50). Instant reservations via Delhi: UB-38, Antriksh Bhawan, 22 K.G. Marg, New Delhi 110001 (☎ 011-3322322; fax 011-3723145).

Talk about charming places! **Negi's Mayflower Guest House** (☎ 2104), a gray stone building with aqua trim set in an orchard, has to be placed high on any list. There are pansies blooming in flower boxes and potted plants along the stairs indoors. The pine-paneled rooms have built-in desks, vanities, working fireplaces, and modern attached bathrooms. Rooms in the annex are a bit better than those in the older section. Doubles range in price from Rs 700 ($23.33) to Rs 900 ($30). Across the road is a huge tree said to be the oldest of its species in the world.

To experience Manali's charm the way it was before all the developers came in, try **John Banons Hotel,** Manali Orchards (☎ 2335; fax 2392), surrounded by lawns and apple orchards, with only 12 comfortably furnished, cozy rooms and lovely views. The rates are comfortable, too, and include meals—which adds to the good deal since the food is another plus here. Rates are Rs 700 single ($23.33), Rs 1,000 ($33.33) double, Rs 1,400 ($46.66) suite.

Doubles for Less Than Rs 2,390 ($79.66)

Most of the hotels in this section fall into our upper budget limit of $50 for a double.

At ITDC's **Manali Ashok,** Manali, 175131 (☎ 2331), 10 doubles and family suites recently spruced up have comfortable, modern furniture and all the comforts you need and more. Some deluxe rooms have little separate sitting rooms. Doubles from Rs 2,190 ($73) to Rs 2,390 ($79.66). Nice views and tasty food.

Also in this price range is **Shingar Regency,** Dungri Road (☎ 2251-53; fax 01901 2253), a promising newcomer offering central heating, room service, a restaurant, and car rental. Doubles are priced at Rs 1,390 ($46.33).

Madhu Gurung is the energetic manager of the 42-room sleek, spacious **Ambassador Hotel,** Sunny Side, Chadiyari, Manali 175131 (☎ 2173). For bookings contact: Ambassador Resort, Dhalpur Maidan, Kulu, 175101 (☎ 2286). Set on five landscaped acres, the architecture of the red-roofed hotel was inspired by the pagoda-shaped Hadimba Devi Temple. Rooms have window seats where you can relax and admire views of mountains and meadows. The decor incorporates local textiles and other crafts. Rates for doubles begin at Rs 2,100 ($70). Frills include a 24-hour coffee shop, health club, and jogging track. Discounts of 30% are offered in off-seasons.

The most recent Banon addition: **Banon Resort** (☎ 2490; fax 2378), comfortable and clean, but more commercial than the typical Banon property, with a coffee shop, restaurant, and CCTV. Doubles without meals run Rs 1,700 ($56.66)

Out O Town, Aleo (☎ 2375), among the newer places in Manali, is centrally heated and modern with some outstanding views.

Worth a Splurge

Often reserved months in advance by vacationing families, HPTDC's 12 vine-covered **Log Huts** (more accurately "cottages") are surrounded by flower beds. Each hut has two neatly furnished bedrooms with carved bedsteads and cushy settees, a kitchen, pantry, and two bathrooms. Rates for cabins 1, 2, and 3—lower down the hills and, therefore, less tiring to reach—are priced highest. Cabins 4 to 12 cost less. Rates are according to size and location; 1, 2, and 3 are lower down the hill and easier to reach, and therefore among the highest priced; cabins 4 to 12 cost less. At Rs 750 ($25) for a small hut, to Rs 2,500 ($83.33) and Rs 3,500 ($116.66) for a little cottage, they range from budget-right to manageable if you share with friends. *Note:* If you don't want to cook, you might hire a local cook, or have meals sent from a nearby cafe. A sweeper is provided at no additional charge to tidy up each day. (Be sure to tip him at the end of your stay.) Smaller log huts—still with two bedrooms—cost less.

Note: Reservation authority for all HPTDC-run accommodations is Area Manager, HPTDC, Manali, H.P. (☎ 77646 or 78311). Be sure and specify which place you're interested in. Book far in advance.

Located on the Kulu–Manali National Highway about 5 kilometers from town is **Manali Resorts,** P.O. 63, Manali 175129 (☎ 2274 or 2175; fax 2174), built of gray stones and accented with stained glass and landscaped gardens that run to the riverbank. The hotel's 39 attractively furnished rooms have balconies facing the river. Doubles range in price from Rs 2,190 ($73) for a standard, to Rs 2,390 ($79.66) for a deluxe room. There's a health club, tennis courts, fishing, and a rec room for children; also a bar, restaurant, coffee shop, and separate Gujarati kitchen. Discounts of 30% are available during the off-season.

Holiday Inn, Manali, Prini, Manali Highway (☎ 2262; fax 3312), has 55 rooms and suites with functional, modern furniture. Prices for doubles, depending upon size and view, go from Rs 2,000 ($66.66) to Rs 4,200 ($140). There is a gym and table tennis; you'll also find fishing, trekking, conference, and secretarial services. There's a children's playground. The restaurant features Manali cuisine, a bar, and 24-hour coffee shop. The hotel has a tie-in with the U.S. chain.

Quality Inn Snowcrest Manor (☎ 3188; fax 3353), has new sleek, modern accommodations with all possible amenities only 2 kilometers from bus stand. Rooms range in price from Rs 3,000 ($100) to Rs 6,000 ($200), the latter for a suite. There is a tie-in with the U.S. chain.

Where to Eat

Eating out here should mean eating outdoors in the glens and groves. Some hotels and guest houses will pack a picnic lunch for you, or you can buy foods in the market. Eating in the top hotels can be pricey, but you can find budget-minded meals in the smaller restaurants around town. The cafes and restaurants near the tourist information office are good bets for budget meals: **Monalisa** and **Mayur, Ardash** among these. For Western treats, such as quiche, cakes, and good coffee, try **Pete's Wholefood,** near the State Bank. Some of the top hotels have bars. The local drink of choice is apple juice, especially fine when fresh pressed in the fall.

Ladakh

7

Think of going someplace remote, and Ladakh (pop. 120,000)—India's highest region, north of the Himalayas nudging into Tibet, closed by snow from November to May, open to tourists only since 1974—would seem to fill the bill.

Well, think again. With tour buses and taxis rumbling regularly in over the mountains from Manali and several jet flights daily, Ladakh, called the rooftop of the world, is now high on the list of must-visit places for adventurous tourists. Such large numbers of Germans pass through these parts that a sign on an antique store in Leh, the main city, is written *Antiken* to attract Teutonic travelers.

Yet despite sizable inoculations of Westernism, Ladakh remains a place apart from all others. It is as rich a repository of Tibetan culture as you're apt to find in this day and age. In the towering mountains of Ladakh, Buddhists have meditated since three centuries before the birth of Christ, and in this country the purest form of Tibetan Buddhism is practiced to this day.

Long before Tibet was converted, Buddhism was introduced in Ladakh in the 3rd century B.C. by missionaries sent from India by the great Emperor Ashoka, ruler of the whole of non-Tamil India, Afghanistan, Kashmir, and Nepal. By A.D. 400 a Buddhist monk

Travel Advisory: About Kashmir

From the days of the Mughal emperors until the late 1980s, Kashmir—beautiful and cool—was one of the most often visited states in India. Since 1989, however, recurring violence by militant separatists has stopped virtually every one from going there. As a result of this situation, visitors are advised **not** to travel to Kashmir until these hostilities cease.

Those who insist on visiting Kashmir—despite this tense situation—are advised to check conditions in Delhi with their embassies and the India Tourism authorities before taking off. They must register with the **Foreigners Registration Office** immediately upon arrival in Kashmir. We have removed coverage of the area in and around Srinagar from this edition.

Meanwhile, the remote Buddhist outpost of Ladakh, far removed from the tempestuous areas around Srinagar, is considered safe.

named Fahsein, traveling as a pilgrim from monastery to monastery, reported on Buddhist rites, and tooth and bowl relics of Buddha in Ladakh. Later came the Tibetan influence, dominant today. Now travelers make pilgrimages to marvel at gompas (monasteries) built on sheer rock faces and decorated with masterpieces of art hundreds of years old.

Since 1947 Ladakh has been part of Kashmir and Jammu—a not altogether happy arrangement. There are complaints that Kashmiris don't understand the Ladakhi's culture and that progress in farming and irrigation has been too slow. Now, as in centuries past, melting glaciers are the main source of irrigation for the patches of green that stand out against a background as barren as the moon.

Ladakh's scanty rainfall averages between five and nine inches a year. Where the sun shines brilliantly 320 days out of the year, there is little cloud cover, and temperatures go up and down like bouncing balls—it can be extremely hot in the midday summer sun and downright cold by the middle of that same night. In the winter the temperatures drop to –60°F (–50° C). That's in a few parts of the warmer areas. Up in the mountains it goes even lower.

The dazzling sun may be Ladakh's salvation: The use of solar energy for cooking and heating is getting underway in Leh. Presently, so little of Ladakh is electrified that the lights in Leh come on for only three hours each night.

Ladakh today is a sensitive border area between India, China, and Pakistan, with the barest traces of the ancient splendor described by early silk traders. Yet this old land of gompas, apricot groves, and ancient rites still weaves a spell around visitors.

1 Ladakh Essentials

GETTING TO LADAKH

Many people are heading for Leh when they go to Ladakh. But no matter how you go, it's an adventure. If you come by bus from Manali, the surrounding mountains are rugged and roads potholed and winding. It's exciting, but a relief to arrive in good shape. If you fly from Delhi, it means taking a 6:40am plane (waking during the night to check the clock—"Will they remember to call me in time?"—and rushing out thinking you've left something behind). Then the plane may be delayed because of weather conditions.

But once you're there and acclimatized (and you've had a stroll around), there's a feeling of happiness in finding such a place.

BY ROAD The direct road from Srinagar, once open June through September, is not advised because of the violence in Kashmir. Nowadays the two-day road journey (485 kilometers) begins in Manali, and goes over the Tanghlangla Pass, a trip that can make some reach for prayer beads, while others delight in every twist, turn, and high-altitude view. It is a long, tough, hard journey. It should be undertaken only by the physically fit and with the knowledge that food and accommodations will be basic: There are food stops in tents; and you need a sleeping bag.

It's possible to break the journey in Keylong, 115 kilometers from Manali, a main town of the Lahaul and Spiti district, where there are monasteries to see and simple government-run and private accommodations.

Regular and ordinary **buses** from Manali run from mid-June to early October. The deluxe fare is about Rs 300 ($10). A **taxi** from Manali is about Rs 3,500 ($116.66) one way; Rs 6,500 ($216.66) round-trip, which you must pay if the taxi returns without a fare. (***Penny-wise tip:*** When leaving Leh en route to Manali, look for a taxi going back empty and pay only a one-way fare.)

About the Airport Security

Airport security is thorough everywhere in India, but more so in Ladakh, a sensitive border area and a major military post. If you have sharp implements—scissors, Swiss army knife, whatever—or even small batteries for tape recorders, radios, or shavers, put them in your checked luggage. Don't even think about carrying them aboard. Elsewhere, you might slip by, but in Ladakh, if these items are in your hand baggage or pocket, they'll be taken from you and given to the pilot for you to retrieve from him upon arrival. The pilot is last off the plane, and you'll have to wait and hunt him down. On a good day, he may have many Swiss army knives. Ever notice how they all look alike?

BY PLANE **Indian Airlines** flies in from Delhi (75 minutes) for $86; from Chandigarh (one hour) for $54; from Jammu (one hour) for $39. It's interesting to watch the landscape below change abruptly from fertile green fields to barren rockscapes as you approach dry Ladakh. Indian Airlines office in Leh is in the Dak Bungalow (☎ 2276).

Flying is faster but has one major drawback: You may not get in or out as planned. The Leh flight goes only when the weather is perfect, which it isn't all the time. Even on a cloudless day, conditions over the Himalayas can disintegrate rapidly, so the flight is often delayed or canceled. You might be stuck for hours or have to hire a taxi to your next destination. This, too, can turn into quite a production: If you're leaving the state, the driver must have special interstate permits, fill up on gas, and, above all, be in top-notch condition to navigate the mountain roads. Not all taxis in Leh meet these criteria.

You'll have to take an airport taxi when you arrive. Taxi fares are fixed from point to point. From the Leh airport (11 kilometers from town) by *Ambassador* car to your hotel or to the tourist office can run about Rs 300 ($10). You can usually share and pay only about a quarter of this fare. Check with the Ladakh Taxi Operators Union when hiring a car or jeep or if you have a question about fares.

GETTING AROUND

Buses have seen better days. Fares are cheap for short or long hauls to stops near the monasteries and other sites mentioned below. Service can be one, two, or three times daily depending on the route: For instance these frequencies—Hemis (one bus daily); Shey (three); Spituk (three); Stok (two); Thiksey (three); Tibetan Refugee Camp (three); Alchi (two times a week)—give you some idea of the scheduling. Be sure to check bus schedules, and plan your trip to allow time for hiking to the monasteries and looking around. You may not be able to return the same day, so you'll want to be prepared to spend the night in a village home or camp out. Remember to take water and snacks. Check with the **Ladakh Taxi Operators Union** when hiring taxis, jeeps, and tongas. Fares are price-fixed from point to point; for the traveler with little time, a hurried day trip from Leh to Hemis, Shey, Thiksey, Stakna, or Stok should run about Rs 550 ($16.66); it's about same price from Leh to Alchi, Rizong, or Likir—something to consider if you can round up a party of five or six or have a tight schedule. The **Tourist Office** has information on ponies and mules for hire (☎ 2294).

FAST FACTS: Ladakh

Altitude The altitude here is 11,554 feet. Take it **very easy** until you're accustomed to the elevation: at least a day resting if you've flown straight from Delhi.

Alcohol Generally, beer is about Rs 30 ($1) per liter in the better hotels. Remember: In this altitude, a little alcohol goes a long way. Sometime during your stay, you might want to try chang (rice beer), the local intoxicating drink.

Bags Take a plastic sack when shopping for fresh apricots or apples (also good here) or you'll get them wrapped in a newspaper cone that falls apart, scattering fruit everywhere. Dried apricots are usually sold in plastic sacks. Be sure and soak them in treated or boiled water before eating them. (For other food and drink safety tips see "Where to Eat," below.)

Clothing and Cosmetics Dress in layers. When the sun's up, you'll want to strip down; in the shade, you'll reach for a sweater. You'll need sturdy shoes with non-skid soles for hiking up the steep trails to monasteries. You'll need a hat, sunglasses, sunblock, moisturizer, and lip protector. Take insect repellent. The gardens and groves are beautiful but buggy.

Courtesies and Customs *Jullay* is the all-purpose greeting used all the time; shoes are removed at monasteries.

Electricity In Leh, it is usually on from late afternoon to 11pm (it sometimes goes off earlier).

Flashlight Don't leave your hotel without it if you want to see the works of art inside the gompas, where the lighting is minimal if there is any at all. You'll also need your flashlight if you intend to prowl around at night outdoors or read once the electricity goes off.

Food and Water There are almost no clean places to eat when you're out at the monasteries on day trips. Some hotels will pack box lunches for these outings. But if yours doesn't, be sure to buy something for the road. Fruit (take a knife to peel it) and Ladakhi bread (bakeries are behind the mosque) are always good munchies. Also remember to take lots of bottled or boiled water whenever you go on an outing. Thirst is almost a constant companion in Ladakh's extremely dry climate. Bottled water is expensive—Rs 20 (66¢) to Rs 40 ($1.33) per liter in some places in Leh. But better to pay up than to be laid up. A local favorite food is thupka, a cereal.

Money Bring lots of small bills with you. No one ever seems to be able to make change in Ladakh. Not having change is common all over India, but in Ladakh it's even difficult to cash traveler's checks. In Leh, you can change money at the State Bank of India (☎ 2252). Take something to read, though; there can be a wait—and don't bank on army payday.

Passport *Always* take your passport with you. There are checkpoints on some routes.

2 Leh

The main city, Leh (pop. 10,000) is virtually a main street at a spectacularly high 11,554 feet, where Kashmiri merchants rent stores and pursue you relentlessly to sell merchandise you can get more cheaply in Srinagar, and where you can wander aimlessly, poking into Tibetan shops lining numerous fascinating but untidy lanes.

In the long open market you can watch Ladakhis smoking, drinking butter tea, socializing, and haggling over bangles, prayer flags, beads, bells, mittens, and shawls. All day they come and go in the market—married women in their high hats and full skirts; the unmarried, hatless, with simpler robes; men with deeply lined faces; ragged kids; stray dogs; and old men turning their prayer wheels round and round. Produce sellers turn up evenings with eggplants, peppers, and golden apricots (the last an acclaimed delicacy, to be eaten only after washing in treated water and peeled, or, if dried, soaked in treated water before eating).

ESSENTIALS

VISITOR INFORMATION

Off Main Street, the **Jammu and Kashmir Tourist Office** (☎ 2294 or 2297), open from 8am to 8pm in summer and 10am to 4pm in winter, provides maps and pamphlets on Ladakh.

You should also check in at the **Foreigner's Registration Office,** Superintendent of Police, Leh.

CITY LAYOUT

In the main bazaar is the mosque that was built in 1594. Islam was introduced in Ladakh more than 300 years ago. The Muslim religion is still prominent today.

Up the hill beyond the Moravian Church, next to the Tsemo La Hotel, the Ecological Centre uses solar energy and has related exhibits, a library, dehydrated foods and dehydrators for trekkers, as well as a restaurant (sometimes closed). Across the road, little boys skinny-dip in the town tank and then stretch out along the retaining wall like chubby seals drying off in the sun.

Don't worry about getting lost in the labyrinth of old streets—you'll eventually reach the center again. And wherever you wander you'll find Ladakhis smiling, helpful, and willing to point you in the right direction.

GETTING AROUND

There are jeep taxis and a few Ambassador cars about. The jeeps are preferable for the unpaved side roads, which often turn into streamlets. You get taxis at the stand in Leh. Their fares are price-fixed; consult with the Ladakh Taxi Operators Union before making any deals. Figure on about Rs 700 ($23.33) for a one-day tour by taxi of the monasteries including fee for a guide. (Always take a Ladakhi guide.)

WHAT TO SEE & DO

Looming above the town, **Leh Palace** is the town's main sightseeing attraction. Built around 1600 on a granite ledge shaped like an elephant's head, it's a smaller version of the Potala built around the same time by the fifth Dalai Lama in Lhasa, Tibet. A remnant of magnificence now, the decaying Leh Palace, dwarfed by the mountains, is dazzling in the morning sun and a ghostly guardian by moonlight. The palace was badly damaged during the Dogra Wars of the last century, when the royal family fled to Stok where their descendants live to this day. Centuries of abandonment and vandalism have further added to the deterioration of the once grand Leh Palace, until the best thing about it is the view below. The Archeological Survey of India is working on its restoration, so you can see it as it undergoes renovation.

The palace is supposed to be open from 6 to 9am and again from 5 to 7pm. But don't be surprised if it doesn't open at the appointed hours—or any others for that matter—and you have to be contented only with the view from below.

High above the palace are the even more ruined older **palace-fort** and what little remains of the **Temple of the Guardian Divinities,** which houses a big Buddha (sightseeing for those who dote on great views and long hikes). **Sankar Gompa** (monastery), a pleasant short walk from the town center (open from 6 to 8am, and 5 to 7pm), has a multiarmed and multihanded Avalokiteshvara, or Buddha of Compassion.

This is the only monastery in the valley and home to the chief Lama of Spituk and 20 lesser lamas. Hours are 7 to 10am, and 5 to 7pm. Prayers are at 6pm.

Back in the main market, stop at **Leh Mosque,** built in 1594 by Singe Namgyal to honor his Muslim mother.

WHERE TO STAY

With tourism becoming a major factor in Ladakh, not surprisingly, perhaps, everyone in town seems to be going into the hotel and guest house business. Tariffs are lower off-season.

Keep a flashlight handy since electricity is erratic; it is usually on in the afternoon until 11pm. Unless otherwise indicated, the hotels below have attached bathrooms with (not always dependable) hot and cold running water.

DOUBLES FOR LESS THAN RS 600 ($20)

Behind an iron gate and high brick wall **Hotel Bijoo** (☎ 2131) is a two-story white building trimmed with brown wood. The best rooms have double exposures; all have attached bathrooms.

Hotel **Ri-Rab,** Changspa, has clean, simply furnished rooms in a quiet location away from the bazaar. The hotel's garden provides the vegetables for the restaurant.

Dragon-Leh's (☎ 2139) 16 simply furnished doubles are almost always filled with trekking parties, whose cooks and porters pitch tents outside. Minimal comforts and cleanliness.

Himalayan Hotel (☎ 2104) is tucked in a shady willow grove near a brook. The ramshackle building houses 16 simply furnished, fairly clean, twin-bedded rooms—12 with attached, Western-style bathrooms, four with a common bathroom—all overlooking a courtyard where young children play and the women do laundry in tubs. Travelers also camp out in the courtyard.

Near the Moravian Church, the **Methokling** has neat, clean guest rooms, set in a garden, and a restaurant.

DOUBLES FOR LESS THAN RS 1500 ($50)

Shamba La (☎ 2267), recently spruced up, has 15 larger-than-average rooms and a restaurant with cornices, pillars, and delicious Chinese and Western food. The giant fireplace in the lounge is nice to curl up in front of on a chilly day. It's half a mile to town.

New, neat, and recommended is **Omafila** (no phone), with 30 rooms and good food. At the edge of town, it's a pleasant stroll from the center.

Half-hidden by gigantic sunflowers and cosmos, the cheerful **Tsemo La,** Karzoo (☎ 2284), has rooms in renovated old villas; alas, maintenance has declined here. Two upstairs rooms in the main building have balconies with splendid views. Rooms in annexes look out on the garden, which also houses the restaurant. The hotel caters to tour groups, so the food is bland to please timid palates. It is located near the solar-heated library and ecological center.

Kangri, Nehru Park (☎ 2251), has 22 Ladakhi-style doubles—deep-pile Tibetan rugs and floor cushions for lounging at low carved tables. Beds are the Western-style with box springs. All rooms are doubles; attached bathrooms have hot and cold running water. The restaurant serves good Ladakhi, Indian, and Chinese food. The hotel is near a noisy generator which shuts down at 11pm.

Peerless K-Sar Palace (☎ 2548), in white stucco with distinctive wood trim, has 23 carpeted, clean, comfortable, spacious rooms with mountain views (front) or field views (back). There's an attractive, multiethnic restaurant and enough warm service to take the chill off the coolest days. The top price is Rs 1,118 ($37.26) for double with meals.

Nearby **Rafica** has 24 rooms, some with views.

Lharimo (☎ 2101) has 30 double rooms. The attractive lobby and restaurant have bright red, lacquered, wooden-beamed ceilings. The white-walled rooms are clean and furnished in blond woods, with views and balconies from which to admire them. The spacious lobby is unusual for Leh.

Hotel Kanglachen (☎ 2144), near the Moravian Church, has 24 rooms surrounded by a garden with a big apple tree; rooms are pleasant and attractive, but some are without private bathrooms. The restaurant decor utilizes ornate painted wood pillars to divide up the space.

Guest Houses

Guest houses open and close like wildflowers; what you see listed below may not be there when you are, but there will be others. Prices rise and plummet like the temperature, seasonally and competitively. Bring a towel, soap, sleeping bag, and insect repellent (in case you find some uninvited guests in your room). Hot water is available in buckets; toilets are primitive. Most will be under Rs 300 ($10) for a double.

Behind a white fence, **New Antelope Guest House** (☎ 2286) occupies a white building trimmed in brown. This is a friendly place with 11 sparsely furnished, clean doubles, six with bathrooms attached, the others with common bathrooms, all with Eastern fittings.

Hills View (☎ 2286), near tourist office, offers the basics plus a garden; some rooms, in fact, come with a view.

To reach **Two Star,** around the bend from the Tsemo La, you must cross a little brook to reach the path to the door. The place is very spartan but tidy. Good food is another plus.

Even cheaper and simpler, you can try these: **Larchang Guest House** offers six clean double rooms with cots and hole-in-the floor toilets. Only cold water is available. Another similar choice is **Lung Snon,** Shetnam Chuli. Low in price, comfort, and cleanliness is **Palace View** (☎ 2161), near the Polo Ground, for those who can stay anywhere. It is popular, however.

Finally, there are the government-run **Tourist Bungalows,** with a few doubles and a VIP room, and **Dak Bungalow and Circuit House,** with a few double rooms; all have bathrooms attached, cold water on tap, hot water in buckets. Reserve in advance by writing to: Assistant Director of Tourism, Tourist Office, Leh 194401, and enclose a 50% deposit.

Check with the tourist office for other places to stay if you arrive without a room. I've barely skimmed the surface in this listing.

Accommodations Outside of Town

Located 11 kilometers (7 miles) from town**, Ladakh Sarai** (named after the old tent villages on trader's routes) offers 15 comfortably outfitted yurts (tents) set in a cool and inviting willow grove below Stok Palace. Three tents share one of the five well-equipped bathrooms in separate cement tents. The lounge and two dining areas are furnished Ladakhi style with low benches and tables. Rates are $100 per person double-occupancy, with a single supplement of $40. Rates include airport transfers, activities, room, and board. There is taxi service by **Union Taxi** to Leh and elsewhere; or trek to town and to the gompas nearby. You also can go river rafting from here. For reservations, contact Mountain Travel India Pvt. Ltd., 1/1 Rani Jhansi Road, New Delhi 110055 (☎ 7525357; fax 7777483).

WHERE TO EAT

First, a health advisory: Prevent stomach upsets; drink only purified bottled or boiled water in Ladakh, or opt for hot tea made with boiling water. The water throughout Ladakh is polluted. Eat cooked vegetarian meals; meat and poultry can be unsafe because they have not been properly refrigerated or well-cooked to kill bacteria. If you must eat fresh, raw fruit and vegetables, wash them in purified water, and peel them with a clean, sterilized knife.

You'll find a variety of Indian regional dishes in restaurants, but the tastiest foods are both Tibetan and Chinese. A hearty meal runs Rs 30 ($1) to Rs 50 ($1.66) in a restaurant, more in the top hotels.

One of the oldest and most reliable restaurants is **Dreamland,** a clean place serving mainly Tibetan and Chinese dishes. The water is said to be filtered (don't risk it); the jasmine tea (for a few rupees) is both safe and tasty. For breakfast, there's mango or orange juice and butter pancakes. A specialty for dinner (requiring six hours' notice, for six to 10 people, at Rs 300) is gagok (a variety pot of mutton, eggs, carrots, rice, and momos, which are dumplings). Hours are 8:30am to 10:30pm every day. The restaurant closes in winter.

Mona Lisa is attractively painted and polished, with a liquor permit. The food is generally well prepared. Tibetan specialties are the best choices.

Of the top hotels, **Shambala** has some of the best food; the new **Omafila** is also recommended. For pastries and breads, try the **German Bakery,** run by Germans who have settled here.

SHOPPING

As throughout India, there are firm restrictions here on the export of antiquities more than 100 years old. And it's doubtful that anything of this vintage will be easily found. However, you might locate something worthwhile down the little lane off the main bazaar in the Tibetan shops. **Tibetan Arts** and **Ladakhi Village Curios** have especially good selections of tankas, bowls inlaid with chips of turquoise, bangles, and beads. On Main Street try **Imatz**—owned by Kashmiri merchants with other shops in Srinagar, Agra, and Kovalam Beach—which has some interesting bangles, bronzes, and other curios (they love to bargain!). Stores and street vendors sell warm hand-knit mittens, shawls, and caps.

Generally, prices are high and the merchants reluctant to come down. Hard bargaining helps. Be sure and carry small change and mint-condition bills; merchants never have change and will refuse worn, torn currency.

3 Beyond Leh

The main activity in Ladakh is visiting ***gompas,*** where you get a glimpse of Tantric Buddhism. To put centuries of tradition into a few descriptive lines: Tantric beliefs involve magical, mystical rites with mantras (chants) and yantras (drawings). When used in the right combination they are believed to evoke powers that lead to higher bliss.

One especially well-known mantra is the Six Syllables, *Om mani padme hum* (Praise be to the jewel in the heart of the lotus). In Ladakh this phrase is everywhere—etched repeatedly on the prayer stones left by the pious at the sides of roads, banks of rivers, and especially on top of the many flat-topped walls, called *manis.* There are countless manis all over Ladakh with all kinds of holy inscriptions and drawings—some are hundreds of years old and look like stone tapestries. Like the little prayer flags you'll see above the bridges, the stones are outdoors so that the wind can sweep their blessings through the valley and beyond. Meditation and other techniques are also important to Tantric Buddhism.

Ladakhi Buddhists are united not only by what they believe, but by their powerful rinpoches, or head monks. Rinpoches are more than religious leaders; they cure ills, counsel those in trouble, and, like Solomon, settle marital disputes.

The gompas are architectural marvels, built to conform to steep hillsides and blend with the rocks. You're more or less free to wander anywhere in the gompas, with occasional assistance from a monk who will appear from the shadows to show you special treasures, such as scrolls or prayer books, or a row of jeweled deities with golden bowls in front of them holding something to drink. New offerings are brought by lamas—water in the morning and butter tea in the evening—to please the finicky gods who prefer their refreshments fresh and sanctified. Sometimes you'll be escorted by a lama to the monastery's smoky kitchen for some butter tea, the local favorite drink of mortals as well as gods. It's made, as the name implies, from tea and butter, but also soda and salt, all sloshed about in a big churn. So often have monks at Hemis monastery been photographed making this drink that they'll strike the pose, whether or not you have a camera, and expect a few rupees in return—rupees that go to refurbish the crumbling monastery.

An important note: With jeep and driver, you can cover a lot of ground in a day; also hire a Ladakhi guide to ease your way at the gompas. Otherwise, you might not get in.

SPITUK A good gompa for starters is **Spituk,** about 10 kilometers (6 miles) from Leh and visible from a plane near the airport if you fly into Ladakh. On a small hill above the Indus River, the 500-year-old monastery has a main prayer hall hung with richly decorated tankas and walls with bejeweled gods and goddesses. All this you can see all of the time, but the main statue of the goddess Kali is demurely veiled and revealed only once a year, at festival time.

Going beyond Spituk, the road beside the Indus River leads to monasteries at virtually every turnoff. As if to pave the way with prayers, mantra stones line the roadsides and riverbanks clear to Hemis, the largest gompa and farthest on this route from Leh.

CHOGLAMSAR Five miles from Leh, the first stop is **Choglamsar,** a Tibetan refugee camp, and an important center for the study of Buddhism and the making and sale of handicrafts. Yak-wool carpets woven on the site cost Rs 950 ($31.66) to Rs 1,400 ($46.66) and higher, depending on size and the pattern.

SABU Next, take a detour to **Sabu,** a sprawling village set in the midst of fertile marsh and farmland, where the springs are believed curative. Here's the famous Sabu headache cure: Lie with your head between two rocks—face up, eyes shielded from the sun by a cap—and let someone pour thin streams of icy water from a tin can in the center of your forehead until the pain goes away. At one streamlet, people were drinking and then running around in circles to get sick and throw up their impurities. Having had no headache, I can't attest to the efficacy of the water-on-the-head cure. But I can tell you that the mere thought of drinking water to throw up made me decidedly queasy.

STOK Off the main road again, the suspension bridge to **Stok** village is covered with brightly colored prayer flags flapping overhead and scattering blessings as freely as the dust over the route to the 200-year-old **Stok Palace** (10 kilometers south of Leh; entry fee Rs 25/83¢; open 8am to 6pm). With few vestiges of its prestigious past, the palace is now home to the queen of Ladakh (the king died in 1974). Three rooms are open to the public as a fascinating museum with tankas depicting various miracles of the Buddha, plus some other exploits. The most holy tanka is guarded by a lama who whisks aside the drapes to reveal it to you. The display also includes royal finery, coins, and precious stones. From the summit of the palace, it's a doll's world below of fields studded with chortens (stupas), relics of the saintly, and bright groves against the mountains. In July, there's an archery contest at the palace. Walk behind the palace for a couple of hours for wonderful views.

SHEY **Shey Palace** (open all day; prayer chanting from 7 to 9am and 3 to 6pm) is another 6 or 7 miles farther along. In the 17th century the palace was the sumptuous summer home of the kings of Ladakh, but is now largely in ruins. Some paintings have been restored. Inside, there's a brightly colored, bejeweled and gold-gilded 40-foot-high Maitreya ("future") Buddha, and for Rs 5 (30¢) a lama to show you a library with 1,000 more Buddhas on the walls. Outside, there's the largest victory stupa in the area, with a spire tipped in gold. Chorten (burial vessels for cremation ashes) can be seen in the distance; attention-deserving rock carvings are found at the bottom of the hill.

THIKSEY From the summit of Shey, the 12-story **Thiksey** gompa, about 2 miles away, is a breathtaking sight topping a hill overlooking the Indus. Built over centuries, with a history stretching back 800 years, Thiksey—entry fee of Rs 10 (33¢)—is a series of stupas constructed at various times and various heights. Some of the treasures include a pillar inscribed with Buddha's teachings, an impressive library, and a Maitreya Buddha. You can often see religious ceremonies here. On some festival days the monks have spirited archery contests in the compound behind Skalzang Chamba. There's a refreshment stand at the entrance. Religious ceremonies usually are at 6am or noon; drums and long horns are used to start things off; for special festivals, there's also colorful dancing here.

From Thiksey, you can see **Stakna.** Off the main road, it's not often visited. One of the oldest monasteries in Ladakh, it has some notable 10th-century tankas. **Matho,** also off the beaten path in a side valley, dates from ancient times and is protected by oracles chosen every few years.

HEMIS For many travelers, **Hemis,** 40 kilometers (28½ miles) south of Leh, is the highlight of their visit to Ladakh. It's the largest gompa in Ladakh and probably the best known for its summer festival (each June or July) held at the height of the tourist season. The three days of festival merriment include performances of masked dancers.

The 400-year-old Hemis (open from 7am to 7pm in summer and 9am to 5pm in winter) is an impressive sight. In the dimly lit halls are golden deities decorated with precious stones—each with a little golden bowl filled in front, a turquoise-encrusted stupa, and a large library. There is also a big tanka that is shown only once in every 11 years (the next time is 2002). The walls inside have paintings of Buddha and vengeful and peaceful deities of Tibetan Buddhism in fairly good condition. At this monastery and some others, you can watch and listen when monks chant their prayers, early in the morning is one recommended time.

Below Hemis is a **Tourist Hotel** in dreadful condition. You're better off camping out or bunking with some of the families nearby.

A suggestion: Hemis is 40 kilometers south of Leh, a day-trip from Leh by bus, jeep, or taxi (or a half-day if you're pressed for time). Be sure to pack a snack and water since there's little or nothing to eat here; nice places to picnic, though.

Nearby is **Hemis High Altitude Park.** This park, established in 1981, occupies 600 square miles in the rugged Markha and Rumbak Valleys, inhospitable to all but a few plant species but home to endangered species such as the snow leopard, ibex, bharal, and shapu. Camping sites must be reserved by contacting the Divisional Forest Officer, Wildlife Warden, Leh. Much of the park is in a restricted area, and you need a special Group Permit to visit. See if you can work out something with a local travel agent who might be able to put a group together during your visit.

North of Leh are many other monasteries. Among the most worthwhile are **Lamayuru,** 54 kilometers from Leh, which dates from the 10th century and has caves in back and some artworks indoors; **Rizong,** 29 kilometers from Leh near Khalsi, and the site of a Julichen nunnery and a monastery; and **Alchi,** 70 kilometers from Leh, near Saspul, with remarkable paintings and a huge Buddha. More than 10 centuries old, Alchi monastery is on the lowlands rather than on a hilltop. Not far away is **Likir,** which is a monastery and school.

4 Trekking

No special permission is needed to trek in some of Ladakh's loveliest mountains and meadows alive with flowers and streams, and dotted with monasteries, mantra stones, and chortens. But be sure to take everything you need before you set off. While latos (shrines to the air and wind) will, according to ancient beliefs, protect you—and the landscape and friendly villagers will let you lodge with them—there won't be stores to provide supplies. Supplies are quite limited in Leh, so the best place to get provisions is the last major city you're in before Ladakh—Manali, for instance, or Delhi, if you're coming straight from the plains. In short, trekking requires a good deal of advance planning.

Special trekking permits are usually required for some circuits. Presently, they're needed for three recently opened circuits in Zanskar, a remote area popular with trekkers. Be sure to apply early. Getting these permits can take three weeks. Only a recognized travel agent or tour operator can request these permits, which are issued for groups of four people or more for maximum stays of seven days.

Resources for information on trekking in Ladakh include the **Indian Mountaineering Federation,** Benito Juarez Marg, New Delhi (☎ 671211), and **Government of India Tourist Offices** in New York and India. One resource for treks and tours in Ladakh is the **Students Educational & Cultural Movement (SECMOL)** (☎ 2284), a nonprofit group that organizes treks and tours.

ACCOMMODATIONS Recently opened for foreign tourists at Jespa, Sarchu, and Numbra Valley are **fixed tent camps** for hire on the American plan. Singles are Rs 650 ($21.66); doubles, Rs 750 ($25). For information and reservations contact: Peerless Hotels and Travels Ltd., GF 15 Prakash Deep Building, 7 Tolstoy Marg, New Delhi 110 001 (☎ 3329399).

8 Heading East

"Not Rome, not Athens, not any city I have ever seen appears to me so striking and beautiful as this, and the more I gaze, the more its beauties grow on me," said William Howard Russell of Lucknow in 1875. Although Lucknow (pop. 1.65 million), the capital of Uttar Pradesh, has remained off the main tourist circuit and little has been done to maintain the monuments, tombs, mosques, parks, and views, there are delightful surprises for those who venture here. But here's something to remember: Wanderers can now stay in a new, 110-room Taj Mahal Hotel. Could the end of Lucknow's nontouristy days be far behind?

1 Lucknow

While Jawaharlal Nehru, India's first prime minister, spoke of Lucknow as a seat of many cultures, the strongest influence on the city has been Muslim. The Nawabs of Oudh, who reigned from Lucknow during the 18th century and built the majority of the monuments we see today, were Shiites when most Indian Muslims were Sunnis. The city still has the largest number of Shiite Muslims in India, and festivals reflect this special heritage.

Muslims first arrived in this area in the 10th century and established a settlement around their fort, which became known as Lucknow. The city became the capital of the Nawabs of Oudh (often written as *Avadh*) in the 18th century. Upstarts as far as Indian history is concerned, they initially ruled from Delhi. Among the earliest of these Nawabs was Safdarjang, whose tomb is a familiar landmark in New Delhi. After Safdarjang's death, the Nawabs moved to Lucknow.

The fourth Nawab, Asaf-ud-Daula (1775–97), was largely responsible for transforming Lucknow from a dusty village into a glittering capital city said to be as luxurious as Hyderabad. Lucknow became famous for its social refinement, which extended to every aspect of life: manners, conversation, gastronomy, and calligraphy. All the arts, especially poetry, flourished under the Nawabs. The city today is still a center for scholarship in Urdu, once the main language of North India.

Between the death of Asaf-ud-Daula in 1797 and the accession of Wajid Ali Shah (1847–56), the last of the line, there were five other

Nawabs. Each one enjoyed magnificence and luxury, and continued to add palaces and mosques to the elegant city. The last Nawab was so entirely immersed in fun and frolic—his main accomplishment was building Kaiser Bagh for his harem of 300 wives and as a place for poetry readings—that the British deposed him, deported him to Calcutta, and annexed the remainder of Oudh in 1856.

The Mutiny (now referred to as the First Indian War of Independence, although there was no Second War) began on May 30, 1857. The Residency was besieged for 87 days by rebellious local troops, only to be besieged again for another 60 days after being relieved. During these days, the entire British population of Lucknow took refuge in the extensive Residency compound. Several thousand British men, women, and children died in the two long sieges, and their graves are in a nearby cemetery. After the Mutiny, the East India Company no longer had sovereign control over India, which was thereafter ruled by a colonial government from London, Queen Victoria eventually being named "Empress of India."

ESSENTIALS

GETTING THERE

BY PLANE **Indian Airlines** has regular flights to Lucknow from Delhi for a fare of $46; from Bombay for $152; from Patna for $47; and from Calcutta for $92. The city office of Indian Airlines Offices is in Hotel Clark's Avadh (☎ 244030), open 10am to 1pm and 2 to 4:30pm. **Sahara Airlines** also flies in from Delhi for $46.

BY TRAIN Lucknow is on the Northern and North-Eastern Railway network. The best train from Delhi is the speedy *Shatabdi Express,* departing Delhi daily at 6:15pm, arriving in Lucknow at 9:50pm. Fares are Rs 405 ($13.50) by AC Chair, Rs 815 ($27.16) for Executive. ***Penny-wise tip:*** Take AC Chair and save $13.66. From Delhi, the *Gomti Express* takes 8 1/2 hours, with a fare of Rs 865 ($28.33) AC First, Rs 101 ($3.36) Second. From Bombay, traveling time is 28 1/2 hours; from Calcutta, 28 hours; from Agra, 8 1/2 hours; from Varanasi, 8 3/4 hours. For railway inquiries in Lucknow call 1331 or 1332; for reservations 259932 or 285182.

BY BUS The main UP State Road Transport Corporation bus stand is at Charbagh, opposite the railway station. For local and some out-or-town reservations, contact bus stands at Charbagh (☎ 50988); call Kaiserbagh for long-distance travel (☎ 242503). Left luggage lockers are accessible at Charbagh Bus Stand from 6am to 10pm, for 25 paise per article.

VISITOR INFORMATION

The **U.P. Government Tourist Office** is located at Hotel Gomti, 6 Sapru Marg (☎ 246205); another office is at 10/4 Station Road (☎ 226205); hours at both are 10am to 5pm. You can also stop by or call the **State Information Bureau,** Hazratganj (☎ 244728), open from 10am to 5pm. There's a good selection of books and periodicals at **Ram Advani Bookseller,** Hazratganj (☎ 43511).

GETTING AROUND

Affordable tempo rickshas run on popular routes; Rs 3 (10¢) is the minimum fare. There are few auto rickshas, and many tongas and bike rickshas. Bargain for rates before getting aboard.

WHAT TO SEE & DO

The **Residency,** built between 1780 and 1800, remains as it was at the end of the final siege, a blackened ruin of shattered walls, pockmarked by bullets and torn open by cannonballs, a surrealistic sight in a serene park with well-tended lawns and sprightly floral borders. Inside the building is a rather musty model of the Residency as it was in 1857. The Residency has no set hours; the model room is open from 8am to 5pm, Rs 2 (7¢) entry fee.

Among the other main attractions in Lucknow is the **Bara (Great) Imambara** (open 6am to 5pm; modest entry fee), which shares a large walled compound with an impressive mosque and formal gardens. Built by Asaf-ud-Daula in 1784 to provide work for his subjects during a famine (the same claim is made about the Umaid Bhawan in Jodhpur), the Imambara is an oblong building blending European and Arabic styles. The central hall, site of Asaf-ud-Daula's tomb, is 162 feet long, 53 feet wide, and 50 feet high without supporting pillars. It is said to be one of the largest vaulted chambers in the world. Under this gallery are a series of passages that have been closed off.

From the ground level, a narrow stairway leads to a complicated labyrinth that zigzags the full length of the building to disperse the weight of the huge roof. Tourists gingerly pick their way through this intricate maze with the help of guides (tip Rs 5 or Rs 6). Local youngsters use passageways as a playground, screeching with joy as they scamper through the narrow halls. To the left of the Imambara, steep stone stairs can be mounted (for a modest fee) to the roof, from which there is a terrific view of all of Lucknow with its graceful domes and minarets. Behind the Imambara, you can see old Lucknow, with the Aurangzeb Mosque punctuating the distant skyline and the medical school in the foreground.

Beside the Bara Imambara—also constructed by Asaf-ud-Daula—is the remarkable **Rumi Darwaza (Roman Gate),** said to be copied from a similar structure in Istanbul. Slim and graceful, it rises 60 feet, straddling a busy road, and is most notable of the city's gates.

Passing through the Rumi Gate, it's a short distance to your next stop, the **Clock Tower and Tank.** The tower, built in the 19th century, stands 221 feet high. Facing the tank is the **Picture Gallery** with portraits of the former potentates. This was once a small summer palace built by Ali Shah. It is open 24 hours.

Nearby is another imambara, the **Husainabad** (or **Chota,** meaning *small*) **Imambara** (open 6am to 6pm), topped with a main dome of gold and other smaller domes. This mixture of buildings was constructed in 1837 by Muhammad Ali Shah as his mausoleum. The ornate main structure faces a pool flanked by two small Taj Mahals—the tombs of his daughter and her husband. The tombs of Ali Shah and his mother are inside, where there are mirrored walls and crystal chandeliers. The Nawab's silver throne is also here and can be seen upon payment of a few rupees. The figures of a man and woman in copper near the gates are quaint Victorian lightning rods.

The **watchtower** across from the Chota Imambara is called the seven-story tower but fails to live up to its name. Builders stopped its construction after the fourth story in 1840 at the death of Ali Shah.

To the west, with two minarets and three graceful domes, is the **Jama Masjid,** begun by Muhammad Ali Shah and completed by Malika Jahan Begum after the former's death. Most mosques in India are open to non-Muslims; this one is not.

A curious sight on the outskirts of town is **La Martinière.** Built at the end of the 18th century as Constantia, the private home of French soldier of fortune Claude Martin, it is now a fine private school. Supposedly designed by Martin, the building looks like an architectural joke with its gargoyles, classic columns, open archways, porticoes, and turrets clashing with each other.

The interior was designed to permit Martin to live comfortably year-round in a series of apartments at different levels: the cool cellar for the summer; the upper story during the monsoon when the Gomti River causes ground flooding; and in the middle section in the winter.

Born in Lyons in 1732, Martin came to India in 1757 as the bodyguard of Count de Lally, governor of Pondicherry. After defecting to the British, he was transferred to Lucknow where he eventually attained the rank of major-general while serving first in the British East India Company Army, later in the forces of the Nawab Asaf-ud-Daula.

Martin also became manufacturer of the first hot-air balloons to float over Asia, and, as such, attracted the attention of the Nawab, who delighted in any kind of novelty. Thereafter Martin's fortunes also rose. Appointed Asaf-ud-Daula's confidential advisor, he became immensely wealthy over the years from lucrative business deals and gifts from those who wished to extract favors from the Nawab.

Martin died in Lucknow in 1800, before his home was completed, and left most of his huge fortune to establish charities to aid the poor of Lucknow and to set up this school, which opened in 1840, and those similar to it in Calcutta and in his native Lyons. The school is in a little park about 2 kilometers from the Tourist Bungalow. Entry is free, and you are permitted to look around the grounds as long as you don't disturb the students.

Near the Tourist Bungalow is **Shah Najaf Imambara** (open 8am to 5pm), the tomb of Ghazi-ud-din Haidar Khan, who died in 1827, and his wives. Furious fighting took place here at the time of the Mutiny. The tomb is named for a town in Baghdad where Hazrat Ali, the Shiite leader, was laid to rest. Rather severe-looking, its dome is said to have been gold-covered.

The modest **zoo** (open from 5am to 7pm), about half a mile from the Tourist Bungalow, houses a large snake collection and is located in a park. In the same park is the **state museum** (open Tuesday through Sunday, 10:30am to 4:30pm) which has some interesting sculptures. Near the bus station are **Kaiser Bagh,** a park with a baradari—a pavilion in the middle of a pool. Built by the last Nawab, Wajid Ali Shah, the park contains both his tomb and that of his wife. Here also is the **Archaeological Museum** (open 10:30am to 4:30pm, closed Mondays; entry Rs 1.50(5¢). The **National Botanical Research Institute,** originally Sikandra Bagh, was another site of fierce fighting in 1857. The gardens are open from 6am to 5pm.

Guided Tours

UP Tours (UP State Tourism Development Corporation) Hotel Gomti, 6 Sapru Marg (☎ 232659 or 220624), conducts local sightseeing tours to the main sights for Rs 60 ($2) adults, Rs 30 ($1) children, plus entry fees. Tours include Shah Najaf Imambara, Picture Galleries, Clock Tower, Rumi Darwaza, Shaheed Amarak, Residency, and Bara Imambara. Pick-up is at the Gomti or your hotel starting at 8:30am. UP Tours also helps tourists with hotel bookings, air tickets, rail reservations, and car rentals.

Shopping

In Lucknow's old bazaar at Aminabad (closed Thursday) are fascinating shops bordering narrow lanes and bulging with merchandise. This is the place to look for chikan work, the famous intricate hand embroidery done mainly on cotton but also on silk, lawn, muslin, and terry-cotton, a synthetic. This stitchery art probably was imported to India from Persia during the Mughal period and flowered under the patronage of the nawabs. Look for simplicity, regularity, and evenness of stitchery;

barely visible knots denote fine chikan work. Designs can be subtle, as if woven into the fabric; raised or arranged in a mesh pattern, they can be floral or geometric. Chikan enhances long shirts (kurtas), salwar-kamiz (tunics and trousers), linens for the home, scarves, children's wear, yard goods, and saris.

Zari, embroidery with gold threads and semiprecious stones, is another famous Lucknow craft; look for slippers, coin purses, and evening bags.

Lucknow is renowned for attars made of rose petals and other flowers, and for clay figures, which must be carefully wrapped or they will be broken in travel.

In addition to the old bazaar, other shopping areas include Hazratganj (closed Sunday); Chowk (closed Thursday); Janpath, Mahanagar, and Nishatganj (all closed Wednesday). Market hours are 10am to 8pm. UP Handloom, Hazratganj (☎ 223252) is open from 10am to 4:30pm.

WHERE TO STAY

Since Lucknow has remained off the main tourist route, hotel development has not been a priority. The hotels below have attached bathrooms, hot and cold running water, TV, and telephones; they have foreign exchange permits, and, at the upper end, accept international credit cards, unless otherwise indicated.

DOUBLES FOR LESS THAN RS 350 ($11.66)

Hotel Deep, 5 Vidhan Sabha Marg, Husainganj (☎ 236441), has 52 rooms, some air-conditioned, a restaurant and bar. Nearby, **Hotel Raj,** 9 Vidhan Sabha Marg, Husainganj (☎ 249483), has some AC rooms and offers room service. These hotels are probably the best among many in this price range. Neither is for the fussy.

DOUBLES FOR LESS THAN RS 500 ($16.66)

Hotel Deep Avadh, Aminabad Road (☎ 236521-25), has 79 rooms in need of care, some air-conditioned. The highest price is Rs 435 ($14.50). There is a restaurant and bar.

Hotel Charan International, 16 Vidhan Sabha Marg (☎ 247219), has 57 rooms that need better maintenance. Rs 500 ($16.66) for a suite.

Charan Guest House, C-6 Nirala Nagar (☎ 71538), offers 18 rooms, topping off at Rs 425 ($14.16) for a deluxe double.

Mohan Hotel, Charbagh (☎ 54283; fax 51955), has AC, deluxe doubles for Rs 450 ($15) and non-AC singles as low as Rs 100 ($3.33); there is restaurant, also a desk for travel services.

DOUBLES FOR LESS THAN RS 700 ($23.33)

Hotel Gomti, 6 Tej Bahadur, Sapru Marg, Lucknow, UP 226001 (☎ 232291), with 84 rooms, is run by the Uttar Pradesh State Tourism Development Corporation and is a cut above others in this price range. A pink marble floor and crystal chandelier dress up the reception area, which also displays a wooden mural that was inspired by the town's landmarks. Halls are not well maintained. Highest rate is for an AC double, Rs 640 ($21.33); prices are lower for non-AC. Restaurant, bar.

Considered adequate, **Kohinoor Hotel,** 6 Station Rd. (☎ 237693), has 52 rooms, recently spruced up, and is centrally AC. Nicely priced, the highest rate is a double for Rs 650 ($21.66).

DOUBLES FOR LESS THAN RS 1,200 ($40)

Welcoming travelers since the days of the Raj, the rambling **Carlton Hotel,** Rana Pratap Marg, Lucknow 226001 (☎ 244201-14; fax 249793), has seen better days. It's set in a nice garden where you can enjoy tea or a meal in fair weather. The rooms are a bit threadbare and dark, having been built to keep the sun from entering in the days before AC. Many travelers like the feeling of history that staying here evokes. The highest rate is Rs 1,000 ($33.33) for an AC suite. A standard AC double is Rs 850 ($28.33). Some prices are lower without AC. There's a restaurant serving Indian, Chinese, and Continental cuisine, also an open-air barbecue and a bar.

Arif Castle, 4 Rana Pratap Marg, Lucknow 226001 (☎ 231313; fax 231360), is an attractive property with central AC, two restaurants, and a high rate of Rs 1,100 ($36.66) for a double.

In this price range, the intimate **Amba Guest House,** BI/11E Mahanagar (☎ 71780), has 21 rooms in passable condition. The highest price is Rs 800 ($26.66) for an AC suite.

Worth a Splurge—Doubles for More Than Rs 2,400 ($67)

On 30 handsomely landscaped acres on the banks of the Gomti, **The Taj Mahal Hotel,** Gomti Nagar, Lucknow 226010 (☎ 3939391; fax 392282), in the Taj Group, has 110 richly decorated rooms and service to please a Nawab. A multicuisine cafe and restaurant featuring famous local kebabs and other specialties, a poolside barbecue, and a host of other frills such as a health club pamper and please. Singles are $80, doubles $85.

Clark's Avadh, 8 Mahatma Gandhi Marg (☎ 240131), offers all manner of modern amenities and dishes up some of the best Lucknawi food in town at the Falaknuma rooftop restaurant. The hotel decor is sleek and modern, and its 98 rooms are often booked, so reserve in advance. Rates are Rs 1,650 ($55) single, Rs 2,400 ($80) double, and Rs 3,500 ($116.66) suite.

Where to Eat

The Nawabs elevated eating to an art and rewarded their chefs with flashy jewels in appreciation of their culinary skills. Their most famous creations were delicious kebabs and roomali rotis (paper-thin soft breads), which are still enjoyed today. Dum puhkt, slow-cooked foods, also originated way back when and hold their own today. It's a local custom to drink tikrick matha (a yogurt drink) with these foods. Lucknow is home to two of India's richest sweets, gilgori (creamy pastry filled with chopped nuts and topped with edible silver) and lal peda, a milk fudge. They are rarely served at the hotels and restaurants, but you can buy them at **Chaudhary's** in Hazratganj and other sweet shops.

Some chefs in Lucknow today are said to be descendants of those who rated huzzahs from the nawabs. Perhaps they are found in these places.

Shame Avadh (near Hotel Clark's Avadh), 2 Mahatma Gandhi Rd., is an outdoor cafe, with umbrellas to shade benches, where a number of vendors sell kebabs and roomali roti. Open 10am to around midnight. Kebabs start around Rs 10 (33¢).

A number of hotels serve local dishes in their restaurants: **Oudhyana,** The Taj Mahal Hotel; **Falaknuma** at Clark's Avadh, with rooftop view; **Nawabeen** and **Ab-o-dana,** Hotel Arif Castle; **Mehrab,** Hotel Gomti. Figure on Rs 200 ($6.66) to Rs 300 ($10) for a three-course meal at all but the top two hotels, where you'll pay double these amounts or more. (For hotel addresses and telephones, see "Where to Stay," above) For buffets, check out the top hotels as well as the **Carlton.**

For snacks and coffee, you get by with much less; at a place like the **Indian Coffee House** at Hazratganj, Rs 20 (66¢) will buy a snack and a drink. You might spend a bit more at **Royal Cafe,** Hazratganj, or **Janata Coffee House,** Kaiserbagh; for Indian-style fast food try **Spicy Bites** in the Tulsi Cinema Building, Hazratganj. Chaat (spicy grain mixtures and other snacks) are famous in Lucknow and the featured attraction at **King of Chaat,** near the Stadium, Hazratganj; **Chaudhary's Sweet House** in Hazratganj, **Kwality Chaat House,** and others. Serving an array of delicious ice creams and kulfis are **Kwality,** Hazratganj; **Go Go Ice Cream,** 10 Shivaji Margj; **India Kulfi,** and **Prakash Kulfi,** both in Aminabad.

Note: The first and seventh days of the month are "dry."

2 Varanasi

At about 6 o'clock every morning, just as the sun is beginning to rise, thousands of people can be found lining the banks of the muddy River Ganges. They are bathing in its sacred waters, washing their clothes or themselves; filling ornate brass jugs to take home; exercising, stripped to the waist, on the broad stone steps (ghats); or simply sitting, lotus-legged, gazing at the emerging sun with their hands clasped and their minds pure.

Most of them are older people, for Hindus (and others) come to Varanasi (pop. 1.03 million) to die, and to spend their last few years in religious works. But there are younger people too—certainly children, holding the strings of their flat, blue kites; always holy men; and innumerable goats, cows, pigs, pigeons, even an occasional camel.

The ghats of Varanasi (often called by its former name, Benares) have been described as the roots of the city, and most Hindus hope to visit the city during their lifetime. There are pilgrim houses all along the waterfront, and visitors can stay in them for up to four days with no charge. Then, if they can find the space, they can move from one to another for four days at a time. Countless pilgrims who have come for a visit have ended up dying and being cremated on one of the burning ghats (crematoria) along the very same waterfront. The fires and smoke can be seen all day, as can the occasional body, wrapped in a shroud and lashed to a green bamboo stretcher.

Six o'clock in the morning is the magical hour to visit the waterfront, just as it is beginning to stir. Pilgrims, after a visit to one of the scores of priests who sit under rows of straw umbrellas, have their eager faces turned toward the eastern sun's watery rays.

You can take one of the regular morning tours at that hour operated by ITDC—whose office is in the Hotel Varanasi Ashok (☎ 46020)—or you can walk over to the main steps at the Dasaswamedh ghat, and for about Rs 35 ($1.16) to Rs 50 ($1.66) per hour (after bargaining) hire a small skiff to transport you up and down the waterfront. The steady creak of ancient oars, the slap of wet cotton garments on the rocks as professional laundrymen ply their trade (Rs 1 to RS 5 per cotton piece), the shrill cries of bathers testing the tepid water, and the tinkling of scattered temple bells disturb the morning calm. A clash of cymbals comes from a red house where widows sing hymns, their plain, white saris unrelieved by any pattern.

Down the river, near the **Someshwar** ghat, a more or less permanent group of travelers shares a brightly decorated houseboat; farther up is a Nepalese temple, richly decorated with erotic carvings. And between these not-dissimilar phenomena sits the elegant home of the caretaker in charge of burning at one of the major crematoria. Tigers flank the roof—a symbol that one is never far from death.

The broad and holy River Ganges, which generally flows southeast, in Varanasi reverses its course and flows north. People tell you that this is a tribute to the holiness of the city. But, alas, the scientific explanation is less miraculous: Like many old rivers on a flat flood plain, the Ganges is a meanderer and flows in huge U-shaped loops. Varanasi is in one of the loops, so on one side of the city the river flows south and on another it flows north. Despite its dirty color, the river's sulfur-filled water is pure—some people drink nothing else—but it's not always harmless. White marks along the walls above the riverbank testify to the height of occasional floods.

ESSENTIALS

GETTING THERE

BY PLANE There are daily **Indian Airlines** connections to Delhi for $74; to Agra for $57; to Khajuraho for $39; and to Kathmandu for $71; there are also connections to Bombay. The Indian Airlines city office is at 52 Yadunath Marg, Varansi Cantonment (☎ 43746). **Modilift** also flies to Varanasi; their city office is at the Hotel Vaibav, Cantonment (☎ 46466).

Babatpur airport is 22 kilometers from the city. **Coach transfers** to and from the airport by Indian Airlines Coach run twice daily for Rs 25 (83¢) via the Government of India Tourist Office. **Tourist taxis** from the airport to hotels in town cost about Rs 275 ($9.16); local taxis cost about Rs 115 ($3.83) to Rs 125 ($4.16), but you must bargain to set a price before you get in.

BY TRAIN Varanasi is a key point for the Northern and North-Eastern Railways and connects to all major cities, such as Delhi, Agra, Lucknow, Patna, Calcutta, Ahmedabad, Bombay, and Triupati. Some trains to keep in mind are the *Poorva Express* (12½ hours) and *Neelachal Express* (13¾ hours) from Delhi (764 kilometers); the fare is Rs 1,222 ($40.73) AC First, Rs 141 ($4.70) second. Among the trains from Calcutta (700 kilometers), there's the *Amritsar Howrah Express* (14½ hours), which costs Rs 1,120 ($37.33) AC First, and Rs 130 ($4.33) Second. From Bombay (1,509 kilometers) go via the *Mahanagri Express* (27½ hours) or *Bombay-Varanasi-Ratnagiri Express* (30 hours); the fare is Rs 1,980 ($63.33) AC First and Rs 209 ($6.96) Second. Trains from Kanpur take 7½ hours. **Varanasi Cantonment Railway Station** is in the heart of the city. For reservations call 348031.

BY BUS Varanasi is at the junction of three national highways: NH2, NH7, NH29. The **UPSRTC Bus Stand** is on Sher Shah Suri Marg, Varanasi Cantonment (☎ 43476). No advance reservations are required. UPSRTC and MPSRTC connect Varanasi to such cities as Allahbad, Jhansi, Lucknow, Lumbini (Nepal), Lucknow, and Patna.

VISITOR INFORMATION

The **India Tourist Office,** at 15B The Mall (☎ 43770), adjoining the Hotel de Paris, is very helpful and courteous. Help can be obtained there each day from 9am to 5:30pm (closed Sunday), and they will happily assist you in hiring taxis or booking tours for sightseeing or give information on local activities; there's another counter at Babatpur Airport (open only during flight timings). **UP Tourism** has an office on Parade Kothi (☎ 48486), and an information counter at the Railway Station (☎ 43670).

GETTING AROUND

Among the budget traveler's best bets are tempo rickshas Rs 1 (3¢) per stage and auto rickshas for around Rs 200 ($6.66) for 2 hours (15 kilometers), but you must bargain hard for this rate. Cycle rickshas and tongas are also widely available. Rates are negotiable. There are no yellow-top taxis, but you can pick up private taxis at the hotels or through travel agencies. Basic rates range from Rs 3.50 (12¢) to 11.50 (38¢) per kilometer. A half-day city tour (45 kilometers/4 hours) by AC car is usually Rs 400 ($13.33) to Rs 600 ($20); for river and airport, Rs 970 ($32.33). A non-AC car is about one-half these prices. Minimum bus fare is 50 paise.

When to Visit

The best time to visit is from October to March; it's very hot and dry in summer. During the monsoon, flooded streets can make it almost impossible to get around, especially the low-lying parts of the city. Cycle rickshas are handy for plying the water-filled streets.

Special Events

The major religious festivals Diwali, Dusshera, Holi, and Basant Panchami are celebrated here. Local festivals happen almost every month; check with the tourist office during your visit. There are music festivals (this is Ravi Shankar's home base) in the winter. This also the area where kathak, one of major forms of Indian dance, originated. Dance performances are sometimes featured at festivals.

WHAT TO SEE & DO

Visiting temples is the main occupation for Hindu visitors, and although you don't need to follow their example quite so slavishly, there are a few special places that are worth your attention.

Fairly new is **Bharat Mata Mandir,** dedicated to Mother India on the campus of Kashi Vidyapath University, one of three universities in the city. Started by followers of Mahatma Gandhi in 1921, it was inaugurated by Gandhi in 1936. The main reason to stop here is to see the marble relief map of India designed by Shiva Prasad Gupta, a noted freedom fighter.

The Mother India Temple lies en route to a temple that tourists in particular enjoy, the **Durga Temple,** which looks something like a cluster of oversized brown asparagus tips clustered around a giant one in the center. Worshippers consider the smaller pointed spires to represent individual souls, the larger one to be the universal soul. Monkeys clamber all over the spires, and for this reason it has earned the nickname "the monkey temple."

Just a peanut's throw away is the **Tulsi Manas Temple,** built in l964, a pristine marble structure believed to be on the site where the great saint and poet lived and wrote his epic poem *Ram Charit Manas.* The text of this great work is inscribed around its interior walls. This temple is open from 6:30 or 7 to 11:30am, again from 3 to 10pm.

A short ride from downtown, all three temples can be reached by taxi, and they are at least two-thirds of the way to the magnificent, tree-lined campus of the famous **Benares Hindu University,** among the largest in the world, where the impressive **New Visvanath Temple** is located. One of the tallest in India, this one, of beautiful white marble, rears its lofty head into the sky like a junior-league Chrysler Building. It's very eye-catching, both outside where a rhinoceros fountain spouts water from its head, and inside where water drips persistently onto a flower-decked lingam signifying that "every moment one should be conscious of God." The Hindu "God" is basically formless, one who nevertheless takes many different forms.

The walls of this Shiva temple, like many of its kind, are inscribed with basic tenets of the Hindu faith, including these: "There is no fire like lust, there is no grip like hatred, there is no net like delusion, there is no river like craving"; and "The senses are the horses, they say, the objects of the senses, their path, the man with mind well reined reaches the highest place of God."

One man whose mind was obviously well reined was the founder of the 1,100-acre university (hours are 11am to 4:30pm, except Sundays and holidays), in which the temple sits. More than 20,000 students now attend the university, two-thirds of them living on campus in pleasant, tree-shaded buildings that overlook spacious playing fields. Madan Mohan Malaviya, the founder, was a lawyer who left his profession to raise money for the university and once described himself as the greatest beggar in the world. Among the donations he received was a loaf of bread from a beggar; it was later auctioned for Rs 12,000, and the beggar's name listed first among the donors.

Also on the university campus—and definitely worth a visit—is the **Art Gallery (Bharat Kala Bhawan),** which has an extensive collection of fascinating medieval miniatures, some on palm leaves, with such favorite themes as red, white, and blue cows, corporal punishment in the harem, peacocks in trees, and a blue-faced Krishna in various guises. The pictures in the gallery deserve several hours of close scrutiny—there's a lot going on there. Summer hours are 8am to noon; winter hours 9:30am to 4:30pm; closed Sundays and holidays.

Across the river is **Ramnagar Fort,** the once-grand former home of the Maharaja of Varanasi; of interest is the Durbar Hall and the royal museum, housing such memorabilia as grand palanquins, clothing, furniture, and arms. The fall festival of Dusserha is celebrated with gusto here. Hours are 9am to noon, and 2 to 5pm; there is a nominal entry fee.

Fourth and last of the not-to-be-missed temples is the holiest one of all, the **Viswanatha,** more commonly referred to as the "Golden Temple" for its gilded spires. It is particularly hard to find, being tucked away amid a maze of shops and homes in the crowded Chowk area near the river. A narrow shopping lane leads off the main street, Dasaswamedh, up to the temple; it's lined with tiny stores and knick-knack stands, some selling holy Ganges water in tiny sealed brass pots (look into the **Cottage Industries** store, up to the left, for bargains.) The view of the temple roof is up a sudden alley—there'll always be somebody who wants to guide you there and hold candles to the narrow, stone staircase so you won't get lost. You'll have to settle for views of golden spires on the rooftop opposite, though (for Rs 5) since non-Hindus are not permitted in the temple.

For those who still want more, there's the nearby **Annapurna Temple,** with a golden goddess within; the unusual **Nepali temple,** on Lalita Ghat, was constructed by the late King of Nepal out of wood from his native land. The walls have robust carvings that have earned it the nickname "mini Khajuraho." Finally, there are 56 **Vinayaka Temples** dedicated to Ganesha throughout the city, to name a few more.

Guided Tours

Two tours round up the sights for you. **UP Roadways Tour 1**—a Ganges River trip, with stops at key temples and Benares Hindu University—costs Rs 45 ($1.50). Summers it is conducted at 5:30 to 11:45am; winters from 6am to 12:15pm. **UP Roadways Tour 2**—Sarnath and Ramnagar Fort—also costs Rs 45. Summer it is conducted from 2:30 to 6:25pm, winters at 2 to 5:55pm. Both tours start from the UPTDC Tourist Bungalow, Parade Kothi (☎ 43413). You also can board at the Government of India Tourist Office, The Mall, a few minutes after departure from the bungalow. Tickets are sold on the bus only. *Note:* Neither tour was operating during my recent visit.

Shopping

Varanasi is renowned for its silks woven with pure silver and gold; their elaborate designs and brocades have evolved over centuries. The city also is a place to buy gold jewelry, brassware, sandalwood, carpets, and ivory wares (not from elephants). The **main shopping areas** are the Chowk, Godowlia, and Vishwanath Lane; you might try the **UP Handlooms Emporia** at Lahurabir, Nadeshwar, and Neechi Bagh; **Tantuja,** at the Bengal Emporium, Dasaswamedh Road; and **Mahatex,** Maharashtra

Emporium, Godowlia. Some other places to shop are **M/s Bhagwan Lila Exports,** Sindu Nagar Colony, Sigra; **M/s Mohan Silk Stores, Bhawagan Stores, M/s J. R. Ivories and Curios, and Brijraman Das,** all four in Vishwanath Gali; **M/s Chowdhary Brothers,** Thatheri Bazar; and **Oriental Arts Emporium,** 10/252 Maqbool Alam Road, Chauki Ghat.

WHERE TO STAY

Be sure and ask about off-season discounts, usually beginning in April and going through July or August. For a town as popular with tourists as Varanasi, it's surprising there are not many good hotels. Finding a nice, clean, neat room in Varanasi to fit the budget in this book is a challenge. The spartan low-budget hotels along the Ganges are sometimes cleaner than the mid-priced hotels. When looking for a place to stay, check with the tourist office. Don't let a ricksha wallah select your digs. He'll collect a commission, and you might end up in a place you hate. Unless otherwise indicated, the following facilities have attached bathrooms, televisions, and telephones. Credit cards and foreign exchange facilities will be found in the mid- to upper ranges.

DOUBLES FOR LESS THAN RS 250 ($8.33)

The best bargain for low-budgeteers is probably the 39-room government-run **Tourist Bungalow,** just off Parade Kothi, Grand Trunk Road (☎ 43413), an efficiently operated two-story stone building, rather plain, in an H-pattern around three sides of two small gardens. It has a shady verandah, minuscule restaurant, and plain clean rooms, with ceiling fans and stone bathrooms with hot and cold running water, some Western and some Indian-style. For rock-bottom budgeteers, there's a dorm. Meals are a bargain here: Rs 15 (50¢) is the average price for a vegetarian entrée. Rs 30 ($1) for non-veg. Beer is Rs 55 ($1.83); Indian whisky Rs 50 ($1.66) per peg.

Near the Hotel de Paris, the simple privately owned **Dak Bungalow,** The Mall (☎ 42182)—actually two or three little bungalows set in a not well-tended garden—offers clean, basic accommodations. In some rooms, hot water comes in buckets; good, cheap food. Top price is about Rs 150 ($5).

DOUBLES FOR LESS THAN RS 550 ($18.33)

Diamond Hotel, Bhelpur, Varanasi 221005 (☎ 310696), was undergoing renovation when I looked in, and its 40 rooms should be sparkling by now. Always pleasant in the past, it's more so with fresh decor: New velvet settees were in the lounge and finishing touches were being put on the spacious rooms, some with lovely garden views. Some rooms are non–air-conditioned, however. There's a restaurant. Diners and Bob cards only.

Hotel Vaibhav, 56 Patel Nagar, Varanasi 221002 (☎ 46477; fax 348081) is neat and clean, with comfortably furnished rooms and a convenient location near the Varanasi RR station, Indian Airlines offices, and the India Tourist Office. Another plus is the price: a double runs about Rs 500 ($16.66).

Hotel Malti, Vidyapith Road (☎ 64708), is white with verandahs all around for sitting out after a tough day of sightseeing. The 33 rooms are comfortably furnished with neat, attached bathrooms. There is a dining hall for hotel guests. The management arranges sightseeing in town and around the area by boat. An AC double is Rs 450 ($15); rooms without AC are less.

Near Lahurabir and the Sanskrit University, the **Hotel Pradeep,** Jagatganj, Varanasi (☎ 44963), is neat, clean, and newly renovated. There are beds with brocade headboards and dressing tables in the rooms, which are also carpeted. The lower-priced, non-AC rooms are less well furnished. An AC double runs Rs 400 ($13.33). The hotel's **Poonam** restaurant serves delicious food. The hotel is walking distance from the Ganges, temples, and other tourist attractions.

Near the Pradeep is **Gautam Hotel,** Ramkatora, Varanasi (☎ 46239), with rundown corridors and 37 simple, all-right rooms and a popular restaurant. An AC double is Rs 450 ($15). There are room phones and attached bathrooms. It's a fair location, between the railroad station and Chowk.

Downtown in Godaulia, **Hotel Ganges,** Dasaswamedh (☎ 321097), has 32 rooms and the popular Temple Restaurant (see "Where to Eat," below), managed by the pleasant and friendly S. Dutta. The rooms have the basic necessities, but cleanliness varies (look before signing up); some have views of the endlessly fascinating parade on the road below.

A stone's throw from Clark's (see below), **Hotel Surya,** S. 20/51, A-5 Nepali Kothi, Varuna Bridge, Varanasi Cantonment, 2212002 (☎ 43014), is surrounded by a beautiful lawn, but it's rundown entrance makes a shabby first impression. Inside, its attractive, newly renovated rooms are wallpapered with floral patterns and coordinated with rust carpeting. British tourists staying here liked it a lot. "It's a good buy," they said; doubles are Rs 450 ($15) with AC. Non-AC as low as Rs 90 ($30).

Barahdari, Maidagin (☎ 330581), is a six- to seven-minute walk from the ghats; a simple, clean, vegetarian hotel, it has 16 rooms, some with AC, and a nice garden.

Doubles for Less Than Rs 900 ($30)

Just down the street from Clark's (see below), the **Hotel de Paris,** 15 The Mall (☎ 46601-8), holds onto its colonial charms architecturally, but has modernized, air-conditioned interiors with sleek furniture. There's a pleasant garden, dining room, and bar. Doubles cost Rs 715 ($23.83).

Pallavi International Hotel, Hathwa Palace, Chetganj, Varanasi 221001 (☎ 56939-43; fax 322943), is right in the heart of town. The 40 rooms (about 10% without AC) have motel modern furniture and all amenities. A double costs about Rs 525 ($17.50), a suite about Rs 1,000 ($33.33). There's a big garden, restaurant, and coffee shop.

Hotel MM Continental, The Mall, Cantonment, Varanasi 221002 (☎ 348379; fax 0091-5414-25345), is a cozy 27-room hotel near Clark's (see below). It is lean and clean, with a salmon, rust, and pink color scheme. The hotel is sparingly furnished but has everything you need for a comfortable stay including central air-conditioning. The rooftop garden and coffee shop are pluses. Doubles top off at about Rs 800 ($26.66).

India, 59 Patel Nagar, Cantonment (☎ 45127), has 33 rooms and charges Rs 600 ($20) for a double. The furniture is functional modern; there's a bar and a popular restaurant. Some cheaper rooms are not air-conditioned. Request the new wing. The garden is nice.

Doubles for Less Than Rs 2,000 ($66.66)

Eighty-four rooms, all with central air-conditioning, each with a good view and private balcony—these are the attractions of the **Varanasi Ashok Hotel,** The Mall, Varanasi Cantonment, Varanasi 221002 (☎ 46020-30; fax 348089), run by India Tourism Development Corporation (ITDC). The hotel is well situated on the banks of the Varuna River, from which the city derives its name. The rooms are twin-bedded (some have settees that convert to a third bed) and have small refrigerators. There's a restaurant and bar, nearly 8 acres of landscaped grounds, and a swimming pool. Expect to pay Rs 1,195 ($39.83) single, Rs 2,000 ($66.66) double, Rs 2,500

($83.33) suite; these rates are without meals. Eating at the hotel is pricey. ***Penny-wise tip:*** Have breakfast in the restaurant and take your other meals outside at the inexpensive places to eat, mentioned later on.

Hotel Best Western Ideal, The Mall, Cantonment, Varanasi 221002 (☎ 348091-92; fax 348685), is new, neat, and modern. The lobby has a marble floor inlaid with diamond patterns and crystal-beaded ceiling fixtures. All 40 rooms have huge windows set at angles so that each has a view. And you'll like the rates (even if they are slightly higher now): single for $28, doubles for $38. The Haveli restaurant serves Indian, Chinese, and Continental cuisines in a white-walled, exposed brick setting somewhat reminiscent of a haveli (grand old home). This hotel has a tie-in with the U.S. chain.

Hotel Hindustan International, C-21/3 Maldhiya, Varanasi 221002 (☎ 57075; fax 57505), has such deluxe touches as refrigerators and closed-circuit TV in the rooms, which cost about $70 for a double. There's a restaurant, coffee shop, bar, and swimming pool.

Worth a Splurge

The following hotels have air-conditioning and every conceivable amenity, such as restaurants and coffee shops, swimming pools, shops, and bars. They take most credit cards.

Taj Ganges, Nadesar Palace Compound, Varanasi 221002 (☎ 42481; fax 348186), is decorated with a lotus motif (symbol of cosmic creation, important to Jains, Hindus, and Buddhists) incorporated into the highly polished floors, staff uniforms, carpets, and around the elevators. The 130 rooms are comfortably furnished, in restful cool greens and soothing browns. Bathrooms are brown and white. Rates are $75 single, $90 double.

The most famous hotel in town is **Clark's Varanasi,** The Mall, Cantonment, Varanasi 221002 (☎ 348501/10; fax 348186), opened more than 100 years ago as an intimate, 81-room colonial-style hotel. It has been enlarged (140 rooms) and become sleek and modern. The decor in the rooms contrasts bright patterned textiles with neutrals. Singles are Rs 1,187 ($39.56), doubles Rs 2250 ($75). About the only old things around are the antique musical instruments in the coffee shop, a few colonial-style sitting rooms, and pleasant old-time service. Green plants in copper planters add color to the muted lounge filled with big contemporary settees and club chairs placed near windows so that guests can sit to admire the view of the well-manicured lawns.

Ghat Hotels, Guest Houses & Others

Hotels on the ghats or tucked amid the winding lanes near the temples can be hard to find. These are low-budget accommodations, with prices that range from Rs 100 ($3.33) to Rs 250 ($8.33) for a double. There's always someone who pops up to show you the way (a tip is in order). (Some might try to steer you someplace where they get a commission.) Be sure to come to an understanding before you set off.

A few places only: **Vishnu Rest House,** D24/17 Pandey Ghat, Varanasi 22101, next to Vishnu Temple, is spartan, clean, and strict (no drugs, weapons, or cooking; doors lock at 9pm) with verandah for watching the endlessly fascinating river; hot water in buckets. The entrance is from the river, and a walk up the ghats.

Ganga Fuji Home is easy to find in the labyrinth of riverside lanes because its exterior is rose-colored with golden trim. This is a new place to stay and as such in top condition. The small room on the rooftop was to become a roof garden restaurant.

Well identified by prominent signs along the river, **River View,** Brahma Ghat (☎ 334565) offers some rooms with private baths, a terrific view, and nice staff. Fagins restaurant serves good vegetarian food.

Sandhya Guest House, near Shivala Ghat, has simple rooms with attached bathrooms and attentive management. There is a rooftop restaurant.

The popular **Yogi Lodge,** D8/29 Kalika Gali, near the Golden Temple (☎ 53986), has basic rooms, a dorm, and shared baths. The rooms are not up to my standards of cleanliness, but they're always jammed with backpackers and other young travelers. **Yaffles** restaurant is pleasantly located on the roof terrace. There's also an indoor place to eat, but it's gloomy.

(Don't mistake this place for **Yogi Guest House,** B21/7 Kamaccha, which is not as good.)

The 26-room–plus dorm accommodations at **Temple on Ganges,** Assi Ghat (☎ 312340) are pleasant and clean. Some rooms have private bathrooms. Food is dished up with a view in the rooftop restaurant.

WHERE TO EAT

All the top hotels have restaurants and/or coffee shops; **Taj Ganges** and **Clark's** have buffet meals especially in season when tour groups visit.

INDIAN CUISINE

Temple Restaurant, one flight off the street on Dasaswamedh Road, Godowlia (☎ 321097), is a triple treat: good food, decent prices, and a great view of a fascinating bazaar. Many tourists stop here for breakfast toast and tea after their early morning boat rides on the Ganges, but this is a full-fledged restaurant where a special chicken curry—Rs 30 ($1)—and vegetarian biryani—Rs 32 ($1.06)—are among the highest-priced items on the menu. Vegetarian thalis, offering a little bit of a lot of things, are Rs 30 ($1) to Rs 35 ($1.16). Or you might just stop for tea and sahi tukra, a favorite Varanasi sweet bread. Open from 6:30am to 11pm.

Also on Dasaswamedh Road is **Ayyar's Cafe,** with vegetarian South Indian food. This is a small place with a clean, stone floor and no decor, known for delicious South Indian vegetarian thalis for about Rs 25 (83¢) and rich South Indian coffee. Open 8am to 9pm.

South Indian foods are also good at **Kerala Cafe,** Bhelpura. **Tulsi,** Chetganj, also serves good vegetarian Indian foods in a moderate price range.

OTHER CUISINE

Win-Fa, Prakash Cinema Building, Lahurabir, has plain uncovered tables, a stone floor, and Chinese and Western background music. The menu offers a range of chow meins and chop suey for about Rs 25 (83¢), and prawns (in season), fish, pork, chicken, and cheaper vegetarian dishes in various Chinese combinations. Entrees top off around Rs40 ($1.33). Open every day from 11am to 10pm.

SNACKS & SWEETS

Ashiyana, Varuna Bridge (☎ 43164), has good pakoras (fritters) and tea. Although it's at a noisy intersection, eating outdoors is more pleasant than the stuffy indoor section.

"I knew nothing of the American place," explained the owner at **Burger King** about the name of his fast food shop near the Taj Ganges. "I only found out later that Burger King was a famous U.S. place." Here are veg, mutton, and chicken burgers, and a range of snacks, none higher than Rs 20 (66¢). No tables; eat standing at counters. Open from 10am to 10pm.

VARANASI AFTER DARK

"Have an enchanting evening," is the phrase Clark's Varanasi uses to describe its evening cultural program in and about an 11th-century palace on the banks of the Ganges. The program starts with the *Ganga Aarti* (prayers) and includes traditional folk dances, scenes from the *Ramlila,* and Indian classical dances. The price of $10 includes transportation to and from Clark's Varanasi; the show lasts from 5:30 to 8:30pm. For reservations (☎ 348501-10, or fax 348186).

3 Sarnath

5 miles (8 kilometers) north of Varanasi

Sarnath, an important city for Buddhists, can be easily visited in a day-long excursion from Varanasi or as part of a guided tour originating in Varanasi.

GETTING THERE

Since buses are jam-packed in Varanasi, **auto rickshas** make a good alternative. You can go to Sarnath by auto ricksha in 45 minutes. You'll find scooters at Kacherhari Crossing, across from Varuna River or near the railway station in the center of town. Going back, get scooters in front of Deer Park. One way should cost about Rs 25 (83¢), and round-trip Rs 50 ($1.66). But you have to bargain to get that rate!

You can also visit Sarnath on a guided tour from Varanasi (UP Roadways Tour no. 2, described under "Guided Tours," above).

Or hire a car and driver for Rs 225 ($7.50) to Rs 300 ($10) round-trip.

WHAT TO SEE & DO

In some ways Buddhism could be said to have started at Sarnath, a sleepy town 5 miles north of Varanasi. Here the young Buddha sat in the lotus position and gave a famous lecture, which seems to have been amply documented. The enormous brick-and-stone **Dhamekh Stupa,** 100 feet high, built in the 5th and 6th centuries, marks the alleged spot of this first lecture to five disciples. The stupa is reminiscent of earlier Gupta architecture. Intricate carvings cover its exterior.

The impressive stupa dominates the grounds of the **Moolgandha Kutir Vihara** (a Buddhist temple), one of three, and the most ornate, in the town. Its interesting murals, painted by the Japanese artist Kosetsu Nosu in 1936, depict the life story of Buddha. East of this vihara, the statues of Buddha and his first five disciples, crafted by a Burmese monk Yumand Chariya, were added in 1989.

Sarnath is also venerated by Jains as the place where the 11th Jain Tirthankara died. The **Digambar Jain Temple,** southwest of the Dhamekh Stupa, is dedicated to him.

The walk from the red sandstone temple to the stupa is lined with evergreen trees, the greenest things in an exceptionally green garden. Farther back are the excavated remains of a Buddhist monastery that once sat on the site (four pillars supposedly mark the room where Buddha stayed), as well as innumerable smaller stone stupas built by various pilgrims up to about the 4th century.

Across the street is the **Archaeological Museum,** whose pride and joy is the glazed, mud-covered **Lion Capital,** the most valuable piece of sculpture in India, dating back to Ashoka's era. Wheels and elephants sit around the base, above which are four lions looking outward in every direction and joined at the center. The Lion Capital (which originally sat atop Ashoka's stupa) was long ago adopted as the Indian national symbol. Other interesting exhibits include the earliest example of a swastika, considered auspicious since ancient times in India; a section of a wall from the 1st century B.C.; and an A.D. 5th-century statue of Buddha, sitting cross-legged on a lotus flower—it appears to smile only when you view it from the side, but then, oddly enough, continues to smile when you move around (do you recall those pictures of Jesus whose eyes follow you around the room?). The museum is open from 10am to 5pm, closed Friday. Admission is 50 paise.

In recent years a deer park has been established adjoining the temple, replacing the one that existed on the site when the monastery was in existence. Buddhists believe that Buddha was reincarnated as a deer. Hundreds of deer roam in the park.

There are two other **Buddhist temples** in Sarnath: a fairly austere Chinese one with a pleasant garden, and an extravagantly decorated Tibetan one with the Dalai Lama's portrait on the altar and hundreds of paintings of Buddha in different postures around the gaily decorated walls. The face on the big seated statue of Buddha bears a Tibetan cast, reflected in the faces of the maroon-robed Tibetan monks who live in rooms around the temple. Many old Tibetan manuscripts and scriptures are stored in the temple, and more are constantly added by new arrivals so that it has become a repository for keeping alive Tibetan culture.

The **Central Institute of Higher Tibetan Studies,** near the ruins, offers a variety of courses from high school to post-graduate levels. The university is engaged in research of Buddhist manuscripts and their restoration; its library is a rich repository of Tibetan manuscripts. Students from universities all over the world come here to stay for long periods and do research and study.

SHOPPING

Vendors near the ruins sell stone, terra-cotta, and metal statues of Buddha and the stupas.

WHERE TO STAY

Sarnath has a **Government Tourist Bungalow,** set in a park a short stroll from the temples. It's in need of repair and care. Rooms are not air-conditioned, but they all have overhead fans. Rates are Rs 75 ($2.50) to Rs 150 ($5); all have attached bathrooms; the higher priced rooms also have an air-cooler and hot water geyser. Rs 20 (66¢) per person in the eight-person dorms. To reserve, write: Uttar Pradesh Tourist Development Corporation Tourist Bungalow, Sarnath 221007 (☎ 42515).

4 Darjeeling

Darjeeling (7,000 feet above sea level) is delightful. It's the mountain town par excellence, with fresh, clean air and happy, healthy-looking people. Physically, it's built in a series of steps hanging precariously onto the sides of the lower Himalayan Mountains. From the moment the old porter grabs your luggage from the taxi and, hanging it around his neck as if it were a bag of feathers, goes leaping up the hillside to the hotel, you know you're among a race of Sherpas. (There are also Bhutias, Tibetans, Lepchas, Nepalese, and other tribes from mountain and plain.)

Darjeeling's population is listed at 73,000, many of whom work in the 140 tea estates of the district, picking and packing the tiny leaves that have made the town literally a household word all over the world. You're never far from nature in the lower Himalayas, and in addition to 4,000 species of plants and ferns and 600 types of birds, there are all kinds of lovely animals—monkeys, leopards, civets, jackals, bears, otters, hares, deer, bears, and elephants, to name but a few—that have been recorded here.

The town's name comes from Dorje-Ling—place of the Dorje, or magnificent thunderbolt—a familiar term in the Lamaist religion. Because of the influx of

Nepalese and refugees from Tibet, Buddhism is strong in the area, but Darjeeling also possesses Hindu temples, Muslim mosques, and Christian churches.

The British made Darjeeling their favorite hill station in 1835, and today it remains not only a popular choice of foreigners but also of Indians escaping the heat of the Bengali plains and Calcutta to the south.

A PAUSE AT KURSEONG

EN ROUTE TO DARJEELING

Twenty miles from Darjeeling, at 4,800 feet, is a less lofty, low-key resort, known primarily as a tea stop for taxis and buses and a way station for the toy train going to Darjeeling. There's the pleasant **Kurseong Tourist Centre** on Hill Cart Road, with a teak-paneled restaurant for transients. The center also houses the **WBTDC Tourist Bungalow** (☎ 409), with 16 neatly furnished, wood-paneled rooms, which cost Rs 300 ($10) for a double with attached bathroom. The bus to Darjeeling from here is about Rs 20 (66¢); a taxi seat should run about Rs 50 ($1.66). The trip takes one hour.

The main reason to tarry a while here is to trek and walk through lush, wooded hills and well-tended tea estates. For information and assistance contact the **Kurseong Tourist Centre,** Hill Cart Road (☎ 409).

ESSENTIALS

GETTING THERE

BY PLANE The nearest airport to Darjeeling is in Bagdogra, to which there are direct flights on **Indian Airlines** from Calcutta, for $50, and from Delhi, for $128.

FROM THE AIRPORT From Bagdogra there is a scenic 3½-hour (90 kilometer) mountainous road trip to Darjeeling, which can be made in a private taxi for Rs 500 ($40.10); in a shared taxi, which carries seven people for a negotiable rate, about Rs 100 ($3.33) per seat; or by West Bengal government bus, for Rs 55 ($1.83). Should this not work out, you can grab a shared taxi—for Rs 40 ($1.27) per seat, a private taxi—for Rs 70 ($2.33), or an auto ricksha—for Rs 20 (67¢), and head l0 kilometers to Siliguri. From there, a private taxi to Darjeeling costs about Rs 600 ($20), a shared taxi about Rs 100 ($3.33) per seat, or a six-passenger minibus about Rs 40 ($1.33). The trip takes about 4½ hours. From New Jaipalguri, a few miles from Bagdogra, the price is the same as at Siliguri; and from Kurseong, 59 kilometers from Bagdogra, it costs about half of the above for either a bus seat and or shared taxi.

There is an **Indian Airlines** office in Darjeeling at Bellevue Properties, Chowrasta (☎ 54230), open weekdays from 10am to 5pm, Sundays 10am to 1pm.

BY TRAIN The famous **"Toy Train"** started operating in the 1880s and is still the most interesting (and crowded) way to get to Darjeeling. It starts from Siliguri and is a once-in-a-lifetime ride through the mountains. The trip takes 7½ hours—twice as long as the ride up by road—of twisting and turning to climb the 77

Phone Numbers in Darjeeling

The telephone system in Darjeeling is currently undergoing a technological update. Therefore, the numbers given in this chapter may no longer be accurate by the time of your arrival.

kilometers through steep passes, most of the way running not only parallel to the road, but actually on it. It's a bargain when it comes to memorable experiences: Rs 250 ($8.33) in first class (there is no second class). One thing more: This train doesn't run regularly; occasional landslides and other mishaps put it out of action.

The best train **from Calcutta** is the *Kanchenjunga Express,* which leaves Howrah at 6:25am daily and covers the 588 kilometers to New Jaipalguri, nearly 12 hours, arriving at 6:10pm The fares are Rs 992 ($30.06) AC First, Rs 114 ($3.80) Second. Returning, it leaves New Jaipalguri at 8am and arrives in Calcutta at 8:35pm. **From Delhi,** the *Avadh Assam Express* is your best bet. It's approximately a 19-hour trip. The fares are Rs 2,197 ($73.23) AC First, Rs 223 ($7.43) Second. The *Avadh Assam Express* **from Guwahati** takes about nine hours, and costs Rs 785 ($26.16) AC First; Rs 185 ($6.16) Second.

For railway reservations and inquiries in Darjeeling call 2555 from 10am to 4pm.

BY BUS The best bus connection to Darjeeling from Calcutta and vice versa is the **North Bengal State Transport Corporation's** *Rocket Service,* departing Calcutta at 9pm and arriving in Siliguri at 7am; on the return it departs Siliguri at 9pm and arrives in Calcutta the following morning at 7am. The fare is Rs 125 ($4.85). Departures and information are from the NBSTC booking offices, Esplanade Bus Stand, Calcutta (☎ 281854), and NBSTC City Booking Office, Burdwan Road, Siliguri (☎ 20531).

Another bus route via **Bihar Transport** connects Patna to Siliguri; it departs at 4am, arriving at 4pm, and the fare is Rs 65 ($3.70). From Siliguri, you can connect with the Toy Train or other transportation to Darjeeling.

Visitor Information

For help with planning your visit and other touristy things, you can contact the **Tourist Bureau,** 1 Nehru Rd. (☎ 54050), which is exceptionally helpful—a must for intelligent travelers. Other resources include the **Tourist Assistance Booths** at the Railway Station and Laden La Road; the **Tourist Information Centre,** Government of West Bengal, New Car Park, Laden La Road; and the office of the **Assistant Director Tourism,** DGHC, Silver Fir, Bhanu Sarani (☎ 54214).

Getting Around

You can rent **ponies** in town near the tourist bureau for Rs 30 ($1) an hour for sightseeing. Jeeps, taxis, and Land Rovers can be hired for local and outstation trips. Negotiate the fare before starting your trip. Taxis congregate at the Main Market Taxi Stand; porters carry baggage for fixed rates; if seats are available on long-distance buses, they'll take passengers to local destinations. The Toy Train is also an interesting way to reach Ghoom.

When to Go

You can visit Darjeeling throughout the year. But the peak season is April to mid-June and mid-September to November. Winters can be damp and cold. In the summer, heavy rains cause landslides that sometimes cut off the highway as well as the famous Toy Train that winds its way up the mountain from Siliguri, 60 miles away, and fog covers the famous peaks.

WHAT TO SEE & DO

Seeing the Sunrise

The big deal in Darjeeling—and the first item on most people's schedule—is to get up at four o'clock in the morning (that's right, 4am) to see the sunrise from **Tiger**

Hill. The habit is so ingrained in the heads of the hotel porters that they'll probably wake you at 4am anyway on your first morning unless you specifically ask them not to. Then, shivering under all the blankets you can wrap around you, there's a 40-minute ride in a jeep (rates negotiable, or take the tour) through sleepy villages, climbing higher and higher until your vehicle struggles up the last quarter mile to the top of Tiger Hill (8,482 feet), about 7 miles from the town.

You can also forget the wheels and trek up to Tiger Hill. But allow a full day, and leave in the wee hours for the sunrise. Of several routes, the easiest starts from Chowrasta and goes via Jorebungalow, Aloobari Monastery, Ganesh, and Toongsoong (9 kilometers, four hours one way) and is almost level all the way. There are no vehicles on this route. Another route takes Gandhi Road near the Darjeeling Club motor stand, goes parallel to Hill Cart Road, meeting Hill Cart Road near Ghoom Railway, and from there ascends to Tiger Hill.

These and other routes offer lovely views of the lush forests lining the mountain slopes, filled with wildflowers and shrubs. Many exotic birds call Darjeeling home at various seasons, so take your binoculars along—and don't forget food and bottled water.

You'll find a two-story concrete pavilion at Tiger Hill, the roof and stairs probably already crowded with shawl-wrapped Indians, most of whom have walked up the mountain for the big moment. The ground floor is a small cafe, just as cold as outdoors, where you can sip some coffee; the first floor is an unheated antechamber, doors and windows wide open, where VIPs (Western visitors) can sit and shiver.

At first, the black sky is merely suffused with a dull red glow, but as time wears on the upper clouds begin to reflect a rust-colored incandescence, which spreads and spreads until the entire eastern sky shines with reddish gold, the horizontal bands of color being gradually interspersed with streaks of lightening sky. To the northwest, the snow-capped Kanchenjunga Range is beginning to take on the glow. Suddenly, the upper tip of the sun appears from the horizon, like a red-hot saucer pushing its way up out of the fire. Within five minutes it is over; the sun has risen and turned yellow, all traces of red have disappeared from the sky, and the chattering crowd atop Tiger Hill is dispersing.

If you drive, most likely you'll return to your hotel for breakfast (you'll pass Darjeeling's golf course—certainly one of the highest in the world), and make the customary two or three sightseeing stops en route. The first is usually beautiful **Senchal Lake,** a favorite picnic spot around the reservoir that provides Darjeeling's water supply.

If you don't stop en route back to town, be sure to visit **Ghoom Monastery,** the most famous in the area, where half a dozen Tibetan monks faithfully preserve centuries-old manuscripts and the padded, silken cushion on which the Dalai Lama sat on one of his visits to the monastery. Heated air from candles in copper bowls keeps prayer wheels perpetually turning. Around the outside of the temples are 38 heavy brass prayer wheels, which everybody spins as they pass; on the roof, in a small hut, are gilded Buddhas and ornate paintings of the type common to Buddhist temples. Star of the temple is the 15-foot image, gaudily painted, of the *Maitreya,* or coming Buddha, its legs spread instead of in the more customary lotus position. The Toy Train chugs up here, too (from April through June and October through November). There is an Rs 10 (33¢) camera fee.

The narrow road that runs up through the village to the monastery is as fascinating as the shrine itself: early morning glimpses into homes, the community gathering beside the water pumps, shopkeepers setting out their wares.

Your next major stop should be the **Tibetan Refugee Centre** (described below), about 3 miles out of town on the way to **Lebong** (where the world's smallest and fastest racetrack—no races anymore, but you can walk around it—is situated). On the way you'll pass **St. Joseph's College** and, just adjoining, **India's first ropeway,** a cable-car that takes you for a breathtaking, 30-minute joyride down the mountainside from the Top Station to Tukvar Station. The round-trip cost is around Rs 20 (66¢). It operates from the top on the half-hour from 8:30am to 12:30pm, and from Tukvar on the hour from 9am to 3pm. For ropeway seats, contact the Officer-in-Charge, Darjeeling, Rangeet Valley Ropeway Station, North Point (☎ 2731). Share taxis from the Market Motor Stand to the Ropeway Station run about Rs 5 (15¢) per person.

The **Tibetan Refugee Centre** is always ready to welcome visitors, and it's an inspiring place to visit. Essentially, it's a mountainside community, centered around a main courtyard in which everybody strolls, basks in the sun, or watches the children play. All around the yard are workshops—cobblers, painters, metalworkers, weavers, even a communal kitchen where all the food is prepared for the 560 or so Tibetan refugees who live here. There's a nursery in which numerous tiny babies with woolen caps snooze in individual cribs beneath brightly colored bedspreads; a weaving shop where the wool is woven into shawls, garments, and magnificent carpets; and a dyeing area in the rear where berries, tea leaves, and other natural products are used to make the lovely dyes. Raw wool sits drying on the roof of the sheds and new looms hang in the carpenter shop.

Most of the residents of this happy community (you never saw so many smiles in one place) fled from Tibet along with the Dalai Lama when the Chinese invaded in 1959 and finally found a home here when American Emergency Relief Committees joined with the Indian government to establish a community which one day would be self-sufficient. Taking shortcuts across the hills, it's possible to walk to the community from Darjeeling in about 40 minutes; a taxi would charge about Rs 150 ($5) round-trip—but make sure before you get in. The center is closed Sundays.

Several times each year, Indians and Westerners who want to study mountain climbing can attend take courses at the **Himalayan Mountaineering Institute** just outside the town—Westerners' fees are about Rs 1,500 ($50). For years the institute was headed by the late Tenzing Norgay, the Sherpa guide who accompanied Sir Edmund Hillary on his conquest of Everest (29,028 feet) in 1953 and who is recorded to have reached the summit at 11:30am on May 29. One of the exhibits in the institute's **Everest Museum**—admission is Rs 1 at the gate and Rs 1 for the museum—which is a must-see for tourists. On display is the original manuscript of the expedition written by Sir John Hunt. It begins: "This the story of how two men, both endowed with outstanding stamina and skill, inspired by unflinching resolve, reached the top of the world and came back to join us, their comrades . . .." Also on view in the museum are such fascinating pieces of memorabilia as electric socks, a high-altitude tent, Tenzing's reindeer-skin boots, ice clamps, clothes, equipment, and a glass case full of the interesting items of food carried by members of such an expedition.

The Everest Museum is open from 8:30am to 5pm in summer, 9am to 4:30pm in winter (closed Tuesday and for lunch, 1pm to 2pm). Admission is 50 paise (16¢). It can be reached either by walking from town or by taxi, at Rs 150 ($5) round-trip, but make sure before you get in. It's cheaper to take a tour, but you won't have enough time to see it properly.

Adjoining the institute is a very interesting **mountain zoo** (entry Rs 1), which boasts all kinds of local black bears, yaks, pandas, civets, and leopards, as well as some magnificent tigers, which were the gift of the Soviet Union's Khrushchev many years ago. The tigers, like the Indians themselves, have a meatless day once a week, and watching them being fed the day afterward is a terrifying spectacle. The zoo is open daily from 8am to 4:30pm.

You can, if you wish, visit a tea estate. The usual one that's visited is the **Happy Valley** tea estate, off the main Lebong Cart Road, about a 2-kilometer (1-mile) walk or ride from the main bazaar. It's open during daylight hours every day except Sunday, when it closes at noon, and Monday, when it's closed all day. Admission is free. Most of the tea processing goes on from May to October.

A Special Tea Tour: For more of the "Champagne" of the East, there's DGHC's Darjeeling–Hima Falls, Marybong Tea Estate–Chongtong-Bijanbari six-hour tour to a number of famous gardens. For more information, contact the **Tourist Bureau,** 1 Nehru Road (☎ 54050).

Various other local sightseeing spots are recommended for those who can't find enough satisfaction merely in walking aimlessly around town. The ones most commonly mentioned are the century-old **Lloyds Botanical Garden,** with its 40 acres housing hothouses, lofty birch, ash, maple, and magnolia trees and a collection of representative Himalayan plants and flowers, just below the Market Motor Stand bazaar (market days are Saturday and Sunday); and **The Shrubbery,** another lovely garden with splendid views of the Singla Valley and Kanchenjunga range.

Other interesting sights around town include the **Natural History Museum,** closed a half day on Wednesday and all day Thursday, fee Rs 1 (5¢); innumerable temples, especially **Shri Mandir** and **Dhirdham;** and the **Temple of Mahakal** to Lord Shiva as well as the **Buddhist Shrine** on Observatory Hill, from which there's a marvelous view of the surrounding mountains. A 15-minute walk from The Mall on C. R. Das Road, takes you to a **Bhutia Busty Monastery,** a great spot for photography.

Guided Tours

The **Tourist Bureau,** 1 Nehru Rd. (☎ 54050), operates tours in season—March to mid-June and mid-September to November. Tour I: "7:30am Tiger Hill tour," from 4 to 7:30am, costs Rs 40 ($1.33) and includes Senchal Lake, Ghoom Monastery, and the Loop; minimum of eight. Tour II: "Local Sightseeing," from 9:30am to 12:30pm and again from 1:30 to 5pm, costs Rs 40 ($1.33) and covers the Mountaineering Institute, Ropeway, Lebong Race Course, Zoo, Tibetan Centre, Happy Valley, Dhirdham Temple, Ava Art Gallery, and Manjusha Bengal Emporium; minimum of eight. Tour III: "The Chrysanthemum Tour (Fall)," lasts six hours and costs Rs 75 ($2.50) for transportation only; Tour IV: "Mirik," from 8:30am to 5:30pm, costs Rs 75 ($2.50); minimum 12; Tour V: "Cinchona/Orchid Tour," includes the summer home of poet Rabindranath Tagore for Rs 75 ($2.50) for transportation only.

Travel agents conduct tours around town throughout the year, providing they can get a full car.

Near the ropeway you can often find share taxis to popular places around town. For instance, the fare from the ropeway to the Market Motor Stand is Rs 5 (17¢).

Trekking & Other Activities

Trekking

There are several trekking agents in Darjeeling who can provide everything you need for a successful trek. The most experienced among them is **Clubside Tours,** 16 Laden La Road (☎ 2122). **The Tourist Bureau,** 1 Nehru Rd. (☎ 54050), also plans treks, from getting your gear and guides to booking accommodations. Some hoteliers plan treks. The Youth Hostel rents trek-wear and other necessities.

Himalayan Treks, a booklet published by the Directorate of Tourism, Government of West Bengal, and available at the Tourist Bureau, has everything you need to know about trekking in the area—and it's free! Included are main routes, where to stay, and what to take. Directions are given for one-day treks as well as much longer treks. Don't leave your Darjeeling home base without it. The Youth Hostel keeps a book of comments on treks by past trekkers; useful reading when planning your own adventure. The best advice is to plan carefully and consult experts in the field before you decide to go.

Water Sports

For the adventurous there's **rafting** on the mighty Teesta River. It's not for the inexperienced. Packages in the budget, economy and luxury classes, ranging from Rs 300 ($10) to Rs 1,000 ($33.33) per person, include transportation, gear (sleeping bags, mattresses, tents, food), and rafting from 25 kilometers to 65 kilometers. Get information on either treks or rafting from: Assistant Director of Tourism, DGHC, Silver Fir, Darjeeling (☎ 54214), or the Tourist Assistance Booths (see the address under "Visitor Information," above).

Other Activities

You can play table tennis, billiards, cards, or use the library at the **Darjeeling Club** for a modest temporary membership fee. The **Darjeeling Gymkhana Club,** The Mall, also issues temporary memberships for around Rs 15 (5¢). The club's facilities include roller skating, snooker, squash, badminton for about Rs 5 (16¢) per hour.

SHOPPING

Tea is high on the list, of course. At **Dinesh Tea Stores,** Chowk Bazaar, Shop 26, Gujmer Dinesh will give you a lesson in quality testing to help you make a good selection.

Also look for tankas (Tibetan scrolls), bold jewelry, bronze figures, beads, woven belts, shoulder bags, sweaters, gloves, and caps. Bargain everywhere except the following: **Manjusha Bengal Emporium,** near Cart Road; **Gram Shilpa,** Khadi and Village Industries Commission, for textiles; **Hayden Hall** (☎ 3228), a cooperative offering woolen carpets, caps, sweaters, and cotton bags; and the **Tibetan Self-Help Center,** for woven coin purses and belts for a few rupees and intricate carpets for a few thousand, plus many wares at prices in between (all of these are price-fixed). At the **Main Market,** off Cart Road, you haggle.

Nehru and Chowrasta roads are the main shopping centers and full of gift shops. **Nepal Curio House,** Nehru Road, has an amazing assortment of wares—bronzes, tankas, jewelry—and honest owners who tell you when an antique-looking piece is not truly antique at all, but a convincingly made fake. Try **Sikkim Art Palace,** Gandhi Road, for interesting bangles and colorful woven bags.

Habib Mullick, Chowrasta Road, is a 100-year-old shop with a remarkable assortment of curios: a Tibetan singing bell made of five metals, for instance; a precious old Diwali lamp for Rs 2,500 ($142.45); and countless little take-away gifts at reasonable prices. Health bracelets, always a good gift, are made of several metals to ward off disease. The proprietor enjoys talking about the items in the shop and is well informed and honest about antiquities. A couple of other shops to try are **Art Emporium** and **Dorjee,** both on Laden La Road. **Das Studios,** Chowrasta, sells old black-and-white photos of the Raj heyday here. Shop early; getting the photos takes a day or two.

WHERE TO STAY

Most hotels offer a discount of 10% to 50% off-season, June 15 to August 31, and December 1 to March 15. Advance reservations are recommended for in-season visits. Keep a flashlight handy in your room and when ambling around town in the evenings. Darjeeling is troubled with power outages.

DOUBLES FOR LESS THAN RS 100 ($3.33)

A bit out of the way, but pleasant and one of the best **Youth Hostels** in India is Darjeeling's, Dr. Zakir Hussain Road (☎ 2290), especially popular with trekkers. It's a three-story concrete building with wrap-around balconies at the very top of town, with views of both sides of the mountains. Dormitory rooms have large, open fireplaces. Bathrooms are large and shared, with lots of showers. Rates are Rs 20 (66¢) for nonmembers, Rs 10 (33¢) for members. There's a big dining room with plenty of windows so you can see the view. Reserve by writing to the Warden, Youth Hostel, Darjeeling 734101

Among the other acceptable places to stay in this price range are **Ailment,** below the Youth Hostel, with clean rooms and a restaurant. The government-run **Lewis Jubilee Complex,** Dr. S. K. Paul Road (☎ 2217), has 30 rooms as well as a dorm; breakfast and dinner are compulsory. Rates are Rs 40 ($1.33) per head.

There are a few more Western-style hotels and more than 50 Indian-style hotels and lodges in this lowest price category. The latter offer basic accommodation for rates ranging from around Rs 25 (83¢) to Rs 150 ($3) and variations in between. They also vary with the season and occupancy rate. The Tourist Bureau, Government of West Bengal, 1 Nehru Rd., The Mall, Darjeeling 734101 (☎ 54050), has a list and will be able to steer you in the right direction. The Tourist Bureau staff can also advise on off-season rates. Check there if you're in doubt about room charges, keeping in mind that some increases are expected by publication time.

DOUBLES FOR LESS THAN RS 250 ($8.33)

The West Bengal Tourist Development Corporation's **Maple Tourist Lodge,** on Kutchery Road (☎ 54413), is an old, pleasant but simple building, slightly run-down but okay if you're not too fussy. The view is outstanding!

Prestige, Laden La (☎ 3199) is both clean and simple.

DOUBLES FOR LESS THAN RS 700 ($23.33)

Bellevue Hotel, The Mall (☎ 54075; fax 54330), has 52 clean rooms. Doubles run Rs 700 ($23.33) in the main building and about 50% less in the bed-sitters in the old Victorian econo-block. Some of the nicest rooms in the main building have cushioned window seats, comfy for admiring the constantly passing parade in the fascinating mall below, and working fireplaces. Rates do not include meals. Cafe and snack bar on site. Each floor in the main building has a rudimentary kitchen if you care to cook, or you can eat at one of the nearby restaurants.

Hotel Polynia, 12/1 Robertson Road (☎ 2826), has 34 spacious, simply furnished rooms, some with Western-style toilets, in a lot better condition than the run-down halls would lead you to expect.

Nearby, **Alice Villa,** H. D. Lama Road (☎ 2381), is one of those places with no frills—just 21 simple, clean rooms. There is a long, pleasant lounge with striped seats along the front of the building. The brightly painted rooms have wood floors, rugs, fireplaces, and attached bathrooms; hot water in buckets. Rs 680 ($22.66), bedtime tea and meals included.

Also on H. D. Lama Road, **Mohit** (☎ 2723; fax 54351), has 28 rooms and a convenient location near the railway station. There's a restaurant. The terrace garden has a powerful telescope for viewing the peaks and valleys. Deluxe doubles run Rs 750 ($25) without meals.

The West Bengal Tourist Development Corporation operates the 15-room **Tourist Lodge,** Bhanu Sarani, The Mall (☎ 54411-2), with splendid mountain views and much less grand maintenance. A single or double runs Rs 480 ($16). To reserve write to Reservations Counter, West Bengal Tourism Development Corporation Ltd., 3/2 B. B. D. Bagh (East) Calcutta 700001, or the lodge manager.

Tiffany's, Franklyn Prestage Road (☎ 2850), has only seven rooms (six with bath attached) and a restaurant. Rates are high for the state of the rooms, even if they do have nice fireplaces. Doubles, Rs 350 ($11.66); the Gymkhana Club is beneath the hotel.

Downtown, the new and convenient **Hotel Seven Seventeen,** 26/H.D. Lama Road (☎ 2265; fax 54358), has 15 rooms and the Jain channel on the 8-channel TVs in the rooms. Rates are Rs 450 ($15) single, Rs 650 ($21,66) to Rs 750 ($25) double. There's a multicuisine restaurant.

Pineridge Hotel, The Mall, Darjeeling 734101 (☎ 54074), has such charming touches as original artwork, antique furniture, fireplaces in every room, gardens, sun deck, a library, and a special counter for trekking information. Highest price is Rs 550 ($18.33).

Aspara, 61 Laden La Rd. (☎ 2983), is a modest 31-room vegetarian hotel where a suite is Rs 650 ($21.66); regular rooms are less.

Doubles for Less Than Rs 1,000 ($33.33)

Chancellor, 6 Rockville Rd., Dr. S. M. Das Road, off Laden La Road (☎ 2956; fax 54330), centrally located, with central heating, this is a fairly new three-story, 50-room hotel. While it lacks pizzazz, the rooms are clean and comfortable, some with Kanchenjunga views; every floor has a lounge. There's good food with an equally fine view from the rooftop restaurant and a fine Chinese restaurant also. For pastry lovers, the hotel's bakery sells luscious treats. Double without meals run Rs 1,000 ($33.33).

The 17-room, centrally heated **Hotel Valentino,** 6 Rockville Rd. (☎ 2228), is owned by the New Embassy Chinese Restaurant in Calcutta and here, too, has a well-appointed Chinese restaurant on the premises, open to outsiders as well as to guests. All rooms have plush carpeting and neat furnishings; those on the top floor overlook the bustling market. Rates range from Rs 600 ($20) to Rs 950 ($31.66). The sundeck and roof garden are pleasant features.

For recalling the Raj, try the **Darjeeling Club** (formerly the Planter's Club) Nehru Road (☎ 3260), which issues foreigners temporary membership; it's a bit down at the heels, but pleasant enough, with such frills as billiards and a log fireplace—handy in the winter. Write to the Secretary for reservations.

Doubles for Less Than Rs 2,200 ($73.33)

Hotel Sinclairs Darjeeling, 18/1 Gandhi Road (☎ 54355), billed as a top hotel, offers nothing "tops" at all except top prices for its 54 rooms. Doubles run Rs 1,900 ($63.33) including meals, and there's a good view. The hotel's brochure must have been written by an aspiring novelist; it's pure fiction. The place is definitely not centrally heated, as described.

New Elgin Hotel, H. D. Lama Road (☎ 3314 or 2882), is in a white building strangely resembling a Methodist church. It has a cozy lounge with big windows, a small bar, and a dining room offering Chinese, Nepalese, Indian, and Western cuisines. All 23 rooms are bright, sunny, and have bathrooms; most have fireplaces. Family antiques accent the entire place. There is a sensational view from the top floor. Some rooms in an annex are not as cheerful. Maintenance could be better throughout. American plan only: Rs 1,800 ($60) is the top price.

Mahakal Palace, near The Mall (☎ 2026), an intimate, 22-room hotel, has a roof garden, restaurants, and central heating. Doubles are Rs 1700 ($56.66) with meals. A bungalow is Rs 3,500 ($116.66)—meals not included.

A Heritage Hotel, the atmospheric **Windamere Hotel,** Observatory Hill (☎ 54041; fax 54043), began in 1882 as a boarding house but has operated as a hotel since 1938. It's a charming place with comfortable rooms and big, old fashioned bathrooms. There are also beautiful gardens with flowering vines, ferns, and well-trimmed shrubs, where you can sit out and admire the mountains. Afternoon tea is served outdoors when it's warm, indoors near the fireplace when it's chilly. Rates include meals: $59 to $65 single, $89 double, $98 for suites. Service charge is 10%.

The delightful **Central Hotel,** Robertson Road (☎ 2003; fax 2746), has a garden, great view, and 52 well-kept rooms in either a three-story, 85-year-old building or a new, five-story annex. The old building has spacious suites with period furniture and fireplaces. Annex rooms are light, airy, modern, and cheaper. Rates include meals. Highest price (a deluxe suite in the old wing) is Rs 2,200 ($73.33); new wing rooms are Rs 1,500 ($50). Tour groups often stay here.

WHERE TO EAT

Most people who visit Darjeeling settle for the American Plan and take all their meals in their hotels—in the busiest season many hotels insist on this. But there are a few interesting places to eat in town, so try to be flexible enough to give one or two a try during your stay.

Glenary's, on Nehru Road (☎ 3335), for many years has been a home away from home for lots of young Western travelers who scribble postcards as they sip soft drinks and meet friends here. This cheerful place is known for its Western dishes and tempting home-baked desserts and breads. You'll want to pay a visit while in town. A light meal should cost Rs 50 ($1.66). Hours are 9am to 9pm.

The restaurant with the best view is **Keventer's** (☎ 2026), on Nehru Road opposite the Darjeeling Club. You can sit outdoors and survey the entire valley while eating simple snacks and sandwiches. Try the delicious, local cheddar-type cheese, or have a big breakfast of eggs with sausage or bacon. Treat your sweet tooth to ice cream. Prices are about the same as Glenary's. Hours are 9am to 9pm.

You might also try the pleasant **Lunar,** on Gandhi Road, for light meals and snacks. **Amigos,** Chowrasta, serves fast food.

Stardust, Nehru Road (☎ 3130), beside the Tourist Bureau, is a small, outdoor cafe with blue-topped tables and good vegetarian food. Try the masala dosa or pakoras or idli. For something more substantial, tuck into vegetable curry. If you've got a craving for a cup of coffee in tea plantation territory, they make espresso here. **Tripti,** B. M. Chatterjee Road, and **Jain Marwari Bhojanalaya,** N. C. Goenka Road, serve good vegetarian food.

Penang, Laden La Road, near the main post office, *serves moo-moos* (dumplings), chow mein, and thupka (Tibetan grains); very inexpensive. Hours are noon to 8 or 9pm.

Delicious Chinese dishes are found at **Shangrila,** Nehru Road; for North Indian, go to **Gol Ghar,** in the Main Market.

5 Kalimpong

52 kilometers (32 miles) east of Darjeeling

The most popular excursion from Darjeeling is to Kalimpong, 52 kilometers (32 miles) east of Darjeeling and about half as high (4,100 feet), a one-time part of the Rajah of Sikkim's domain; later, it was headquarters of the Bhutan government until the British took over. Once the beginning point of the trade route to Tibet, Kalimpong still has flourishing Saturday and Wednesday markets where Bhutias and Tibetans come to trade as well as shop. Today there is little to see in Kalimpong (pop. 41,000), but loads of quiet charm make it a relaxing place worth a day or two.

The 2½-hour drive down from Darjeeling to Kalimpong is a delightful ride through an Eden of japonica, cherry, teak, and magnolia trees, cardamom plants (the spice is exported from here), and terraced tea estates. On the way, there's a scenic viewing stop to admire the wild confluence of the Teesta and Rangeet Rivers, where river rafting is offered to tourists. Your passport and visa are checked along this route. Kalimpong can also be a stopover before you go to Darjeeling.

GETTING THERE

Kalimpong can be reached in 3½ hours **from Bagdogra Airport,** Rs 600 ($20) by private taxi, Rs 60 ($2) by bus. Locally, **Indian Airlines** is handled by Mintri Transport (☎ 55741) in Kalimpong. Buses, taxis, and jeeps ply the route **from Siliguri:** A shared taxi from Siliguri runs Rs 25 (83¢), a private taxi Rs 500 ($16.66). **From New Jalpaiguri,** a shared taxi runs Rs 35 ($1.16); **from Gangtok,** Rs 50 ($1.66). **From Darjeeling,** a shared taxi will run Rs 45 ($1.50), a private taxi Rs 600 ($20). Check with the tourist office in Darjeeling on Kalimpong tours, which sometimes operate in season.

WHAT TO SEE & DO

Main attractions are two monasteries: the 20th-century **Tharpa Choling Monastery** (1837), a stroll away at Tirpal, for the yellow-hat sect to which the Dalai Lama belongs; and the **Thongsa Monastery** (Bhutan Monastery), below Tharpa Choling. Founded in 1692, it is the oldest in the area, now refurbished and painted brilliant colors. Prayer wheels surround the shrine, and visitors are invited to turn each one chanting, "Om mani padme hum," to ensure long life, good health, and strength, as they go around the building. At **Durpin Dara,** are outstanding views as well as the **Brang monastery** (Zang-dog-Palri-fro Brang), with links to a medical institution in Tibet. En route to Durpin Dara, you'll find **Gauripur House,** a retreat for Rabindranath Tagore, who wrote some of his works here; it is now a Cooperative Training Institute.

Kalimpong nurseries grow some of India's finest amaryllis, orchids, gladioli, roses, and cacti and are enjoyable to visit. Among the best are **Universal Nursery,** 8th Mile (☎ 55387), Shanti Kunj, Dr. B. L. Dikshit (☎ 55293), and **Shri Ganesh Mani Pradhan and Son,** Ganesh Villa, 12th Mile (☎ 55389); there are others. The Tourist Bureau in Darjeeling can arrange visits.

Some other attractions include **Deolo Hill,** at 5,500 feet, the highest point in Kalimpong and also site of **Dr. Graham's Home.** Started in 1900 by a Scottish missionary for indigent children, it now has 700 students, with its own dairy, poultry farm, and bakery.

Walking & Trekking

Starting from Kalimpong, there are numerous possible treks that head into the scenic surroundings for one to four days. Check with the **Gorkha Hills Council Tourism** or the **Tourist Bureau,** both in Darjeeling.

Shopping

The Wednesday/Saturday market, billed as a big attraction, is nothing of the sort. It's for you if you're into housewares, fruit, Sly Stallone posters, chili peppers, yak cheese, and dense crowds—it's not the place to hunt for arts and crafts to take home. You go to see it only because it's here and so are you.

Kalimpong Arts and Crafts Centre, on Malli Road within walking distance from the Motor Stand, is a better bet. Look for Lepcha and other Sikimese and Bhutanese embroidered coin purses, place mats, dresses, and wall hangings. Store hours are 9am to 3pm weekdays, 9am to 1pm Saturday; closed Sunday.

Where to Stay

The season here is March to June and September to February; be sure to ask about off-season discounts. Unless otherwise indicated, the following have every comfort; the top hotels accept major credit cards and will plan tours and arrange for rafting and other activities.

Doubles for Less Than Rs 300 ($10)

The Government of West Bengal's **Shangrila Tourist Lodge** (☎ 55280), in an old British building, has three doubles, two eight-bed dorms, and one three-bed room. It's reasonably clean and basic. Breakfast and dinner are included in the rates.

Doubles for Less Than Rs 600 ($20)

Kalimpong Park Hotel, Ringkingpong Road, Kalimpong 734301 (☎ 55304), consists of 20 rooms in an old British bungalow, which was the summer home of the Maharaja of West Dinajpur, and a modern annex on the grounds. The rooms are spacious and simply but adequately furnished. Doubles run 600 ($20) without meals; Rs 1,250 ($41.66) with meals, which keeps it just a hair outside our budget. There's a 10% service charge. A rock garden is an attractive feature.

Three kilometers from town, the 1940s country home of a former British jute magnate is now the **West Bengal Tourist Lodge,** Morgan House (☎ 55384), and quite a place. A stone building with casement windows and a Burmese teak roof, it has seven rooms overlooking a huge garden. Doubles run Rs 450 ($15). A walk connects to Tashiding, the six-room annex, an impressive gray stone country house dating from 1935, formerly the summer hideaway of the prime minister of Bhutan. Some of the original furnishings remain here, too.

The Top Hotels (Doubles for Less Than $60)

Hotel Silver Oaks (☎ 55296; fax 55368), in town, has the ambience of a country estate and is filled with owner Diamond Oberoi's valuable collection of Daniels lithographs and Douglas paintings from the days of the Raj when this resort was the rage. Oberoi, also owner of the New Elgin in Darjeeling, is an avid collector who uses antiques judiciously everywhere. Each of the 25 rooms has an individualized decor. Typically, there are chintz-covered chairs, bedspreads, and drapes, but the colors vary and so do the old dressing tables, wardrobes, desks, chairs, and artworks. There's a restaurant and bar. Alas, maintenance has declined. And there are no silver oak trees here. The big terraced garden out back has plenty of silver firs and many other lovely plants and flowers, though. The peak price for a double with meals is Rs 1,800 ($60). There's a 10% service charge.

The famous **Himalayan Hotel,** Upper Cart Road (☎ 55248), was originally the home of David MacDonald, who turned it into a hotel in 1924. Its drawing room and verandah conjure up that past quite nicely. There are 12 clean, simply furnished rooms in the main building and a small annex on the grounds. Interesting tankas decorate the restaurant. There's a 10% service charge. Good food and a lovely garden and lawns are other lures. Top price is Rs 1,600 ($53.33) double.

WHERE TO EAT

Most people stay on a room-with-meal plan, but should you venture out, try the restaurants in the **Silver Oaks** or **Kalimpong Park Hotels** for nappery and good food. The low-priced **Gompu,** off Main Road (☎ 55818), in the modest hotel of the same name, has good, cheap food in the usual Indian, Chinese, and Continental styles. Chinese food is the specialty at **Mandarin,** near the taxi stand. Buy sweets and breads at the bakeries for nibbles.

9 Calcutta: The Eastern Gateway

Everything you've ever heard about Calcutta—its crowds, its poverty—is true. But despite it all, the city is one of the most fascinating on earth, and one of the largest. It's the heart of India's industry, its main port, and until just after the turn of the century its capital. Then it got a little rough for the British, who made it what it is today, and administration shifted to Delhi. But Calcutta has never stopped growing, and today its population is about 11 million, most of whom seem to be in the streets at the same time.

What gives the city vigor and inimitable excitement is the outdoor life. It's as if somebody had built an enormous rambling city as a stage set and then invited the inhabitants of a thousand different villages to act out their lives on it.

What little space is left, in the center of the road, is contested for by aging cars, trucks, buses, taxis, horse-drawn surreys, bullock wagons, rickshas, mangy dogs, the ubiquitous wandering cows, and the most motley collection of human carriers—men, women, children—ever seen. Before seeing Calcutta, it is impossible to conceive of how many different loads can be carried by human beings, and the innumerable modes and methods by which they carry them. It's an unforgettable spectacle, so varied and kaleidoscopic that one hesitates to blink for fear of missing an important vista.

For more than 200 years Bengali and Bihari peasants have been migrating to Calcutta for economic opportunities, and additional enormous waves of refugees arrived from neighboring Bangladesh (formerly East Pakistan), during both the 1947 Partition and the 1972 Pakistan-Bangladesh war. Although the pace of refugee influx has slowed somewhat in recent years, the city is finding it hard to cope. Everything in Calcutta is overloaded. There is not enough housing, the traffic is snarled, the power-generating system produces outages so frequently that everyone has some alternative source of power—candlelight in private homes, backup generators in hotels and at other businesses—and perennial labor unrest shuts businesses periodically. This last instability is changing as Calcutta establishes the necessary stability to attract foreign investment to revitalize the city.

None of these problems need concern visitors, except to help explain what has made the capital of Bengal what it is and to instill in them a sense of admiration for the way life rumbles on with more than a degree of dignity despite all the difficulties.

Portions of the city are, of course, calmer than others. The areas around **BBD Bagh (Dalhousie Square),** with its crumbling old Victorian office buildings, and around **Chowringhee** (Jawaharlal Nehru Road) are more or less white-collar sections, and their appearance is not all that different from what you've known before. But it's hardly necessary to go to the suburbs to see the panorama described above; about 90% of Calcutta is the suburbs, and any of the side streets in even the most "dignified" part of town will lead you to a different world.

For some observers the best way to get around is either by taxi or by hand-pulled ricksha. And however you feel about rickshas, they're an intimate way to see the action. (To socially conscious Westerners who complain about how rickshas "exploit human dignity," one local editor replied succinctly, "Well, if everybody refuses to hire them, the problem will solve itself: then they'll all starve to death.") Calcutta is the only big city to have human-pulled rickshas, and when the local authorities tried to convert them to cycle rickshas some years ago, the owners would have none of it. So, still on foot, they continue to negotiate the city's incredible traffic faster than most people can drive. (Recently, there have been renewed drives to rid the city of human-powered rickshas as the current crop of pullers dies out; however, there are still 40,000 pullers.)

Of course, Calcutta has other distinctions. It has been the birthplace of the great religious reform movement started by Ramakrishna Paramanhansa. A Brahmin, he renounced his heritage to embrace all religions and preach unity of all mankind, without regard to caste or color. Ramakrishna's disciple, Vivekananda, traveled widely to spread this message, and in 1897 founded the Ramakrishna Mission, which now has 119 branches in India and abroad (his memorial is at Cape Comorin/Kanya Kumari). You can visit the **Ramakrishna Mission Institute of Culture,** Gol Park (☎ 7413035), an arm of the mission, which seeks to promote international understanding with an emphasis on interpreting the cultural heritage of India. There you will be shown the 90,000-book library and universal prayer room. Also to be visited in north Calcutta is **Belur Math,** the mission's headquarters. This unusual structure resembles a temple, church, or mosque, depending on how you look at it, and is open from 6:30am to noon and again from 3:30 to 7:30pm every day. Across the Hooghly is a group of 13 temples; in the one dedicated to Kali, Sri Ramakrishna had his vision of religious brotherhood.

The city has been home to two Nobel Prize winners. Most recently, in 1979 Mother Teresa received the Nobel Peace Prize. To experience some of Mother Teresa's good works, visitors can call at **Mother House,** 54A Lower Circular Rd., and attend prayers (from 6:30 to 7:30pm on Monday, Tuesday, Wednesday, and Friday; from 6 to 7:30pm on Thursday and Sunday). There you can get a list of Missionaries of Charity centers throughout the city, what they do, where they are, how to get to them, and when they are open for visitors.

The other Nobel Prize winner (in 1913 for literature) is Rabindranath Tagore, a key figure in Calcutta's great cultural scene. His house, now a small museum, is discussed later in this chapter. Tagore is credited with inspiring new forms of music, drama, dance, and prose.

Since Tagore's time, Calcutta has also had a strong tradition of filmmaking. Calcutta-made films deal realistically with life rather than take the escapist outlook of other Indian-made films. The filmmaker who first brought Bengali life to the attention of the world was the late Satyajit Ray, the Academy Award winner who lived and worked in the city all his life.

French author Dominique Lapierre, inspired by Calcutta, wrote his now famous account of life in a fictional Calcutta slum named in the title of the book *City of Joy.*

When visitors regularly ask at the tourist office where they can find this "City of Joy," the staff replies, as many a Bengali might: "Here, it is here—everywhere in Calcutta." And while *joy* may be stretching it a bit when it comes to Calcutta, *resiliency* is right on the mark.

1 Orientation

ARRIVING

BY PLANE Calcutta is connected by air to all of India's major cities (and some less prominent ones), and to such points outside of India as Kathmandu, Chittagong, Dhaka, and Bangkok. From Delhi, the approximately two-hour flight costs $132; from Bombay, it's approximately 3 1/2 hours and costs $157; from Madras, the three-hour flight costs $137; from Bagdogra (gateway to Darjeeling), the flight takes one hour and costs $50. (Airfares are cited in dollars for foreign travelers.)

Nataji Subhas Chandra Bose International Airport is about 20 kilometers from the city. Airport transfers by **Ex-Serviceman's Link** non-AC bus to various important hotels costs Rs 40 ($1.33). **City Link** AC bus costs Rs 75 ($2.50). **Taxis** are prepaid, and fares vary according to destination. **Chauffeur-driven car** from the airport to the city is Rs 300 ($10) to Rs 450 ($15), the higher rate for an AC car. A seat in a **minibus** is Rs 8 (26¢). Driving time between the airport and city is up to an hour.

Indian Airlines city office is at Airlines House, 39 Chitteranjan General Inquiry, open from 9am to 5:30pm (☎ 263390); Indian Airlines is also located in the Great Eastern Hotel (☎ 2480073) and HHI (Hotel Hindustan International (☎ 2477062). Should **Vayudoot** begin operations again, the city office telephone number is 2477092. **Air India** is at 50 Jawaharlal Nehru Rd., Chowringhee (☎ 2422256). **Jet Airways** also flies into Calcutta; 230A A. J. C. Bose (☎ 5518811).

BY TRAIN Trains arrive and leave from two stations, Howrah and Sealdah, which connect Calcutta to major cities throughout India. Be sure to check from which station your train will depart. The best (and most expensive) train **from Delhi** is the *Rajdhani Express,* which makes the trip overnight (leaving Delhi at 5:15pm and arriving in Calcutta at 10:45am); the train runs five days a week, and costs Rs 2,440 ($81.33) for AC First, Rs 705 ($23.50) AC Chair. The *Kalka-Howrah Mail* leaves Delhi at 7:30am and arrives in Calcutta (1,441 kilometers) about 25 hours later. The fare is Rs 1,913 ($63.76) First, Rs 209 ($$6.96) Second. **From Bombay** (1,187 kilometers) the *Gitanjali Express* leaves at 6:05am and takes about 32 1/2 hours. The fare is Rs 2,564 ($85.46) AC First, Rs 308 ($10.26) Second. **From Madras** (1,663 kilometers), among the best trains is the superfast *Coramandel Express* (27 hours), which costs Rs 2,099 ($69.96) AC First, Rs273 ($9.10) Second. If you're coming **from Darjeeling,** catch the *Kanchenjunga Express* for Rs 976 ($32.53) AC First, Rs 143 ($13.76) Second. The 566-kilometer journey takes about 10 hours.

Reservation offices for trains are open from 9am to 6pm weekdays, 9am to 2pm Sundays and national holidays: Fairlie Place, 6 Fairlie Place (☎ 2206811); New Koilaghat, 14 Strand Rd. (☎ 2203496); Old Koilaghat, 3 Koilaghat St. (☎ 2489494); Rabindra Sadan, 61 J. L. Nehru Rd. (☎ 247143); Howrah 1st Floor, New Howrah Station and Sealdah, 1st Floor (☎ 3503496).

BY ROAD Calcutta is connected by national highways to important cities. If you are interested in itineraries, road maps, and information such as where to stay along the way, write to: **Automobile Association of Eastern India,** 13 Ballygunge, Circular Road (☎ 4755513); you also will need a car, a driver, and a lot of time.

Calcutta

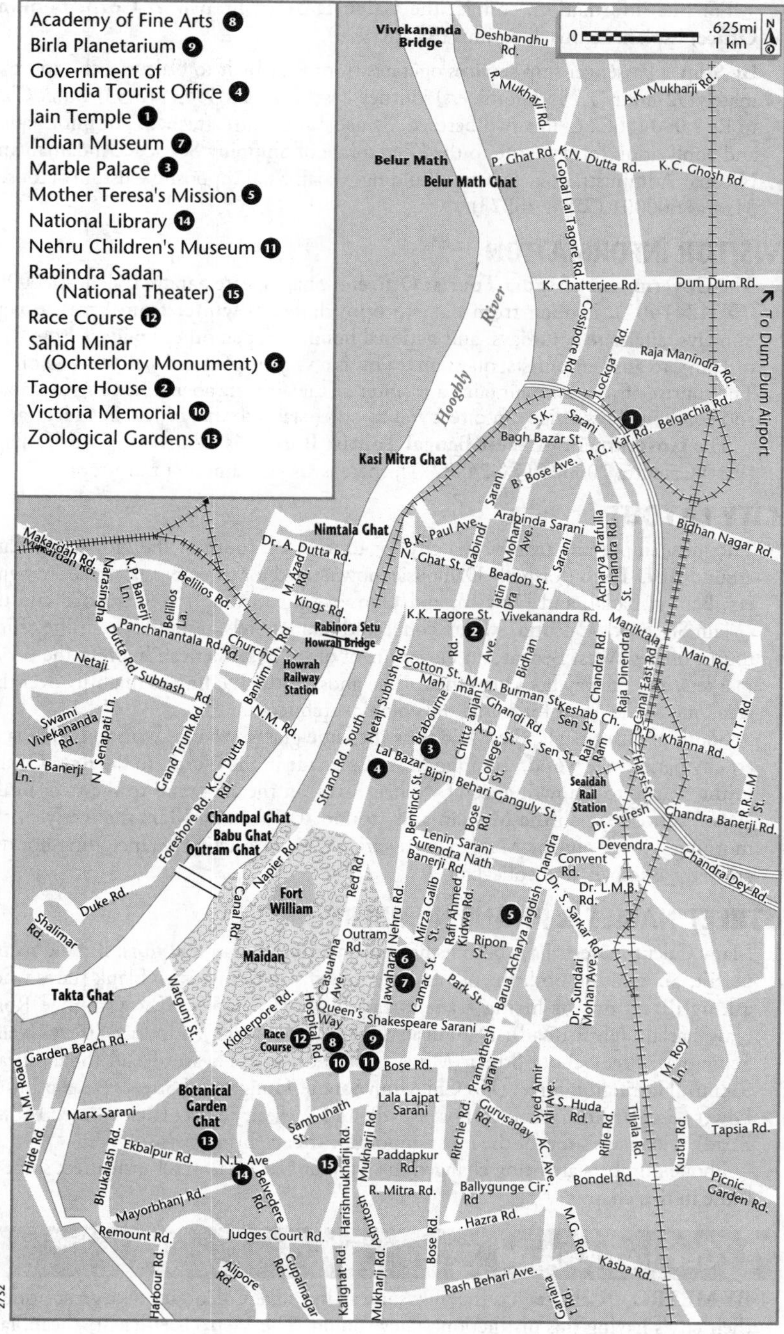
Academy of Fine Arts 8
Birla Planetarium 9
Government of India Tourist Office 4
Jain Temple 1
Indian Museum 7
Marble Palace 3
Mother Teresa's Mission 5
National Library 14
Nehru Children's Museum 11
Rabindra Sadan (National Theater) 15
Race Course 12
Sahid Minar (Ochterlony Monument) 6
Tagore House 2
Victoria Memorial 10
Zoological Gardens 13
0
.625mi
1 km
N
Vivekananda Bridge
Deshbandhu Rd.
R. Mukharji Rd.
A.K. Mukharji Rd.
Belur Math
Belur Math Ghat
P. Ghat Rd.
K.N. Dutta Rd.
K.C. Ghosh Rd.
Gopal Lal Tagore Rd.
K. Chatterjee Rd.
Dum Dum Rd.
To Dum Dum Airport
Hooghly River
Cossipore Rd.
Lockga' Rd.
Raja Manindra Rd.
S.K. Sarani
Belgachia Rd.
Bagh Bazar St.
R.G. Kar Rd.
B. Bose Ave.
Kasi Mitra Ghat
Arabinda Sarani
Bidhan Nagar Rd.
Nimtala Ghat
B.K. Paul Ave.
Rabindra Sarani
Mohan Ave.
Acharya Prafulla Chandra Rd.
Makardah Rd.
Dr. A. Dutta Rd.
N. Ghat St.
Beadon St.
Jatin Dra
Sarani
K.P. Banerji Ln.
Belilios Rd.
Belilios La.
M. Azad Rd.
Kings Rd.
K.K. Tagore St.
Vivekanandra Rd.
Maniktala Main Rd.
Narasingha Dutta Rd.
Panchanantala Rd.
Church Rd.
Bankim Ch. Rd.
Rabinora Setu
Howrah Bridge
Howrah Railway Station
Netaji Subhash Rd.
Ave.
Bidhan
Chandra Rd.
Raja Dinendra St.
Canal East Rd.
Netaji Subhsh Rd.
Cotton St.
M.M. Burman St.
Keshab Ch. Sen St.
Mahatma Gandhi Rd.
Swami Vivekananda Rd.
N.M. Rd.
Brabourne Rd.
Chittaranjan Ave.
A.D. St.
S. Sen St.
D.D. Khanna Rd.
C.I.T. Rd.
Strand Rd. South
College St.
Raja Ram
A.C. Banerji Ln.
N. Senapati Ln.
Grand Trunk Rd.
K.C. Dutta Rd.
Lal Bazar
Bipin Behari Ganguly St.
Seaidah Rail Station
Harsi St.
R.R.L.M. St.
Foreshore Rd.
Chandpal Ghat
Babu Ghat
Outram Ghat
Bentinck St.
Bose Rd.
Dr. Suresh Chandra Banerji Rd.
Lenin Sarani
Surendra Nath Banerji Rd.
Devendra
Convent Rd.
Chandra Dey Rd.
Napier Rd.
Red Rd.
Dr. L.M.B. Rd.
Duke Rd.
Canal Rd.
Fort William
Mirza Galib St.
Rafi Ahmed Kidwa Rd.
Acharya Jagdish Chandra
Dr. S. Sarkar Rd.
Shalimar Rd.
Outram Rd.
Ripon St.
Maidan
Jawaharal Nehru Rd.
Casuarina Ave.
Camac St.
Park St.
Barua
Dr. Sundari Mohan Ave.
Takta Ghat
Watgunj St.
Kidderpore Rd.
Hospital Rd.
Queen's Way
Shakespeare Sarani
Garden Beach Rd.
Race Course
Bose Rd.
Pramathesh Sarani
M. Roy Ln.
N.M. Road
Botanical Garden Ghat
Lala Lajpat Sarani
Sambunath St.
Syed Amir Ali Ave.
S. Huda Rd.
Marx Sarani
Ritchie Rd.
Gurusaday Rd.
Rifle Rd.
Tiljala Rd.
Kustia Rd.
Tapsia Rd.
Hide Rd.
Bhukalash Rd.
Ekbalpur Rd.
N.L. Ave
Harishmukharji Rd.
Mukharji Rd.
Paddapkur Rd.
Belvedere Rd.
R. Mitra Rd.
Ballygunge Cir. Rd
A.C. Ave.
Bondel Rd.
Picnic Garden Rd.
Mayorbhanj Rd.
Ashutosh
Hazra Rd.
Remount Rd.
Judges Court Rd.
M.G. Rd.
Alipore Rd.
Gupalnagar Rd.
Kalighat Rd.
Mukharji Rd.
Bose Rd.
Kasba Rd.
Rash Behari Ave.
Gariaha Rd.
Harbour Rd.
2732

For **bus** information, contact the **Calcutta State Transport Corp. Booking Office,** Esplanade Bus Terminus (☎ 281916).

By Ship Passenger ship services operates from Port Blair to Calcutta, the approximately 52-hour (1,255 kilometers) journey costs from Rs 550 ($18.33) Bunk Class to Rs 2,000 ($66.66) in a two-berthed, deluxe cabin, bath attached. For information and application forms, write to the Directorate of Shipping Services, Andaman and Nicobar Administration, Jawaher Building, Rajaji Salai (opposite Customs House), Madras 600001 (☎ 5226873).

VISITOR INFORMATION

The **Government of India Tourist Office,** 4 Shakespeare Sarani, Calcutta 700001 (☎ 4241402), is open from 8am to 6pm daily (in winter from 9am), except Sundays, alternate Saturdays, and national holidays (open other holidays from 8am to 1pm), to answer tourists' questions. This is a very helpful and well-stocked office. The tourist office also maintains a counter at the airport, open when flights depart and come in. This office can direct you to other states tourist offices in Calcutta.

The **Government of West Bengal Tourist Bureau** is located at 3/2 BBD Bagh (East) Calcutta 700001 (☎ 2488271); there is also a counter at the airport.

CITY LAYOUT

The most important areas of the city for tourists are south of the Howrah Bridge, around **BBD Bagh** (formerly Dalhousie, now named for three Bengali freedom fighters: Benoy, Badal, and Dinesh), and **Chowringhee** (now J. Nehru Road and the "Main Street" of Calcutta), where you'll find many hotels, restaurants, airline office, tourist offices (West Bengal and Government of India), American Express, the GPO, markets, and railway booking offices. The ghost of the Raj lingers mightily over this area, one of the finest for seeing old colonial architecture.

South of BBD Bagh, **the Maidan** is the large grassy expanse (said to be the largest city park in the world), running from Esplanade in the North, to the Race Course in the South, to Chowringhee (J. Nehru Road) in the East, and to the river in the West. You can stroll the Maidan and around the Victoria Memorial early in the morning. Check out the Maidan for a variety of sports activities, including hockey, cricket, basketball, and volleyball.

STREET NAMES & PHONE NUMBERS

Many Calcutta streets have been rechristened within the past few years. But old names persist. So mention both the old and the new if you're met with blank stares when asking directions or hiring transportation. For instance: Chowringhee Road (Jawaharlal Nehru Road); Dalhousie Square (BBD Bagh); Lindsay Street (Nellie Sengupta); Free School Street (Mirza Ghalib Street); Theater Road (Shakespeare Sarani); Harrington Street (Ho Chi Minh Sarani; Hungerford Street (Picasso Bithi); Lower Circular Road (A. J. C. Bose Road); and Wellesley Street (Rafi Ahmed Kidwai Road). These are a few of the most important streets for tourists.

Phone numbers are being changed throughout Calcutta, which will affect some of those in this chapter.

2 Getting Around

BY METRO Calcutta has the only subway in India. Calcuttans take great pride in their city's having this distinction. They should! The Metro is efficient, cheap, fast, clean—just what the budget tourist and Calcuttans need. The Metro runs between Esplanade and Tollygunge, with eight stops en route, a trip that takes 16 minutes, and from Belgachia to Dum-Dum (more routes are to come). The Metro operates weekdays from 8am to 9:16pm, and 2pm to 9:17pm on weekends (later on some holidays). It gives easy access to south Calcutta, site of most hotels, restaurants, bars, and many top tourist attractions. The fare is Rs 2 (7¢) and Rs 3 (10¢) one way. Timetables are available free at stations.

BY TAXI **Yellow cabs** can make suburban journeys; **black-and-yellow** taxis cannot. Taxi meters start at Rs 5 (17¢), and you add 50% to the meter reading at the end of your journey (the meters have not been reset since 1991). Ask for fare card if in doubt. Taxi fares in Calcutta are among the cheapest in India.

By Auto Ricksha On auto rickshas, meters are also out of date, and you will pay about 60% over the meter reading. When in doubt about any metered fare, ask to see the rate card before paying up.

BY HUMAN-POWERED RICKSHA There's no fixed rate for manually operated rickshas, but the asking rate for foreigners is about Rs 4 (13¢) to Rs 5 (17¢) per kilometer—Indians pay Rs 2 (7¢) to Rs 3(10¢). You must bargain and set a fare before you get in.

BY BUS Minibuses operate from BBD Bagh and the Esplanade north to Dunlop, south to Gariahat, southwest to Thakurpukur, and east to Tangra. These are clean and not so crowded as the usual Calcutta buses (no one is supposed to hang outside, for instance), but the fare is slightly higher. There is a minimum of Rs 1.20 (3¢) and you can spend as much as Rs 3 (10¢) depending on where you're going.

BY TRAM Calcutta is the only Indian city to still have trams; (which run from 4am to 11pm). They can be cheap and convenient, but are also crowded, except on Sundays or off-off peak hours. Fares often no higher than Rs 1.

BY FERRY Ferries cross the Hooghly River from Chandpal Ghat and Babughat to Howrah; service is also available to the Botanical Garden, Baghbazar, Kasipur, and Baranagar. They run every 15 minutes, from 8:15am to 8pm, less frequently on Sundays.

3 Useful Information

MONEY CHANGING

Banks are open Monday to Friday from 10am to 2pm, until noon on Saturday. A few banks open on Sundays. **American Express,** located on Old Court House Street opposite the Great Eastern Hotel (☎ 2488570), is open for money changing only from 10am to 2pm; for all other business, from 10am to 2pm and 2:30 to 5pm, Monday through Friday, to 2pm on Saturday. Calcutta International Airport's bank is open 24 hours a day. Top hotels change money for guests.

WHEN TO GO

The best time to visit Calcutta is October to March; the rainy season is June to early September. A special time to visit is during Dusshera (in September/October) when the entire area is festive with displays everywhere depicting the forces of good and evil represented by deities and demons.

4 Where to Stay

Finding a good budget hotel in Calcutta isn't easy, and can be nearly impossible if you arrive without reservations during the peak season, roughly October to March, or during the Durga Puja, celebrated in September or October (the dates for the latter change slightly from year to year). Many top-quality budget hotels are located on **Sudder Street,** which people will tell you is possibly not safe at night. You can, of course, hear this about many areas in the world's larger cities these days, but it's worth keeping in mind when staying at the Sudder Street hotels.

When budgeting for Calcutta, remember that taxes levied by the West Bengal and national government can add as much as 35.5% to your hotel bill. Remember that some hotels cite rates only in dollars for foreign travelers.

Paying Guest Accommodations Lists of families who welcome paying guests are available through the Government of India Tourist Office, 4 Shakespeare Sarani, Calcutta 700071 (☎ 2421402), and West Bengal Tourist Office, 312 BBD Bagh (East), Calcutta 700001 (☎ 2488271).

DOUBLES FOR LESS THAN RS 350 ($11.66)

Off Sudder Street on Stuart Lane are two well-known, cheap hotels popular with backpackers and other young wanderers. **Modern Lodge,** 1 Stuart Lane (☎ 444960), has singles, doubles, and a dorm. **Paragon,** 2 Stuart Lane (☎ 242445), has rooms upstairs that are light and airy, and that face a roof terrace that seems perpetually full of young travelers doing laundry in the sinks. Rooms on the ground floor are dark, little cells, some without attached baths. At the Paragon, rent is collected every day. At both Modern Lodge and Paragon, foreign guests are suspected of using drugs—whether it's true or not.

Back on Sudder Street, **Hotel Maria,** 5/1 Sudder St. (☎ 243311), is always crowded with budget travelers—sometimes among them are workers for Mother Teresa. The rooms are plain and fairly clean, but need sprucing up. The pleasant proprietor, Ismail Abbasbhai, puts guests on the roof under a tin canopy when all the 21 rooms and the 11-bed dorm are full. No meals are served at the Maria. Drugs and alcohol are prohibited.

Just across the street from the Fairlawn and Lytton hotels is the **Red Shield Guest House,** 2 Sudder St., Calcutta 700016 (☎ 2450599), run by the Salvation Army, with 70 beds (a few double rooms, but mainly dorm-style). Rates run Rs 120 ($4) to Rs 150 ($5) for a double with attached bath; rooms with a common bath are Rs 80 ($2.66); beds in the dorm are Rs 30 ($1). The gate is locked at midnight; to get in after that, you have to inform the gatekeeper in advance. Breakfast is the only meal served here. For Rs 10 (33¢) per day, nonresidents can leave their luggage while they go off exploring. There is a seven-day limit. Popular with young travelers, it is often full.

The **YMCA,** 25 Jawaharlal Nehru Rd., Chowringhee, Calcutta 700016 (☎ 292192), takes in men, women, families, and groups; it's the oldest YMCA in Asia. Some attached baths, some AC. There are also dorms. For rooms with an attached bath, figure on Rs 250 ($8.33) to Rs 500 ($16.66) without AC, Rs 400 ($13.33) to Rs 650 ($21.66) for AC; dorm rooms are Rs 150 ($5). There is a modest temporary membership fee. Tariff includes bed, bedtime tea, breakfast, and dinner. I've had complaints that it isn't clean enough, but it's nearly always full.

The 75-room **YWCA Gallaway House,** 1 Middleton Row, Calcutta 700071 (☎ 297033), has 75 rooms, 38 for transients. It takes in single travelers, married couples, and sometimes families with children under 12. Most of the rooms are off a verandah; all have attached baths (some shared with an adjoining room) with big tubs or showers. Non-AC rates from Rs 250 ($8.33) to Rs 500 ($16.66) for a single, and Rs 400 ($13.33) to Rs 600 ($20) for a double; these rates include all meals. There is a large lounge and a utilitarian dining room. The front door is locked at 10pm, but a porter on duty will let you in up to 1am. Rates include breakfast. To reserve write: Secretary, YWCA, 1 Middleton Row, Calcutta 700071.

Hotel Heera (not to be confused with Heera International), 28 Grant St., Calcutta 700013 (☎ 2488516), near the Elite Cinema, has decent, clean, and cheap rooms. Doubles are Rs 350 ($11.66), and its rooms are often filled by young travelers.

DOUBLES FOR LESS THAN RS 600 ($20)

On its second floor, **Gujral Guest House,** 8B Lindsay (☎ 2240260), has six simple, clean rooms. The top price is Rs 480 ($16) for double with attached bath.

Marble Palace, 5 Beck Bagan Row, 700019 (☎ 2478180), is no such thing, just a reasonably okay, simple guest house. The price for a double was not yet established during my research trip, but you should expect to pay around Rs 400 ($13.33).

Akash Ganga Guest House, 1 Orient Row, Calcutta (☎ 2473341; fax 2474285), has 36 simple rooms—Rs 550 ($18.33) for a double—with many amenities associated with full-fledged hotels, such as attached baths with hot and cold running water and room telephones.

DOUBLES FOR LESS THAN RS 1,000 ($33.33)

A striking, old red mansion is now **The Astor Hotel,** 15 Shakespeare Sarani, Calcutta 700071 (☎ 2429957-50), with bright and cheerful rooms in the main building, and with slightly higher rates than those in the budget-priced but gloomy annex. Some street noise, and the rooms could use a touching up. Wonderful Kebab-E-Que in the garden (see "Where to Eat," below). Rates range from Rs 675 ($22.50) or Rs 875 ($29.16) for a standard AC single or double, respectively, to Rs 1,175 ($39.16) for an AC suite.

Under renovation when I stopped in, **Astoria Hotel,** 6/2 and 6/3 Sudder St. (☎ 2449679; fax 250190), seemed promising (ask for a newly renovated room); there are 30 air-conditioned rooms in all in a much altered old mansion. Expect to pay Rs 500 ($16.66) for a single, Rs 700 (($23.33) for a double.

Hotel Heera International, 115 Ripon St., Calcutta 700016 (☎ 295594), has 31 neat, decently priced rooms—doubles are Rs 700 ($23.33)—near the Metro and the Birla Planetarium.

Rutt-Deen, 21-B Dr. U. N. Brahmachari Sarani (formerly Loudon Street, off Park Street), Calcutta 700016 (☎ 2475240; fax 2475210), has fairly clean if uninspired rooms. Expect to pay Rs 700 ($23.33) to Rs 800 ($26.66) for a standard single, Rs 850 ($28.33) for a standard double, Rs 900 ($30) to Rs 950 ($31.66) for a deluxe double.

In the busy BBD Bagh (Dalhousie Square) area—location of the G.P.O. and American Express—is **Shalimar Hotel,** 3 S. N. Banerjee Rd., Calcutta 700013 (☎ 2485030). The hotel has an orange and white lobby with stainless-steel trim. The 22-rooms are modern and compact, but hardly serene because of the busy street below. There is a restaurant for residents only. Cottage Industries Emporium is steps away.

About the same price, **Hotel Circular,** 171/A Acharya Jagdish Chandra Bose Rd., Calcutta 700014 (☎ 2441533/7641; fax 2450263)), is a white, boxlike building in front of Mother Teresa's Missionaries of Charity. Fairly neat and clean, it has 12 singles and 14 doubles with amenities associated with higher-priced hotels, such as a color TV in your room, 24-hour hot and cold water, and AC. A double runs Rs 675 ($22.50) in 90% of its rooms.

Executive Tower, 52 Ananada Palit Rd., Calcutta 700014 (☎ 2451338; fax 2441284), has 28 attractive well maintained rooms in a convenient location. Singles rates range from Rs 500 ($16.66) to Rs 675 ($22.50), doubles from Rs 650 ($21.66) to Rs 725 ($24.16). There is room service, but no restaurant. There is a florist.

Lindsay Guest House and Hotel, 8B Lindsay St., Calcutta 700087 (☎ 2448689), is, as far as I know, the only guest house in the city with a star rating—one star, in this case. The reception is at street level, and the hotel on floors six, seven, eight, and nine is what to aim for (skip the guest house portion on the lower floors). The halls could use a coat of paint, but the rooms are okay. Who needs frills? In numbers 901, 902, and 903 you get million-dollar city views at moderate prices. Doubles with AC are Rs 800 ($26.66). There's a terrace garden. The Lindsay is popular with Indian men traveling on business.

DOUBLES FOR LESS THAN RS 1600 ($53.33)

In a superb location steps from the Maidan and Park Street—and possibly the best value for the doubles' buck—is the 123-room **Quality Inn,** 12 J. L. Nehru Rd. (Chowringhee Road), Calcutta 700013 (☎ 2430301-7; fax 2486650). Once upon a time, this was The Ritz, but it has been closed for years by labor trouble. Newly renovated, the hotel's spacious granite lobby has a clean, spare, modern look and the rooms are modern, too, but cheerful with printed bedspreads and drapes. Doubles run Rs 1,600 ($53.33), a little over our budget, but worth it. The hotel has two restaurants (see "Where to Eat," below), a coffee shop, and a bar.

Easily the most colorful hotel in Calcutta, the **Fairlawn,** 13A Sudder St., Calcutta 700016 (☎ 2451050; fax 2441835), is still owned by Violet Smith, an Armenian woman whose family has run this 20-room hotel for more than 50 years. Today, it still retains a lot of its pre-Independence character; however, it's become a seedy over the years, rather than nostalgic. But is still enormously popular. Enter through the garden and the open verandah full of red and green plants, and you will quickly see that Mrs. S. is trying hard to provide a warm and spotless home away from home. Plants abound inside as do cozy lounges full of brightly painted furniture and knickknacks. Not everyone's cup of tea. Doubles are $45 to $50, singles $35 to $40 with AC. All rates include three meals, which makes this a bargain. There's a 5% service charge, 20% discount from April 1 to September 30.

Next door, the **Lytton Hotel,** 14 Sudder St., Calcutta 700016 (☎ 2491875 or 2491747; fax 2491747), is less spectacular than the Fairlawn, but its 65 renovated rooms—blonde pine and clean, painted walls—are a cut above many others in this price range. All rooms have AC, as well as telephones and piped-in music, attached bathrooms with modern fixtures, and hot and cold water. This is a good buy. The top priced double is Rs 1,200 ($40). There are two restaurants and a bar.

A calm little oasis in this bustling city, with 107 rooms, **The Kenilworth,** 1 and 2 Little Russell St., Calcutta 700071 (☎ 2428394-5; fax 2425136), is well maintained, with both an old (rarely used) and a new wing, and a broad, green peaceful lawn. In the marble-walled reception and lounge are comfortable brown leather armchairs and area rugs in shades of green on sparkling, clean marble floors, which run throughout the hotel. The restaurant, also resplendent in marble, is called the Marble Room; and there's also the cozy Alcove Bar in beige, pink and gray; and Crystals, the open-air coffee shop. The well-maintained rooms ($53 for a double) are airy and spacious, with tasteful furnishings and large windows; they are a fine value in this city. The hotel's suites ($80 to $90) are huge and have Jacuzzis in their bathrooms. This hotel still falls within our budget unless you book a suite; then, it's a splurge.

Great Eastern Hotel, 1-3 Old Court House St., Calcutta 700069 (☎ 2482331; fax 2480289), an elegant establishment of moneyed travelers in the old days, is a bit threadbare now. Run by the government of Bengal, it is popular with government officials and often fully booked by them. Most of the rooms are spacious, with attached bathrooms; some seem to be a page from the past, with Art Deco furniture and old, whirling ceiling fans. The management is always promising to renovate and improve this hotel, and perhaps by now there's been some sprucing up. Rates for AC rooms are Rs 970 ($32.33) single, Rs 1,350 ($45) double; economy rooms without AC are Rs 275 ($9.16) single, Rs 500 ($16.66) double.

WORTH A SPLURGE

Big spenders make a beeline for luxury at the **Taj Bengal,** 34B Belvedere Rd., Alipore, Calcutta 700027 (☎ 2483939; fax 2481776), a commanding white building, topped by red-tiled roof, and set in a splendid garden, across from the zoo. Stately palms and other plants adorn the spacious, airy atrium lobby where towering clay figures, folk art, and antiques create one of the most dramatic settings in India. Valuable works of art and antiques grace the halls as well as the 250 rooms, as do local crafts and textiles. A village-style Indian restaurant, a teak-paneled and mother-of-pearl-accented Chinese restaurant, and a 24-hour coffee shop with an old railway theme, a swimming pool, a health club, and swift, attentive service are among some of the hotel's other amenities. Standard singles are $180, doubles $190. The rates include bedtime tea and Continental breakfast. There are also a nightclub and a tea lounge.

Tops since the Raj years is the venerable old **Oberoi Grand,** 15 Jawaharlal Nehru Rd., Chowringhee, Calcutta 700013 (☎ 2492323; fax 291217), right across from the grassy Maidan (central park). With its elegant shops, lovely garden, swimming pool, and some of the most gracious service in all of India, this is a winner. The 230 attractively refurbished rooms recall the old days and are big and comfortable, with ample space to spread out and move around. Suites are especially evocative of the British period. Standard singles run $200; doubles $220. Tea lounge, pool, and discotheque.

The modern **HHI (Hotel Hindustan International),** 235/1 A. J. C. Bose Rd., Calcutta 700020 (☎ 2472394; fax 2472824), with 212 rooms, was completing a massive renovation, adding amenities such as an executive floor with business services. Some new rooms were almost ready for occupancy with light and airy decor, white painted furniture, and rose and gold upholstery, spreads, and drapes. The hotel's Palm Court, a 24-hour coffee shop, has a gently splashing waterfall. The hotel has two other restaurants, a discotheque, bar, and swimming pool. Standard singles run $110, doubles $140.

At the **Park Hotel,** 17 Park St., Calcutta 700016 (☎ 297336; fax 2497336), recent renovations have given a Regency look to the lounge and added interesting paintings by local artists as focal points. Its 150 rooms are typically done up with light woods and blue-green color schemes; the odd-numbered rooms on the fourth floor have spectacular views. Hallways have planters in niches and strategically placed little works of art. The hotel has a swimming pool, restaurants, coffee shop, and confectionery. Singles are $110, doubles $120.

AT THE AIRPORT

ITDC's **Hotel Airport Ashok,** Calcutta Airport, Calcutta 70052 (☎ 5529111; 5520137), is neat, clean, efficient, and fine if you're in transit and overnighting; otherwise it doesn't make sense to stay here (18 kilometers from town). There is a swimming pool, restaurant, coffee shop, and bar.

A CLUB

Fashionable playground of the British, the 100-year-old **Tollygunge Club,** 120 Deshapran Sasmal Rd., Calcutta 700033 (☎ 46-3106), on a former estate of the descendants of Tipu Sultan, is still attracting the rich and famous. The neatly furnished rooms in bungalows and a new, 32-room hotel block— doubles Rs 1,500 ($50), taxes included—are always booked far in advance. Guest memberships cost Rs 50 ($1.66) per week. There's an 18-hole golf course, pool, riding, tennis, and grand gardens—all 5¹/₂ miles from Park Street, a Rs 50 ($1.66) taxi ride. Buses and the Metro come out this way in case you want to look around or have meal (reserve in advance). The price-fixed lunch and dinner menus—Rs 100, $3.33 each—are British bland. Better is the South Indian breakfast (every day but Sunday when there's brunch; see "Buffets," under "Where to Eat," below).

5 Where to Eat

Before listing notable Calcutta restaurants, here's a little trivia: Calcutta claims to have more bars outside of hotels than any other Indian city. From all appearances this could be true. Certainly you see a lot more bars around this town than around others, and in the evenings they're filled with men hoisting a few with their buddies. But Westerners wonder why there are rarely any women on the scene, and here's the explanation. Generally, Indian women are nondrinkers. Often when they go out, it's a family affair with the kids along, and they'll head to a vegetarian restaurant where no liquor is served. But this is changing, and today some modern women accompany men to restaurants where drinks are served.

Running diagonally off Jawaharlal Nehru Road, just below the Oberoi Grand Hotel, is **Park Street,** one of the places to head when you're hungry. There are a dozen or more restaurants, most air-conditioned, all near each other, and one or more has music at night. Many restaurants in Calcutta are closed on Thursday, which is both a meatless and a dry day. When they are closed, hotel restaurants are always open. Chinese and vegetarian restaurants are also likely to be open when the others are closed. Wherever you choose to eat, at least once during your stay be sure to try hilsa, a local white fish. It's bony but delicious! Bhekti fry (fried fish), chingri malai (a local prawn curry), and ruhi macher kaha (carp curry) also rates a taste.

Bengali sweets are famous throughout India; try rossogolla and sandesh. Calcutta-Mughlai cuisine is rooted in the elaborate dishes of the former Nizams that traveled here with their cooks when on visits in Calcutta.

Now for the less-appetizing news: Taxes on food, alcoholic drinks, and entertainment (music live and canned) can heft your bill to double the menu charges.

MULTICUISINE RESTAURANTS

ON PARK STREET

Mocambo, 25B Park St. (☎ 294152); **Trinca's,** 17B Park St. (☎ 247978); **Magnolia,** 12K-N Park St. (☎ 298997); **Blue Fox,** Park Street (☎ 29-7948); and the slightly run-down **Moulin Rouge** (298480)—all are dimly lit, open similar hours (around 11am to midnight, closed Thursday), and have similar menus. They all feature Indian, Continental (such culinary antiquities as lobster thermidor), and a smattering of Chinese foods in about the same price ranges: Rs 30 ($1) for vegetarian to Rs 50 ($2.30) for nonvegetarian main dishes. At **Trinca's,** a number of the Chinese dishes are Szechwan style, rather than the Cantonese found elsewhere. Adjacent to Trinca's (and under the same management) is the **Tavern,** with the same menu, but its Arthurian decor and swords and shields makes it look different from the other restaurants. On top of the Tavern is the **Other Room,** again with the same owners but serving the same foods at slightly higher prices. Trinca's also runs the **Ming Room,** in the same complex, good for its Chinese menu. **Big Bite,** on the street level, is Trinca's fast-food eatery.

Continuing along Park Street, the **Sky Room,** 57 Park St., Park Mansions (☎ 294362), open from 10:30am to 11:30pm (closed Tuesday), serves a similar menu but in a tonier ambience (stars twinkle on the sky-blue ceiling) and at slightly higher prices. Recently closed by a strike, it may be open now. It was very popular for Continental food.

Peter Cat, 18 Park St. (☎ 298841), open from 10am to midnight (closed Thursday), has two levels joined by a teak staircase rimmed in copper. Upstairs, the walls have a soft metallic finish, and copper lanterns cast soft light on red and beige banquettes. Downstairs, stained-glass lampshades throw colorful shadows on the textured white stucco walls. Specials of the day are in the Rs 48 ($1.60) range, in addition to the copy-cat menus found everywhere else on Park Street. Desserts include ice creams and special sundaes.

Golden Dragon, 40 Park St. (☎ 293507), makes delicious Manchurian chicken for Rs 50 ($1.66). It is open from 11am to 11pm daily.

A pleasant change of pace, **Maple,** 15 Park (☎ 299192), is vegetarian, with stone and wood decor. About the highest priced item on the menu is a rich, creamy navratan curry for Rs 65 ($2.16); a hearty club sandwich costs Rs 40 ($1.33); and snacks such as pakoras are less.

There are two **Kwality** restaurants in Calcutta: one at 17 Park St. (☎ 297941), open from 10:30am to midnight (closed Thursday), and another at 2A Gariahat Rd. (☎ 4751982), open 10am to 10:30pm (closed Wednesday). Both are popular family places and go way back when it comes to good food and value in pleasant surroundings. On Park Street, the decor includes modern paintings and brass accents. Dinner for two with chicken or fish accompanied by a vegetarian biryani costs about Rs 150 ($5)—not cheap, to be sure, but good value.

Oasis, 33 Park St. (☎ 299033), open from 11am to 11pm (closed Thursday), is a popular family place with decently priced dishes. A couple of winners from the Indian side of the menu are vegetables navratan, made with dried fruit and vegetables, and jhalfrazy, which is made with chiles.

For Calcutta-style Mughali, go to **Shiraz Golden Restaurant,** 56 Park St. (☎ 2477702), with prices and hours about the same as the other restaurants on the street.

Away from Park Street

With tables covered with snowy linens and set among lovely waterfalls tumbling over rocks, **Zaranj,** 26 J. L. Nehru (Chowringhee) (☎ 2490369), next to the Indian Museum, is classy and upscale. The menu features Northwest Frontier foods (with a detour to Hyderabad), prepared in a glassed-in kitchen. Sip jeera pani (spiced water) or something stronger while studying the menu and the well-heeled crowd. (This is no place for jeans.) A typical meal might include such main dishes as Zaranj raan (the chef's special tandoori lamb) or murgh nawabi (boneless chicken), with an order of khum bhara dhania (mushrooms with spring onions) and a Bengali sweet for about Rs 600 ($20) for two without a drink, tax, or tip. Hours are 12:30 to 2:30pm, and 7:30 to 10:45pm.

Two of the town's best-known restaurants are **Amber,** on two floors at 11 Waterloo St. (☎ 2486746), open from 11am to 11pm (closed Thursday), and **Sagar,** 1/1 Meredith St. (☎ 277979), open from 11am to 11pm. Both have the same menu of snacks and meals. Amber is more attractive, and one of the city's best for a variety of such famous Indian dishes as tandoori prawns with thick and tender tandoori roti, tikka kebab (chicken skewered and tandooried), chicken sag (chicken with a spinachlike vegetable), and kulcha (bread). With some single portions large enough to share, figure on Rs 150 ($5) to Rs 200 ($6.66) for a three-course a meal for two.

Elfin Bar and Restaurant, 5 Meredith St. (☎ 274199), is open from 11am to 11pm daily. It's dark and cozy with some stone decorations, slatted wood walls hung with paintings of English merrymakers, and tile floors. The cuisine is Indian and Chinese. Elfin serves a non-veg thali with chicken, nan, rice, and condiments for about Rs 30 ($1). You can get a Chinese lunch for the same price. Unfortunately, the bar seems to get the upper hand at times here.

At 2A Middleton Row, adjacent to the YWCA, **Shenaz** (☎ 298385), has dancing figures made of wire along one wall and usually a group waiting to get in at the door. Reservations are a must in this small, cozy place where the Indian food is delicious. Among the highest-priced specialties is chicken Baghdadi (stuffed with minced mutton, eggs, and cream sauce) for at Rs 60 ($2). Less pricey (but not less delicious) is the fish tandoor kebab and mutton kebab for Rs 26 ($1.50); both dishes are a good meal for two along with plain rice pulao. Open from 10am to midnight, closed Thursday.

Kebab-E-Que, in the garden at The Astor Hotel, 15 Shakespeare Sarani (☎ 2429917), elevates kebab-making to a high art. Whether chicken, mutton, fish, or vegetarian, all 14 kebabs on the menu are deliciously prepared. Prices from Rs 50 ($1.66) to Rs 75 ($2.50). Beer goes great with them. Open from 4pm to midnight. Indoors at The Astor, **Serai** serves good Indian food with main dishes priced from Rs 38 ($1.26) to Rs 48 ($1.60), with menu explanations in English. It is open from 8am to midnight. Some of the dishes in both Kebab-E-Que and Sarai have interesting histories, but the delicious anecdotes about them are, unfortunately, not on the menu. For example, the story is that murgh kasturi so delighted a former maharaja that to express his compliments, he gave the chef his weight in pearls.

For the ultimate in kebabs Calcutta-style, head to **Nizams,** 22 and 25 Hogg Market, a simple but spacious tile-walled cafe, and try a kathi kebab—a kebab and wrapped in a paratha (thin bread) or a famous Nizam roll—a grilled kebab rolled in a paratha with onions and chilies and sauces; you can also have your rolled kebab fried. Prices are about half what you pay in one of the more upscale restaurants.

BENGALI CUISINE

It seems an obvious thing: a top restaurant dedicated to fine Bengali cuisine here in Calcutta. But until the recent opening of **Aaheli** ("Authentic City"), in the Quality Inn, 12 J. L. Nehru Rd. (☎ 2472394), there was no such showcase. Relax in gracious room of gold and black accented by clay murals from Vishnapur while studying the menu and enjoying an aam poraa sharbut (smoked, raw mango drink). Delicious among the many topnotch dishes are taatkaa mochaar ghonto (banana florets and potatoes cooked in khas paste); chingri jogey chamot kaar (prawns in a smooth coconut gravy); bhekti with green chiles and mustard oil baked in a banana leaf; and baashmoti (basamati) rice. End with rossogulla (a milk sweet) and manolobhs malpoora (crepes with sweet syrup). An à la carte meal for two can cost $20; there are thalis on the menu for Rs 100 ($3.33) and Rs 125 ($4.16) to give your taste buds a treat from dal to dessert. Hours are 12:30 to 2:30pm, and 7:30 to 10:30pm.

Home cooking Bengali style—nothing fancy, just the typical dishes you'd get if you dropped in unannounced on a local family—is served at the plain and clean **Suruchi,** 89 Elliot Rd. (☎ 291763). Run by the All Bengal Women's Union, it's open from 10am to 8pm weekdays (until 3pm Saturday and Sunday). Profits from the restaurant go to charity. Daily menu prices are market-driven. Vegetarian thalis might cost Rs 17 (56¢), Rs 22 (73¢) to Rs 24 (80¢) with fish; a lunch with rice and dal and subji (vegetables) is about the same price.

CHINESE FOOD

Calcutta boasts of India's only Chinatown. Although many of the city's Chinese residents are now concentrated in Tangra, a neighborhood of Chinese-owned tanneries en route the airport, traces of the old Chinatown still can be found in its original location near the Tiretta Bazar, in the BBD Bagh (Dalhousie Square) area. Connoisseurs of Chinese foods today search out the tiniest restaurants in Tangra's lanes and frequent the stalls on Blackburn Lane across from Tiretta Bazar for a Chinese breakfast of soup and steamed pork buns or fried wontons hot from the sizzling woks. Here are some of the more traditional places to eat Calcutta's famous Chinese foods.

The **Waldorf,** 24B Park St. (☎ 297514), has red-lacquered pillars, dragon motifs, lanterns, and delicious Cantonese food. The highest-priced dishes are around Rs 35 ($1.16) for such tasty items as prawns in tomato sauce or garlic, sweet-and-sour chicken, and an un-Cantonese, Indian/Chinese chile chicken. These dishes are very good with special fried rice. The Waldorf's menu offers both large and small portions, the latter about one-third less. This restaurant is not air-conditioned, but big, whirling overhead fans and breezes from the open windows keep it comfortable. Open from 11am to 11:30pm, closed Tuesday.

New Embassy Restaurant, 53-A Jawaharlal Nehru Rd. (☎ 2426760), open from noon to 10pm (closed Tuesday), has the same owners as Valentino's in Darjeeling and the Sunflower Beauty Parlor here in Calcutta. It's a vest-pocket-size restaurant, dimly lit and pleasant, with shiny, blue-and-green striped walls, blue plastic upholstered chairs, under a Chinese-design and polka-dotted ceiling. Forego the familiar and slightly cheaper Cantonese dishes in the Rs 40 ($1.33) to Rs 50 ($1.66) range, and opt for the house specialty—five delicious duck preparations, each Rs 50 ($1.66) and not often found in town. Combine them with the special chow mein made with pork, prawns, chicken, and chicken liver.

Eau Chew, P32 Mission Row Extension, 12 Ganesh (☎ 272003), is hard to find but worth the search up a flight of dingy stairs above a gas station. For here in a simple, spotless restaurant are some of the city's most unusual Chinese dishes. Try the chimney soup, a satisfying mixture of fish, meat, and vegetables topped with a poached egg and served in a handsome copper tureen, its central chimney stuffed with coals to keep the pot bubbling while you eat. This costs around Rs 75 ($2.50) and will easily serve four or more. Other Chinese dishes average Rs 20 (66¢) to Rs 50 ($1.66).

For splurging in a Chinese restaurant, try the hushed and elegant **Chinoiserie,** Taj Bengal, 34B Belvedere Rd. (☎ 2483939), open from 10am to midnight. Teak walls form a handsome background for mother-of-pearl pictures and quietly swaying beaded curtains. Szechwan dishes are the specialties, and the average main dish is Rs 125 ($4.16). About the same prices and hours are observed at the well-appointed **Ming Court,** in the Oberoi Grand, Jawaharlal Nehru Road (☎ 2492323).

Extending the Asian repertory beyond Chinese is **Zen,** Park Hotel, 17 Park St. (☎ 2497336), the only restaurant in the city serving, dishes from Indonesia, Burma, Thailand, Singapore, and Hong Kong, plus the Chinese mainland.

VEGETARIAN CUISINE

Vineet, 1 Shakespeare Sarani (☎ 440788), opposite the tourist office in the Air-Conditioned Market, is open from 11am to 3pm, and 7 to 11pm serving minimeals such as nan and curry of the day for about Rs 35 ($1.16); less expensive are Western sandwiches, such as cottage cheese with pineapple, and a host of Indian sweets for less. It's neat, clean, unfancy, and a place for a refreshment break while shopping.

For South India's dosas, idlis, and other vegetarian dishes, try **Jyothi Vihar,** 3/A Ho Chi Minh Sarani (☎ 2429791).

FRENCH & MEXICAN

Calcutta's only French restaurant is **La Rotisserie,** at the Oberoi Grand; it's definitely a splurge. **The Atrium** at the Park Hotel is the city's only Mexican restaurant, and it is also a splurge.

BUFFETS & SALAD BARS

In general, hours for buffets are 6:30 to 11am, 12:30 to 3pm, and 7:30 to 11pm; there are variations, so check in advance. The prices below do not include taxes or gratuities.

Taj Bengal's **Esplanade** (coffee shop), 3-B Belvedere Road (☎ 2483939), has buffets for breakfast—Rs 125 ($4.16)—and lunch—Rs 195 ($6.50). In **La Brasserie** at the Oberoi Grand, 15 Jawaharlal Nehru Rd. (☎ 2492323), the buffets are indeed grand at both breakfast—Rs 125 ($4.16)—and lunch—Rs 175 ($5.83). At **Sujata,** at the Park Hotel, 17 Park St. (☎ 2497336), buffets at lunch—Rs, 150 ($5)—and dinner—Rs 175 ($5.83)—feature Indian and Continental foods. There's a salad bar in the Park Hotel's sleek modern **Atrium**—Rs 60 ($2) for either lunch or dinner—with 10 salads and cold dishes.

In the HHI (Hotel Hindustan International) A. J. C. Bose Road (☎ 24723947), the buffet's in the **Palm Court**—Rs 150 ($5) for breakfast, Rs 200 ($6.66) for lunch or dinner. HHI's **Oriental** restaurant offers a three-course "executive lunch" for Rs 175 ($5.83).

At the **Crystal Room** in the Hotel Kenilworth, 1 and 2 Little Russell St. (☎ 2428394), there's a lunch buffet—Rs 175 ($5.83). At **Trinca's,** 17-B Park St. (☎ 298947), you get Continental and Indian dishes—Rs 59 ($3.35)—from 12:30 to 2:30pm, and Chinese and Indian dishes—Rs 100 ($3.33) each—from 5:30 to 7:45pm, both daily except Sunday when everything is a la carte and Thursday when the restaurant is closed.

Sunday is buffet day at the wonderful 100-year-old **Tollygunge Club,** 120 Deshpran Sashmal Rd. (☎ 4732361). The price is Rs 100 ($3.33). "There's no food we can't do," said the catering manager. If you miss your usual bagels and lox, let the catering manager know in advance, and they'll be specially ordered for you (à la carte, of course).

SWEETS & SNACKS

Sweet shops open as early as 7 or 8am and close around 10pm. They also carry delicious savories—grain snacks made fresh every evening.

Bengalis are famous for the variety and richness of their sweets. A local favorite is a milk-and-syrup sweet rossogolla (also rasgoola) a cottage cheese–type sweet, and a version known as raskadamba (dipped in shredded fresh coconut and chopped almonds). You can taste this treat, as well as another favorite, sandesh (a fudgelike confection), and others at **K. C. Das,** 11 Esplanade East (☎ 2485920).

The only place to find another rich Bengali treat, shor bhaja (another milk-based sweet), is said to be **Mukherjee Sweets,** 29/B Ballygunge Place. **Ganguram and Sons,** 159 Vivekananda Rd. (with branches all over the city), is known for excellent mishti doi (sweetened yogurt).

Buy sweets by the piece, or get an assortment to take out to nosh as you please. Expect to pay a price for some of these rich Bengali treats. Rasgoolas might cost Rs 75 ($2.50) for 875 grams (about eight pieces). Sandesh, when made with chopped nuts and topped with a shadow-thin layer of edible silver, must surely be the Tiffany-priced of the sweets at around Rs 400 ($13.33) per kilogram. Shedding its glistening silver coat and nuts, plain sandesh is less expensive at around Rs 10 ($1) per piece. If you're invited to a Bengali home for a meal, sweets are such an appreciated gift that they'll undoubtedly get you invited again. The demand is so great around festival times that sweets are rationed. This is to make sure there will be enough to satisfy the enormous Bengali sweet tooth, as well as to ensure enough milk for more nutritious uses (since Bengali sweets are milk-based).

TEA & SNACKS

When Indians from other cities visit Calcutta, they eat Western-style sweets and take some back home, for these are well-known specialties of this bustling business and industrial center. Famous for more than 60 years for Western sweets is **Flury's,** 18 Park St. (☎ 297664), where tea for two with cakes (try the famous Black Forest cake) and sandwiches costs Rs 70 ($2.33) to Rs 100 ($3.33). It's also pleasant to drop in at 11am when everyone from chief executives to clerks stop by for a break. Sunday is fun as well, when families turn out for treats. Open from 6:30am to 8pm, closed Monday.

Some 70 years ago, an Iranian immigrant founded **Nahoum's,** F-20, in New Market, off Lindsay Street (☎ 243033), a confectionery shop, which is the first name off the lips of sweet lovers in Calcutta. Few shoppers in New Market can pass by Nahoum's without buying a pastry to nibble on the spot or a selection to take home. For Rs 100 ($3.33) you can get generous an assortment of rich, cream-filled, fruit-stuffed, or chocolate-covered pastries, tarts, and cakes. By the piece they cost around Rs 10 (33¢) to Rs 25 (83¢).

For traditional teas with nappery and silver, treat yourself to the **Tea Lounge** on the balcony at the Oberoi Grand or **Palm Lounge** at the Taj Bengal.

COFFEE

Coffee House, Albert Hall, College Square, and **Coffee Board Coffee House,** 5 Chittaranjan Ave., serve coffee and inexpensive snacks. These are favorite student hangouts.

6 What to See & Do

The best possible thing to do in Calcutta is to walk around aimlessly and watch the life around you. If this is too rich for your blood, try sitting on a streetcar (sit on the side nearest the sidewalk) and ride as far as it goes. Sooner or later it will get hopelessly stuck in a traffic jam, but meanwhile you'll get a superlative close-up view of the streets. A hand-pulled ricksha—if your conscience allows—is marvelous for even closer viewing. Bargain with the ricksha driver *before* you get in, and remember that a fair fare is Rs 2 to Rs 3 per kilometer. Or try a ride in one of those stately, horse-drawn, hansom carriages. Don't worry about getting lost; when you're tired of looking around, hop into a taxi and head back to your hotel. Make sure the taxi has a meter and the driver turns it all the way back to Rs 5 (16¢) for the first 2 kilometers. However, you must add 50% to reflect an increase not shown on the meters—or ask for the rate card.

Among the top sights in Calcutta is the **Victoria Memorial** (☎ 2485142), which sits in majestic splendor at the bottom end of the big green space called the Maidan, and should certainly be looked at even if not visited. An immense palace of white marble, it's a fitting reminder of the days when pomp and ceremony were more important than money. The 25 galleries inside are chockablock with 3,500 exhibits, including lithographs, furniture, firearms, portraits, statues, manuscripts, and other historical evidence of Britain's reign in India. Outside the ornamental gate, you'll most assuredly see ice cream vendors and performing monkeys. The memorial, which cost around a million dollars to build back in 1920, is open daily except Monday from 10am to 4pm.

A new **son et lumière** show effectively casts the history of Calcutta against the Victoria Memorial every evening, from November to January; note the wonderfully catchy Calcutta theme song. Admission is Rs 5 (16¢) back, Rs 10 (33¢) front. After the performance, visit the musical fountain, near one of the main gates to the memorial, which plays all kinds of tunes to dancing waters; it's illuminated at night.

In the complex just across the greensward from the memorial are other places of interest. The **National Theater Rabindra Sadan** (outside is a lovely fountain whose jets constantly change color) presents plays and musical and dance concerts almost every evening at 6:30pm. The **Birla Planetarium** (☎ 2481515), biggest in the world after the one in Russia, has two shows in English daily (check the *Statesman* for a schedule of this and other events). The **Academy of Fine Arts** (☎ 2484302) is open from noon to 7pm daily, 3 to 7pm Sundays, closed Monday. The museum was built in 1847 in the Indo-Gothic style, with its fine selection of miniatures, Kashmiri shawls and carpets, old engravings, mica paintings, Bengali and Varanasi saris, and Tagore paintings. The ground floor usually shelters a temporary show of contemporary art. It's on Cathedral Road next to St. Paul's Cathedral.

Behind the National Theater is the **Nandan Complex** devoted to cinema, a fitting tribute to Calcutta's reputation as a leading filmmaking center.

On the western side of the Maidan is the **Ochterlony Monument** (now **Sahid Minar**), a 158-foot tower honoring Sir David Ochterlony, who won the Nepalese war (1812–14) for the British. The monument, built in 1828, is a strange mixture of Turkish, Syrian, and Egyptian architectural styles. Supposedly, you can climb it to view the city, but first you have to get permission from the chief of police.

Behind the Victoria Memorial, in the other direction, is the **race course**—office at 11 Russell St. (☎ 291104)—and behind that to the left down Belvedere Road are the **Zoological Gardens,** covering 41 acres. The zoo (open 6am to 6pm) is worth a visit in any case, partly because it's extremely attractive with flower beds and pools, is easy to walk around, and has lots of distractions, and also partly because it owns some rare white tigers, descendants of Neeladri and Himadri, who were born on the premises in 1963 from an ordinary-colored mother and a valuable white tiger caught and donated to the zoo in 1951 by the Maharaja of Rewa. Admission is Rs 2 (6¢) for adults, Rs 1 (3¢) for children, and it costs another 50 paise to get into the special tiger enclosure. The zoo is very crowded on Sundays. Be sure to buy peanuts before you enter the zoo; you'll have lots of opportunities to give them away, if not to the ostrich, deer, chicks, or peacocks, then to the ubiquitous black crows that line the fences of every cage awaiting such a generous gesture.

Opposite the zoo is the rather elegant former Residence of the Governor of Bengal, with an enormous banyan tree entirely sheltering its rear garden. The building now houses the **National Library,** India's largest library with eight million books in a multitude of languages.

The biggest banyan tree in the area, and probably in the world, is the more famous one in the 273-acre **Botanical Gardens** (open from dawn to dusk), on the other side of the River Hooghly (merely a continuation of the Ganges, which, 80 miles to the east, finally empties into the Bay of Bengal). You can also take a bus (no. 55, or 59 from Esplanade bus stand and jam-packed with people) or taxi across the massive **Howrah Bridge (Rabindra Setu),** third largest in the world, or ferry over to the gardens.

At the other side of the bridge is one of India's most famous landmarks, the **Howrah Railroad Station,** where any hour of the day or night you'll see families virtually living (sleeping and cooking) on mats spread on the station's stone floor. As many as 210 trains arrive or depart from here every day.

Calcutta, as mentioned above, is the birthplace of Rabindranath Tagore, one of India's greatest poets, who was born and died (in 1941) in Calcutta in a lovely old house known colloquially as **Thakur Bari.** With its cupolas and balconies, its style is not unlike the houses in old New Orleans. At one time, this was the nerve center of Bengal's cultural life. Located at K. K. Tagore Street, off Rabindra Sarani, it is today part museum and part university. You'll see students milling about in its corridors and relaxing on the flower-fringed lawn. The **Rabindra Bharati Museum** (open from 10am to 5pm, until 1:30pm on Saturday), is an invaluable trove of photos, letters, and portraits pertaining to the Nobel Prize winner (who subsequently turned his hand to plays, drama, short stories, and a poem called "Morning Song," which later became the Indian National Anthem).

Up a nearby little alley, Muktaram Babu Street, Chorebagan, is the **Marble Palace,** once a private collection of art and now open to the public from 10am to 4pm (closed Monday and Thursday). It houses a mixed bag of artworks, paintings by Rubens and Reynolds, Roman fountains, and Grecian clocks. Admission is free, but you must get a visitors permit from the **West Bengal Tourist Office,** BBD Bagh (East), which requires 24 hours notice. Remove your shoes before entering.

Over at 94/1 Jawaharlal Nehru Rd., the **Nehru Children's Museum** (☎ 2483517) has, among other things, delightful displays of the *Ramayana* and *Mahabharata*—an easy way for adults to bone up on these epic poems. Admission is Rs 2 (6¢) adults, Rs 1 (3¢) for children; it is open from 11am to 7pm, closed Monday.

At 27 Jawaharlal Nehru Rd., the **Indian Museum** (☎ 2496941) is one of the oldest and most comprehensive in the country; it's also said to be the largest museum in Asia. Especially fascinating are the archaeological relics located on the southern side of the main floor; upstairs on the second floor is a small, interesting Mammal Gallery. Worth seeing also are the Art and Textile collection and the collection of 50,000 coins, the latter requiring a special viewing permit. Newer portions include the Egyptian Gallery and the air-conditioned Theme Gallery, dedicated to rare maps and other Calcutta memorabilia. The museum is open 10am to 5pm from March to November; 10am to 5:30pm from December to February, closed Mondays. Admission is Rs 1 (3¢) for adults.

The **Asiatic Society,** 1 Park St. (hours are 10am to 8pm weekdays, 10am to 5pm weekends; admission is free), opened its doors in 1784 (to Indians in the 19th century) and is the oldest institution of its kind in the world. It houses many books and other documents in Asian languages, some dating as far back as the 7th century. The small museum, opened in 1814, has valuable coins and European paintings.

Before leaving South Calcutta, take a walk through **South Park Street Cemetery,** and read some of headstone inscriptions as an unusual history lesson about the early settlers who came to Calcutta from distant lands. The cemetery is partially maintained by APHCI (The Association for the Preservation of Historical Cemeteries in India), which has relocated historic tablets from other cemeteries here. Their office is in the Bishop's House.

In northeast Calcutta, the **Jain Temple,** on Budree Das Temple Street, is open from 6am to noon, and 3 to 7pm. You wouldn't call it beautiful, but nobody could deny that it's extraordinary. How to start describing it? It's like a combination of New England rococo, with Victorian gingerbread, plus the entire contents of your grandmother's attic tossed in for good measure. Silver statues of men on horseback, flower-inlaid marble tiles, cut-glass chandeliers, stained-glass windows, mirrors and walls encrusted with semiprecious stones—these are but a handful of the things the tourist has to contend with on first inspection. As you walk around the temple, which was built in 1867 by the court jeweler, things seem to fall more into place. The temple belongs to the Jain sect, a Buddhist extremist faction founded by Mahavira, a noted ascetic. It is dedicated to Sri Sheetalnathji, the 10th of the 14 Jain reformers. One wonders what these men would have made of this ostentatious display. It's set in a formal garden.

GUIDED TOURS

The **West Bengal Tourist Bureau,** 3/2 B. B. D. Bagh (East) (☎ 2488271), operates guided coach tours daily from 7:30am to 5:30pm, and 8:30am to 5:30pm. Each tour costs Rs 75 ($2.50) without food. These tours take in the Commercial Area, Belur Math, Indian Museum, Victoria Memorial, the zoo, Jain Temple, Botanical Gardens, and other key museums and points of interest. In some seasons, half-day tours are also available. Inquire when you book your ticket at the **Government of India Tourist Office,** 4 Shakespeare Sarani (☎ 242402). Departure is from the tourist office. Private tour operators also conduct city tours.

WALKING TOURS

Walking tours of historic North Calcutta are conducted by **Conservation and Research of Urban Traditional Architecture (CRUTA)** to see old palaces and other interesting buildings. For information write or phone them at 67B Beadon St., Calcutta (☎ 306127). The walk takes about two hours to cover the old sites and streets from which Calcutta started. There is no fixed charge for the walks, but a contribution is appreciated.

7 Shopping

THE MAIN MARKET

The main place to bargain for assorted wares is the **New Market** (formerly Hogg Market), off Lindsay Street. This is a huge market of more than 2,000 stalls where you can find everything you need to sustain life and then some, arranged according to merchandise category. Still, if you get lost meandering around, don't worry—there is always someone to tell you how to find the shop you want or how to get out to the street again. Parts of the market open early, others not until 10am. Bargaining is essential here. And stay away from so-called "market guides"; they lead visitors only to places where they get commissions.

OTHER SHOPPING AREAS

Burra Bazar is the wholesale market with lower prices than some others; **B. B. Ganguly Street** is the jewelry bazaar with shop after shop offering silver, gold, and precious and semiprecious stones. Not far from BBD Bagh, there's **Bentinck Street,** renowned for its roughly 100 Chinese shoemakers. Custom-made shoes for men start at around Rs 250 ($8.33), and ready-made styles and sizes cost a little less. Ready-made sandals are Rs 200 ($6.66)—not cheap, but it's good-quality merchandise.

Bargain here, too. Looking for a book? On **College Street** there are more than 200 second-hand bookshops.

GOVERNMENT EMPORIA

In Chowringhee, at 7/1 D Lindsay St., the **West Bengal Emporium** is, as the name implies, devoted to items made in West Bengal, such as the famous terracotta toys and handlooms in cottons and silks. Some of the prettiest textiles are from Murshidabad. At **Central Cottage Industries Emporium,** 7 Jawaharlal Nehru Rd. (☎ 2484139), open weekdays from 10am to 6:30pm, on Saturday to 2pm (closed Sunday), there is merchandise from West Bengal and a number of other states. The emporium has an excellent selection of ready-made salwar kamiz in the latest as well as in traditional styles. Nearby **Priyadarshini Handlooms** (Karnataka Handloom Development Corporation, Ltd.), 7 J. L. Nehru Road (☎ 2482104), has lustrous silks from Karnataka. Several other Indian states also have emporia in Calcutta in Chowringhee, Lindsay Street, Gariahat Road, and elsewhere.

8 Calcutta After Dark

Calcutta, like the other major Indian cities, has little in the way of traditional nightlife. But in this cultural capital there is an evening life. Around 6 or 6:30pm you can almost always find a cultural event somewhere in town—a dance or music recital, or other artistic discipline. They are listed in ***Calcutta This Fortnight,*** a free pamphlet available from the tourist office. The office sometimes has a limited number of free tickets for these events, so be sure to ask when you're there.

Also at 6:30pm every evening, there's *Dances of India*, an introduction to various styles, with commentary, in the Moghul Room of the Oberoi Grand Hotel, 15 Jawaharlal Nehru Rd., for a modest fee. Or you might go to a pop history lesson on Calcutta at the **son et lumière** (see "Victoria Memorial" under "What to See and Do," above).

Disco devotees will find discotheques/night clubs in the following hotels: **Pink Elephant** (Oberoi Grand; ☎ 2492323); **Incognito** (Taj Bengal; ☎ 2483939); **Someplace Else** (Park Hotel; ☎ 2497336); **Anticlock,** HHI (Hotel Hindustan International; ☎ 2472394). They're open from about 9pm to 3am (call to double-check times) and closed on Thursdays. Most are free to hotel guests and open for a fee to nonresident foreigners. Some have rules about admitting unaccompanied men and women; check before you go.

The top hotels and several restaurants have bars where you might head for a nightcap before 11:30pm or midnight, when they close down.

You might also catch a movie. Elite, Lighthouse, Metro, Minerva, New Empire, Tiger, and Jamuna cinemas show English-language films, censored to remove the steamy parts; sometimes Satyajit Ray's films have special showings here, as might be expected (in Bengali).

10 The Andaman Adventure

If you think you've gotten away from it all before, you haven't really until you've been to the little-known Andaman and Nicobar Islands. This distant strip of land in the Bay of Bengal is over 610 miles east off the coast of India. The northern tip of the Andamans is in fact 117 miles off the south coast of Burma, and the southern tip of the Great Nicobar Island is only about 88 miles from Sumatra in Indonesia. It's almost like not being in India at all! Of the 293 islands stretching 500 miles into the sea, 274 are in the Andamans and 19 are in the Nicobars. Only 26 of the Andamans and 12 of the Nicobars are inhabited. Very few of these islands are open for tourism because of various restrictions.

In ancient mythology the islands were the monkey-god Hanuman's stepping stones over the ocean, and they bore his name. Historically, the islands were split off from India by the Marathas in the latter part of the 17th century. They were a base for the indomitable 18th-century Admiral Angre, noted for skirmishes against Europeans. During the British colonial period, these peaceful islands were a penal colony for Indian freedom fighters.

From the plane, the Andaman and Nicobar Islands are a vast ribbon of greenery stretching as far as the eye can see into the sea. Over 90% of the area is covered with evergreen species and tropical rain forests of incredible beauty, filled with some of the most rare flora in the world.

The capital of this lush archipelago, **Port Blair,** the tourist's entry point, is little more than a main street, with houses scattered about the hillsides and a couple of good hotels (one on the beach, the other up on a cliff overlooking the sea). Less than a quarter of a century ago these islands had about 50,000 inhabitants—aborigines, Burmese settlers, and convicts and their keepers. The population has swelled since then to 180,700, due largely to the central government's encouragement of immigration and the offer of land as repatriation for property losses by Bangladesh refugees. Obviously with this kind of growth and a push to attract tourists, the sooner you visit, the better your chance of seeing the Andamans and Nicobars at their most beautiful and unspoiled.

One-fifth of the current inhabitants are tribal. They are divided into two main groups. The first are of Negreto stock (the Andamanese, Onges, Sentinelese, and the Jharawas), who live in the Andamans. The second group are Mongoloid in origin, and include the inhabitants of the Nicobar Islands (the Shompens and Nicobarese). Except for the Nicobarese, the others live in "Special Primitive Tribal Reserve Areas," described in the fact sheets as a means of encouraging development while protecting their way of life.

The closest the average tourist comes to seeing tribes living traditionally is in photos in the small Anthropological Museum in Port Blair, one of the attractions described below. Otherwise, you stand little chance of firsthand observation, as the government does not permit visits to restricted areas. Rare exceptions are made to this rule for those who get permission from the Indian Ministry of Home Affairs in New Delhi. You would be well advised to make any special request six to eight weeks in advance of your trip and have some credentials warranting such a visit. Before making an application, check with your nearest Indian embassy or consulate to get the necessary forms. You can also file for your permit through these authorities, who will forward your application to New Delhi.

1 Essentials

ENTRY PERMITS

Permission to visit areas open to foreign tourists is given upon arrival at the airport in Port Blair. Ask the duty officer to stamp your passport with the necessary 30-day permit, or you'll waste a lot of time trying to get one later. Foreign tourist permits can also be obtained at Indian missions overseas and **Foreigners Regional Registration** offices at Delhi, Bombay, Madras, and Calcutta, and from the immigration authorities at airports in these cities. Getting your permit in Port Blair is by far easiest.

Presently, foreign tourist permits are restricted to Port Blair Municipal Area, Jolly Buoy and Cinque Islands. However, foreign tourists in groups of six to 20 can visit Grub, Red Skin, Snob, and Boat islands with special permission of the chief secretary of Andaman and Nicobar Administration and when accompanied by a liaison officer.

Indians do not need special permits to visit the Andamans and Nicobars, with one exception. To visit Car Nicobar, Indian tourists must get special permission from the Home Ministry (Union Territories Cell), South Block, New Delhi, or the Deputy Commissioner Car Nicobar or Chief Secretary, (Andaman and Nicobar Administration, Port Blair).

GETTING TO PORT BLAIR

BY PLANE Regular flights operate to Port Blair from Madras (1,191 kilometers, 727 miles) on Tuesday, Thursdays, and Saturdays for around $136, and from Calcutta (1,255 kilometers, 765 miles) on Mondays, Wednesdays, Fridays, and Sundays for around $134. Flying time from either is about two hours.

BY SHIP Passenger ships operate from Calcutta, Madras (every 10 days), and Visakhapatnam (1,200 kilometers); the journey takes about 52 hours. Fares range from Rs 550 ($18.33) bunk-class to Rs 2,000 ($66.66) for a two-berthed deluxe cabin, bath attached.

For application forms and other information, in Madras contact Directorate of Shipping Services, A&N Administration, Jawaher Building, 1006 Rajaji Salai (opposite Customs House), Madras 600001 (☎ 5226873); in Calcutta, Shipping Corporation of India Ltd., 13 Strand Rd., Calcutta 700001 (☎ 284456); in Visakhapatnam, M/s A. V. Bhanojiraw and Gupta Pattahiramayya, PB17. Start early. Tickets are issued on a first-come, first-served basis, and making arrangements takes time.

GETTING AROUND

Buses are operated throughout the city and suburbs by both the State Transport Services or private lines from Central Bus Stand near the Aberdeen Bazaar. **Bikes** can be rented for about Rs 15 (50¢) per day at the cycle shop between Sapna Photos Studios and M. Permual General Merchants in the Aberdeen Bazaar. Be prepared for some very hilly pedaling. **Taxis** operate within the main parts of Port Blair, Rs 6 (2¢) plus 30% for the first kilometer, and Rs 3 (1¢) plus 30% thereafter. **Commuter Ferries** are operated by the Directorate of Shipping Services from Phoenix Bay, Junglighat, and Chatham jetties (information ☎ 20528).

Getting Around Between Islands The Directorate of Shipping Services also operates passenger cum cargo ferry services from Phoenix Bay Jetty to a variety of islands. (Information on ferry schedules and tariffs contact the Director, Shipping Services, Port Blair (☎ 20528). **Motor boats and dinghies** are available for hire from the Marine Department or Oceanic Company, Mahatma Gandhi Road, Middle Point. For Big Spenders, there are **helicopters** for hire for island-hopping. Check with tourist office for helicopter hire information.

VISITOR INFORMATION

The **Government of India Tourist Office,** 189 2nd Floor, Junglighat, Main Road, Port Blair 744103 (☎ 21006), is open from 8:30am to 5pm Monday through Friday, and 8:30am to 12:30pm Saturday. Information on sights and tours is available here. Government of India Tourist Offices also operates an information counter at Lambda Line Airport, during flight times.

Tourism Office, A&N Administration, Secretariat, Port Blair, 7441-1 (☎ 20694), is another source of information; A&N also operates at the airport during flight times. (☎ 20414).

2 What to See & Do

The main reason for visiting Port Blair is for some R&R. Unless you are one of the very rare few who get to visit the tribes, sightseeing is limited to the following attractions.

The **Cellular Jail,** which was built between 1886 and 1906 by the British for criminals, was ultimately used to incarcerate freedom fighters. Now it houses interesting exhibits and memorabilia showing life within the jail. Open 9am to noon, and 2 to 5pm. There is a **son et lumière** show, daily in Hindi at 6pm; one in English, at 7pm Wednesday, Saturday, and Sunday.

Chatham Saw Mill is one of the oldest and largest mills in Asia; tours show the various steps in turning logs into seasoned planks. No photography is permitted. There is also a small museum.

The displays at the **Anthropological Museum** (open 9am to noon, and 1 to 4pm; closed Saturday and public holidays) illustrate life of the Aborigines; the **Marine Museum** (open 8:30am to 4pm) shows 350 species of marine life; the **Zoological Garden** and **mini-zoo** (open from 7am to noon, and 1 to 5pm; closed Monday) houses rare and endemic birds and animals of this region.

3 Excursions on South Andaman

Corbyn's Cove Beach (10 kilometers from Port Blair) Near the Andaman Beach Resort, for swimming in crystal clear waters. There is a snack shop. Rs 40 ($1.33) taxi from Aberdeen bazaar.

Sippighat Farm (14 kilometers) See agricultural research in farming of spices. Open 6 to 11am, and noon to 4pm daily; closed Mondays.

Wandoor Beach (28 kilometers) Good snorkeling; the wooden jetty is the boarding place for ferries to Jolly Buoy, Red Skin, and other islands. Pack a picnic and take the ferry for one hour to Jolly Buoy for lunch. Don't forget your snorkeling gear.

Chiriyu Tapu (30 kilometers) Also known as Bird Island, a one-hour drive from Port Blair, at the southern most tip of South Andaman, is famous as a tropical rainforest haven for birds and butterflies, with mangroves and driftwood in fantastic shapes, as well as a fabulous view.

Mount Harriet (55-kilometer drive or 15-kilometer ferry ride plus half-hour walk) Offers unusual trekking opportunities and fine view at the summit, 1,200 feet (about 35 meters).

Madhuban (75 kilometers–50 kilometers by boat, plus 15 to 20 kilometers on foot) A treasury of flora and fauna and part of Mount Harriet National Park. Elephants are trained here for lumbering timber.

4 Excursions on Other Islands

MAHATMA GANDHI MARINE NATIONAL PARK

(See "Entry Permits" for restrictions; usually travel agents can put together groups where needed.)

Such islands as Grub, Redskin, Jolly Buoy, Pluto, and others dotting the surrounding waters are part of **Mahatma Gandhi Marine National Park,** 30 kilometers southwest of Port Blair and full of exotic tropical flora and fauna. All around these islands is a magic kingdom of natural marvels, fields and forest of corals with fish in a rainbow of colors, like the palette of a painter run amok, dart between these formations. While a bit of this fantasy is visible in pools near the surface, you need snorkeling gear to fully appreciate it. (Collecting of corals and shells is not permitted.) Pack a lunch in Port Blair, and spend the day seeing the underwater paradise. On the ferry over, you'll probably make a number of new friends, some eager to share their life stories and snacks with you.

OTHER POSSIBILITIES

At **Cinque Islands Sanctuary** (40 kilometers from Port Blair), coral and white beaches are the winning combination. Get permission to ferry over from the forest department. **Ross Island,** across from the Aberdeen Sports Complex, was formerly the seat of British administration, and ruins from those days can be seen. Take the boat from Phoenix Bay. On **Havelock Island** (54 kilometers from Port Blair), you'll enjoy the lush forests and Radha Nagar Beach. Take the interisland ferry from Phoenix Bay Jetty. Radha Nagar has been slated for resort development by the government.

5 Nicobar Islands

Limited access to the **Car-Nicobar** islands is provided on an island-to-island cruise calling on the huge rubber plantation at Katchal; Nancowry, which is famous for its harbor; Indira Point, southern-most point in India; and Campbell Bay in Great Nicobar Island. The Nicobarese are, among other things, great swimmers. Their housing is unusual— dome-shaped, thatch-covered huts on stilts about three feet above ground.

GUIDED TOURS

Government-operated tours depart from Goal Ghar, Delanipur and Haddo. Book tours and buy tickets at **Tourist Information Centre,** Tourist Home, Haddo (☎ 20380), in advance or day of departure. Tours of **Port Blair**—Tuesday, Wednesday, and Friday from 1:30 to 5:30pm, costing Rs 12 (40¢)—cover major sights. Another tour operates to **Corbyn's Cove Beach**—Wednesday through Sunday from 9am to 12:30pm, costing Rs 12 (40¢). There is also a **harbor cruise** (Tuesday, Thursday, and Saturday, lasting about 2½ hours, for Rs 20 (66¢) adults, Rs 12 (40¢) children. For reservations and exact times, contact the Marine Department, Port Blair (☎ 20725).

A variety of tours also are offered by travel agents, including **Island Travels,** Aberdeen Bazaar, Port Blair (☎ 21358); **Shompen Travels,** 2 Middle Point, Port Blair (☎ 20425); and **Andaman Beach Resort,** Corbyn's Cove (☎ 20599). If you book a day tour, check to see if lunch and bottled water are provided in the fee; if not, order a lunch in advance at any of the top hotels. At the Bay Island Resort a satisfying non-vegetarian lunch of chicken, finger sandwiches, fruits and other dishes runs about Rs 100 ($3.33), veg is less.

SHOPPING

Cottage Industries Emporium (open from 9am to 1pm, and 1:30 to 5pm; closed Monday and Friday) is next to the Tourist Office and sells local crafts including textile hangings and shell work. Prices are fixed. Shops in **Aberdeen Bazaar** also have shell-studded souvenirs. Bargain here.

6 Where to Stay

There is not an abundance of budget-priced accommodations, but new hotels and lodges open now and then, so there may be more choices by the time you use this book. Lack of maintenance is a big problem in the lowest-priced hotels. Off-season discounts of 20% to 30% are in effect from roughly May to September 15.

DOUBLES FOR LESS THAN RS 700 ($23.33)

The following accommodations are run by ANDICO: **Megapode Nest,** Haddo, Port Blair (☎ 20207), has 10 adequately furnished rooms; with AC the price is Rs 400 ($13.33) for a double. Nearby is **Nicobari Cottage** (☎ 23080), where rooms cost Rs 700 ($23.33). For reservations and information, contact: General Manager, New Marine, Dry Docks, Port Blair (☎ 20076)

The three following hotels in Aberdeen Bazar provide simple and acceptable accommodation: **Hotel Dhanalakshmi,** Aberdeen Bazaar, Port Blair 744101 (☎ 21953), has 16 double rooms with attached baths; the restaurant serves Indian and Chinese foods; **NK International** (☎ 21066); and **Hotel Shalimar** (☎ 22963). Rates for AC doubles are about Rs 300 ($10).

The following are basic accommodations run by the directorate of tourism: **Teal House** (☎ 20642); **Hornbill Nest** (☎ 20018); **Dolphin Yatri Niwas,** Havelock. Rates are $10 for foreigners, Rs 150 ($5) for Indians. For reservations and information, contact Director of Tourism A&N, Administration Secretariat, Port Blair (☎ 30933 or 20747; fax 20656).

The following less-expensive places (under Rs 300 for a double) are generally untidy and have little but price to recommend them. Better look at the rooms before checking in. **Sampat Lodge** (☎ 21752) has six rooms, all doubles; two have attached bathrooms. **Ram Niwas Lodge,** Aberdeen Bazaar, Port Blair 744101

(☎ 21717), has 16 simple rooms, four doubles with attached bathrooms. You might also try these three: **Tourist Cottage,** Babu Lane (☎ 21021); **Central Lodge,** Goalghar (☎ 21632); and **Modern Lodge** (☎ 21054). These are a few of the inexpensive places in this part of Port Blair, but typical of many.

DOUBLES FOR LESS THAN RS 1,500 ($50)

In this price range, the rooms have attached baths and many amenities of international resort hotels. Air-conditioning is an option in a number of places.

Andaman Beach Resort, Corbyn's Cove, Port Blair 744101 (☎ 21463; fax 293381), painted cream and rose, has 48 double rooms with balconies and four cottages. Centrally air-conditioned, the hotel overlooks a natural beach and an 18-acre garden with mammoth crotons, huge daisy-like gerberas, magnificent hibiscus, cascading bougainvillea, and other species. Flowered chintz cushions on furniture carry the garden look into the lobby, which has a bold black-and-white, geometric-patterned granite floor and plants here and there. The clean, cheerful rooms have functional modern furniture and bright flowered drapes and bedspreads. Rates range from Rs 1,100 ($36.66) single to Rs 1,500 ($50) double, and Rs 1,800 ($60) for a cottage, without meals; add about Rs 450 ($15) per person for meals.

Hotel Sinclairs Bay View, South Point (☎ 20644; fax 20425), has 24 rooms facing the sea with balconies in need of better maintenance. Rates range from 400 ($13.33) for a non-AC single to Rs 700 ($23.33) for an AC double, without meals. Meals add Rs 430 ($14.33) per person.

Hotel Shompen, Middle Point (☎ 20360; fax 20425), has 45 passable rooms with balconies and harbor view. Doubles with AC are Rs 750 ($25).

WORTH A SPLURGE

The top hotel is the **Welcomgroup Bay Island,** Marine Hill, Port Blair 744101 (☎ 20888; fax 21389). A striking white stucco structure with a sloping wooden roof, it was designed by prize-winning architect Charles Correa of Bombay. The multilevel hotel is partially air-conditioned (designed to catch sea breezes) and built to blend with the contours of a cliff overlooking the sea. The huge open lounge has cut-log furniture covered with brown and beige hand-woven cotton, and low tables decorated with stencilled designs and inlays. There's also a big wooden bar that's a popular meeting place. The rooms have comfortable furniture made from local materials and offer smashing views. Highest price double is $123. Meals are à la carte. There's a seaside pool.

7 Where to Eat

Your best bet is a hotel restaurant; most of them welcome nonresidents. Meals are costly here compared to other places in India because many ingredients are imported from the mainland, miles way. Fresh caught seafood, fresh tropical fruits, and venison are local specialties. Bengali and South Indian foods are available. **Andaman Beach Resort** and **Welcomgroup Bay Island** serve Indian and Continental dishes. One of the less-expensive places to eat is the restaurant in **Hotel Dhanalaxmi.**

11 The Route to the South

The journey runs southward now, through country and city celebrated for attractions, both natural and fabricated: flourishing wildlife, sparkling lakes, ancient temples, immense mosques, sturdy bastions, triumphal arches, delicate glasswork, heady perfumes, and golden filigree.

1 Bhubaneswar

The beautiful east-coast state of Orissa has as its capital Bhubaneswar (pop. 411,500), a city with a split personality: an old town of crowded, narrow streets, and ancient temples surrounded on three sides by a newer settlement of modern architecture and California-style habitations. Many of the buildings are composed of the reddish lava blocks that are characteristic of the region.

Most tourists give it one night en route to Konark and Puri, and, in truth, this pleasant capital doesn't have much to detain you longer. The area around Rajmahal Square (intersection of the main roads to Calcutta and Puri) contains some stores, restaurants, and hotels. In the old town, you'll find mud homes decorated with white lacy paintings as a tribute to Lakshmi, the goddess of wealth.

Orissa is well known for its filigree silver and gaily colored hand-woven cottons. Also widely sold are soapstone reproductions of erotic scenes from the temples, often inset neatly into matchboxes. The state government maintains an excellent low-cost store for local handicrafts at Bhubaneswar airport and in Bhubaneswar and Puri.

ESSENTIALS

GETTING THERE

BY PLANE **Indian Airlines** flies to Bhubaneswar from Delhi ($128); from Calcutta ($41); from Madras ($116); from Nagpur ($83); and from Hyderabad ($95).

Taxis to town should cost Rs 90 ($2.85) to most hotels, but more to the Oberoi, which is out of town. You may have to bargain to get this kind of a fare. For transportation questions call 401084 or 406472.

BY TRAIN Bhubaneswar is located on the main Calcutta–Madras line of the **South Eastern Railway** and reachable from the rest of India. Here are a few of the better trains. **From New Delhi,** a once-a-week, totally air-conditioned *Rajdhani Express* (1,248 kilometers, about 25½ hours) costs Rs 3,215 ($107) First, Rs 1,820 ($60.66) two-tier sleeper; or the *Kalinga Utkal Express* (about 29½ hours), which also goes on to Puri (another 65 kilometers), costs Rs 1,913 ($63.77) AC First, Rs 207 ($6.90) Second. **From Hyderabad (Secunderabad),** the *Faluknama Express* (1,154 kilometers, about 20 hours), costs Rs 1,635 ($54.50) First, Rs 200 ($6.66) Second. **From Madras,** the *Coramandel Express* (1,226 kilometers, almost 20 hours) costs Rs 1,635 ($54.50) First, Rs 230 ($7.66) Second.

BY BUS **OSRTC** operates interstate bus services; other state bus corporations and private buses operate to virtually everyplace in Orissa and many locations in the nearby states. Deluxe services are available to and from Calcutta, Rourkela, Bijapur, and Visakhapatnam; some sleeper services also available. The **Capital Bus Stand,** Unit II (Old Bus Stand), is in the heart of the city (☎ 400540); the reservations desk is open from 8am to 12pm. The **New Bus Stand** is 6 kilometers from the city.

GETTING AROUND

A frequent choice of penny-watchers are **cycle and auto rickshas.** Rates are negotiable. A leisurely tour by cycle ricksha to the temples in town and the caves costs about Rs 75 ($2.50) after bargaining. Some auto rickshas offer point-to-point fares, but this is rarely the case. Metered taxis are nonexistent; the shortest ride can run Rs 50 ($1.66); tourist taxis cost Rs 2.50 (8¢) within the city.

You might consider a **hired car** for the day for Rs 600 ($16.66), non-AC within the city. Outside the city, rates for an *Ambassador* (eight hours/80 kilometers) are Rs 3.50 (12¢) per kilometer; for a *Maruti* Rs 7.50 (25¢) per kilometer. Cars can be booked from OTDC, Panthanivas, Lewis Road, Transport Service (☎ 55515) and Swosti Travels (☎ 408738).

As in other cities in India, buses are very crowded. There are two bus stands. Capital Bus Stand, called the "old" bus stand, located in Unit 2 (off Rajpath), is the main bus stand and right in the heart of the city. OSRTC (☎ 400540) is the "new" bus stand, located approximately 6 kilometers from town. The reservations desk is open from 8am to noon.

Before busing it, be sure to check timings and routes. For instance, you can grab a **bus** in town at the bus stand around 9am and go to Khandatri Traffic (where four roads converge), then walk 300 yards to the caves. Return to the circle to get another bus around 11am on to Nandankanan Park, and later on to Puri. Or you can take a 7am bus from Puri, near the hospital, go to Bhubaneswar to see the caves and the park, and return to Puri on the late-afternoon bus.

Minibuses to Puri also leave from Rajpath near the old bus stand and near the petrol station opposite Kalinga Ashok Hotel.

VISITOR INFORMATION

The **Government of India Tourist Office,** B-21 Kalpana Area, Bhubaneswar 751014 (☎ 54203), is open from 9:30am to 6pm weekdays.

The **Government of Orissa Tourist Information Office,** near Panthanivas (☎ 50099), is open from 10am to 5pm. There's also an Orissa Tourist Information Counter at Bhubaneswar Railway Station, which is open around the clock (on holidays from 6am to 10pm) and at the airport, open during flight hours.

WHAT TO SEE & DO

TEMPLES

Despite the ravages of time—and deliberate destruction over the years—there are still several hundred ancient temples in the region of Bhubaneswar. Most visitors content themselves with visiting a cluster of the older ones, which happen, conveniently, to be fairly close together. Oldest of all is the one called **Parasurameswar,** built in the 7th century and dedicated to Lord Shiva. It is elaborately carved on the exterior with hundreds of figures: natives catching wild elephants, gods sitting on lotus flowers, a lingam being draped with garlands of flowers. Nearby, sticking out of the ground, is a similar stone lingam that present-day worshippers have decorated with real flowers. All this artistry is even more remarkable when you know that this early temple predates the use of mortar. Proper balance and weight hold it together. The temple's projecting roof stones keep both harsh sun and rain from getting inside.

The magnificent temple called **Mukteswar,** built in the 9th century, shows both Buddhist and Hindu influences in its carvings. The interior has a beautifully carved ceiling, including a fully open lotus flower; on the exterior walls, numerous examples of the mythical animal Gajasimha—half lion, half elephant—identifies the architecture as Kalingan in period. A famous legend, illustrated in several carved panels, is of the frolicking monkey who lived in a tree beside a river and ate blackberries all day. The monkey's friend, the crocodile, shared these daily feasts until one day, taking some blackberries home for his wife, he was urged by her to bring the monkey home for dinner. (The wife wanted tender monkey heart for dinner.) On the way home, the crocodile asked the monkey, who was riding on his back, if he'd donate his heart to Mrs. Crocodile for dinner. Thinking fast, the monkey replied, "Why, if you'd only told me before, I would have brought it with me instead of leaving it in the tree trunk." And back he went to get it.

A third temple nearby is **Rajarani,** built of red sandstone in the 9th century. Most interesting here are the elegant pairings of deities about three feet high carved into the lower section of the main tower, guarding the structure. The sculptures above the main doorway represent the nine planets.

To the east of Rajarani is another temple jewel, **Brahmeswar,** from the 10th century, frequently overlooked and not on any tour. You can only peer in the incense-filled hall at the lingam. But the big show's on the outside for everyone to see in the intricately carved friezes of slender-waisted beauties and their handsome lovers, noble warriors, a nursing mother, parading pachyderms, prancing monkeys, and watchful birds.

The other temple that should be seen—but that cannot be visited by non-Hindus—is the 10th-century **Lingaraj Temple,** built successively by three kings. Surrounded by a high wall, it comprises a 170-foot-high main shrine with the traditional four separate chambers, plus 20 smaller temples in the grounds. The numerous stone lions peering pensively from among the moss-covered stones are representative of the Keshari (lion) dynasty. Though the temple cannot be entered by non-Hindus, it may be observed from a stone platform nearby. Unlike the other temples mentioned, it is not away from the town but right in the center of the old city, not far from the sacred tank, Bindu Sagar, which is supposed to contain water from all the holy rivers and tanks throughout India.

The other main sightseeing activity is to visit the **caves** cut into the twin hills of Udayagiri and Khandagiri, about 4 miles from town. The caves were excavated about 2,000 years ago as a Jain monastery and are impressively decorated outside with numerous carvings. The caves are a series of hollowed-out living cells with a stone ridge on the floor of most to act as a pillow. Despite the fact that the overhanging stone roof has survived for 20 centuries, the Indian government has recently added stone pillars for additional support.

Farther up the hill is the Hatigumpha cave, with its famous rock on which is inscribed the year-by-year diary of events during the reign of King Kharavela, who ruled the area, then known as Kalinga, in the 2nd century B.C.

A Wildlife Park

A little over 18 miles from town, **Nandankanan** (named for "Nandan Van," the pleasure garden of the gods) is indeed a pleasurable experience. This vast tract is part zoological park and part biological park, divided by a big lake, and carved out of a generous swath of jungle. Rare even here among the many exotic beasts such as panthers, lions, rhinoceros, pangolin, barking deer, and sambar—all in their natural settings—are five white tigers, the unusual offspring of tiger parents of the usual brilliant stripes. There is also a lion safari park (African lions, as there are not enough Indian lions to stock a park).

In the botanical garden are more than 100 species of trees and plants. The huge lake is a sanctuary for dozens of birds, including cranes, storks, pelicans, pea fowls, parakeets, and wild ducks.

There is a modest entry fee; modest fees also apply to touring by car, rides on the toy train and on elephants, and to view the lions on a safari trip.

Other Interesting Sights

Ekambarkanan is a garden with 500 roses, which are the centerpiece of a festival held here in December/January.

Indira Gandhi Park, opposite the Secretariat, honors the late prime minister with a statue. She gave her last speech in this city.

The **Orissa State Museum,** Gautam Nagar, opposite the Hotel Kalinga Ashok is open from 10am to 5pm every day but Monday. It is worthwhile for its local and statewide exhibits and artifacts such as palm leaf manuscripts, coins, and arms.

The **Handicrafts Museum,** Secretariat Road, open 10am to 5pm, closed Sundays, is also worth a visit. On display are star handicrafts such as patta paintings, horn objects, toys, silver filigree work, sculpture, and brass castings.

The **Science Museum,** Regional Science Center, Secretariat Road, Unit 9, has displays dealing with scientific progress as well as working models of advanced machinery.

The **Tribal Museum,** CRP Square, features fascinating displays on Orissa's tribal culture and exhibits covering all manner of tribal life, including housing and ornaments.

Guided Tours

The easiest way to round up all the Bhubaneswar sights and Nanadankanan park as well is on an **OTDC tour. Tour 1** is offered daily from 7am to 7pm, for Rs 75 ($2.50)—Rs 100 ($3.33) for superdeluxe AC. The tour covers Nandankanan, caves, temples, and Dhauli. **Tour 2** is also offered daily, from 9am to 7pm, and goes to Konark, Pipli (applique village), and Puri for Rs 85 ($2.83), Rs 130 ($4.33) superdeluxe AC. Both tours leave from Panthanivas, Jayadev Marg (Lewis Road) (☎ 54515). Bookings are made through the manager, OTDC Transport Unit, at Panthanivas (☎ 55515).

OTDC also offers package tours (30-person minimum) with overnights at various Panthanivas. Check with OTDC Head Office, Jaydev Marg, near Panthanivas (☎ 50099).

One of the most interesting out-station tours is the nine-day Swosti Tour to tribal villages; for more information, contact Swosti Tours, Swosti Hotel, 103 Janpath (☎ 404178)

Shopping in Bhubaneswar

Orissa is noted for more than 30 different handicrafts, and there are half a dozen or so hand looms associated with the area. Among the best known craft items are silver filigree jewelry from Cuttack, paintings on silk panels, painted palm-leaf items such as bookmarks and wall hangings, and soapstone carvings of deities, many of these originating in Puri. But the most famous Puri crafts are the charming, primary-color paintings of gods and goddesses, animals and birds, from playing-card size to huge and custom-designed works, and the papier-mâché statues of Jagannath, his brother Balaram, and his sister Subhadra. From Pipli come vivid colored appliqués made into large items such as garden umbrellas and small packable coin purses and fans. Orissa has eight different types of textiles. Bold designs with animal and floral motifs distinguish many of the most striking saris from those of other regions. Some of the loveliest hand looms are subtle flame-stitch patterns, and one of the most elegant silks is tussar, woven from hand-reeled silk (non-mulberry silk) with a natural color and unique luster. This kind of silk is beloved in the West by fashion designers.

Main shopping areas in Bhubaneswar are on Janpath and in the Market Building Complex on Rajpath. Bargain in all but government-run emporia. Temple shops are overpriced.

A favorite bargaining place for everyone in Bhubaneswar is the **daily market** on Rajpath, Unit 2, near Utkalika (government emporium), where you can find everything from household items to silk saris. The market is especially diverting in the evenings when there is little else to do.

You can get an overview of handicrafts in Bhubaneswar at **Utkalika,** Market Building (☎ 400187), open 9am to noon and 4 to 9pm, closed Thursdays; or try the Orissa State Handloom Cooperative, J. N. Marg, "Bayanika" Market (☎ 400741), closed Thursdays. Some other government-run or price-fixed shops for textiles are **Orissa State Handloom Development Corporation,** Janpath, Unit 9 (☎ 403038); **Sambalpuri Bastralaya Handloom Weavers Society,** Kalpana Square; **Orissa State Tussar and Silk Cooperative,** Janpath, "Amlan" Sahidnagar (☎ 54852).

The **Gift Shop** in the Oberoi Hotel (price-fixed) and **Swosti Crafts** in the Swosti Hotel have good craft selections; you might also check out **Kalinga Art Palace** near Ravi Talkies.

Where to Stay

Budget travelers get a break in Bhubaneswar; your budget goes a long way when it comes to creature comforts here.

Western-Style Hotels

Most Western-style hotels have everything you need for comfort—attached bathrooms, air-conditioning, TV, telephones; some have swimming pools and tennis courts; one has a jogging track. Recently, the top-priced hotels have added conference rooms and business service centers. *Note:* Telephone numbers are being changed in Bhubaneswar, and those changes may affect numbers in this chapter.

Doubles for Less Than Rs 700 ($23.33)

Tops in this price range, **Hotel Meghdoot,** 5B Sahid Nagar (☎ 405802), has halls in need of painting. The 43 rooms are passably clean. Larger than most, they have brightly flowered bedspreads and drapes. Very nice management makes up for the lack of decor. Highest price doubles run Rs 700 ($23.33), with AC. Lower-priced rooms do not have AC.

Doubles for Less Than Rs 1100 ($36.67)

Centrally air-conditioned **Swosti,** 103 Janpath, Bhubaneswar 751001 (☎ 404178; fax 407524), has a lobby dominated by huge Puri-style murals of gods and goddesses. The 60 double rooms are efficiently rather than imaginatively done up. In the hotel are two restaurants, a bar, and Brown and Cream Parlour, a pastry shop that sells fabulous cakes and Indian sweets that can do serious harm to the waistline. Doubles run Rs 1,100 ($36.67).

ITDC's **Hotel Kalinga Ashok,** Gautam Nagar, Bhubaneswar 751014 (☎ 53318; fax 410745), started out many years ago as 12 simple rooms off a courtyard and now has 64 rooms furnished in motel modern in dire need of better maintenance. Expect to pay Rs 750 ($25) for a single, Rs 950 ($31.66) for a double. Some interesting Orissan artworks line the halls on the way to the restaurant. The coffee shop is said to be the most reasonably priced in town; its service is among the slowest.

Hotel Prachi, 6 Janpath, Bhubaneswar 751001 (☎ 402328; fax 403287), has 48 clean, cheerful renovated rooms with print drapes and solid spreads; others were under renovation and should be mint-fresh by now. You'll pay Rs 800 ($26.66) for a single, Rs 1,000 ($33.33) for a double. There's central AC, a restaurant where Indian music is played on Sundays, a swimming pool under swaying palms, gardens with a terrace for barbecues, and tennis courts. Next door, Prachi Pub is a restaurant run by the hotel.

A replica of a the Sun Temple wheel stands outdoors at the **Hotel Kenilworth,** Gautam Nagar, Bhubaneswar 751014 (☎ 56543; fax 56147). The spacious marble lobby is dominated by a bold Puri-style mural of Lord Krishna in ceramic tile prominent on the staircase landing. There are 65 air-conditioned modern rooms, with standard doubles about Rs 1,000 ($33.33). Rooms in front are noisy. For refreshment after sight-seeing, you can enjoy a swimming pool, treats in the pastry shop, or a delicious meal in the hotel's restaurant or coffee shop. It's convenient to temples, the train station, and the tourist office.

Worth a Splurge

The top hotel, **Oberoi Bhubaneswar,** Nayapalli, Bhubaneswar 751013 (☎ 56116; fax 56269), is surrounded by 14 landscaped acres away from the center. Architect Sathesh Grover's style blends traditional temple and modern designs. Within the spacious white lobby are gleaming, red granite floors, red sandstone pillars, and, throughout the hotel, paisley wall hangings and local works of art. Orissa woven spreads, drapes, and upholstery fill the rooms with restful, subtle colors. The courtyard swimming pool is surrounded by a shady terrace for drinks and snacks. There are floodlit tennis courts and a jogging track. Singles (rates are cited in dollars for foreign travelers) are $38, doubles $75.

Indian-Style Hotels & Lodges

These are the cheapest. If those below are full or don't appeal, check others on Station Square, Cuttack Road, or Kalpana Square. Don't expect much in the way of cleanliness or comforts.

The modest **Hotel Anarkali,** 110 Kharavela Nagar, Unit 3, Bhubaneswar 751001 (☎ 408801), near the railway station, is often all booked. The reception area looks neater than the rooms, some with balconies. Rates are Rs 375 ($12.50) for a double with AC.

Pushpak, Kalpana Chowk, Bhubaneswar 751014 (☎ 50896), is fairly clean, well lit, and pleasant. The floors are tiled with mosaic patterns. Twenty-one doubles and two singles, some with Western bathrooms. AC doubles are about Rs 375 ($12.50).

A Penny-Wise Choice

If you're conserving rupees, your best bet is the OTDC's **Panthanivas Tourist Bungalow,** Jayadev Marg (Lewis Road) (☎ 54515), right across from the State Government Tourist Office, about 3 miles from the airport, 1 mile from the railway station, and walking distance from some of the temples. There are 52 rooms. Those in the new block are recommended. All rooms have attached bathrooms, with hot and cold running water; big overhead fans swirl the air in the non-AC rooms. There are no single-occupancy rates: Rooms cost Rs 175 ($5.83) to Rs 325 ($10.83) without AC, Rs 325 ($10.83) to Rs 375 ($12.50) with AC. There's a no-frills bar and restaurant, where you can get an Indian vegetarian thali meal.

Where to Eat

Delicious Orrisan curries are made with fish or prawns. Also try chhenapodapitha, a long name for what, in short, is a delicious local delicacy: baked cheesecake.

Of the hotels, the **Oberoi Bhubaneswar** is your choice if you're in the mood for a splurge. Entrées average Rs 120 ($4) à la carte. Surroundings are elegant except for the overly bright lighting. Although Oberoi food doesn't deviate much from the standard Indian and Continental dishes, it's well prepared. The hotel also serves Indian and Continental buffets at breakfast for Rs 70 ($2.33), Rs 150 ($5) for lunch or dinner; the **Kenilworth Hotel** has good Chinese food; the **Prachi Hotel** serves dosas and other South Indian dishes; sometimes they have buffets. Panthinivas has bargain-priced thalis.

A beacon for vegetarians is **Hare Krishna,** upstairs in the Lafchand Market Complex (left of Swosti Hotel and through a narrow passageway), indeed, run by a Hare Krishna devotee. Very relaxing soft lighting bounces off a too-low copper ceiling. The interesting menu has dishes named for Hindu gods and goddesses, each described in detail, plus a delicious "Radha Raul's Surprise," a dish of mixed vegetables. Entrées run Rs 24 (80¢) to Rs 36 ($1.20); breads, Rs 4 and Rs 5 (about 15¢); stuffed parantha, Rs 12 (40¢). Open daily from 11am to 3pm and 7 to 11pm.

For coffee and snacks there's an **Indian Coffee House** in New Market. For sweets, it's Dama Maharaja, Satya Nagar, near Ram Mandir.

Bhubaneswar After Dark

The favorite local activity is going to the cinema; some of the better known movie houses are **Sriya, Swait,** and **Stuue**—all in Unit 3. Check the daily paper to see if they are showing English-language films.

Performances of famous Odissi classical dance, music, and dramas based on folk or mythological themes are presented occasionally and worth attending. Check at **Soochana Bhawan** (☎ 402594), **Rabindra Mandap** (☎ 401777), and **Bhanja Kala Mandap** (☎ 50945). **Odissi Research Centre** (☎ 406797) is the headquarters for the famous Odissi dance.

En Route to Konark & Puri

About 8 kilometers (5 miles) south of Bhubaneswar at Dhauli, off the Puri Road to the right, are **edicts** carved into a rock slab in the 3rd century by Emperor Ashoka. In these, Ashoka describes the horrors of the Kalinga war from which he emerged the victor and his conversion to the peaceful beliefs of Buddhism. So well have they withstood the ravages of time that you can read them clearly today.

The well-preserved rock edicts stand below a **Peace Pagoda** built in 1972. It's a popular place at sunset for its beautiful view of the surrounding countryside.

Farther south by some 7 kilometers (4 miles) is **Pipli,** a village known for its appliqué work, where little shops line the road selling dozens of colorful items from minuscule coin purses to mammoth wedding tents. The craft is said to have been once used exclusively by the Jaggannath Temple. Unfortunately over the years, as this work has become commercial, it has parted company with its once carefully constructed designs. Still you'll undoubtedly find some bright little trinket to take home.

2 Puri

37 miles (60 kilometers) south of Bhubaneswar

Sitting comfortably on the coast of the Bay of Bengal is the town of Puri (pop. 125,000), a sleepy place in between the numerous holy pilgrimages and festivals that, especially in June and July, draw visitors from all over India.

ESSENTIALS

GETTING TO PURI

BY TRAIN From Bhubaneswar, there are numerous trains to Puri, 64 kilometers, two hours) for around Rs 197 ($6.56) First, Rs 33 ($1.10) Second. For train inquiries call 402233; for reservations call 402042 from 9am to 4:30pm.

Additionally, the *Kalinga Utkal Express* makes a stop in Puri (see "Getting There" under "Bhubaneswar," above for more information).

BY BUS There is regular bus service to Bhubaneswar from Puri, and the trip can sometimes be faster by bus than by train. Buses to Puri leave from the **Capital Bus Stand,** Unit 2 (Old Bus Stand) (☎ 400540); the reservations desk is open from 8am to 12pm.

Minibuses to Puri also leave Bhubaneswar from Rajpath, near the old bus stand and near the petrol station opposite Kalinga Ashok Hotel.

BY HIRED CAR If you wish to make the entire Puri/Konark trip in one day, the round-trip by car between Bhubaneswar and Puri (65 kilometers) with stops in Pipli and Konark (70 kilometers) can run from Rs 1,500 ($50) non-AC to Rs 3,000 ($100) AC. There are lower-priced deals as well, but make sure your car is up to the trip before settling for the cheapest deal. The excursion takes about six to seven hours, including a one-hour stop at Konark and 15 to 30 minutes at Pipli. Check with OTDC, Swosti Travels, Sita, or other travel agencies in town on car rentals. Hotels in Bhubaneswar can also help with transportation arrangements.

WHEN TO VISIT

The season is September through March. But many people come in June or July for the important festival Rath Yatra (Cart Festival) at Puri, when Lord Jagannath and his brother and sister are taken from the temple, placed on carts, and pulled down the main street to their summer garden. Jagannath's cart is about five stories high with 16 enormous wheels. The other carts are only slightly smaller. It takes 4,000 professional draggers to drag the deities one mile to their summer house, where they spend seven days before being dragged back to their home shrine again. Other festivals and fairs take place throughout the year.

WHAT TO SEE & DO

Although the region is rich in temples, the **Sri Jagannath** is one of the most visited in India. Built in the 12th century by a king of Orissa, it celebrates the cult of

Jagannath, a reincarnation of Vishnu, and entry is barred to non-Hindus. The traditional thing for tourists to do is climb onto the roof of the Raghumandan Library (which, by the way, contains interesting and ancient palm leaf paintings), at one end of the big square opposite the main entrance to the temple. You need to get the keys from the librarian to get to the top; ask for both keys so you can go to the highest platform and ask for the stick he keeps around to tap in front of you to frighten off any monkeys. (Alternatively, you can climb to the roof of the Jaya Balia Lodge, after asking permission and giving a few rupees.)

From the roof of the library, outside the 34-foot-high pillar **Aruna Stambhe** (brought from Konark), you can see through the main gates of the gaudily decorated temple.

It's a distinctive structure, with a cone-shaped tower, 192 feet high, surrounded by several buildings that seem to go up in steps. According to legend, the unfinished wooden images that stand on the altar inside (unseen, unfortunately, from outside) were carved by God himself, in the guise of an old carpenter, after many other carpenters had broken their chisels on a holy log fished out of the sea.

From your rooftop perch, you can see acolytes and helpers at work outside the temple's enormous kitchens. At festival times they feed 10,000 people—steaming rice and curries for thousands of temple servants who traditionally are fed on the premises.

Library hours are from 9am to noon and from 4 to 8pm, closed Sundays and holidays. The librarian will show you some of this private library's treasures, manuscripts written on palm leaves, centuries old, many in Sanskrit. He will also ask for a small donation for the library. This donation is, of course, not compulsory, although you will be made to feel it is. The librarian also cooks the books, adding zeros to contributions so you believe that you must give a huge donation: Rs 10 (33¢) to Rs 20 (66¢) maximum, don't be coerced. But it's for a good cause, if the money helps preserve this treasury of old manuscripts.

If you long for outdoor activity, Puri's long, golden **beach** is a lovely place for watching the sunrises and sunsets. The waters take on the colors of the sky. Night markets spring up on the beach after sunset. But walking along the beach to nearby fishing villages is not especially aesthetic. (People mistake certain areas of the beaches for bathrooms.) Take a flashlight and great care.

Guided Tours

From Puri, the **OTDC** conducts two tours. **Tour 1**—daily from 7am to 7pm, Rs 75 ($2.50)—covers Konark, Dhauli, the caves, and Bhubaneswar's temples. **Tour 2**—6:30am to 7:30pm (check on frequency of tour), Rs 85 ($2.92), with extra fees for boating—goes to Chilika Lake and Kaliji Temple. Book tours through the Manager, Transport Unit, **OTDC,** Puri, in the **Panthanivas** (☎ 22562).

Shopping in Puri

Grand Road, Station Road, Mochi Sahi Chowk, and the beach market are the best places to bargain-hunt in Puri. But haggle here; everything is overpriced, and the merchants are hard-sellers. You can always turn to the price-fixed markets: **Utkalika Government Emporium** at Mochi Sahi Chowk, the **Crafts Complex** at the same location, the **Weaver's Co-op Society** on Grand Road, and **Sudarshan Crafts Emporium,** Station Road (☎ 23882).

Where to Stay

At various scenic spots along the 22-mile Marine Drive connecting Konark and Puri are resorts and camping grounds in addition to accommodations in town. Discounts usually apply from July to September.

Doubles for Less Than Rs 100 ($3.33)

Very popular with backpackers and fairly clean, the **Youth Hostel,** Puri, 752001, south of Chakra Toth Road, behind the Boat Club on the Bay of Bengal (☎ 22424), charges minimal rates. There are 49 beds in all: 31 for men, 18 for women. In the hostel's restaurant, you can get a tasty vegetarian thali. There's a 10pm curfew. For reservations, contact the warden at the Youth Hostel, or Tourist Officer, Tourist Office, Puri.

Doubles for Less Than Rs 450 ($15)

Best of the many Indian-style hotels along the beach is **Puri Hotel,** Swargadwar (☎ 2114). Opened in 1947, it has expanded slowly to its present 127 rooms in five connected buildings. Rooms in the newer building are nicest—and slightly higher priced—as they face the sea. Though undecorated except for a fairly fresh paint job and an occasional tile floor, the premium-priced rooms look right out over the ocean across 50 yards of beach. You can lie in bed and watch the sunrise hit the sea. Attached bathrooms are all Indian-style; you get hot water in buckets. If you ask in advance, the restaurant serves Indian and Chinese vegetarian food and welcomes non-residents. There is a 10% service charge. Bus service is available to and from the railway station.

Moderately priced and the best buy for penny-wise budget crunchers, OTDC's **Panthanivas Tourist Bungalow** (☎ 22562), is right on the beach. This is a simple, clean, pleasant place. In the 27-room new wing—the best rooms, nearer the sea, although they are smallish—there's wicker furniture and sea views. The top rate is Rs 350 ($11.66) for an AC double. Moderately priced vegetarian and nonvegetarian meals are available in the restaurant. Lots of backpackers stay here.

Doubles for Less Than Rs 900 ($30)

Hotel Vijoya International, Chakratirtha Road, Puri 752002 (☎ 22702), has 44 rooms, some with AC. Furniture in the rooms is modern, and the look is a cookie-cutter version of a lot of other hotels, but the views are nicer than some since all rooms face the sea. An AC double costs Rs 600 ($20). There's a nice open terrace and restaurant with sea views. There's a 6% service charge. Good in this price range; there is an off-season discount from July to September. Located next to the Mayfair.

Hotel Nilachal Ashok, V.I.P. Road (☎ 23639), is centrally air-conditioned, with 36 rooms off an atrium with wooden balconies. The hotel is run-down, but still enjoys 35% occupancy. A few rooms have sea views. From October to March, you'll pay Rs 500 ($16.66) for a single, Rs 800 ($26.66) for a double; there is a discount from April to September. There's a restaurant and coffee shop. Access to the beach is via the basement. Nice front garden.

The **South Eastern Railway Hotel,** Puri 752001 (☎ 22063), was posh when built in 1925 and stands in a small garden, across from the beautiful beach. The hotel's 35 rooms, some with AC, others with fans to stir the breezes, all face a shady verandah. Rooms are clean but in need of renovation, which seemed underway when I looked in. Some rooms have two attached bathrooms—one with a bathtub and the other with a shower. You'll pay Rs 600 ($20) for an AC single, Rs 900 ($30) for a double. There's a billiard room, bar, lounge, and library. The food is bland old England; outsiders are welcome in the dining room but are advised to ring up and make arrangements before coming in. Lunch and dinner are about Rs 125 ($4.16) each.

DOUBLES FOR LESS THAN RS 2,000 ($66.66)

The **Mayfair Beach Resort,** Chakratirtha Road (☎ 24041; fax 24242), has 34 doubles, some with AC, in the main block with balconies as well as cottages surrounded by a lovely eight-acre garden with a small temple where a priest makes a morning puja. Everything is light and beachlike with modern rattan furniture (some deluxe rooms have mirror-spangled headboards) and well maintained. An AC double costs Rs 1,100 ($36.66), with an off-season discount from July to September. The restaurant keeps you well fed with vibrantly flavored Indian food and Chinese selections. There's a swimming pool and small health club. Service charge is 20%. Pick-up service from the railway and bus stations is available upon advance request.

On Marine Drive, **Toshali Sands,** P.O. Baliguali, Puri-Konark 752002 (☎ 22888; fax 57365), is 7 kilometers from Puri, and 23 kilometers from the Sun Temple at Konark, and a short ride via the hotel's minibus from a beach. A 12-acre garden makes a vivid centerpiece for this attractive resort surrounded by coconut and casuarina groves, next to dense private woods. In the big, open reception area and lobby are a huge, clay planter and a floor mural showing aspects of Hindu mythology by a village artist. There is also Ganesha in bold Puri colors and many plants in clay planters. Guests stay in 50 four-room and two-room, simply furnished garden suites and villas, all with little patios overlooking the well-kept grounds. An AC cottage rents for Rs 900 ($30) single, Rs 1,090 ($36.33) double. Add Rs 450 ($15) to the price of a single for all meals; add Rs 720 ($24) to the price of a double for the same (there are options in between as well). There's a swimming pool. The restaurant, inspired by village huts, has deep brown walls decorated with white graffiti. Often there is a buffet lunch. Service charge 10%. Tour groups stop here.

One of the two Patra brothers is usually around to see to guests' comforts at their **Hotel Holiday Resort,** Sandy Village, Chakratirtha Road, Puri 751002 (☎ 2440). They are well-known as exporters of Orissan lobsters and prawns to Europe, and not surprisingly seafood appears as stars on their menu. A magnet for families, the 100-room hotel and 26 cottages with sea views, are set in a neat garden, a few steps from the beach. Dark wood furniture, taupe spreads, and rose-colored ceilings are typical of the decor in the cottages, and a similar look prevails in the main-wing rooms. Potted plants around the hotel are changed with the seasons, and the foods offer variety as well—dishes from all over India are served in the restaurant. Lots of kids.

Hans Coco Palms, Swargadwar ("Gateway to Heaven") Gourbarsahi (☎ 2638; fax 3135), is a branch of the Hans Plaza in Delhi. The 36-room, centrally air-conditioned hotel right on the beach and 1 1/2 kilometers from Lord Jagannath's Temple, was closed for renovation when I looked in. It should be spruced up and filled with guests by now. Doubles should be about Rs 1,100 ($36.66).

WHERE TO EAT

Chung Wah, near Puri Hotel, is about the only restaurant outside of a hotel. All the recommendable eating places are in the hotels. Try the **Mayfair, Holiday Resort, Hans Coco Palms, Toshali Sands,** and **South Eastern Railway Hotel.**

3 Konark

20 miles (33 kilometers) from Puri, 40 miles (64 kilometers) from Bhubaneswar

Konark, which can be visited from either Puri or Bhubaneswar, is not much more than a few souvenir shops surrounding a fascinating temple. It is usually visited as a day trip, but you can spend a night there if you want.

ESSENTIALS

Getting to Konark

From Bhubaneswar The bus from Bhubaneswar takes 1 1/2 hours along banyan- and mango-shaded roads to cover 64 kilometers (40 miles) for Rs 15 (50¢).

From Puri Buses from Puri cost Rs 7 (23¢).

On a Guided Tour Alternatively, you can take the OTDC tour every day (at least in season), which goes all the way to Puri and covers Konark on the way (a similar tour leaves from Puri, including Konark—see "Guided Tours" under "What to See and Do," above, for more information). Reservations and information at the OTDC Transport Counter, Panthanivas, Bhubaneswar, or Puri.

When to Go

The **Annual Konark Dance and Music Festival** usually takes place from December 1 through 5 at Konark Natya Mandap, Arka Vihar, Kanark, Orissa. (However, check for specific dates; recently it was held in February.) Contact Eastern Zonal Cultural Centre and Orissa Dance Academy (☎ 408494 or 400638). Tickets are sold at many hotels in Puri and Bhubaneswar, at Panthinivas in these locations, in Konark, and the Orissa Dance Academy, 78 Kharvelanagar, Unit 3.

WHAT TO SEE & DO

The Sun Temple (Black Pagoda) Virtually in the middle of nowhere, Konark is a shrine built in the 13th century by King Langula Narasimha Deva. According to legend, 1,200 architects took 12 years to build the temple under the direction of a master architect named Bishnu Maharana, who had left his native village to stay at the site and work. When the temple was almost ready for completion, calculations proved that the tower could not be added until corrections were made. Just then, Bishnu's son arrived in search of him, made the necessary adjustments, and finished off the job. However, to atone for his father's shame, he jumped off the newly completed tower into an adjoining river and died.

Whatever the truth of the story, the tower, once over 200 feet high, no longer exists. Speculation is that it fell in an earthquake several centuries ago. But even without it, the temple rises almost 100 feet and can be seen from 5 miles away. It is ornately decorated with thousands of carved animals, larger-than-life erotic groupings, statues, and honeycombed rock.

While erotic groupings are usually seen as decorative friezes on Indian temples, these are exceptionally explicit. Many theories have developed about their true meaning. One is that they portrayed the temple devadasis; another is that they represented the provocative worldly as opposed to the austere spiritual life. More probably, scholars today believe they represented an element of sexual mysticism grounded in the Indian religious beliefs.

At ground level, on each side, are 12 immense stone chariot wheels, each spoke of which is intricately inset with sculpted scenes of animals and people, and on the top level are various statues of Surya, the sun god, to whom the temple is dedicated. In the morning sun, the statue of Surya looks peaceful; in the evening he looks tired (he's on horseback).

This Sun Temple, a 24-wheeled chariot pulled by seven stone horses, is sometimes known as the Black Pagoda and sits majestically in a semiwooded area about a mile from the coast. It's a beautifully peaceful spot (with a few too many vendors)—the ideal place to get away from everything for a day.

When you leave Konark Temple, don't leave the compound immediately. Do as many Indian visitors do: Turn left and walk north to the little unprepossessing yellow building, a 20th-century structure, housing a nine-planet temple with 12th-century deities. For about Rs 11 (37¢), buy an offering and go inside; you'll come out with your personal blessing by the priest and a flower. Give the priest another Rs 2 as you leave.

The Sun Temple is open from 6am to 5pm. It is illuminated with floodlights from 5:30 to 9:30pm in summer, 6 to 10pm in winter.

Other Things to See and Do About half a mile from the temple, right next to the Travellers Lodge, is a **museum** operated by the Archaeological Survey of India, containing statues and carvings from the Black Pagoda, images of the sun god, animals, celestial musicians, nymphs, etc. Publications are for sale. It is open from 9am to 5pm every day but Thursday and it's free.

WHERE TO STAY

Most travelers treat Konark as a day trip, staying in Puri or Bhubaneswar. Plans to develop beach resorts in this area are underway by major hoteliers. Presently, if you would like to stay here longer, there are two choices.

There are modest tourist accommodations adjoining the temple site. The **Travellers Lodge** (☎ 8823) is rarely used and has four run-down rooms. Rates are from Rs 110 ($3.66) non-AC, to Rs 220 ($7.33) with AC for a double room. **Panthanivas** (☎ 8831) is cleaner than the lodge and charges about the same. For reservations, contact the Manager, Panthanivas and Travellers Lodge, Puri District, Orissa.

If you plan to stay, take along some bottled water, fruit, and cookies, and also something to read, because, aside from shopping at souvenir stalls, there are no diversions and nowhere to buy things you need in the "village" nearby. There are plenty of coconuts available, though.

4 Hyderabad

What the late Pandit Nehru described as the "meeting place between north and south" is Hyderabad (pop. 4,280,000), capital of Andhra Pradesh and India's seventh-largest city. It is actually twin cities—**Old Hyderabad,** founded by Mohammad Quli Qutb Shah in the late 16th century, and modern **Secunderabad,** which owes its origin to the British in the early days of occupation. The two cities, usually regarded as one, sprawl for a considerable distance over relatively flat, rocky countryside about 1,200 feet above sea level.

The climate is pleasant, except for the overly humid spring months, and the city is luxuriant in trees, plants, and flowers.

It really is a meeting place in a sense, for 16 languages are spoken by the natives of the region (the major ones are Telugu and Urdu). Minarets and beautifully graceful spires and towers form the skyline, and combined with the Musi River, which winds through the old city, the panorama makes for one of the most attractive cities in India. There are thousands of bicycles and motorbikes in the city, which is apparent to anybody trying to negotiate rush-hour traffic.

An important educational center, Hyderabad is the location of five universities: Osmania, founded by the Nizam in 1917 and built in an interesting Indo-Sarecenic style; the University of Hyderabad; the Jawaharlal Technological University; the Agricultural University; and the Andhra Pradesh Open University.

ESSENTIALS

GETTING THERE

BY PLANE **Indian Airlines**, **East West, NEPC,** and **Jet Airways** operate daily and have weekly flights connecting Hyderabad with Delhi (one hour, 50 minutes) for $124; Bombay (one hour, 10 minutes) for $74; Madras (one hour) for $57; Calcutta (two hours) for $134; Visakapatnam (one hour) for $55; and Nagpur (one hour) for $55.

Begumpet Airport is in the residential area of the twin cities. Driving time to most hotels is about 30 minutes; a prepaid taxi costs about Rs 85 ($2.83), metered auto ricksha about Rs 25 (83¢). For Indian Airlines questions call 599333 in the city, at the airport 844422-33; for Jet Airways 231045 in the city, 840382 at the airport.

BY TRAIN Hyderabad/Secunderabad is a major rail center. **From Delhi,** fares on the AC *Rajdhani Express* (1,666 kilometers, 23 hours) run Rs 2,655 ($88.50) First, Rs 1,530 ($51) two-tier sleeper. From Delhi you can also take the *A.P. Express* (1,666 kilometers, 26 hours) for Rs 2,081 ($69.36) AC First; Rs 218 ($10.90) Second; **from Madras,** the *Charminar Express* (793 kilometers, 15 hours) costs Rs 1,252 ($41.73) AC First, Rs 144 ($4.80) Second; **from Bombay,** the *Hyderabad-Bombay Express* (800 kilometers, 14 hours) costs Rs 1,252 ($41.73) First, Rs 144 ($4.80) Second; the best train is the *Rajdhani Express* (400 kilometers, 12 hours), or you can take the *Bangalore-Hyderabad Express* (17 hours) for Rs 992 ($33.06) First, Rs 114 ($3.80) Second, to name only some trains. City bus service operates from the railway station.

The busiest railway station is in Secunderabad; for centralized railway questions call 135; for reservations from Secunderabad 75413, 75045, or 76444. In Hyderabad call 231130, 235623, 231044, or 237133. Reservations are computerized.

BY BUS Hyderabad and Secunderabad are at the junction of two major national highways: NH-7, which goes all the way from Varanasi to Kanya Kumari, and NH-9, which goes from Bombay to Vijayawada. The twin cities are also well connected by road to major tourist centers throughout India. **APSRTC,** Musheerbad (☎ 64571), operates regular bus services to all centers in the region; the main bus station for Andra Pradesh is Gowliguda Bus Station.

Within Andhra Pradesh, buses are available to and from such sites as Bidar (ancient tombs and home of Bidriware), Nagarjunasagar Dam (museum housing archaeological finds at Nagarjunakonda), Tripupathi (an ancient temple), and Vijayawada (a former Buddhist site now noted for toys). For information on deluxe coach service to some of these places, contact **Ashok Travels** (☎ 522971).

GETTING AROUND

Auto rickshas are metered and start at Rs 3.70 (13¢) per 2 kilometers and Rs 1.85 (6¢) per kilometer thereafter; from 11pm there are double charges. **Black-and-yellow taxis,** of which there is a shortage, are not metered and get what traffic will bear. If you're going around town or out of town by taxi, bargain for the best fare before setting off. The drivers will invariably try to get more from Westerners. **Bicycle rickshas** charge by the district, but seem to have a Rs 5 (17¢) minimum charge and an additional charge of about Rs 1.50 (5¢) for each additional kilometer. But set the rate before you set off.

APTTDC provides diesel *Ambassador* cars for Rs 2.50 (8¢)per kilometer; Rs 350 ($11.66), eight hours/80 kilometers; Rs 275 ($9.16), four hours/40 kilometers. Prices are probably higher now. Other car rental resources are **Ashok Travels,** Lal Bahadur

Stadium (☎ 230766), and **Travel Express,** Safiabad (☎ 234035). Rates are about the same.

Bike rentals are inexpensive at shops around town.

Local buses are best boarded at the terminus; otherwise they are so crowded you probably won't be able to squeeze in. You might, however, try to board near the Char Minar buses no. 94 or no. 95, which go to the zoo. But I'm willing to bet you'll give up and take an auto ricksha.

Visitor Information

The **Government of India Tourist Office** is located in the Sandozi Building, No. 1 Himayatnagar (☎ 666877). The **Andhra Pradesh Department of Tourism** is on the first floor, Gagan Vihar, M. J. Road (☎ 557531). **The Andhra Pradesh Travel and Tourism Development Corporation (APTTDC),** Yatri Nivas, S. P. Road, Secunderabad (☎ 843931), also runs tourist information counters at the airport and railway stations in Secunderabad and Hyderabad.

FAST FACTS: Hyderabad

Books Try A. A. Hussain, M. G. Road, especially for travel books; Waldens, Raj Bhawan Road, for all kinds of books.

Banking Hours These vary. Some banks are open Monday to Friday from 10am to 2pm, and Saturdays, from 10am to noon; others are open from 9 to 11am and 4 to 6pm; some even have Sunday hours, from 10:30am to 12:30pm.

Cinemas Hyderabad has more cinemas than any other Indian city. There are more than 125 cinemas in the twin cities, some showing English-language movies.

Cultural Experiences Regular cultural programs or film shows are organized at **Ravindra Bharati Indoor Theater,** Safiabad (☎ 233672); **Lalit Kala Thoranam,** Public Gardens; **Kala Bhavan,** Secunderabad; and **Max Mueller Bhavan,** Eden Bagh (☎ 43938).

Film For film and other photographic needs, Byas and Co. Basheerbagh; Murthy and Sons, Nampally; Ganry's and Studio, Abids; and Jyothi Photo Studio, Secunderabad.

Swimming You can swim for a fee at these hotels' pools: Nagarjuna (☎ 237201); Parklane, Secunderabad (☎ 70148); Ritz (☎ 233570); and Deccan Continental (☎ 840981). Telephone each hotel for more information before plunging in.

When to Visit

The high season is from October to March. Summer temperatures can be in the 90s (°F) or higher; winter averages a pleasant 70°F, but can get higher. The rainy season is June to September. Frequent festivals add color to almost any visit. Particularly colorful is the **Harvest Festival** in January, when everyone flies a kite.

WHAT TO SEE & DO

The Bazaar Visiting Hyderabad without taking a look at the bangles in the **Lad Bazaar** would be like traveling to Agra and not looking around the Taj Mahal: It just isn't done. The bazaar is on the street that leads down from the famous Char Minar, and the numerous stores with which it is lined contain enough brightly colored bangles to line the wrist of virtually every woman in the world. For a handful of rupees—maybe a dollar's worth—you can festoon your arm with a dozen or more delicately spun glass circles. Down another street of this bazaar you'll find heady perfume oils, jasmine soaps, incense, and oil lamps—indeed, clusters of stalls selling everything from the frivolous to the practical.

Hyderabad is also renowned for its pearls and gold filigrees. Almost as famous is Hyderabad Bidriware, which is silver inlaid in zinc-copper alloys. (See "Shopping," below, for more information).

Char Minar The heart of ancient Hyderabad—and an absolute must for the first-time visitor—is the immense arch called **Char Minar** ("building with four minarets"), something referred to as the "Arc de Triomphe of the East." It is so closely associated with the city that it is also the name of a local brand of cigarettes that displays the monument on its yellow packet. The arch is illuminated from 7 to 9pm daily (with a market on Thursday); there is a modest entry fee.

Almost 200 feet high, the Char Minar was built to celebrate the ending of a plague in 1591 by Quili Qutab Shah, the fifth of seven kings whose dynasty ruled the region during most of the 16th and 17th centuries. All around it are the streets of the bazaar, including the famous "Street of Bangles" mentioned above.

Mecca Masjid Traffic of all kinds—vehicular, human, and animal—flows around the Char Minar from all these streets and alleys into a perpetually busy area in front of the Mecca Masjid, one of the biggest mosques in Asia, which reputedly can accommodate 10,000 worshippers at one time. As with most mosques, there are impressive historical statistics to recite to newcomers: The immense door arches are made from solid slabs of granite, mined in a stone quarry seven miles to the north and brought here with the pulling power of 1,400 sweating oxen. It was started in 1614 and completed in 1657.

Salar Jung Museum To most people Hyderabad's outstanding possession would be the Salar Jung Museum (☎ 523211), surely one of the world's most amazing collections. What adds to its fascination is the fact that the museum's contents were the collection of one man, Mir Yusuf Ali Khan Salar Jung III, who, before his death in 1949, had briefly acted as the Nizam, or prime minister, of Hyderabad. He was a bachelor and seems to have been single-mindedly devoted to acquiring representative treasures from all cultures of the world, ancient and modern. There are 35,000 exhibits in 35 rooms, ranging from junk to great treasures.

Originally displayed in one of the palaces (now a supermarket), it was relocated to its lackluster government building in the north of the city in 1968. While there are interesting captions explaining the exhibits, the semi-circular layout is confusing, and maintenance at the moment needs improvement. Still it's not to be missed.

Among the exhibits are extensive collections of European art (mediocre) glass, Chinese jades, ivory (chairs, inlaid tables), bronzes, porcelain, fine illuminated manuscripts, and jeweled weapons (look for Empress Noor Jehan's dagger and the Nawab's diamonds-studded sword). The collections include an early model flying boat, fine bidriware, Indian miniatures from major schools, modern Indian paintings, and more.

The museum is open from 9:30am to 5:30pm; closed Friday. Entry fee is Rs 2 (7¢) children Rs 1.

Other Sights in Hyderabad Buses leave for various places from the general area around the Char Minar, the first destination being the **Nehru Zoological Gardens** (bus no. 94 or 95 from outside the Madina Hotel, three blocks from Char Minar), which is one of the biggest, and certainly among the nicest, zoos in India. Covering 300 acres of seemingly undeveloped land, the zoo houses about 1,800 animals, most roaming in their natural habitats. Open from 9am to 6pm; closed Monday. There is a modest entry fee; cars are an additional Rs 10 (33¢).

Inside the zoo grounds is a **Natural History Museum** (with the same hours as the zoo) guarded by a stuffed bear whose paws hold the sign "Please Do Not Touch the Exhibits." Most of the exhibits are life-size reproductions in glass cases of incidents in the life of a tiger. One label reads, "To see a tiger striding on velvety paws across a meadow of grass with the fading rays of the setting sun harmonizing with its tawny black-striped coat, the very symbol of physical beauty, strength and dignity, is surely one of the greatest aesthetic experiences in nature."

There is also a 10-acre **prehistoric animal park** with creatures 25 feet high and 50 feet long, a **Lion Safari Park** (additional small fee) housing rare Asian lions in 30 acres of hills and forests, and a children's train.

Nampally Public Gardens (formerly Bagh-e-aam), also housing the State Legislative Assembly and Archaeological Museum and Art Galleries, is another place to take a break amid lotus ponds and handsome landscaping. For more archaeological finds, check out the **Birla Archaeological Museum,** Malakpet, with displays of artifacts from local digs in Asman Ghad Place, 9 kilometers from town.

Naubat Pahad encompasses two hillocks north of the gardens; proclamations were read from their summits in the old days to drumbeats, a tradition that continued until Aurangzeb's days. In 1940, two pavilions were placed on them, and a hanging garden adorns one, while a temple to Sur Lord Venkateswara (Birla Temple) sits on the other. The temple is modern and interesting for its carvings and decorations. Non-Hindus are allowed inside.

Birla Planetarium, one of the most modern in India, near the Birla Temple, has six shows daily; eight on Saturday, Sundays, and holidays.

Faleknuma Palace, a castle-looking building crowning a lonely hill, was built in 1870 in the days of sixth Nizam. They say it will be turned into a hotel some day. Presently, private tours to see its fading grand interiors and those at a few old havelis can be arranged by getting permission from the Nizam's office in Hyderabad.

As a break from sight-seeing **walk along Tank Bund,** the popular promenade that dams Hussain Sagar. It's lined with 33 statues of the states notables; at the center of the lake is a huge Buddha. The lake itself is site of many sports events. A children's park is located at the flyover end of the lake.

Sights Outside the City

Golconda Fort and Qutb Shahi Tombs A little more than 11½ kilometers (7 miles) west of the city, the remains of the almost-impregnable Golconda Fort sprawl over a hillside about 1,000 feet above the surrounding countryside. Built originally of mud, it was converted into a stone bastion by the seven kings of the aforementioned Qtub Shahi dynasty (1518–1687), each of whom added to and strengthened it during the years of his reign. The early use of sophisticated acoustics in architectural design is one of the features of the fort. Sounds made at the entry gate can be relayed to the top (61 m) without any modern amplification devices, something guides delight in illustrating. There are many legends concerning the fort. One of the most haunting tells of two beautiful dancers, Taramati and Pemamati, sisters who danced on ropes strung between their rooms and those of the king (their patron), Abdulla Qtub Shah. Then there's the last king, Tana Shah, who bathed in a fountain filled with rosewater.

The three walls enclosing the fort are still intact, the fort having fallen but once—when Aurangzeb, after an eight-month siege, bribed a traitor to open what is now called the **Victory Gate.** The conqueror, believing rumors about hidden gold, ripped the roofs from the palaces on the grounds, but otherwise the structures are much as they were almost 300 years ago.

Outside the fort, visit the **Qtub Shahi tombs,** distinctively designed with sensuously shaped domes. There are seven altogether, all with accompanying little "tomblets" to house their queens—but the seventh is unfinished because the seventh king, Abul Hassan, was conquered and captured by Aurangzeb and imprisoned in Daulatabad before he had a chance to complete his own tomb. The tombs have graceful Naksh inscriptions and bits of the once-lovely glazed tiles that covered them. They are surrounded by graceful gardens.

Note: There is a fascinating **son et lumière** at Golconda Fort, with narration by famous film star Amitabh Bachchan (from March to October at 7pm, from November to February at 6:30pm; in Hindi Tuesday, Friday, and Saturday; in English Sunday and Wednesday; in Telugu Thursday; closed Monday). For tickets contact the **AP Travel and Tourism Development Corporation** (see "Visitor Information" under "Essentials," above). Bus no. 119 or 142 go from Nampally to the Fort and tombs. Go early before the tour buses arrive.

Guided Tours

Andhra Pradesh Travel and Tourism Development Corporation (APTTDC), Yatri Nivas, S. P. Road, Secunderabad (☎ 84394312), conducts a comprehensive daily tour from the Yatri Nivas office, commencing at 7:40am (times change seasonally) to the Public Gardens, Buddha Purnima boating complex, Qtub Shahi, Golconda Fort, Osman Sagar (Gandipet), Salar Jung Museum, Char Minar, Mecca Masjid, Zoological Gardens, and Birla Mandir. The tour allows 60 minutes for the Golconda Fort, 90 minutes for the Salar Jung Museum, Char Minar, and Mecca Masjid. It is rushed, but gives the essence of the sites. If you have time, you can return to your favorites on your own.

You can also get information and make reservations for the tour through the **Government of AP Tourist Office,** 5th Floor, Gagan Vihar, M. J. Road (☎ 55753132). It's best to book in person the day before the tour of your choice.

Shopping

Hyderabad is renowned for pearls (from the Persian Gulf) in various guises, silver jewelry, and bidriware in black metal inlaid with silver. Glass bangles from Hyderabad circle the wrists of women all over India. From the tiny town of Pochampalli come lustrous printed saris and cottons; kalamkari, an old art of vegetable dying prints, produces all kinds of lovely things, including saris and wall hangings. Keep an eye out also for colorful crafts from all over Andhra Pradesh—Kondapalli toys from Vijaywada, carpets from Warangal and Eluru. Most shops are open from l0am to 9pm, closed on Sunday.

Main shopping areas are Abids, Basheerbagh, Nampally, and Sultan Bazar in Hyderabad, and M.G. Road and Rashtrapati Road in Secunderabad. The markets around Char Minar feature both bangles and pearls as well as herbs, spices, attars, and silver and gold laces. In Chor Bazaar merchants resell what the rich have pawned—gold-encrusted saris, Venetian glass lampshades, imported Meissen, and large nude statues that once graced a former palace.

Bidriwares (originated in Bidri, site of ancient tombs) can be found at **Lepakshi Handicrafts Emporium** (Gun Foundry; ☎ 235028), starting at about Rs 50 ($1.66) for small boxes, and going up to the Rs 1,000 ($33.33) range for elegant carafes. Rugs inspired by Persian motifs and some of the attractive, translucent decorations carved from animal horns are also available locally. For the budget-souvenir hunters, there are brightly painted and lacquered animal toys costing Rs 15 (85¢) to Rs 30 ($1.70) apiece. The emporium consists of two gigantic floors crammed with all the above, plus silver filigree, yard-long sticks of incense, saris, Nirmal ware (hand-painted teak trays from the village of the same name)—most of the best handicrafts produced in Andhra Pradesh State. Open till 8pm; closed Sunday. Everything is price-fixed.

There are **APCO Handloom Houses** on Mukharam Jahi Road, Abids, M.G. Road, Amerpet Khoti, and elsewhere; **Khadi Bhandar** is in Sultan Bazar. For handicrafts try **Khadi Crafts,** Municipal Complex, Rastrapati Road, Secunderabad. **Nirmal Industries,** Raj Bhavan Road, as the name implies, showcases Nirmal ware (hand-painted teak items). Various other emporia feature regional handicrafts, including **Kairli** (Kerala), **Gangotri** (U.P.), **Tantuja** (West Bengali Hand looms), and **Coptex** (Tamil Nadu Hand looms).

Among the pearl merchants is **Mangat Rai,** Basheerbagh (☎ 235728), opposite the Hotel Nagarjuna. This 70-year-old firm has pearls in a great variety of colors and shapes, from about Rs 600 ($20) up, and also sells coral, emeralds, rubies, and lapis. You can see the store's artisans stringing pearl necklaces and designing striking jewelry. Some other pearl and jewelry shops are **Sri Omprakash and Sons,** 7-1-938 Kingsway Circle, R. P. Road, Secunderabad; **Jagadhamaba Jewellers and Pearls,** Gupta Estate, Basheerbagh; and **P. Satyanarayanan and Sons,** opposite the Gandhi Medical College, Basheerbagh. There are also reputable pearl shops in some of the hotels (expect to pay more).

WHERE TO STAY IN HYDERABAD

Among Western-style hotels are a former palace up in the hills overlooking the twin cities as well as hotels with push-button modernity. Whichever your choice, be sure to book in advance. There are a limited number of hotels in Hyderabad and Secunderabad. The hotels below, unless otherwise indicated, have rooms with attached bathrooms, hot and cold running water, room service, room telephones, and other amenities. Pricey hotels have central air-conditioning, business facilities, and accept international credit cards.

Indian-style hotels in Hyderabad (they get much better farther south) are simple places, cheap by Western standards but catering to fairly affluent Indians. Their kitchens are usually vegetarian and the plumbing generally Indian-style (sans commode).

Note that most tourists stay in Hyderabad to be near the main attractions. If you stay in Secunderabad, be prepared to spend 20 minutes or more, depending on the traffic, and many rupees going by bus, auto ricksha, or taxi to and from Hyderabad. Stuck in a traffic jam on Tank Bund Road skirting the lake, you can, if it's election time, marvel at incredible political slogans scrawled everywhere on retaining walls, and, at any time, admire the statue of Lord Buddha, rising from Gibraltar Rock in the middle of the lake. The 63-foot-high statue weighs 350 tons and took from 1985 to 1989 to complete; it is purportedly the world's tallest monolithic statue of Buddha. In addition to their inconvenience, the acceptable Secunderabad hotels tend to be expensive, and are grouped together at the end of this section.

Taxes can add as much as 20% in the mid- to top-priced hotels, 10% at less expensive hotels. As elsewhere in India, some hotels quote foreigners rates in dollars.

LOWEST BUDGET

Doubles for Less Than Rs 100 ($3.33)

Rock-bottom–rated hotels are clustered in a compound near the railway station at Nompally. They are **Royal Hotel** (possibly the best), **Neo Royal, Gee Royal Lodge,** and the **Royal Home**—but you'll see these are only for deposed royalty when you note their down-at-the-heels condition. However, you're apt to find within each of these hotels some rooms that are cleaner than the others. If you want to stay in any of these places, ask to see more than one vacant room before settling in, Private, attached bathrooms are a rare find. If you're backpacking, you'll undoubtedly have what you need to be comfortable. If not, bring a sheet and towel.

Another group of rock-bottom accommodations can be found around on Kachiguda Road, near Kachiguda Railway Station, Hyderabad 50027. A cut above some others are **Tourist Hotel** and the **Tourist Home.** Plate meals in the dining room cost under $1. Indian-style plumbing predominates at both.

INDIAN-STYLE HOTELS

Doubles for Less Than Rs 600 ($20)

The **Taj Mahal Hotel,** Abid Road (☎ 237988), is a pleasant place with wicker chairs, shade trees, and a porch to sit out on. There are 69 rooms, 22 with AC, a few with Western-style toilets, split between old and new annexes. Rates are Rs 110 ($6.25) single, Rs 150 ($8.55) double, without AC; singles with AC are Rs 175 ($9.95), doubles Rs 250 ($14.25) to Rs 325 ($18.50). In the Taj Mahal's big, popular, noisy restaurant (open from 6:30am to 9:30pm), you can get snacks and plate meals, South Indian–style. The cost is Rs 7.50 (45¢) for a plate meal; there's a separate room for women dining alone.

A marble reception area and latticework screens and ceilings add decorative touches to the **Hotel Jaya International,** P.O. Box No. 264, Abids, Hyderabad 500001 (☎ 232929), situated in a little lane right in the center of town. The rooms are large, with adequate furnishings but uninspired decor. The restaurant serves both North and South Indian vegetarian dishes.

Hotel Sarovar, 5-9-22 Secretariat Rd., Hyderabad 500003 (☎ 237638), across from the Secretariat, has 77 rooms, some with Western-style toilets, and within walking distance of Hussain Sagar. The rooms could use a paint job, but are passable otherwise. The restaurant is known for top-notch vegetarian food.

Hotel Rajdhani, 15-1-503 Siddiamber Bazar, Hyderabad 500012, has 88 simple rooms, some with AC. The restaurant serves South and North Indian vegetarian cuisine.

WESTERN-STYLE HOTELS

Doubles for Less Than Rs 850 ($28.33)

At the **Guest Line Days-Hotel Golkonda,** 10-1-124 Masab Tank Rd., Hyderabad 500028 (☎ 226001; fax 222564), the lobby looks to the Golconda Fort for inspiration, with a 66-foot-high atrium encircled by 156 functionally furnished rooms. Centrally air-conditioned, with all the modern amenities, the hotel is a good value in Hyderabad, one of India's more expensive cities. Doubles are Rs 750 ($25). There is a restaurant, coffee shop, and bar.

Nagarjuna, Bashir Bagh 500029 (☎ 237201; fax 236789), has fairly clean rooms, with doubles from around Rs 600 ($20). Enjoy a view with your meal in the rooftop restaurant (hours 11am to 3pm and 7 to 11pm). The menu is Indian, Chinese, and Continental, with main dishes in the Rs 30 ($1) to Rs 60 ($2) range. There's a ground-floor coffee shop and a swimming pool.

Viceroy, Viceroy Tank Bund Road, 500380 (☎ 618383; fax 618797), has central AC, 150 comfortable doubles, a swimming pool, 24-hour coffee shop, and restaurant. Rates are Rs 850 ($28.33) doubles.

The Central Court, 6-1-71 Lakdi-ka-pul, Hyderabad (☎ 233262; fax 232737), offers central AC, 77 acceptable rooms, coffee shop, restaurant, and barbecue. Doubles are Rs 600 ($20).

Hotel Krystal, Lake Hills Road, Hyderabad 500483 (☎ 237574), is under the direction of M. J. Sujanani, formerly with the well-regarded New Kenilworth in Calcutta. The intimate 26-room Krystal is a clean and homey place. Some rooms are without AC, but there are balconies to catch Hyderabadi breezes. Doubles run Rs 250 ($8.33) without AC, Rs 450 ($15) with AC. The restaurant serves Indian and Chinese cuisine.

Your best choice near the old city, **Hotel Sampurna International,** Mukramjahi Road, Hyderabad 500001 (☎ 40165), has a mirrored Indian pageant mural in the lobby, along with black bucket armchairs and a marble floor. The halls are badly maintained, but the rooms are cleaner than many others and more attractively done up in sleek, modern, Western motel-style furniture. Figure on about Rs 600 ($20) for the hotel's best doubles; cheaper rooms come without AC.

Hotel Ashoka, 6-1-70 Lakdi-ka-pul, Hyderabad 500004 (☎ 230105; fax 230088), has shabby halls and sinister lighting, but the rooms are not half bad. The hotel is busy, noisy, and budget-right. An AC double is about Rs 500 ($16.66). The air-conditioned, vegetarian Saptagiri Restaurant is a real find for penny-wise travelers; they can get an unlimited plate meal (curry rice with refills, served on a dinner-size plate) here for about $1. There's also a moderately priced nonvegetarian restaurant (see "Where to Eat," below).

Doubles for Less Than Rs 1,500 ($50)

High in the hills, with a stunning view of Hussain Sagar Lake, is the **Ritz Hotel,** Hill Fort Palace, Hyderabad 500463 (☎ 233571), a former palace of the Nizam's second son. Behind a stark, white facade topped with turrets and crenellations, is a plant-filled courtyard with swimming pool shaded by tall trees and a tennis court amid spacious lawns. Although this hotel is delightfully atmospheric, the rooms look a bit weary. They have all amenities associated with high-priced places. Standard doubles are Rs 900 ($30).

Behind the star-shaped glass walls of **Bhaskar Palace,** Road No. 1, Banjara Hills, Hyderabad 500034 (☎ 397987), is a severe marble lobby with almost no seating except two circular conversation areas topped with golden canopies. Guest rooms have three different color schemes—rust, blue, or burgundy. Topping the hotel is what is said to be the world's biggest revolving restaurant (see "Where to Eat," below). There is also a coffee shop, swimming pool, and health club. Highest doubles are Rs 1,400 ($46.66).

Neat and new **Quality Inn Green Park,** Greenlands, Begumpet, Hyderabad 500016 (☎ 291919; fax 291900), has 148 modern, functional rooms with more comforts than imagination. Rates are Rs 625 ($20.83) to Rs 775 ($25.83) single, Rs 850 ($28.33) to Rs 950 ($31.66) double. The no-smoking rooms are a novelty in India. This place caters to business travelers. Coffee shop, restaurant, and bar.

Doubles for Less Than Rs 1,900 ($66.66)

Perched at the edge of a little lake, the **Gateway Hotel on Banjara Hill,** Road No. 1, Banjara Hills (☎ 399999; fax 392218), in The Taj Group and one of the top hotels in town (five stars), has 124 rooms furnished in modern international style and a lobby-lounge that's a lively meeting place. There is a swimming pool, a patio barbecue, coffee shop, bar, and restaurant serving delicious Andhra dishes. (See "Where to Eat," below). The rates are $39 single; $60 double.

Holiday Inn Krishna, Road No. 1 Banjara Hills (☎ 223347; fax 222684), has 150 rooms, central AC, a no-smoking wing, and wheelchair access (new in India). Rooms are attractive, modern, and functional, with every convenience, and the restaurant serves Italian cuisine, as well as Chinese, Continental and various Indian cuisines. Doubles run Rs 1,900 ($63.33), including breakfast but not the 20% expenditure and luxury taxes. The hotel is affiliated with the U.S. chain.

Worth a Splurge

The **Krishna Oberoi,** Road No. 1, Banjara Hills, Hyderabad 500034 (☎ 222121; fax 223079), has fortress-inspired architecture and a wealth of amenities. This is a 262-room bastion for luxury. Everything is grand—the huge lobby, chairs, spacious restaurants (see "Where to Eat," below), and public rooms. Many guest rooms have grand views of Hussain Sagar. There's a swimming pool and health club. Rates are $100 single, $110 double; suites, some with private swimming pools and gardens, are much higher.

In Secunderabad

Indian-Style Hotels

Your best bet is the **Hotel Taj Mahal,** Sarojini Devi Road, a branch of the Hyderabad Taj, with near similar accommodations and moderate prices. Most rooms have private attached bathrooms; some of the lowest priced are shared-bath accommodations. Rates are about the same as the Taj Mahal in Hyderabad. Similarly, you can get a modestly priced plate meal of curry and rice in this outpost of the Hotel Taj Mahal.

Western-Style Hotels

At the APTTDC's **Yatri Nivas,** Sardar Patel Road, Secunderabad 500003 (☎ 843931), all 16 rooms have balconies and attached bathrooms, with hot and cold running water; some are air-conditioned. A double runs around Rs 250 ($8.33). Meals and snacks are served. From here, an auto ricksha to Hyderabad should run about Rs 15 (50¢), depending on traffic; bus no. 87 goes from Secunderabad Railway Station to Char Minar. ***Penny-wise tip:*** This is the best buy for the true budget traveler, content with cleanliness and basic comforts.

The following hotels are air-conditioned and have multiple comforts.

At the entrance to the 75-room **Hotel Baseraa,** 9-1-167/168 Sarojini Devi Rd., Secunderabad 500003 (☎ 823200; fax 832745), is a replica of a wheel from the Sun Temple at Konark in Orissa, where the owners are headquartered. Behind the modern main building, an old minipalace has a few rooms, including a honeymoon suite all done up in red—a red flower petal–shaped headboard on a king-size bed and a spangled, velvet wall hanging of lovers. More subdued rooms are also well furnished and comfortable. Singles run Rs 500 ($16.66) to Rs 525 ($17.50), doubles Rs 750 ($25) to Rs 800 ($26.66). **Daawat** restaurant serves South Indian vegetarian dishes and snacks; **Mehfil** serves Mughlai, Indian, Continental, and Chinese dishes (see "Where to Eat," below).

Hotel Deccan Continental, Sir Ronald Ross Road, Secunderabad, 500003 (☎ 840981; fax 840980), with a panoramic view of Hussain Sagar, has a nice view of the city (admired from the room balconies). The decor is modern at this 74- room hotel, convenient to the airport. Singles are Rs 550 ($18.33), doubles Rs 750 ($25). After sight-seeing, relax in the pool or health club or restaurant, bar, or coffee shop.

Not far from the main shopping area is the **Hotel Parklane,** 115 Park Lane, Secunderabad 500003 (☎ 840466), with a copper and brass mural behind the reception desk. The hotel's 47 rooms have all the amenities, except good maintenance.

Singles run Rs 400 ($13.33), doubles Rs 500 ($16.66). There are both vegetarian and nonvegetarian restaurants, a coffee parlor, swimming pool, and garden.

Asrani International Hotel, 1-7-179 Mahatma Gandhi Rd., Secunderabad 500003 (☎ 842267), has sleek, modern rooms with such amenities as satin spreads and little refrigerators in all the rooms. The maintenance could be better. A single runs Rs 450 ($15), a double Rs 650 ($21,66). The hotel has both vegetarian and nonvegetarian restaurants.

WHERE TO EAT

Geographically, this is South India, but typical foods have Muslim overtones. Be sure and try the local biryani (rice with meat or chicken and spices) and bhaghere baigan, made with eggplant. Another typical local dish, haleem, mates wheat and mutton. Kebabs are local favorites. Try them with the unusual sweet bread, sheer maal. Many South India dishes also are served, as are spicy Andhra and Deccan delicacies.

HYDERABAD

Multicuisine Buffets

Figure on buffets costing around Rs 50 ($1.66) to Rs 150 ($5).

For the least expensive buffet it's **Pick 'n' Move,** Amrutha Estates, Himayatnagar, across from the Blue Fox (☎ 233226), a clean fast-food place, where the items on the menu are illustrated in color photos on the walls, as you might see in some Japanese restaurants in the states. The buffet has eight Indian vegetarian dishes, including a sweet. Open from noon to 3pm. A popular place with office workers.

You get not only a choice of foods but a selection of views at Bhaskar Palace (☎ 226141, ext. 150), where the buffet is served in **Revathi** ("Star"), the revolving restaurant topping the hotel, from noon to 3pm. At night from up here, the city is quite a sight, and the menu is à la carte. You can figure on Rs 400 ($13.33) to Rs 700 ($23.33) for a nonvegetarian, three-course meal for two, without beer or wine.

At the Gateway Hotel on Banjara Hills (☎ 399999), the buffet's in **Dakhini,** from 12:30 to 2:30pm. Hotel Krishna Oberoi (☎ 222121), serves buffet in **Firdaus,** an Empire setting, where handsome antique ceiling fans accent the ceiling; the buffet is served from 12:30 to 3pm Monday through Saturday. On Sunday, brunch is in this same room. Dinner is à la carte; figure on Rs 500 ($16.66) to Rs 1,000 ($33.33) for a three-course dinner for two, the lower price for vegetarian foods.

For other buffets, try **Quality Inn Green Park** (☎ 291919) and **Guestline Days Hotel Golkonda** (☎ 226001).

Restaurants Featuring Deccan Delicacies

At splurge-priced **Dakhini,** in the Gateway Hotel on Banjara Hill (☎ 399999), foods from the different regions of the Deccan are featured in a cozy setting combining wood pillars and cushioned banquettes. Figure on about Rs 600 ($20) for a three-course meal for two, without drinks. A one-liter bottle of beer will cost about Rs 55 ($1.83). A dinner of Deccan dishes might start with such appetizers as tamatar ka shorba, a spicy consomme with red peppers floating in it and chapa bajjilu, a fritter made of fish, poppy seeds, and spices. It is then followed by Andhra-style (among the hottest of all Indian cuisines) dishes such as chicken stir-fried with herbs and chiles, or a local lake fish in coconut-and-onion gravy, accompanied by the tamer-tasting dal pundi phalliya (made with nuts and spices and gangura leaves), lemon-and-tomato rice, and Andhra bread. Skip the sweet desserts—fresh fruits are more refreshing after such a hotter-than-hot meal.

For less expensive Hyderabadi food, try **Hotel Akbar,** 1-7-190 M. G. Road, Secunderabad; **Azizia Hotel,** 11-6-225, Station Rd., Nampally; and **Hotel Madina,** Madina Building, Patthergatti, where a nonvegetarian meal for two will run about Rs 150 ($5).

Two simple cafes in the old city have inexpensive, well-prepared local dishes such as kebabs and haleem. They are **Niagara Cafe,** Chaderghat, where you can buy a picnic to take out, and **Chaheran,** on Gulzar Hauz, near Char Minar, where you can eat in. A meal costs about Rs 100 ($3.33) to Rs 150 ($5).

Multicuisine Restaurants

At most of these places, figure on Rs 400 ($13.33) to 800 ($26.66) for a three-course meal for two, the lower price for vegetarian foods.

Generous portions, good quality, and a great view make the **Palace Heights,** 8th floor, Triveni Complex, Abids, Hyderabad worth a visit. Inside the oblong dining room, the white walls are hung with paintings of former Nizams and harem dancers, and there are handsome antique sideboards and statues. The menu features familiar Indian, Chinese, and Continental dishes. Beer runs about Rs 50 ($1.66) for a liter. Reservations are suggested, especially in the evening, if you want a window table. Open from noon to 10:30pm.

Nearby on Abid Road is the quiet, dignified **Golden Deer** (☎ 240497), open from 11am to 3pm, and 7 to 11pm, a place to enjoy a few dishes not found everywhere. The mirrored pillars and archways entwined with golden vines gleam softly under crystal fixtures, as do dark wood chairs, upholstered in green leather. One of the specialties is chicken aashiana, made with tomatoes and a cream sauce; another is mutton Golden Deer, made with fruits, nuts, and coconut gravy.

Next door on Abid Road is **Golden Gate** (☎ 232485), open from 11am to 11pm, with sophisticated decor combining a dark wood-paneled ceiling and walls with light metal murals. On the menu are well-known North Indian dishes such as kebabs and tandooris.

The dimly lit **Blue Fox,** in the Hotel Minerva, Himayatnagar (☎ 241574), is owned by the Palace Heights and is, in fact, older than that establishment. The menu is more or less predictable: Indian and Chinese. Open from 11am to 11pm, and only 2 kilometers from Salar Jung Museum.

Prices are also a bit lower at the pleasant nonvegetarian restaurant in the **Hotel Ashoka,** 6-1-670 Lakdi-ka-pul (☎ 230105). Few Westerners know about this cozy hideaway. Chinese food is featured.

For a splurge-priced Chinese meal in a quiet dignified setting, try **Szechuan Garden** at the Hotel Krishna Oberoi (☎ 222121), where expensive, well-prepared foods come with a dramatic view of the waterfall, which plays on one of the outside walls after sunset. Figure on Rs 300 ($10) to Rs 800 ($26.66) for a three-course meal for two.

For less expensive Chinese food, try **Hai King,** 3-2-276 Himayatnagar, or **Chung Hua,** 5-9-30 Basheerbagh.

Indian Vegetarian Cuisine

Opposite the Birla Temple, **Kamat Hotel,** 60/1 Saifabad, is open from 7 to 10am, 11am to 2pm, and 7 to 9pm. By government order, some items in this restaurant and a few others around town are especially cheap at various times of day. They are posted on a board outside, and you get coupons for them in the restaurant. Even without the coupons, the Kamat thali is reasonably priced for generous portions of rice, puri, curds, two curries, and rasam; a sweet is extra.

Three popular hotel restaurants are tops for vegetarian foods for budget-watchers: the **Taj Mahal** hotels in Hyderabad and Secunderabad, and **Sarovar Hotel** in Hyderabad. **Tanjore,** 41 Vasavi Colony, near Kharkhana Police Station, Section 15, serves Chettinad cuisine, the delicious peppery dishes of a small community in Tamil Nadu.

Fast Food, Snacks & Sweets

Juke Box, 66 Rasthrapathi Rd., serves fast-food Mexican specialties, with a real juke box spinning out tunes. There's also **Pick 'n' Move,** Amrutha Estates. The immensely popular **Liberty,** Abid Road, with Statue of Liberty logo and colorful tiled walls, serves pizza, burgers made of mutton, chicken, or vegetables, fast-snack Indian foods, and ice creams. It is open from 11am to 10:30pm.

Hyderabad is famous for kalakahn and two places to try this sweet and others made with cashews and almonds are **Pulla Reddy,** Station Road, a tiny, sparkling clean shop, and the equally clean but larger **Almond House,** Lingapur Building, Himayatnagar, with a huge array of sweets and snacks. You can taste sweets at either shop before you purchase them—but only if you buy something. The shops are open from 8am to 10:30pm.

In Secunderabad

At **Daawat** in Baseraa Hotel (☎ 823200), South Indian specialties are served from 7am to 10pm in a pretty setting combining mosaic walls, mirrored archways, and marble floors. Idlis, "the best in the twin cities," says the maître d', and a crispy, delicious masala dosa (rice pancake stuffed with nuts and potatoes) are good choices here. Thalis are priced according to the variety of dishes, starting around Rs 30 ($1). In the same hotel, the mirrored and brass-muraled **Mehfil** serves well-prepared Mughlai foods, from 11am to 11pm. An à la carte meal for two, consisting of soup, boneless tandoori chicken, and pulao will cost about Rs 600 ($20), excluding beer or cocktails. Pastries and ice creams are available at all times in the hotel's **Havmor Ice Cream** parlor.

Kwality, at 103 Park Lane (☎ 847735), open from 11am to 11pm, serves Mughlai, Continental, and Chinese dishes in the Rs 30 ($1) to Rs 175 ($5.83) range for main dishes.

For Chinese food in Secunderabad, try **Lung Fung,** Sardar Patel Road, APHB Commercial Complex, and the **Golden Dragon,** near Park Lane Hotel.

12

Madras: Where the South Begins

The capital of Tamil Nadu and its largest city (pop. 5.36 million), Madras is regarded as the gateway to South India. Unlike the rushed atmosphere in the North, the pace is slower here, as is characteristic of southern climes; the climate is invariably humid and conducive to leisurely living.

The British were here fairly early in their occupation of India and have left traces of their military (Fort St. George), commercial (banks), and religious presence (the oldest Anglican church in India). Since Independence, Madras, once known primarily as a textile center (cottons and silks), has continued its prominence producing hand looms but is also known for leather wares, as well as both large industries (automobiles, railway cars) and a considerable number of small-scale industries. It's also a major filmmaking center.

One of the curiosities of this spacious city—it is India's fourth largest—is that despite its vast population, there always seems to be room to spare. The large, wide beach known as Marina is almost always deserted (except in late afternoon), and the streets and stores are never as crowded as could be expected.

There are not many things to disturb the compulsive sightseer. A climb up the new lighthouse at the end of Marina Beach will give a good perspective of the city, dotted with open green spaces and lush palmy vegetation; Fort St. George has an interesting museum, and the official Government Museum is worth a couple of interesting hours.

Try to see some of the lovely, big houses in the suburbs (probably on a visit to Elliot's Beach) and drop by the enormous grounds of the Theosophical Society to stand under the gigantic banyan tree.

1 Orientation

ARRIVING

BY PLANE Madras is served by several international carriers including Air India, Lufthansa, Gulf Air, Saudi, Air Lanka, British Airways, Singapore Airlines, and the Malaysian Airlines System. Indian Airlines, East West, Jet, and Damania connect Madras to major cities within India: from Delhi, it costs $162; from Bangalore, $33; from Bombay, $110; from Calcutta, $137.

Indian Airlines, 19 Marshalls Rd. (☎ 8251677), ticketing and reservations office is open from 8am to 8pm, closed Sundays and holidays. At the same address, **Air India** (☎ 474477) is open 9am to 5:30pm. Other Indian Airlines booking offices are located in the Mena Building, 57 Dr. Radhakrishnan Rd., Mylapore (☎ 8279799); 7 Umpherson St. (☎ 583321); and Adwave Towers, T. Nagar (☎ 4347555). Hours for all three are from 10am to 5pm, with a lunch break from 1 to 1:45pm. Here are other airline offices: **East West,** Mootha Centre, 9 Kodambakkam High Rd. (☎ 8277007); **Jet**, Gems Court, B-5, 14 Khader Nawaz Khan Rd. (☎ 8259804); **Damania** Airways, g-A/2, No. 17, Khader Nawaz Khan Road (☎ 2348418).

Both airports—**Kamarajar National** and **Aringar Anna International**—are situated 12 kilometers southwest of the city center in one large complex at Trisoolam in Meenambakkam. The prepaid taxi fare between the airport and the city is determined by distance, and fares range from Rs 120 ($5) to Rs 150 ($5). Allow 30 minutes for travel by taxi to the city center.

Cars with drivers, booked in advance, cost Rs 250 ($8.33) to or from the terminals to the city.

Aviation Express airport coaches between the airport and principal hotels cost Rs 50 ($1.66) per head. (However, there is no coach service from hotels to airport.) An **auto ricksha** to the airports will run about Rs 80 ($2.66) from the city center, but you must bargain.

Penny-wise tip: If you're traveling light, take the commuter train to Thiruslam (also Tirusoolum) and you'll be minutes from the terminals at Meenambakkam; the same line also takes you to Egmore and Fort stations in town. This fare is set according to station, but should cost about Rs 4 (13¢).

BY TRAIN Many a tourist has missed his or her train by not showing up at the right station. Madras has three stations: **Madras Central** for broad-gauge trains to other places in India; **Egmore** for meter-gauge to other southern towns. A minibus takes passengers between the two stations. **Beach** station handles suburban trains.

For **Madras Central Station** inquiries, call 563535; for arrivals 567575; for first-class reservations 563545; for second-class reservations 564455; and for meter-gauge (☎ 563344). For **Egmore Station** general inquiries and current reservations, call 566565; for first-class reservations 564010; for second-class 543344. Reservation hours are 8am to 2pm, and 2:15 to 8pm, 8am to 2pm Sundays.

From Delhi, the best train is the *Rajdhani Express* (2,195 kilometers, 30 hours) for Rs 2,885 ($96.17) AC First, Rs 1,510 ($50.33) two-tier sleeper, Rs 690 ($23) Second. Another choice is the *Tamil Nadu Express* (36 hours) for Rs 2,564 ($85.47), AC First, Rs 246 ($8.20) Second. **From Bombay,** take the *Dadar Madras Express* (1,279 kilometers, 24 hours) for Rs 1,725 ($57.50) AC First, Rs 191 ($6.65) Second. **From Ernakulam,** trains include the *Madras-Alleppey Express* (700 kilometers, 13 hours) for Rs 1,139 ($37.97) AC First, Rs 135 ($4.50) Second. **From Bangalore,** the *Shatabdi Express* is the best train (362 kilometers, 6 1/2 hours) for Rs 670 ($22.33) Executive; Rs 335 ($11.17) AC Chair.

BY BUS Dr. J. Jayalalitha (JJTC) interstate express buses operate frequently **from Bangalore** (351 kilometers, 8 1/2 hours) for Rs 77 ($2.57); **from Video** or **Omni** for Rs 120 ($4); **from Ernakulam** (Cochin) (700 kilometers, 9 hours) for Rs 143 ($4.77); and **from Trivandrum** (752 kilometers, 12 1/2 hours) for Rs 250 ($8.33). The Andrha Pradesh (APSRTC) superexpress **from Hyderabad** runs Rs 203.50 ($6.77). For interstate bus inquiries call 560753. Reservation hours are from 4:30am to 9pm.

Within Tamil Nadu, frequent daily TTC bus connections can be made to and from **Madurai** (448 kilometers, 9 hours), **Ooty** (465 kilometers, 13 hours), and

Madras

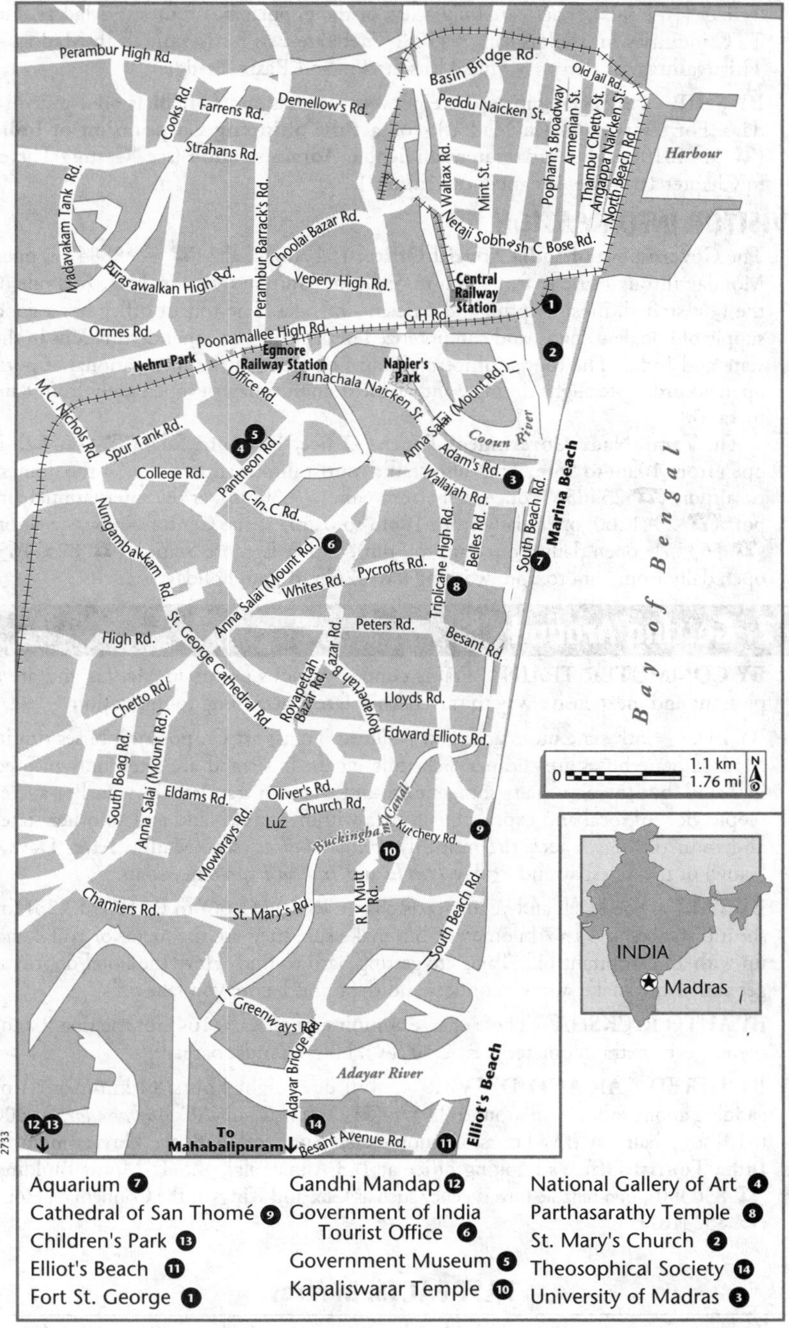

Perambur High Rd.
Basin Bridge Rd.
Old Jail Rd.
Cooks Rd.
Farrens Rd.
Demellow's Rd.
Peddu Naicken St.
Popham's Broadway
Armenian St.
Thambu Chetty St.
Angappa Naicken St.
North Beach Rd.
Harbour
Strahans Rd.
Waltax Rd.
Mint St.
Madavakam Tank Rd.
Perambur Barrack's Rd.
Choolai Bazar Rd.
Netaji Sobhash C Bose Rd.
Purasawalkan High Rd.
Vepery High Rd.
Central Railway Station
G H Rd.
Ormes Rd.
Poonamallee High Rd.
Nehru Park
Egmore Railway Station
Napier's Park
Office Rd.
Arunachala Naicken St.
Anna Salai (Mount Rd.)
M.C. Nichols Rd.
Spur Tank Rd.
Pantheon Rd.
Cooun River
Marina Beach
Adam's Rd.
College Rd.
Wallajah Rd.
Bay of Bengal
C-In-C Rd.
Belles Rd.
South Beach Rd.
Nungambakkam Rd.
Anna Salai (Mount Rd.)
Pycrofts Rd.
Triplicane High Rd.
Whites Rd.
Peters Rd.
High Rd.
St. George Cathedral Rd.
Besant Rd.
Royapettah Bazar Rd.
Royapettah Bazar Rd.
Chetto Rd.
Lloyds Rd.
Edward Elliots Rd.
South Boag Rd.
Anna Salai (Mount Rd.)
Eldams Rd.
Oliver's Rd.
Church Rd.
Luz
Buckingham Canal
Kutchery Rd.
Mowbrays Rd.
0
1.1 km
1.76 mi
N
Chamiers Rd.
St. Mary's Rd.
R K Mutt Rd.
South Beach Rd.
INDIA
Madras
Greenways Rd.
Adayar Bridge Rd.
Adayar River
Elliot's Beach
To Mahabalipuram
Besant Avenue Rd.
2733
Aquarium 7
Cathedral of San Thomé 9
Children's Park 13
Elliot's Beach 11
Fort St. George 1
Gandhi Mandap 12
Government of India Tourist Office 6
Government Museum 5
Kapaliswarar Temple 10
National Gallery of Art 4
Parthasarathy Temple 8
St. Mary's Church 2
Theosophical Society 14
University of Madras 3

Trichy (10 hours). These are only a few of the popular bus routes to Madras. For TTC inquiries in Madras call 564108. There are two bus terminals in Madras—**Thiruvalluvar** at Parry's Mofussil Bus Station and **Basin Bridge.**

BY SHIP Passenger ships operate between Madras and Port Blair once every 10 days. For reservations (in Madras), contact the **Shipping Corporation of India** (☎ 5144010) or the **Andaman and Nicobar Administration** (see "Getting There" in Chapter 10, "The Andaman Adventure").

VISITOR INFORMATION

The **Government of India Tourist Office,** 154 Anna Salai (☎ 8278884), is open Monday through Friday from 9am to 5:45pm, Saturdays 9am to 1pm. It is one of the best staffed, most helpful, and efficient in India. The tourist office has a good supply of booklets, maps, and computerized information on other destinations in the state and India. The tourist office maintains counters at the international airport, open according to flight timings, and at the domestic airport (open daily from 8am to 1am).

The **Tamil Nadu Government Tourist Office,** 143 Anna Salai (☎ 840752), is open from 10am to 5pm. They also staff a tourist information center at the domestic airport (☎ 2340569; open daily from 6am to 9:30pm), at the international airport (☎ 2341260; open daily from 10pm to 6am), at the Central Railway Station (☎ 563351; open daily from 7am to 7pm), and at Egmore Station (☎ 8252165; open daily from 7am to 9pm working days, 2pm to 9pm holidays.)

2 Getting Around

BY COMMUTER TRAIN Trains connect various points in Madras and are a pleasant and inexpensive way to travel. Your fare is according to the station.

BY BUS Both state buses and Thiruvalluvar Transport Corporation buses run in Madras. State buses are cheaper. Schedules at the bus stand are often only printed in Tamil, but there's usually someone around who can translate for you. For a telescopic view of local and express bus routes within Tamil Nadu and to other states and train timings, check the monthly *Hallo Madras* (see "Madras After Dark," below) or the Tuesday and Friday *Hindu* and *Indian Express* newspapers.

BY TAXI The black and yellow taxis charge Rs 50 ($1.66) to Rs 100 ($3.33) for short distances of 5 to 7 kilometers, but make sure they use the meter or you'll end up with an exorbitant bill. Taxis are getting hard to find. Have the hotel doorman get yours, and make sure you understand the terms before you take off.

BY AUTO RICKSHA These charge a minimum of Rs 5 (16¢) for the first 2 kilometers; each extra kilometer is Rs 2.50 (8¢), but you must bargain.

BY HIRED CAR AND DRIVER A full day (eight hours/80 kilometers) of gadding about should run around Rs 470 ($15.66) in a non-AC *Ambassador,* Rs 300 ($10) for a half-day (five hours/50 kilometers). But check with the **Government of India Tourist Office's** booking office at 143 Anna Salai, V.S.T. Motor Building (☎ 830390), or a reliable travel agency such as **Cox and Kings** at the Connemara Hotel (☎ 8520162).

FAST FACTS: Madras

The best overall view of the city and harbor is from the 150-foot-high new **lighthouse** at the southern end of Marina Beach. It is open between 2 and 4pm each day. (But double-check, as this may not be possible any more.)

Guides Tour guides can be hired from the Government of India Tourist Office for about Rs 250 ($8.33) for a half-day and Rs 350 ($11.66) for a full day, including the lunch allowance.

Money Exchange Traveler's checks can be cashed at Thomas Cook and Co., Eldorado Building, G/4-112 N. H. Road from 9:30am to 4:30pm, although the office stays open until 6:30pm; and at **American Express,** G-17 Spencer Plaza, Anna Salai. Most big hotels cash traveler's checks for guests, and some have banks on their premises for residents and nonresidents; there are also banks at the airport.

Pharmacy (late night) **S. S. Day and Night Chemists,** 106 D Block, First Main Road, Anna Nagar (☎ 615263), is a drugstore open as the name implies—day and night.

Post Office The Mount Road Post Office on Anna Salai (Mount Road), is open from 8am to 8:30pm.

Telephones Public phones, of which there used to be a shortage, can now be found on many corners in red and yellow booths in Madras and throughout Tamil Nadu. The average call costs Rs 1.50 (5¢) to Rs 2 (7¢) for three minutes.

Visa Extensions These are granted at the Foreigners Registration Office, Shastri Bhavan Annexe, Haddows Road (☎ 8275424). Hours are 9:30am to 6pm, Monday through Friday.

Weather The temperature in Madras and other lowlands never goes below 70°F, and often rises to the 90s even in the winter months, which are, by the way, the most pleasant. The rainy season is June to September. It's always summer in most of Tamil Nadu, with the exception of the hill resorts where it's comfortably cool.

3 Where to Stay

India's fourth-largest city is her least Westernized, so Madras is an ideal place for staying in an Indian-style hotel, where the prices are fine for budget travelers. These hotels are among the best in the South, and the prices are lower simply because the style of life on the premises is not imported, as it is in a hotel catering to Western visitors. Be prepared, therefore, for granite floors and rooms that are rather bare in appearance. You will have all the necessities of life but may lack such Western frills as wall-to-wall carpeting, a well-appointed lounge, and central air-conditioning (some Indian-style hotels have window units). The service in these South Indian hotels is generally very good, however, and the standard of cleanliness is high.

Above all, there are wonderful touches of personal luxury: In the Hindu religion cleanliness is next to godliness, and bathing several times a day is so much a part of life that almost every room in a South Indian-style hotel has an attached bath and toilet. There are two styles of plumbing in these places: Western, with a commode; and Eastern, without. Some Indian-style hotels have Western fixtures, but always specify when you make your reservations to be sure of getting just what you want. Also, do book in advance, for while some of the Western-style hotels in Madras may have an occasional vacancy if you just drop in, these Indian-style places are enormously popular and booked throughout the year.

The one big difference at these Indian-style hotels is the food. In accordance with orthodox Hindu beliefs, not one shred of meat can cross the threshold, so the food is vegetarian but so deliciously prepared as to make you forget all that nonsense about the plainness of any such diet.

On the other hand, beach buffs might prefer relaxing in a well-appointed cottage by the sea at Mamallapuram (Mahabalipuram), 40 miles to the south and 1 1/2 to two hours away by car, coming into Madras to sightsee. The beach accommodations are described in "Excursions from Madras," below. So, take a look before deciding.

Also, keep in mind that luxury taxes can add to your hotel bill in Madras: 10% to 20% or perhaps more.

LOWEST BUDGET CHOICES

Among these lowest-budget accommodations, you will not find any rates above Rs 400 ($13.33) for a double.

Clean, but 30 minutes from town, the **Tourist Hostel** (Andra Mahila Sabha), 38 Adayar Bridge Rd., Madras 600028 (☎ 838311), is run by an organization engaged in welfare services. The hostel, built in 1964, has the comforts of a private home and is popular with budgeteers craving peace and quiet. There are six singles, 14 doubles, and some larger rooms that can accommodate three or four. In the new wing are Western toilets, if you care about such things. Some rooms have air-conditioning.

The **YWCA International Guest House,** 1086 Poonamalle High Rd. (☎ 39920), is pleasantly situated in a garden compound, and the building itself is full of green plants. In the main lobby is a small lounge, and an attractive dining room opens off the verandah. The rates include breakfast (lunch and dinner can also be had inexpensively) but not the modest, temporary membership fee. There are 60 spotlessly clean rooms with attached bathrooms, a few with AC; others have mosquito netting for the beds. Preference is given to women and families, but men can stay for a minimum of three days. This place is popular, so reservations are recommended. Write to Secretary at address above.

Sharing the Y's compound, **Laharry Transient Youth Hostel,** accepts females under 30 for up to 15-day stays. There are two dorms with eight beds and two-bed rooms. Rates are under Rs 100 ($3.33).

There is also a **Youth Hostel,** 2nd Avenue Indira Nagar, Madras (☎ 412882). Students and members pay Rs 7 (23¢); others pay Rs 14 (47¢). There is also a camping site, vehicle park, and meeting hall. For reservations, write to the warden.

World University Service Centre, Spur Tank Road (☎ 663991), offers rooms and a dorm. An international student card is required for admission. It is centrally located. For reservations, write the director.

Hotel Broadlands, 16 Vallabha Agraharam St., Madras 600005 (☎ 845573), a rambling, old, pastel-painted Victorian building with pink gingerbread trim, caters to budget-conscious young Westerners. There are 50 tiny, basic rooms, a few with attached baths. Top-floor rooms preferred. Penny-watchers love this place, so reserve in advance, give an arrival time, and show up on the dot or your room will the reassigned. Bring a towel and soap. Tea and coffee are available, but no meals are served. It's a 10- to 15-minute walk to Anna Salai, or you can rent one of the hotel's seven bikes for a modest fee. Buses from Esplanade Road outside the express bus terminus or Egmore Station go to and from the hotel.

Nearing the lowest budget, but slightly above, **Transit House,** 26 Venkataraman St., T. Naggar, Madras 600017 (☎ 8281346), is owned by the popular Silversands Beach Resort at Mamallapuram, and is used primarily by guests in transit to or from the resort for short stays. But anyone can stay here, and many people do enjoy the budget-right rooms and dorms.

If you're still looking for a cheap place to stay, head north on Anna Salai (Mount Road) to the area around Parry's Corner and the surrounding streets. Good luck!

INDIAN-STYLE HOTELS

DOUBLES FOR LESS THAN RS 400 ($13.33)

Fairly new, the **Hotel Garden,** 68-A Puraswalkan High Road, Madras 600007 (☎ 6422677), has 49 functional rooms, a roof garden for tea or dinner, and partial AC. Low price is another attraction, with doubles in the range of Rs 250 ($8.33) to Rs 275 ($9.16), with AC. No credit cards.

The **Hotel Ramprasad,** 22 Gandhi Irwin Rd., Egmore, Madras 600008 (☎ 8254875), with 32 fairly neat rooms, is conveniently near the Egmore Railway Station. It faces a busy street, so the rooms get a lot of traffic noise. Some singles share a common bath. The rate for an AC double is Rs 265 ($8.33). The hotel's dosas (rice pancakes) and idlis (steamed rice cakes) are some of the best in Madras and a must for breakfast. There's a roof garden. No credit cards.

DOUBLES FOR LESS THAN RS 1,000 ($33.33)

The **New Woodlands,** 72–75 Dr. Radhakrishnan Rd. (formerly Edward Elliot's Road), Madras 600004 (☎ 8273111), is the top choice and a favorite for Indian weddings. You can play table tennis or swim in the pool, set in a flower-filled garden. A pool-side snack bar is open from 7am to 7pm. The hotel has 56 singles (25 non-AC) and 63 doubles, with balconies and Western-style bathrooms, and 51 suites. A colorful mural of dancers and elephants brightens the reception area. This very nice hotel is clean and well maintained. No wonder it's so popular. AC singles run Rs 300 ($10), AC doubles and cottages Rs 375 ($12.50) to Rs 950 ($31.66). Service charge is 5%, and to that you add the luxury tax. If there's a wedding going on, ask the manager, K. Shankar Rao, and he'll try to get you invited. No credit cards. See "Where to Eat," below, for the hotel's restaurant.

Dasaprakash, 100 Poonamallee High Rd., Madras 600084 (☎ 8255111), has nine landscaped roof gardens, each one different from the other and interspersed with eating spots. Copies of the Bhagavadgita (the "bible" of Hinduism) instead of the Gideon Bible are in the rooms; a statue of Lord Krishna stands in the garden, where there is also a playground for the children beneath a huge acacia tree. Rooms are very attractive but a little dark (they were built before the days of air-conditioning to keep the sun out), with highly polished wood walls, wardrobes, and small sitting rooms. There are 52 singles, 43 doubles, and 5 suites, all with private baths and mostly Western toilets. AC singles run Rs 250 ($8.33) to Rs 300 ($10); AC doubles Rs 350 ($11.66) to Rs 450 ($15). The hotel will pack a picnic lunch of soup, vegetarian sandwiches, fruit, and barfi (a rich, fudgelike sweet). There's a 10% service charge. No credit cards. See "Where to Eat," below, for the hotel's restaurant.

Madras Hotel Ashoka, 33 Pantheon Rd., Egmore, Madras 600008 (☎ 8253377; fax 8256597), is not quite as nice as the two above; it needs TLC. Architecturally, the 109-room Ashoka is unusual because its main building is circular. AC singles are Rs 275 ($9.16), doubles Rs 400 ($13.33) to Rs 425 ($14.17), cottages Rs 600 ($20); there are some lower-priced non-AC rooms. All have Western-style plumbing. The hotel is popular for Indian wedding receptions and, as Indians are extremely hospitable, they will usually enjoy sharing the occasion with a foreigner. Speak to the hotel manager first, though. The restaurant room at the Ashoka serves vegetarian foods in the Madras, Bombay, and Andhra styles. No credit cards.

A six-foot high woodcarving of Shiva dances at one end of the otherwise undistinguished lobby at the **Hotel Maris,** 9 Cathedral Rd., Madras, 600086 (☎ 8270541;

fax 8254847). You can find touches like this throughout the 70-room hotel. On the exterior, for instance, an ordinary yellow building is given some life by extending support beams on every other floor and painting some of these extensions in bright colors, too. All rooms have balconies, and some railings and panels are brightly painted. Inside the rooms, there is occasional wood paneling and wallpaper above the beds. All are clean, but the walls need fresh paint jobs. The highest-priced double is Rs 400 ($13.33). In the restaurant, from 6 to 10am, you can get a price-fixed vegetarian breakfast for about $1.

Hotel Palmgrove, 5 Kodambakkam High Rd., Madras 600034 (☎ 8271881), despite its name, has no grove. But it's very neat and clean. Although it's an Indian-style hotel, all rooms have Western-style bathrooms, and the more expensive double rooms have bathtubs. Some of the 88 rooms have small balconies and sitting rooms, and there are also nine cottages. The highest-priced room is Rs 744 ($24.80) for a deluxe double with AC. Two dining rooms serve vegetarian foods. Of these, Oorvasi, on the top with AC, is most pleasant; it is open from 11am to 2:30pm, and 7 to 11pm. There's a "permit room" (a bar) also. No credit cards.

Hotel Kanchi, 28 Commander-in-Chief Rd., Egmore, Madras 600105 (☎ 8271100), has 64 functional rooms, partially air-conditioned. There is a rooftop restaurant. This is a pleasant place with doubles for Rs 395 ($13.16).

WESTERN-STYLE HOTELS

DOUBLES FOR LESS THAN RS 1,000 ($33.33)

Unless otherwise mentioned, they're air-conditioned, have baths attached, plus restaurants, bars, room service, and other amenities. Overall, decors are serviceable rather than innovative or exciting. Most accept international credit cards.

Merit Inn, 2 Montieth Rd., Egmore, Madras 600008 (☎ 8257770; fax 8251793), is a simple place with 55 rooms, sharing space with the Merit-Swiss Asian School of Hotel Management. There are a coffee shop, dining room, and lawns where weddings sometimes take place. Rooms have functional furniture and wall-to-wall carpeting. Doubles are Rs 700 ($23.33). At the same address, **Hotel Atlantic** (☎ 8260461) has 36 simple, no-frills rooms, some non-AC, two restaurants, and a bar. An AC double, is about Rs 500 ($16.66).

New Victoria Hotel, 3 Kennet Lane, Madras 600008 (☎ 8253638), is a pleasant place with gleaming white marble floors grand enough for a palace, a roof garden, and ornate grillwork. But the maintenance has declined over the years. Some of the 43 rooms need paint jobs. Doubles and suites are in the $28 to $40 range. Front-facing rooms have balconies. The dining room has grillwork doors and a glass wall.

The modern, fully air-conditioned, 63-room **Madras International Hotel** is at 693 Anna Salai (formerly Mount Road), Madras 600006 (☎ 8524111; fax 8523412), an excellent location in the commercial center of the city and within walking distance of the main market. Rooms are small; the best are in the new wing. Doubles are $38 to $42.

Hotel Shrilekha Inter-Continental, 564 Anna Salai, Teynampet, Madras 600018 (☎ 453132), has 200 rooms and is the choice between the two Shrilekha hotels in town. Rooms, while not inspired, are clean. Doubles with AC are Rs 650 ($21.66); there are some dark and dreary non-AC rooms. The other **Shrilekha** is down-at-the heels, located at 49 Anna Salai (☎ 830521). It has 77 rooms and no restaurant.

The modern, boxy **Hotel Pandian,** 9 Kennet Lane, Egmore, Madras 600008 (☎ 8252901; fax 8258459), has 90 rooms, 36 with AC. Rooms are snug; the halls need care. Price and location—Rs 450 ($15) to Rs 600 ($20) for doubles, half a kilometer from Egmore Station—are main attractions. The sleek, modern Shaanthi restaurant serves vegetarian and nonvegetarian dishes, but the emphasis is on the vegetarian side; the highest-priced main dish is about Rs 70 ($2.33).

Gold leaf murals and a rock garden with fake vines and flowers trailing into a pool accent the lobby at the **Residency,** G. N. Getty Road, Madras 600017 (☎ 8253434; fax 8250085). This well-run, pleasant 112-room hotel has neat, clean rooms with mirror-studded, headboard-backed beds, floral bedspreads and drapes in soft muted earth tones. A standard single goes for Rs 800 ($26.66), a double for Rs 950 ($31.66). **Tinto,** the hotel's bar, has a Mexican motif; other restaurants serve Indian, Continental, and Chinese cuisine, plus there's a 24-hour coffee shop (see "Where to Eat," below). Conference hall.

At the intimate, 54-room **Windsor Park,** 349 Poonamalee High Rd., Amjikarai, Madras (☎ 600029), there's a lot of decor; in the lobby, red-and-blue print chairs are reflected in shining granite floors; halls are lined with lace-patterned wallpaper; and the elevator's interior is silk-paneled. Rooms have functional, modern furniture and soothing color schemes. Live it up in a suite for around $40; doubles run $27. Rejuvenate in the swimming pool or small health club, and enjoy a restaurant and coffee shop. Business facilities.

The four-story **Hotel Chandra Towers,** 9 Gandhi Irwin Rd., Egmore, Madras 600008 (☎ 8258171; fax 8251703), has a stylized, tower-shaped front entrance, and the silhouette of a l'hirondelle (swallow) is its logo and inspiration. Why? According to the brochure, each winter swallows take shelter in the eaves of French homes, where they are so well cared for by the residents they return year after year. Get it? Clean, tidy, and attractive, it's indeed a swallow type of place. In a typical room, star-spangled, patchwork-quilt spreads cover the beds and coordinate with the drapes and tweed upholstery on comfortable chairs. The lowest-priced single is Rs 595 ($19.83); the highest-priced double Rs 795 ($26.50); a suite goes for Rs 950 ($31.66). There are two restaurants—one multicuisine and one pure vegetarian.

Nilgiris Nest, 58 Dr. Radhakrishnan Rd., Mylapore (☎ 8275111; fax 8260214), a cozy 44-room all-double hotel, is notable for having a department store on its premises. Rooms are small, compact little nests, but could be tidier. It's slightly less expensive than the other newish hotels. A standard double is around Rs 600 ($20), a fine buy at that price.

Doubles for Less Than Rs 1,800 ($60)

There are a number of fairly new hotels in Madras where you can get a double for $40 or $50 (or the equivalent in rupees). Centrally air-conditioned, with every comfort, most accept international credit cards. All have restaurants; most also have coffee shops (specialties, if any, are noted below) and bars. They court the business traveler with conference rooms and business services. Whatever your reason for visiting, I strongly recommend reservations. Acceptable hotels at these prices almost always fill up. Here are a some of the most promising.

At **Quality Inn Aruna,** 14 Sterling Rd., Nugambakkam, Madras 600034 (☎ 8259090; fax 8258282), the lounge combines cream walls, taupe club chairs and settees, and glossy granite floors. The 100 rooms also have neutral color schemes and tasteful modern furniture. The fourth is the nonsmoking floor. Expect to pay Rs 1,280 ($42.66) for a single, from Rs 1,780 ($59.33) for a double; prices include breakfast. The coffee shop right off the lobby allows you to people-watch while enjoying your meal; there's also a North Indian restaurant. There are a swimming pool and business facilities. This hotel is affiliated with the U.S. chain.

The Sindoori Hotel, 24 Greams Lane, off Creams Road, Madras 600006 (☎ 8271164; fax 8275838), has a deep gray and off-white color scheme in the lounge, which is echoed in the rooms. Maintenance could be better. A standard double goes for $40. The hotel has its own confectionery shop, a rooftop barbecue restaurant (see "Buffets" under "Where to Eat," below), and a light and airy 24-hour **Gazebo** coffee shop with a fish tank and decorative bird cages.

Breeze, 850 Poonamallee High Rd., Madras 600010 (☎ 6428202; fax 6413301), has a spacious, white lobby with a sculpture of dolphins to one end, an oddly named coffee shop, **Kane 'n' Abel,** where there's a fine daily buffet (see "Buffets" under "Where to Eat," below) as well as a multicuisine restaurant, open-air ice cream parlor, and a pastry counter with luscious desserts. The 90 rooms are pleasant, not innovative, with avocado, brown, and cream color schemes. Some bathrooms have both Western and Indian-style toilets. Expect to pay $25 to $35 for a single, $28 to $43 for a double; executive rooms are about $5 more in either single or double occupancy. The halls needed a paint job.

At **Savera Hotel,** 69 Dr. Radhakrishnan Rd., Madras 600004 (☎ 474700), the severity of the lobby is relieved by stone statues of deities. In the halls are full-length mirrors with baroque frames. Renovations were underway when I stopped in. The typical, newly decorated room is quietly tasteful and, in addition to beds and chests, has a comfortable little settee and a new granite bathroom. Rooms on higher floors have terrific city views. Expect to pay Rs 1,100 ($36.66) to Rs 1,195 ($39.83) for a single, Rs 1,500 ($50) for a double. Beside the swimming pool, and visible in a palm grove through the glass wall in the living room, is a statue of Buddha said to be 2,000 years old. There are two restaurants, the **Minar** on the 11th floor serving Mughlai foods, and the **Chakra,** site of the lunch buffet (see "Where to Eat," below), plus the **Chariot** coffee shop, Bamboo Bar, and Sweet Touch pastry shop.

Ambassador Pallava, 53 Montieth Rd., Madras 600008 (☎ 868584), is owned by the Ambassador, a Bombay hotel long known for its antique appointments. The tradition continues here with a handsome, antique mirror in the lobby with a stone grotto to one side and an ornate, lotus-patterned ceiling overhead. The Cinderella-style, silver-trimmed coach is a rich travel relic of long ago. Rooms, while not imaginatively furnished, are comfortable and cheerful. A typical room on the 6th floor was more spacious than some others in town and with a fine view. The duplex suite has carved furniture. Singles start at Rs 1,435 ($47.83), doubles at Rs 1,850 ($61.66). Hotel buffets are memorable feasts (see "Where to Eat," below).

Worth a Splurge

Doubles in the following splurge hotels will be priced in the $100 to $200 range (all tariffs are quoted in U.S. dollars). These hotels are air-conditioned and have an array of amenities such as swimming pools, health clubs, restaurants, and bars; one has a special tea lounge, another a Saturday night disco.

Above the reception desk of the high-priced **Welcomgroup Chola Sheraton,** 10 Cathedral Rd., Madras 600086 (☎ 8280101; fax 878779), is a large mural by the contemporary artist Krishan Khanna. It shows the voyages of the Chola kings, the difficulties they met, and their thanksgiving when they reached their destination. The message is clear for any traveler, and indeed the Chola is a haven for which even a king would give thanks. Doubles are $110 to $175. Don't miss the Northwest frontier cuisine in Peshwari.

The **Taj Coromandel,** 17 Nungambakkam High Rd., Madras 600034 (☎8272827; fax 8257104), has been spiffed up recently in a style recalling the Raj, with a tea lounge beside the potted palms, as have the 200 rooms, some with fine views. There's a no-smoking floor. Throughout the hotel, beautiful Tanjore paintings and antique pieces recall the cultural riches of Tamil Nadu. A standard double is $155.

Glass stalactites, fountains, a console organ player, and white wicker furniture decorate the main lobby of the **Welcomgroup Park Sheraton and Towers,** 132 T. T. K. Rd. (formerly Mowbrays Road), Madras 600018 (☎ 4994101; fax 4997101), a haven for both the tourist and the business traveler. Set apart from the main hotel is the Sheraton Towers at the Park, with its own elegant lobby and rooms tailored to the poshest traveler and special Executive accommodations for those on business. Doubles are $110 to $185. There's a Saturday night disco as well as Dakshin restaurant with excellent South Indian regional cuisine (see "Where to Eat," below).

The style of an earlier era is still echoed in the atmosphere of the **Connemara,** Binny Road, Madras 600002 (☎ 8520123; fax 8523361), in The Taj Group, which was formerly a grand mansion. Some rooms might welcome Madras movie glamour queens to their oversized beds with quilted, half-circle headboards with tiaras of chunky, smoky, topaz mirrors, white silk-quilted spreads, white deco-style lacquered furniture, deep gray carpeting, and frosted glass windows. Standard doubles run $95. **Raintree** restaurant is a must for Chettinad cuisine. The red Victorian building next door once housed Spencer's Department Store, dating from the Raj days and flourishing today in a new building. Across Anna Salai is the India Tourist Office.

AT THE AIRPORT

The Trident, 1/24 G. S. T. Road, Madras 600027 (☎ 2344747; fax 2346699), in the Oberoi group, only 3 kilometers from the airport, is a perfect place to spend the night if you've got a wee-hours flight. The white hotel with its red-tiled roof, trailing vines, and gardens looks like a hacienda in some tropical Mexican town. Light streams through frosted-glass skylights, making this a most appealing indoor space. Doubles are $95. There is shuttle service to the airport. It's 9 kilometers from the center of town, 19 kilometers to the railway station.

4 Where to Eat

The state of Tamil Nadu is famous for spicy, South Indian vegetarian dishes, and the capital, Madras, is a great place to taste them. (In the South, food tends to be hotter, less rich, and includes more rice and coconut, which are abundant locally.) There are more orthodox Hindus in this area too, and therefore a greater proportion of strictly vegetarian restaurants (not even eggs served on the premises) to cater to them. The best cooks, by repute, come from a small town called **Udipi,** and many eating places incorporate this word into their names.

Restaurant hours for lunch generally are 11am to 3pm, and for dinner 6 or 7 to 10pm. In the top hotels, there are 24-hour coffee shops, and restaurants in hotels tend to stay open later at night to accommodate visitors.

MULTICUISINE BUFFETS

As in other major cities, Madras's top hotels serve bountiful buffets at some meals. They feature Indian and Western main dishes, salads, and desserts—all for a fixed price, no matter how full your plate the first time or how often you return for more. While their prices have risen over the years, they are still a penny-wise buy when it comes to hearty eating. You can eat so abundantly at these lunches (and breakfasts) you might easily skip your next meal.

At the **Connemara,** Binny Road (☎ 8520123), the buffet on Saturday and Sunday evenings features Chettinad cuisine at the **Rain Tree,** located in the hotel's courtyard (the buffet moves indoors to a handsome, villa-inspired restaurant during inclement weather), where the centerpiece is a huge, more than 100-year-old rain tree.

Chettinad food is prepared with black pepper, fragrant spices such as mace and saffron, rose petals, and marinades. It's not as hot as recipes made with chile peppers, but then it's not exactly tame either. The Chettinad buffet is Rs 210 ($7), served from 7:30 to 11:30pm. There's also Indian dancing. Connemara also has a daily lunch buffet in the **Verandah** coffee shop.

At the **Taj Coromandel,** 17 Nungambakkam High Rd. (☎ 8272827), buffets take place in the **Pavilion.** Breakfast, 7:30 to 10am, is Rs 100 ($3.33); lunch, 12:30 to 3pm, is Rs 225 ($7.50); and dinner, 7:30pm to midnight, with a variety of cuisines—Monday is Mongolian, Wednesday is seafood, Friday is Italian—is Rs 275 ($9.16).

At the **Ambassador Pallava,** 53 Montieth Rd. (☎ 8268584), the buffets are in **The Other Room:** breakfast, 7:30 to 10:30am, is Rs 75 ($2.50); lunch, 12:30 to 3:30pm, is Rs 150 ($5).

At the **Savera,** 69 Dr. Radhakrishnan Rd. (☎ 474700), the lunch buffet is in **Chakra,** noon to 3pm, for Rs 165 ($5.50).

At the **Welcomgroup Park Sheraton and Towers,** T. T. K. Road (formerly 123 Mowbrays Rd.) (☎ 4994101), there are buffets daily in the **Residency**—12:30 to 3:30pm, Rs 290 ($9.66)—and **Gatsby's**—for dinner, Rs 175 ($5.83).

The **Welcomgroup Chola Sheraton,** 10 Cathedral Rd. (☎ 8280101), serves its lunch buffet with a great view in **Sagari,** the city's most attractive rooftop restaurant, from 12:30 to 3pm, and **Mercara,** the 24-hour coffee shop for dinner, from 7:30 to 10pm. These buffets top off at about Rs 200 ($6.66).

More buffets: At the **Sindoori Hotel** (☎ 8271164) every day but Sunday, for lunch in the delightful **Gazebo,** Rs 110 ($3.66); at **Quality Inn Aruna** (☎ 8259090) in **Colombia,** the coffee shop, Rs 117 ($3.90), including taxes. Breeze offers buffets in **Kane 'n' Abel** at breakfast—Rs 70 ($2.33)—and lunch—Rs 150 ($5)—daily, and for dinner on Saturday and Sunday—Rs 150 ($5). Also try the buffets at **The Residency** (☎ 8253434), **Windsor Park** (☎ 4839999), and **Chandra Towers** (☎ 8257181). Cool and inviting, marble-lined **Mathsya** in the **Udipi Home** (☎ 8251515), has daily buffets for breakfast, 7:30 to 10:30am, for Rs 30 ($1).

THALIS & OTHER VEGETARIAN FEASTS

To try a little bit of a lot of things, order a traditional thali meal (platter) or banana leaf (instead of a platter) with an array of dishes. You should also try tiffin snacks. Although available all over India, they originated here. Tiffin is served from breakfast onwards in spotlessly clean snack shops and restaurants. Most popular among these light, vegetarian dishes, served with chutney and a lentil sauce, are masala dosas (crisp, rice-flour pancakes stuffed with potatoes and spices), idlis (steamed rice pancakes), and vadus (doughnut-shaped bean fritters).

One of the best, most expensive, and elaborate thalis is at the **Welcomgroup Park Sheraton,** 123 Mowbrays Rd. (☎ 8280101), in the **Dakshin,** a handsome room modeled after the residence of a renowned high priest, Raja Guru. Here, the banana leaf–lined thali is a splurge at around Rs 150 ($5) vegetarian, Rs 175 ($5.83) nonvegetarian, including a sweet. The chef here also makes delicious appam (rice and toddy pancakes from Kerala), good with sabjzi (mixed vegetables). Reservations recommended, especially on weekends.

At the **Savera,** 69 Dr. Radhakrishnan Rd. (☎ 8274700), in the **Chariot,** the jeweled mural shows famous charioteers from the Bhagavadgita, Arjuna, and Krisha, and the thali is about Rs 70 ($2.33) with tax.

At the **Mathsya** in the **Udipi Home,** 1 Halls Rd. (☎ 8251515), there's an abundance of marble and trellis dividers, and a warmth of atmosphere. The waiters seem eager to please and offer seconds on thalis that range from Rs 22 (73¢) to Rs 55 ($1.83). You can get dosa, idli, and other snacks. Offered from 7:30am to midnight daily.

Excellent tiffin is served at **Woodlands Drive-In,** 29/30 Cathedral Rd. (☎ 8271981). Everything tastes top-notch, especially when nibbling a dosa under the mango trees in what once was a beautiful botanical garden. There is no set menu outdoors, but apart from specialties in the Rs 6 to Rs 7 range (about 2¢), there are many tiffin items such as dosas and idlis, various chutneys, sambar (vegetable sauce), and vadus (fritters), all decently priced. There are two indoor sections; one is air-conditioned and has a full menu. The self-service counter is open for breakfast, lunch, and dinner. On Sunday, Woodlands is full of families eating and keeping a watchful eye on their kids who ride ponies in the children's park. Open from 6am to 9pm every day.

Both tiffin and thalis are delicious in the very popular, white, inviting, and no-smoking restaurant in the **New Woodlands Hotel,** 72/75 Dr. Radhakrishnan Rd. (☎ 8273111). Figure on Rs 55 ($1.83).

Another choice for tiffin is **Dasa Dozza,** a unit of Hotel Garden, 94/3 T. T. K. Rd., Alwarpet, where two dosas, with two limes and sodas, cost Rs 172 ($5.73) with tax. Served from 12:30 to 3:30pm, and 7 to 11pm.

REGIONAL INDIAN SPECIALTIES

Four different, regional cooking styles make up South Indian cuisine: Tamil Nadu, Kerala, Karnataka, and Andhra Pradesh, and each has its own ethnic specialties. These local cooking styles, once put down as unrefined, have found themselves stars of the culinary scene over the past few years. One of these enjoying a current revival is the Chettinad cooking of the Chettiars, the famous merchant bankers of Tamil Nadu, which is featured at the Connemara (see "Buffets," above).

Here are other places to taste Chettinad and other regional dishes.

Try the **Kaaraikudi,** 84 Dr. Radhakrishnan Rd. (☎ 8269122), decorated with Chettiar antiques, where a complete meal with such dishes as kozhi melagu varvul (fried peppercorn chicken) or kola urundai kozhambhu (minced meatballs in a hot sauce) served with pilau (a rice dish) and other dishes, will cost around Rs 400 ($13.33); there's a thali for Rs 30 ($1).

At **Aachi,** 24 Commander-in-Chief Rd., Chettinad-style yeral (shrimp) or crab curries cost about Rs 30 ($1) and can be part of your Chettinad-style meal. Traditionalists say the most authentic Chettinad foods are found in the modest branches of the **Velu Military hotels** and **Madurai Muniyaandi hotels** around the city. Wherever you eat Chettinad foods, be sure to try the unusual Chettinad dessert made from banana flowers.

The hottest of the southern regional foods is fiery Andhra Pradesh cooking. If you are not going to Hyderabad, you can try it in Madras at **Amaravati,** 1 Cathedral Rd. (☎ 476416). Your complete meal will be arrayed on a banana leaf and include chicken as well as rice and side dishes for about Rs 60 ($2).

For sampling a variety of South Indian cuisines, it's **Coconut Grove,** 95 Harrington Rd., Chetpet (☎ 8268800). Here, it is most pleasant outdoors in one of three pavilions with red tile roofs seemingly guarded by terra cotta elephants holding flowers in their trunks. You might try one of the Kerala thalis for Rs 50 ($1.66) vegetarian, or Rs 75 ($2.50) nonvegetarian, or any of a host of other regional dishes. About the highest-priced item on the menu is jumbo prawns for Rs 150 ($5). Open daily, from noon to 3pm, 7 to 11:30pm.

A Special Thali Vegetarian Meal

Annalakshmi ("Goddess of Plenty"), 804 Anna Salai (☎ 8525109), is a haven for well-prepared foods, gracious service, and beautiful artifacts with a twist. In this restaurant, charmingly hosted by followers of Swami Shantanand, exceptional vegetarian dishes are prepared from treasured old family recipes and presented on silver thalis by devotees in silk, jewel-tone saris. Menus change daily. Their idea is to realize a 10% return for the restaurant and plow the rest back into their charities dealing with the arts, culture, and health services to the poor. The first few weeks guests were allowed to pay what they thought appropriate for their meals. Fees must be in place by now. Reservations are a must. They serve both lunch and dinner. The artworks you see are for sale.

If your favorite region is Northern India, there's good Mughlai food at **Moghul,** upstairs at 83 Anna Salai (☎ 840391), a dimly lit restaurant run by **Buhari's,** the restaurant downstairs. The latter has been famous for pastries for more than 40 years. Mughlai dishes here run from about Rs 40 ($1.33) to around Rs 100 ($3.33); there are Western dishes as well. Don't leave without checking out the luscious sweets at Buhari's, which also serves light meals. Other Buhari's around town and in the surrounding area are at 14 Beach Rd., on N. S. C. Bose Road, on Poonamalee High Road, and at the Blue Lagoon Resort.

For a splurge Northeast Frontier meal, try **Peshawri,** in the Welcomgroup Chola Sheraton.

CHINESE & THAI

Especially good Chinese food (with lovely views) is served at **Sagari,** in **Welcomgroup Chola Sheraton** (☎ 8280101); at the elaborate **Golden Dragon,** in **Taj Coromandel** (☎ 8272827) for Szechwan specialties; and at **Shanghai,** in **The Trident** (☎ 2344747). Chinese, Thai, Malay, and other Far Eastern dishes are headliners at **The Cascade,** in the **Kakani Towers** (basement), 15 Khaderi Nawaz Khan Rd. (☎ 8272514). All restaurants are splurge-priced.

SNACKS, SWEETS & FAST FOODS

Traditional South Indian sweets, such as badaam halwa (almond pudding), adirasam (a sugary, cardamom-flavored fried sweet), and others, are made fresh and served outdoors at **Grand Sweets and Snacks** on Main Road. About Rs 30 ($1) will buy more than one kind of sweet. Sweets are also highlighted at the air-conditioned **Bombay Halwa House,** Anna Salai Road, to the left of Khadi Gramodyog Bhavan, where halwa and other sweets run about Rs 20 (66¢). Delicious South Indian coffee is also served here.

Eskimo, 827 Anna Salai (☎ 827840), is a funny name for a restaurant in perpetually warm, warmer, warmest Madras. But this air-conditioned little place is cool as an igloo and serves good quality food at a fair price. Right near the shops and movies, it serves meals but is most well-known for its snacks, from 9am to 10pm. Snacks, sandwiches, kebabs, and such cost Rs 25 (83¢) or Rs 50 ($1.66). More substantial dishes are also offered, such as tandoori chicken or chicken do piaza (curry with onions) at slightly higher prices.

HIGH TEA

A not-to-be missed treat, unique in India, is the splash-out tea at the elegant **lobby tea lounge** at the **Taj Coromandel** from 7am to 11pm. Choose from 22 different

Assam teas (the lounge is run in cooperation with Assam tea interests), served in delicate china cups, as well as snacks, sandwiches, and sweets from a well-edited menu. Even non–tea takers can enjoy themselves downing richly delicious ice cream sundaes or cold drinks—a splurge, though.

5 What to See & Do

A preliminary exploration of Madras might start in the northern area along Poonamallee High Road, near the majestic **civic buildings** of the Municipal Corporation and the Madras Central Railway Station. Just past there, taking the right fork of the road, you'll come to what's left of old **Fort St. George,** a major cog in the city's defenses when the British were in power two centuries ago, its buildings now used for various administrative and garrison purposes. This was the home of legendary British Empire builders such as Robert Clive (originally an obscure clerk in the East India Company, later a 1750s governor of Bengal), and Colonel Wellesley, later duke of Wellington (of the Battle of Waterloo fame).

Part of the fort itself is now a **museum** (open from 9am to 5pm every day but Friday and some holidays), which contains portraits of these famous figures as well as those of various governors and such English kings and queens as could be said to have ruled India. The signatures of King George V and his wife, Mary, written when they visited here in 1906, are still preserved in the visitors' book. In glass cases downstairs are stamps from that period bearing the heads of British sovereigns, and, by contrast, the infinitely more interesting stamps issued when India became independent (August 15, 1947), when Gandhi was murdered (January 30, 1948), and on the inauguration of the Republic of India (January 26, 1950). A scale model of the fort, as it was centuries ago, demonstrates that the sea used to lap at the walls where the road now runs past.

Also on the grounds is **St. Mary's Church,** built by the East India Company between 1678 and 1680, when Streynsham Master was the governor, with its near-copy of Leonardo da Vinci's *Last Supper,* done by some unknown French artist early in the 18th century. One of St. Mary's generous benefactors was Elihu Yale, a former governor, and yes, donor to the American university of the same name.

You're now on South Beach Road, parallel with the sea but separated from it by dockyards. Up to your left are the stalls of the **Burmese Bazaar**—lots of bargains here—but we'll head south, past the stately **government buildings** and campus of the **University of Madras,** past the thatched mud huts of the fishermen displaced years ago by a hurricane (they've been offered better homes but prefer to stay near the sea), and past the **aquarium** and almost-deserted sandy beaches. It's quite a lengthy walk, this stretch along the **Marina,** and maybe you'd prefer to get a taxi or cycle ricksha. Our destination is the **Basilica of San Thome,** a small gray church where earlier it was believed that St. Thomas, one of the 12 apostles, was buried; its crypt contains a small hand bone of the apostle and head of a lance, which is said to have been used in an attack on him.

The church had several incarnations. It had so deteriorated in the 14th and 15th centuries that the Portuguese moved St. Thomas to a new tomb and built a new church, which was given the status of a cathedral in 1606. That church was also demolished when the present Gothic-style cathedral was built in 1896; it was elevated to Basilica status in 1956. It's a pleasant place, patches of color from the stained-glass windows casting patterns on the shiny wooden pews.

Just around the corner, so to speak, life is busier near the incredible **Kapaleeswarar Temple,** its wedge-shaped gopuram, or tower, covered with tier after tier of exceptional carvings. The centuries-old temple is dedicated to Lord Shiva, and the palm-fringed tank at its rear is the scene of an annual festival (early spring), when the temple images are taken out and floated upon the water.

Your next destination is about a mile to the south. **Elliot's Beach** has developed into one of the poshest areas of Madras. Though not as secluded as it once was, it's still worth a visit. Bus no. 5E from Vadapalani to Besant Nagar (or no. 5M from Parry's to Adyar B.S.) will take you there.

Inland from the beach, we're now in the suburbs, as a glance at the surrounding houses and gardens will prove. On the way you'll see the elegant mansion and extensive grounds of the **Theosophical Society,** with its enormous banyan tree. (Visitors welcome from 8am to 11am, and 2 to 5pm Monday to Friday, from 8 to 11am on Saturday). There are two other landmarks on the highway out here: a delightful **Children's Park** with playground, midget railway, deer, cranes, monkeys, bears, panthers, and an elephant; and a simple, attractive park, **Gandhi Mandap,** where some of the ashes of the great pacifist are enshrined.

The Children's Park is located on the vast grounds of **Raj Bhavan,** the governor's estate, itself at the edge of Guindy National Park—open from 8:30am to 5:30pm—the only national park in India within a city's limits. There are two other parks within this park: a **deer park** houses rare black buck and spotted deer in their natural habitat, and a **snake park,** home to some 500 snakes—including cobras and pythons—that slink around in natural-looking surroundings. The animals and reptiles make good photographic subjects. City buses no. 18E from Parry's Corner, no. 45 from Periyar Bridge, and no. 46 from Anna Square go to Guindy (but double-check since routes and numbers change). Or grab a commuter train from Egmore or Beach Station.

If Indian classical art forms interest you, while you're out this way, make a point to visit **Kalakshetra,** founded by Rukmini Devi Arundale in 1936, which is devoted to the revival of classical arts. Students from all over the world study and live with their gurus (in the ancient Indian tradition), learning classical dance, music, traditional textile design, and weaving in natural surroundings on a 100-acre campus. The institution is expected to be named a university momentarily. It's best to call for an appointment before visiting.

Stargazers might want to stop at the **B. M. Birla Planetarium** (☎ 4167511) in Kottur before heading to midtown. Shows are on Tuesday through Saturday at 10:45am, 1:15pm, and 3:45pm (in English), at noon and 2:30pm (in Tamil); entry is Rs 7 (23¢), children under 12, Rs 3 (10¢); it is closed Monday.

Going back to the midtown area in Egmore, the **National Gallery of Art** (open from 9am to 5pm; closed Friday and national holidays; entry free), with an interesting collection of both ancient and contemporary works, is housed in a pleasant, red stone building on Pantheon Road, between the two midtown areas represented by Anna Salai (Mount Road) and General Hospital Road.

Adjoining the art gallery is the infinitely more time-consuming **Government Museum** (open from 9am to 5pm; closed Friday and national holidays), with its collection of bronze statues (a repetitious set of god images dating back to the 4th and 5th centuries), but also much more absorbing galleries devoted to anthropology and natural history.

Some attention should also be given to the armory in another of the galleries, devoted not only to ancient weapons but also to relics from old Indian tribes: bamboo and coconut utensils, pipes, bows and arrows, equipment for igniting fires, and musical instruments.

Visitors spend so much time checking out ancient stuff in India that they forget to investigate the modern arts. While in Madras, you might also want to check out a few of the **art galleries** lining Khader Nawaz Khan Road, opposite the Taj Coromandel Hotel. Among these are **Saakshi, Le Gallerie,** and **Vimonisha.**

GUIDED TOURS

Half-day sightseeing tours are conducted daily by the **Tamil Nadu Tourism Development Corporation (TTDC)** from 7:30am to 1:30pm and from 1:30 to 6:30pm. The cost is Rs 65 ($2.16). Places covered include Fort St. George, Government Museum, Valluvar Kottam (a memorial to poet Saint Thiruvalluvar, fashioned after a temple cart and engraved with couplets), Snake Park, Kapaleeswarar Temple, Elliot's Beach, and a drive along Marina Beach. (The Government Museum is closed on Friday, so Birla Planetarium is a stop on Fridays only.) TTDC's full-day tour, from 8:10am to 7pm, costs Rs 145 ($4.83), including a vegetarian meal. The tour covers the points above and beyond to Muttikadu Boat House and VGB Beach Resort.

The full-day **Mammalapuram Tour,** from 6:10am to 7pm, costs Rs 150 ($5) non-AC, Rs 220 ($7.33) AC, and includes breakfast and lunch. The tour covers Kanchipuram, Mamallapuram, Crocodile Bank, Muttukadu Boat House, and VGP Golden Beach Resort. Pick-up points are the Central Railway parking area, the Express Bus Stand (I.T.C. Esplanade), and the TTDC office at 143 Anna Salai. Seats are on a first-come, first-served basis, upon payment.

Sales counters for these tours are at TTDC (☎ 830498 or 830390), the Express Bus Stand (☎ 5341982); Central Railway Station (☎ 563351); Youth Hostel (☎ 589132); Tourism Information Egmore Station (☎ 8252165); and TN Information Counter, Airport (☎ 2340569). You can book tours at many hotels.

The **India Tourism Development Corporation (ITDC)** also conducts a daily sightseeing tour of Madras, from 1:30 to 6:30pm, which costs Rs 50 ($2.55) per person. The tour covers all of the above sights. On Friday the Government Museum and National Gallery are closed, so the tour goes to the Botanical Garden and Parthasarathi Temple. For reservations, contact ITDC, 29 Victoria Crescent D-in-C Rd. (☎ 8278884); Government of India Tourist Office, 154 Anna Salai Mount Rd. (☎ 8278884); ITDC's Reservation Counter at the Express Bus Stand, Esplanade (☎ 561830); or its counter at the Central Railway Station (☎ 567451).

6 Shopping

Shopping complexes are developing in Anna Salai and Parry's Corner areas and are similar to malls in the West, with many shops under one roof. Department stores, while smaller than their Western counterparts, manage to do what department stores do: have every kind of merchandise under one roof. It is still possible to pleasurably shop in small stores where you'll be treated to a cold drink or cup of tea while you decide on your purchases with the owner. Hours are generally 9am to 9pm, with a lunch break between 1 and 3pm (though some stores do not close for lunch). Local holidays often disrupt these hours. *Note:* Many merchants still refer to Mount Road addresses, although Anna Salai has been officially the name for many years. I've heeded their wishes below.

Look for a round-up of South Indian crafts in Madras, ivory inlay, sandalwood, distinctive local vegetable-dye paintings and leather ware; and, of course, fabulous cotton, which put Madras on the map in the first place, and the lustrous silks that keep the state famous among textile connoisseurs.

The following is a mere sampling of shopping opportunities in Madras, one of India's great marketplaces. For bargain hunting, keep in mind that certain markets in Madras have specialties: **Sri Theyagaraya Road** for gold and silk; **Anna Salai (Mount Road)** for textiles, also **Rattan Bazaar** and **Parry's Corner.** The **Burmese Bazaar** is the place to bargain for imported products, but it's also a place to be careful. Your bargain may turn out to be nothing but a cheap imitation of an expensive item, worth less than you paid.

Books The best bookstore in town is **Landmark,** Apex Plaza, 3 Nungambakkam High Rd. (☎ 827637), open from 9am to 8:30pm; one of the oldest is **Higginbothams Ltd.,** 814 Mount Rd. (Anna Salai) (☎ 831841), open from 9am to 7pm, with a branch in the Varsa Arcade, F-39 Anna Nagar East, near Chinthamani Market, open the same hours. Also on Anna Salai are these choices: **Kennedy Book House** 1/55 Mount Rd. (Anna Salai) (☎ 831797), open 9am to 9pm; and **The Bookshop at Spencer Plaza,** 769 Mount Rd. (Anna Salai) (☎ 8522701).

Most of the top hotels have bookstores. **Danai's** has branches at the Taj Coromandel, Sindoori, open 8:30am to 10:45pm, and Adyar Park, 8:30am to midnight. Tiny **Giggle's** in the Connemara is an amazing place—floor to ceiling fully stocked with stuff to read.

Fruits and Flowers To be enveloped by the sweet scent of jasmine, visit the **Fruit and Flower Bazaar** on N. S. C. Bose Road. This is where Madras women buy single blossoms for their hair and devotees select garlands for worship. Nearby stalls display bananas, custard apples (they look somewhat like artichokes), and other luscious fruits. Wash and/or peel before you eat.

Handicrafts For handicrafts, try the **Cottage Industries Exposition** (not to be confused with the government-run Cottage Industries Emporia in other cities; this one is privately owned), 118 N.H. Rd., across from the Taj Coromandel, where you'll find items in rosewood, sandalwood, ivory, bronze, silver, and leather, as well as textiles, carpets, and precious jewelry. Open from 10am to 1pm, and 4 to 9pm. **Sri Karpaga Vinayaka Kalai Koodam,** S 9-D, 2nd Floor, Spencer Plaza, 769 Mount Rd. (Anna Salai)(☎ 582549), has an unusual assortment of prayer articles, gems, and natural medicines. Another choice is **Tiffany's Antiques** 520A, Second Floor Spencer Plaza, Mount Road (☎ 8256701). **Indian Arts Museum,** Agarchand Mansion, 151 Mount Road (Anna Salai) (☎ 8268683), has a good assortment of handicrafts, Kashmir carpets, Indian silks, and stone jewelry. And the government-run **Poompuhar,** 818 Mount Rd., has an extensive selection of objects made in Tamil Nadu, price-fixed.

The 100-year-old **Victoria Technical Institute,** 765 Anna Salai (☎ 863131), open from 9:30am to 7:30pm weekdays and from 9:30am to 2pm Saturdays, has a special room for antiquities and unusual items made especially to be sold here. It's the place to look for a one-of-a-kind souvenir. Less special, but very nice, are the VTI's rosewood elephants dangling from a key chain and hand-embroidered easy-to-pack linens.

Jewelry Before visiting any of the many jewelers in town, drop in at the India Tourist Office, 154 Anna Salai, for an approved list to make sure you're dealing with a reputable merchant. Among the well-established jewelers are **Vummidi Bangaru Jewellers,** Rani Seethal Hill, parallel to Gemini Flyover, 603 Anna Salai (☎ 8279652); **Bapalal and Co.,** 24 Cathedral Rd. (☎ 8273030); **Prince Jewellery,** 13 Nageswara Rao Rd., Pangal Park, T. Nagar (☎ 446783); and **Ranee Jewellers,** 5 Cisons Complex, 150 Montieth Rd. (☎ 8266069).

Silks and Cottons Silks woven in the temple city of Kanchipuram, not far from Madras, are good buys at many stores. Some stores known for the best quality include

India Silk House, 846 Mount Rd. (Anna Salai) (☎ 833830), open from 9am to 8pm; and **Radha Silk Emporium,** 1 Sannathi St., Mylapore, near the Sri Kapaleeswarar Temple, where tourists get a brochure on how to wrap, wear, and care for a sari. The latter has Western items as well, such as shirts in famous Madras-plaid crepe cotton and scarves that make easy-to-pack gifts. Ready-mades also include salwar kamiz for women. Hours are 10am to 8pm Monday through Saturday, closed Sunday. Also try **Nalli Chinnasmai Chetty,** opposite Pangal Park, T. Nagar (☎ 4344115), open from 9am to 9pm; and **Apsara,** Spencer's Building, 769 Mount Rd. (Anna Salai) (☎ 8263740).

The famous cotton plaids of Madras are well represented at **Handloom House,** 8 Rattan Bazaar, and **Khadi Gramodyag Bhavan,** 844 Anna Salai, where there are also tailors to make your fabrics into fashionable clothing. Hours are 9:30am to 7:30pm, closed Sunday.

7 Madras After Dark

Every day the two local papers, the *Hindu Express* and the *Indian Express* (mornings) carry a list of local entertainment. *Hallo Madras,* a monthly magazine available for Rs 5 (16¢) at bookstores, contains information on current events of all kinds.

Indians love **films,** and there are dozens of movie theaters—at least four or five showing English and American films regularly (movie timings are usually 3:30, 6:30, and 9:30pm). Like Bombay, Madras is a filmmaking center, and local Tamil-language films are, like most India-made films, romantic boy-meets-girl-loses-girl-gets-her-back or religious-theme stories. It is advisable to book movie seats in advance.

In addition to films, quite often there are dance concerts of the South's beautiful **classical dance,** Bharata Natyam, and singing and music—most especially from mid-December through January, locally known as "the season," when the city is the site of a music festival, and in February when there's a dance festival. These events attract renowned artists from all over India. Two Indian instruments, the stringed veena and the drumlike mridangam, are popular locally. Check with the Government of India Tourist Office, 154 Anna Salai, about the arts festivals. Reserve hotels far in advance.

The top hotels have **bars.** And such rooftop hotel restaurants as the **Minar** at the Savera (where ghazals, North Indian songs, are sung), the **Oorvasi** at the Palmgrove, the **Sagari** at the Chola Sheraton, and the **Regal** at Madras International provide pretty views as well as dinners and music too.

The Taj Coromandel's, Mysore Room (which was to be renamed) showcases **Indian and classical music** and dance in the evenings at 8:45, 9:45, and 10:45pm, but double-check (☎ 8272827); the hotel has a live band in the 24-hour Pavilion coffee shop. At the Connemara there's classical Indian music and dance at the Rain Tree restaurant and a live band in the 24-hour coffee shop.

There's a **poolside barbecue** at the Welcomgroup Park Sheraton and Towers, and a **disco** in The Gatsby on Saturday nights (very young crowd and rather tame stuff).

8 Excursions from Madras

The major, and virtually indispensable, excursion from Madras is to the small town of Kanchipuram and the coastal village of Mamallapuram (Mahabalipuram), which are famous for their memories of the Pallavas, a dynasty that ruled this part of India more than 1,000 years ago. The former, which is still filled with well-preserved temples, was their capital, while the latter was their port and today is visited to see the ancient monuments of the Pallavas and as a relaxing resort.

KANCHIPURAM

Kanchi (pop. 170,000) is a typical rural town of southern India. The mud streets are dotted with groups of people winding and sorting colored thread—this is a big weaving center—amid a kaleidoscope of animals, women carrying brass pots to the well, cycle rickshas, and holy men with ash-covered faces. It's a very holy town, in fact one of the group of seven holy places that an ardent Indian pilgrim will try to cover on his crusade around India. For the visitor on a leisurely schedule, it might be very pleasant to spend a quiet night there, returning to Madras or moving on after a day or so.

ESSENTIALS

Getting to Kanchipuram

There are two **trains** a day from Madras to Kanchi (as it is called for short), and **bus** nos. 76, 76B, PP76, 79, and 130 from Madras go there every 20 minutes (from 3:30am to 10pm), the trip taking two hours. There are buses every half hour starting at 10pm—nos. 119A, 188, 188K. A **car and driver** for a one-day round-trip to Kanchipuram (eight hours/180 kilometers) is Rs 900 ($30) in a non-AC **Ambassador,** Rs 1,500 ($50) with AC.

Guided Tours

It is also possible to join the daily **TTDC** or **ITDC** guided tours from Madras to see the sights.

From Madras, **TTDC** (☎ 830498) offers one daily tour, from 6:10am to 7pm, which combines Kanchipuram and Mamallapuram. The cost is Rs 150 ($5) to Rs 220 ($7.33), including breakfast and lunch. **ITDC** (☎ 8278884) offers a similar daily tour from 7:30am to 7pm for Rs 100 non-AC, including breakfast (see "Guided Tours" under "What to See and Do," above).

Festivals

Kanchipuram ratha (temple carts with gods being drawn to Kamaskshi Amman) festivals are held in January, April, and May, the dates changing from year-to-year. Throughout the year, there are special days when the gods are taken out for a breath of air on their vehicles.

EN ROUTE TO KANCHIPURAM

On National Highway 4, 22 kilometers from Madras, is **Motel Highway,** 89 Bangalore Trunk Rd. (☎ 6272420), with tables under the trees where you can sit and have breakfast or a snack going to or coming from Kanchipuram. There's also an indoor AC restaurant. The dosas, idlis, vadus, and coffee here are truly delicious and cost only Rs 8 to Rs 10 (about 30¢) per order. There's food service 24 hours a day. And if you want a nibble for the road, there's a little shop where you can buy juices, mineral water, and biscuits.

Or you might spend the night if you're traveling on to Bangalore (about six hours) and it's late in the day. Clean, basic doubles cost Rs 225 ($7.50) with AC, Rs 180 ($6) without.

WHAT TO SEE & DO IN KANCHIPURAM

Temples Most of the 70 (some say 1,000) temples were built by the Pallavas in the 8th century, and, although time and the weather have chipped away their ancient carvings, they are still splendidly decorated with, as in the case of the **Kailasanatha Temple,** some traces of the ancient colorings. This is said to have been the first stone temple in India and the most important in Kanchi. At this place in particular (but also at many others), you'll encounter a self-appointed priestly guardian who'll suggest a donation (often off-the-wall exorbitant) for temple funds in return for illuminating the interior sculptures: Donate Rs 5 to Rs 10.

The most interesting temple is **Ekambareswara,** dating from a later period, with its 188-foot-high gopuram, or ornamental tower. This is decorated in steps with excellently carved blue and yellow figures and stands beside a small, stone pool in which the neighborhood women wash their clothes. A larger tank, however, behind the main hall of the compound, is much more the center of action. Here, half a dozen small boys carrying buckets of puffed rice will focus their attention on you. For a rupee they'll tip a measure of the rice into your hands and accompany you down the steps of the tank to feed the fish. Beside the bottom step the water is so thick with these small fish that it seems all you need to do is reach in a hand to pick one out. They're too fast for the average visitor but easy for the boys to catch barehanded. They're always tossed back into the water, though. The building flanking the tank is held up by scores of stone pillars, all intricately carved.

According to Hindu mythology, Ekambareswara marks the spot where Shiva forgave Parvati for a prank in which she covered his eyes for one second. This tiny blindness plunged mortals into darkness for years, and for this, Shiva made Parvati atone until he forgave her here.

Visitors usually include a third temple in their tour, the one dedicated to **Varadarajaswamy,** scene of an annual pilgrimage. Built in the 12th century, its main hall, also adjoining a holy tank, is supported by enormous pillars, each carved from a separate rock. The pillars are covered with a wealth of tableaux: horsemen, lions, and even a man carrying what must have been one of the earliest known rifles. The extreme right-hand pillar, nearest the tank, does have one special curiosity: a tableau of three men with four legs between them but carved in such a way that it seems each man has two legs.

Two less visited sites deserve your attention. The first is **Devarajaswamy** (3 kilometers from town), built by the Vijayanagara kings, with a fine 100-pillar hall. Look for severed halves of a great chain stone sculpted out of a single boulder (broken up by Muslim invaders) and the figures of the God of Love and consort astride a swan and parrot.

The second is **Kamakshi Amman Temple** (located in the center of town), which the Cholas built in the 14th century. Dedicated to Parvati, it is one of the three of the most holy places for Shakti worship—the others are Madurai and Varanasi. There's a golden gopuram.

The temples open at the crack of dawn and close between noon and 4pm and reopen in the evenings. You can probably manage these few above in a day.

Weavers Most of the weaving in Kanchi is of the cottage-industry type, with several looms in one house operated as a family business. If you visit one of the homes (and this can be arranged through the **Weavers Service Centre,** 20 Railway Station Rd., west of the station), you're likely to see two barefoot boys sitting at a small loom with such an intricate array of threads, strings, wooden bars, slats, and metal weights that it takes several days to set it up for production of the particular design. Working almost as fast as the eye can see, the boys dexterously pass the shuttle under and over the taut threads, the bare toes of the operator manipulating the strands. Working together, a pair of weavers can complete a sari in about 15 days, including the time for setting up. For this, the retail price in the stores is Rs 900 ($30) or more.

Where to Stay & Eat in Kanchipuram

Very few tourists stay in Kanchipuram overnight, but if you'd like to, there's the TTDC's **Hotel Tamil Nadu,** Kamatchi Amman Sannathi Street, Big Kanchipuram 631502 (☎ 22553), near the railway station, which has been improved and enlarged over the years. The 24 rooms are clean and basic but fine for an overnight stay, and each has a bathroom attached. Twelve have AC; rates are Rs 320 ($10.66) to Rs 420 ($14); the higher rate provides a television set. Non-AC doubles are Rs 300 ($20). To these rates, taxes must be added. There's an air-conditioned restaurant where you can get both vegetarian and nonvegetarian meals. It's the best place to eat if you find yourself here at meal times or want a snack. It's probably a good idea to telephone in advance to make sure there's food on hand, in case there are no other guests.

Your other choice is **Baboo Soorya,** 85 East Raja Veethi, Kanchipuram 631501 (☎ 22555), a relative newcomer to the area. With 38 rooms arranged around an atrium, 20 AC, rates are Rs 275 ($9.16) single, Rs 350 ($11.66) double. Renovation was planned to upgrade the non-AC. Too bad the plan doesn't include better maintenance. There's a vegetarian restaurant; a special thali costs Rs 32 ($1.06), including tax.

Shopping in Kanchipuram

The shops in this little town feature locally woven silks. Prices are generally high, but so is the quality. Bargaining is almost nonexistent, at least with Westerners. If you don't want anything as ambitious as a sari, pretty silk scarves start around Rs 200 ($6.66) and go up. Easy to pack, they make both good gifts and good souvenirs. **Sri Swami Silks,** 116 T. K. Nambi St. (☎ 2716), is one of several well-stocked stores.

MAMALLAPURAM (MAHABALIPURAM)

Until recently, Mamallapuram (Mahabalipuram, pop. 9,500) was isolated and almost unvisited, its temples and monuments forgotten or ignored. It had once been a busy port but was now merely a small fishing village so remote that visitors could get there only by boat or on foot from the nearest road. Then the town was "rediscovered," and now tourists come not only to sightsee but also to stay. It's a charming little place with a vast unused beach and attractive accommodations right beside the sea. At Mamallapuram (Mahabalipuram), the sights to be seen are a famous temple on the beach, a group of enormous carved monuments called *rathas,* some rock-cut cave temples, and what is said to be the largest bas-relief in the world.

En Route to Mamallapuram (Mahabalipuram)

As you leave Madras by the coastal road, the landscape glistens with paddy fields, fanned by palms. There's a stop to be made only 18 kilometers from the city, either en route to Mamallapuram or as an excursion itself. This is the **Cholamandal Artists' Village,** a thriving artists' community established in 1966 by artists for artists. A large number of sculptors and painters live and work here today, and their works are on display and for sale. However, unless you see something you simply can't live without, you might be wise to wait and make your sculpture purchases in Mamallapuram itself, where there's a bigger selection. There you will find numerous artisans chipping and hammering away at stone blocks to create souvenirs inspired by local landmarks, hoping you will want to buy their wares.

Essentials

Getting to Mamallapuram (Mahabalipuram)

The Tamil Nadu State Transport **buses** no. 119A, 68, and 19C take off from 6:30am to 8:30pm for a 2½-hour trip to Mamallapuram. For splurgers, a round-trip by **taxi,** covering Mamallapuram and back in a day (140 kilometers), costs about Rs 680 ($22.66) in an *Ambassador,* non-AC, and Rs 1,200 ($40) with AC. The nearest railway station is **Chingelput,** 29 kilometers from Mamallapuram.

Visitor Information

The **Government of Tamil Nadu Tourism** office, East Raja Street, open from 10am to 5:30pm, is near the post office and bus stand. Guides are best hired in Madras. However, should you need help in Mamallapuram with ticketing, tours, taxis, or telephone calls, contact Francis at Metro Tours and Travel 137 East Raja St. (☎ 42456).

Getting Around Mamallapuram

Bikes cost Rs 20 ($66¢) a day; if you're foolish enough, motorbikes rent for Rs 100 ($3.33) a day. There are signs around the little town, or ask at the tourist office about where to find rentals.

A Festival

In January, a dance festival draws dancers from all over India who perform with Arjuna's Penance as their backdrop.

What to See & Do in Mamallapuram

Entering the village, the first thing that catches the newcomer's eye is a bunch of enormous rocks casually strewn around the landscape. One of them, often referred to as **Krishna's Butterball,** is a tremendous, egg-shaped rock, which at first appears to be balanced precariously on the hillside but has actually been stationary there for several hundred years. At least a thousand years ago there was a big tidal wave in these parts, which may account for the random position of some of these stones. It's known that the wave washed away several of the seashore temples, but one attractive temple remains right on the beach, the waves lapping against its surrounding walls.

This **Shore Temple,** surrounded by about a score of big stone bulls, contains a few stone carvings, but the walls of the temple itself are also sculpted, and its charm lies more in its location than its content. The major attraction is the group of five blocks of stone called *rathas.* They were carved in the form of temple chariots by the Pallavas and named after five Pandava princes' wives (Yudhishtira, Bhima, Arjuna, Nakula, and Sahadeva). Each of the rathas is carved, decorated, sculpted, and hollowed out so that it seems more like a decorated building than a work of art carved from solid rock. Adjoining the group are three life-size animals—a lion facing north, an elephant south, and a bull on the eastern side.

Back inside the town is a **lighthouse** (not open for climbing), but behind it on the hill is a much older lighthouse that was once a Shiva temple and is heavily carved. Naturally, from the ledge surrounding it, there is a panoramic view of the town and the beach. Down a few steps, around and under the lighthouse, is what's known as the **Mahishasuramardini Mandapam** (a cave), in which is carved the legendary story of the fight between the goddess Durga, mounted on a lion, and an evil buffalo-headed demon.

Down below, at the side of the main road, is another cave, the **Krishna Mandapam,** in which is carved a lovely pastoral scene of a man milking a cow plus other aspects of rural life.

Not far away from this is the famous bas-relief known as **Arjuna's Penance.** This is a huge boulder—part of the cliff face—that is 90 feet long and 30 feet high. Carved on it are more than 400 beautiful figures, including an old hermit, arms outstretched, doing penance; a standing cat, paws outstretched, mimicking the old man; a deer scratching its face with its hind leg; elephants sheltering baby elephants; and a host of gods, snakes, lions, leopards, monkeys, and mice. Down through the center of the panel is a natural gap representing the Ganges and through which, it is believed, water once flowed.

To wind up your sightseeing, stop at the **Government College of Architecture and Sculpture,** near the Youth Hostel, where you can see how students are trained in the various aspects of temple art and architecture, according to ancient traditional methods. On display is an exhibit of student sculpture, open from 9am to 2pm, and 2 to 6:30pm, closed Tuesdays.

Farther Afield

For a worthwhile side trip, accessible by bus from Mamallapuram and about 17 kilometers (10 miles) inland, there is calm and peaceful **Thirukkazhukundram (Thirukalikunram).** The name means "hill of the sacred kites" (in this case birds, not playthings), and sights include a hilltop temple where around noon every day, two sacred kites come to get lunch from the hands of the temple priest. This practice is believed to have been started ages ago, and according to legend the two birds are saints in disguise and on their way south to Rameswaram from Varanasi.

Back on the road to Madras, about 4 kilometers from the main monuments, is **Tiger's Cave,** an ancient open-air theater where performances were held for Pallava royalty.

A few miles farther on, you'll see a big sign for the **Crocodile Bank,** where there are endangered species of Indian crocodile. More accurately, it's a savings bank, for it was set to breed and restore rare crocodile species. There is a modest entry fee; hours are 8:30am to 5:30pm daily. Buses to and from Madras will drop you near both the Tiger's Cave and the Crocodile Bank.

Where to Stay in & Around Mamallapuram (Mahabalipuram)

In Mamallapuram

If you're looking for truly low-budget accommodations—under Rs 250 ($8.33)—you have a few, though limited, choices.

For years, **Mamalla Bhavan** (☎ 42250), a short walk from the bus stand, has offered clean and basic bargain accommodations right in the center of Mamallapuram. The lodging is a stone's throw from the tourist office and Pallava sites. Spartan rooms with bathrooms attached cost Rs 45 ($1.50). While there is no AC, they have fans and windows facing the sea, so you get the breezes. The one hitch is that this place is often booked up. Delicious vegetarian meals are served in the restaurant at Rs 9 (30¢) South Indian-style, Rs 10 (33¢) North Indian, on an unlimited-plate basis.

The proprietor of **Tina Blue View Restaurant,** Ottavadai Street (see "Where to Eat in Mamallapuram," below), G. Souriappan, also has a few clean, cell-like non-AC rooms to rent at around Rs 100 ($3.33). You'll be better off here than in the similarly priced, unkempt lodges near the bus stand in town.

Nearby, **Ramakrishnan,** 8 Ottavadai, has rooms with showers, the basics only, but is cleaner than some in this bracket. **Surya Drive-Inn,** near the tourist office and the sea, has fairly clean rooms in simple cottages, some with AC. A sculpture garden is a bonus.

Calling it "A Sequel to a Legend," the owners of the Mamalla Bhavan (described above) run the more upscale **Mamalla Bhavan Annexe** (☎ 42250 and 42260) next door. The tidy, two-story, cream-colored building with red trim, on a small lawn, houses 43 neatly furnished rooms, 12 with AC, ranging from Rs 190 ($6.33) to Rs 400 ($13.33); an additional 12 might be ready now. A major plus is **The Golden Palate,** the AC restaurant where a top-notch thali, for Rs 33 ($1.10), features four to five curries, pooris (puffy bread) or chapatis (flat bread), soup, pappadums, curd, rasam (lentil based consommé), sambar (vegetable stew), and a sweet.

Hotel Veeras (☎ 42288), new, pleasant, and more ambitious, has deluxe doubles for Rs 450 ($15), boasting such big-town hotel amenities as AC and minirefrigerators; there are lower-priced rooms too. Features include non-veg and veg restaurants, a bar, and conference room. International credit cards are accepted.

Only one hotel in the following group has rates in excess of Rs 600 ($20). Ask about off-season discounts if booking from April through September.

Silversands, Mamallapuram (Mahabalipuram), Madras 603104 (☎ 2228 or 2283, fax 2280; in Madras 8277444), was the pioneer, opening the first resort out this way in 1968 with six simple, thatched-roof cottages. Now this friendly, pleasant place has 65 suites and rooms at prices ranging from Rs 250 ($8.33) for a standard AC single to Rs 1,150 ($38.33) for a sea-facing beach villa. Especially fine seafood is served here. There's a separate vegetarian kitchen. Varied events include demonstrations by potters and sculptors, Bharata Natyam dancers, and classical musicians. Lowest-budgeteers are accommodated in **Silver Inn** away from the beach. There is free shuttle service to Madras for long stays. In Madras, Silversands runs Transit House (see "Where to Stay," above).

My mail bulges with raves over **Ideal Beach Resort,** Mamallapuram 603104 (☎ 4113, 42240, or 424434; fax 42243), where the cheerful, friendly P. M. Dharmalingam and his wife, son, and daughter-in-law see that guests are happy and well looked after. The 27 rooms are clean and simply furnished, fine for a casual beach vacation. Tariff peaks at Rs 525 ($17.50) for an AC cottage. The swimming pool is something else! With its gazebo to one end and classical statues here and there, this could be an Indian film set—and it often is for Madras filmmakers. The resort's menu features both vegetarian and nonvegetarian foods.

Golden Sun Hotel and Beach Resort, 59 Covelong Rd., Mammalapuram (☎ 42245; reservations in Madras ☎ 841020); the reception hall's pillars and archways are covered with trailing bougainvillea. Here are 69 cheerful rooms with basic furniture and straw matting on the floors. Avoid the gloomy stone cottages near a dump. Sea-facing doubles run Rs 600 ($20); suites are higher. There are some cheaper, non-AC rooms. Nice swimming pool.

Only half a mile from the ancient shore temple, the air-conditioned ITDC **Temple Bay Ashok Beach Resort,** Mamallapuram 603104 (☎ 2251; fax 2257), offers a choice between 29 well-appointed stone cottages equipped with sundecks and kitchenettes and seven simply furnished rooms in the main building, all in a lovely garden with cool, inviting swimming pool. Doubles run Rs 1,550 ($51.66), making this a fraction of a hair over our budget. If you're stuck for a place to stay, management might let you camp on the grounds. You'll need a ticket, though. Check with the receptionist at the desk.

TTDC's **Shore Temple Beach Resort** (☎ 235) is comprised of 48 architecturally varied cottages, some resembling modernized English row houses, others looking like American Indian teepees. Their AC doubles are Rs 500 ($16.66). Another group has a low Mediterranean look and is known as **Hotel Tamil Nadu II.** They are more basic, cheaper, and share extensive grounds with the 42-bed **Youth Hostel.** The restaurant specializes in Chinese food—the only one on the beach to do so. It's open to outsiders, too, from 7am to 11pm.

Hotels Between Madras & Mamallapuram

About 19 kilometers (12 miles) south of Madras on the Bay of Bengal is **VGP Golden Beach Resort,** East Coast Road, Enjambakkam Village, Madras 600041

(☎ 4926445), with 60 landscaped acres dotted with fantasy pavilions, sculptures, and a 60-foot waterfall. It's an extravagant, but not altogether successful, attempt at a theme park. Imagine a cottage that looks like a yacht. For casual visitors who want to look around, there's a modest entry fee, deductible from charges for any food purchased on the premises. Very popular with Indian tour groups and a lunch stop on both TTDC sightseeing tours from Madras. Cottages cost Rs 300 ($10) to 900 ($30). About half a mile away from Cholamandal Artists' Village, mentioned earlier, Madras city buses (route 19) go out here every 15 minutes, in case you just want to look around.

Elegant and pricey place is **Fisherman's Cove,** Covelong Beach, Chingleput District (☎ 2304; fax 2303), a Taj Group hotel. In the main building are 42 rooms; of the 28 cottages on the beach, 10 are nestled right in the dunes. All make tasteful use of local textiles. The laid-back need only to get up to grab some barbecue or dip in the swimming pool. For those who thrive on activities, there are walks and bike tours to sights in Mamallapuram. Double rates only: from December 12 to January 20, $105; other times, $80.

Where to Eat in Mamallapuram

Your best bets for vegetarian food are the **Mamalla Bhavan** and **The Golden Palate** at Mamalla Bhavan Annexe. The restaurants at **Hotel Veeras** are worth a try for crisp dosas on the veg side and non-veg foods, too.

A standout among the nonhotel restaurants is the lively **Gazebo,** on East Raja Street (☎ 42525), a place to connect with other foreigners and all kinds of visitors. Known for its seafood, the menu offers tasty grilled prawns, lobsters, and curries, for Rs 35 ($1.16) to Rs 40 ($1.33). It is open from 7am to midnight. Ask for the helpful G. Bernard.

Tina Blue View Restaurant, 152 Ottavadai St., on a balcony with a sea and temple view, is pleasant with wicker chairs painted blue and covered with blue striped cushions, lantern-lit at night. There is a reasonably priced breakfast (try the idlis), lunch, or dinner. There's nothing unexpected on the menu—your typical seaside stuff: lobsters, prawns, and that sort of thing from the nearby fishing village, and the usual Indian and Western standards. Refreshing fresh fruit juices are a plus. Open 7am to 10pm.

Honey Falls, on Shore Temple Road in a cottage covered by thatch, has many fish and prawn dishes from Rs 35 ($1.16) to Rs 50 ($1.66). Open from 8:30am to midnight.

There are a number of other restaurants on Shore Temple Road and Raja Street, all with almost identical menus, prices, ambience, and dirty tablecloths, not worth mentioning by name.

Shopping in Mamallapuram

The government-run **Poompuhar,** near the Shore Temple, and stalls near the five rathas sell handmade baskets, soapstone statues, and sea shell curios. The **Government College for Architecture and Sculpture** is another resource.

Southern India: Pondicherry & Tamil Nadu

13

Beyond Pondicherry lies the Dravidian southland of Tamil Nadu, which has remained relatively unaffected by foreign incursions. A pleasant place with a leisurely pace, this land is green-spangled, with rice paddies cooled by palms. But the memories you'll retain most vividly about this part of India are the templed cities of long-past dynasties whose rulers were undoubtedly among the world's greatest temple builders. Like much of India, the splendid temples present the visitor with a surfeit of riches. It is necessary, therefore, to be selective to see even some of them. Now, to cover these centuries, let's start with French-accented Pondicherry, then dig deeper into the past and end with the ghost of the Raj in the hill station of Udhagamandalam (Ootacamund).

1 Pondicherry

Pondicherry (pop. 401,000), the headquarters of the Union Territory of Pondicherry (made up of Pondicherry, Karaikal, Yanam, and Mahe), was developed by the French, who relinquished their rule in the 1950s, but Pondicherry still retains a soupçon of French flavor. The policemen wear red kepis, and there are statues of Deuplix and Jeanne D'Arc; you hear some people speaking French and see some French street signs and names. The city is oval-shaped, and the streets of Pondicherry are neatly aligned at right angles. This is said to make them unique among streets in Indian towns.

By the time the French arrived in 1673, the settlement had been in the hands of several South Indian dynasties—Pallavas, Cholas, Vijayanagar kings, and Nayaks. Even they were upstarts in this part of India: Legend has it that in 1500 B.C., Sage Agastya set up a hermitage here.

The coconut palms of the Coromandel coast fringe the community right up to the seafront, and the roar of the waves is a perpetual accompaniment to all who stay or pass by the eastern side of the town.

Except during the winter monsoon season, Pondicherry slumbers under an almost constant sun, its streets tranquil but humid. There are few taxis, so cycle and auto rickshas are the major means of getting around. The famous Tamil poet Bharathiar lived here, and later came Sri Aurobindo, a young revolutionary turned yogi, whose ashram is now the town's major attraction. Auroville, a developing town of international residents 10 kilometers (a nice day-trip) from Pondicherry, is a fascinating glimpse at an experiment in living.

ESSENTIALS

GETTING TO PONDICHERRY

BY PLANE There are no direct flights. The nearest airports are in Madras (239 kilometers) and Tiruchirappalli (172 kilometers).

BY TRAIN The closest main-line railway stations are **Villupuram** (62 kilometers away) and **Madras** (239 kilometers away). Villupuram is connected to Pondicherry by a meter-gauge line (allow 1½ hours for this trip) and is easily accessible from Madras, Madurai, or Tiruchirappalli.

Trains from Madras Egmore include the *Pallavan Express,* which departs at 3:10pm, arriving in Villapuram at 9am; the *Pandyan Express* departs Madras at 7:10am, arriving in Villapuram at 3pm; the *Vagai Express* departs at 12:25pm, arriving in Villapuram at 11:45am. Fares are Rs 1,370 ($45.66) for AC First, Rs 785 ($26.16) for AC sleeper, and Rs 88 ($2.93) for Second. From Villapuram, it's necessary to change to a meter-gauge train (about 1½ hours) or take a bus (approximately a half hour) to Pondicherry.

In case you want to retrace your steps to Madras, here are some connections. There are two daily trains from Pondicherry to Villupuram: 8:15am and 10:30pm. The evening train connects to the *Pandyan Express,* departing from Villupuram at 3:15am and arriving Madras at 6:45am; the *Vaigai Express* departs Villupuram at 11:50am, arriving Madras 2:20pm; and the *Pallavan Express* departs 9:05am and arrives Madras 11:35am. Remember that trains can be late when making your plans. Reservations are made at the Madras Railway Station for trains leaving from Villupuram and Madras.

BY BUS The easiest way to reach Pondicherry is by **TTC Express** bus from Madras's Central Bus Stand, leaving every five minutes from 4:20am to about 10:20pm. The fare for the four-hour journey is about Rs 15 (50¢), and if you book in advance, there's a Rs 10 (33¢) reservation fee. There is frequent bus service also from Chidambaram, Coimbatore, Tiruchirappalli, Madurai, and Thanjuvar (Tanjore), and Villupuram to name a few.

If you're moving on from Pondicherry, remember that there are two bus stands, both on Maraimalai Adigal Salai: the **Municipal Bus Stand** and the **TTC Bus Stand;** the former receives all bus companies, the other only TTC. Make sure you are in the right place if you are taking a bus onward from here. The bus stands are generally frenetic, and you'll have to be very patient to find out what's what.

BY HIRED CAR A car and driver round-trip from Madras will cost a minimum of about Rs 1,000 ($33.33), not including the driver's overnight fee.

VISITOR INFORMATION

Before you begin your visit, you'll want to stop in at the **Tourism Information Bureau,** 19 Goubert Salai (Beach Road) (☎ 39497), open from 8:45am to 1pm, and 2 to 5:45pm, to get pamphlets and a map. This is also where you get **the Pondicherry Tourism and Transport Development Corporation** minibus tour to the ashram and around town and Auroville—there is a tour from 8am to 1pm, another from 2 to 6pm—for Rs 25 (83¢), provided a minimum of 10 people show up.

You will also want to call at **Auroville Information Centre,** 12 Nehru St. (☎ 25128), for information on visiting Auroville, and the **Ashram Reception Service, Main Building,** Rue de la Marine (☎ 24836), for programs at the ashram.

Getting Around

Auto rickshas are not metered; bargain for your fare before setting off. You can usually negotiate two hours of city sightseeing for about Rs 50 ($1.66). **City buses** are very cheap, 40 paise or so for a minimum fare. They will take you to all places of interest. With **cycle rickshas** haggle for your rate.

Vikram-Tempos (large auto rickshas) and **minibuses** ply fixed routes and charge on a point-to-point basis per stage, usually about Rs 1.50 (5¢). **Car and driver rentals** from PTDC run somewhere in the neighborhood of four hours/50 kilometers for Rs 200 ($6.66), Rs 400 ($11.40) for eight hours/100 kilometers. Before hiring a car, check out the **Pondicherry Union Territory Taxi Owners Association** fixed rates, listed on the bulletin board at the International Guest House and perhaps elsewhere, or call 38437.

WHAT TO SEE & DO

Sri Aurobindo Ashram

The heart and soul of Pondicherry is the Sri Aurobindo Ashram, focal point for pilgrims not only from India but from all parts of the world. It is an unusual ashram in the sense that its buildings are spread all over the town, and some of its businesses provide employment and services for other residents of Pondicherry. It includes, for example, its own laundry, perfumery, printing press, and travel agency, as well as a bakery, tailors, furniture factory, oil mill, and handmade paper workshop. The ashram also sponsors cultural and educational activities in the community.

In the Education Centre of the ashram, almost every evening you can go to a film, slide presentation, or lecture. Tourists, residents at the ashram, and local people can attend these programs, which are usually without charge. You might be asked for a donation, but you won't be hounded.

The founder of this movement, which combines the two disciplines of yoga and science, Sri Aurobindo, was born August 15, 1872, in Calcutta. Educated at Cambridge, he became a writer and revolutionary in the extremist wing of the Indian Independence Movement early in the century. Jailed by the British in 1908 for his involvement in a bomb plot, he studied yoga and meditation during his year in prison and by 1910 was in Pondicherry continuing his silent divinations and rejecting political overtures from the increasingly active independence parties. He died on December 5, 1950, but his philosophical essays, translated into many languages, influence and inspire many people today.

On the other hand, the woman who became known as the Mother of the Sri Aurobindo Religious Movement was born Mira Alfassa, in Paris, to wealthy parents of Egyptian ancestry. From her earliest days she was exposed to different spiritual and religious systems. In 1914 she accompanied her second husband, Paul Richard, a French diplomat, on a journey to India and had an audience with Sri Aurobindo. The meeting changed the course of Mira Richard's life.

She left India when World War I broke out, but returned, alone, six years later. When Sri Aurobindo went into seclusion in 1926, the Mother, as she was then called by all, took complete charge of the ashram and all activities, encouraging its economic independence. She remained as head of the ashram until her death, at age 95, on November 17, 1973. Nolini Kant Gupta, oldest disciple of Sri Aurobindo, succeeded the Mother.

All during the Mother's life, everyone connected with the ashram in any way, and many of the people in the town, regarded her with reverence. When problems or doubts arose, it was automatically assumed by all that the Mother could solve them.

Also a prolific writer, her widely translated essays have influenced people throughout the world. At her death, thousands of mourners streamed into the ashram to pay their final respects to this remarkable woman.

The samadhi (meditation place) of Sri Aurobindo and the Mother, in which their bodies are now entombed, is open to all visitors between 8am and 6pm daily. If there are enough visitors, the Reception Service in the ashram's main building (open from 8am to noon, and 2:30 to 5:30pm) at Rue de la Marine (☎ 24836) will arrange a conducted tour of the ashram any day but Sunday, darshan (blessing) days, and other special days. The tour starts at 8:45am, guided by a member of the reception staff, and lasts about three hours; it covers the highlights. The Mother's meditation chamber can be seen at 11:30am for 15 minutes, but only by appointment.

Meditation

To experience something of the spiritual side of Pondicherry, spend one evening (or more) attending collective meditation at Sri Aurobindo Ashram, Rue de la Marine (Monday through Wednesday, and Friday, 7:30 to 7:45pm). It takes place in the main building compound around the marble samadhi holding the remains of Aurobindo and the Mother. Arriving about 10 minutes before meditation permits you to join in offering incense and flowers as the others do upon entering the courtyard. When everyone is seated, the lights are switched off, and everything becomes so utterly still it's hard to believe you're in midtown Pondicherry. Sitting there and getting into a meditative state, something quite wonderful happens in this courtyard—momentarily you switch off the rickshas and passersby, and magically become serene. You have escaped completely the cares of the day.

Dolphin Watching

A very different experience is available nearby. On a backwater of the River Chunnamber (8 kilometers away) you'll find a boathouse where a variety of craft are for hire. From February on, the *Sea Queen* takes visitors cruising to see dolphins for Rs 350 ($11.66) per person. Go early in the morning. Book this tour through **Seagulls** restaurant.

Shopping

Anyone who loves food and spices will enjoy the **Pondicherry Market** off MG Road. It is liveliest on Mondays.

More conventional shopping might begin with a visit to **Kospalayam,** in the suburbs, or any of the town's handicraft emporia to purchase a Pduucheri bommai, one of the famous handcrafted dolls made of terra-cotta, papier-mâché, or plaster of paris. Some of the places in town to look for these are the government-run **Poompuhar,** 15 Nehru; **Co-optex,** 28 Nehru; and **Khadi** and **Village Industries,** 10 Amber Salai.

Pondicherry has some upscale boutiques selling the delightful wares of the ashram and Auroville craftspeople: marbled silk and hand-dyed fabrics, perfume, incense, handmade paper, hand-loom rugs and bedspreads, and pottery. Look for these at **Boutique d'Auroville, Harmonie Boutique, Ashram Exhibition Centre,** the **Handloom Centre, Aurocreation,** and **Auro-Tibetan Handicrafts.** Bronze and brass objects, wooden sculptures, and korai (mats woven from grass) are other items to buy.

Where to Stay

Doubles for Less Than Rs 300 ($10)

Many people who visit Pondicherry want to stay in one of the guest accommodations run by the Aurobindo Ashram, which is a wise choice. No alcohol or smoking are permitted on the premises, and kitchens are vegetarian. The doors close at 10:30pm, but there's usually a watchman to let you in later.

The best choice is **Park Guest House,** Goubert Salai (☎ 24412), with 80 small, neat, monastic rooms and dorms next to the town beach. These rent for Rs 200 ($6.66) with attached bath. Upstairs rooms have wonderful sea views. Vegetarian meals are available. The staff is very pleasant. It's very popular, so book in advance.

Cottage Guest House, Periarmudaliarchavadi (☎ 28434), 6 kilometers from town on the beach, offers rooms in cottages and a restaurant on a peaceful, palm-fringed beach. Bike rental is available on the premises for getting into town.

Two other ashram guest houses, Bureau Centrale (day rest house) and New Sweet Home, are generally not used by foreigners.

There are several other guest houses available in Pondicherry that are comparable in price.

International Guest House, Gingee Salai (☎ 26695), is a pretty, three-story modern building with a profusion of potted plants and 57 clean, simple rooms with attached Western-style bathrooms and fans overhead to stir the breezes. Expect to pay from Rs 50 ($1.66) to Rs 250 ($8.33) for a double, the highest price for an AC room in the new wing. There is no restaurant. International is popular; advance reservations advised.

Other places to stay include the **Aristo Guest House,** 50-A Mission St., Pondicherry 605001 (☎ 26728). It's clean, has a friendly management, and is one flight up off the street. Some rooms have AC. They are priced from Rs 70 (($2.33) to Rs 90 ($3).

Ajantha Guest House, 22 Goubert Salai (Beach Road) Pondicherry 605001 (☎ 28927), has tidy rooms, some with terrific sea views, all with attached bathrooms (some with Indian-style toilets). Rooms range in price from Rs 200 ($6.66) to Rs 250 ($8.33). There's an AC restaurant and an open-air roof garden (where service is snail paced when it's crowded).

Wallpaper and linoleum cover the walls of the 523-room **Ram International,** 212 West Blvd. (☎ 27230). Rooms have attached bathrooms with either Western- or Indian-style toilets. Non-AC rooms have no frills. Rooms need paint jobs, but are otherwise okay. Non-AC rooms range in price from Rs 80 ($2.66) for a single, to Rs 115 ($3.83) for a double; for AC rooms, expect to pay Rs 140 ($4.66) to Rs 190 ($6.33).

The **Government Tourist Home,** Uppalam Road (☎ 226376 or 26378), is right behind the railroad station (turn right, then right again, and walk across the tracks). It's a modern, three-story building in its own small compound, with airy balconies and 45 rooms—eight with AC—all fairly clean and simple. Rooms come complete with fans and bathrooms. Rooms are priced at Rs 20 (66¢) for a non-AC single, Rs 30 ($1) for a non-AC double; expect to pay Rs 45 ($1.50) for an AC room. Neighboring it is the **Excursion Centre** with dorms for groups. There's a dining room.

The **Tourist Home Annex,** Indra Nagar (☎ 26145), in the suburbs near the hospital, has 12 fairly clean doubles (one with AC) with balconies overlooking a palm grove. There is a small canteen for simple meals.

Doubles for Less Than Rs 600 ($20)

Newish but in need of TLC, **Hotel Surguru,** 104 Sardar Vallabhai Patel Salai (☎ 39022), has a mirror-studded ceiling at reception and gleaming marble floors. The 57 rooms, some non-AC, are furnished in simple, light woods but need better maintenance. An AC single is Rs 220 ($7.33), a double from Rs 380 ($12.66) to

Rs 430 ($14.33). Much nicer is the hotel's AC **Arugraha** restaurant with a wide range of vegetarian dishes, including tandooris. Thalis are Rs 22 (73¢) to Rs 40 ($1.33). It is open from 7 to 11am, 11:30am to 3:30pm, and 4 to 10pm (for snacks), 6 to 10pm dinner.

Doubles for Less Than Rs 1,500 ($50)

Anandha Inn, S.V. Patel Road (☎ 30711; fax 31241), with 70 centrally air-conditioned rooms, has an upscale, big-city ambience. The spacious lobby has Raj sofas and a huge wall mural showing the tableau of Jesus in an 18th-century setting with plenty of chubby angels overhead. The standard rooms handle king-sized beds, brocade chairs, and tasteful printed fabrics for spreads and drapes. Deluxe rooms have minirefrigerators and tubs in addition to showers. Expect to pay Rs 600 ($20) for a standard single, Rs 750 ($25) for a standard double; deluxe doubles are Rs 850 ($28.33). There are two restaurants: **Surabi** is South Indian vegetarian; **L'Heritage** is a dressy, multicuisine restaurant, with elegant ambience and French, Indian, Chinese, and Continental cuisines and taped Bach to eat by.

Hotel Pondicherry Ashok, Chinakalapet (☎ 85460), has sleek, modern decor and is located on a lonely strip of beach 12 kilometers from town. Centrally air-conditioned, all rooms face the sea. A single is Rs 950 ($31.66), a double Rs 1,150 (($38.33); off-season, the same rooms go for Rs 700 ($23.33) or Rs 800 ($26.66). The usual three cuisines—Indian, Chinese, and Continental—parade to the table. The best meal is an abundant thali. Location can be a drawback if you like to roam around town. (Cars here cost Rs 50 ($1.66) per hour plus Rs 1 per kilometer and must be telephoned in advance.)

On the same long strip of beach **Mass Classique Beach Resort** has cottage-style accommodations, which were under renovation during my last visit; rates were not yet set. The restaurant was operating, featuring a French menu with such bistro classics as coq au vin and poulet estragon, as well as a few Chinese dishes and fresh spinach noodles. Entrees top off at Rs 70 ($2.33).

Youth Hostel

The most dramatic sea views and sunsets can be seen from the roof of the Kuppam **Youth Hostel,** Solaithandavan (☎ 23495), north of the city, 5 kilometers from the bus stand and railway station. There are 56 beds in six dorms for Rs 25 (83¢) per person. Sheets are provided. There is a restaurant where a vegetarian thali costs about Rs 10 (33¢).

Where to Eat

Very pleasant and popular is the **Hotel** (meaning restaurant) **Aristo,** 36/E Nehru St. (☎ 6728), run by the Aristo Guest House. Both the roof garden and indoor restaurant serve well-prepared, decently priced food in Indian, Chinese, and Western styles. Rs 20 (66¢) is the average price for a main dish.

Bon Ami, 224 Rue St. Louis (☎ 24457), serves an array of nonvegetarian foods in the same price range as Aristo (closed Tuesday).

From the rooftop of the bistro-ish **Rendezvous,** 30 Rue Suffren Louis (☎ 39132), you can feel the pleasant night breezes. During the day when it's hot, you can also dine indoors in the white-walled restaurant. Friendly owners Jessica and Vincent Mathias serve a lobster and mushroom quiche, pizzas, a host of fish dishes, an array of vegetarian foods, and delicious fresh fruit juices, too. Entrées top off around Rs 80 ($2.66). It is open from 8:30am to 3pm, and 6pm to midnight.

Satsanga/La Table Francaise, 13 Rus Lal Bahadur Shastri, in a lovely old colonial building with ceiling beams indoors and a tiled verandah, offers French cuisine such as steak au poivre, soups, and salads. Prices range from Rs 50 ($1.66) to Rs 80 ($2.66). Order wine in advance. Hours are from noon to 2pm, and 7 to 10pm.

27 St. Louis St. (☎ 38598), at its epynonymous address, opposite the Governors Building, is a vest-pocket sized AC restaurant with red checked tablecloths and tandoori specialties, including a mixed plate of tandoori items for Rs 80 ($2.66), about the highest price on the menu. Cochin curry is another dish. The restaurant is open daily from 11:30am to 3pm, and 6:30 to 11pm.

Seagull's off Goubert Avenue (☎ 23627), is near the Park Guest House and overlooks the new pier. The terrace is pleasant, the indoors stuffy, and the waiters huffy. The menu features the usual dishes in Continental, Indian, and Chinese styles. Hours are 10am to 10pm.

Oceanic, 112 Lal Bahadur Shastri, is a cool, air-conditioned oasis that serves fish plus the usual Indian, Continental, and Chinese dishes. The highest entrée price is around Rs 50 ($1.66) for something from the tandoor. It is open daily from 9am to 3pm, and 6 to 11pm.

Blue Dragon, 30 Rue Dumas, dishes up the usual Cantonese Chinese dishes amid attractive antiques.

For simple vegetarian meals prepared from freshest possible ingredients, nothing beats the **Ashram Dining Room,** north of Government Place. You must buy tickets for three meals at Park Guest House.

For cheap snacks such as toast and jam and dosas all day long, try the **Indian Coffee House,** 41 Nehru St. For the cheapest thali in town, head to the **Youth Hostel.**

For a splurge meal, it's the stylish, air-conditioned **L'Heritage** restaurant at Anandha Inn (S. V. Patel Road), or the veg **Surabi** in the same hotel. For an upscale vegetarian meal there's also the air-conditioned **Arugraha** in Hotel Surguru (104 Sardar Vallabhai).

PONDICHERRY AFTER DARK

Ratna Talkies shows **English-language films,** as do some other theaters. There are **bars** at most of the tonier hotels. **Alliance Francaise (Goubert Salai)** stages occasional French cultural programs, including films.

AN EXCURSION TO AUROVILLE

To carry its experiment in international harmony further, the Sri Aurobindo Ashram, during the Mother's lifetime, conceived the idea of an international city in which people from all races and nationalities could live and work together. The new city, Auroville ("City of Dawn"), was greatly hailed in 1968 at its ground-breaking. The president of India and dignitaries from around the world attended and brought soil for an urn to symbolize the city's high ideals of harmony. From the initial dedication ceremony, you can see today the crater-shaped amphitheater with a lotus center containing the earth from the 125 countries participating in the inauguration festivities.

GETTING TO & AROUND AUROVILLE

The first thing to do is to stop at **La Boutique d'Auroville** on J. Nehru Street in Pondicherry, to get advice on visiting. You can also join a conducted tour here three times a week and get information on where to rent bikes or hire taxis or rickshas. The PTC's tour gives good coverage of Auroville as well as Pondicherry (see "Guided Tours" under "What to See and Do," above).

Whatever transport you use to get to Aurovillle, keep it while you're looking around; the distances are too great to cover on foot, and you'll need some way to return. You can bike out and back, but keep in mind that there are miles of unpaved roads that can be hard to navigate over the beautiful rural setting—hard for a good biker in good shape. You can also motorbike, but the ruts in the unpaved roads also make it a risk (helmets in Pondicherry are rare).

For **bike rentals,** several shops on Gingee Salai in Pondicherry, including **Jaypal Cycle Store,** charge about Rs 15 (50¢) to Rs 20 (66¢) for a day, plus a refundable deposit of Rs 200 ($6.66). Some shops have **motorbikes** at Rs 80 ($2.66) to 100 ($3.33) for a day, plus a substantial refundable deposit. The asking price for an **auto ricksha** is usually Rs 200 ($6.66) round-trip, but you can probably settle for Rs 150 ($5), including waiting charges. A **taxi** round-trip to Auroville is supposed to cost Rs 400 ($13.33), according to the fixed rates posted by the Pondicherry Union Territory Taxi Owners Association.

ABOUT AUROVILLE

In the original design (seen at the settlement's "Auromodel") by French architect Roger Anger, the 800-acre city spirals out from a center core into five main zones: Work, Dwelling, Education, Society, and the World. While there was to be light industry, Auroville has remained as envisioned—in close contact with nature, with plentiful fruit orchards and other food crops—now seen along with a blend of modern architectural styles.

As the first settlers came from France, England, the Netherlands, and North America, funds were contributed to the community by the central and state governments and by UNESCO. Work then began on the "soul of Auroville," the golden spherical Matrimandir ("concentration" hall—beyond the usual meditation and symbolizing the birth of the new consciousness) and continues today, along with agriculture, energy, and other developmental projects. Visitors to the Matrimandir must request a pass 24 hours in advance at the Matrimandir reception. Passes can be picked up at 3:15pm the day of the visit, which takes place from 4pm and 5pm. Complete silence is required; cameras, bags, and shoes are left outside. For more information, call 2268 from 9am to noon.

From the beginning, the settlers faced considerable challenges, a lack of energy resources and soil erosion major among them. To solve the most formidable problems, they constructed windmills and a solar reflector for energy, and planted more than a million trees on 2,000 acres as a land-reclamation project. Giant steps since then have been taken to set up such essential services as schools and a health center to satisfy the needs of the residents living in the settlement. Contributing to further self-sufficiency are successful, income-producing ventures in the computer sciences and handicrafts. The well-designed handicrafts are sold in La Boutiques in Auroville and Pondicherry and shops in the major cities of India. (**La Boutique d'Auroville** in Bhara Nivas is open from 9am to 1pm and 3 to 5:30pm.) Presently, the city, which was to have housed 50,000, has about 1,000 residents living in more than 50 communities sprawled across 50 square kilometers and remains in a largely unfinished state. But no one who visits can fail to be impressed by how much has been accomplished over the years.

Much of the delay in development can be traced to the long conflict that began soon after the Mother's death in 1973, pitting the Sri Aurobindo Society and Auroville's residents against each other in a battle for control of the new community. The society claimed it owned the land and therefore the town on it; and indeed it did control the funds, which it often delayed and eventually refused to transfer to

Auroville. Thus work had to be severely curtailed and ultimately stopped for a while. It has resumed again.

The people in Auroville, recalling the Mother's word, insisted that Auroville was a "city of the world, belonging to everyone." The society continued its attack by charging that drug abuse (actually, drugs and alcohol are not permitted) and promiscuous sex at Auroville vilified the Mother's ideals. To this the Aurovillians counterattacked by accusing the society of misusing funds intended for the new city. When word of the wrangling spread around, fundraising efforts—and therefore outside funds—greatly declined.

Despite the conflict's escalation, the Aurovillians managed to get by for a time by pooling their resources and doing some successful outside fundraising. But ultimately the situation between the two factions grew so grave that in 1976, the ambassadors of the United States, France, and Germany stepped in to provide food and supplies to the residents. Soon after this occurrence, the central government took over Auroville temporarily, and today it is calm and peaceful again. The residents continue to be determined to achieve success for their idealistic experiment, whatever the future holds.

STAYING AT AUROVILLE

Some residents will take in guests for fees of Rs 35 ($1.16) to Rs 150 ($5) per person per day. Reservations should be made in advance by writing the Auroville Guest Program, Auroville 605104, Kottakuppam, India (☎ 413862248). Mention whether you require a host who speaks English. A list of accommodations is available in Auroville and the Auroville Visitors Centre (near Bharat Nivas) or the La Boutique d'Auroville, 12 Nehru St. (west of the canal) in Pondicherry.

EATING IN AUROVILLE

There's a **food store** (open from 10am to noon) at Auroville where you can buy cardamom-scented tea, lassi, lemon juice for lemonade sweetened as you wish, homemade macaroons, and other biscuits. The **kitchen,** open from 1 to 2pm, feeds residents primarily, and occasionally five or six visitors—but don't count on it. If you plan to be out here a while, you might want to bring some fruit or other foods to nibble on. Be sure to dispose of all garbage in an appropriate fashion in a waste bin, or take it out with you.

On the outskirts of Auroville is **New Creation Cafe,** open from 8am to 1pm, and 2 to 6pm. It is spotlessly clean and offers snacks, soft drinks, and excellent local mineral water. *Note:* Pondicherry's mineral water is one of the few in India from a mineral spring rather than created in a purification plant. It's also delicious.

2 Chidambaram

From Pondicherry, a 65-kilometer (40-mile) coastline drive south takes you back in time to a temple begun in the 9th century and built over hundreds of years at Chidambaram. This town (population 69,000) is one of Tamil Nadu's great holy places.

ESSENTIALS

GETTING TO CHIDAMBARAM

BY BUS Private and government **buses** operate frequently from the **Central Bus Stand** in Pondicherry for a 1½-hour ride. There are also buses from Madras, Cuddalore, and elsewhere.

BY TRAIN Chidambaram is 232 kilometers from Madras and lies on the Madras-Tiruchirapalli main line of Southern Railways. Trains to the South connect with Tiruchirapalli, Madurai, and other cities, and to the North to Madras and Bangalore, to name only two. There are no direct connections to Pondicherry; you have to take the meter-gauge train to Villapuram and connect there to a Chidambaram-bound train from there.

VISITOR INFORMATION

The **Tamilnadu Tourist Office** is next to the Tamilnadu Hotel on Station Road (☎ 2939). It is open from 10am to 1:30pm, and 2 to 5:30pm, closed Saturday and Sunday.

GETTING AROUND

Auto rickshas are available, but you must bargain. From the Hotel Tamilnadu, expect to pay about Rs 10 (3¢) to the bus station and Rs 8 (27¢) to the temple. **Bikes** can be rented from shops in town for about Rs 10 (33¢) a day, but, again, bargain.

FESTIVALS

Of several festivals, the most memorable for visitors is the **Natyanjali Festival,** dedicated to the Cosmic Dancer, which is held annually during February through March. Dancers perform at the Natraja Temple. Another festival is **Uthiram Festival,** March and April, in which devotees skewer themselves in ritual thanksgiving for answered prayers.

WHAT TO SEE & DO

The huge **Natraja Temple** has enormous impact on visitors. It covers 32 acres of land stretching between two rivers, and has a tank measuring 315 feet by 170 feet. Two of the temple's four 160-foot-high gopurams—which face north, south, east, west—are covered with carved figures showing the 108 poses of Indian classical dance. Indeed, the temple is dedicated to Shiva as the Cosmic Dancer. The east gopuram (entrance for visitors) is the oldest, constructed in 1250; the north gopuram rose between 1509 and 1530.

Within the temple are five halls surrounded by high walls. Two of these are roofed with a total of 21,600 golden tiles, *each tile* said to be worth Rs 2,500 ($83.33) today; the halls make up the main sanctum. In one, the *Kanaka Sabha,* is the Natraja statue, cast of five metals, depicting Shiva as the Cosmic Dancer. In two of his hands are the insignia of his diverse powers: the drum of creation and the flame of destruction. His left leg is raised and his right foot rests on a dwarflike figure to represent stamping out illusions. The other hall, *Chita Sabha,* houses the presiding deity of the temple, representative of air, one of the five elements and known as "Akasa Lingam." There is no idol in this sanctum, the absence of which symbolizes that God exists in open space.

Of the other memorable halls, *Rajah Sabha,* built between 1585 and 1685, is the hall of 1,000 (actually 999) pillars, 340 feet long and 190 feet wide. This was the site of victory ceremonies held by the Pandyas, Cholas, and other rulers who helped build the temple. The most beautiful hall, *Nritta Sabha,* resembles a chariot drawn by horses and has 56 pillars sculpted with dance motifs that some art historians believe are the most elegant and graceful dance figures in all South India. Lately, this hall has been used again, as in ancient times, for dancing during Natyanjali, the February-March festival dedicated to the Cosmic Dancer. Ask about it if your visit is during these months.

In the temple are shrines to Parvarti (look for ceiling murals depicting a cure for leprosy and a plan of temple) and Subramanya. Ganesha also has a shrine, said to be the largest to the elephant-head deity in India. There's a temple to Vishnu as well, where he reclines on a bed of snakes. Nandi, Shiva's mount, waits patiently in the courtyard, peering toward his lord and master.

The temple hours vary with holidays and other celebrations, but generally the main shrine is open from 5am to noon, and 4 to 10pm. Subshrines are open from 5 to 8pm. The best time to visit is during any of the six daily pujas, when the temple reverberates with drums and chanting and smells sweetly of sandalwood paste and floral offerings.

Temple etiquette and notes: Shoes are removed; be sure to take small bills and coins with you. No authorized guides are allowed inside. The temple is full of Brahmin priests (at least one even willing to take a visitor on a fascinating tour for a small fee, set in advance), and every time you step up to a shrine, someone will put holy ashes on your forehead and ask for sizable donation. This can be both puzzling and annoying, but less so if you know the temple has never had landed benefactors. It belongs to a local sect of Brahmins who support it by asking alms in the communities and from visitors.

The tiny **Thillai Kali temple** at the northern end of town was built in the 13th century by a Chola king, Kopperunjingan. The best time to visit is for the 4pm puja, in which you will be allowed to participate. Hours are 9am to 1pm, and 3 to 6pm. Offer the priest a few rupees.

WHERE TO STAY & EAT

The pleasant, government-operated **Hotel Tamilnadu,** Station Road, Chidambaram 608001 (☎ 20056-60), needs better maintenance but has warmth and friendliness. Non-AC singles and doubles cost Rs 100 ($3.33) to Rs 160 ($5.33), and AC rooms are Rs 300 ($10). All have Western bathrooms attached. There's an 18-bed dorm, for Rs 30 ($1) per person, with a common bath and toilet. The restaurant serves simple but adequate meals. A big breakfast costs Rs 38 ($1.26).

P. M. Lodge, 15 S. Sanathi, is fairly clean. Some top-floor rooms have good views of the temple; others are dark. Rooms cost Rs 33 ($1.10) to Rs 60 ($2) with Indian-style bathrooms.

The **Star Lodging Complex,** 101-102 S. Car St.(☎ 2743), is made up of both a lodge and a restaurant. The lodge has simple, no-nonsense, clean rooms for Rs 150 ($5) double. The cheerful, crowded **Star Restaurant,** with striped walls and pink marble tabletops, serves excellent vegetarian food—worth a visit while you're in town. It's Rs 12 (40¢) for a vegetarian thali.

Ramanathan Mansions, 127 Bazar St., has simple rooms, with baths attached, in a quiet area of town, away from the temple.

3 Kumbakonam

At any time you might see a temple elephant lumbering along the road as you near the next destination, Kumbakonam, which is 75 kilometers (46 miles) from Chidambaram. This peaceful town at the juncture of the Cauvery and Asarlar rivers in Thajavur district is one of the oldest in South India. A busy, modern commercial center as well, the town has also held fast to its traditional side, as seen in the lovely copies of old jewelry displayed in shop windows.

GETTING TO KUMBAKONAM

BY TRAIN There are trains from Chidambaram, Thanjavur (Tanjore), and Madras. The Kumbakonam station is 2 kilometers from town. **From Chidambaram** (69 kilometers) the fare is Rs 210 ($7) AC First, Rs 22 (73¢) Second. **From Thanjavur (Tanjore)** (38 kilometers), the fare is Rs 169 ($5.63) AC First, and Rs 15 (50¢) Second; **from Tiruchirapalli** (24 kilometers), the fare is Rs 149 ($4.96) AC First, Rs 33 ($1.10) Second; **from Madras** (313 kilometers), the fare is Rs 721 ($24.03) AC First, Rs 84 ($2.80) Second.

BY BUS There is frequent TTC bus service from Madras, Chidambaram, Thanjavur (Tanjore), and Tiruchirappalli.

WHAT TO SEE & DO

Kumbakonam is known for its 18 temples. Four are immense and quite important: Nageswara Swami, Sarangapani, Kumbesware, and Ramaswamy.

Nageswara, circa 886, is oldest, but much altered over the years. Its namesake Natraja shrine resembles a chariot, a popular architectural metaphor in this region. There are some notable carvings on the exterior of the main shrine.

The largest gopuram, at **Sarangapani,** soars 147 feet high. Look closely at the intricate jewelry on the handsomely carved figures, and you'll see that it provides the inspiration for the pieces seen in the jewelry shop windows.

The approach to **Kumbheswara Temple,** the largest Shiva temple in Kumbakonam, is a wide avenue of shops thronged with shoppers and devotees. I was greeted by a great procession: Everything stopped when the temple gods, dressed in silks and jeweled finery and comfortably propped up on cushioned palanquins, were escorted by musicians sounding horns and drums as they took their charges out to call on gods at another temple, which was built mainly in the 17th century in the Nakayan style. Such spectacles are routine events.

Built in the same era, the **Ramaswamy** temple has some murals with Ramayana scenes and handsome horse sculptures.

Also famous here is the **Mahamaham Tank,** site of a festival every 12 years, when it is believed that the Ganges flows into it. Thousands of devotees flock here to bear witness, bathe, and wash away their sins. The last festival was in 1992.

All temples are closed from noon to 4:30pm, so plan accordingly.

WHERE TO STAY

Best is the recently opened **Hotel Athitya,** U-12 Thanjavur Main Road, Kumbakonam 612001 (☎ 217945), a white building with neat and tidy modern rooms, some with AC, and friendly, helpful manager S. Rajagopal, who goes out of the way to help foreign visitors. AC doubles are Rs 325 ($10.83), Rs 150 ($5) non-AC.

The pleasant **Hotel A. R. R.,** 21 T. S. R. (Big Street), Kumbakonam 612001 (☎ 21234), is painted in bright colors like the deities on South Indian temples. There are 46 rooms in all. The AC suite is Rs 360 ($12); other non-AC rooms start at Rs 150 ($5). See more than one room if you plan to stay here; they vary greatly. Walls throughout are unsightly, but management is friendly and nice. Good restaurant (see "Where to Eat").

WHERE TO EAT

Delicious vegetarian food in simple, clean, air-conditioned surroundings make the vegetarian restaurant at **Hotel Athitya** the most popular place in town. An abundant thali, served on a banana leaf, offers generous portions and unlimited refills.

An excellent buy for Rs 20 (66¢). Snacks and other dishes are served for breakfast, tea, and dinner.

INTERESTING TEMPLE EXCURSIONS FROM KUMBAKONAM (OR THANJAVUR)

The best way to enjoy these temples is to pack a picnic and some bottled water, strike a bargain with a taxi driver, and make one or two day trips, returning to stay at Kumabakoman. Alternatively, you can base in Thanjavur (see p. TK) and visit these temples, taking into account that the drives will be longer from there. If you have only a limited amount of time, the first temple and fourth on the list below are not to missed.

In Dharasuram, a modest village 5 kilometers (3 miles) south of Kumbakonam, is one of the three most important Chola Temples (others are Thanjavur, Gangakondai Cholapuram; see below). **Airvateswara** was built by Raja Chola II. Now restored and protected by the Department of Archeology, the granite temple has beautiful sculptures. If you can find the caretaker, he'll show you how the granite slabs on the temple sound like the seven different tones of Karnatic music and tell enchanting legends about the sculpture. The intricate carvings can also be appreciated on their own as works of artistry in stone. Almost the entire temple is so richly covered with carvings that it looks like a tapestry, but the northwest mandapa (porch), a dancing hall, is richest of all. There is a small museum. The temple is open from sunrise to sunset.

Swamimalai, located 6 kilometers (4 miles) west of Kumbakonam and dedicated to Lord Subramanya, marks the spot where he explained to Shiva the meaning of *Om,* which precedes all Hindu prayers. The temple is at an elevation about 100 feet. Visitors are permitted to join the pilgrims in making pujas (prayer ceremonies). Sculptors here are famous for their metal statues of deities.

Tirubuvanam, 8 kilometers (5 miles) from Kumbakonam, another Chola temple at Kampahareswara is dedicated to Shiva and dates from the 13th century. This village is an important silk-weaving center.

Gangaikondacholapuram, 32 kilometers ($19^{1}/_{2}$ miles) north of Kumbakonam, was constructed in the 13th century by Rajendra Chola, son of Raja Chola and builder of the Brihadeshwara temple at Thanjavur (Tanjore). Here, he strove to build a bigger and better copy of it. Its tower is visible for miles around. The temple has beautiful inscriptions and sculptures, but it is far less restored than the more famous Brihadeshwara Temple. Be sure and see the Ganesha shrine at the southwest corner before you leave.

4 Thanjavur (Tanjore)

A quiet, romantic refuge almost at the delta of the Cauvery River, the pleasant town of Thanjavur (Tanjore) had its glory days during the reign of the late Chola kings from the 10th to the 14th centuries, when it was a noted center of learning and culture. In the Thanjavur district are some of South India's most celebrated temples built by the Cholas, including the foregoing and others.

Thanjavur (pop. 200,200) is known today as the "rice bowl" of Tamil Nadu, and historically income from Thanjavur's fertile paddies financed the initial Chola building sprees. They were later supplemented with funds derived through a flourishing trade with China. Later dynasties, the Nayaks and Marathas, ruled from the vast palace, which today is a library and museum, and a playground for birds enjoying games of hide and seek in the vaulted halls.

Not only rice, but fertile fields of sugar cane and bananas surround Thanjavur and fill the entire district, which is best visited in winter. In January, throngs arrive for the music festival in the village of Thiruvaiyaru, 7 miles away, which celebrates the anniversary of one of South India's greatest composers, Saint Thyagaraja, at the Thyagarajaswami Temple, a place of great importance for devotees of Karnatic music.

ESSENTIALS

GETTING TO THANJAVUR

BY TRAIN There are 13 trains daily between Tiruchirapalli and Thanjavur (52 kilometers) from 4am to 10:30pm; fares are Rs 169 ($5.63) First, Rs 17 (56¢) Second. Thanjavur is also served by the Madras-Tiruchirapalli meter-gauge line, along with Madurai; to the trip to Madras (340 kilometers) takes about 8¾ to 9½ hours, depending on the train, and costs Rs 636 ($21.20) AC First, Rs 50 ($1.66) Second.

BY BUS Buses from Tiruchirapalli leave every five minutes to Thanjavur, for Rs 5.50 (18¢) for a trip of about an hour through the famous southern rice paddies. Buses also depart every 10 minutes from Kumbakonam for the hour-long trip. You can also go from Madras via Pondicherry, an eight-hour trip; from Madras via Villapuram takes nine hours.

GETTING AROUND

Taxis are not metered and are few and far between; the same goes for **auto rickshas.** You must bargain for your fare before you get in. Also, if you do find a taxi, keep it while sightseeing as you may not get another. A **tourist taxi** charges about Rs 2 (10¢) per kilometer, but they're not easy to find here either. **Buses** can take you to most points of interest.

VISITOR INFORMATION

The **Tamilnadu Tourist Office** is in Shop 3, adjacent the Tamilnadu Hotel; it is open from 8 to 11am, and 4 to 8pm.

WHAT TO SEE & DO

Soaring from the flat South Indian plains is the 13-tiered tower of the **Brihadeshwara (or Brahadeeswara) Temple,** built by the Chola emperor Rajaraja the Great in the first decade of the 11th century. Polychromed brightly in the 16th century, the temple has now been restored to its natural reddish color (thanks to sun, rain, extreme age, and loving care on the part of archaeological experts). The temple is open from 6am to noon, and 4 to 8:30pm. The main shrine houses a huge lingam and some ancient sculptures and frescoes. These Chola wall paintings were uncovered only around 300 years ago when layers of paint the Nayaks applied were stripped away. You can get close enough to see the 13-foot-high lingam, measuring 54 feet around its massive base and 26 feet around the top, covered with silver and floral offerings—Rs 5 (17¢) is usually given to the priest. The doors on each side of the sanctum lead to the frescoes. However, their reproductions are on view in the little museum in the temple complex, along with explanations of the Archeological Survey of India's conservation program. Inscriptions on the walls of the temple document gifts by patrons to local peasants, who helped care for the temple.

Note: Should you want to try to get rare permission to see the real frescoes, write to the Archeological Survey of India, Fort St. George, Madras 600001, far in advance of your visit with an excellent reason for wanting to see them. No groups are allowed.

To get the full impact of the Brihadeshwara Temple, take a few minutes to sit outdoors on a stone ledge at one of the entrances. Then let the breezes restore you as you take time to contemplate the great glory of this remarkable architectural work.

You can wander freely (barefooted, please) in the courtyard after entering through a 90-foot-high gopuram guarded by two huge, striking statues of dwarapalakas (doorkeepers).

Commanding the courtyard, facing the shrine, sits a huge image of Nandi, Shiva's sacred mount, almost 13 feet high and 16 feet long, all carved from a single block of granite, the second largest Nandi in India (the first is at Mysore). Anointed daily for centuries by the pious, the effigy now gleams as if it were made of bronze. The figures in the friezes on the pavilion are believed to be from the 16th century.

Shiva's bull sits patiently in front of the vimana, its 216-foot-high, geometric-shaped tower crowned with an invisible tympanic plate of granite (80 tons) under the dome. The Cholas, inventive engineers, had their workers push this huge plate and dome slowly into place along an inclined ramp (as the Egyptians did with the Pyramids), which began in a village 4 miles away—a distance four times the length of the Golden Gate Bridge. They also placed it so it never casts a shadow on the ground.

Northeast of the temple is the **Palace**—with an entry charge of Rs 2 (6¢), an extra charge for cameras—on a street that used to run through the Great Fort. It is a vast structure built mainly by the Nayaks in 1550. One of the buildings, the former armory, is 190 feet high and was used until 1885 as a military lookout. In the palace is a research and reference **library,** where there are more than 30,000 valuable, painted palm-leaf and paper manuscripts in Indian and European languages. The library is open from 10am to 1pm, and 2 to 5pm (closed Wednesdays). The expansive **Darbar Hall** (closed Thursday) is acoustically perfect.

But all other palace sights pale in comparison with the small **Raja Chola Art Gallery** (open daily, except national holidays), full of choice sculptures—113 in granite and 250 in bronze, dating from the 9th to the 12th centuries. Some of the best pieces in the collection were salvaged from village fields where they were abandoned when old temples fell to ruin. An excellent book, written some time ago by the gallery's most knowledgeable staff member, which you can purchase in the gallery, can give you details. Hours are 9am to 1pm, and 3 to 6pm (closed Fridays).

To the western side of the art gallery is the **Royal Museum** with exhibits of apparel and household appointments. There is an admission charge of Rs 2 (6¢)

Nearby is **Tamil University,** established in 1981, with a collection of coins and old musical instruments, The university is engaged in the research and advanced study in Tamil.

East of the palace is **Schwarz Church,** honoring Danish missionary C. V. Schwarz, and built in 1779 by Rajah Serfoji to commemorate their friendship. A fine relief of marble figures depicts the missionary's death.

WHERE TO STAY

The following two hotels have the usual amenities, such as attached bathrooms; they also have room telephones, televisions, conference facilities, and accept international credit cards.

DOUBLES FOR LESS THAN RS 400 ($13.33)

The **Hotel Tamilnadu,** Unit 1, Gandhi Road, Thanjavur 613001 (☎ 21421), framed by a bright mural and set in a small garden surrounded by big trees, has

32 clean rooms with attached bathrooms— Indian-style downstairs and Western-style upstairs. Most rooms have balconies; all have big ceiling fans; a few have AC. They start at Rs 100 ($3.33) for a non-AC single to Rs 400 ($13.33) for an AC double. The restaurant serves both vegetarian and nonvegetarian meals.

The **Hotel Tamilnadu,** Unit 2, Trichy Road, Thanjavur 613001 (☎ 20365), is clean but too far out of town, and few people stay here. Rates are Rs 70 ($4) single, Rs 90 ($5.15) double.

Ashoka Lodge, 93 Abraham Pandither St., Thanjavur 613001 (☎ 20021), in a pink, ochre, green, and blue building, has very helpful management and 75 tidy rooms, the best of which are upstairs. Ask to see a room or two before settling in. Cheapest rooms share a bath. Rooms with baths attached range from Rs 77 ($2.56) for a non-AC single to about Rs 400 ($13.33) for an AC double. This place is very popular.

Doubles for Less Than Rs 1,500 ($50)

Tops in town, the **Hotel Parisutham,** 55 G. A. Canal Rd., Thanjavur 603001 (☎ 21601; fax 22318), has a waterfall at the entrance, an antique grandfather clock in the lobby, gleaming marble floors, and beautiful plants inside and out from its own nursery. The 48 neat, efficient, cheerful rooms and two suites have printed spreads and drapes. AC doubles are about Rs 1,500 ($50), singles Rs 1,200 ($40). Restaurants, a 24-hour coffee shop, and poolside barbecues welcome guests and nonguests. (See "Where to Eat," below.) The palm-shaded swimming pool has a bar at the shallow end.

Hotel Oriental Towers, 2889 Srinivasam Pillai Rd., Thanjavur 603001 (☎ 24724; fax 22770), with 160 rooms, looked promising as finishing touches were being put in place. New, sleek, and modern, the hotel is centrally air-conditioned. Rooms range in price from $32 for a single to $42 for a double. There will also be two restaurants, a shopping arcade, health club, and 24-hour coffee shop.

WHERE TO EAT

The air-conditioned restaurants in the **Hotel Parisutham** are recommended for a special meal: a delicious vegetarian thali, with unlimited refills, featuring about 10 little dishes plus chapati, papad, rice, and coconut cake for Rs 50 ($1.66). There's also a non-veg version for Rs 125 ($4.16) and many à la carte dishes.

The restaurants at **Oriental Towers** looked promising as they prepared to open. The simple **Padma Hotel** (the Padma Restaurant), on Gandhi Road opposite the Hotel Tamilnadu, is clean and cheap for tasty vegetarian foods.

SHOPPING

Thanjavur craftsmen excel in unusual metalwork that combines burnished copper, brass, and gleaming silver into all kinds of objects—trays, plates, bowls, and boxes. Bell metal is another process for making figures and small decorative objects. Thanjavur paintings (the genuine antiques are rare, but there are some convincing copies) make heavy use of gold leaf and fake or real gems while depicting various deities in a stylized way. Local silks are lovely, lustrous, and heavy—six yards would be enough for a long dress or sari. Other items are papier-mâché dolls, objects made from unhusked paddy and sandalwood paste, and musical instruments such as the veena, the latter quite a challenge to get home. For a survey, see **Poompuhar,** the government emporium on Gandhiji Road, a few steps from the Hotel Tamilnadu and the shops in **Gandhiji Road Bazaar.**

5 Tiruchirapalli (Trichy)

The overwhelming thing about Trichy (pop. 711,100) is the centuries-old Rock Fort that looms almost 300 feet overhead and completely dominates the city. Characteristic views of Trichy show the fort with the Cauvery River in the foreground, but actually most of the city sprawls over the crowded streets behind.

Artificial diamonds are manufactured locally, and the region is also known for its cigars, glass bangles, hand-loomed cloth, and toys made from wood and clay.

Winter is the best time to visit, especially during the three-day harvest festival in January, when cows and bullocks are painted and decorated. An interesting pilgrimage takes place nearby in December, when visitors from all over India stream to the temple on Srirangam Island, three miles upriver.

ESSENTIALS

GETTING TO TRICHY

BY PLANE The airport is 7 kilometers from city. **Indian Airlines** flights connect this city with Madras, for $34; and Madurai, for $16. For confirming ongoing plane tickets, Indian Airlines is on 4A Dindigul Rd. (☎ 41433; at the airport ☎ 27563).

BY TRAIN Trichy is a major junction on the Southern Railway. Meter-gauge trains connect Trichy to Madras, Thanjavur, and Madurai as well as Rameswarum. Broad-gauge trains connect Trichy with Bangalore, Coimbatore, Udhagamandalam (Ooty), Cochin, and Kanya Kumari.

From Madras, the *Pandhyan Express*—six hours, 37 kilometers (205 miles)—costs Rs 636 ($21.20), AC First, Rs 76 ($2.53) Second. **From Madurai,** the *Vaigai Express*—2½ hours, 155 kilometers (94 miles)—costs Rs 342 ($11.40) First, Rs 77 ($2.56) Second. **From Pudukkottai,** the *Madras-Rameswaram Express*—one hour, 55 kilometers (33 miles)—costs Rs 197 ($6.56) AC First, Rs 18 (6¢) Second. These are only a few examples.

BY BUS From Madras, buses take about eight hours and go via Villupuram, Sivaganga, or Eral for fares under Rs 60 ($2) by government bus, Rs 75 ($2.50) deluxe. The bus from Thanjavur to Trichy costs Rs 5.50 (18¢); from Villupuram to Trichy, Rs 24.50 (82¢); from Madurai to Trichy, Rs 30 ($1), to name just a few of the connections.

GETTING AROUND

Taxis are unmetered. Bargain to get a fair fare; bargain also for auto rickshas; expect to pay Rs 30 ($1) to the Fort; Rs 48 ($1.58) to Sangam; Rs 40 ($1.32) to Jambukaswaram. South India Travel Agency, Sangam Hotel (☎ 40685), is a friendly, experienced travel agency that can help you with car-driver rentals and other aspects of getting around or out of town.

VISITOR INFORMATION

After stopping at the TTDC Tourist Office (☎ 40136) next to the Hotel Tamilnadu, Cantonment, for pamphlets and a map, step across the street to the bus stand and grab bus no. 1, which departs frequently to stops near the main monuments. You can also board this bus at the railway station.

FESTIVALS

Target the last week of December and first week of January for **Mohini Alangaram, Vaikunta Ekadasi, Garuda Sevai,** the **Flower Festival,** and the **Car Festival** all at

Srirangam. During March and April, the **float festival** is held at Teppakkulam; in April, Samayapuram Mariamman Temple has a **Poorchoirthal** festival.

WHAT TO SEE & DO

Artificial diamonds made locally, bangles, and other souvenirs are best sought in the **Big Bazaar,** around the section called **Woriyar,** or at stalls near the **Srirangam Island Temple.** The tourist office can probably arrange for you to visit a local cigar factory (there are several) or an artificial diamond factory.

The major sightseeing attraction, of course, is the **Rock Fort**—open from 6am to 9pm; entry is 50 paise; camera fees are Rs 10 (33¢) to Rs 50 ($1.66). You must climb barefoot (434 steps), and it is advisable to make the climb early in the day or late in afternoon for the spectacular sunset. The view from the top is worth the climb even though the various shrines are barred to non-Hindus.

Local historians are somewhat vague as to the fort's origin, although it is believed the Pallavas first built a temple at the rock's base more than 1,200 years ago. Until 1772, when it was almost destroyed by an explosion, there was a hall containing 1,000 pillars near the main entrance.

Once at the top, you can step out and see the views: **Srirangam Temple** and the Cauvery River, a mere trickle to the North, except during the rainy season; the modern suburb of **Golden Rock,** to the South, where the French were defeated in a celebrated 18th-century battle; and to the East and North, respectively, the **Green Hills** and the 4,000-foot mountain called **Kollimalai.** Be sure to see the cave temples constructed at its base by the Pallavas 1,200 years ago.

Near the foot of the fort is the **Teppakulam,** or sacred tank, with a pavilion in the center of it. Southeast is a house in which Clive is supposed to have stayed, now part of **St. Joseph's College;** northwest is **Christ Church,** built by a Danish missionary in the 18th century. Stop at the **museum** on Bharatayir Road for an interesting display of sculpture and other artifacts, and walk along the Cauvery to see the **funeral ghats,** turning off at A. Mandapam Road for a visit to the **Heritage Art Emporium,** among the most interesting places in Trichy to shop (see "Shopping," below).

Srirangam Island, 3 miles upriver, is attached to the mainland by a bridge with 32 arches. The water surrounding the island is considered holy. The 11th-century Chola kings built a great stone dam, 1,000 feet long and 60 feet wide, which still sends sacred streams through a series of canals to irrigate the fields.

About 1 mile from the bridge is the 17th-century **Ranganathaswamy Temple** (open from 7am to noon, and 4 to 8pm), dedicated to Vishnu. The temple is almost a town in itself, most of the houses tucked within the mile-long walls of the three outer enclosures. The main entrance, 48 feet high, is tall enough to admit a multistoried temple cart. Before entering the fourth enclosure to see the temple, you must check your shoes (tip 25 paise when you pick them up) and pay a camera fee from Rs 10 (33¢) to Rs 50 ($1.66), the latter for a movie camera. Then stop at the temple's rudimentary museum and buy a ticket for Rs 2 (6¢). This will permit you to climb a flight of stairs—a guide will show you where to go and unlock the gate—so you can stand on a landing and get a panoramic view of the surrounding countryside and see soaring gopurams at close range. You must make this climb before 5:45pm; otherwise, the temple is open from 6:15am to 1pm, and from 3 to 8:45pm.

In the temple under a golden-roofed sanctum, a bejeweled, beautifully groomed Vishnu lies resting on his bed of serpents. Who could be more deserving of relaxation? Remember it was Vishnu who saved the world from the demons who had defeated the gods. Perhaps he is resting in preparation for some puja when he undoubtedly will be dressed in his best and taken in a procession to see and be seen. Thousands of people turn out for such a spectacle in December and January, during Vaikunta Ekadasi festival.

Ranganathaswamy Temple is said to date from the Ramayana. In the 1600s, King Achutharaya, to commemorate a victory over a Chera king, began work on a seventh tower to crown the outermost gateway, but he died before it could be completed. The tower was not finished until 1987, so it is a contemporary addition. And what a tower it is! Standing 236 feet high with 13 richly decorated tiers, it is said to be the tallest temple tower in all of Asia.

Like a number of other temples, this one has a 1,000-pillared hall, and through it is a porch supported by handsomely carved rearing horse pillars, not found in such artistry elsewhere. Look closely at the figures and you will see a Portuguese soldier spearing a Nyack; approved guides can be found in the temple, and they will be happy to show you the "magic sculpture," which is either an elephant or a bull, depending how you look at it. While in the fourth enclosure courtyard, see the small shrine to Krishna with his faithful graceful gopis (milkmaids), one of whom is depicted applying a tilak (dot) to her forehead.

Before you leave, visit the temple elephant that undoubtedly will be surrounded by adoring fans offering cookies and sweets. For Rs 1, she'll raise her trunk to touch your head in a gentle blessing.

Farther Afield

About 7 kilometers (11 miles) away is Tiruvanaikaval, where there is a Shiva temple, **Jambukeswaram,** which has a lingam almost completely submerged in water from an underground spring. The name is derived from a legend that an elephant once worshipped Shiva under the Jambu tree here. The temple is surrounded by four walls and has several gopurams. Beautiful sculptures of birds, flowers, monkeys, and almost every living thing are to be seen on the structure—but, unfortunately, you won't see the submerged lingam in the inner sanctum, which only Hindus can enter. Open from 6am to 1pm, 4 to 9:30pm.

Shopping

Khadi Kraft, opposite the railway station, and **Poompuhar,** near Main Guard Gate, are sources for brassware and silks; and also try the shops in **Big Bazaar Street,** near the Srirangam Temple, for brass and other items. For imaginative jewelry and other rare pieces, try **Heritage Art Emporium,** 5 A. Mandapam Rd. (near the Cauvery). If nothing in stock appeals, the owner, Pandian, will make something to order for you. Shopping for your future? There are many palm readers in Trichy to help you; their English may be limited, however.

Where to Stay

Unless otherwise indicated, hotels below have attached bathrooms, telephones, and televisions in rooms, and accept international credit cards.

Western-Style Hotels

Doubles for Less Than Rs 250 ($8.33)

Hotel Tamilnadu, Unit 2, Race Course Road (☎ 23498), is inconveniently located away from town. The four double rooms need much TLC. Unless it's renovated, go here only if everyplace else is booked.

Midland Lodge, 20 MacDonald's Rd., Cantonment (☎ 23911), is basic. **Hotel Kanchana Boarding and Lodging,** 13 Williams Rd., Tiruchirapalli 620001 (☎ 40473), has 13 simple doubles and two restaurants—veg and non-veg.

Doubles for Less Than Rs 800 ($26.67)

At **Ramyas Hotels,** 13-D/2 Williams Rd., Tiruchirapalli 620001 (☎ 41128; fax 42750), every room has a little verandah. A single goes for Rs 350 ($11.66), a double for Rs 425 ($14.16), a deluxe room for Rs 550 (($18.33). There are both vegetarian and non-vegetarian restaurants as well as an ice cream parlor. This is a convenient location near the bus stand and train station.

Painted in lemon, beige, pink, and green pastels like some of the South Indian temples, the **Hotel Aristo,** 2 Dindigul Rd., Tiruchirapalli 620001 (☎ 41818), is a modern, Western-style hotel with 23 rooms, some non-AC. Best are the seven stone cottages in the garden, each with AC and special decor; the honeymoon cottage has a round bed surrounded by mirrors; another, "Mogul Maison" is especially spacious. For the cottages, rates are Rs 225 ($7.50) single, Rs 325 ($10.83) double; room rates range from Rs 75 ($2.50) for a non-AC single to Rs 200 ($6.66) for an AC double. Eat in the garden or the indoor restaurant.

Clean, with a streamlined modern look, the 66-room **Hotel Gajapriya,** 2 Royal Rd., Cantonment, Tiruchirapalli 620001 (☎ 32400), has pleasant rooms, some non-AC. Expect to pay Rs 375 (($12.50) for a double. There are veg and non-veg restaurants.

Run by the Tamil Nadu Travel Development Corporation, the **Hotel Tamilnadu,** Unit 1, Cantonment, Tiruchirapalli 620001 (☎ 40383), has 36 pleasant, functionally furnished rooms and would benefit from better maintenance. You'll pay about Rs 400 ($13.33) for a double.

Doubles for Less Than Rs 1,500 ($50)

At **Jenney's Residency,** 3/14 MacDonald's Rd., Tiruchirapalli 620001 (☎ 41301; fax 42584), the reception and lobby glow with crystal chandeliers and mirrored columns. Have a seat on a red plush chair or settee. Swim in the pool, or pump iron in the health club. Quieter decor prevails in the 72 rooms, and some of the 12 suites with pearlized furniture seem suitable for a movie star. Service is smooth and swift. Rates are Rs 550 (($18.33) for a single, Rs 700 ($23.33) to Rs 750 ($25) for a double. The hotel's vegetarian and Chinese restaurants are recommended for good meals. There is a disco.

The 60 rooms at **Hotel Sangam,** Collectors Road, Tiruchirapalli 620001 (☎ 44700; fax 41779), have modern furniture without much personality. Maintenance could be better, management more professional. Overall, a so-so three-star hotel. Doubles are quoted in U.S. currency at around $45. Swimming pool, restaurant, bar.

Indian-Style Hotels

Doubles for Less Than Rs 900 ($30)

The best choice is the 116-room **Femina Hotel,** 14-C Williams Rd., Tiruchirapalli 620001 (☎ 41551), with balconies in every room, some with Rock Fort views, and a swimming pool and vegetarian restaurant, which features South and North Indian and Continental selections. Upscale and well-run, with AC doubles for around Rs 600 ($20). Some rooms are non-AC. Street noise can be a problem.

At the **Abbirami Hotel,** 10 MacDonalds Rd., Tiruchirapalli 620001 (☎ 460001; fax 42584), non-AC rooms are neat, clean, and priced at Rs 220 (($7.33) double; double rooms with AC have settees with bolsters suitable for relaxing on; some glitzy rooms have bedside mirrors! Prices for AC rooms are Rs 290 ($9.66) single, Rs 340 ($11.33) double; Rs 390 ($13) to Rs 450 ($15) deluxe. There is a vegetarian restaurant.

Clean, but small, the rooms at **Hotel Aanand,** No. 1 Racquet Court Lane, Tiruchirapalli, 620001 (☎ 40545), could do with less furniture in them. Some rooms are non-AC. Prices range from Rs 150 ($5) to Rs 210 ($7) without AC, from Rs 300 ($10) to Rs 330 ($11) with AC vegetarian restaurant, ice cream parlor. Convenient location near bus and train stations.

WHERE TO EAT

At Jenney's Residency, **The Peaks of Kunlun** has Chinese characters and silk scrolls to set scene for well-prepared Chinese food. Rs 50 ($1.66) is an average entrée price. Hours are 12:15 to 2:30pm, and 7:15 to 11:30pm. In the same hotel, **Suvai** is a sleek, modern vegetarian restaurant.

At **Abbirami Hotels,** a vegetarian thali costs only Rs 15 (50¢). **Vasanta Bhavan,** near the Rock Fort and opposite the Tourist Office, serve tiffin (snacks), such as crispy, delicious dosa, as well as thalis.

EXCURSIONS FROM TRICHY

The byways between Trichy and Madurai are an archeological treasure trove. I have space here for only a few highlights.

Kodumbalur is 42 kilometers (26 miles) south of Trichy. At the 38-kilometer stone go left, and left again at a huge figure of Nandi, to the **Muchukundeswara Temple,** from an early Chola period. You are a short walk from **Muvacoil,** where there are two Chola shrines with magnificent sculptured figures in fairly good condition, although time and the weather have taken their toll. Adjacent is a small museum of recently excavated objects, which you can see if the attendant is on duty—unfortunately a rare occurrence.

Continuing the journey south of Trichy, about 58 kilometers (36 miles) north of Pudukkottai is **Sittannavasal,** a fascinating Jain hideout from the 2nd century B.C. The attendant is stationed near the trees below the monument, and he'll accompany you to the caves, which are up 245 steps over the rocky terrain, tufted with lemon grass but otherwise as barren as the moon. Once at the caves, sit in their shade, enjoy the view, and see what remains of some ancient wall paintings.

Pudukkottai is a town with a long history interwoven with the usual South Indian cast of characters—the Pandayas, Cholas, and Pallavas, to name a few leading players. The modern town, originally a fort, has some old buildings, such as the palace, but most interesting to you will be the small museum housing displays about the area. On sale in the museum is a *Guide to the Important Monuments in and Around Pudukkottai;* at Rs 30 ($1) it is an indispensable reference for any travelers interested in South India's long history as chronicled in temple architecture.

While in Pudukkottai, there's a clean little **cafe** near the Vashanta Lodge (itself not worth bothering about) for coffee and dosas.

Tirumayam, 21 kilometers (13 miles) from Pudukkottai toward Madurai, is a fort-temple dating from the 12th and 13th centuries with many interesting shrines and an adjoining fort, part of which is well preserved.

HOW TO GET TO THE TEMPLES

Getting to any of the above is not the easiest thing in the world (unless you splurge on a taxi), but the truly dedicated can manage by taking the bus from Trichy to see Kodumbalur and Muvacoil; then doubling back to Trichy and getting a bus to Pudukkottai.

From Pudukkottai, a bus can take you close to Sittannavasal, but you must ask the driver to make the stop. From here, you can get buses to Muvacoil that go back to Trichy, or you can return to Pudukkottai and get a bus either to Trichy or farther south to Madurai, making a stop en route to see Tirumayam. Be sure to ask for directions about taking the buses, and make note of their numbers, as the schedules are in Tamil. Bus connections may keep you waiting around, but I discovered no clean lodges or hotels en route for overnighting or even relaxing for a while with the exception of the cafe at Pudukkottai (described above).

6 Madurai

The second-largest city in Tamil Nadu, Madurai (pop. 1.09 million) is at an inland location almost equidistant between the east and west coasts and the southern tip of India. It is an important textile center and an interesting city in its own right, with several special attractions, including a museum devoted to Gandhi and one of the most incredible—and probably the largest—temples in India.

ESSENTIALS

GETTING TO MADURAI

BY PLANE **Indian Airlines** links Madurai to Trichy, Madras, and Bombay. Daily nonstop flights **from Madras** ($46) take about 50 minutes, **from Trichy** ($16) about 30 minutes, and from Bombay ($128) about two hours (the plane stops in Coimbatore).

East-West's daily flight connects Madurai with Bombay and Trivandrum (Tiruvanathanpuram). **From Bombay** ($124) it is about 70 minutes, from Trivandrum (Tiruvanathapuram) ($29) about 50 minutes. The airport-to-city **Pandyan Roadways** coach transfer costs Rs 25 (83¢) per person and stops at Pandyan, the Madurai Ashok Hotel, the Tamil Nadu II Hotel, and the Indian Airlines office. Taxis and auto rickshas are also available.

Indian Airlines office is located in the United Building, 7-A West Veli St. (☎ 37234), open from 10am to 1pm, and 2 to 5pm. **East West** has an office at 119 West Perumal Maistry St., First Floor (☎ 22795; airport ☎ 37433).

BY TRAIN Trains from Madras include the *Vaigai Express* (491 kilometers, 7¾ hours); the *Pearl City* (11 hours); and the *Pandyan Express* (10½ hours); fares are Rs 890 ($29.66), AC First, Rs 138 ($3.60) Second. The *Pandyan Express* also stops in Trichy (155 kilometers), departing at 3am, arriving Madurai at 6:15am. Another possibility is the *Nellai Express,* departing Trichy at 1:25am and arriving in Madurai at 4:40am. The fares are Rs 342 ($11.40) AC First, Rs 41 ($1.36) Second. There are other possible trains.

BY BUS Madrai is well connected on busy bus lines. **From Madras** (450 kilometers), more than 30 **TTC** buses daily depart, with an ordinary fare of Rs 67.50 ($2.25); semideluxe Rs 78.50 ($2.61); superdeluxe Rs 88.50 ($2.95). **From Pondicherry** (340 kilometers), there are four semideluxe buses with a fare of Rs 51 ($1.70). **From Trichy** (103 kilometers), the fare is Rs 24.20 (81¢). **From Bangalore** (451 kilometers), the fare is Rs 71.50 ($2.38). **From Mysore** (via Ooty) (450 kilometers), the fare is Rs 95 ($3.16) to name a few popular routes. Buses **to Kodaikanal** depart from 4:45am–4:55pm, and the fare is about Rs 17.50 (58¢). Be sure to get there early in peak season, from April to July.

There are four bus stations in Madurai: **TTC Bus Stand** (☎ 25354)—also at this stand are **PRC** (Private Bus Companies) (☎ 35293); **Arapalayam Bus Stand**—RMTC buses (☎ 603740); and **Palankantham Bus Stand** (☎ 600935). All are centrally located on West Veli Street; **Anna Bus Stand** (☎ 43622) is 3 kilometers from town.

Visitor Information

Whether you arrive by plane or train or bus, you will find a **Government Tourist Information Centre** ready and willing to serve you—at the airport; the railway station (☎ 33888), open from 7am to 8pm (government holidays from 7 to 10:30am, and 5 to 8pm); and near the Central Bus Stand in the **Tourist Office** in the Hotel Tamilnadu Complex on West Veli St. (☎ 34757)—this is the main office, open from 10am to 5pm, closed Saturdays, Sundays, and government holidays. The offices have a useful brochure incorporating a map. The tourist office is well stocked with brochures and well staffed with knowledgeable helpful people.

Shree Meenakshi Tours, 97 Vakil New Street Madurai (☎ 39339), is a knowledgeable, friendly, local travel agent who can help with car rentals or other mechanics of getting around or out of town.

Getting Around

If you're staying in the center of town, you can walk to Meenakshi Temple and Tirumali Nayak Mahal. Otherwise, **Bus** nos. 1 and 2 go to the Gandhi Museum and nos. 4 and 4A go to Mariamman Theppakulam. Bus 44 goes out to Alagarkoil Road, where two top hotels are located.

Both **taxis** and **auto rickshas** have meters, but, like baby shoes in the West, they are strictly decorative. Instead you set your fare before you get in. For auto rickshas figure on something like Rs 25 ((83¢) to Rs 50 ($1.66) for 5 kilometers; and Rs 100 ($3.33) for taxis. Taxis on a daily basis cost about Rs 275 ($9.16), plus the Rs 2 to Rs 2.25 (7¢) per running kilometer. **Cycle rickshas** charge something like Rs 8 (27¢) to Rs 10 (33¢) per kilometer. Some samples: A cycle ricksha to Meenakshi Temple, Vishnu Temple, Tirumali Nayak Mahal, and Handloom House runs about Rs 40 ($1.33).

Special Events & Festivals

There's a one-hour, daily **son et lumière** show at the Tirumala Nayak Palace at 6:45pm in English, at 8pm in Tamil. Tickets cost Rs 2 (6¢) to Rs 5 (17¢). Tickets on sale 15 minutes before the performances.

Pongal, a January harvest festival, is marked in various places throughout the South. But unique in Madurai at this time is the **Jallikatu**—a bullfight with a big difference. For this contest the bulls get all primped up, their horns polished and painted and pointed, to be pursued by bullfighters who catch the animal, tame it, and claim the cash reward tied to its razor-sharp horns.

The **Float festival,** at the Teppakulam Tank in January or February, is when the deities are treated to a trip around the tank on a raft decorated with flowers and little lights. The most important festival is **Chitirai,** celebrated for 10 days in March and April, and marked with many processions that celebrate the marriage of the goddess Meenakshi to Lord Sundereswarar.

What to See & Do

Despite its size, Madurai is in some ways a small town, as are almost all cities in southern India, with most of the action in the streets. Here and there you'll see men and women stretching the brightly dyed threads that eventually go into some of Madurai's beautiful saris (this industry supports almost half the local population), and judging by the bright colors seen on the local women, many of these saris never leave the town where they are made.

The city was founded more than 2,500 years ago and is by far the most famous and most ancient home of the Tamil culture. To Hindus it is a holy place, and thousands of them flock from all over India to visit the fantastic **Meenakshi Temple,** whose present form dates from the reign of the Nayak kings in the early 16th century. The temple occupies a vast plot of land in the center of the old part of town, south of the River Vaigai. Its major masterpieces are four vast, terraced gopurams (towers), each more than 150 feet high and ornately decorated all the way to the top with stair after stair of brightly colored statues and carvings. There are many smaller gopurams dotted around the temple grounds. The tallest gopuram (the one on the south, at 160 feet), has a series of interior stairs that open into smaller and smaller chambers, all leading eventually to a narrow trap door on the roof—and a fantastic, dizzying view of the surrounding countryside. At the time of my last visit, unfortunately, climbing was no longer permitted.

Down below, in the center of the temple, a shallow tank is the magnet for pilgrims bent on immersing themselves in the holy water. All around are worshippers carrying bowls of coconuts and flowers; a ceaseless chatter ascends to the recently repainted psychedelic ceilings aglow with eye-popping mandalas and those historical/mythical scenes of which Hindus are so fond. Many of the visitors, their foreheads caked with white ash, gather excitedly around what looks like a cashier's cage, waiting to participate in the numerous weddings that are always taking place under the immense stone pillars. A cage full of green parrots adds to the clamor. Demure young girls in gold-threaded saris restrain their younger sisters, who gaze curiously at the random non-Hindu strangers, who must stop short at the entrance to the inner temple. The entrance hall leading to the tank bears brightly painted murals of age-old scenes, beside which ever-enterprising vendors offer bangles and cheap toys. There are flower vendors and incense peddlers—a bustling bazaar inside the temple itself.

To the rear of the temple is what is known as the **One Thousand Pillar Hall,** now turned into a museum open from 7am to 7:30pm for an entry fee of Rs 1 (3¢). Originally the perspective, looking past the pillars, was one of geometrical intrigue, but today cases of photos and relics interrupt the natural lines. On closer inspection, however, many of the exhibits turn out to be quite fascinating—for example, the colored pictures of goddesses, each with full breasts and four hands holding symbolic objects. There are paintings of old Tamilian ships with animal-shaped prows; elephant-headed figures (Lord Ganesh) sitting on dragon-type lions; delicate wire sculptures demonstrating lotus postures; and intriguing charts explaining "Life in Colors" (black equals malice; lilac stands for fear; pure blue indicates pure religious feeling; orange means pride; fuchsia, pure affection; light violet equals love for humanity; light green stands for sympathy). Another display is devoted to rituals. The consecration of a temple, it explains, requires 64 different rites, the first of which is to pour—into the first hole that is dug—liquid from the seven seas (symbolized by brine, water, milk, curd, ghee, cane juice, and honey). One particular section emphasizes the contribution the Tamil race has made to the world. There are samples of spices (smell), pepper (taste), peacock feathers and pearls (sight), and hand looms (touch).

Despite the hall's name, it is alleged, there are only 997 pillars. But all are different, and the ones just to the left of the museum exit are even more so. If tapped with a stick they respond with musical notes.

The temple is open every day from 5am to 12:30pm. At 4pm the temple reopens and stays open until 9:30pm, on Friday until 10:30pm. ***Note:*** Don't pay the fee to climb the South Tower; this has not been permitted for some years and probably never will be again. In the One Thousand Pillar Hall you must pay an Rs 1 (3¢) entrance fee and an extra Rs 5 (17¢) photography fee if you plan to take a camera inside. You'll need a flash for inside photography here (no video cameras are permitted).

You should also return to the temple at night between 9 and 10pm for the centuries-old ceremony that gives Westerners a rare glimpse of Indian religious life. This rite signals the time when Shiva leaves his chamber to spend the night with his wife, Parvati, in her chamber. It happens almost every night, although it's not confirmed in advance. (Get there about 8:30pm. You'll see other people near Shiva's sanctum waiting for the ceremony to begin.)

A crash of cymbals and blaring of horns announces the procession that forms around the concealed Shiva held aloft in a jewel-encrusted silver litter on the shoulders of dhoti-draped priests. Other priests stir the incense-filled air with giant peacock-feather fans. A stop is made to anoint the litter's step with sandalwood paste in preparation for Shiva's feet. Then the cortege passes by to music that seems loud enough to wake all the gods in the world before it disappears through the shadowy corridors leading to Parvati's room. Shiva goes back to his room at 5am, when there's another similar ceremony. If, on rare occasion Shiva doesn't go out to see Parvati, the temple is always abuzz with fascinating activity to make your evening visit worthwhile.

A few blocks southeast of the Meenakshi Temple is what remains of the **Tirumali Nayak Mahal,** a palace constructed in 1636 in the Indo-Saracenic style by one of the Nayak kings who ruled Madurai for almost 200 years; this king built a succession of fortifications, dams, aqueducts, and the celebrated Meenakshi Temple itself.

European writers of that era compared Tirumala's Nayak Mahal with the ancient monument of Thebes. Although much of it was destroyed late in the 17th century by Tirumala's grandson, who recycled some of it to build himself a palace at Tiruchirappalli, there still survives today an enormous roofed arcade supported by 40-foot-high stone pillars elaborately carved and painted. Griffins, lions, gargoyles, and other monsters can be seen everywhere. The most memorable sight is the Swarga Visalam, once the audience hall; its dome was a remarkable engineering feat for the time, rising to a height of 200 meters without support of any kind. The covered arcade encloses an enormous, sandy courtyard, in the center of which is a small garden.

Today the palace is a protected monument and museum. It's open from 9am to 1pm, and 2 to 5pm; the entry fee is Rs 1 (3¢) per person. The small museum focuses on Madurai vis-à-vis the Nayak kings and their art and architecture. There's a **son et lumière** show here in the evenings (see "Special Events" under "Essentials," above). The palace is a 10- or 15-minute stroll from Meenakshi Temple, or squeeze onto the crowded no. 17 or 17A buses.

There are many traces of the late Mahatma Gandhi all over India, but here in Madurai, at the **Gandhi Memorial Museum and Library,** it is possible to study Gandhi's life in all its facets. Opened by India's late great prime minister Nehru in 1959, the museum, ensconced in 300-year-old **Mangammal Palace,** is open every day except Wednesday from 9am to 1pm, and 2 to 5:30pm. To get there, take bus nos. 1, 2 or 3 from the train station—they run every 15 minutes—or a taxi, which costs about Rs 60 ($2) from anywhere in town. The museum contains room after room of touching mementos of Gandhi's life—a white woolen shawl, a pair of rimless glasses, an eating bowl—as well as innumerable letters he wrote to world-famous figures who influenced him (Tolstoy) or whom he hoped to influence (Hitler, FDR). He was never averse to fighting for anybody who needed help, even to the extent of sending letters to schoolteachers pleading for mercy for students who had been barred from school for taking part in the fight for independence. One of his most famous sayings was: "In my opinion noncooperation with evil is as much a duty as is cooperation with good."

Sharing the same compound is the **Government Museum,** open 10am to 1pm, and 2 to 5pm (closed Fridays), which has archaeological exhibits. Admission is free.

Mariamman Theppakulam (5 kilometers from Meenakshi Temple), built in 1636, is a tank with a shrine in the middle; it's most famous for the Floating Festival held here in January and February. Take bus no. 4 or 4A from the train or bus station.

Sights Nearby

At **Kochadai,** a few miles south of the city, the fat, ferocious-looking village deity lives in a park surrounded by smaller deities and a rearing horse. The more famous **Thiruparankundram** is 8 kilometers (5 miles) south of Madurai and the site of a temple to Subramanya (also Subramnian). Behind it is an ancient rock-cut temple, particularly beautiful at sunset when peacocks strut their stuff. (Take bus no. 5 to both these sights, or take an auto ricksha and keep it for the return.)

On the **River Vagai,** west of Madurai near Vandiyoor, is the oft-overlooked **Nayak-era mandapam**, supported by 24 pillars. It's in rather dilapidated condition but looks pretty good for its 400 years.

Yanai-Malai (Elephant-Rock) is located on the Trichy-Madurai road right outside the city. Indeed, it looks like a seated pachyderm. You can admire the formation in passing or climb to the top; start early before the sun gets too hot; wear sturdy, rubber-soled shoes. It becomes evident, after you run out of well-worn rock cut stairs, that you are in nontenderfoot territory—on a steep, stepless path. If the climb hasn't already taken your breath away, the view from the top will. Have your own seat on the elephant's rocky back.

SHOPPING

Look especially for textiles (cotton, silks, Sungudi saris, embroideries), jewelry, wood, stone carvings, brass deities, and wooden toys. Many shops are in and around the temple, where you can get small souvenirs or an entire outfit made to order. Opposite the Eastern Tower of the Meenakshi Temple are hundreds of tailors in a huge hall ready, willing and able to stitch up a salwar kamiz or something more western in a few hours. They'll supply the fabrics, or you can bring your own. Also look for stores on Town Hall Road and Avanimoola Street.

Beautiful, hand-loomed textiles can be found at many stores, including **Co-optex,** a group of shops at South Chithirai and West Tower streets; **Handloom House,** on East Veli Street; and **Sri Bhagyalakshmi Silks** on South Avanimoola Street.

For handicrafts, try **Poompuhar,** West Veli Street. You can also find handicrafts at **Madurai Gallery,** at Cottage Expo Crafts, 19 North Chithrai St., where you'll find interesting jewelry and accessories—an amber-lapis necklace for Rs 6,001 ($200), emeralds at Rs 12,000 ($400) per karat; silk scarves for Rs 150 ($5) to Rs 850 ($28.33). The store offers customers and browsers a rooftop view of the famous golden dome of the Meenaskshi Temple. Ask before going up.

Cottage Industries Exposition, a privately owned company, has high-priced, good-quality merchandise, at 142-44 Netaji Rd., near the temple. Handicrafts, jewelry, kurtas, and small statues are only a few of the items sold here. From the shop's roof you can get a terrific view of the temple, whether you buy or not—ask permission first. Open daily from 9am to 10pm.

WHERE TO STAY

Unless otherwise indicated, the hotels below have attached bathrooms, room phones, TVs and all kinds of services from room service to laundry. In the upper price ranges, they accept international credit cards and have money-changing permits.

DOUBLES FOR LESS THAN RS 250 ($8.33)

Lack of maintenance is a problem on most of the following hotels. Some manage to be run-down yet remain clean. They are not for fussy travelers. Room telephones, TVs, and money-changing permits are no longer de rigueur.

Hotel Keerthi Pvt. Ltd., 40 West Perumal Maistry St., Madurai 625001 (☎ 31501), is very modest and in need of fresh paint; but the bedding is clean. Bathrooms are dark. Some rooms have AC—Rs 408 ($16) (with tax) for a double. With its shortcomings, this is still a cut above others in this price range.

Hotel International, 46 W. Perumal Maistry St., Madurai 625001 (☎ 31552), has 35 acceptable, non-AC rooms in need of a paint job, all of which open off balcony corridors. But imagine a deluxe double for Rs 201 ($6.70). Good location close to the bus and railway stations and the Meenakshi Temple. There's 24-hour room service but no restaurant.

Indian-style **New College House,** Town Hall Road, Madurai 625001 (☎ 24311), was built years ago as housing for Madurai College students. The 193 down-at-the-heels rooms are clean, spare, and very popular with young backpackers. Some AC rooms have telephones and Western-style plumbing. Rates are Rs 312 ($10.40) for an AC double, Rs 138 ($4.60) for a non-AC double. The vine-covered building faces a cheerful, bustling courtyard, which can get to be noisy. Vegetarian food is recommended for the cheap thalis, about Rs 10 (33¢).

DOUBLES FOR LESS THAN RS 500 ($16.66)

A great view of the Meenakshi Temple from the upper floors is an attraction at the pleasant, friendly, 72-room **Hotel Aarathy,** 9 Perumalkol West Mada St., Madurai 625001 (☎ 31571). There's also a small temple across the street. Upstairs, where the views are best, there's no AC. There are overhead fans and breezy little balconies off the neat, simply furnished rooms. Lower down you lose the view but gain AC, where rates are Rs 250 ($8.33) single, Rs 350 ($11.66) double. Eat indoors in the restaurant or in the outdoor cafe. This is a good buy for the price

There are two **Hotel Tamilnadus** in Madurai, both run by the Tamil Nadu Tourism Development Corporation (TTDC). The first is on Alagarkoil Road (☎ 42465), where the well-appointed rooms are pretty decent and a good value: Doubles have AC, TVs, and balconies, all for Rs 350 ($11.66). The dining room serves Indian and Western foods. The location is 4 kilometers (2½ miles) from town.

At the **Hotel Tamilnadu,** on West Veli, Madurai (☎ 37470), there are similar rates and less distinctive decor. The AC rooms are in the best condition. Rates for rooms with AC range from Rs 250 ($8.33) single, to Rs 350 (($11.66) double. The restaurant serves both vegetarian and nonvegetarian foods. The location is a 10-minute walk from the station and the Meenakshi Temple.

Hotel Prem Nivas, 102 W. Perumal Maistry St. (☎ 37531), has a small lobby with a dome-shaped ceiling, light-wood reception counter, and ear-splitting tapes of Indian film music. Rooms are smallish and need TLC, but they are better than many others in this price range. The rate for an AC double is Rs 309 ($10.30). The tiled bathrooms have dark-green fixtures; half the toilets are Western, half Indian. Rooms open off a breezy hall. In the hotel's AC restaurant, a thali costs about Rs 18 (60¢).

TM Lodge, 50 W. Perumal Maistry St., Madurai 625001 (☎ 37481), has 55 small, fairly clean rooms on four floors. Eight AC doubles with attached, Western-style bathrooms are Rs 290 ($9.66), plus 20% tax. One of the better places in this price range.

Doubles for Less Than Rs 1,500 ($50)

The following hotels are air-conditioned and accept international credit cards.

ITDC's **Madurai Ashok,** Alagarkoil Road, Madurai 625002 (☎ 42531; fax 42530), surrounded by gardens, has 43 functionally furnished rooms; those facing the road are slightly larger, with crewel-print spreads and drapes; the others have solid color decor. You'll pay Rs 1,200 ($40) single, Rs 1,350 ($45) double. Maybe it's the heat, but a lack of energy pervades this place. There are a swimming pool, a bar, and a restaurant, which is open to non-residents.

Pandyan Hotel, Race Course, Madurai 625002 (☎ 42470; fax 42020), with 57 rooms, is sleek and modern. Halls need spiffing up, but the rooms look good with fresh paint jobs, print spreads, and tweed chairs. Works of art by local artists dress up the walls. You'll have temple views from rooms on the north side. Rates are Rs 1,000 ($33.33) single, Rs 1,200 ($40) double. Like the Ashok, this hotel is away from the center— 5 kilometers (3 miles) from the railway station and about the same distance from the shopping area. There's good food in the hotel's restaurant (see "Where to Eat," below).

Park Plaza, 114-115 West Perumal Maistry St., Maudurai 625001 (☎ 32112; fax 23654), has 55 rooms and stands out in its price range. You'll pay Rs 550 ($18.33) single, Rs 650 ($21.66) double for an AC room. The second floor is non-AC—a double here is Rs 325 ($10.83). The lobby is decorated with elaborate Diwali lamps, white wicker furniture, and modern murals; the smart uniforms on the staff and above average maintenance make a positive impression. (The loud, Western music does not.) Service is better than some higher priced places. You can see the Meenakshi Temples from the rooftop restaurant. There are also a bar, a boutique, and a book shop. The hotel is centrally located.

Nearby, the similarly priced **Hotel Supreme,** 110 West Perumal Maistry St., Madurai 625001 (☎ 36331; fax 36637), is another good buy. Here is a cozy lobby with comfortable chairs and a welcoming Diwali lamp. The 69 rooms (39 with AC) are clean and attractively furnished. Some have balconies. Economy rooms with AC are Rs 405 (($13.50) double. The Queen Suite, at Rs 1000 ($33.33), not only has a balcony and a temple view, but a plush red bed with a mirror to the side of it(!). From the rooftop restaurant eat a variety of vegetarian cuisine and enjoy the panoramic view.

Worth a Splurge

At Madurai's top choice, **Taj Garden Retreat,** Pasumalai Hill, Madurai 625004 (☎ 88256), some rooms are in what once was the elegant home of a wealthy British businessman. The extensive gardens, which house a swimming pool and tennis courts, are luxurious. In addition to the original main house and an annex, individual cottages make a total of 30 tastefully furnished rooms. Rooms range in price, from standard (doubles in the annex—$70 to $85) to old world (rooms in the original building—$80 to $85) to deluxe (the cottages, $100 to $115). There's a fine view of the city from here (you're 6 kilometers from the center). The kitchen, however, is ready and willing but not always able.

WHERE TO EAT

Typical South Indian dishes are tops in Madurai: Try idlis, dosa, vada, sambar, and chutney. Many restaurants ("hotels") are on Town Hall Road or West Masi Street.

Food is top quality, delicious, and decently priced at **New Arya Bhavan,** 241-A West Masai St. (☎ 345777). Downstairs, it is bustling and open to the street; upstairs there's air-conditioning. A local friend and I had tandoori roti, dal fry, paneer (cheese) chops with fresh lime, and soda and coffee for Rs 77 ($2.56) for two, plus a Rs 15 (5¢) AC charge. Another time, we returned for some of their famous sweets and South Indian coffee. Ask for Devendar Kumar Gupta or Surinder Kumar Gupta if you need help deciding on your menu. Anything you order will be good. Hours are 7am to 11pm. Arya Bhavan by Night, on E. Veli Street, is a rooftop restaurant, open from 4pm to 2am.

Inexpensive and tasty meals also can be found at the clean, simple **Ashok Bhavan,** TTC Bus Stand (☎ 27418), where a South Indian thali will cost around Rs 12 (40¢), and a North Indian thali about Rs 15 (50¢). Or drop in for a cup of delicious South Indian coffee and a snack—at about Rs 6 (2¢) each—for dosas and other delights. Hours are 5:30am to 11pm. Similar prices prevail at the **Hotel Aarathy,** 9 Perumalkoil West Mada St. (☎ 31571).

North Indian, non-veg is served in air-conditioned comfort at the dimly lit **Mahal,** 21 Town Rd. (☎ 33700), which serves the by-now familiar Indian, Chinese, and Continental dishes such as biryani, spring rolls, and boneless tandoori chicken, all well prepared. Top priced entrées are Rs 55 ($1.83). Hours are 7am to 11pm.

There are North Indian dishes on the non-veg menu at the **Taj Restaurant,** 10 Town Hall Rd. (☎ 37650) , named for the famous Agra monument. Mughali chicken is Rs 25 (83¢); the highest-priced dish is Rs 30 ($1) for prawns.

Among the most popular places for non-veg are the **Madurai Muniyandi Vilas Hotels** around the city; the food is prepared to local taste and can be spicy for timid palates. Just ask anyone for the nearest one; they're spread all over the city.

For a good veg meal plus a fine view, try either the rooftop restaurants at the **Hotel Park Plaza,** 114-115 West Perumal Maistry St. (☎ 32112), or **Hotel Supreme,** 110 West Perumal Maistry St. (☎ 33448). Pricey thalis run Rs 30 ($1), or order à la carte. Both serve only dinner.

The **Taj Garden Retreat** is where you can eat in a garden (buffet dinner and live dance music on weekends); the **Madurai Ashok** and **Pandyan Hotels** feature multicuisine menus in the upscale range. Pandyan's **Silver Spring,** with a waterfall and small canal, offers a daily lunch buffet of delicious dishes for Rs 125 ($4.16), a good buy. Address for both are given under "Where to Stay," above).

7 Kanniyakumari (Cape Comorin)

The multicolored sands of Kanniyakumari (Cape Comorin), according to Hindu legend, were formed when Kanya (an incarnation of Parvati), daughter of the king of the Himalayas, was stood up at the altar by Lord Shiva and angrily tossed the uneaten wedding feast into the waters, where it was transformed forever into the sands of brown, yellow, silver, orange, blue, purple, and russet. (Another legend is the gods sprinkled colored rice over the couple at their wedding and it was transformed into the Technicolor sands.) The sands aren't the only mind-blowing natural phenomena of the cape: Wait until you see the unforgettable sunrises and sunsets! And if you hit a full moon day, you will see the sunset and moonrise almost simultaneously.

Three bodies of water meet here at India's southernmost point—the Arabian Sea, the Indian Ocean, and the Bay of Bengal—and the tip of land has been famous among navigators for centuries. Ptolemy's maps mention it (as "Comaria Akron"), and Marco Polo also marked it on his charts. Today, Kanniyakumari (pop. 189,500) is revered by Hindus not only for the Kanniyakumari Temple, but by all Indians, and many others, for its Gandhi Mandapam (memorial).

ESSENTIALS

GETTING TO KANNIYAKUMARI

Although in Kanniyakumari is located in Tamil Nadu, it is only 86 kilometers (54 miles) from Thiruvananthapuram (Trivandrum) and most easily approached from Kerala's capital. Keep this in mind when planning your itinerary. Note also that there is a chronic shortage of train and bus seats to Kanniyakumari from Thiruvananthapuram, so book well in advance.

BY PLANE The nearest airport is in Thiruvananthapuram, 86 kilometers (54 miles) away.

BY TRAIN The journey can be made pleasantly and inexpensively by train **from Thiruvananthapuram.** There are three trains a day each way, taking 2½ hours in either direction. Take any of these express trains: *Him Sagar Express, Kanniyakumari-Bombay Express* or *Kanniyakumari-Banglore Express.* Fares are Rs 259 ($8.63) in AC First, Rs 25 (83¢) Second. **From Madras,** the *Him Sagar,* takes 24 hours; **from Bombay,** the *Kanniyakumari-Bombay Express* takes 47 hours.

BY BUS There are 11 buses a day from Thiruvananthapuram's Central Bus Station, Thampanoor, near the railway station in Thiruvananthapuram, between 4am and 9pm. You can also take a bus from the stand near the Ashok Beach Resort in Kovalam four times a day, at 6:45am, 9:50am, 1:45, and 6:40pm. The express bus fare is around Rs 55 ($1.83).

If you take the bus from Thiruvananthapuram and want to see Padmanabhapuram Palace (see "Thiruvananthapuram," in Chapter 14), you must board a bus that stops at Thircklay, then get off and walk 10 minutes to the palace, returning to get another bus. Check these arrangements carefully before you leave Thiruvananthapuram and find out which buses make this stop so you can continue if you break your journey.

If you go to Kanniyakumari from Madurai in Tamil Nadu, the 232-kilometer road trip takes about 4½ hours.

BY TAXI Taxis will take you to Kanniyakumari from Thiruvananthapuram or Kovalam, but set the rate before you get in and make sure your driver has a permit to cross into Tamil Nadu.

A GUIDED TOUR

The easiest way to see Kanniyakumari is **KTDC's** daily tour from Thiruvananthapuram, which leaves at 7:30am and returns at 9pm. The price is Rs 120 ($4) per person, excluding meals. For information and reservations, contact: KTDC Tourist Reception Centre, Thampanoor, Thiruvananthapuram 695001 (☎ 75031). (For information on other KTDC tours in and about Thiruvananthapuram, see Chapter 14, "Kerala.")

VISITOR INFORMATION

The **Government of Tamil Nadu Tourist Office,** Beach Road (☎ 71276), is available to serve you. There is also an **Information Centre** (at the Vivekanand Rock Memorial), Beach Road (☎ 71250).

Getting Around

You'll find taxis and cycle rickshas. Bargain for your fare.

WHAT TO SEE & DO

The **Kanniyakumari Temple** is built at the place where Parvati supposedly awaited Shiva. The goddess who guards India shores wears an unusually grand, faceted diamond nose stud, which is said to emit powerful rays that can cause ships to stray off course and crash on the rocks near the shore. So the temple's seaside door is closed and opened only on rare occasions. Hours are 4:30 to 11:30am, and 5:30 to 8:30pm. Non-Hindus cannot enter the inner sanctum. Men must wear dohtis. Shoes are, as always at temples, removed.

The **Gandhi Mandapam** (memorial) is a yellow structure trimmed with blue and encircled by a walkway that you can climb. From there, gaze into the waters into which the great statesman's ashes were cast after his cremation in 1948. Inside the memorial is a simple chamber, a black marble marker indicating the spot where the ashes rested. Above this marker is a minute hole in the ceiling, cleverly designed so that once a year, on Gandhi's birthday (Oct. 2), the midday sun casts one long beam on the marker.

Offshore, almost directly opposite the Gandhi Madapam, are the two rocks on which the 19th-century philosopher Vivekananda sat in meditation before he set sail to preach love and brotherhood to Americans. It took 500 workers to build the **memorial dedicated to Vivekananda** that stands on the site and is a structure of ancient and modern inspiration, incorporating a variety of Indian regional styles; it houses a statue of the Vivekananda. A mammoth statue of the poet-philosopher Thiruvalluvar was also erected on this site recently. Hours for the memorial are 7 to 11am, and 2 to 5pm. Entry is Rs 3(10¢); the ferry Rs 5 (17¢). Nearby is another revered rock, **Sri Pada Parai,** meaning "blessed by footprints of the goddess."

The best view of land's end is from **lighthouse** near the Youth Hostel. The lighthouse hours are 3 to 7pm.

Nearby Attractions

Suchindram, 13 kilometers away, has a fine collection of treasures from many periods, from the Pandyans to Travancore kings. This temple is one of a handful in India dedicated to the trinity, Shiva, Vishnu, and Brahma. Its 7-story gopuram is fantastically ornamental; there are musical pillars and an 18-foot statue of the monkey god Hanuman, in addition to artifacts from several eras. Some inscriptions in the temple date from the 9th century. Sunset services are on Friday.

Padmanabhapuram, 45 kilometers away, was the capital of Travancore in 1333. The architectural calling cards from those days are a fort, which encloses a palace with interesting art relics, a temple, and some other buildings. While located in Tamil Nadu, this site is most frequently toured from Thiruvananthapuram or Kovalam (see "Kovalam Beach" in Chapter 14, "Kerala").

Shopping

Curios made of seashells and palm leaves, packets of colored sands are what to look for at Poompuhar, Sannathi St. and Khadi Krafts, S. Car Street; for textiles, check out Co-optex, near Gandhi Mandapam.

WHERE TO STAY & EAT

There are simple, clean accommodations at all of the following; reserve far in advance. The state-run accommodations are especially popular. Since Kanniyakumari is a holy place, you might get in if you believe in miracles and make your reservations very far in advance. Most are bath-attached but in some hot water comes in buckets.

Government Accommodations

TTDC's Hotel Tamilnadu (☎ 71257), has 14 rooms with attached bathrooms and balconies overlooking the sea, three with AC double rates only, range from Rs 250 ($8.33) without AC to Rs 350 ($11.66) with AC. Two second-class bungalows are Rs 115 ($3.83); two family rooms (with six beds each) are Rs 225 ($7.50). Eight twin cottages without AC are Rs 250 ($8.33), and four cottages with AC are Rs 400 ($13.33).

TTDC also runs a **Youth Hostel,** where doubles without attached baths (they are communal and shared with the other rooms) are Rs 75 ($2.50), and a dorm bed is Rs 25 (83¢).

TTDC's Cape Hotel (☎ 71222), has nine rooms, two with AC. Rates are Rs 250 ($8.33) to Rs 325 ($11.66). The accommodations are simple, the sea views smashing.

Meals are taken at the TTDC's cafeteria for both Hotel Tamilnadu and Cape Hotel. Direct dorm reservation inquiries for all properties to the Manager, Hotel Tamilnadu, Kanniyakumari 629702. TTDC's accommodations are usually booked to overflowing.

Hotels

Rooms at the **Hotel Samudra** (☎ 71162-67), have sea views and attached baths. Doubles range from Rs 350 ($11.66) non-AC to Rs 550 ($18.33) with AC. This place is cleaner than most; there is a restaurant.

Hotel Sangam (☎ 71351), opposite the post office, is very modest. Prices range from Rs 75 ($2.50) to Rs 100 ($3.33), all non-AC.

Guest Homes & Lodges

A nice, old, low-budget standby, **Kerala House** (☎ 71229), is a cream-colored building with a bright red roof and a wonderful sea view from its dozen rooms. The sparsely furnished rooms have bathrooms attached, most with Western bathrooms. Rates are Rs 45 ($2.55) non-AC, Rs 50 ($2.85) with AC (there are three AC rooms). This simple place is a better choice than many of the unkempt guest houses and lodges.

Of the modest tourist homes, **Manickam Tourist Home,** North Car Street, Kanniyakumari 629702 (☎ 71387), has simple, modern rooms with attached bathrooms (some cold water only), tidy enough for a short stay. Every room has a balcony from which you can watch the sunrise, sunset, and moonrise, which are big deals around here. Rates are Rs 150 ($5) to Rs 250 ($8.33), the higher rate for AC. There's a restaurant and room service.

On Main Road, **Sankar's Guest House** (☎ 71360) is not for everyone. The rooms cost about the same at Manickam's, with attached bathrooms and balconies, some with sea views. There's a decent vegetarian restaurant.

In the same price range, **NTC Lodge,** Bus Stand, has fairly clean rooms and a restaurant.

A Hotel Outside of Town

Nineteen kilometers away from Kanniyakumari, in Nagercoil, is **Hotel Rajam,** M. S. Road, Vadasery, Nagercoil 629001 (☎ 04652- 24581), with 32 neatly furnished rooms, 60% with AC. Doubles with AC are Rs 350 ($11.66), Rs 180 ($6) without. It's a good place to break your journey, have a meal or snack, use a clean bathroom, or, if need be, spend the night. While in town, you should see the Nagaraja Temple. The temple's unusual entrance architecture resembles a Chinese Buddhist Vihara.

There is frequent bus service to Kanniyakumari from Nagercoil.

8 Udhagamandalam (Ootacamund)

Ootacamund (in Tamil, *Udhagamandalam*), or "Ooty" for short, is the fading remains of a 19th-century English community in the flower-strewn hills of Tamil Nadu's Nilgiris ("Blue Hills"). The hills were so named for the distinctive bluish halo that surrounds them (similar to that seen in the Great Smokies in the United States).

Today, Ooty (pop. 8,700, elev. 7,500 feet) has old, gabled manor houses and vast gardens that rival Kew, flower shows, and a town center called Charing Cross. Yet it's quite a different place from what it was when John Sullivan, a collector from Coimbatore, built the first bungalow—the Stone House—here, now quarters for the head of the Government Art College nearby, which led to the Duke of Buckingham and other swells making their summer headquarters here.

Tucked in one little corner of Wenlock Downs, a massive tract of grassy lawns, hills, and dales, is Hindustan Photo Films, India's only manufacturer of sensitized photographic materials. (You can visit the factory.) Fortunately, the downs extend for some 50 miles, so despite the light industry there is still plenty of room for picturesque beauty and outdoor activities.

Beyond, the roads climb through forests of teak and eucalyptus and the terraced slopes of the south's renowned tea and coffee estates set into this junction of Western and Eastern ghats. Indeed, eucalyptus oils and other extracts from cinchona trees, introduced in 1842, have become a thriving local industry. Pungent wintergreen, geranium, and other oils are for sale in the marketplace.

Though Ooty's past may seem rooted mainly in England, it truly goes deeper, back to the aboriginal Toda tribes that once roamed the walnut and teak groves. Their descendants can be seen today herding cattle along the roads, as can their animist shrines in the fields nearby.

Light industry aside, Ooty hasn't changed in one respect since the days when the Madras government moved here for the summer. Now, as then, it is a delightful place where the average temperature, between 50° and 60°F, makes it an ideal escape from the heat of the plains. To take a trip to Ooty is to step away from the rigors of travel and relax before digging more deeply into other treasures and pleasures of India.

Ooty's center of town has, alas, lost it's charm, having become a congested mess due to overbuilding. New regulations have restricted development since l993. You can find the old-fashioned peace and quiet by heading out of the commercial center.

ESSENTIALS

GETTING TO OOTY

BY PLANE The nearest airport is Coimbatore (105 kilometers away). Taxis are available at the airport. A most convenient flight connects Madras to Coimbatore ($53, daily, departs 6:20am; arrives 7:35am), from which you can take a taxi or bus or train to Ooty. Buses leave every half hour, from 6:30am to 8:30pm, from Coimbatore's Central Bus Stand at Gandhipuram. They also meet the express trains from Madras (to combine with train travel to Coimbatore, below).

BY TRAIN Most convenient is to take the *Nilgiri Express* from Madras overnight to Coimbatore and on to Mettupalayam (538 kilometers; departs 9:05pm; arrives

7:20am) for Rs 929 ($30.97) AC First, Rs 109 ($3.63) Second. This train connects with the Blue Mountain Railway, the famous blue- and banana-color narrow-gauge train, which departs at 8:45am and arrives Ooty around 12:20pm. The Blue Mountain fares are about Rs 140 ($4.66) First, 70 ($2.33) Second.

While the **Blue Mountain Railway** does not traverse the road like Darjeeling's "toy train," the train—on a 45-kilometer, 4½-hour journey—chugs along tracks cut into steep slopes to offer a fascinating ride with plenty of heart-stopping views into deep wooded valleys, passing en route through 16 tunnels and 250 bridges. The first stop is Coonoor. So if you're in a time bind, hop aboard here for a memorable minitrip to Ooty. Or take the little train from in Ooty to Conoor during your stay. (Updating of the wooden coaches and changing from coal to oil-fueled locomotives is expected in 1996.) Additional Blue Mountain Railway departures are scheduled during the season; alternatively you can take the afternoon Blue Mountain Railway from Ooty around 3pm and connect with the *Nilgiris Express* for an overnight trip to Madras. (Service may be interrupted during the monsoon.)

There are also three trains connecting from Bangalore and four from Coimbatore, on a daily basis.

BY BUS The government-run Cheran Transport buses ply the roads between Bangalore and Ooty (about a nine-hour trip), departing **from Bangalore** at 6:30am, 10:30am, noon, and 8pm. The 160-kilometer ride **from Mysore** to Ooty takes 5½ hours. Buses depart Mysore at 1:45am, 9am, and 7pm (there may be more frequent departures during the season). From Ooty buses depart for Mysore at 8, 9, and 11:30am, and 1:30 and 3:30pm. Ooty departures are from the Central Bus Stand (☎ 2770). Some Mysore-Ooty buses go via **Bandipur,** the wildlife sanctuary. These buses can also be taken as far as **Mudumalai Sanctuary;** this 2½-hour ride costs about half the fare to Mysore.

The circuitous road to Ooty goes through an Eden of areca nut palms (fruit used in pan digestive) and pine trees, with monkeys swinging in the trees or seated on the retaining wall watching the traffic go by.

Visitor Information

The **tourist office** is located in the Supermarket Building, Charing Cross Road (☎ 3964), and has a limited supply of brochures, one of them with a little map.

Getting Around

Taxis, cycle rickshas, and unmetered auto rickshas are available. Bargain for your fare. Bicycles can be rented in town.

When to Go

The best time to visit Ooty is in May, during the annual Flower and Vegetable Show at the Botanical Gardens, the Dog Show, or the Lake Pageant and Boat Race.

WHAT TO SEE & DO

The main attraction in Ooty is the **Botanical Gardens,** which were started in 1847 by an English marquis. They are laid out in spacious terraces, graded one on top of the other almost like a tea estate. The gardens' dramatic backdrop is Doddabetta Peak. In the pretty 50-acre park are huge shade trees, 650 species of plants, and, near the little lake, a fossil tree trunk dating back some 20 million years. A fairly late addition is a world map in plants, made from contributions sent from many nations.

From the garden, Ooty's **artificial lake,** 2 miles wide and 45 feet deep, is a little over a mile away. It was created by John Sullivan, the first European to have a summer house here, in 1819. Unfortunately, the lake has become polluted and water hyacinth—incredibly fast multipliers—have tried to claim it as their home. A clean-up has commenced, including weeding the voracious plants and setting up a new system to pump waste to a treatment plant. The boat house is open from 8 to 6pm; row boats are for rent. Beyond the lake is a train that runs a few kilometers—a great favorite of children.

Doddabetta Peak is 10 kilometers (6 miles) outside of town. It's a short bus ride from the Central Bus Stand (the bus stays about 20 minutes before returning). It's also an easy climb for anyone in reasonably good shape. At 8,650 feet, this is the highest peak in Tamil Nadu and offers a spectacular panoramic view of the surroundings. There's a viewing platform to ooh and ah from. This is only one of several viewing points, some named for illustrious English citizens, scattered between Ooty and Coonoor, 30 kilometers (18 miles) away.

Another point of interest is **St. Stephen's Church,** the first church in Ooty. It was built in 1820s—clock tower first, gallery bells later—in the Gothic style, on the site of a Toda Temple. The wood used in the church is said to have come from Tipu Sultan's palace at Srirangapatna. Interiors are interesting, but best is the adjoining cemetery with some of the oldest British headstones in town, including those of John Sullivan and family.

Guided Tours

Tamil Nadu Tourism and Development Commission (TNTDC) conducts two tours of Ooty and the surrounding area. Tour No. 1 leaves at 8:30am, returning at 7pm, and costs Rs 75 ($2.50). It covers Ooty Lake, the Botanical Gardens, Doddabetta Peak, and Mudumalai Sanctuary, via the Kalhatty Waterfalls.

Tour No. 2 also leaves daily at 8:30am, returning at 6:30pm, and costs about Rs 80 ($2.66). It takes you to Ooty and Coonoor Kotagiri, Kodanad View Point, Lamb's Rock, Dolphin's Nose, and Sim's Park.

For reservations, call the **Tamil Nadu Tourist Office** (☎ 3964) or any of the hotels in town.

Shopping

Poompuhar and **Kairali** have emporia in Ooty. Don't miss the **Toda Showroom,** which displays and sells tribal jewelry and textiles. The **Municipal Market** and **Super Market** are the main places to bargain and worth a visit.

WHERE TO STAY

Only a fraction of Ooty's hotels are listed below because maintenance in many others was not up to the standards of this book. Off-season discounts, roughly from July 1 through March 31, bring the highest-priced accommodations within range of our budget. Keep in mind that luxury taxes add from 10% to 20% to hotel bills.

There was virtually no place to recommend wholeheartedly in the lowest price hotels around Commercial Road and Ettines Road. They were singularly unkempt, in a congested noisy part of town. I had only slightly better luck in the midprice range in the popular Charing Cross area. The most pleasant places are removed from the center of town.

Doubles for Less Than Rs 350 ($11.66)

Garden View, Lake Road (☎ 3369), has 26 rooms that are cozy, but down at the heels and acceptably tidy. Next door, **Gaylord** (☎ 2378) has modest rooms, a dorm, and a rooftop restaurant. **Sanjay Hotel,** Charing Cross (☎ 3160), is a standout in this price range. The rooms are clean; they have balconies; the people who work here are nice. And there's a restaurant. Street noise is a problem, though.

Karnataka State's **TDC Hotel Mayura Sudarshan,** Fern Hill (☎ 3828) has simple, fairly clean rooms for about Rs 200 ($6.66).

YWCA Guest House, Anandagiri, Ootacamund (☎ 2218), takes men and women and is nicer than you would expect a Y to be. The highest rates are for cottages, at around Rs 250 ($8.33). The dorm costs Rs 60 ($2). It's a bit out of the way, but young backpackers don't seem to mind at all.

The **TTDC Youth Hostel,** Charing Cross Rd. (☎ 3665), is in run-down condition but cheap. Dorm rooms are Rs 50 ($1.66) in season, Rs 25 (83¢) off-season. Three non-AC doubles are also available for Rs 150 ($5) to Rs 200 ($6.66) throughout the year.

Usually reserved by train travelers, **Railway Retiring Rooms** (☎ 2246) sometimes have vacancies.

Doubles for Less Than Rs 750 ($25)

Hotel Lake View, West Lake Road (☎ 3904; fax 3579; in Bombay ☎ 2874532), has 95 doubles and 25 suites in bright yellow cottages standing side-by-side on an eight-acre site. Only front cottages overlook the lake. Suites with fireplaces are around Rs 600 ($20) in season—a buy. There is a restaurant. This is an okay place despite its similarity in looks to a suburban tract development.

Stone walls and stained glass windows are unusual at **Hotel Khems,** Shoreham Palace Road, off Ettines Road, Ooty 643001 (☎ 4188), a hotel that needs better maintenance. The bedrooms have little sitting areas, pleasant if uninspired furniture, and nice modern bathrooms. Rates are Rs 450 ($15) to Rs 650 ($21.66) in-season, Rs 275 ($9.16) to Rs 475 ($15.83) off-season. Service charge is 10%. The mood is rather formal for a hill resort.

Across from the tourist office, **Nahar Hotels,** 52-A Charing Cross Rd., Ooty 643001 (☎ 2173; fax 2405), is a fairly clean, Indian-style hotel with 75 acceptable rooms, some of them papered in wild patterns. It's one of the better places in this part of town. Standard doubles are in the Rs 500 ($16.66) to Rs 800 $26.66) range. Deluxe doubles and suites are higher. All rooms have both Indian and Western facilities. Inexpensive thalis are available in the hotel's restaurant.

With a lake view, the rambling yellow structure trimmed in red is the Indian-style **Hotel Dasaprakash,** South of racecourse (☎ 2434), in the famous Dasaprakash chain, but not nearly as nice as the others. The rooms I saw were gloomy and in need of TLC. There are 100 rooms, some perhaps better than the ones I saw. Doubles are about Rs 500 ($16.66). Service charge is 5%. There are two good vegetarian restaurants and a nice outdoor snack bar with a fine lake view, as well as a children's playground.

The Nilgiri Woodlands, opposite racecourse (☎ 2551), has a comfortable, homey atmosphere; there rooms both in the old building and in newer cottages on the grounds. A standard double is Rs 500 ($16.66), more for a cottage. Very nice in this price range, with services and facilities associated with posher spots, such as the tennis courts.

Regency Villa Hotel, Fernhill Post Office (☎ 2555), is located near Fernhill Palace and is, in fact, its old hunting lodge. Eighteen rooms are available in the villa and surrounding cottages. Rates range from Rs 180 ($6) for a cottage to Rs 400 ($13.33) for a villa. The lawns are nice. Overall, an interesting and atmospheric place.

Doubles for Less Than Rs 1,500 ($50)

The following hotels accept international credit cards.

With a heated, indoor swimming pool, health and fitness center, and discotheque, **The Monarch,** off Havelock Road (☎ 4408; fax 2455), is a whole new world to explore when it comes to Ooty's hotels. What more could you want? A bit better maintenance. But the atmosphere is pleasant overall. Rates are Rs 750 ($25) to Rs 850 ($28.33) for a standard double; Club Class rooms are Rs 1100 ($36.66); service charge is 10%. You'll also find 63 up-to-the minute rooms, convention facilities, a multicuisine restaurant, and table tennis and pony rides for those who like activities.

Sterling Holidays, P. B. No. 25, R. K. Mutt Road, Elk Hill, Ramakrishnapuram (☎ 4263-5; fax 2093), has 103 rooms and suites, the highest rate about Rs 1,050 ($35). And with its conference facilities, this hotel has business visitors in mind. There's a restaurant, bar, coffee shop, golf, and tennis in case you want to relax between deals.

TTDC's **Hotel Tamilnadu,** behind the supermarket and tourist office and near Charing Cross Road (☎ 4010), is clean and a good buy. Rooms have balconies facing the hills. There are steep penalties—from 50% to losing your whole deposit—for canceling in-season reservations less than three days in advance. Consider yourself lucky if you can get in. The top price in-season is around Rs 850 ($28.33). For reservations, contact The Manager, Hotel Tamilnadu, Ooty, 634001, or The Commercial Manager, TTDC, 143 Anna Salai, Madras.

The atmosperhic **Fernhill Palace,** Fernhill Post, Ootacamund 643004 (☎ 3910), in a 42-acre park, formerly was in the 1800s a 51-room summer palace of the Maharaja of Mysore. Now under Taj management, Fernhill has been partially renovated over the past few years and enhanced by professional management. Rates begin at Rs 800 ($26.66) and go to Rs 1,500 ($50). It's an enjoyable place for a meal if you don't stay here.

The following three places have rates from Rs 900 ($30) to Rs 1,600 ($53.33), which places them squarely in our budget if two are sharing.

Comfort Inn Aruna, Gorishola Road (☎ 4308/9; fax 4229), has old-fashioned charm plus views and central heating, which give this 88-room hotel special old/new appeal. The rooms are clean and comfortable; doubles range from Rs 1,200 ($40) to Rs $2,500 ($83.33); service charge is 10%. There's a multicuisine restaurant and a pastry counter hard to pass for serious sweet lovers.

Holiday Inn, Gem Park, Sheddon Road (☎ 2955), a newcomer to Ooty, is pleasantly modern. Expect to pay Rs 1,450 ($48.33) to Rs 1,600 ($53.33) for a double. The hotel is affiliated with the U.S. chain.

Ramanshree Inn Southern Star, 32 Havelock Rd. (☎ 3601), 67-modern, functional, pleasant rooms. The hotel is located on a hill about 2 kilometers above the town and has a nice view. Doubles are Rs 1,145 ($38.16). The garden is popular for tea. The restaurant has good food. Greatly improved under new management.

Savoy Hotel, 77 Sylks Rd., Ootacamund, Tamil Nadu 643001 (☎4142-7; fax 3318), dating from 1877 and now in the Taj Group, is loaded with old-fashioned charm. Cozy rooms, suites, and cottages with fireplaces and terraces set around a spacious garden are just bit above our basic budget, but not much since meals are included. Rooms with meals (the American Plan) begin at $53 and go up to $105. You name it, they'll arrange it: tours, treks, fishing. Or if you want to be left alone with a drink in your hand while admiring the sunset in the garden, that's all right, too.

WHERE TO EAT

Many people eat at their hotels, but you don't have to unless you've opted for the American plan. Most hotels welcome outside visitors to their restaurants. To step back to Ooty of the old days, have a meal at either the **Savoy** or **Fernhill Palace;** for a modern setting and good food, try **Ramanashree Southern Star** or the **Holiday Inn.**

Cheap, tasty, vegetarian thalis are available at **Nahar;** for Chinese food try **Shinkows** (near the Collector's Office). There's an ice cream parlor at the **Dasaprakash Hotel** serving famous Dasaprakash ice creams.

AN EXCURSION TO MUDUMALAI WILDLIFE SANCTUARY

Most people plan to spend a day in Mudumalai, the 114-square-mile wildlife sanctuary 65 kilometers (40 miles) from Ooty, nudged up against both Karnataka and Kerala. Elephants are most frequently seen, and there are also bison, tigers, panthers, and hyenas, plus a number of snakes and rare birds. In addition, a main attraction for visitors takes place at 6pm at the Elephant Camp at Kargudi (5 kilometers away)—the elephant puja, when a trained baby elephant actually lumbers through a puja in honor of the evening. Late afternoon is also the best time to watch the camp elephants being fed and to learn fascinating facts about what and how much they eat and how camp diets differ from elephant foraging in the wilds. Elephants in this camp are tamed and trained to work in the lumber industry and others.

Mudumalai is open from 6:30 to 10am, and 4 to 6pm. The elephant puja and elephant feeding are daily at 6pm. Elephant riding hours are 6 to 8am, and 4 to 6pm. Elephant rides cost Rs 35 ($1.16) per person. Camera fees are Rs 5 (17¢) still, Rs 50 ($1.66) video.

If you wish to ride an elephant, you should make a reservation two days in advance of your sanctuary visit by contacting the Wildlife Warden, Mahalingam and Co., Conoor Road, Ooty.

Some Ooty-Mysore buses can be taken as far as **Mudumalai Sanctuary;** this 2½-hour ride costs about half the fare to Mysore (see "Getting to Ooty" under "Essentials," above).

ACCOMMODATIONS NEAR MUDUMALAI

Seeing the sanctuary properly takes overnighting. However, there are so few accommodations that you absolutely *must* reserve in advance, especially in season.

LOW-BUDGET CHOICES

Accommodations maintained by the forest department are all ultrasimple. The first three are in Theppakadu: **Log House** and **Silvan Lodge,** both Rs 80 ($2.66) per room; **Minivet Dormitory,** Rs 20 (66¢). **Abayaraniyam Guest House** and **Annexe A, Abayaraniyam,** Rs 80 ($2.66) per room. For inquiries and reservations for forest department accommodations, write: Warden Wildlife Bldg., Coonoor Road, Ooty, (☎ 4098).

TTDC's Youth Hostel (☎ 86249) in Theppakadu, costs Rs 50 ($1.66) per head, Rs 25 (83¢) off-season. There are three blocks of beds, one with 16 beds, two with 12 each. Meals are in the canteen. To make reservations, check with the tourist office on Charing Cross Road in Ooty, in the Supermarket Building (☎ 3964), or contact the manager at the hostel.

DOUBLES FOR LESS THAN RS 700 ($23.33)

The following three are about 13 miles away from Mudumalai.

Bamboo Banks Farm Guest House, Musinigudi P.O., Nilgiris 643223, The Nilgiris, Tamil Nadu South India (☎ 86222), is, as its name implies, a working farm as well as a small, family run guest house. Owners Siasp T. and Zerene Kothavala are always around to see to guests' comforts (Mr. Kothavala is quite a talker). Bearing some resemblance to a hacienda in the U.S. Southwest, the rose-colored main building with red-tile roof houses the lounge/dining room and two of the six guest rooms. The others are in cottages in the garden. Rooms are clean and tastefully furnished in a simple, homey style. Rates are Rs 1,820 ($60.66) double, with meals, which puts it well within our budget. The food is good. Swim in a natural pool. View game from van or elephant.

Hidden in a valley, **Jungle Hut,** Musinigudi P.O., Nilgiris 643223, Tamil Nadu, South India (☎ 86240), run by Joe and Hermie Mathias, offers 12 clean, simply furnished rooms with attached modern bathrooms, in three hand-hewn stone cottages. Meals are served in an enclosure outdoors. There's an indoor lounge. Rates are around Rs 600 ($20) for a double. Jeep trips are available to Mudamailai.

Jungle Trails/Mavinhalla Village, Musinigudi P.O., Nilgiris 643223, Tamil Nadu, South India (☎ 86256), has four clean bedrooms, each with two to four beds and basic furniture, set around a lounge. Guests share a bathroom. You're near an important elephant migratory route, so often a parade of pachyderms lumbers by the open verandah. Rates are comparable to those at Jungle Hut.

The Monarch Safari Park, Bokka Ram, Masinigudi, The Nilgiris, Tamil Nadu (☎ 86343), offers 14 adequate doubles, baths attached, and a range of activities including trekking, rock climbing, table tennis, and jogging, plus a children's playground and a meditation center. Doubles run Rs 500 ($16.66).

9 Coonoor

The hill station Coonoor (pop. 99,600) is 30 kilometers (18 miles) from Ooty, at an altitude of 5,600 feet. Here are Sim's Park and a number of view points. It's much quieter than Ooty, and some travelers prefer it for that reason. Buses go from Ooty to Coonoor from 7:20am to 7pm.

ESSENTIALS

GETTING TO COONOOR

BY TRAIN See the description of the Blue Mountain Railway, under "Getting to Ooty," above).

BY BUS There is frequent service between Ooty and Coonoor and frequent service to Coimbatore. The road trip from Coimbatore is scenically beautiful, with dew-spangled palms, emerald forests, terraced tea estates, awesome views, and monkeys doing what monkeys do—frolicking in the trees and carrying their young on their backs.

There are also a number of buses to and from Kotagiri via an equally pretty drive.

GETTING AROUND

Rickshas: Don't bargain, haggle for a fair fare. Taxis are available; check at your hotel.

WHAT TO SEE & DO

Sim's Park, started in 1874, displays as many as 330 rose varieties, many quite rare and a eucalyptus more than 180 years old. A newer attraction is a map of the world made from plants sent by various countries, much like Ooty's. During the third week in May there's a fruit fair, when growers come from everywhere to exhibit their produce.

You'll want to see **Law's Falls** (7 kilometers away), at the junction of Kateri rivers on the Coonoor, on the road to Mettupalayam ghat road; there are various view points, such as **Lamb's Rock** (6 kilometers) or **Dolphin's Nose** (12 kilometers). You can explore **The Droog** (13 kilometers; alt. 1,917 meters) to see the ruins of a 16th-century **Fort,** built by Tipu Sultan as a lookout; it's a 3-kilometer trek to the summit. You can also visit the **Pomological Gardens** at Wellington (3 kilometers), one of three experimental fruit gardens in the Nilgiris (others are at Burliar and Kallar), maintained by the State Agricultural Department. Among the fruits grown here for research purposes are apples, plums, peaches, and lemons. Fresh fruit is on sale. The town, Wellington, named for Arthur Wellesley, is famous as the headquarters of the Madras Regiment, the oldest in the Indian army, founded more than 250 years ago. Today, the Indian Defense Services College is located here and still uses the barracks built in the mid–19th century.

To **visit a local coffee or tea estate,** contact United Planters Association of South India (UPASI), "Glen View," Coonoor. TTDC's Coonoor-Kotagari tour takes in Sim's Park and major viewpoints. Check with the tourist office (☎ 3964) in Ooty and specifics (also see "Guided Tours" under "What to See and Do," above).

FARTHER AFIELD

At **Kotagiri,** another small hill station 19 kilometers (12 miles) from Ooty, even quieter than Coonoor, and a bit higher at 6,500 feet, there's **Kodanad View Point, St. Catherine Falls,** and **Rangaswamy Pillar and Park.** Buses from Ooty run on the half hour from 7:30am to 6:30pm and cost about Rs 10 (33¢).

SHOPPING

There's a bazaar bulging with bargains, a branch of **Spencer's Department Store** with many essentials under one roof, and many smaller shops

WHERE TO STAY & EAT

The cement-block and red-brick facade of the **Vivek Tourist Home,** Figure of Eight Road, near Upasi, Coonoor (☎ 7292), is back to basics. The halls are awful. The rooms are clean and bright. High-season rates top off at about Rs 250 ($8.33) for a double.

Better than most of the lowest-priced hotels and guest houses is Coonoor's **YWCA Guest House,** Wyoming, Coonoor, with 12 tidy rooms, a dining room, and a garden.

The top place to stay is the **Taj Garden Retreat** (formerly Hampton Manor Hotel), Upper Church Road, Coonoor, Nilgiris 643101 (☎ 20021; fax 22775). This 33-room, 108-year-old hotel has a main lounge, dining room, and accommodations in white stucco cottages topped with red-tile roofs and surrounded by a well-manicured lawns and neatly trimmed hedges. Rates are $53 single, $95 double on the American plan (including meals). You can eat outdoors in the garden or indoors in the brick-and-beamed dining room.

The '40s-style, 24-room **Monarch Ritz Hotel,** Orange Grove Road, Coonoor 643101 (☎ 620084), right near Sim's Park, also is nice with a lot a charm. The rooms have balconies overlooking the gardens and lawns. Rates are Rs 425 ($14.16) double, Rs 950 ($31.16) suite; service charge is 10%. There's a restaurant and bar.

The **Hotel Blue Hills,** Mount Road, Coonoor (☎ 20103), has 40 clean rooms furnished motel-modern, and a nice view from the terrace. There's a small garden with a topiary, and the very pleasant management is eager to please visitors. Doubles cost around Rs 400. ($11.40) in season, Rs 100 ($5.70) off-season; singles are Rs 176 ($10) in season, Rs 89 ($5) off season. Indian vegetarian and nonvegetarian foods are served in the restaurant.

10 Coimbatore

Coimbatore, the third-largest city in Tamil Nadu (pop. 1,135 million), has so many textile mills that it has been nicknamed the "Manchester of South India." Coimbatore's rich, black soil produces such abundant cotton that a textile industry was begun here. The first few textile mills were humming in the 1800s; now there are more than a l00. The industry's expansion is tied to harnessing the waters of Pykara Falls to create energy resources to power the plants. Sometimes people call Coimbatore "The Detroit of the South" because pumps in Indian-made automobiles are made here, but that's stretching it.

ESSENTIALS

GETTING TO COIMBATORE

BY PLANE **Indian Airlines** flies from Madras, Bombay, and Bangalore. **Jet, East West,** and **NEPC** also fly from Bombay (NEPC operates from Madras). Sulur Airport is 30 kilometers from the center; Cheran Transport buses will take you to hotels for Rs 20 (66¢). Taxis charge Rs 100 ($3.33) to Rs 125 ($4.16), and auto rickshas cost around Rs 70 ($2.33).

Indian Airlines office is located on Trichy Road; for inquiries and reservations (☎ 213569); for **Jet** reservations ☎ 212034; **East West,** Gowtham Centre, 1055 Avinash Road (☎ 210286); **NEPC,** Trichy Road, Ramanathapuram (☎ 216741-42).

BY TRAIN Two trains connect Madras and Coimbatore: the *Kovai Express* (484 kilometers, 8³/₄ hours) and the *Cheran Express* (eight hours). Fares are Rs 865 ($28.83) AC First, Rs 50 ($1.66) Second. Several other trains, including the *Trivandrum Mail, Cochin Express,* and *West Coast Express,* originate in Madras and pass through Coimbatore every day. There are trains from Bangalore (9¹/₂ hours); Madurai (5¹/₂ hours); Rameswaram (11 hours). From Ooty, the Blue Mountain Railway narrow-gauge goes to Mettupalayam for a change to broad-gauge trains to Coimbatore and beyond.

For Combatoire Junction Railway Station inquiries call ☎ 36224-5; railway reservations (☎ 131); station superintendent (☎ 212224).

BY BUS Coimbatore is well served by buses from **TTC** (Madras) and **Kerala State** and **Karnataka State Road Corporations,** as well as **Cheran Transport** and other private lines. Regular services operate to and from Trichur, Cochin, Mysore, Tripati, Trichy, Pondcherry, Salem, Udhagamandalam, Ooty, Coonoor, Madras, and many other places in and around Tamil Nadu.

GETTING AROUND

Buses cover the city. Cheran Transport bus takes passengers from the airport to most city hotels for Rs 20 (66¢); in town, bus no. 12 links the bus station with the Coimbatore Junction Railway Station. Taxis cost Rs 2 (6¢) per kilometer in the plains and Rs 2.50 (8¢) on ghat roads (hills); taxis have a minimum charge of Rs 30 ($1). Auto rickshas have an Rs 3 (10¢) minimum. All are metered, but set the price before you get in.

WHAT TO SEE & DO

Coimbatore's main interest to tourists is as a place to connect with trains or taxis to Ooty or gateway to Kerala. However, for those with time and curiosity, here are a few sights east to see on a brief stopover.

If you have some time, **Perur Temple** (7 kilometers/5 miles away) is an interesting excursion. Dedicated to Shiva, the temple was constructed by Karikalan Chola more than 1,500 years ago. Particularly noteworthy are richly carved sculptures in the Kanagasabai Hall, a pillared corridor, which show Shiva in various poses. The temple is the site of Panguni Uthiram festival each year in March.

WHERE TO STAY AND EAT

DOUBLES FOR LESS THAN RS 600 ($20)

The TTDC's **Hotel Tamilnadu,** Dr. Nanjappa Road, Coimbatore 641001 (☎ 36311-324), has 49 rooms and an assortment of rates, starting with Rs 150 ($5) for a non-AC single to Rs 400 ($13.33) for an AC double deluxe. There's a restaurant and bar.

DOUBLES FOR LESS THAN RS 1,200 ($40)

One of the tallest buildings in the city, **Hotel City Tower,** P.B. 2418, Coimbatore (☎ 230981; fax 230103), has 100 sleek, modern functional rooms (56 with AC), including singles, doubles, and suites. A double runs about 600 ($20). Two restaurants, one vegetarian and one (on the rooftop) nonvegetarian.

Hotel Surya International, 105 Race Course Rd., Coimbatore 641018 (☎ 217755; fax 216110), has 44 modern rooms and a bar, restaurant, and lawns. Doubles are around Rs 800 ($26.66).

Kerala: City Life & Wildlife

14

The southern tip of India can make a strong claim for being its most attractive and interesting part. Certainly it is one of the least-visited areas (but for how long?). Thiruvananthapuram has an international airport, which in itself makes it especially enjoyable for the tourists who do get there.

The lush and lovely state of Kerala has always gone about its business pretty well undisturbed by the rest of the world. In its capital city of Thiruvananthapuram visitors do not need conducted tours. They can discover their own treasures, perhaps with the aid of the local tourist office or a couple of quaintly printed local guidebooks. Conducted tours are available, however, and they can be a helpful orientation to the city and budget-stretchers in outlying areas.

1 Thiruvananthapuram (Trivandrum)

Thiruvananthapuram (pop. 827,700) is a delightful city, tropical and sleepy as southern communities are apt to be, yet with some modern buildings, wide avenues, and the inevitable liveliness of a state capital. It's not quite on the water, although the Arabian Sea is only a mile or two away, and $11^1/_2$ kilometers (7 miles) to the south, at Kovalam, is one of the best-known beaches in all of India—its fame spread far and wide by Chester Bowles, a former U.S. ambassador to India, who used to vacation annually in the century-old palace nearby.

Thiruvananthapuram—its tongue twister name derived from the thousand-headed serpent's home Tiru Ananatha Puram—was the capital of Raja of Travancore in 1750, who shifted it here from Padmanabhapuram.

Like the rest of Kerala state, Thiruvananthapuram is best avoided during the monsoon season (June and July, and to a lesser extent in October) and is at its coolest in November and December. Its busiest season is November to January and during the festivals at the local temple in March to mid-May. Exact dates vary from year to year, but it's always the hottest time of the year. Temple deities are paraded through the streets and exotically dressed performers re-create ancient Hindu legends via kathakali, the dance-drama for which Kerala is famous. If you plan to visit Thiruvananthapuram at festival time, make sure you have advance reservations.

ESSENTIALS

GETTING TO THIRUVANANTHAPURAM

BY CANAL BOAT Easily the most enjoyable way to get to Thiruvananthapuram is to travel as far as possible by boat through Kerala's famous backwaters, getting a close-up of life along the palm-fringed lagoons.

Buy a ticket at Ernakulam's Main Boat Jetty for the tourist office's daily backwaters trip, which lasts from 8:15am to 6pm, and costs Rs 125 ($4.16), which includes a coach transfer to Alappuzha (Alleppey), where you shove off for a leisurely tour of the backwaters ending up at Kollam (Quilon). (For reservations: Tourist Office, Main Boat Jetty, Ernakulam.) If you plan to stay at Kollam for a while to sightsee, check your plans in advance with the tourism people since you may have to make special arrangements to transport your baggage. (For staying on to sightsee, see "Sights Out of Town" under "Kochi," below.) There is frequent bus and train service from Kottayam (81 kilometers) or Kollam (Quilon) to Thiruvananthapuram (75 kilometers).

This is an exceptionally fine experience. There are whitewashed houses, whose rose-tiled roofs glow in bits and pieces under towering palms; neat yards, where graceful women kneel preparing a family meal; children waving (do not throw candies, pennies, or pens); country boats propelled by boatmen in dhotis tied high; a kingfisher nibbling a fish. There are patches of lavender-flowering water hyacinths, banana or mango groves, and perhaps a stop to observe craftspeople at work and to sip some thirst-quenching juice out of a gigantic fresh-picked coconut—a perfect toast to Kerala, India's coconut state, and an idyllic journey's end.

BY PLANE Thiruvananthapuram has an international airport (6 kilometers from town) with flights arriving from and departing to all over the world via **Air India; Indian Airlines** connects from Sri Lanka and the Maldives. **East-West** also flies between Bombay and Thiruvananthapuram.

Domestic service on **Indian Airlines** flies in from Delhi (five hours, $219); from Bombay (two hours, $124); from Madras (one hour, $65); from Bangalore (one hour, $69); and from Kochi (30 minutes, $23).

A prepaid taxi to the city is Rs 110 ($3.66); by auto ricksha Rs 50 ($1.66). The trip takes 20 to 30 minutes depending on traffic.

For reservations and flight information, you can contact **Air India,** Velayambalam (☎ 64837; airport ☎ 71426); **Indian Airlines,** Mascot Junction (☎ 66370; airport ☎ 73537); and **East-West** (☎ 355242, in Kochi).

BY TRAIN Thiruvananthapuram is a major terminus on the Indian Railways system, with train links to all parts of the country. Both broad- and narrow-gauge trains operate to the city. A popular train **from Madras** is the *Thiruvananthapuram Mail* (920 kilometers, 12¾ hours); fares are Rs 1,323 ($44.10) AC First, Rs 159 ($5.30) Second. **From Delhi,** a good choice is the speedy *Rajdhani Express* (less than 45 hours); fares are Rs 1,340 ($44.67) to Rs 4,304 ($143.47). **From Bombay,** take the *Kanniyakumari Express* (45½ hours); fares are Rs 2,440 ($81.33) AC First, Rs 238 ($7.93) Second. And **from Calcutta,** it's the *Trivandrum-Guhawati Express* (49 hours); fares are Rs 3,866 ($128.66) AC First, Rs 327 ($10.90) Second. Or you might consider the scenic coastal route on one of the express trains toThiruvananthapuram **from Kochi** (221 kilometers/135 miles); fares are Rs 482($16.07) in AC First, Rs 56 ($1.86) Second. For information, call the Thiruvananthapuram Central Railway Station, 69266, ext. 131; for reservations ext. 132.

BY BUS **Kerala State Road and Transport Corporation (KSRTC)** buses ply routes through the state and Tamil Nadu. There are several express buses between 4am and 9:30pm **from Ernakulam** to Thiruvananthapuram for around Rs 50 ($1.66), the 221-kilometer (135-mile) journey takes a little over five hours via express buses. Fast passenger buses from Ernakulam cost less and take longer—about 6½ hours to Thiruvananthapuram. From north Kerala, buses leave **Kozhikode** at 9:30pm.

There are two bus stations: KSRTC Central Bus Station, Thampanoor (☎ 63886); and City Bus Stand, Fort (☎ 71029).

Visitor Information

If you need help upon arrival or in town, here's where to turn: the **tourist information counters** at Thiruvananthapuram Airport (☎ 451085), railway station (☎ 67224), or Central Bus Station, Thampanoor (☎ 67224).

Government of Kerala Tourist Information Centre, Park View, opposite the museum (☎ 61132), is open 6am to 5pm. **Tourism Development Corporation Information Centre,** near Central Bus Station (☎ 330031). They have a good selection of maps, pamphlets, and guide books, and they can assist with hotel reservations and book conducted tours. The **Government of India** also has a tourist information counter at the airport (☎ 451498).

Getting Around

Yellow-top **taxis** charge about Rs 3 (9¢) per kilometer; **auto rickshas** are metered and supposedly charge Rs 3.50 (12¢) per kilometer (but you usually have to bargain).

Cars with drivers can be hired from **KTDC,** Transport Division, Chettikulamkara (☎ 61783); **ITDC,** Transport Section, Chettikulamkara (☎ 61783), or Moullassery Tower, Van Ross Junction (☎ 484374962); or from reliable travel agents.

When to Go

The best season is November to March; the rainy season is May to November. Summer temperatures are usually above 90°F, and winter temperatures rarely go below the high 60s.

Ulsavom (March to April and October to November) is celebrated at Padmanabhaswamy Temple for 10 days. The temple elephants go out in processions around the town, and there are folk music and dancing performances.

The **Great Elephant March**—promoted as the world's largest gathering of elephants (about 100)—takes place annually from January 17 to 20, when elephants, resplendent in golden caparisons and shaded by purple and scarlet silk umbrellas, wend their majestic way from Thrissur (Trichur) to Thiruvananthapuram via Kochi and Alappuzha. The event begins at Thrissur with a ceremonial feeding of the elephants and concludes with a grand salute by the elephants at Thiruvallan, near Kovalam Beach. The festivities also showcase snake boat races, dance, and martial arts displays. At each point, visitors can not only observe the elephants, but can also ride and feed them.

WHAT TO SEE & DO

There are two mandatory tourist attractions: the famous Sri Padmanabhaswamy Temple and the Public Gardens, the latter containing the Napier and Sri Chitralayam museums. Of passing interest are the Kaudiyar Palace, once the residence of the local maharaja; the ancient observatory; and the Oriental Library, with its historic palm-leaf manuscripts.

The **Padmanabhaswamy Temple** was probably built during the 18th-century reign of Raja Marthanda Varma, although legends say there was some sort of temple on the site as far back as 3000 B.C. At any rate, its 300 pillars and imposing seven-story tower make it by far the most impressive landmark around town, and it's not hard to believe the story that 4,000 stonecutters, 6,000 other workers, and a few hundred elephants were employed in its construction. The temple is devoted to Vishnu, who is seen inside resting on Anantha, the serpent god. Non-Hindus aren't allowed inside the gates but will find it most interesting to peek in between 6 and 8am and 5 and 7pm when most of the worshipers gather inside.

Thiruvananthapuram's **Public Gardens** will consume most of your time, partly because it's pleasant to meander among the tropical plants and flowers and visit the moderate-sized zoo (the animals are housed as much as possible in their natural habitat), but also because it contains the town's two museums. The **Napier Museum,** a monumental piece of Victorian architecture, with a striking red-and-white exterior, is devoted mainly to stone sculptures, bronzes, and woodcarvings, the oldest relics dating from between the 2nd and 9th centuries. There are ancient musical instruments, a reconstructed tharawad (a typical Nair family dwelling), and a natural history section with the usual showcases of everything from stuffed owls to whale skeletons. The museum is open from 10am to 5pm (closed Monday and on Wednesday morning), and admission is Rs 2 (6¢). You enter from the 50-acre zoo—admission is also Rs 2—that can be toured without getting out of your car upon payment of a few rupees. There is a range of fees for cameras, depending on their type. The zoo is open from 9am to 5pm.

Also in the gardens, not far from the Napier, is the smaller **Sri Chitra Art Gallery,** which is renowned for its great collection of paintings by Raja Ravi Varma of Travancore as well as its varied collection of art from China, Japan, and Tibet; miniatures from northern India; gold-leaf and gem-studded pictures from Tanjore; works from Bali and Java; copies of Ajanta frescoes; and contemporary works by local artists. Admission is Rs 2 (6¢); hours are 9am to 5pm, closed Monday and on Wednesday morning. Next door is a modern art museum.

Thiruvananthapuram's most rewarding shopping spots are **Chalai Bazaar, Connemara Market,** and **M. G. Road,** from Palayam to Fort, where you can haggle to your heart's content; **Sree Gram,** the village art and crafts center, and the state-run **S.M.S.M.** (Central Handicrafts Emporium), in Kairali opposite the secretariat, have fixed prices and are among the better places to shop. Among the local merchants, **Natesan's** on M. G. Road has some valuable and attractive artifacts.

GUIDED TOURS

KTDC conducts several coach tours, departing from and booked through **KTDC Tourist Reception Centre,** Thiruvananthapuram (☎ 330031). Tour 1, the Thiruvananthapuram City Tour, departs daily at 8am, returning at 7pm; the cost is Rs 60 ($2). It covers Padmanabhapuram Palace, Shankumugham Beach, the aquarium, SMSM Institute, Aruivkkara Dam, Neyyar Dam, Kovalam Beach, museum and art gallery, and the zoo. (The itinerary changes on Monday, when the zoo, museum, and institute are closed.) Tour 2, a half-day tour of Thiruvananthapuram, departs at 2pm, returning at 7pm; the cost is Rs 40 ($1.33). It covers Veli Lagoon, Shankumugham Beach, and Kovalam Beach. Tour 3, to Kanniyakumari, departs at 7:30am daily, returning at 9pm; the cost is Rs 120 ($4). It includes Kovalam Beach, Padmanabhapuram Palace, Suchindram Temple, Kanniyakumari, and the Vivekananda Memorial. Tour 4, to Ponmudi and the hill station, departs daily at 7am, returning at 7pm; the cost is Rs 100 ($3.33). Tour 5, to Thekkady, is a two-day tour, departing Saturday (except the last Saturday of the month) at 6:30am, returning Sunday at 9pm; the cost is Rs 275 ($9.16). It includes boating at Thekkady. Be advised that this is a tough (but scenic) nine-hour drive each way—not worth the effort unless it's your only alternative. Tour 6, to Kodaikanal, including Thekkady and Madurai, is a three-day tour, departing on the last Saturday of each month at 6am, returning Monday; the cost is Rs 450 ($15). Tour 7, to Courtallam and the curative falls, leaves each Saturday and Sunday in season (June–September) at 7am, returning at 9pm; the cost is Rs 100 ($3.33). Prices do not include entrance fees, food, or accommodations.

BACKWATER TOURS

A **canal-village tour** through the Thiruvananthapuram backwaters by country boat costs about Rs 300 ($10) for two to four hours and can be booked through the Tourist Reception Centre in Thiruvananthapuram.

WHERE TO STAY

Most tourists don't stay in town (it's a major business center), but at beautiful Kovalam Beach, 16 kilometers (10 miles) and a 20-minute taxi ride from town. The beach is an especially good choice for low-budget travelers, who will find a better choice of less pricey places out there than in town. No matter where you stay, remember that service charges at some hotels are 10% and luxury room taxes at all hotels run from 7.5% for non–air-conditioned rooms to 10% to 15% for air-conditioning. Sales taxes generally run 6% on food.

DOUBLES FOR LESS THAN RS 250 ($8.33)

Here are some modest places recommended mainly for price; all have a few air-conditioned rooms.

Silver Sand, Thampanoor Flyover (☎ 70318), has 38 rooms and a restaurant. **Paramount Tourist Home,** Aristo Junction (☎ 63474), has 24 rooms and no restaurant. **Lal Tourist Home,** near the railway station (☎ 68477), has 40 rooms. **Mas. Overbridge Junction** (☎ 78566) is cleaner than most in this price range. **KTDC's Yatri Nivas,** Stadium Road, Thriussur (☎ 332333), has 16 rooms, some dorm style, and is almost always full; rates range from Rs 100 ($3.33) to Rs 400 ($13.33), the most expensive room with seven beds.

Still looking? Follow the golden rule of finding cheap accommodation in India: Check the simple Indian-style hotels near the bus and railway station. Target on Manajalaikulam Road and Station Road, both in Thampanoor.

The **YWCA Guest House,** Palayam, behind Secretariat (☎ 68059), offers modest accommodations. The **Youth Hostel,** 10 kilometers (6 miles) from town, is pleasantly situated on a shady lagoon in the Veli Tourist Village. A restaurant, water sports, and cheap accommodation should be a winning combination, but these two are inconvenient to almost everything. You must take a ricksha or bus to town, thus using up both your savings and precious time.

DOUBLES FOR LESS THAN RS 850 ($28.33)

In the heart of town, the 52-room, **Hotel Pankaj,** M. G. Road (opposite the Secretariat), Thiruvananthapuram 695001 (☎ 76667; fax 76255), is modern and well maintained, with 52 rooms and two restaurants—the one on the rooftop has a terrific view. The brick-accented reception makes a nice first impression. Room color schemes emphasize green tones (even the furniture is lacquered green). Some rooms are non-AC. Standard rooms with AC are Rs 600 ($20) single, Rs 850 ($28.33) double; deluxe rooms with AC are Rs 650 ($21.66) single, Rs 900 ($30) double. This one is good in its price range.

The **Jas Hotel,** P.O. Box 431, Thycaud/Aristo Junction, Thiruvananthapuram 695014 (☎ 64881), boasts the highest rooftop restaurant in the city and is a great place to enjoy typical Kerala foods and a panoramic view (see "Where to Eat," below). The 45 busily wallpapered rooms (some non-AC) need some TLC but are a good buy. Doubles are around Rs 500 ($16.66); suites Rs 600 ($20) to Rs 800 ($26.66).

Nice and new, **Hotel Residency Tower,** South Gate of Secretariat, Press Road, Thiruvananthapuram 695001 (☎ 331661; fax 330849), is a cozy, 49-room, partially AC hotel with a quiet, tasteful cream and taupe color scheme. Rates for AC rooms are Rs 430 ($14.33) single, Rs 600 ($20) double, Rs 700 ($63.33) suite. There are also a restaurant, bar, and conference hall.

Plants accent the modern functional lobby at **Hotel Geeth,** near the General Post Office, Pulimoodu Junction (☎ 71941). The partially AC hotel has 52 uninspired rooms. AC rates are Rs 300 ($10) single, Rs 400 ($13.33) double, Rs 480 ($16) suite. Its nicest feature is the Pamir rooftop restaurant open from 7 to 11pm.

KTDC's **Hotel Chaithram,** Thampanoor, Thiruvananthapuram (☎ 75777), has an atrium-style lobby with a cushioned conversation pit and 88 clean rooms (some non-AC). AC doubles are Rs 550 ($18.33). After you're settled in, check out the two restaurants—vegetarian and nonvegetarian—the bar, and the lawns. Services include a travel agency and currency exchange. This is a penny-wise choice near the bus and railway stations, next to the Tourist Information Centre.

Highlands, Manjalaikulam Road (☎ 78440), has 85 acceptable rooms, a few with AC. Doubles run Rs 350 ($11.66). There is no restaurant, but several are nearby.

The 23-room **Hotel Amritha,** Thycaud, Thiruvananthapuram 695014 (☎ 63091), has modest, fairly clean rooms; it is conveniently located near the railway station.

Doubles for Less Than Rs 1,200 ($40)

An old standby, the Kerala Tourism's 44-room **Mascot Hotel,** Mascot Junction, Trivandrum-Thiruvananthapuram 695033 (☎ 438990; fax 434406), is about half a mile from downtown. One wing of this rambling hotel was an office building more than a century ago. Halls lined with fresh plants lead to comfortable rooms, some with dressing rooms and high ceilings. Rates for doubles with AC range from Rs 995 ($33.16) to Rs 1,195 ($39.83). All share a shady verandah and look out over well-maintained lawns. Enjoy a 24-hour coffee shop, outdoor barbecues, swimming pool, and health club.

The lively **Hotel Luciya Continental,** East Fort, Thiruvananthapuram 695023 (☎ 463443; fax 67642), has 100 rooms, central AC, and a diverse crowd of locals and foreigners mingling in the popular Zodiac restaurant. Spend a night in China, Arabia, or old Kerala in one of the exotic suites—for Rs 2,200 ($73.33)—or sleep in a tailored, uninspired standard double for about Rs 900 ($30). The only discotheque in town and a bar are diversions.

South Park, M. G. Road, Thiruvananthapuram 695034 (☎ 76667; fax 68861), has been done in the more-is-more school of decor. The lobby is all mirrors and crystal chandeliers, marble floors, and cushioned banquette seating with plants here and there; even the elevators are gussied up with copper and brass. Calm prevails in the rooms, which are comfortably but not imaginatively furnished. Rates range from Rs 1,095 ($36.50) to Rs 1,195 ($39.83) double. (Reservations through the

Welcomgroup.) Caters to the well-heeled business traveler. For restaurants, see "Where to Eat," below.

Hotel Horizon, Aristo Road, Thiruvananthapuram 695014 (☎ 66880), has 46 (some non-AC) uninspired, modern rooms and a spacious atrium-style lobby, where planters and marble floors contrast with stone-block walls. Maintenance and staff have drifted downward here. Presently Rs 800 ($26.66) seems high for a double at this hotel.

WHERE TO EAT

BUFFETS

Hotels offering budget-stretching buffets include: **Luciya Continental,** East Fort (☎ 463443); breakfast, from 6 to 11am, is Rs 110 ($3.66); lunch, from noon to 3pm, and dinner, from 7:30 to 11pm, are each Rs 175 ($5.83). **Hotel Pankaj,** M. G. Road (☎ 76667), has lunch buffet in the Sandya on the fifth floor, where there's a lovely view, from 12:30 to 3pm (not served Sundays and holidays). **South Park,** M. G. Road (☎ 65666), serves buffet lunch and dinner in the elegant Regency Room amid mirrors, pillars, and lantern lighting; lunch, from 1 to 3pm, and dinner, from 7:30 to 11pm, are around Rs 150 ($5)each. The **Mascot Hotel** (☎ 438990) has a lunch buffet.

OTHER HOTEL RESTAURANTS

Savor Kerala curries or Continental food in rooftop restaurants with stellar views. **Jas Hotel,** Thycaud (☎ 64881), has a plant-decked, open-air roof garden and offers a panoramic view and Kerala-style curries and other dishes in the Rs 55 ($1.83) to Rs 60 ($2) range at lunch and dinner. The top-floor restaurant at **Hotel Pankaj,** M. G. Road (☎ 76667), serves an à la carte dinner in addition to the previously mentioned buffet lunch. At the **Hotel Geeth,** Pulimoodu (☎ 71941), Pamir, a roof-garden restaurant, serves moderately priced à la carte meals from 7 to 11pm. **Horizon's** (☎ 66888) handsomely landscaped roof garden was not functioning recently but was expected to again.

OUTSIDE OF THE HOTELS

Atmospheric **Nalukettu,** opposite the Inspector General's Office (☎ 69287), is in a traditional old Nair home, with high ceiling, wooden beams, a generous covered porch, and Kerala specialties; entrées are in the Rs 20 (66¢) range. There's lawn service at night, an indoor air-conditioned section, but most people eat on the covered porch. Open from 11am to 11pm; reservations recommended.

Lowest-budget travelers make a beeline for the two modest **Indian Coffee Houses** (both on M. G. Road near Spencers and near East Fort Bus Stand), where there's delicious coffee and snacks rarely higher than Rs 8 (27¢). Both are open from 8:30am to 8:30pm. The nonatmospheric **Azad,** M. G. Road, has non-veg North Indian dishes. **Arul Jyothi,** opposite the Secretariat, is famous for its mammoth dosas. **Parthas,** T.C., 38/1520 Power House Road, has delicious seafood and typical South Indian dishes. **Arya Bhavan,** near the railway station and the Central Bus Station, has cheap vegetarian meals.

NIGHTLIFE & ENTERTAINMENT

The discotheque at the **Luciya Continental** is open Fridays and Saturdays from 10pm onwards; most of the top hotels have bars. For arts and cultural events, contact **C.V.N. Kalari,** East Fort (☎ 74182), which specializes in kalaripattu, Kerala'a ancient martial art; the **Indian Council for Cultural Relations,** Vellayambalam

(☎ 62489); and other organizations such as **Thiruvananthapuram Kathakali Club** about dance and other cultural events.

2 Kovalam Beach

About 11 1/2 kilometers (7 miles) south of Thiruvananthapuram is Kovalam Beach, so fabulous it's almost a cliché: age-old black rocks, towering palms, pale sands, and gentle surf (take care—there can be an undertow!). It has remained peaceful as it develops into a popular resort. Although Kovalam has its overtouristed side, Lighthouse Beach being a prime example with shops, cafes, and hotels, and tourists who leave more than their footprints in the sands (butts, plastic bags), Kovalam has much to offer, even on this wildly popular stretch of beach and elsewhere. For those who enjoy a beach holiday, there's good food, views, decent prices, friendly ambience, and a chance to try some Ayurvedic massages. And, recently, the addition of lifeguards has made it safer, too.

Below are only a few of the hotels in various price ranges; by the time you get there, new hotels undoubtedly will have opened. Most hotels offer off-season rates or will negotiate in season if they're not fully occupied. It literally pays rupees to ask about special rates. It can vary, but generally off-season is May 1 through September 30.

ESSENTIALS

GETTING TO KOVALAM

The **bus** from Thiruvananthapuram runs frequently from around 6am to 9pm. You get it at the East Fort Bus Depot and Central Bus Stand, Thampanoor. Early and later buses are the least crowded, although all of them become less crowded as you make stops along the way to the beach. Coming back from Kovalam, buses run often, from around 6am to 10pm. The bus stand is near the Kovalam Ashok Beach Resort. Rickshas and taxis also congregate there.

VISITOR INFORMATION

Kerala Tourism's office is near the entrance of the Kovalam Ashok Beach Resort. The staff here are knowledgeable and helpful.

PADMANABHAPURAM PALACE

Usually visited en route to Kanniyakumari (Cape Comorin) (see Chapter 13, "Southern India") and part of the Kanniyakumari Tour, Padmanabhapuram Palace can also be an interesting excursion from Thiruvananthapuram or Kovalam.

The palace, dating mainly from the 17th century, looks like one structure. But it's actually a series of buildings with peaked pagoda roofs blending as one. Dark teak from the local forests was the basic building material. The mirror-shiny floors look like highly polished stone but are actually a rock-hard compound of pulverized coconut shells and raw egg whites. The rooms and their accouterments are impressive—a dining hall that could hold 1,000 guests at a time, a stone dancing hall with delicately carved stone screens at one end, behind which the ladies of the court used to watch discreetly, and vivid orange, green, and brown murals depicting epic poems.

A century or two ago the palace served as the ancient capital of the Rajas of Travancore. The maharajah's bed, composed of 64 different kinds of medicinal wood and given to him by Portuguese visitors, can still be admired, as can the ivory-inlaid bed of his queen.

The palace, about 53 kilometers (33 miles) south of Thiruvananthapuram, and about 12 kilometers (20 miles) from Kovalam, is open daily except Monday from 9am to 5pm. (The last ticket is sold at 4:30pm.) Entry is Rs 2 (6¢), camera fees range from Rs 5 (17¢) for a still camera to Rs 500 ($16.66) for a video camera. Well-informed guides at the entrance accompany visitors.

Ten miles farther south, another landmark is the **Suchindram Temple,** but non-Hindus are not allowed inside (see "Kanya Kumari" in Chapter 13).

Shopping

Almost everyone with something to sell, from Tibetans to Kashmiris and Karnataka gypsies, beats a path to Kovalam; find them near the Ashok Beach Resort and all along Lighthouse Beach. Buy a carpet for your living room, or have a kurta (a loose-fitting shirt) made. Look for metalware, woodcarvings, and interesting costume jewelry (not especially well made).

WHERE TO STAY

Seasonal rates can vary somewhat from hotel to hotel, but are generally lowest from May to July; and highest from December to February. There are sometimes different rates from August to November, and March to April. Below are the most frequently quoted rates. Don't be shy; if the place isn't full, negotiate a better rate whenever you visit.

Many of the lower-priced hotels are not air-conditioned. Try to get a room on an upper floor and/or facing the sea for cooling breezes. Bring insect repellent for non-AC night visitors and request mosquito netting.

Doubles for Less Than Rs 250 ($8.33)

A Kerala home has been converted into the **Blue Sea,** near telegraph office (☎ 480401), with modest rooms and a garden. The best room is on the top floor with a view. Offering more than you'd expect in this price range, **Wilson's Tourist Home** has 20 rooms (some with Indian-style toilets), an outdoor restaurant, and nice service. Almost always full, **Sergeant Guest House,** Lighthouse Beach, is run by a former sergeant. Clean and interesting, lots of young travelers stay here.

Doubles for Less Than Rs 700 ($23.33)

Samdura Tara, Lighthouse Beach (☎ 480653), and **Orion** are under the same management. Samudra Tara charges Rs 800 ($26.66) for an AC double in season. Orion's eight simple, upstairs rooms have great views and are Rs 600 ($20); four lower-floor rooms are Rs 400 ($13.33); there's a suite for Rs 1,000 ($33.33). Consider these prices guidelines; frankly, the rate structure seemed negotiable.

One of the first to open out this way in the '70s, **Raja Hotel,** Kovalam Beach (☎ 480355), is still going strong, offering 20 no-frills, clean rooms with bathrooms attached, but hot water in buckets, for Rs 400 ($13.33) in season, Rs 300 ($10) off-season. There's a restaurant and bar.

Restful and slightly lower-priced, the **Al Italia Beach Resort,** Samudra Beach (☎ 480319), is situated in a quiet spot with plain, clean rooms, good food, and friendly ambience.

About 5 kilometers (3 miles) from Kovalam on a strip of beach, Kerala Tourism is developing **Lagoona Beach Resort,** Pachalloor (☎ 443738), a resort without such intrusions as TV or loud music. Peace and quiet stretching on to infinity will be coupled with daily backwater village tours. Kerala curries and apam will be served in the restaurant. A welcome respite. You might want to see how far this has progressed.

Simple, basic, and clean is the formula that makes **Hotel Seaweed,** Lighthouse Road, Kovalam 695521 (☎ 480391 in Vizhinjam, 0471-60806 in Thiruvananthapuram), a top choice for budget travelers. There are 35 rooms, a few of them air-conditioned, for Rs 700 ($23.33) double in season; for non-AC doubles,

Rs 600 ($20) is the top price; cheapest rooms, about Rs 200 ($6.66), do not have balconies. There's a rooftop restaurant, open 7am to 10pm. Ayurvedic massages here are around Rs 100 ($3.33) for one hour.

Doubles for Less Than Rs 1,600 ($53.33)

Rockholm, Lighthouse Road, Vizhinjam (☎ 695521), perched on a rocky ledge overhanging the sea. The large, simply decorated rooms have big attached bathrooms and balconies to catch the soft sea breezes. The feeling overall is that of a gracious, well-cared-for private home. Steps lead down to the beach, from which it's a pleasant 15-minute walk to a string of outdoor cafes. Rockholm rates are Rs 775 ($25.88) single, Rs 800 ($26.66) double. Rockholm food is delicious, and the view from the dining room to the sea crashing on the big rocks adds a feast for the eyes. The fish dishes offered in the restaurant are especially recommended, as are reservations for dinner, which are usually required in season for nonresidents. Main dishes are in the Rs 60 ($2) to Rs 120 ($4) range. The highest-priced dishes are for prawns, which are the most popular choice here.

Near Rockholm, **Aparna,** Lighthouse Road (☎ 74367), has eight rooms (two per floor) with no decor to speak off, but views focus your attention outside, especially from the upper floors. Doubles go for Rs 800 ($26.66) in season. There's no restaurant; you can eat at the Rockholm next door.

Also on Lighthouse Road is the hotel **Palmshore (formerly Palmanova),** Vizhinjam (P.O.), Thiruvananthapuram District 695521 (☎ 0471-481481 in Thiruvananthapuram), with 24 air-conditioned, clean, and simply furnished rooms with sundecks and a semiprivate beach, just about perfect for a beach holiday. Peak season is December 21 to January 10, when rates are $50 for an AC single or double; in-season—October through March, except for the December/January peak—the rate for single or double is $40; from April through September, rooms are $40 and $35. Non-AC rooms (an option if you prefer sea breezes) are $5 to $10 cheaper, depending on the season. Adding appeal are herbal massages and complete beauty services.

Set in a palm grove, **Hotel Neptune,** Lighthouse Beach, Vizhinjam (☎ 54222; ☎ 79933 in Thiruvananthapuram), has 37 clean, simply furnished rooms. Three with AC are $25 in season, and some with balconies; non-AC rooms are $15 and face an interior garden courtyard filled with lush potted plants. Traditional rice and curry meals served on plantain leaves (freshly picked leaves are considered cleaner than plates, which gather dust on shelves) cost Rs 40 ($1.33). In season, Kathakali dancers perform here from 6:30 to 8:30pm; nonresidents are welcome. Just call to check times and dates of performances. Nonresidents can also book Ayurvedic oil massages at the Neptune—here around Rs 75 ($2.50).

Moon Light Tourist Home, Kovalam Beach (☎ 480375), has improved. Its 10 rooms (two with AC) range from modest, with mosquito netting for Rs 350 ($11.66), to an AC double for Rs 900 ($30). The hotel organizes backwater boat trips for Rs 500 ($16.66) for two.

Back in Kovalam on Samudra Beach, KTDC's **Samudra Hotel,** G.V. Raja Road, Kovalam 695527 (☎ 0471-62089 in Thiruvananthapuram), has 50 pleasant, modern, functional rooms in the main building and cottages. The room rates vary with the seasons, as well as their locations on the site. You can pay as much as Rs 1,600 ($53.33) for an AC double in season. A fish-curry lunch or dinner costs about Rs 25 ($1.40) in the restaurant.

Worth a Splurge—The Top Spots in & Near Kovalam

Beautiful, elegant **Surya Samudra Beach Garden and Ayurveda Spa,** Pulinkudi Mullur, P.O. Thiruvananthapuram (☎ 480413; fax 471-481124), is about 10 kilometers (6 miles) from Kovalam on a rocky cliff with an exquisite view. There are 14 rooms (a few more were under construction), the most memorable in old Kerala houses that were dismantled, rebuilt, and fixed up with just enough furniture, lovely textiles, and works of art; wait till you see the enclosed, open-air bathrooms. The restaurant is in a separate pavilion and specializes in seafood; a private beach in a secluded cove, cleaned every day with a lifeguard in attendance, gives you some idea of the maintenance. Doubles are Rs 4,000 ($133.33) in season, Rs 1,000 ($33.33) off-season. The hotel is run in cooperation with Toptour GMbH, Piusalle 108, D-48147, Muenster, Germany (☎ 0049-251-23559), and you can reserve there or at the address above. Very romantic.

Somatheeram Beach Resort, Chowara P.O. (☎ 04723-600), 10 kilometers (6 miles) from Kovalam, combines an extensive selection Ayurvedic treatments with a resort atmosphere and a handsome setting. Accommodations are new made-to-look-old well-appointed cottages. Doubles start at Rs 4,000 ($133.33) and go up.

ITDC's **Kovalam Ashok Beach Resort,** Kovalam Beach, Vizhinjam (☎ 480101; fax 48152), offers 189 centrally air-conditioned rooms, most of them in Charles Correa's handsome white structure terraced into landscaped gardens and cliffs jutting over the sea. Every room has a little sundeck and staid, modern furniture. Other rooms are in cottages, and the curious old Victorian castle houses sumptuous suites. A sea-view double goes for Rs 2,800 ($93.33) in season. Castle suites are much higher. Marble graces the spacious lobby floors. There's Shells Restaurant, with huge shell chandeliers, a coffee shop, and outdoor beach snack bar. Two swimming pools, tennis courts, a health club, and a shopping arcade are among the diversions. Nonchalance is elevated to an art form here when it comes to room service and the front desk.

WHERE TO EAT

Most visitors eat in their hotels, but there are some other possibilities, such as the restaurants and Sunday barbecue at the **Kovalam Ashok Beach Resort,** where the average price of main dishes ranges from Rs 60 ($2) vegetarian to Rs 120 ($4) nonvegetarian. At the **Palmanova,** there are always Kerala specialties on the menu (or made to order upon request). Excellent fish dishes are also Rs 60 ($2) to Rs 120 ($4) at **Rockholm** (reservations are a must). Reservations are also necessary for a meal at the atmospheric **Surya Samudra.**

Eating out can be literally eating "out" at the cafes and stalls that line the beach, serving light meals and snacks. Many of these open only in the season when there is enough traffic to make it worthwhile. Some of the cafes blare Western music, show videos, and present live nighttime entertainment. Barbecued fish is a specialty; among those doing it right are **Shell's Bar** and **Velvet.** During the day, vendors hawk fruits and drinks for beach-goers, just as they do at many beaches the world over. The main difference at Kovalam is that even a papaya is not price-fixed—you bargain for your snack.

3 Kochi (Cochin)

If Kerala is India's most beautiful state, which many tourists believe, then the lovely port of Kochi is its jewel. It's heard its share of superlatives—Queen of the Arabian Sea, Venice of the Orient, etc.—but earns most of them simply by being inimitably its unspoiled, relatively unvisited self.

Yet Kochi has everything the average tourist usually seeks—true tropical, palm-studded surroundings, constant sunshine, a harbor that rivals that of Hong Kong, hotels with swimming pools and good food, endless backwater boat trips to eavesdrop on life and work that has not changed for centuries, and cheerful, good-natured people as yet uncorrupted by the corroding tide of tourism.

Kerala is a luxuriant garden state, the fabled land of incense and myrrh—to which King Solomon's ships sailed a thousand years before Christ—and Kochi is the port from which such exotic cargoes as pepper, spices, ivory, and coir are still exported. When the Portuguese established the first European colony in India here in the early 16th century, it had already known the Romans, the Greeks, and the Chinese.

Kochi owes its modern status as an important port to a British admiralty engineer, Sir Robert Bristow, who opened up its backwaters in 1929 by cutting a long, deep channel in the ocean bed.

ESSENTIALS

GETTING TO KOCHI

By Plane The airport is on Willingdon Island, 5 kilometers from Ernakulam. **Indian Airlines** links Kochi with Bombay (1¾ hours, $109); with Delhi (four hours, $200); with Thiruvananthapuram (40 minutes, $23); with Goa (80 minutes, $68); with Madras (65 minutes, $69); and with Bangalore (50 minutes, $40). **East-West** and **Jet** also connect Kochi to Bombay. A prepaid taxi from the airport to Ernakulam costs Rs 50 ($1.65).

For flight information and reservations, you can call **Indian Airlines** (in the city ☎ 352065; at the airport ☎ 364433); **East-West** (in the city ☎ 362111; at the airport ☎ 666509); **Jet Airways** (in the city ☎ 369879; at the airport ☎ 666509).

By Train The *Madras-Kochi Express* leaves **Madras** Central (7:35pm; arrives 8:45am); at Ernakulam Junction it goes on to Willingdon, arriving Kochi H.T. at 9:10am. This 708-kilometer trip to Kochi H.T. costs Rs 1,188 ($39.60) AC First, Rs 137 ($4.56) Second. From **Thiruvananthapuram,** most trains stop only at Ernakulam; among these is the *Kanya Kumari Express,* from Thiruvananthapuram (221 kilometers; departs 7:35am, arrives 1:10pm), for a fare of Rs 482 ($16.07) AC First, Rs 56 ($1.86) Second. For a most scenic coastal ride, local trains connect Thiruvananthapuram, Quilon, Kottayam, and Kochi.

For information, in town call (☎ 353920); Junction (☎ 369119); Terminusk, Willingdon Island (☎ 6050).

By Bus **KSRTC** fast, superfast, and superexpress buses ply the roads to and from Ernakulam and major cities in Kerala; for instance, from Alappuzha (1½ hours) the fare is Rs 20 (66¢); from Kottayam (2½ hours) the fare is Rs 25 (83¢), from Thekkady (6¾ hours) the fare is Rs 50 ($1.66); from Thiruvananthapuram (five hours) the fare is Rs 54 ($1.80), all superfast.

Other KSRTC fares are based on regions. From Bangalore (15 hours) the fare is Rs 155 ($5.16); from Madras (16½ hours) the fare is Rs 132 ($4.40). From Kanniyakumari, via Alappuzha, Kollam, and Thiruvananthapuram (8¾) hours the fare is Rs 70 ($2.33); from Madurai (nine hours) the fare is Rs 70 ($2.33). Many more buses ply this route, operated by private operators as well as KSRTC.

The Central Bus Station is on Stadium Road, near Ernakulam Junction; for KSRTC information call (☎ 352033).

VISITOR INFORMATION

The KTDC **Tourist Reception Centre,** Shanmugham Road, Ernakulam (☎ 353234), open from 8am to 7pm, should be your first stop in town for information, advice on hotels, maps, and tour reservations. The staff are very helpful and well-informed. Ask for a copy of *Kerala Travel Facts* when you stop by.

The **Government of India Tourist Office,** Willingdon Island (☎ 666045), open from 9am to 5pm, shares the Malabar Hotel compound and is another helpful resource. Guides can be hired through the tourist office.

An absolutely indispensable aid to the traveler in Kochi is the *Jaico Time Table (Travel and Tourist Guide),* available for Rs 5 (15¢) at bookstalls and the Tourist Reception Centre. It lists the latest bus, train, and air timings, entertainment, and dozens of other facts of interest.

City Layout

Kochi (Cochin) (pop. 1.14 million) is not just a town but a complex of islands grouped off the mainland town called **Ernakulam.** One of the islands, **Willingdon,** named after Viscount Willingdon (a former governor), 12 square miles, was created in 1900 by a dredge and is where most of the port facilities are centered, also the airport and Kochi Harbor Railway Terminus.

If you arrive by air or some trains, Willingdon will be your debarkation point, and it also contains the main tourist office and, next door, Kochi's most famous hotel, the Malabar.

Also in the harbor are **Gundu Island,** site of the coir factory, and **Bolghatty Island,** with one hotel. To the south are **Mattancherry,** with such attractions as the 16th-century synagogue and Dutch palace and Fort Kochi, site of what is supposed to be the oldest European settlement on the Indian subcontinent. Even from the briefest of descriptions, you can see that Kochi has a fascinating blend of cultures. To the north is **Vypeen,** of little interest to tourists. On the mainland are many hotels, the Ernakulam Junction Railway Station, the Kochi Cultural Centre, main post office, Indian Airlines office, and Kerala State Transportation bus station, and the Tourist Reception Centre, where you can book sightseeing tours.

All the locations are connected by ferries, easily the most pleasant and least expensive way to go from island to island (fares average Rs 1 per trip). A good road and bridges also link Willingdon and Fort Kochi/Mattancherry and Ernakulam.

Getting Around the Islands & Town

BY FERRY Willingdon is connected by ferry to the mainland town of Ernakulam (Rs 1, 25 times a day in either direction). The first ferry from Ernakalum leaves at 6:50am and the last at 9:40pm; from Mattancherry, the first ferry leaves at 6am and the last at 9:10pm. After the last ferry, the trip to and from Ernakulam can be made by taxi or auto ricksha—all the way down the island, across the bridge, and back up the mainland on the other side. The Perumanoor ferry also goes to Willingdon, but is not conveniently located for tourists; it's handy if you're going to or from Air India, which is near the Perumanoor jetty.

Willingdon and Mattancherry are also connected by ferry, running from 6am to 9pm. The trip takes 10 minutes. There is no ferry service between Fort Kochi and Willingdon. You can hire a rowboat for this trip, which should cost Rs 5 (16¢) or Rs 10 (33¢), but invariably the boat owners ask more from foreigners.

Fort Kochi is connected with Ernakulam by ferry service, about a 20-minute crossing, with more than 20 trips a day in either direction, from Ernakulam beginning at 6:30am until 9:40pm, and from Fort Kochi beginning at 6:50am until 9pm.

Ernakulam and Vypeen Island ferries operate all day: beginning at 5:30am from Ernakulam until 10:30pm; from Vypeen, beginning at 6am to 10pm. Between Fort Kochi and Vypeen, there is service about every 10 minutes from 6am to 9pm for a five-minute trip. You can change at Vypeen for the ferry to Fort Kochi. There's also a private ferry between Willingdon and Fort Kochi, every 20 minutes from 6:30am to 9pm; buy tickets at the jetty next to Malabar Hotel.

Ferries to Bolghatty Island run every 20 minutes from High Court Jetty Ernakulam, from 6am to 10pm.

There is no ferry service to Gundu, which can be seen on the sightseeing tour.

BY PRIVATE BOAT Private boats operate between Ernakulam and Varapuzha from 7:40am to 5pm. Take this 40-minute ride if you wish to cruise leisurely for two hours to get a superb close-up look at village life. (Skip Varapuzha if you plan to do a longer backwater cruise described in "Getting to Thiruvananthapuram," above.)

BY TAXI Taxis in Kochi/Ernakulam try to charge what they think the traffic will bear. You must bargain to set a fair fare before you get in. Yellow-top and tourist taxis—those with white license plates—charge about Rs 3 (10¢) per kilometer and Rs 50 ($1.66) per hour. There are extra charges for waiting.

BY AUTO RICKSHA Auto Rickshas have meters, but don't use them. They charge about Rs 4 (13¢) per 1½ kilometers, but fix charges before you get in. Waiting charges are extra.

BY HIRED CAR Cars with drivers can be hired through the **KTDC's Tourist Reception Centre,** Shanmugham Road (☎ 353234), **Great India Tour Co.,** Flat 39/5750, Chiramel Chambers (☎ 373962), and other travel agents and taxi operators around town.

When to Go

The most popular visitor season is October to March. The rainy season is June to October. **Onam** (August and/or September) is a statewide harvest festival, but particularly colorful in the lagoon communities such as Kochi, and especially Alappuzha, where "snake boats" (carved, decorated boats) compete in races for the prime minister's trophy. Also, much cymbal and drum beating, lots of gorgeous floral decorations on the homes, and many graceful dancing girls in white saris make this festival memorable. Also, the **Great Elephant March** in Thiruvananthapuram begins north of and passes through Kochi.

WHAT TO SEE & DO

The island known as **Fort Kochi,** with its settlement named **Mattancherry,** probably has the most to intrigue the tourist. Supposedly, it was the first place in India to be settled by Europeans (Portuguese), and in numerous landmarks their memory remains. Not far from the ferry dock is the **Mattancherry Palace** (open from 10am to 5pm, closed Friday and national holidays), which was built by the Portuguese in 1555, later taken over and altered by the Dutch, and finally handed over to the local maharajas, who added the ambitious *Ramayana* murals that cover the walls of the royal bedchamber. The building itself, low slung and with gently sloping, red-tile roofs, is quite incongruous in Indian surroundings and therefore all the more interesting to see. Its carved teak ceilings could have come from any wooden warship of the period. Apart from the brightly colored Shiva and Vishnu scenes and some stray weapons hung on the walls, the chief interest centers on some elegant ivory palanquins (enclosed litters) with the family motto "Honor Is Our Family Treasure" painted on the side and gold-embroidered coverlets, and that celebrated piece of Indian furniture, the howdah, for riding on the back of elephants. Referred to locally as the "Dutch Palace," the building was never used as a residence, only for a coronation. It is really four buildings in one, arranged around a central courtyard. Two of the buildings are Hindu temples, one dedicated to Vishnu and one to Shiva. A high wall, with entrances to the east and to the west, surrounds the complex.

Not far away is the area where the descendants of a centuries-old **colony of Jewish refugees** from Roman-dominated Jerusalem still live. There were a lot of them originally, once protected by one of the local kings (who gave them a charter to the land, inscribed on copper plates), persecuted later by the Portuguese, and finally once again allowed peace under Dutch, British, and Indian rule. In December 1968, they celebrated the 400th anniversary of the founding of their lovely Chinese-tiled **synagogue;** the ceremonies were attended by the late Prime Minister Indira Gandhi, who stood amid the silken drapes and under the colored lanterns and chandeliers and wished the community—now under 100—long life. The synagogue is open to visitors from 10am to noon, and 2 to 5pm every day but Saturday.

Another religious shrine is Fort Kochi's **St. Francis Church,** built by the Portuguese in 1503, converted into a Dutch Reform and then later an Anglican church. Tombstones of members of all three faiths line the aisles, the most famous of which is the Portuguese explorer Vasco da Gama, who died here in 1534, his remains later being removed to Lisbon. Locked up in the church office are Dutch baptism and marriage records dating back to the 1730s. The church is closed Sundays.

Get your camera ready for one of Kochi's popular "Kodak moments"—the graceful **Chinese fishing nets** at the entrance to the harbor. North of St. Francis Church along Calvetty Road is a good place to get a good shot. Though used elsewhere, they have become almost synonymous with Kochi. They were introduced to Kerala by traders from the courts of Kublai Khan.

GUIDED TOURS

A pleasant guided **Kerala Tourism Development Corporation (KTDC)** tour takes in the major landmarks—synagogue, Dutch Palace, etc., plus Bolghatty—for Rs 40 ($1.33) per person. Usually there are two tours a day, at 9am and 2pm, lasting 3½ hours each. Departures are from the Sealord Hotel's jetty.

KTDC's other guided tours include the following: a daily Sunset Tour, from 5:30 to 7pm, which costs Rs 25 (83¢) per person; twice-daily Backwaters Village Tours, at 8am (mornings are cooler) and 2pm, for Rs 300 ($10) each, which are conducted in a country boat and is an exceptionally interesting two-hour expedition through narrow channels to a coir village, a famous Shiva temple, and performance of kalaripattu, the traditional marital art of Kerala. A daily coach tour, leaving at 9:30am, returning at 7:30pm, which costs Rs 75 ($2.50), includes the city sights and those beyond such as the Museum of Kerala History (10 kilometers) at Edappally, Tripunithura (10 kilometers), the hill palace of the maharaja of Cochin (now the Hill Palace Museum), and Kalady (48 kilometers), the birthplace of Shankaracharya, the renowned 8th-century philosopher.

KSTD also runs outstation tours. A 2-day tour to Thekkady costs Rs 200 ($6.66), departing at 7:30am Saturdays and returning 8pm on Sundays; overnighting in Periyar. A three-day Cochin-Velankanni Tour leaves at 8am every second Friday of the month for Rs 525 ($17.50), and takes in Thekkaday, Madurai, and Thanjavur. The one-day Cochin-Arthirappally-Vazhachal Tour, for Rs 100 ($3.33), visits some famous waterfalls.

Reservations for all tours can be made through the **KTDC Tourist Reception Centre,** Shanmugham Road, Ernakulam (☎ 353234), open from 8am to 7pm.

SHOPPING

Look for coir items (mats, carpets), carved rosewood objects, water buffalo horns, elephants of sweet-smelling sandalwood, incense, beads, Kerala's beautiful white and gold saris, shawls, and unusual coconut-shell spoons, egg cups, etc. Places to bargain hunt include the **Kerala Government Handicrafts Store,** Kairali; and **State Handicrafts emporium,** Saurabhai; and **Apex Society,** Khadi Bhavan, all on Mahatma Gandhi Road, Ernakulam; open most every day but Sunday, from 10am to 1pm and from 3 to 8pm. Convent girls' intricate embroideries on clothes, napkins, and place mats are sold at **Our Ladies Convent** (near Mattancherry), Palluruthy P.O., Kochi (☎ 230508); **Kasav Kada** (near Fine Arts Society) (☎ 372395), open from 9am to 8pm, except Sundays, sells the famous white cotton woven with real gold and/or silver bridal saris so elaborate they each can take 20–30 days to make. One sari can run Rs 7,000 ($233.33) or more (a small fortune to some in India) and might be made also into fabulous evening wear or bridal dress in the West. They are woven in Balaramapuram, a village near Kovalam en route Kanniyakumari.

WHERE TO STAY

Luxury taxes add 5% to 15% to most room tariffs quoted below. Some hotels also add a 10% service charge, as well as a 10% to 15% service charge for room service. Some offer off-season discounts. All add sales taxes for food and beverages.

All hotels, unless otherwise indicated, have attached bathrooms, with hot and cold running water, room telephones, radios, TVs, restaurants, and/or bars and coffee shops. Most have gift counters or shops, travel facilities, and accept international credit cards.

ON WILLINGDON ISLAND

On Willingdon are the famous five-star Malabar, three-star Casino and very modest Maruthi Tourist Home.

The splurge-priced 100-room **Hotel Malabar,** Willingdon Island, Kochi 682003 (☎ 666811; fax 668297), a Taj Group hotel, has a great location right on the waterfront overlooking the harbor, bay, and backwaters. The hotel has spacious lawns, a swimming pool, bar, and restaurants. Dating from colonial days, the Malabar has been refurbished and expanded but still retains its old-fashioned charm and ancient Dutch-influenced Kerala architecture. Rates range from $80 for a double to $250 for a lavish suite. The Government of India Tourist Office is on the grounds.

Set back from the street, the homelike **Casino Hotel,** Willingdon Island, Kochi 682003 (☎666821; fax 668001), is situated only a couple of hundred yards from the Kochi Harbor Railway Terminus. It's light and airy, with colored coir carpeting and other local furnishings. There's a swimming pool, restaurant in an adjoining building (the hotel began from this restaurant), a top-notch outdoor seafood cafe, and a bookstore. Rooms are attractively and comfortably furnished, with refrigerators and air-conditioning among their amenities. Singles cost $35; doubles $65—plus the expected taxes. No views, waterfront or otherwise.

Next to the Casino Hotel, the **Maruthi Tourist Home,** Willingdon Island, Kochi 682003 (☎ 668069), has 26 rooms (some non-AC) that are almost always full of business travelers who congregate in the bar. The rooms are simple and worn, with attached, Western-style bathrooms. The air-conditioned rooms at Rs 200 ($6.66) are best. Non-AC rooms need TLC. You can get a good thali meal in the vegetarian restaurant for Rs 14 (47¢). There a slightly pricier, non-veg AC restaurant.

IN ERNAKULAM

M. G. (Mahatma Gandhi) Road is lined with hotels, shops, restaurants and other businesses. Following are a few hotels.

Doubles for Less Than Rs 300 ($10)

Hotel Luciya, Stadium Road, near the State Bus Stand, Ernakulam, Kochi 682011 (☎ 354433), has 106 rooms (eight AC). The hotel has declined over the years, but the rates are attractive and management is nice. Non-AC rooms run Rs 60 ($2) single and Rs 102 ($3.40) double. Here, as elsewhere, if rooms are non-AC, they have ceiling fans. AC singles are Rs 125 ($4.16) and doubles Rs 220 ($7.33). It has a bar and restaurant (recently under renovation) on the premises and serves both vegetarian and nonvegetarian food.

Among the best of the low-priced places is **K. K. International,** opposite the Ernakulam Railway Station, Kochi 682016 (☎ 366010), with 75 rooms, eight air-conditioned. This is a simple place, and although careworn, it is also clean and pleasant. The rooms have patterned wallpaper or painted walls and furniture that's been painted white with a brown trim; they have attached bathrooms with cold running water and hot water in buckets. Considering how hot it is in Kochi at times, a cold shower might be quite the thing. Rates for AC doubles are Rs 275 ($9.16); non-AC doubles are Rs 135 ($4.50); non-AC singles as low as Rs 80 ($2.66). South and North Indian dishes, and Chinese and Continental vegetarian and nonvegetarian foods are served in the restaurant.

Hotel Mercy, M. G. Road, Ravipuram, Fort Kochi (☎ 367040), offers fairly clean rooms and is a good buy in this price range. Rates are Rs 180 ($6) AC double, Rs 100 ($3.33) non-AC double. The rooftop restaurant has good views and thalis for Rs 40 ($1.33) non-veg, Rs 22 (73¢) veg. There's a bar where whiskey is Rs 40 ($1.33) per peg; beer Rs 40 ($1.33). The small garden has a golden statue and swings for children.

Bijus Tourist Home, Market Road, near Canon Shed Junction, Ernakulam (☎ 369881), has 28 clean rooms, some with AC, for Rs 280 ($9.33) to Rs 300 ($10); there's room service, but you'll have to go out for a restaurant.

On Shanmugham Road, the low-priced **Hotel Sea Shells,** Ernakulam, Kochi 628031 (☎ 353807), has 10 Spartan rooms, those facing the street with great sea views; the two AC rooms, at Rs 108 ($3.60) have attached bathrooms with hot and cold running water. In others, for Rs 80 ($2.66), hot water is supplied in buckets. The staff is friendly and helpful. Sea Shells has a bar and small dining room serving veg and non-veg dishes. In modest places such as this, vegetarian food is not only cheapest, but safest, requiring less care in storing or preparation than non-veg.

Almost as simple as Sea Shells, and nearby, is a low-budget travelers' favorite—**Hotel Hakoba,** Shanmugham Road, Ernakulam, Kochi (☎ 353933), with its 12 double rooms, for Rs 108 ($3.60). From rooms 31, 35, and 39, you'll have fine sea views from huge windows; some have attached bathrooms with Western-style plumbing and running hot water. The halls could be a lot tidier, but the rooms are clean, and the service is friendly and efficient. There's a dark bar always filled with men; the restaurant offers the usual Indian, Chinese, and Continental menu. Near the ferry dock.

Possibly one of the best buys in the low-price range is **Piazza Lodge,** conveniently near Ernakulam Railway Station (☎ 367408), with attractive rooms; AC doubles go for Rs 200 ($6.66); non-AC doubles are Rs 110 ($3.66).

The **YWCA,** Chittor Road, Ernakulam (☎ 355620), has five rooms for guests (men only): two singles and three doubles, all under Rs 100 ($3.33). Meals are served in the big dining hall, where you get inexpensive vegetarian and nonvegetarian fare. Contact: general secretary.

Doubles for Less Than Rs 600 ($20)

Penny-wise tip: The non-AC rooms in the hotels below can cost as much as Rs 100 less than the AC-double rate. If a ceiling fan will do for you, these can be very good buys.

Hotel Excellency, Nettipadam Road (☎ 374001; fax 370397), is new, next to the ritzy Avenue Regent, steps off M. G. Road, and a seven-minute stroll to the South Junction Railway Station. It has small, neat, and clean rooms, with doubles Rs 450 ($15). Complimentary coffee and newspaper are delivered between 6 and 7:30am. Elegancy restaurant serves Kerala, Chinese, Continental, and tandoori cuisine until 11:30pm. No liquor, but you can bring your own.

Hotel Joyland, D. H. Road (☎ 367764; fax 370645), has 40 rooms (4 with AC). AC doubles, with rates of Rs 375 ($12.50), have painted white furniture and printed drapes and spreads that are much better maintained than the scruffy halls. The hotel was renovating its reception to make room for a shopping arcade. The rooftop restaurant was not operating; room service only. Conveniently located to railway station and transport bus stand.

Among the best buys on M. G. Road is the Indian-style hotel **Woodlands,** Woodlands Junction, M. G. Road, Ernakulam, Kochi 682011 (☎ 351372; fax 368795), a friendly place with 65 rooms (23 AC)—spacious, not elaborate, but clean and with such amenities as attached bathrooms with either Western- or Indian-style toilets. Some rooms have balconies; those with AC have fancier furniture. Doubles with AC are around Rs 450 ($15). For about Rs 26 (86¢) you can get an unlimited thali meal in the Lotus Cascade restaurant.

Two hotels popular with Westerners are the **Sangeetha,** Chittor Road, Ernakulam, Kochi 682016 (☎ 368736; fax 354261), and the **Gaanam Hotels Ltd.,** 36/1675 Chittor Rd. (☎ 367123; fax 354261), behind the one-star, partially AC Sangeetha, in the same compound. At the all-vegetarian Sangeetha, there are 45 functionally furnished rooms, all with bathrooms attached and hot and cold running water. A nice feature is the complimentary Indian-style breakfast for each guest, offering a selection of traditional South Indian dishes (try the idli). Rates for standard double with AC—Rs 250 ($8.33)—are slightly lower than those at the Gaanam. Service charge is 10%.

The 40-room (24 with AC) **Gaanam** is a two-star hotel. All rooms have phones, piped-in music, and modern attached bathrooms with marble flooring. Deluxe rooms have closed-circuit TV. Tariffs for pleasant, comfortable standard AC rooms are about Rs 500 ($16.66). Service charge is 10%. The Gaanam offers guests a choice of complimentary vegetarian or nonvegetarian breakfast, and both vegetarian and nonvegetarian food in the two restaurants. There is also a pleasant rooftop restaurant open in the evenings.

Near the bus terminal on Durbar Hall Road, the 92-room **Bharat Hotel,** Ernakulam, Kochi 682016 (☎353501; fax 370502), is also next door to Indian Airlines and a short stroll from the ferry terminal and Ernakulam Railway Station. Bharat is a vegetarian hotel set in a pretty little garden. There's a mural featuring a village woman in the reception area, which is decorated with a chairs covered brocade prints and patterned area rugs. Doubles with AC cost Rs 500 ($16.66). The two restaurants (covered later in "Where to Eat," below) serve both South and North Indian vegetarian foods. There is also a coffee shop for drinks and snacks. The rooms overall are nice, especially those with sea views; although some need paint jobs, they are clean.

Also on M. G. Road, the **Grand Hotel,** Ernakulam, Kochi, 682001 (☎ 353211), is a pleasant, tropical-style building with 24 rooms. Rooms are large and clean; doubles cost Rs 400 ($13.33), some with balconies. There is a 10% service charge. Meals are served in the large, airy dining room. There is also the AC Peacock restaurant. The cozy little round bar with wood-slatted walls, booths, and a marble top is open from 10am to 11pm. There's lawn service in the evenings.

M. G. Road is also the location of tidy and pleasant Indian-style **Dwaraka Hotel,** Ernakulam, Kochi 682016 (☎ 352706), with 42 rooms; central AC is a recent addition to the third floor. New wing rooms are best, big and clean with tile floors and new wood furniture and printed drapes. An AC double is Rs 350 ($11.66). Dwaraka's two AC vegetarian restaurants serve both South and North Indian dishes.

A hotel with bigger than average rooms is **Sun International,** Rajaji Road, Kochi (☎ 364162). The halls could use a paint job, but the rooms, while modest, are clean and the price is right; AC doubles go for Rs 350 ($11.66).

Doubles for Less Than Rs 1,000 ($33.33)

On Shanmugham Road, the splurgey-feeling, 40-room **Sealord Hotel** (☎ 352682), has all kinds of amenities and a pleasant rooftop restaurant, and a sunbathing terrace in the shape of a ship's deck, both with wonderful views. The Princess Room restaurant serves well-prepared food on the first floor (see "Where to Eat," below). Sealord's rooms are modern and functional. Doubles, Rs 700 ($23.33), let also as singles, for Rs 500 ($16.66). Some cheaper non-AC rooms are available.

Among the outstanding buys is centrally air-conditioned **Abad Plaza,** M. G. Road, Kochi 682035 (☎ 361636; fax 370729), which has a hint of old Dutch in its architecture. Marble floors gleam under a glistening crystal chandelier in its small lobby and reception area. The 80 tastefully furnished rooms and suites have varied color schemes; soft earth tones or crisp, white, green, and blue are among them. Good maintenance starts with the hotel's owner, who will touch up hall walls himself if they show wear. Highest doubles go for around Rs 850 ($28.33). The elegant Regency Room (see "Where to Eat," below) is open from 12:30 to 3pm and from 7:30pm to midnight; there's a rooftop swimming pool and health club.

On M. G. Road, the **International Hotel,** P.B. 3563, Ernakulam, Kochi 682035 (☎ 353911; fax 373929), is spacious and clean, with a big upstairs lounge, Persian-style carpets on the stairs, and most rooms with all amenities and balconies. There is a bar, dining room, roof garden, and nice outdoor terrace. The hotel is centrally air-conditioned. The highest double is around Rs 900 ($30), plus a 10% service charge. The Coq D'or Restaurant serves both vegetarian and nonvegetarian meals, Indian, Continental, and Chinese, from 7am to 12:30am. The Belle Bar, with leatherette booths and a jug-of-wine, loaf-of-bread theme mural, opens from 10:30am to 10:30pm.

Doubles for Less Than Rs 2,000 ($66.66)

On a prime waterfront location, at the **Taj Residency,** Marine Drive, Ernakulam 682011 (☎ 371471; fax 371481), you see fantastic sunsets and sunrises from nicely furnished rooms, with rates of $38 to $78 per night. There are also views from the 24-hour bar and Indian restaurant. The hotel's pitch is to the "businessman" (tsk, tsk, Taj Group, how about all those businesswomen?), but despite this, equal attention is given to tourists. No stay is complete without a stop at the La Patisserie for a luscious pastry. There's a pool.

The ritzy new **Avenue Regent,** 39/1796A, M. G. Road (☎ 353003; fax 228640), has Fragonard-style art at reception and a French period atmosphere in the lobby, with 62 spacious centrally air-conditioned rooms upstairs. Double rates range from $40 to $47. This two-year-old hotel seems off to a good start when it comes to maintenance and service. There's a good buffet in the restaurant (see "Where to Eat," below).

Hotel Presidency, Ernakulam Town, Kochi 682018 (☎ 363100), has a world map on the wall in the reception area, and Kerala-style lamps hang from the lofty ceiling in the lounge, which is furnished with comfortable wicker armchairs set off by tropical plants. Centrally air-conditioned, with a three-star rating, the hotel makes extensive use of rosewood in the decor of the rooms, where beds have fancy carved headboards and colorful coverlets. Rates are Rs 1,000 ($33.33) for a double.

In Fort Kochi

The best hotel in Fort Kochi is **Hotel Abad,** Chullickal Junction, Fort Kochi 682005 (☎ 282111), on the main highway between Fort Kochi and Ernakulam, under the same ownership as the pricier Abad Plaza in Ernakulam. Abad is centrally air-conditioned, its 20 rooms clean and cheerful with printed spreads and drapes and all the amenities. Doubles are about Rs 400 ($13.33). Both the restaurant coffee shop serve good seafood dishes (see "Where to Eat," below).

Seagull Hotel , Calvathy Road, Fort Kochi (☎ 228128), set in old buildings back from the street and on the waterfront, has six rooms, two with baths attached and AC. The AC rooms run Rs 350 ($11.66), while non-AC rooms are priced from Rs 175 ($5.83) to Rs 250 ($8.33). All are simple, but recently spruced up. The attached bathrooms on the ground floor have cold running water, and hot water is ordered by the bucket. The rooms are modest and the views from them are not spectacular. But the entire front of the hotel is a glass-walled dining room/lounge facing the sea. The restaurant's fish curry and seafood are considered some of the best in town (see "Where to Eat," below). There's an air-conditioned bar.

Tharavadu Tourist Home, Quiros Street, Fort Cochin 682001 (☎ 2266894), has eight no-frills rooms, two with a common bathroom, in a charming 300-year-old building with solid teak floors and beamed ceilings. Rates are Rs 75 ($2.50).

On Bolghatty Island

On the island of Bolghatty, the **Bolghatty Palace Hotel,** Kochi 682504 (☎ 355003), has a commanding position facing the outlet to the open sea to one side and the High Court Jetty in Ernakulam, a brief ferry boat ride away, to the other. The building, set on great lawns dotted with big trees, was once a governor's palace, soundly built by the Dutch in 1744, and later the home of British governors. It has timbered ceilings, polished plank floors, and teakwood staircases to enchant the tourist snowed by history, and its enormous rooms with vast bathrooms could each accommodate a cricket team. Unfortunately, much of this elegance is seedy now. The cottages on the grounds bear no relationship to the architectural grandeur of the main building. Their rooms are as small and compact as train compartments; their nicest feature is a verandah overlooking the water. Rates range from Rs 300 ($10) for a non-AC single, to Rs 1,250 ($41.66) for a suite. The cottages, priced from Rs 625 ($20.83) to Rs 725 ($24.17), have fared better than the rooms in the main building. There's ferry service between the island and mainland every 20 minutes, or you can hire a rowboat for the journey. Sightseeing tours stop here, and nonresidents are welcome at the evening kathakali show at 6:30pm (but there are better shows on the mainland).

WHERE TO EAT

BUFFETS

In Willingdon

Budget-stretching buffets featuring a wide array of Kerala-style and Continental foods, cool salads, and rich desserts are served at the **Malabar Hotel** (☎ 666811) in **The Waterfront Cafe** for Rs 175 ($5.83); hours are 12:30 to 3pm, Monday through Saturday for lunch, with dinner on Sunday from 7 to 11pm. **Casino** (☎ 66821) serves buffets at breakfast, from 6:45 to 9:30am for Rs 90 ($3), and at lunch, from 12:30 to 3pm for Rs 140 ($4.66) daily in the **Tharavad** (which means "ancestral home").

In Ernakulam

The **International Hotel** (☎ 353911) has a lunch buffet daily from 11am to 3pm for Rs 106 ($3.53), including tax. **Hotel Abad Plaza,** M. G. Road (☎ 361636), has a daily lunch buffet for Rs 125 ($4.16) in the **Regency Room,** aglow with mirrors and rosewood pillars, lacy drapes, and stucco walls. **Taj Residency's** (☎ 371471) **Utsav,** an Indian restaurant with a temple decor incorporating copper canopies, wood carvings, and enjoyable views, has a lavish daily lunch buffet for Rs 145 ($4.83). The **Sealord Hotel** (☎ 352682) has buffets on Saturday and Sunday from 8 to 11:30pm, for around Rs 100 ($3.33).

THALIS

Here's another penny-wise tip: Eat budget-priced thalis for nutritious, delicious meals.

On Willingdon Island

Thilakam Food, Harbour Gate, Willingdon Island (☎ 667526), run by Bharat Tourist Home, has a delicious thali for Rs 28 (93¢), and dishes such as idli and dosa—fast food India style.

Fort Cochin is the name of the outdoor thatch-covered restaurant at **Casino Hotel** (☎ 666821), where seafood is the specialty. Have a lovely meal of fresh grilled fish, Indian bread hot off the griddle, vegetables, and dessert for around Rs 150 ($3) to Rs 200 ($6.66). The meal is pricey but delicious and well served.

In Ernakulam

The **Bharat Hotel,** D. H. Road, Ernakulam (☎ 353501), offers a vegetarian thali meal for Rs 23.50 (78¢), tax included, in the AC restaurant, a few rupees less in the non-AC section.

Maduban in Dwaraka Hotel, Ernakulam (☎ 352706), is attractive, with rosewood furniture with pink-and-gray striped upholstery, sparkling, pink-and-gray marble floor, and soft, restful lighting. A South Indian thali costs Rs 33 ($1.10), a North Indian thali Rs 40 ($1.40). Open 6am to 10pm.

Lotus Cascade, in the Woodlands Hotel, M. G. Road (☎ 351372), is sleek, modern, and charges Rs 25.45 (85¢) for an unlimited thali meal, tax included—a good buy. Dosas here, from Rs 8.50 (28¢) to Rs 13.50 (45¢), are exceptionally fine.

At cheerful **Sathya** (above Bimbis), M. G. Road, big windows are attractive and Rs 25 (83¢) to Rs 30 ($1) buys a thali meal.

Plain but clean, **Suraam,** Railway Station Road, serves a plate meal (not a thali, a meal on a plate, no refills) for Rs 15 (50¢); fish curry is Rs 16 (53¢).

Among the cheapest thalis in town is the one at **Arun Joythi,** Shanmugham Road (☎ 351747), for Rs 7 (23¢); hours are 7am to 9pm.

In Fort Kochi

At **Hotel Abad,** Fort Kochi (☎ 282111), you can get an "executive" thali for Rs 37 ($1.23) from noon to 3pm.

OTHER RESTAURANTS

On Willingdon Island

For a delicious splurge-priced Chinese meal in an regal setting try the Szechuan specialties at **The Jade Pavilion** at the **Malabar Hotel** (☎ 666811).

Fort Cochin is the name of the outdoor thatch-covered restaurant at Casino **Hotel** (☎ 666821), where seafood is the specialty. Have a lovely meal of fresh grilled fish, Indian bread hot off the griddle, vegetables, and dessert for around Rs 150 ($3) to Rs 200 ($6.66). The meal is pricey but delicious and well served.

In Ernakulam

At **Pandhal,** M. G. Road, Ernakulam (☎ 367759), which is owned by the Casino Hotel, the dark wood ceiling and white walls serve as backdrops to the chairs upholstered in rust-colored fabric, and an abundance of potted palms. Pandhal (which means "archway") is popular with foreigners, and they most often order Chinese fried rice and noodles for Rs 42 ($1.40) to Rs 50 ($1.66), or a variety of pizzas with tomatoes, onions, cheese, mushrooms, and a smattering of Indian cheese (not like mozzarella) on a cookie-style crust for Rs 40 ($1.33) to Rs 42 ($1.40)—only a distant relative of pizzas in the United States. Some make a beeline for the gooey ice cream sundaes and rich, Western pastries, the latter available in an adjoining shop, but also served at table for Rs 20 (66¢) to Rs 40 ($1.33). Pandhal also serves low-cholesterol, high-fiber, and diabetic meals. It is open from noon to midnight.

For a colorful array of Indian sweets and snacks, **Bimbis,** M. G. Road, Jose Junction (☎ 360357), clean and crisply decorated in red, white, and black, is always a top choice. It's one of three places to eat sandwiched into one building. Above Bimbis, and under the same management, is **Khyber,** an attractive, lantern-lit place selling North Indian dishes, including tandooris. The highest-priced items on the menu are around Rs 45 ($1.50). One flight above is cheerful **Sathya,** a multicuisine restaurant where entrées top off at about Rs 55($1.83) and where there are thalis (see "Thalis," above) for less.

Across from Bimbis is the **Indian Coffee House,** for cheap coffee for around Rs 2 (6¢), such snacks as masala dosa for Rs 5.50 (18¢), and dubious hygiene.

Attractive and midpriced is the **Peacock Restaurant,** in the Grand Hotel, Mahatma Gandhi Road, Ernakulam (☎ 353211). It has a fancy floral-patterned ceiling, teak and leather booths, gold drapes, and wood paneling—all this and AC too. The chicken Afghani (made with nuts and white sauce) and the poached prawns are two of the specialties. Prices rarely rise higher than Rs 70 ($2.33) for main dishes. It is open for lunch and dinner, from 11am to 3pm and 5 to 11pm.

Try the **Princess Room** at the **Sealord Hotel,** Shanmugham Road (☎ 352682), for delicious seafood from Rs 55 ($1.83) to Rs 70 ($2.33); fish Veronique (with grapes), for Rs 60 ($2), is among the highest-priced dishes on the menu. There's also steak, grilled prawns, and, for an unusual dessert, fried ice cream—coconut-coated ice cream that is deep-fried and dished up on a bed of sweet vermicelli—a Sealord special at Rs 40 ($1.33). Beer costs Rs 50 ($1.66) to Rs 55 ($1.83). There's a band and dancing at night. Open from 7am (for the breakfast menu) to midnight every day. Another possibility at the Sealord is the restaurant on the rooftop, open from 7:30pm to midnight.

The **Regency Room** at the **Hotel Abad Plaza** (☎ 361636), where, in addition to the buffet at lunch, there is an à la carte menu where main dishes average

Rs 60 ($2) but can go higher. Seafood is a specialty. Dinner is served from 7:30pm to midnight.

You can have a meal in a village setting at the **Hotel Presidency's** (☎ 35372) rooftop restaurant, a pretty setting with a lovely view. A meal for two should run Rs 300 ($10) to Rs 500 ($16.66); add another Rs 55 ($2.85) for beer.

In Fort Kochi

For a panoramic water view with Chinese fishing nets and the mainland thrown in, it's hard to beat the down-to-earth–priced rooftop or outdoor garden restaurants at the **Seagull Hotel,** Fort Kochi (☎ 223172), open from 8:30am to 10:30pm. A three-course meal of soup, entrée, and dessert runs about Rs 50 ($1.66) to Rs 60 ($2). Choose karameen (a famous Kerala fish) or crab masala or mullet as your main dish for an authentic meal. Or go for just tea and to see the sunset—Rs 20 (66¢) for tea and toast, the sunset is free.

At **Hotel Abad** (☎ 228211), between Fort Kochi and Ernakulam, you'll find one of the more varied menus around town in the **Pavilion Restaurant,** done up with wood trellis dividers and red-draped windows. Here are Japanese tempura and well-prepared seafood. Lobsters in season (January, February, and March) are sold by the kilogram. For a 1-kilo lobster that looks big enough to ride, the price is around Rs 800 ($26.66), and it can easily serve two. Heavier lobsters can run even more and feed you and some friends. Another less pricey specialty is black tiger prawns, cooked in the tandoor.

Ice Cream Parlors

Keralans are crazy about ice cream and ice-cream parlors—and bakeries, another Kerala passion, are everywhere you look. A nice place for ice cream is **Meghadoot** (open from 10am to 1am), in Dwaraka Hotel, where old-fashioned lamps hang over booths with tables topped with flowered cloths. A wide range of ice-cream concoctions includes an American-style banana split, for around Rs 35 ($1.16). The **Caravan Ice Cream Parlor,** C.S.I. Shopping Center, Broadway, South End (☎ 365510) (open from 10:30am to midnight), serves milkshakes, sundaes, and other ice-cream desserts. The house specialty, Caravan, has four flavors of ice cream with fruits, jelly, and cashews for Rs 25 (83¢).

KOCHI AFTER DARK

Presently, there are three places to see fascinating short performances of **kathakali** (*kath* means "story," *kali* means "play"), Kerala's famous dance-drama. You also watch the application of the elaborate make-up that is integral to its performance and receive an explanation of its intricacies. Choose between the **See India Foundation,** Kalathipurambu Lane, Ernakulam Junction (☎ 369471), behind Laxman Theatre, under the direction of P. K. Devan, whose family has a 100-year tradition in kathakali (performance from 6:45 to 8pm; makeup from 6pm, admission Rs 50); **Art Kerala,** XXXV/346 Kannanthodath Lane, Valanjambalam, Ernakulam (☎ 366238), under the direction of T. Radhakrishnan, a disciple of the late Guru Gupanath (daily performances—call for times, admission Rs 50); and the **Kochi Cultural Center,** Durbar Hall Ground (☎ 368153), which is air-conditioned (performances from 6:30 to 8pm; similar admission). The center also holds classes in kathakali and other dance forms and arranges for Ayurvedic oil massages.

Reservations are required wherever you go. And if you find everything is sold out, there are also performances at **Kathakali Dance Club** (near Seagull Hotel, Fort Kochi); monthly performances by the **Kathakali Club** (check dates/times with tourist office); and performances at **Bolghatty Palace Hotel** (☎ 355003), which are not as expert as the others.

Performances usually take place between 6 and 8:30pm, but you should double-check the timings when you book your seat. The shows are merely teasers for visitors compared to traditional performances of kathakali for local audiences. A real performance of kathakali often lasts all night and is usually done outdoors. It is not unusual for some spectators to come equipped with cots so they can nap during the performance and awake later on, refreshed and ready to watch again.

It's also a long time back to the origins of kathakali, which dates from early temple worship. The performers dip into an endless supply of story materials from the nearly 3,000-year-old tales in the *Ramayana* and *Mahabharata.* It even takes a long time to train an actor (no women) for kathakali—about eight years, in fact. Starting at age 12, he's ready to go on stage by age 20. He's been trained to be both flexible and strong enough to leap about nimbly under excessively heavy makeup and costumes for many hours.

Four or five hours are needed to apply makeup on the actors. They lie flat on the floor while their faces are covered with rice-flour paste and then painted in bright colors in stylized representations of the gods, goddesses, demons, and kings they portray. Even the whites of their eyes must be part of their makeup—they are irritated especially for the performance by placing eggplant seeds under the lids and blinking the eyes until the whites are red.

You can see some of this makeup artistry and learn more about kathakali before performances at 6pm. Bring your camera.

For other entertainment, several **movie theaters**—among them the **Sreedhar** on Shanmugham Road and **Shenoy's** on Mahatama Gandhi Road—show English-language movies, usually at 3:30, 6:30, and 9:30pm.

There's music nights and weekends for listening or dancing in the top hotels. Some hotels also accompany dinner with Indian music.

EXCURSIONS FROM KOCHI

VARAPUZHO

It is only a short trip by boat to Varapuzho, two hours from Kochi, and you can return the same day. Ferries run frequently, from 7:40am to 3pm. This is an option if you cannot take a long backwaters journey.

ALAPPUZHA

In under two hours, you can bus to Alappuzha (60 kilometers), a center for boat traffic in Kerala. The train also takes two hours. Alappuzha is a scene of great activity during the festival of Onam (August/September), when snake boat races take place on the canals, and especially, the second Saturday in August every year during the **Nehru Trophy Boat Race**—the most colorful snake boat race in Kerala.

Getting to Alappuzha

The nearest airport is Kochi; trains connect from Kochi; you can get a KSRTC bus from Ernakulam (62 kilometers) for Rs 14 (6¢) to Rs 20 (66¢), and from all major centers in South India.

Information

A **KTDC Tourist Office,** recently in the planning stages, should be open on the jetty by now.

What to Do in Alappuzha

Some people are so enchanted by Alappuzha, they stay here for a while to enjoy the beach and lazy life, venturing into Kochi or cruising the lagoons when the spirit moves them. The town's greatest influx is during the Nehru Trophy Boat Race.

The town is known for **Vembanand Lake,** the longest in India, and its position on the backwaters, where boats are available. If you want to arrange a backwaters tour from here contact: **Alappuzha Tourism Development Co-operative Society,** at Karthika Tourist Home, near the central bus stand (☎ 3462). They arrange special backwater trips upon request. The society also offers boat cruises to Kollam (Quilon) on Mondays, Wednesdays, and Fridays, at 9:45 am. The trip lasts eight hours, and the fare is Rs 70 ($2.33). The ATDCAS also operates a cruise from Kollam to Alappuzha on Tuesdays, Thursdays, and Saturdays.

There are few essential sights, and the most interesting are out of the city: a **Syrian Christian Church,** seen on a backwaters trip or by road; the rather distant **Krishnapuram Palace** (47 kilometers) en route to Kollam, a double-storied palace with large murals and historic artifacts; and **Karumadikkattan** at Karumadi, 3 kilometers from Ambalapuzha (also visited from Kollam), where there is an 11th-century statue of Buddha.

Where to Stay & Eat

The best hotel in town is the **Alappuzha Prince Hotel,** A. S. Road (N.H. 47), Alappuzha 688007 (☎ 375257), a neat white building about 1 1/2 kilometers from the beach, with 30 clean, pleasant rooms. The hotel is centrally air-conditioned. Singles cost Rs 400 ($13.33), doubles Rs 500 ($16.66). If you take all your meals—and you probably will since there are few restaurants nearby—it will add around Rs 300 ($10) to Rs 350 ($11.66) per person to your bill. There's a swimming pool. During the Nehru Trophy Boat Race, the rates increase by Rs 100 ($3.33). The hotel organizes backwater trips for guests in its own 40-person double-decker boat. The boat is usually booked by tour groups, which means independent travelers have to organize their own trips.

KOLLAM (QUILON)

Kollam is one of the oldest ports in these parts and well known for **Ashtamudi Lake,** rimmed with palms and promontories, where, if you haven't had enough boating on your backwaters trip, you can go rowing. The town itself is still a market center, but not the important port it was when the ancient Phoenicians, Greeks, Persians, and Romans called here for spices, sandalwood, and ivory. The Chinese also traded here from the 7th to the 14th centuries, and so did the later-arriving Dutch, Portuguese, and British. Three kilometers (2 miles) from town you will also want to explore the ruined fort, old lighthouse, and European graveyards.

Short excursions can be taken from Kollam to **Kapapuzha** and to **Guhandapuram.** You can also cruise up to **Alappuzha** on the Alappuzha Developments backwaters cruise on Tuesday, Thursday, and Saturday; the cruise lasts for eight hours, costs Rs 80 ($2.66), and you'll see the major sights on the way.

Getting to Kollam (Quilon)

The nearest airport is in Thiruvananthapuram; Kollam is an important railhead of the Southern Railway; KSRTC buses arrive regularly from Ernakulam (150 kilometers), with fares ranging from Rs 33 ($1.10) to Rs 45 ($1.50).

Where to Stay in Kollam (Quilon)

All these accommodations are modest (ask for mosquito netting or coils). Wherever you stay, remember rates go up during the Nehru Trophy Boat Race when advance reservations are a must.

Sudarsan, Paramesar Nagar, Hospital Road (☎ 75322), has 38 rooms, with AC doubles for Rs 305 ($10.16) and non-AC doubles for Rs 160 ($5.33), all with attached baths; there are two restaurants and a bar. **Hotel Shah International,**

T. B. Road, Kollam (☎ 75362), has AC doubles for Rs 240 ($8). **Karthika,** Paikada Road, Kollam 691001 (☎ 76240), has non-AC doubles as low as Rs 100 ($3.33) and AC rooms for up to Rs 175 ($5.83); they're nothing to rave about, though. **Hotel Sea Bee,** Jetty Road (☎ 75371), has 40 rooms ranging from Rs 80 ($2.66) for a non-AC double to Rs 150 ($5) for a double with AC; there are four restaurants and a bar.

KOTTAYAM

Getting to Kottayam

From Alappuzha's jetty near the bus stand, boats leave for Kottayam 14 times a day, about every hour from 5am until 10:30pm, for the three- to five-hour trip. Buses and trains connect from Thiruvananthapuram; trains also connect from Kollam, as do buses.

In Kottayam, you can see an old Syrian Christian churches and rubber, tea, pepper, and cardamom plantations. Kottayam's business district is a hectic place; for a welcome change, head for wildlife in the hills, a bird sanctuary, or the neighboring backwater resorts.

Kottayam is the place to get the bus to the **Periyar (Thekkady) Wildlife Sanctuary,** 114 kilometers (71 miles) away. The bus to Thekkady takes four hours through scenic spice groves. There, you can make arrangements for a boat tour, at Rs 50 ($16.55) per person for two hours. You should book your accommodations in advance during the peak season.

Where to Stay

Kottayam's best mainland hotel is the **Anjali Hotel,** K. K. Road, Kottayam 686001 (☎ 5633661), near downtown. The centrally air-conditioned rooms cost Rs 440 ($14.66) single and Rs 570 ($19) double. Restaurants; bar; boat cruises arranged.

Located right at the jetty, 2 kilometers from town, is **Vembanad Lake Resort** (☎ 564298), with an outstanding outdoor restaurant, **Lake Lane,** where fish is cooked to perfection. Lunch or dinner for two costs about Rs 200 ($6.66) for a meal consisting of generous portions of fish with mixed vegetables, parotta (rich Kerala bread), and fresh lime, soda, and coffee. There are also a few modest rooms here, at Rs 375 ($12.50) for an AC double with bath attached. The resort also has an AC restaurant, barbecue, ice-cream parlor, bar, and children's playground. The hotel arranges tours around the lake, famous for its bird sanctuary.

KUMARAKOM

Twelve kilometers from hectic Kottayam, your destination is the **Kumarakom Tourist Center** (open from 9am to 6pm) to arrange a visit to the 14-acre bird sanctuary and take a KTDC boat tour, for Rs 60 ($2), on surrounding backwaters and the lake.

Where to Stay

The best way to soak up the serenity of the backwaters is to spend a few lazy days staying in their midst, as in the old days. The Baker Bungalow, a stately cream-pillared mansion with a typical red, Kerala sloping roof, was such a retreat 130 years ago. Well situated on the banks of the Vembanad Lake and neighboring bird sanctuary, it has been refurbished as a **Taj Garden Retreat,** 1/404, Kumarakom (☎ 377), retaining all its old charms: high ceilings, shining teak floors, and period furnishings. New cottages, built to blend, and two thatch-covered country boats moored on a pond, converted into cozy, textile-lined rooms, make 58 rooms in all. Rates are $65 to $75 ($95 to $115 from December 20 to January 10). The hotel is accessible by road or by a 45-minute boat ride (provided by the hotel) from the Thaneerkuman jetty.

Neighboring **Coconut Lagoon,** Kumarakom, Kottayam (☎ 491; in Kochi ☎ 666221), run by the Casino Group, is accessible only by hotel boat, which passes you like royalty under a Venetian-style bridge before docking at the steps to the reception of this swanky hideaway. Here, nestled amid towering coconut trees and bridge-crossing canals your accommodations, restaurant, and Ayurvedic Centre are in meticulously rebuilt, old Kerala teak houses. Rates are $65 to $75 from October through March, and $50 to $60 from April through September. The swimming pool is on a pavilion overlooking the lake. The food is fine, and if you don't stay, you might call ahead and reserve for a meal en route to Periyar or Kochi. Call to arrange a boat from the jetty, or cruise the backwaters from Kochi (contact the Casino Hotel) to the resort. From Periyar, visitors are received at the hotel's Kumarakom boat landing.

KTDC's Kumarakom Tourist Village, Kavanattinkara, Kumarakom North P.O., Kottyam (Dist) (☎ 92258), located on a finger of land jutting into Vembanad Lake and bordering the 14-acre bird sanctuary, has six modest, acceptable AC doubles in an old villa for Rs 300 ($10), with a restaurant, bar, and assistance in seeing local sights.

4 Periyar Wildlife Sanctuary

Roughly halfway between Madurai and Kochi, just inside the borders of Kerala State, is the Periyar Wildlife Sanctuary—a large artificial lake filling a series of related valleys and all surrounded by dense forest—where many varieties of Indian animals roam. It's not very accessible, the last stage being reachable only by car or bus, but worth the trip for those who seek a quiet rest.

The drive to Periyar is singularly beautiful and interesting. As you corkscrew up the Western Ghats roads, green rubber and pepper plantations pass by. Then the scenery changes to coffee, tea, cinnamon, and nutmeg plantations. Here and there are gingerbread cottages, and finally you come to a steep incline lined with fragrant spice shops. Stop to buy something to help you remember this place. Beyond, in the dense jungle, roam the animals of Periyar.

The dense, moist deciduous forests around the lake here were declared "Reserved Forests" in 1899 by the Maharaja of Travancore; they were turned into a sanctuary in 1934 and made a Tiger Reserve in 1978.

ESSENTIALS

GETTING TO PERIYAR

From Ernakulam, take **KSRTC** fast passenger bus to Thekkady—there is only one a day (the trip takes six hours)—for Rs 46 ($1.53). Regular buses also connect from Kottyam (four hours) for Rs 30 ($1); also from Trivandrum, Kovalam, and Madurai.

Alternatively, from Kochi you can take a bus to Alappuzha and ferry the canals to Kottayam, then connect with a bus for Periyar.

Or from Kochi/Ernakulam take the KTDC's conducted **tour.** It departs every Saturday at 7:30am and returns the next day after lunch, arriving in Ernakulam at 8pm. The cost is Rs 200 ($6.66). For reservations, contact the **KTDC Tourist Reception Centre,** Shanmugham Road, Ernakulam (☎ 353234), open from 8am to 6pm. A similar KTDC tour operates from Thiruvananthapuram.

WHEN TO GO

The season for Periyar is September to May, when it's dry and the animals come out to look for water. Be sure to take your binoculars to view the animals too shy to come close. There's a machan (viewing tower) for a long-distance look around. Dawn and dusk are the best times to see the animals.

GAME VIEWING

By Boat

A small motor-powered vessel, looking a bit like a houseboat, sets off around the lake, nosing its way past the tips of lifeless trees that protrude above the surface and into quiet backwaters. It is always hoped that a herd of elephants will be found drinking at water's edge, but more usually three or four of the great gray beasts are seen on a hillside in the distance. An occasional wild pig can be spotted snuffling in the foliage, and gaur (Indian bison) are not uncommon. Cutting the motors and gliding quietly up to the water's edge, the boat is sometimes lucky enough to come within sight of a pack of red foxes that have killed an elk and are drinking unsuspectingly, trying to drag its body out of the water. Sometimes tigers and leopards pad down to the lake for a drink, but glimpses of them are highly unlikely. There are always beautiful waterfowl to watch—graceful darters and little cormorants skim the water and whole families of snakebirds stare down from the trees.

The two-hour tours by boat operate from 7am to 4pm. Sunrise and sunset are best times to see animals. The upper deck (best for viewing) on the **KTDC launch** is Rs 50 ($1.66) per person, lower deck is Rs 25 (83¢). Launches sometimes are delayed if they do not fill up. They hold about 60 people and putter around the lake, making enough noise to inhibit the animals.

Hotel Aranya Niwas has smaller passenger boats for rent that quietly prowl the waters and are advised. Reservations for either launch or boats are made through the manager at the Aranya Niwas and other hotels. There are additional camera fees.

Trekking with a Ranger

Alternatively, you can trek the forests with a ranger viewing game from machans (platforms). Make arrangements through the forest department. Elephant rides can be arranged.

Wherever and however you go game-viewing, take some bottled water; there's no place to get anything hygienic to drink in the wilds.

WHERE TO STAY & EAT

Serene **Spice Village**, Kumily-Thekkady Road (☎ 2231415)—you can also book through the Casino Hotel in Kochi (☎ 666821)—is a series of cottages, patterned after primal forest dwellings, with continuous verandahs all around with borders of pepper vines and cardamom bushes, and wooden furniture, all in complete harmony with the environment. Sipping tea outdoors here is exquisite. The food is excellent; service efficient and cheerful. There's a swimming pool. Singles are $60, doubles $65. Meals add approximate $25 additional. (In summer, from April through September, rates drop to $50 and $55.)

The **Lake Palace** (☎ 22023; fax 22282), once the palace of the Maharaja of Travancore, on an island in the lake, is now a Heritage Hotel run by KTDC, with old-fashioned charm and handsome old furnishings. Six nicely renovated rooms are clean, comfortable, atmospheric, and have great views of the lake. Look carefully and you might see wild boars congregating on the shore. You get here by boat from the Aranya Nivas Hotel; the room rates are Rs 1425 ($47.50) for a single, Rs 2875 ($96) for a double, all rates on the American plan (meals included).

Aranya Niwas (same telephone as Lake Palace, above), also run by KTDC, sits right beside one end of the lake, about 2 miles past Kumili village. A solidly built stone pavilion on the hillside, refurbished with simple, tasteful, modern furnishings, it still retains some Old World charm. There are 30 rooms ranging in price and comfort from non-AC doubles for Rs 200 ($6.66) to a deluxe AC suite for Rs 1,995 ($66.50). This hotel is on the European plan (meals not included). There is a small shop, and a pool is planned.

Hotel Ambadi (☎ 22192) is down the road from Spice Village at the Forest Checkpost; here are ornate, dark interiors, with some duplex rooms and basic cottages, all clean and acceptable. A double runs Rs 500 ($16.66). There is a restaurant.

Leelapankaj Resort has Lilliputian-size cottages. Prices about the same as the Ambadi.

Another less-expensive possibility is KTDC's **Periyar House** (☎ 22026), a short walk through the woods from the boat landing, modern, two-storied, and recently under renovation—but should be in shape by now. Room rates range from Rs 300 ($10) to Rs 350 ($11.66). Doubles have attached bathrooms with Indian or Western toilets; single rooms have shared bathrooms. Good vegetarian food.

15 The State of Karnataka

From Bandipur, a wildlife sanctuary at the southern tip, to Bijapur in the North, and including the capital, Bangalore, the entire state of Karnataka (formerly Mysore) is a delight. There are temples so amazingly decorated that they appear to be lace or carved ivory (Somnathpur, Belur, and Halebid); distinctive Muslim tombs (Gumbaz and Gol Gumbaz); and an impressive palace in Mysore City itself.

For a rest from such manufactured riches, there are forests of teak, ebony, and sandalwood. Abundant flowers make the entire state seem to be one huge garden; indeed the name *Karnataka,* chosen in 1973, means "plateau land" or "rich black soil."

At Bandipur and Nagarhole you can see bison, elephants, deer, and black-faced monkeys; at Ranganathittu (a bird sanctuary) there are ibis, storks, and egrets. Dams and waterfalls are refreshing sights in Karnataka, and the unusual rock formations are purported to be among the oldest in the world. Chandragupta, the emperor who adopted Jainism 300 years before Christ, spent his last years here. Ashoka, the grandson of Chandragupta, once ruled part of this state. It was the Hoysalas (11th to 14th centuries) who put all of what is now Karnataka State under one ruling house and left some of the most memorable monuments. The Hoysalas' capital was destroyed in 1327, and four centuries of Hindu-Muslim struggles followed, until Hyder Ali became victorious overall in 1761. He and his son, Tipu Sultan, whose former capital is now on the tourist route, ruled until 1799 when the British defeated Tipu and restored an old Hindu dynasty.

1 Bangalore

The best starting point from which to see the state is the capital, Bangalore (pop. 5.2 million). October through February are the finest months to visit, although March is still quite bearable. April to June is very hot, and July to the end of September is rainy. In general, though, the climate in Bangalore (alt. 3,250 feet) is salubrious, so many Indians choose to retire here. And this wonderful climate has been a boon to attracting businesses, too. A sizable migration has made Bangalore India's fifth-largest city, the position once held by Hyderabad. A major industrial and commercial center, with considerable scientific and research capabilities, Bangalore is, according to some sources, the second-fastest-growing city in the world.

In its development, Bangalore has been called India's "Silicon Valley," but it is beyond that now. Such intense high-density, hi-tech activity helped create a gold-rush atmosphere for other businesses and industries looking for technically qualified people. A number of multinationals and some of India's largest companies have opened plants and offices here, and more are expected to do same. Since employees of top-notch businesses have the reputation for upscale lifestyles, new shopping, entertainment, and leisure opportunities also have been adding color to the city (which is good for tourists, too).

Land has been available for new businesses to grow outward into multiacre industrial estates, so there's no profusion of tall buildings in the town; however, there has been some loss of distinction. Many charming Victorian buildings have been razed for glitzy shopping complexes. And green swaths, Bangalore's trademark since Hyder Ali's 18th-century heyday, are also disappearing under the city's growth. Now, everyone wonders if Bangalore's expanding business development will be able to coexist with its beauty and charm.

The name *Bangalore* means "baked beans," but, of course, it's as different from Boston as you can possibly imagine. Bangalore was founded in 1531 by Yelahanka Prabhu chieftain Kempegowda, who was given the land by a Vijayanagar emperor. But the city is quite modern, having been built mainly in the 18th century, and, despite all the development, still spacious, well planned, dotted with graceful parks, and surrounded by pretty suburbs and sprawling industrial estates. The city's horticultural department aims to keep it this way. There's nothing here to detain you for very long, but it's a good place for a brief visit.

ESSENTIALS

GETTING TO BANGALORE

BY PLANE Regular flights connect Bangalore to Delhi ($161), Bombay ($88), Calcutta ($159), and Madras ($33), as well as Thiruvananthapuram ($65), Hyderabad ($56), Goa ($52), and other cities, via **Indian Airlines** and private airlines.

The airport is 8 kilometers from M. G. Road. The bus from the airport to important hotels costs Rs 15 (50¢); a tourist taxi to the city takes about 20 minutes and costs Rs 200 ($6.66); prepaid taxi service is also available. An auto ricksha costs about Rs 80 ($2.66) to the city.

Indian Airlines has an office at Cauvery Bhawan, Kempegowda Road (☎ 2211914; airport ☎ 566233); hours are from 10am to 1pm, and from 1:45 to 5pm. Private airlines with offices in the city include **Modiluft,** near Armravathi Restaurant, off Residency Road (☎ 5582202; airport ☎ 5561136); **Damania,** Manipal Centre, Dickenson Road (☎ 5586779; airport ☎ 5588666); **Jet Airways**, Sunrise Chambers, Unit GW 0107,22 Ulsoor Road (☎ 5588354); **East West**, M. G. Road (☎ 5586095; airport ☎ 5586494); and **Sahara,** Church Street (☎ 55886976).

BY BUS Bangalore connects with Bombay and Pune via NH 4; to Hyderabad (565 kilometers), Kanmiyakumari (719 kilometers via NH 7); Mangalore (349 kilometers) on NH 48; and Madras via Dharmapuri and Vellore (340 kilometers). Bus lines of **Karnataka, Andhra, Tamil Nadu,** and **Kerala State Road Transport Corporations,** as well as many private buses, connect Bangalore to major centers of the country.

The interstate bus terminus is located in Subash Nagar, near Majestic Circle, and faces the Railway Station Roadways. For information call 2871261 or 2876974.

BY TRAIN The best train **from Delhi** (2,444 kilometers/12 hours) is the *Rajdhani Express,* for Rs 3,155 ($105.17) First, Rs 800 ($26.67) Chair. **From Bombay,** the *Udyan Express* (1,210 kilometers/24 hours) has rates of Rs 1,725 ($57.50) AC First, Rs 239 ($7.96) Second. **From Madras,** the *Brindavan Express* (917 kilometers/six hours) or *Bangalore-Madras Express* (seven hours), have rates of Rs 1,323 ($44.10) AC First, Rs 159 ($5.30) Second. Better is the *Shatabdi Express,* departing Madras at 6am and arriving Bangalore at 11am, for Rs 670 ($22.30) Executive, Rs 335 ($11.17) Chair; *Shatabdi* departs Bangalore at 11:10am, arriving Mysore City at 1:30pm, for 330 ($11) and Rs 185 ($6.17). ***Penny-wise tip:*** Take the *Shatabdi* Chair and save Rs 335 ($11.17) on the Madras-Bangalore sector and Rs 145 ($4.83) from Bangalore to Mysore.

There are prepaid taxis from the railway station; an auto ricksha to M. G. Road runs about Rs 80 ($2.66). Make sure before you get in that the meter is on. Foreigners are often overcharged.

Railway reservations can be made by phone: first class (☎ 76351); second Class (☎ 74172/4). Counter 1 in the new building is especially for foreigners and disabled.

Visitor Information

The **Government of India Tourist Office,** KFC Building, 48 Church St., Bangalore 560001 (☎ 5585917), is open from 9:30am to 6pm, Monday through Friday, from 9am to 1pm on Saturday. It is closed Sundays and holidays. The staff is eager to help with pamphlets, maps, and advice. You can book guides from the tourist office at Rs 250 ($8.33) for a half-day (four hours), Rs 350 ($11.66) for a full day (eight hours), for a party of one to four persons (the fee includes a lunch allowance for the guide). If you take a guide out of the city, there's an overnight, outstation charge. There's an additional Rs 100 ($3.33) for a foreign language guide (a guide that speaks a language other than English). Be sure to stock up in Bangalore on pamphlets for Mysore and other places you're going in Karnataka. There's no comparable tourist office in the state.

The **Government of Karnataka Tourist Information Centre** is located at 64 St. Marks Road (☎ 2236854); there are also Government of Karnataka Tourist Information Counters at HAL Airport (☎ 5268012), open from 9am to 7:30pm; and at the Bangalore City Railway Station (☎ 2870068), open from 7am to 10pm.

The **Directorate of Tourism** maintains an office in F-Block, 1st Floor, Cauvery Bhawan, Kempegowda Road (☎ 2215489).

The **KSTDC Information Counter,** is located at Nadami House, N.R. Square (☎ 2275883), open from 10am to 5:30pm.

Getting Around

Yellow-topped **taxis** are scarce in the city; if you find one, it will cost Rs 15 (50¢) for first 2 kilometers and Rs 8 (27¢) per kilometer after that (meters are rarely used, so bargain). **Tourist taxis** are easily available through rental agencies, hotels, and at stands. **Auto rickshas** are plentiful and metered in Bangalore and charge a minimum of Rs 4 (13¢) for the first kilometer and Rs 4 per kilometer after that. There are plenty of **buses** and plenty of people on them.

A full day (eight hours) or 80 kilometers (48 miles) with an **air-conditioned car and driver** in Bangalore costs Rs 600 ($20); **non-AC** car and driver will run Rs 450

($15). If you hire an AC car and driver for an outstation trip, the charge will be Rs 6.50 (22¢) per kilometer (minimum of 400 kilometers), about half that for non-AC gasoline car, slightly less for diesel. But you'll have to bargain because drivers try to charge Westerners more; or go to a reputable travel agency such as **Cox and Kings,** B.M.H. Complex, K.H. Road (☎ 2239192), or one of the car-rental agencies, such as **Karnataka Tourism Transport Unit,** Mayura Hotel, Kemprgowda; the **Government of Karnataka Tourist Information;** or **India Tourist Office** for a list of reliable car rental firms.

WHAT TO SEE & DO

You're not apt to miss **Vidhana Soudha;** this extraordinary granite structure in the neo-Dravidian style is located at the north end of Cubbon Park and houses both the Secretariat and the State Legislature; one look and you'll know why it's Bangalore's most well-known landmark.

Cubbon Park, laid out in the 1800s by Lord Cubbon, then Viceroy of India, is as lovely today as it was years ago and appreciated more than ever for its tranquility in this bustling metropolis. Here are beautiful bamboo and shady glens, places to stroll, jog, or cycle. The 300-acre park houses the High Court and the State Central Library. You can visit the Pompeian red **State Central Library,** which houses rare books and enjoy its gothic architecture.

Cubbon Park houses the **Government Museum,** one of the oldest in the country (dating from 1886), which has sections on geology, art, and numismatics, as well as relics from Mohenjo Daro in the North, one of sites dating back 5,000 years to the dawn of Indian civilization; hours are 10am to 7pm, closed Wednesdays.

Next to the museum is **Venkatappa Art Gallery,** named after a famous Indian artist and filled with old works in its permanent collection and host to contemporary shows. The **Visvesvaraya Industrial and Technological Museum** is also here, with displays devoted to the application of science and technology to the benefit of humanity. The museums are open daily from 10am to 5pm.

Lal Bagh, covering 240 acres, is one of India's most celebrated botanical gardens, with one of its finest collections of tropical plants. Tipu Sultan and his son, Hyder Ali, laid out the gardens in the 18th century with lakes, limpid lotus ponds, and rare trees and shrubs from Persia, Afghanistan, and France. It's lovely to walk around, jog, or cycle the paths. What people remember most about the gardens is the extraordinary **Glass House,** inspired by the Crystal Palace in London. It's a showcase for graceful wrought-iron pillars seemingly rising and dissolving into arches and beams and translucent glass roof tiles letting in streams of light. Flower shows are held annually in January and August.

In the 16th century there was nothing in Bangalore except a **mud fort** built by the city's founder, Kempegowda. This fort was rebuilt in stone by Hyder Ali and Tipu Sultan, and what's left of it can be seen today. Near the fort, the two-story former **palace** is now a museum.

The **Gavi Gangadhareshwara (Bull) Temple,** renowned for its massive granite figure of Nandi, Shiva's mount, draws pilgrims from all over India. It's Dravidian and dates from the 16th century, also the date of the temple's cave architecture. Here on the 14th and 15th of January each year, the sun passes through the horns on Nandi, who is posed outside the temple, to cast a spotlight on the figure of the fire goddess Agni inside, testifying to both the astronomical and architectural sophistication of the ancient builders. Great numbers of people show up for this event. The umbrella, moon, and sun disc in the yard look startlingly modern.

Guided Tours

Guided sightseeing tours by coach operated by the **Karnataka State Tourism Development Corporation (KSTDC)** are the most economical ways of seeing these and other sights:

City Sightseeing, twice daily, except Sunday, leaves at 7:30am, returning at 1:30pm; also at 2pm, returning at 7:30pm, for Rs 80 ($2.66) per person. It covers Lal Bagh Sultan and now the Government Botanical Gardens, Bull Temple, Tipu Palace, Cauvery Arts and Crafts Emporium, Gavi Gangadhareshwara Temple, Ulsoor Lake (a popular boating spot), and Vidhana Soudha (legislature, secretariat, and other government offices).

Mysore Sightseeing, leaving daily at 7am, returning by 11pm, takes in Mysore City for a cost of Rs 150 ($5). There are also tours to **Sravanabelagola, Belur, and Halebid**—daily from 7:30am to 10pm, for Rs 200 ($6.66); to **Shivasamdudra, Somnathpur, and Ranganathittu**—Sundays and holidays from 8:30am to 6:30pm, for Rs 170 ($5.66); to **Bannerghatta and Muthyala Maduvu/Pearl Valley,** to see wildlife and waterfalls—Mondays and Wednesdays from 9am to 6pm, for Rs 60 ($2); to **Nandi Hills** and **Muddenahalli,** combining majestic scenery with Sri M. Visvesvaraya's birthplace—Mondays, Wednesdays, and Fridays from 8:30am to 6pm, for Rs 70 ($2.33).

From April 15 through June 15, there are daily, three-day tours to Ooty, which include Mysore and Bandipur Game Sanctuary (they are done Fridays only during the off-season), departing at 7:30 am, returning in three days at 10:30pm, for about Rs 600 ($20). KSTDC also conducts a two-day tour (leaves Friday at 10am, returns Sunday at 10:30pm) to **Mantralaya, Tunghahadra Dam,** and **Hampi,** for Rs 450 ($15). Another three-day tour goes to Tripathi-Mangapura, an important pilgrimage place, leaving Wednesday at 10:30pm, returning on the third night at 9:30pm).

There's also the one-day **Special Hampi Tour** via overnight train; the price includes transfers from the station, breakfast, the ruins, lunch, and return on the night train to Bangalore. Inquire at office below regarding schedules and prices.

For booking and information, contact **KSTDC,** 10/4 Mitra Towers, 2nd Floor. Queen's Circle, Kasturba Road (☎ 2212901) or any of the tourism information resources above.

Outdoor Activities

The **Bangalore Golf Club,** Sankey Road, High Grounds, will allow foreigners to use the club's facilities for $35 a day, any time (Rs 75 to Rs 100 for Indians weekdays). On weekends, the **KGA Golf Course** charges foreigners Rs 200 ($6.66) per day to use the course, Rs 400 ($13.33) on weekends; for outstation Indians, the cost is Rs 50 weekdays, Rs 100 weekends.

The **Ashok Hotel** allows nonresidents to use pool for a fee.

At the **Bangalore Turf Club,** Race Course Road the racing season is May through July, and November through March.

The **Bangalore Tennis Club** is in Cubbon Park.

Shopping

Look for handicrafts in sandalwood and rosewood; elegant silks and hand looms in saris or by the meter or as ready-made or made-to-order salwar kamiz sets (pajamas and tunics) for women; and kamiz and tailored shirts for men. Also sandalwood oils, soap, and charming lacquered toys.

Main **shopping areas** are Mahatma Gandhi Road, Commercial Street, Kempegowda Road, Chickpet City Market, Russel Market, Brigade Road, and

Residency Road. As elsewhere, many hotels have shopping arcades where prices tend to be much higher than in the markets. A number of states, in addition to Karnataka, have boutiques in Bangalore. Government shops are open from 10am to 6:30pm; private shops are open from 10am to 10pm. Some shops close for lunch. Many have started staying open Sundays.

Among the packable items at **Cauvery,** in the Karnataka State Arts and Crafts Emporium, 23 Mahatma Gandhi Rd., are sandalwood letter openers with hand-carved motifs along the handle or edge; silk scarves for Rs 250 ($8.33) and up; and sandalwood and rosewood beads for Rs 50 ($1.66) and up. Toys in wood, such as charming giraffes on wheels at Rs 30 ($1), are just a few of the many made-in-Karnataka souvenirs found in this shop.

The oldest silk store in Bangalore (established in 1920), and one of the best in India, **Vijayalakshmi Silk and Saris,** 20 J/61 Mahatma Gandhi Rd. (☎ 5587937), has opulent temple saris woven with real gold from the temple-sari-weaving town of Dharmavaram, 180 kilometers (110 miles) from Bangalore on the way to Bombay. The store's literature describes having one of these saris as "possessing a precious jewel," and indeed they're gem-high in price—Rs 35,000 ($1,166), or more. Less costly, but absolutely lovely georgette saris heavily embroidered in silver or gold wire work—works of fabric art—range from Rs 1,000 ($333.33) up to the highest realms as well. Lovely silks in vivid colors from Kanchipuram cost Rs 1,500 ($50) per meter without gold and Rs 2,000 ($66.66) per meter with gold. Brocade stoles run Rs 500 ($16.66) to Rs 1,000 ($33.33). These are just a sampling of the store's gorgeous silks, and if it sounds high, everything here is highest quality. Open from 10am to 8pm, including Sunday.

Ashok Silks, Shrungar Shopping Centre, Mahatma Gandhi Road (☎ 5588427), will copy your favorite fashions or work from patterns in one day; price depends on design and type of fabric. Elegant silk shirts for men, ready-made, cost Rs 500 ($16.66) and up; silk-cotton blends and cotton and polyblend shirts are also available for less, as are made-to-order shirts priced according to fabric, workmanship, and size. Ready-made salwar kamiz for women—Rs 250 ($8.33) and up in cotton, Rs 1,500 ($50) and up in silk—are also in stock. Men's ties, too, can delight a fashion-conscious Western woman who loves tailored shirts and suits. Hours are 9am to 8pm (to 2pm on Sunday). The brochure has a good map of Bangalore.

Also in Shrungar Shopping Centre, at no. 26, **Nobles** (☎ 588351) has a good assortment of children's wear; charming dresses to fit fashionable four-year-olds cost around Rs 75 ($2.50). They are open from 10am to 2pm, and 4 to 8:30pm; closed Sundays. **Hidedesign,** 14 Shrungar Shopping Center (☎ 5587679), carries handbags, jackets wallets, chappals (sandals), and travel bags. A similar inventory can be found at **Cose Belle,** 19 Shrungar Shopping Center, plus curios.

Folio, Vittal Mallay Road, Bangalore, 560001 (☎ 2218142), is a showcase for Indian designer clothing for men and women; some things are pricey, but they're also pretty if you're looking for something special. Costume jewelry and accessories and cosmetics also.

Needles, no. 10 Cooper Arch, Infantry Road (☎ 5591409), specializes in plus sizes for both men and women. Open from 10:30am to 8:30pm; closed Sundays.

Some of Bangalore's best bookstores are on M. G. Road: **Gangaram Book Bureau, Higginbothams,** and **International Book House;** as is **Spencer's,** the South Indian department store chain. There's a nice outdoor cafe at Spencer's to take a break. Antiquarian book collectors head to **Select Book Shop,** 71 Brigade Rd., open from 11am to 6:30pm Tuesdays through Saturdays, from 11am to 5:30pm Sundays; closed Mondays.

For pottery objects and other trinkets, try **Raga of Gifts,** Devantha Plaza, Residency Road or Cunningham Road.

On Commercial Street, several jewelers have inexpensive silver chokers and earrings as well as high-priced precious things. The 125-year-old **C. Krishniah Chetty and Sons,** 35 Commercial St. (☎ 5588731), has one of the best selections of fine jewelry ready to go or made to order, and often there are lines three deep to buy it. Custom-made traditional jewelry, such as heavy bangles and delicate necklaces with stones, look great at **Bhushan,** Krishaveni Complex, 31 Commercial St. (☎ 5582204).

Sandals are good buys in Bangalore on Commercial Street, M. G. Road, as well as Brigade Road. You'll find them in many stores. You have to keep trying on pair after pair until you find your size. Good-quality leather thongs should cost about Rs 150 ($5) to Rs 350 ($11.66).

WHERE TO STAY

Accommodations in Bangalore are of a fairly high standard, as even many budget hotels boast of lovely gardens with luscious tropical plants and posies. However, sales and luxury taxes can add as much as 5% to 25% to your room bill. ***Penny-wise tip:*** Bangalore is pleasantly cool, so you might try non-AC accommodations where offered; they can run Rs 100 less than AC rates. Your room will have a ceiling fan and windows to open for breezes; the management provides coils and/or mosquito netting if you want it.

INDIAN-STYLE HOTELS

Doubles for Less Than Rs 500 ($16.66)

Hotel Raceview, 25 Race Course Rd., Bangalore 560001 (☎ 266147), has 48 rooms, 16 with a view of the race course. The rooms comfortably furnished, but not well-maintained—shelves were covered with dust. Ask to have them tidied before checking in. Race course view and deluxe rooms are Rs 375 ($12.50) to Rs 425 ($14.17) with AC; all rooms are doubles. The hotel's Samrat restaurant is air-conditioned, nonsmoking, and vegetarian.

Doubles for Less Than Rs 1,200 ($40)

At **Woodlands Hotel,** 5 Raja Ram Mohan Roy Rd., Bangalore 560025 (☎ 225111; fax 2236963), the approach through a narrow, tree-lined lane leads to well-kept gardens, fragrant with fresh roses and frangipani, where cottages and a seven-story annex (the seventh floor has a Lal Bagh view) spread over 5½ acres have 244 neat and clean rooms. Rooms in the new wing have Western toilets. Doubles with AC are Rs 500 ($16.66); AC cottages run Rs 800 ($26.66) to Rs 1,150 ($38.33)—and a 25% increase is expected. Reserve far in advance. The entrance is highlighted by two huge murals with scenes from the *Bhagavadgita.* Sunheri restaurant serves delicious vegetarian meals for about Rs 30 ($1) to Rs 35 ($1.16), and there's a bar and snack shop.

In the heart of town, **Hotel Maurya Bangalore,** 22/4 Race Course Rd., Gandhinagar, Bangalore 560009 (☎ 26411), has a white marble reception area, contrasted with black sofas and brocade chairs in the lobby. Partially air-conditioned, it has 88 rooms, all clean, with tasteful modern furniture, restful earth tone color schemes, and Western-style bathrooms. AC doubles are about Rs 500 ($16.66). The hotel has vegetarian restaurants, AC and non-AC.

Opposite Natraj Cinema, the **Hotel Gangothri,** 173/1 S.C. Rd., Seshadripuram, Bangalore 560020 (☎ 368316), has a white, marble-floored reception area with red sofas set in alcoves and a striking Arjuna's chariot mural. Sixty clean doubles, some non-AC, and decently priced are the main attraction. Doubles with AC are Rs 500 ($16.66). The restaurant is off the lobby.

A cross between an Indian- and a Western-style hotel, **Ashraya International Hotel,** 149 Infantry Rd., Bangalore 560001 (☎ 2261921), is convenient to Vidhana Soudha (State Legislature and Secretariat), the race course, golf club, and Cubbon Park. The low-ceilinged, marble-lined lobby is decorated with a mural that depicts Krishna and Arjuna from the epic *Mahabharata.* Doubles have dark-wood furnishings and beds topped with chenille spreads, and spotless granite floors. The rate for a double is Rs 675 ($22.50). Some are non-AC. The halls need painting. Shanbhag restaurant offers vegetarian Indian and Chinese dishes. A nonvegetarian restaurant serves the usual Continental, Chinese, and Indian, and tandoori dishes.

Kamat Yatri Nivas, no. 4, First Cross, Gandhinagar, Bangalore 560009 (☎ 2200049), is built in the atrium style; the rooms are comfortable enough, with simple modern furniture. AC doubles are Rs 600 ($20). The hotel's strictly vegetarian restaurant serves a delicious food. A limited (no refill) thali is Rs 18 (60¢); a full meal on a plantain leaf with refills costs Rs 35 ($1.16).

WESTERN-STYLE HOTELS

Doubles for Less Than Rs 600 ($20)

Hotel Abhishek, 19/2 Kumara Krupa Rd. (☎ 2262713; fax 22668953), new but in need of better maintenance, has 36 rooms; an AC double is Rs 600 ($20). The **Banjara** restaurant (☎ 2262756), attached to the hotel, serves veg and non-veg dishes; crab, prawns, and other seafood are specialties. Heineken beer, rare in India, can be ordered here for Rs 90 ($3).

Hotel Chalukya, 44 Race Course Rd., Bangalore 560001 (☎ 265055), has 82 adequately, if not imaginatively, decorated rooms, some with AC, for Rs 400 ($13.33) to Rs 475 ($15.83). Of the two restaurants, **Samrat,** for vegetarian food, is recommended over the nonvegetarian restaurant, **Alampur.**

Nilgiris Nest, 171 Brigade Rd. (☎ 5588401), has an excellent central location and 24 clean, modern rooms (14 with AC) with everything you need for a comfortable stay, but little ambience. Doubles are Rs 400 ($13.33). The hotel, owned by Nilgiris Dairy Farm Ltd., has a dairy store, as well as a restaurant and bar. This hotel is similar to Nilgiris Nest in Madras, which is under the same management.

Hotel Highgates, Church Street (☎ 5597172; fax 260174), has 40 nicely appointed rooms and suites; a delightful patio coffee shop is memorable here. The hotel also has services such as voice mail. Hard to beat at this Rs 300 ($10) to Rs 600 ($20) price range. Central location.

Doubles for Less Than Rs 1,100 ($36.66)

A glitzy, mirrored reception/lobby with gleaming marble floors greets you at **Ramanashree Comforts,** 16 Raja Rammoham Roy Rd., Bangalore 560025 (☎ 2225152). The 67 rooms, set around a triangular atrium, have blond-wood and wine-toned color schemes, quilted print spreads, and botanical prints on walls. Maintenance could be a tad better; still they're quite acceptable. A double is Rs 1,095 ($36.50). Stay-a-day packages offers a dawn-to-dusk concessional rate of Rs 530 ($17.66) and use of the business center. Two restaurants (both with buffets) and a bar.

Great views of the landmarks can be had from the **Ivory Tower,** 12th Floor, Barton Centre, 84 M. G. Rd. (☎ 558933), and balconies to step out and enjoy them are reason enough to stay here. Pleasant ambience and a central location add to its attractions. Doubles go for Rs 900 ($30) and up. Nice views, too, from the **Ebony** restaurant, where the menu includes Parsi cuisine, a rare treat outside Bombay, where many Parsis reside.

Curzon Court, 10 Brigade Rd., Bangalore 560001 (☎ 5581698), is a cozy, centrally air-conditioned hideaway in the main commercial district. The entrance and halls need better maintenance, but the rooms are acceptable with bamboo-backed upholstered chairs, printed drapes and spreads, and carpeting. Standard doubles are Rs 550 ($18.33); deluxe rooms, for Rs 700 ($23.33), are larger and have bigger bathrooms, but are not worth the extra rupees. Street noise is a problem. The sinister-looking **Pub** restaurant is a negative, but there are many attractive places to eat nearby.

Hotel Nahar Heritage, 14 St. Marks Rd. (☎ 2213233; fax 2218735), fully air-conditioned, has 48 rooms, with doubles from Rs 800 ($26.66) to Rs 900 ($30). Neat, nice, and fairly new, it has a restaurant and a pub.

Hotel Rama, 40/2 Lavelle Rd., Bangalore 560001 (☎ 2213311; fax 5580357), occupies an unimposing, three-story, concrete-block building near a main shopping area and next to beautiful Cubbon Park. Rooms are fairly clean and comfortable, with carpeting, built-in desk/vanity, and wardrobe—a good buy at Rs 700 ($23.33) for a double with AC, since it includes a sumptuous veg and non-veg buffet breakfast. There are 36 AC rooms and suites out of a total of 55. Although the **Shilpa** bar and restaurant has no decor, it is modern and clean, with booths and tables. The menu is the usual melange of Continental, Indian, and Chinese foods.

Doubles for Less Than Rs 1,650 ($55)

Gateway Hotel, 66 Residency Rd., Bangalore 560025 (☎ 5584545), is operated by The Taj Group of hotels. The rooms have pastel color schemes coordinated with blond-wood furniture. Rates range from $45 to $55, and include a buffet breakfast. There's a swimming pool. **Karavalli** restaurant has good coastal cuisine (see "Where to Eat," below). The coffee shop gives new meaning to the word slow. The lobby lounge is a popular for drinks and tea (smoky when crowded).

"Allowing you to do business the American way, quickly, efficiently and with a touch of fun," is the slogan promoting **The Central Park,** Manipal Centre, 47 Dickerson Rd. (☎ 5584242; fax 55885594). Centrally air-conditioned, the 129 rooms are furnished in modern-motel style; doubles are about Rs 1,400 ($47); amenities include a coffeemaker in each room, restaurant, bar, and pastry shop, as well as wide ranging business services. The **Orange County** coffee shop strives to serve American dishes.

The Atria, 1 Palace Rd. (☎ 2205205; fax 2256850), centrally air-conditioned, looked promising. Doubles are Rs 1,450 ($48.33), including complimentary breakfast in the coffee shop.

Worth a Splurge

Remember that 25% room taxes are added to the following hotels. Two people traveling together may still be able to manage some of these hotels on our $45-a-day budget.

A turn-of-the century landmark, the **West End Hotel,** in the Taj Group, High Grounds, 41 Race Course Rd., Bangalore 560001 (☎ 2269281; fax 2200010), is surrounded by beautiful 20-acre gardens, for pleasant strolls through rose arbors and under old shade trees. A collection of quaint gingerbread cottages and a rambling, two-story Victorian building house some of the 135 cozy rooms and grand suites, many with verandahs. Other rooms are in the characterless new wing, which has the charm of an American motel, so that's not where you want to be. Rooms and suites cost around $135 to about $400. The **Crazy Horse Bar** is a favorite local meeting place. **Paradise Island** serves a Thai, Chinese, and Continental buffet (see "Where to Eat," below). There's also a poolside barbecue. Shopping arcade, travel agent, three tennis courts, and a post office.

Taj Residency, 41/3 Mahatma Gandhi Rd., Bangalore 560001 (☎ 5584444; fax 5584748), has 125 rooms set around a nice garden; it looks a whole lot more gracious inside than its brick-and-concrete, boxlike exterior. In the handsome, marble-pillared lobby are splashing fountains and comfortable rust and brown settees. The tastefully decorated rooms have all the comforts—chaise lounges in addition to beds, cane-backed chairs, and smallish bathrooms. Rates are $50 single and $65 double for standard rooms. No expense has been spared in the decor of the restaurants and bar, and they are among the highest-priced in India (see "Where to Eat," below). Plus there's a swimming pool and other five-star amenities for guests.

At the **Holiday Inn Bangalore,** 28 Sankey Rd., Bangalore 560052 (☎ 269451), a glass-walled elevator whisks guests to rooms set around a glass-topped atrium. The Regency-inspired decor in guest rooms uses printed drapes and spreads and the dark woods. Second-floor rooms have balconies. Bathrooms have pulsating showers, soothing to the weary. All rooms are doubles: Standard rooms cost $60 and $75. The **Lanai** lobby coffee shop is rimmed with plants for an indoor garden look. There's a swimming pool in the garden and a health club indoors. It is affiliated with the U.S. chain.

Also on Sankey Road, what looks like a beautiful old royal residency is the **Welcomgroup Windsor Manor Sheraton and Towers,** 25 Sankey Rd., Bangalore 560052 (☎ 2969898; fax 2264941), with gleaming marble floors, sweeping staircases, and 240 rooms. There's a nod to Queen Anne in the room decor; some of the best open onto charming interior garden terraces where you can stroll under trellised walks and have tea in a tiny gazebo. In the exclusive Towers wing for the business traveler are butler service as well as latest business technology, such as personal fax machines, private lounges, and a reference library. The hotel's facilities include an authentic English pub, excellent restaurants, a chocolate shop, and a health club for those who had one chocolate too much, plus a pool and a disco. Singles range from $110 to $235, doubles from $120 to $245, suites up to $900.

The pleasant ITDC **Ashok Hotel,** Kumara Krupa, High Grounds, Bangalore, 560001 (☎ 269462), is surrounded by lovely gardens with a swimming pool. The hotel's spacious marble lobby is broken up by intimate conversational groupings. The 181 rooms and suites, recently renovated, combine dark woods with traditional Indian printed textiles. Rates are $55 single and $65 double. Enjoy a fine view from the elegant, expensive Mandarin Restaurant on the rooftop—a good choice for a special meal. There's a daily buffet elsewhere in the hotel (see "Where to Eat," below). Facilities include tennis courts and a shopping arcade.

Built recently in the old Colonial style, the 130 elegantly appointed rooms at **The Oberoi,** 37–39 M. G. Road, Bangalore 560001 (☎ 5585858; fax 5585960), open onto a broad, shady verandah facing a lush garden with giant ferns and gushing waterfalls splashing against black rocks. The priceless antiques decorating all the public rooms include a beautiful Vishnu altar. Frills include butler service, transfers to and from airport, pool, and a business center. Singles are $130, doubles $140. The hotel's excellent restaurants are covered in "Where to Eat," below.

YMCAs—All Under Rs 100 ($3.33)

The **YMCA,** Bourdillon, 65 Infantry Rd. (☎ 572681), offers rudimentary accommodations for men only. Mattresses and pillows are provided for the cots, as are one bed sheet and a pillow case, but no towel. From the looks of things, you might be more comfortable, and far wiser, using a sleeping bag rather than the provided bedding. Also basic, the **YMCA,** 57 Millers Rd. (☎ 57885), houses families. The **YMCA Guest House,** 86 Infantry Rd. (☎ 570997), founded in 1823 and still in the same building, takes families as well as women. The **City YMCA,** Nrupathunga (☎ 211848), functions in association with the Youth Hostel Association of India.

WHERE TO EAT

Among the best budget stretchers are the eat-all-you-like buffets in the high-priced hotels. They're not cheap, to be sure, but they allow you to come back for seconds, so you can eat hearty and make this your main meal of the day. Even more penny-wise in Bangalore (and throughout the South) are the simple, clean South Indian vegetarian restaurants. They offer a delicious breakfast of idli (steamed rice cake), sambar (gravy), and coconut chutney or dosa (crisp rice pancake), and a cup of rich, South Indian coffee, for the equivalent of Rs 10 (33¢) to Rs 20 (66¢); you can also get lunch or dinner plate meals of curries, rice, and Indian bread for around $1.

Breakfast is usually offered from 6 to 10am, lunch from 12:30 to 3pm, dinner from 7:30 to 10pm. Some restaurants stay open to midnight. It's always a good idea to call to check and to reserve at lunch and dinner.

BUFFETS

Buffets at the Taj Residency (☎ 5584444): In **Memories of China,** Chef Jimmy Chu makes delicious dishes, for Rs 180 ($6); in **Southern Comfort,** the coffee shop, lunch and dinner and buffets are Rs 175 ($5.83); and soup and a salad lunch for Rs 100 ($3.33). The West End Hotel (☎ 2259281) lunch buffet in **Paradise Island,** a Victorian pavilion surrounded by a moat, features Thai, Chinese, and Continental cuisine for Rs 245 ($4.55). Gateway Bangalore (☎ 5584545) serves lunch buffet in its light and airy **Peacock Garden,** Rs 140 ($4.66) every day; Saturdays regional foods are offered; and Sundays are family buffets with kids counter and entertainment. Breakfast buffet in **Potluck.**

At the Welcomgroup Windsor Manor Sheraton (☎ 269898), there are lunch and dinner buffets in the **Wellington Room** for Rs 254 ($8.46), including tax, from 12:30 to 3pm; there's also a dinner buffet from 7:30 to 10:30pm. ITDC's Ashok Hotel (☎ 2269462) serves a buffet in the **Lotus,** Monday to Saturday for Rs 175 ($5.83); on Sunday it's in the **Mandarin** and features Chinese foods.

Buffets are served for breakfast—Rs 130 ($4.33), lunch and dinner—Rs 175 ($5.83) in the **Lanai** at the Holiday Inn Bangalore (☎ 2262233). The light and airy **Le Jardin,** at The Oberoi (☎ 5585858), serves a lavish lunch buffet with salad and dessert counters for Rs 248 ($8.26), including tax.

Feeling like Chinese? **Noodles,** at Ramanashree Comforts (☎ 2235250), has a daily Chinese lunch buffet for Rs 100 ($3.33). The hotel also has daily buffets for breakfast and lunch in the **Darpan** restaurant for about Rs 70 ($2.33).

Sixteen dishes for Rs 75 ($2.50) are served at the buffet in the **Victoria Hotel,** 47–48 Residency Rd. (☎ 5584076), from noon to 3pm daily. (For more about Victoria see "Breakfast," below.) A French provincial, Parsi, Mughali, and tandoori lunch buffet is Rs 75 ($2.50) at **Ebony** at Hotel Ivory Tower (☎ 5589333)—a smashing view too.

SOUTHERN & COASTAL COOKING

To explore the unusual cuisine of South India, don't leave town, just go to **Coconut Grove,** 84 Church St. (☎ 5596149), where you'll discover Malabar, Konkan,

Coorg, and Chettinad specialties in a tropical hut-style ambience complete with namesake coconut palms. The well-designed menu is color-keyed to cue you in to the regional delicacies, and a well-written explanation accompanies each dish. Typical main courses average Rs 55 ($1.83) to Rs 74 ($2.46), although you can get by for less. One delicious dish from Coorg, kummu kari, combines oyster mushrooms and coconut gravy, cumin, coriander, and red chiles; appam is a rice pancake bread for scooping up the wet dishes; aviyal is a spicy, coconut-accented dish from the Malabar coast; and nadan cheman curry (with prawns), Rs 75 ($2.50), a native dish along the southern coast, is among the most expensive on the menu. If you have a sweet tooth, save room for an ada prathman, made with milk and nuts or pineapple halwa. ***Penny-wise tip:*** Try the thali for Rs 45 ($1.50) to Rs 60 ($2). Draught beer is Rs 19 (11¢), a premium bottle is Rs 45 ($1.50). Lunch is served from 11:30am to 3:30pm, dinner from 7 to 9:30pm. This place is very popular, often with a line at the door.

Another delightful place for regional cuisine is outdoors at **Karavalli** at the Gateway Hotel (☎ 5585140), where the focus is on coastal cuisine from Goa, Karwar, Malabar, and Mangalore. Fish and seafood are the featured attractions. The menu is coded to indicate origin of the dish—bananas and palms denote Mangalore and so on. A delicious three-course meal will cost around Rs 200 ($6.66) per person; beer will add Rs 50 ($1.66) to your bill. Some dishes to try are duck masala (a Cochin specialty) and Karavalli's mutton curry. The highest priced items on the menu range from Rs 115 ($3.83) to Rs 120 ($4). Thalis cost Rs 70 ($2.33) to Rs 90 ($3).

For spicy Andhra-style foods, try **Amarvathi,** 45/3 Residency Cross Rd. (☎ 5587140); **R.R. Plantain Leaf Brigades,** 55/1 Church St. (586060) serves Andhra food the old-fashioned way, on a plantain leaf; open from 11am to 3pm, and 6:30 to 10:30pm.

Vegetarian Indian Cuisine

Not-to-be missed for South Indian vegetarian foods is **Mavalli Tiffin Room ("MTR"),** 2-C Lalbagh Rd. (☎ 2220022), near the Main Gate. This famous half-century-plus-old restaurant lives up to its acclaimed reputation. Billed as the "world headquarters of the Indian dosa"—they may well also be the most delicious—the restaurant also features a host of other well-prepared South Indian dishes, idlis and wadas (melt-in-the-mouth minidoughnuts made from ground lentils and bathed in spiced curds) to name but two. The specialty, in addition to delicious foods, is a high regard for good hygiene: everything is served on sterilized dishes and plates by waiters in spotless uniforms. They offer coffee and tea in silver services. Most dishes are moderate: Rs 15 (50¢) for superb dosa. One more thing: So popular is the Mavalli Tiffin Room that there is usually a line. You leave your name, wait and wait, and then, when called, take a seat wherever there's a vacancy. Hours are 7 to 11am and 4 to 7pm (closed Monday and holidays). You can also order take-out.

Nonvegetarian Indian & Mughali Cuisine

Mezban, 50/1 Residency Rd. (☎ 545021), across from the Galaxy Theatre, emphasizing rich Mughlai cuisine, offers a welcome change from the usual restaurant menu. A pleasant place with white walls, brown grill work, pillars, and snowy linen. In accordance with Muslim beliefs, neither pork nor alcoholic drinks are served here. Instead, you might try aab-e-bahar (coconut juice, honey, and herbs) or jhoomta mezban (an orange-based punch). Among the tasty appetizers are kebabs, from Rs 50 ($1.66) to Rs 150 ($5); entrées include an excellent biryani made with rice, grated eggs, mint, and spices for around Rs 55 ($1.83). A thali meal that permits you to sample several dishes costs Rs 45 ($1.50) vegetarian and Rs 55 ($1.80) nonvegetarian. Figure on Rs 100 ($3.33) to Rs 250 ($8.33) for a three-course à la carte meal. Open from 12:30 to 3pm and 7pm to midnight.

Another place for Mughlai food is at the **Khyber,** 171 Residency Rd. (☎ 2213758), an elegant place with banquettes set in alcoves along the walls and soft lighting and atmospheric Kashmiri murals, specializing in Mughlai and Northwest Frontier foods. Among the interesting dishes are motki chicken tawa, cooked on a special stone; chicken bharati; stuffed kebabs; and a variety of other kebabs and biryanis; and tandoori prawns. Open daily from 11am to 3pm and 7pm to midnight.

Cool and comfortable, the **Kwality Restaurant,** 44-45 Brigade Rd., upstairs (☎ 5582633), has a beamed ceiling, red banquettes, ceramic-tile walls, soft lighting, too loud music, and tables covered with snowy-white cloths. Specialties are tandoori foods and kebabs, with the most expensive dishes around Rs 60 ($2). Well-known for its rich desserts, the menu features a selection of ice cream and other sweets. Some Chinese selections. Hours are daily from 11am to 3:30pm and 7 to 11pm.

Continental & Multicuisine Restaurants

The coir-carpeted **Oasis,** 1 Church St., Bangalore 560001 (☎ 5586081), is a dark hideaway with coir-inlaid, wood-paneled walls where seafood is the main attraction, from 11am to 3pm and 7pm to 11pm; the bar is open from 11am to 11pm daily. It is specially recommended for curries with seafood, such as prawns or fish, in the Rs 65 ($2.16) to Rs 80 ($2.66) range.

The Only Place, Mota Royal Aaracde, 158 Brigade Corner (☎ 5588678), is a small place with a little rock garden, famous for steaks since 1965. A steak dinner with potatoes, grilled onions, boiled vegetables, dessert, and a soft drink costs about Rs 50 ($1.66) to Rs 70 ($2.33). American-style pies—apple, peach, cherry—are another specialty. If you feel like something Indian, try the kebabs, rotis, or nans, and polish off with pie. Open from noon to 3:30pm and 7 to 11pm.

Chinese Cuisine

Penny-wise tip: Chinese is among the least expensive and more varied cuisine available almost everywhere, including Bangalore. Figure on about Rs 100 ($3.33) to Rs 200 ($6.66) on the average meal for two people at most Chinese restaurants in Bangalore **outside** of the hotels.

Green carpeting and upholstery and a straw-and-bamboo ceiling hung with Chinese lanterns are decorative touches at the **Chinese Hut,** 4105/4106 High Point, 45 Place Rd. (☎ 2267364), where the chef makes Szechuan-style dishes. A meal might consist of the unusual whipped-egg jade soup, with a cloud-light topping, for Rs 40 ($1.33); triple Szechuan rice, noodles, vegetables, and meat for Rs 40 ($1.33) to Rs 45 ($1.50); or you might choose lamb Szechuan or golden fried prawns. At the same address is **Jhopdi,** an Afghan restaurant. Main courses range from around Rs 85 ($2.83) to Rs 95 ($3.16). Hours are noon to 3pm and 6:30 onwards.

Rice Bowl, 215 Brigade Road (☎ 558417), has a range of Chinese specialties, as does **Continental,** Centre Point, 56 Residency Rd. (☎ 5597765), where Chef Charles Ma makes the usual Cantonese, Szechuan, and Hoisin specialties.

Breakfast

For a tasty breakfast, in a memorable setting—a peaked roof Victorian bungalow with mosaic floors, slowly swirling fans, and an outdoor terrace, **The Breakfast Club** at the Victoria Hotel, 47/48 Residency Rd. (☎ 5584076), lets you choose between several cuisines. A Continental breakfast is Rs 30 ($1); other styles include English, Rs 45 ($1.50); Kerala, Rs 35 ($1.16); Goan, Rs 40 ($1.33); and Hyderabadi, Rs 30 ($1). The chef's specialty is a chicken liver, bacon, and cheese omelet. Open Sunday only, 9am to noon.

Especially fine appam (rice pancakes) and sabzi (stewed vegetables) are served Sunday mornings (from 9am to 11pm) at **Koshy's Jewel Box and Restaurant,** 39 St. Marks Rd. (☎ 2213793), which otherwise serves North Indian, Continental, and Chinese cuisine. Regular hours are 9am to midnight.

Pizza, Snacks & Sweets

A restaurant offering pizza and burgers, the **Casa Piccola,** Devantha Plaza, 131 Residency Rd. (☎ 2212907), opposite Cash Pharmacy, is a big hit with both Bangaloreans and visitors. The menu lists a whole range of pizzas with such names as "The Godfather" and "Don Giovanni," as well as burgers, fried chicken, chicken pot pie, soups, salads, pastas, and sweets. The most expensive dish is around Rs 50 ($1.66) for steak au whisky. Very loud music. Hours are 11:30am to 11:30pm. There are branches at C.M.H. Road, Indiranagar, Westminister, and Cunningham Road. I give an A-plus for cleanliness to them all.

Perhaps only in magical, mystical India can "the original taste of American pizza" arrive via Sweden and Mr. Berenjian. **U.S. Pizza,** NG-10, Manipal Centre, Dickenson Road (☎ 559955), has a red, white, and blue color scheme and serves something they call "American-style" pizza (it's tasty but not quite the same; maybe it's the cheese) for about Rs 25 (83¢). But then, what really is "American" about pizza? Mr. B. likes to remind everyone that the dish originated in Italy. **Upper Crust,** 171 Brigade Rd., dishes up something of the West—burgers, panned pizzas—and something of the East—curried peas, dosa, idli, and vada—plus you can make your own ice cream. **Indiana Fast Foods,** no. 9 Ground Floor, St. Patricks Complex (☎ 585966), serves ice cream, burgers, and hot dogs from 11am to 11pm. At 2 St. Patricks Church Complex, Brigade Road, **Stars 'n' Stripes** dishes up burgers, pizzas, and delicious biriyanis in "just about a minute."

Hot Breads, 44 Brigade Rd. (☎ 5583943), also at Infantry Road (☎ 5591848), offers a wide array of pastries and breads. Good if you're heading out on a day trip. Both are open daily from 10:30am to 11:30pm. **Baskin-Robbins,** which serves its 31 flavors in 3,600 stores in 53 countries, has a shop in Bangalore, too, at Residency Chambers, 78/1 Residency Rd. (☎ 5596616).

Worth a Splurge

Figure on Rs 1,500 ($50) to Rs 2,500 ($83.33) for a three- to four-course meal for two at these swank places. Wine can add Rs 500 ($16.66) and upwards to your bill. Chinese portions are usually large enough to serve two.

At the hushed and elegant, wood-paneled **Jockey Club,** Taj Residency (☎ 5584444), scampi gratiné and lobster in mustard and cream sauce are among the highest-priced items on the menu. Some typical dishes include tea-smoked chicken breasts, spinach and cheese soufflé, and asparagus with morels. On the dessert list are passion fruit cheesecake and crème brûlée. Open 12:30 to 3pm and 7pm to midnight. There's a fixed-price, three-course lunch, including coffee or tea, for about Rs 200 ($6.66).

In the same hotel, **Memories of China,** with hand-painted peach silk wall panels and Regency-period Chinese furniture, offers beautifully presented Chinese dishes prepared by a chef from China. Some memorable dishes include prawns in hot garlic; steak and ginger chicken with chiles, baby corn with spinach and vegetable haka noodles, and date pancakes with ice cream. Each dish can be shared by two. Open from 12:30 to 3pm and 7pm to midnight.

Beautiful Chinese screens are focal points of the decor at The Oberoi's **Szechwan Court** (☎ 5585858), which features hot and spicy Szechwan dishes, all cooked to order and served hot from a wok. Hours are 12:30 to 2:30pm and 7:30 to 11:30pm.

You'll find more Chinese elegance—and with a splendid view—at the rooftop **Mandarin Room,** in the Hotel Ashok (☎ 2269462), where mainly Szechuan specialties include crisp lamb, mixed fried noodles, and vegetarian wonton. It's open for lunch and dinner every day; there's a dance band at night.

A view comes with your French provincial, Parsi, Mughlai, or tandoori meal at the **Ebony** restaurant in the Hotel Ivory Tower (☎ 5589333).

At the **Terrace Grill** in the Welcomgroup Windsor Sheraton and Towers (☎ 2269898), there's no menu. Patrons choose from the freshest daily selection of meats, seafood, and vegetables and have them charcoal-grilled on the spot. A complimentary pitcher of sangria, garlic toast, and an open salad bar accompanies each order. Windsor Manor's **Wellington Room** features dum pukht (steamed recipes)—originating with the Nizams of Lucknow, it is one of India's most distinctive regional cuisines—and hearty, Northwest Frontier foods in Royal Afghan.

PUBS

There are more than 100 pubs in Bangalore (all opened since the '80s). Hours are generally from 11am to 2:30pm and 5:30 to 11pm (some are open from 11am to 11pm on weekends). Beer ranges from mugs at Rs 14 (47¢) to pitchers for Rs 80 ($2.66). Pubs attract a younger crowd; the more mature gather at hotel bars. Some pubs serve light meals.

Among the popular pubs are the **Black Cadillac,** Mohan Towers (☎ 2216148), where you can get a good pub lunch; **Pub World,** 65 Residency Rd. (☎ 5585206), with selections from four regional pubs under one roof, plus music and dancing; **NASA,** 1/4 Church St. (☎ 5586512), hi-tech with a space shuttle theme, videos, and karaoke; **The Underground,** Bluemoon Complex, M. G. Road (☎ 5589991), with London tube decor; **Cheers Pub, Bar, and Restaurant** 8-9 S.N.S. Plaza, Kumara Krupa Road (☎ 2633840), which serves an Indian and Chinese menu. **Royal Derby,** in the Welcomgroup Windsor Manor Sheraton Towers, which recreates an English pub (a pub lunch here consists of a Continental meal with a complimentary glass of beer).

BANGALORE AFTER DARK

Top hotels have dinner and or dinner/dance music at night, some have Indian music in their Indian restaurants; at **Gateway Hotel,** there are ghazals (North Indian songs) with dinner.

A new **disco** (first in a Bangalore hotel) should be open by now in the **Welcomgroup Windsor Manor Sheraton and Towers;** discos outside hotels are **Prince's Knock-out Disco,** 9 Brigade Rd., Curzon Complex (☎ 565678), **Time and Again,** Brigade Road, and **Underground;** there are floor shows with dancing girls in and about M. G. Road and Majestic Road. Where restaurants offer meals with floor shows, menus feature the usual Continental, Chinese, and Indian fare. Figure on hefty cover charges or minimums if there's a show.

Most of the better hotels have **bars,** most open from 11am to 11pm or 7 to 11pm. Among the famous is **The Crazy Horse Bar,** the **Taj West End,** and, breathing hot on its trendy neck, the West End's new bar, **Colonnade,** off the new lobby, with soft piano music in the background. Among the most gracious bars is the **Polo Club** at the Oberoi, which opens onto the wide verandah for enjoyment of the lovely landscaped gardens. Some restaurants also have bars: **Pink Panther,** G-7 Ramanashree Chambers, 37 Lady Curzon Rd. (☎ 5592404), where a meal for two is about Rs 150 ($5); **Kwality,** 44-45 Brigade Rd. (☎ 5582263); and **Napoli,** Gupta Market (☎ 2260748), which features one of those dreary floor shows with live music.

Of the more than 90 **movie theaters** in town, **Shankar Nag,** M. G. Road (☎ 57328811); **Pallavi,** Sampangi Tank Rd. (☎ 2223191); **Rex,** Brigade Road (☎ 571350); **Plaza,** M. G. Road (☎ 572282); **BluDiamond,** M. G. Road (☎ 571099); **Sangam,** Tank Bund Road (☎ 2870023); and **BluMoon,** M. G. Road (☎ 576537) have English-language movies. Bangalore's movies are popular, and you're advised to book seats in advance whenever possible. Call the numbers above.

Chowdiah Memorial Hall and **Ravindra Kalakshetra** showcase cultural programs. Check the local newspapers and *Bangalore for Tonight* for events during your visit.

EN ROUTE TO MYSORE CITY

About 18 miles from Bangalore, you can get a glimpse from the bus of the **caves** used in the film *Passage to India,* up in the hills. If you're driving, this is a good place to stretch your legs. Then about 4½ miles before Srirangapatna, there's the **Mayura Highway Restaurant,** with clean toilets and a restaurant. The major stop—one that almost everyone makes—between Bangalore and Mysore City is Srirangapatna.

SRIRANGAPATNA

Getting to Srirangapatna Srirangapatna can be reached by Bangalore-Mysore express trains for Rs 90 ($3) and Rs 25 (83¢) in first and second classes respectively. Regular passenger trains take hours longer and are to be avoided. Buses go all day long to Srirangapatna from either Bangalore or Mysore, about Rs 30 ($1) to Rs 45 ($1.50), depending on the number of seats.

What to See & Do

Srirangapatna, 77 miles from Bangalore, is an island in the Cauvery River where Tipu Sultan died in battle in 1799. Srirangapatna is full of historic sites, among them the remains of the **Old Fort** and dungeons. In a much better state of preservation is the 500-year-old **Sri Ranganatha Temple,** where (after taking your shoes off) you can wander in the cool halls and peer in at gods and goddesses in splendid adornments. Nearby, you can climb to the top of the former sultan's **mosque** and get a glimpse of Mysore's gleaming domes in the distance.

Also on the island is Tipu Sultan's **summer palace,** outside the fort. This is a pavilion of graceful arabesques and pillars, richly decorated in ornamental paintings. The gold-accented walls are covered with murals in a dizzying and dazzling profusion, depicting scenes of court life and battles from the days of Tipu Sultan and his father, Hyder Ali. On the west wall is a realistic rendition of the battle at which Hyder Ali beat the British at Pollilore. This painting was whitewashed in the 19th century but restored by an artist who knew the original. The summer palace also contains a **museum** with portraits, maps, gleaming silver cups, and other artifacts. Admission is 50 paise (2¢), and it's open from 9am to 5pm.

At the eastern end of the island is **Gumbaz,** Tipu's elegant, square-shaped, cream-colored mausoleum, with a graceful dome, surrounded by black pillars as shiny as mirrors. Each of the four corners of the tomb has a tall minaret. Double doors of rosewood inlaid with ivory lead to the interior. Inside you will see the tiger-stripe insignia of **Tipu.**

About $1^1/_2$ miles beyond Srirangapatna is the **Ranganathittu Bird Sanctuary,** best seen June through October when a variety of feathered friends are in residence. The sanctuary is included in the KSTDC Mysore City sightseeing tour. There are entry fees for each car, bike, and person. There are also boating fees and camera fees. The sanctuary is open from 8:30am to 6pm. Prime time is sunset, when the Cauvery, birds, and colorful sky are a beautiful sound and sight.

The best way to explore the sanctuary is by boat. Boats can be rented for a modest sum, which is advised. If you buy a seat in a boat and wait for it to fill up, it may not go at all if other people don't show up. And think twice about going at all if you're not there at the peak season. There have been reports of paying all the fees and not seeing anything.

Where to Stay

Should you want to spend time in and about Srirangapatna examining the fascinating sights, there's the small, simple **Hotel Mayura River View** (☎ 52114), run by the KSTDC, in a splendid setting overlooking the Cauvery. Neat little rooms in cottages with nice verandahs are about Rs 325 ($10.83) double, with private attached bathroom. A restaurant on the premises serves meals and snacks.

Amblee Holiday Resort, Cauvery River (☎ 52326), is well situated, with a terrific view; all rooms have balconies or patios to enjoy it from. This place looked quite promising although it was closed for alterations and the addition of a new wing. The rooms and restaurant that were ready showed simple good taste. Rates are Rs 700 ($23.33) for a double. There are a swimming pool, billiards, and kids playground.

2 Mysore City & Beyond

Mysore City (pop. 652,200) is chock-full of gardens, the streets are wide, there are many grand dwellings and even some of the more mundane buildings (railway offices, Maternity Hospital, and Technical Institute) look very elegant. Most of the buildings in Mysore are painted creamy yellow, and the Maharaja's Palace is by far the most outstanding structure in town.

ESSENTIALS

GETTING TO MYSORE CITY

BY TRAIN From 6:05am to 10pm daily there are **express trains from Bangalore** from the City Railway Station for an approximately three-hour journey of 87 miles for Rs 170 ($5.66) or Rs 35 ($1.16), first or second class respectively. Don't take a regular passenger train. They cover the same distance in six hours, and, though cheaper, are obviously best avoided in the interest of time. Trains are very crowded, and there is hardly an iota of difference between first and second class.

The *Shatabdi Express,* the speedy tourist train, makes it in two hours and 20 minutes, departing Bangalore at 11:10am, arriving Mysore City at 1:30; the fare is Rs 166 ($5.53) AC Chair, Rs 330 ($11) Executive. For train information, inquiries, and reservations, call the following numbers: first class 76351; second class 74172/4.

BY BUS **Express buses** go from Bangalore to Mysore every 15 minutes from around 9:40am to 9:20pm daily, from the City Bus Stand in front of the City Railway Station. The fares are Rs 28 (93¢) ordinary, Rs 40 ($1.33) luxury. They leave Mysore's bus stand with similar frequency if you wish to return to Bangalore. There are huge lines for both train and bus tickets.

BY CAR AND DRIVER A car and driver between Bangalore and Mysore will cost Rs 3.50 (12¢) per kilometer, for a minimum of 250 kilometers plus the driver's overnight allowance. If you book your car through a travel agency, such as **Cox and Kings,** B.M.H. Complex, K.H. Road (☎ 2239192), the driver's allowance is included in the quoted rates. (You're expected to tip at the end of your journey.)

BY TAXI Diesel-fueled **taxis** will also make this trip for Rs 2.50 (8¢) per kilometer.

Near the City Bus Stand, at Sirisi Circle, are **private taxi** operators who sell seats to Mysore; they take six people for Rs 30 ($1) per head to Mysore. The trip can take 4½ hours because they stop to pick up and let off passengers. In Mysore, Try the Metropole Hotel Circle for the same kind of deal.

VISITOR INFORMATION

The **Regional Tourist Office** is located in the Old Exhibition Building (☎ 22096); it's open from 10am to 5:30pm. There's also an office at the railway station.

GETTING AROUND MYSORE

Auto rickshas do not use their meters, so bargain to get a fair fare; for example, from Gandhi Square to Lalitha Mahal (about 8 kilometers), the fare should be Rs 25 (83¢); they'll ask Rs 50 ($1.66). **Tourist taxis** for four hours (40 kilometers) should cost from Rs 225 ($7.50) to Rs 250 ($8.33) for a diesel; for eight hours (80 kilometers), the cost should be Rs 450 ($15) for a diesel; outstation trips will run you Rs 2.50 (8¢) per kilometer for a diesel. Gasoline cabs charge a bit more. But you'll have to bargain to get these rates because Westerners get higher quotes. Go to a reputable car agency to save a lot of hassling.

WHEN TO VISIT

Dussehra is celebrated with gusto here in the fall for 10 days (from the end of September through early October) as it has been since 1610, when Raja Wodeyar led the first festivities. The palace is illuminated like a giant wedding cake, and on the last day golden caparisoned elephants march in a great parade and the festivities extend to evening revelries at Chamundi Hill. From April through May there is a cart festival. August 11 is the **Feast of St. Philomena** when residents give the statue a ride around the town and return her in time for evening services.

WHAT TO SEE & DO

Built between 1897 and 1907, the **Maharaja's Palace** is a mixture of the Hindu and Saracenic styles and also shows some influence of the Hoysalas, who built some temples nearby. Domes, arches, turrets, and colonnades are some of the elements in its extravagant design. During the 10-day fall festival of Dussehra, as well as Sunday nights, the entire palace is outlined with thousands of tiny lights.

One of India's largest palaces, it is well-restored and well-maintained, so an atmosphere of earlier opulence still permeates the interiors. Behind its ornamental facade, age has not dimmed the luster of such elegant treasures as stained glass windows, rosewood doors, murals, beamed ceilings, and gold- and silk-trimmed walls in the rooms open to the public. The immense Durbar Hall holds the gold throne shaded with a pearl-trimmed canopy (on display only Dussehra). Perhaps the soul of the palace is the Kalyana Mandapam (Wedding Hall) hung with the portraits of the family in their finery.

Some of the big paintings depict Dussehra pageantry, showing the maharaja leading a huge procession surrounded by the handsomely costumed members of his retinue. Notice his elephant caparisoned in gold. In the Palace museum is the golden howdah (an elegant elephant "saddle") upon which he used to sit on this occasion.

In November 1973, Maharaja Sri Jaya Chamarajendra Wadiyar Bahadur, member of the ruling dynasty from the 18th to the 20th century, announced he was preparing to turn his elaborate palace over to the government to become "somewhat like Versailles." And so it is. The palace is open from 10:30am to 5:30pm, and admission is Rs 2 (6¢) for each section.

Across from the palace grounds is **Statue Square,** where a statue of the grandfather of the present maharaja sits under a golden canopy.

Then it's up **Chamundi Hill,** where, at the summit, you will be greeted by a grotesque, brightly painted statue of the terrifying demon King Mahishasura, who was slaughtered by the goddess Chamundi after whom the hill is named. The top of the hill is crowned by the **Shri Chamundeswari Temple,** whose tower is a mere 300 years old, whereas the foundation dates from 2,000 years ago. About halfway up the hill is the huge 17th-century statue of Nandi, Shiva's mount, 16 feet high and carved out of one rock from tail to tinkling rock bell and stone-cut garland. The bull has been anointed over and over again and shines like metal.

St. Philomena's Church (3 kilometers from town) has lovely stained-glass windows. In the Gothic style, its Medieval look is rare for India. Hours are 8am to 6pm.

Another highlight in Mysore is the **Shri Chamarajendra Art Gallery,** in Jagan Mohan Palace—open from 8am to 5pm every day, admission Rs 2.50 (7¢). Look for paintings from the Mughal and Rajput schools, gem-like miniatures, each one a jewel.

Mysore's **zoo,** established in 1892, covers 37 1/4 hectares and is one of the best in India. Every effort is made to create natural habitats for the animals in amid spacious gardens. Admission is Rs 1 (3¢). Hours are from 8:30am to 5pm.

Guided Tours

KSTDC offers several tours. The **City Tour** (daily from 8am to 6pm) takes in the city sights, for Rs 60 ($2); the same city tour including Somnathpur (daily from 7:30am to 8:30pm), costs Rs 100 ($3.33); there is a tour to Ooty daily from April through July.

There's also a daily tour to Belur, Halebid, and Sravanabelgola (from 7am to 10pm), for about Rs 140 ($4.66)—this is rushed for those who wish to savor the temples and climb to see Gomateswara. But if you have a lot stamina, and little time, take it. There's also a tour to Hampi, Aihole, Badami, and Bijapur.

For information on these and many other tours, contact, **KSTDC, Transport Wing,** Hotel Mayura Hoysala, Jhansi Laxmi Bai Road (☎ 23652). The tours can also be booked in Bangalore through **KSTDC Conducted Tours,** 10/4 Mitra Towers, 2nd Floor, Kasturba Road, Queen's Circle (☎ 2212901). Bookings and information are also available through some hotels in Mysore.

Shopping

Silks, sandalwood, inlaid objects, soaps, oils, rosewoods carvings, and lacquered toys made in Channapatna can be purchased on the Bangalore-Mysore Road. Main shopping areas are Sayaj Rao Road, Ashok Road, Devraja Market, and Dhanavantri Road. Some places to look are **Cauvery Arts and Crafts Emporium,** Sayaji Rao Road (☎ 21258); **Government Silk Weaving Factory,** Manathody Road (☎ 21803); **KSIC Showroom,** K.R. Circle (☎ 22658); **Lakshmi Vilas,** K.R. Circle (☎ 20730); and **M.V. Bhojaiah,** opposite Indian Bank (☎ 22446). Department stores are **Janathan Bazar,** Nehru Circle (☎ 22010); and **Mohan Bhandar,** Sayaji Rao Road (☎ 22190).

WHERE TO STAY

Sales taxes, luxury taxes, expenditure tax (in higher priced hotels) can make your hotel bill mount, in virtually all price classifications. Unless otherwise noted, the hotels below have attached bathrooms and the amenities you need for a comfortable stay plus a few frills. Some have AC and color TVs, for instance. Some accept international credit cards. Details below.

INDIAN-STYLE HOTELS—ALL DOUBLES LESS THAN RS 700 ($23.33)

Two hotels in the Dasaprakash chain present possibilities. The older is **Dasaprakash,** Gandhi Square, Mysore 570001 (☎ 24444). From the hotel's top floor there's a superb view of Mysore's distinctive domed skyline. Sadly, the maintenance has declined, and the 145 rooms are a bit seedy, but acceptable choices. (Maybe spruced up now.) Those highest up are the most cheerful, and those on the lower floor a bit dark. Fifty rooms have Western toilets in attached bathrooms, the rest are outfitted Indian-style. Highest price is Rs 250 ($8.33) for a non-AC double, but rooms have big ceiling fans to stir the breezes. Food is vegetarian; for around Rs 25 (83¢) you can get a no-refills thali meal in the restaurant.

In the newer, sleek, octagonal **Dasaprakash Paradise,** 105 Vivekananda Rd., Yadavagiri, Mysore 570020 (☎ 5156155), there is a plant-filled lobby, halls that need painting, and 90 spacious rooms, neatly furnished in modern style. The highest price is Rs 700 ($23.33) for an AC double on the top floor with a lovely view. The AC Vishala restaurant serves vegetarian cuisine (see "Where to Eat," below). There's a cozy bar.

While not at all palatial, **Darshan Palace,** Lokaranjan Mahal Road (opposite Regency Theatre) (☎ 520794), is a pleasant place with a plant-filled reception area. The 30 compact rooms (one with AC) are clean and surround a circular staircase. Rates range from Rs 150 ($5) to Rs 500 ($16.66), and they have high-priced frills such as color TV, telephones, and attached baths with hot and cold running water. The chipped hall walls are a turn-off, but this is one of the best in this price range. There's room service for snacks and meals, but no restaurant.

The same management runs **Sudarshan Lodge,** opposite Jaganmohan Palace (☎ 26718), which is clean and comfortable; **Prasanth Lodge,** Santhepet (☎ 521748); **Modern Lodge,** Santhepet (☎ 520082); and **Sri Ram Lodge** (☎ 23348). All are decent places, but not quite in a league with Darshan Palace or Sudarshan Lodge.

Hotel Calinga, 23 K.R. Circle (☎ 313310), has 72 clean, spartan rooms, 8 suites, and low-rates, which range from Rs 180 ($6) for a double, to Rs 220 ($7.33) for a suite. Rooms have Indian-style bathrooms and temperamental hot water, but you can get it in a bucket. A friendly place and popular. There is a vegetarian restaurant.

And if you're really bargain hunting, there are many low-priced hotels and lodges all around Gandhi Square and along Dhanavantri Road, charging about Rs 100 ($3.33) and under. They're in various states of repair, so check them out before checking in.

WESTERN-STYLE HOTELS

All these hotels offer every possible amenity for a comfortable stay and then some: the charm of old colonial buildings, a palace or two, and new modernity. Wherever there is something different and good (a garden, view) or bad (lack of maintenance) it's been noted. Most of these hotels accept international credit cards.

Doubles for Less Than Rs 600 ($20)

A blend of East and West, the **Hotel Mayura Hoysala,** 2 Jhansi Laxmi Bai Rd., Mysore 570001 (☎ 25349), run by the KSTDC, has 21 neatly furnished, clean rooms, with either Indian or Western toilets, off breezy balconies in an old Raj-style bungalow. It's an okay place although improved maintenance would make it better. Rates are bargains at Rs 150 ($5) to Rs 225 ($7.50). There's a restaurant (tour buses stop), bar, and pleasant ambience. It's a popular place.

In the same compound, the new wing, KSTDC's **Mayura Yatri Nivas,** dorms cost Rs 25 (83¢) without a bed and Rs 40 ($1.33) with a bed. A double here is Rs 140 ($4.66). It needs care.

Parklane Hotel, 2720 Sri Harsha Rd. (formerly Curzon Park Road), next to the K.E.B. Building, Mysore 570001 (☎ 30400), is a charming place looking a little like a hacienda with eight small whitewashed rooms above a patio—spartan but smart, with dressing rooms and private bathrooms. The indoor restaurant is white-walled with fern paintings; the rustic outdoor cafe is topped with a red-tile roof. Both restaurants serve the usual Indian, Continental, and Chinese dishes, but the pleasant ambience (especially outdoors) gives them special flavor and makes them very popular. New management had taken over; I hope it's maintained as before.

Also on Sri Harsha Road, at 2716-2-3-7 and almost always fully occupied, is **Maurya Palace** (☎ 27162/7), with clean, ordinary rooms, better than expected in this price range; some have AC. Be smart; book in advance. It is convenient to bus and railway stations.

Doubles for Less Than Rs 1,000 ($33.33)

Ritz Hotel Metropole, Jhansi Laxmi Bai Road, Mysore 570005 (☎ 20871), was once a maharaja's guest house. A circular staircase leads to the rooms, all opening onto a shady veranda overhung with scarlet, fuchsia, and orange bougainvillea. The rooms are big, clean, and comfortably furnished—many handsome, old rosewood pieces are still in use—and they're complemented by tasteful bedspreads, rugs, and drapes. All rooms have dressing tables, nightstands with reading lamps, comfortable chairs, beds with mosquito netting, and attached bathrooms. High ceilings are fitted with fans to help keep even those without AC cool. An AC double is Rs 1,000 ($33.33), a suite Rs 1,200 ($40)—an excellent buy. Some non-AC rooms are cheaper. There is a 10% service charge.

A recent (and welcome) addition to Mysore, **Ramanashree Comforts,** L43/A, Harding's Circle, Mysore 570001 (☎30503; fax 33835), has a glass-domed lobby with black-and-white settees and wine brocade chairs, set off by shiny marble floors. Centrally air-conditioned, with 63 cheerful, modern rooms, many with balconies, the hotel has doubles starting around Rs 1,000 ($33.33), including a buffet breakfast. A good buy. There are two restaurants, **Noodles**—the only Chinese specialty restaurant in Mysore—and multicuisine **Darpan.**

Recently renovated, **Kings Kourt,** Jhansi Laxmi Bai Road, Mysore 570001 (☎ 25250; 563131), has 60 rooms, is centrally air-conditioned, and looks smart with new tailored room decor with clean, white walls replacing the earlier wildly patterned wallpaper. Doubles are about Rs 900 ($30). There's a stylish wood-paneled lobby with step-down conversation grouping; the staff is welcoming. Mirrors gleam at **Memories** restaurant, where the menu is the by-now-familiar array of Chinese, Indian, and Western dishes. There is a bar.

Doubles for Less Than Rs 1,800 ($60)

Quality Inn Southern Star, 13-14 Vinobha Rd., Mysore 570005 (☎ 27217; fax 32175), centrally air-conditioned, has a spacious plant-accented lobby with tapestry-upholstered cane and rattan furniture in intimate groupings. The 108 rooms have cheerful cream and rust color schemes, and modern rosewood furniture. **Gardenia,** the 24-hour coffee shop, is decorated with many botanical prints, but not one of them is a gardenia. **The Derby** cocktail lounge has saddles as bar stools. There's a multi-cuisine restaurant, tea lounge, and barbecue. A pretty good deal considering that the rates—about Rs 1,800 ($60) for a double—include a lavish buffet breakfast (see "Where to Eat," below). There's a 10% service charge. Swimming pool, health club. It is affiliated with the U.S. chain.

Worth a Splurge

One of the roads to Chamundi Hill goes to the ITDC's **Lalitha Mahal Palace,** Mysore 570011 (☎ 27650; fax 33398), once owned by the maharaja and now a delightful 54-room hotel. Inside the 22-room old wing, there are big bedrooms and marble baths, a sweeping marble staircase, and a glittering ballroom with a stained-glass dome; the 32 rooms in the new wing are less spectacular. The restaurant has three stained-glass domes, large pillars, and potted palms. You can sit in splendor while you savor something simple like a bowl of soup or dine more graciously on chicken tikka masala and nan. There are also Continental dishes. The conference room chairs are inlaid with the maharaja's crest. All this opulence understandably comes at splurge prices: Singles are Rs 2,500 ($83.33), doubles Rs 2,700 ($90) and up, suites up to Rs 5,000 ($166.66) a night. Most rooms have verandahs. There is a swimming pool.

Like a jewel box, **Rajendra Vilas Palace,** Chamundi Hill, Mysore 570018 (☎ 20690), sits high atop Chamundi Hill, 14 kilometers (8 1/2 miles) from town overlooking Mysore City. Once a weekend getaway for the Maharaja of Mysore, some years ago it was converted into a sumptuous, intimate, 29-room hotel, with balconies or terraces and picture postcard views. It will be closed until the end of 1996 for renovation, but it should be worth considering then. One hitch: The hotel is about a half-hour drive from Mysore City.

OUTSIDE OF TOWN

Staying at Brindavan Gardens

Outside of Mysore City, 19 kilometers (12 miles) northwest the **Ritz Krish-narajasagar** (☎ Belgula 57222), a charming, old-fashioned hotel is beautifully situated in the Brindavan Gardens, huge and handsomely terraced with symmetrical floral designs, accented boldly with red and yellow flowers, where countless fountains send glistening sprays of water into pools and channels. The hotel rooms have wardrobes, night stands, comfortable chairs, and balconies. Each room has a private bathroom and ceiling fan. Rooms rates range from Rs 495 ($16.50) fora non-AC single, to Rs 700 ($23.33) for a double. There's a 10% service charge.

Adjacent to the Krishnarajasagar is the **Hotel Mayura Cauvery** (☎ Belgola 57552), run by the government of Karnataka, where for under Rs 200 ($6.66) you can admire the elaborate gardens while living in the simplest surroundings. The rooms have balconies from some of which you can see the river. All rooms have attached baths, and five have Western-style toilets. There's a restaurant for guests, or you can eat next door at the Krishnarajasagar.

Under construction is the **Oberoi Brindavan,** a 130-room luxury hotel, which might be ready by now.

Brindavan Gardens The gardens are part of the huge irrigation dam that was built between 1911 and 1927, and the landscaping took six years to create. From the dining room of the hotel you can see the waters harnessed by the dam, gushing forth through the riverbed. Matching the floral display, the hotel's exterior is yellow, trimmed with aquamarine, and there are spacious rotundas from which you can see the gardens and fountains. At night, colored lights play on the fountains and flowers, transforming this setting into an enchantment of shapes and colors. The gardens are open to the public from 6:30am to 10pm, for a modest entry fee. If you're planning to use a camera, there's a camera charge also, depending on the type of camera. There's a light and fountain show at sunset every night: from 7 to 8pm on weekdays, to 9pm weekends and holidays, depending on the time of sunset.

Even if you don't stay out here, make it a point to see the gardens; buses start from Mysore at 2:30am and run until 5:15pm. The fare is Rs 5 (17¢).

WHERE TO EAT

Buffets at the following hotels are open to nonresidents: **Quality Inn Southern Star,** where there is a breakfast and two lunch buffets—Chinese and multicuisine—at the **Ramanashree Comforts.** When group tours are in town (which is often) buffets are available at **Lalitha Mahal;** they will run from around Rs 80 ($2.66) to Rs 200 ($6.66).

The classy **Dasaprakash Paradise,** Vivekananda Road (☎ 27777), serves notable vegetarian food in **Vishala,** decorated in earth tones. It's open from 6am to 10:30pm, with Indian classical music from 8pm onward. The accent is regional here, so you can eat specialties from various parts of Karnataka as well as North India, such as the north's mattar paneer (peas with cheese), kofta curry (ground vegetable balls in a sauce thickened with yogurt and nuts), and elaborate pulaos (rice dishes), as well as South Indian idlis, dosas, puris, and coconut milk–based curries. These dishes à la carte run Rs 9 (30¢) to Rs 25 (83¢). South Indian thali meals cost Rs 35 ($1.16). Recommended desserts are the rich ice creams, from Rs 12 (40¢) for something as mundane as vanilla to Rs 28 ($93¢) for something exotic like mango topped with sauces and fruits, a house specialty.

Samrat, Dhanvantri Road (☎ 23660), run by the Hotel Indra Bhavan, is somewhat of a pleasant surprise. While the hotel has gone downhill and is no longer recommended, the restaurant is clean, neat, and simple, offering vegetarian plate meals and à la carte dishes. The highest price is around Rs 26 (87¢) for a navarattan curry. Hours are 6 to 10:30am for breakfast, noon to 3pm for a North Indian lunch, and 7 to 10pm for dinner.

An old favorite, **Indra/Paras Cafe,** Sayaji Rao Road (☎ 52036), is comfortable and air-conditioned. The wide range of delicious vegetarian dishes includes dosas, ravi dosas (with onion), and idlis, which are delicious here. A South Indian thali (lunch only) is Rs 20 (67¢); a North Indian thali is Rs 42 ($1.40). The owners asked me to explain about their wonderful fresh fruit drinks because many Westerners throw a fit when they find they are made with a little water. The juice is whipped in a special machine, which requires a small amount of water—in this case, hygienic water filtered for drinking—however, you can ask for the juice without ice. Hours are 7:30 to 11am for snacks and breakfast, noon to 3:30pm for lunch, and 5 to 8:30pm for tea, snacks, and dinner; a special North Indian thali and a la carte served from 7:30 to 10pm (closed Thursday). Clean, sparkling **Indra Sweets** adjoins the restaurant.

On Gandhi Square, **Shilpashri** (☎ 25979), open from 9:30am to 11pm (no liquor between 2:30 and 5:30pm), is jammed on fair evenings when you can have a bite on the terrace. There's nothing special about the indoor restaurant, which is in operation throughout the day and evening. Many Westerners eat here. Highest priced entrées, Indian or Western, are around Rs 25 (83¢). There's reason to eat indoors, which is both noisy and unattractive.

Hotel Durbar, Gandhi Square (☎ 20029), is a simple place known for Kerala-style cooking. The menu features some Kerala curries, for Rs 6 (35¢) to Rs 12 (70¢), to be eaten with parotta, a rich, Kerala-style bread, for Rs 2.50 (15¢). Open from 8am to 11pm.

Parklane Garden Restaurant, in the hotel of the same name, is a great place for a tête-à-tête over drinks and snacks; sometimes there's a special seafood barbecue for Rs 40 ($1.33), served from 7 to 11pm.

ilapur 2721/1 Sri Harsha Rd. (☎ 32878), has frosted glass dividers, bright Indian murals, a rust and brown color scheme, and is spotlessly clean and air-conditioned. This new restaurant features "a taste of Andhra" cuisine—biriyani, mutton, prawns, all Andhra-style (some of it very hot!). There are also various curries. tandooris, and Chinese dishes for Rs 30 ($1) to Rs 60 ($2). Most other entrees peak around Rs 55 ($1.83). Hours are 11:30am to 4pm and 6:30 to 11 or 11:30pm.

EXCURSIONS FROM MYSORE CITY

There are a number of places of interest in the general area of Mysore City, many of which offer accommodations in case you want to spend a longer time visiting the temples and other major sights.

SOMNATHPUR

The landscape is dotted with curving palms, farms, bullock carts, and the occasional big banyan tree as the road goes 35 kilometers east of Mysore City.

Getting There

For Somnathpur, take the bus from the Suburban Bus Stand in Gandhi Square to T. Nirasipur, and change there for the bus to Somnathpur. Or you can take the bus at the Central Bus Stand to Bannur (there are six buses daily) and bargain with a ricksha driver to take you Somnathpur.

What to See & Do

The modest village of Somnathpur is best known for its extravagant, 13th-century **Kesava Temple.** The temple stands on a star-shaped platform. Eye-level sculptures depict some of the great Hindu epics, and elaborate friezes are bursting with elephants, swans, scrolls, horsemen, and mythical beasts. The temple was built by Somanatha, an officer under the Hoysala King Narasimha (1254–91). No two friezes are alike. This is but a teaser among temples, leading up to the even more exuberantly carved Belur and Halebid temples.

The on-site guide has only rudimentary knowledge of the temple (at least in English), so take an approved guide from Mysore City.

Where to Stay

KSTDC's **Hotel Mayura Kesav** (☎ 7017), has two run-down rooms costing under Rs 100 ($3.33) each (the manager did not know the rates, which tells you something about how often guests check in). Since relatively few people stay here, it's best to make advance reservations through the KSTDC Head Office, 10/4 Kasturba Rd., Bangalore (☎ 2212901), before taking off, to make sure the place is clean and ready to receive guests. You might also take along some food and bottled water.

HASSAN, BELUR, HALEBID, SRAVANABELAGOLA

North of Mysore are three of South India's major sights: the temples of incredible ornamental carvings (Halebid and Belur) and the solemn, exquisitely proportioned statue at Sravanabelagola, relatively near the town of Hassan.

Hassan

Hassan is in its last gasp as a bustling little city (pop. 108,500) and staging ground for tourists who've come to visit the famous lacelike temples of Belur and Halebid. (You can also visit these sites from Mysore or Bangalore, but staying overnight here permits more leisurely inspection.) Hassan will soon be much more vibrant: Businesses and industries have targeted the city as the next "Bangalore" and plan to push development here.

Getting There Hassan (157 kilometers from Mysore), can be reached by (very slow) passenger **trains,** at Rs 93 ($5.30) First (if it exists) and Rs 28 ($1.60) Second. There are no express trains from Mysore to Hassan. The station is 2 kilometers from the center of town. **Buses** to Hassan from Mysore's Central Bus Stand run from 2:45am to 8pm. The fare is Rs 26 (87¢).

Getting Around Bargain with the cycle ricksha, tonga, or taxi driver for your fare to the temples; a taxi is easiest. They charge Rs 2.50 (8¢) per kilometers. They'll ask for Rs 800 ($26.66) but will probably settle for Rs 500 ($16.66) to Halebid, the Jain Temples, Belur, and Doddaghadavalli (make sure your driver knows you want to stop there). Although Belur and Lakshmidevi Temple predate Halebid, the tour is usually done in this sequence, returning to Hassan.

Buses from Hassan go to Belur in 1½ hours, and from Belur to Hassan in half an hour, but they're not practical.

It's necessary to go back to Hassan to get the bus to Sravanabelagola.

What to See & Do The only sight to see in town is the **District Museum,** Maharaja Park, open 9am to 5pm, closed Mondays; there are coins, weapons, and other artifacts. Admission is free. Most visitors use Hassan as a base for visiting Belur, Halebid, and Sravanabelagola.

Staying in Hassan Hassan's proximity to Bangalore (192 kilometers) and the availability of low-cost land for office and industrial sites have made it a target for business development and the business-class hotels that go with it. Those I saw under construction must be finished by now to add to the following possibilities for tourists.

ITDC's **Hotel Hassan Ashok** on the Bangalore-Mangalore Road, Hassan 573201 (☎ 68731; fax 67154), the top spot in town, is a three-story structure with 46 functionally furnished double rooms, 24 with unreliable AC; rates are Rs 1,100 ($36.66) for an AC double, Rs 900 ($30) without AC. The friendly ambience is a plus. There's a restaurant, bar, shops.

Hotel Amblee Palika, 4724 Race Course Rd., Hassan 573201 (☎ 67145), has 34 clean, simple double rooms, all with attached bathrooms, but no showers in cheaper rooms and hot water in buckets; there's a restaurant. Very nice indeed.

Of the inexpensive Indian-style hotels, the nicest are **Vaishnavi Lodging,** Harsha Mahal Road (☎ 67413), clean, spartan, and cheap, there are 30 singles—Rs 108 ($3.60)— and 12 doubles—Rs 71 ($2.36). Veg snacks are available. **Satyaprakash Lodge,** Bus Stand Road (☎ 68437), is clean and simple; **New Abhiruchi,** Bangalore Mysore Road (☎ 68885), is also clean and has a veg restaurant. All have similar rates.

If none of these work out, the Karnataka Tourist Bureau, also on the Bangalore-Mysore Road, can give you leads on vacancies.

En Route to the Hoysala Temples

Leaving Hassan for a visit to the Hoysala temples, the landscape turns barren with little of interest to see—strange-shaped cacti in the fields, small girls walking to school, their hair tied in big red bows, book straps slung across their shoulders.

About 19 kilometers from the city it gets more fertile, there's a small lake, and 2 kilometers beyond, the road curves into a rutted path to the dusty little village **Doddagaddavahalli,** an seemingly unlikely site for a 13th-century, Hoysala-style temple.

This is **Lakshmidevi Temple,** built in 1113, about the same time as Belur, but without the elaborate exterior sculptures you'll find there. Few tour groups stop here, and there's no government approved guide. The watchman shows visitors the interior: four small shrines off the center hall—to north, Kali, followed to the right by Mahalakshmi (this, according to the watchman, is one of three ancient Lakshmi temples in India), Bhairava (Shiva), and Bhutanatha. The small but well-carved statues were a prelude to future extravgance at the more famous templs. Kids come out to see the foreigners. Do not give pennies, candies, or pens. (It just takes one penny, pen, or candy to turn a little child into a beggar asking for something from every foreigner. When I was here, they hadn't started asking.) Wave, say "hi" and "bye," and take off for Belur.

About the Hoyasalas The road goes on for another 19 kilometers to Belur, once a capital of the Hoyasalas, as was Halebid, to be seen later on. The Hoysalas were great warriors and rulers of a huge chunk of South India between the Krishna and Cauvery rivers, but they also were interested in cultivating the arts. Theirs were peaceful and plentiful times, and they encouraged artisans, even allowing them to sign their works. This was an unheard-of innovation for the times, and it fostered a friendly competition to produce remarkable masterpieces.

The Hoysalas commissioned their extravagantly carved temples as offerings to their gods in return for assistance in combat. Aptly, the legends of the Mahabharata Ramayana and Bhagvata Purana form the friezes, as do images of everyday life. It was as if the artisans decided to leave no stone unsculpted in a burst of creativity and religious fervor.

Hoysala temples, unlike others in the South, are small jewel boxes of intricate design, perched on star-shaped platforms. They are aptly called lacelike. For illustration, guides take a thread through the eye of a figure, and pull it through the nose; the proportions are perfection as the taut string test shows: Place it on the devadasi's forehead, and it falls to her turned up toe.

Every detail is carved in soapstone, which is comparatively soft and malleable when sculpted; when hardened, it looks like metal.

Belur

Almost 900 years ago, Belur was the prosperous capital city of the Hoysala kings. Nothing matters here except the **Chennakesava Temple**—but that matters a lot. Built in the 12th century, this Hindu contemporary of such great European cathedrals as Chartres and Rheims represents medieval architecture at its most exalted level. Belur commemorates the victory of the Hoysalas over the Cholas at Talakad. Krishna's figure is in the courtyard as is winged Garuda, guardian of the temple.

It is star-shaped in plan, as befits Hoysala style. The sculptures are easy to see, most on a level with the eyes. Remove your shoes to inspect the carvings more closely: rows of graceful goddesses bedecked with jewels and surrounded by lacy stone canopies, handsome gods with stone-cut crowns and garlands. You also find a sculptured "novella" of royal life—hunters, dancers, musicians. There are elephants, demons, trees, flowers, and scrolls to delight the eye and to fascinate. The 650 elephants charging around the exterior are a fine example of the artistry—no two are alike.

Belur's temple has three entrances—at the East, South, and North—each worth close inspection. The north doorway is decorated with full-bosomed female statues and nearby is a stone-cut "filmstrip" of the evils of destruction, involving such diverse participants as an eagle attacking a beast, which is trying to get a lion, which in turn is going after an elephant, which is preying on a snake about to down a rat. The south doorway is resplendent with a myriad of gods and goddesses, beasts, and evil demons. The eastern doorway is unusually fine, with eight elaborate friezes. On the right are small musicians. Above are 28 windows carved with star patterns and leafy designs. Be sure to note the 38 bracket figures that support the eaves of the temple. They are beautiful, well-endowed women, striking various poses with a lyrical grace. Can you find the spy? *Clue:* She's the figure with the scorpion at her feet. Here's her legend: She was fed venom with milk until her body was full of it, then she was dispatched to end the lives enemies of the Hoysalas with a kiss of death.

In the dark interior (Rs 5 lighting fee), there are hand-lathed turned pillars decorated with incomparable friezes; note the small barren space on the Narasimha Pillar waiting to be sculpted by someone daring and talented enough to do it. Four bracket figures in the ornate ceiling were inspired by Queen Shantala Devi, a great beauty and talented dancer. Notice the fantasy in these bracket figures each unique—a pet parrot has a peacocklike tail, a dancer's fingers become flowers, still another wrings the water from her hair, the drops seen on the delicate strands. On the platform in front of the shrine, the queen herself dances for Lord Krishna. Because this temple and Halebid do not have towers but others such as the one at Somnathpur do, some scholars think these two were never finished. There are government-approved guides at Belur to offer help, and pesky vendors who hawk souvenirs.

Staying at Belur KSTDC's modest **Hotel Mayura Velapuri,** Temple Road (☎ 9), has two simple rooms with rates under Rs 100 ($3.33), bathrooms attached. If you want to stay here, contact the manager or make your reservations through KSTDC's head office at 10/4 Kasturba Rd. in Bangalore (☎ 2212901), so you'll be expected in Belur. The hotel is near the temple, main market, and local restaurants (called "hotels"), where you can get simple South Indian foods, soft drinks,and coffee. There are also a few simple Indian-style hotels on Main Road in Belur.

Halebid

Fergusson, who documented so much of India's architecture, placed Halebid's **Hoysaleswara Temple** at the extreme opposite pole from the Parthenon. Here there is nothing austere. The sculptors seemed convinced that to leave any surface uncovered would be a lavish waste of space. So, almost 900 years ago they created a rococo structure that looks as if it might be intricately carved ivory with lacy trims, declaring the adoration of their gods in a series of photographically realistic statues. About 10 miles from Belur, and built 10 years after the other temple, Hoysaleswara was never completed. It took 80 years to create what you see now. The material used was soapstone, which hardens with age, but is soft enough at the onset to permit these intricate designs. The Hoysaleswara Temple has two shrines, one to Shiva and the other to Parvati. You must remove your shoes before looking around.

The friezes that surround the building are painstakingly executed and arranged to play off the horizontal elements against the verticals. Time and time again, elephants, symbolizing stability, march in procession on the bottom tier. On top of them are lions, then horses, oxen, and birds. Scrolls curl to set off scenes of religious epics, and there are legendary beasts and swans.

The most outstanding of the friezes show curvaceous, heavenly maidens lavishly adorned with gorgeous jewels and posed arrestingly under sculptured awnings that have provided eight centuries of shade for them. You can also see the entire roster of Hindu gods and goddesses. Look for baby Krishna playing, demon Ravana lifting Mt. Kailasha, Shiva dancing. Be sure to look for Ganesha, the elephant-headed god of good luck, who is especially well turned out in a huge headdress.

Inside, cool, black marble pillars rise like dark stone trees, and more carvings; Queen Shantla Devi seems to invite the visitor to look more closely at the fine stoneworks that here are larger than at Belur and as delicately chiseled in that same sensuous black stone. There are government-approved guides here.

In the courtyard opposite the temple is a small **museum** of sculpture, which is open from 10am to 5pm

Signs at the gate point you to the Jain temples (Jains flourished here, too), about half a mile from Halebid's Hoysaleswara Temple. They are eloquent in their simplicity. The pillars inside gleam like mirrors, as an attendant will demonstrate. Tip him Rs 5 (17¢).

Staying at Halebid There are simple **Tourist Cottages,** Belur 573121 (☎ 08197-3224), where doubles are Rs 50 ($1.66), singles Rs 25 (83¢). Contact the manager for reservations. Call in advance, so that he'll be able to tidy up the place and stock provisions. The cottages are rarely occupied, so you probably won't have any trouble getting in, however. There's always the fixings on hand for an omelet as well as soft drinks. Meals are to order. There are a couple of Indian-style restaurants to eat at nearby, or you can bring some provisions.

Under construction, about 1 1/2 kilometers away, at Pushpagiri Hill, are eight double rooms and a big restaurant with boating, etc.

Sravanabelagola

This is the site of the huge statue of **Gomateswara** (57 feet high), an important saint in the Jain religion. It was at Sravanabelagola that the Emperor Chandragupta was supposed to have lived his final days, after scorning all worldly wealth and possession. To see the statue, you remove your shoes as pilgrims have done for centuries and climb barefoot up 614 steep, smooth, rock stairs that run to the top of the 470-foot-high **Indragiri Hill.** Try to climb early in the day before the steps become too hot, or wear socks to protect your feet. For those who are unable to climb, there are coolies (porters) to help with chairs. The climb gives an incredibly fine view of the surroundings; the higher you go, the more it looks like a fairytale village set out below. There are several shrines on the way up, all 12th century, but one dating from about 200 years earlier.

The statue, carved between 980 and 983 from one immense rock, is a stylized nude gazing serenely into the idyllic valley below. Creeping vines entwine the arms and thighs. They symbolize that the saint meditated so long and deeply that vines grew unnoticed around him. The nudity represents denial of worldly wealth. According to legend, the statue commemorates a young man who exemplified unselfish denial. He fought his older brother and won their father's kingdom. But he turned his prize back to his brother and went into the woods to follow the aesthetic life.

There has been renovation going on at the summit for some time, so the statue's massive head has scaffolding around it. Be sure to see the beautiful murals.

Every 12 years (next in 2006), during the Mastakabhisheka—sacred head-anointing ceremony—pilgrims flock in great numbers to Sravanabelagola from everywhere to bear witness. Priests climb up a specially constructed scaffolding to pour pots of ghee (clarified butter), milk, coconut water, tumeric, paste, honey, vermillion powers, even gold and precious stones over the idol's head. A modern twist involves a helicopter dropping rose petals on the figure below.

You can leave your gear at the Karnataka Tourist Office near the entrance while you climb. It's not easy to ditch the pestering kids selling souvenirs and postcards; like your shadow, they'll go where you do—except up the big climb.

Staying in Sravanabelagola There's a government-run **Tourist Canteen-cum-Rest House** at Sravanabelagola, 48 kilometers from Hassan, charging about Rs 25 (83¢) for a single and Rs 50 ($1.66) for a double. For reservations, contact Manager, Tourist Canteen-cum-Rest House, Department of Tourism, F-Block, First Floor, Cauvery Bhavan, Bangalore 560001 (☎ 2215489). There is also a **Travellers Bungalow,** where you can stay for Rs 10 (55¢) per room. For reservations, contact: Chief Executive Officer, Taluk Board, Chennarayapatna, Hassan District. There are also **dharmashalas** (simple pilgrim shelters) and **cottages.** At Sravanabelagola, the accommodations are usually full of Jain pilgrims visiting one of their immensely important religious sites, so you are advised to book well in advance. In any case, you'd be wise to stay at Hassan, where you'll have both greater comforts and more chance of getting in.

BANDIPUR

Only 80 kilometers (50 miles) from Mysore City is Bandipur, a wildlife sanctuary where you can see such animals as black panthers, wild elephants, deer, bison, black-faced monkeys, sloth, bears, chital, and many rare birds. Bandipur is one of India's tiger reserves.

Game-viewing is a matter of luck. You may spend a day going about with a guide in a minibus and see only one or two animals, or you may see them all on a two-hour trip. The Bandipur setting is pretty, and even if you do not see an abundance of game, it provides a relaxation from Karnataka's extraordinary temples.

The 689-square-kilometer tract is actually part of the larger Venugopal Wildlife Park, established in 1931 by the Mysore maharajahs. It takes in Mudumalai Forest in Tamil Nadu and Wynad in Kerala.

Getting to Bandipur

Buses leave three times a day from Mysore's Central Bus Stand, for a fare of Rs 18 (60¢). Or you can take one of the seven buses to Ootacamund Rs 33 ($1.10) each day and get off at Bandipur.

Making Bandipur a Day Trip

Bandipur can also be day's excursion from Mysore. If you're on the 6:15am Ootacamund bus, you can take the last Bandipur bus back at 3:15pm. It will be rushed, but if you're short on time, you might try it. Or negotiate a flat rate with a taxi and have more time to park it.

Bandipur Basics

The best season for Bandipur is June to October; entry fee is Rs 2 (6¢); there are fees for various still cameras. Game viewing by minibus is Rs 12 (40¢) per head; on elephant back, Rs 25 (83¢) per hour for four persons. Visiting hours are 6 to 9am, and 4 to 6pm. Forest guides accompany viewers on all trips. If you wish to reserve a park tour in advance, call the assistant director.

Staying at Bandipur

Neat, comfortably furnished **cottages,** in clearings under huge shade trees, offer accommodation for Rs 50 ($1.66) per double room and Rs 100 ($3.33) per double VIP room. Each cottage has a cook, who prepares breakfast, lunch, and dinner for modest fees. There are also two dorms, with 12 and 22 beds, where the fee is Rs 10 (33¢) per bed. There are few accommodations, so you must book in advance if you hope to get in. For information and reservations, contact: Assistant Conservator of Forests, Bandipur National Park; or Chief Wildlife Warden, Aranya Bhavan, 18th Cross, Malleswaram, Bangalore 560003 (☎ 361993), for accommodations from one to four rooms; for larger bookings, contact: Field Director, Project Tiger, Government House Complex, Mysore 570008 (☎ 220901).

Kargudi Elephant Camp

Elephants are part of the workforce in South India. Kargudi (5 kilometers from Bandipur) is their finishing school. Here they are tamed and trained to be employed in the lumber industry. They also perform puja (prayers) at the temple at 6 pm, and visitors learn the what of elephants diets and when and how this life differs from theirs in the jungles.

Nagarhole National Park

From Mysore, there's a good road to Nagarhole National Park. Beyond the city you pass a number of electronics industries, a joint U.S.-India Jeep venture, Mahendra and Mahendra, and manufacturers of shovels, dumpers, and bulldozers. But soon the scene is pastoral as you go through villages and paddy fields and near the 572-square-kilometer game sanctuary, south of Coorg and bordering on Kerala.

Getting to Nagarhole

The 96 kilometers trip from Mysore to Nagarhole can be made by **express bus** from Mysore for Rs 16 (53¢) or Rs 20 (67¢) in approximately three hours; or from Bangalore, 215 kilometers away, for Rs 50 ($1.66), a full day's trip. The Mysore-Nagarhole road turns south at Hunsur.

If you hire a taxi—Rs 2.50 (8¢) per kilometer diesel driven, Rs 3 (9¢) per kilometer gasoline-driven—in Mysore for the trip to Nagarhole, get an early start so you can turn west for 34 kilometers (20 miles) and stray into **Madikeri** (formerly Mercara), the capital of the scenic Western ghats, noted for orange groves, coffee plantations, and dense woods. Main attractions are an interesting fort, the terrific view from Rajah's Seat, Omkareswara Temple, and palace. There's a nice place to stay 7 kilometers from town, **Capital Village,** or in Madikeri at the KSTDC's **Mayura Valley View** (☎ 6387).

About the Park

Going into Nagarhole the road deteriorates as it winds through dense, untamed jungles of the lush, wild terrain. The name Nagarhole means "Snake River" in Kannada, the local language, and the namesake river winds through the beautiful park where there are also lakes, swamps, bamboo groves, towering rosewoods, and flowering trees. Entry is Rs 2 (6¢), plus camera fees.

Bordering Kerala, this is one of India's most beautiful sanctuaries now—covering 572 square kilometers—but ruins indicate that years ago it was a thriving settlement. More recently, part of the vast park was the exclusive hunting preserve of the maharajas of Mysore and famous as the site of the kheddas—elephant roundups. They led to the capture of 1,536 wild elephants between 1890 and 1971.

Today the park is a sanctuary for elephants, gaur (among the world's largest oxen), sambar, chital (spotted deer), bison, leopards, and tigers, a few of the species roaming this protected area. Peacocks and storks are among the 250 birds nesting in the park.

Game viewing There are guided, game-watching tours in mini-buses, jeeps, and vans (which last about an hour) at 5:15. There are machans (platforms) to climb for viewing. You may see a whole congress of elephants, as well as a few smaller family groups with babies protected by females bringing up the rear, plus gaur, sambar, and black-faced monkeys. All within a few yards of the vehicle.

Staying in Nagarhole

Best bet for accommodation is at one of the **Forest Lodges** right in the park. Typical is **Gangotri Lodge** with four double rooms, two on the upper floor and two on the ground floor, and all the comforts of home (bedrooms, attached bathrooms, living room-cum-dining room) and more—a bearer to clean, cook, and serve. The charge is about Rs 50 ($1.66) per person, plus modest fees for meals and teas. There are no desserts with the meals (you might want to bring some fruit), but a special treat at sunset is seeing from the forest lodge herds of deer and elephants roaming and grazing around the compound.

To book a lodge: At least one week in advance, contact Chief Wildlife Warden, Aranya Bhavan 18th Cross, Malleswaram, Bangalore 560003 (☎ 341993); or Assistant Conservator of Forests, Wildlife Sub-Division, Vani Vilas Road, Mysore (☎ 221159).

Adjacent to Nagarhole at Karapur, 48 miles from Mysore, is the expensive **Kabini River Lodge,** on the banks of the Kabini Reservoir. The main building was built in the 18th century as the former maharaja's game lodge and still sports his crest, but now it is the reception and administrative area. Two new buildings, built to look like the old one, have 14 twin-bedded rooms usually occupied by tour groups. The cost is about $200 per day per person, including accommodation, meals, game drives, and coracle rides for bird-watching. These rates are for foreign nationals only; Indians pay **less than half** this amount. All rates are due for an increase. For reservations and information, contact Jungle Lodges and Resorts Ltd., Shrungar Shopping Centre, M. G. Road, 560001 (☎ 5586163). You can get a bus from Mysore to Karapur, which is nearby the Kabini River Lodge.

Cauvery Fishing Camp is on the banks of the river Cauvery at Bimeshwari. For reservations, contact Jungle Lodges at the address above.

3 Hampi—The Ruins of Vijayanagar

At first, Hampi seems somewhat surreal—massive, crumbling structures strewn about nine square miles of barren, rocky landscape. These are the still-majestic ruins of the capital of the powerful Vijayanagar Empire (1336–1565), which extended from the Arabian Sea to the Bay of Bengal and from the Deccan Plateau to the Indian peninsula.

The kings and nobles are long since gone from this once-grand city, and so are its half a million inhabitants and the foreign traders who returned home dazzled by its wealth. Today, aside from a handful of priests and bazaar wallahs, it's a showcase for past artisans who transformed the lonely landscape into the vibrant capital of the largest Hindu empire in India's history.

In 1336, when two Hindu princes, Harihara (Hakka) and Bukka, broke ground on this place, they sought to defy the might of invaders by choosing a remote site, protected by the Tungabhadra River to the North and rocky ridges to the other three sides. They surrounded their city with strong fortifications. You still can see mighty crenelations marking the northern outpost of the Vijayanagar Empire above the Tungabhadra River.

Their site selection might also have been made for religious reasons—this was believed to be Kishkindha, the capital of the monkey kingdom in the *Ramayana.* To this day, it's a hallowed home for many monkeys.

The Vijayanagar Empire achieved its eminence under Krishnadevaraya Raya (1509–29), widely known as a patron of the arts, literature, and religion. Its dominance of the spice and cotton trades made the city's treasury bulge, and its markets, glittering with gems and gold, attracted European travelers who were dazzled by such splendor and affluence.

Weaker than their predecessor, the kings who followed Krishnadevaraya wrangled unnecessarily with the Deccan sultans. In 1565, the ruler of Vijayanagar, Ramaraja, was defeated at Talikota by a coalition of these sultans. They ravaged Hampi and brought an end to its glory. The kingdom came under Mughal rule in 1689, and in 1780 it was annexed to the Nizam of Hyderabad.

ESSENTIALS

GETTING TO HAMPI

BY BUS **From Bangalore** (350 kilometers), KSRTC **bus** service departs daily at noon and arrives at 9pm. The return bus departs from Hampi at 6:30am and arrives in Bangalore at 3:30pm. There is frequent bus service **from Hospet** (13 kilometers/ 9 miles) to Hampi to enter at Museum (Rs 4) and near the Bazaar (preferred fare, Rs 3.50). The last bus back to Hospet is around 8pm.

From Mysore to Hospet, there's one bus a day at 7:30pm; the fare is Rs 81 ($2.70).

BY AUTO RICKSHA OR TAXI Auto ricksha drivers will usually settle for Rs 150 ($5) for a day trip to and around the ruins; taxis hired through the hotels and near the bus stand charge about Rs 200 ($6.66) for four to five hours at Hampi, Rs 300 ($10) for six hours, for five to six passengers sharing the vehicle. For a full day at Hampi and a run to Tungabhadra Dam, expect to pay around Rs 400 ($13.33) to Rs 450 ($15). These fares, needless to say, are after hard bargaining. They've increased as more foreigners have given in to higher rates without bargaining. Do your best.

For going around Hospet, cycle rickshas and auto rickshas get what they can; bargain for a fair fare.

BY BICYCLE There are a number of cycle shops in Hospet (ask anyone if you have trouble finding one) where you can rent a bike for about Rs 20 (66¢) per day. Make sure both you and the bike are in good condition before taking this trip. There's a good road for the 12-kilometer trip between Hospet and Hampi. The route through the ruins is unpredictable, and, at times, rough going. And the sun can be very hot. This is physically taxing and should the bike break down, be prepared to fix it yourself or walk.

BY TRAIN Hampi is 13 kilometers east of Hospet, the nearest train station. Auto rickshas and taxis are available. A convenient train, the *Bangalore-Hospet-Hampi Express,* departs **from Bangalore** at 9:55pm, arriving in Hospet at 7:30am, for approximately Rs 700 ($23.33) AC first class, Rs 80 ($2.66) second class. This train departs Hospet at 8:30pm and arrives at Bangalore at 7am. You can also grab trains **from Hyderbad/Secunderabad** and change at Guntakal for Hampi.

VISITOR INFORMATION

Signage at Hampi is minimal, so you'll want to pick up two fairly good publications to guide you with photographs, descriptions, and sketch maps. They are *Hampi,* a pamphlet published by Karnataka Tourism, First Floor, F Block, Cauvery Bhavan, K.G. Road, Bangalore (☎ 560009), available there or at the India Tourist Office, 48 Church St. (☎ 5585917); and *Hampi: A Tourist's Guide,* published by Vasan Book Depot, Bangalore ($1.15), at bookstores in Bangalore or Hospet, the town

13 kilometers from the ruins, or in the Hampi Bazaar near the Virupaksha Temple. Stores may also have an archeological survey map of Hampi. If you need information or require a guide, inquire at the tourist office near this same temple in the Hampi Bazaar.

Note: Take a hat for protection from the sun, sunblock, and bottled water.

WHAT TO SEE & DO

It could easily take several days to really do justice to these ruins, but lacking the luxury of time, the diligent visitor can see the highlights in a day—providing you get an early start.

Hampi has two zones: The sacred center, with many temples, lies along the south bank of the Tungabhadra River. To its south is the royal area, where you'll find palaces, stables, baths, and a few temples. While Hindus predominated in the city, there also are some Jain temple ruins and an architectural blend of Hindu and Islamic styles.

Most visitors start at the sacred center of Hampi, the Virupaksha Temple. Alternatively, you might begin at Museum Temple, especially if you take one of the buses from Hospet, which drops you there. (Try to get the bazaar drop off bus.)

Virupaksha Temple is open 8am to 12:30pm and 3 to 6:30pm; the entry fee is Rs 2 (6¢). This is one of the few temples still in use at Hampi, set at the end of a 700-meter lane once the site of the great bazaar—flourishing today with temple trinkets and handicrafts. The elaborately carved gateway predates the temple, which is dedicated to Shiva; the central shrine is decorated with scenes of Hindu mythology. A pleasant activity is wandering through the warren of temple courtyards dotted with shrines and pillared halls that date from the Vijayanagar kings. The priests are very nice and welcome visitors who wish to look around the small courtyards. They might even show you around some of the tiny shrines. Outside the temple compound, young boys herd family cattle along one of the paths which trails off into a cane field; thus the past and present blend in this unusual setting.

In the sacred zone as well are three imposing idols, each worshipped as a temple. They are the towering four-armed **Narasimha,** Vishnu's lion incarnation, 22 feet high, seated under a cobra canopy; and, next to it, a 10-foot-high **Shiva lingam;** and two imposing statues of Ganesha on the slopes of **Hemakuta Hill**—one is 10 feet high, the other 16 feet high.

But this zone's great star is the elegantly decorated **Vittala Temple** (1513–21), dedicated to Vishnu. Its main feature is a hall of 56 extraordinary columns, sculpted with fantastic creatures and graceful animals. The temple attendants invariably point out to visitors the monkey, cleverly designed to strike five different poses. The carved columns make musical sounds when struck by a temple attendant. Placing your ear near the structures, you'll hear that one of them sounds like a marimba, another like a vina. Each is said to sound like a different musical instrument. A handsome stone chariot stands in the courtyard.

In the royal area, you will find the fascinating 15-foot-tall granite pillars and 12-foot cross beam that held the **Kings Balance,** where rulers were weighed against their weight in gems and gold, which were distributed on auspicious days, and the **Zenana Enclosure,** with its watchtower standing guard over the **Lotus Mahal,** a blend of Hindu and Islamic architectural styles. Named for its graceful petal-shaped archways, it was probably a former palace. Climb the stairs to the side for a close-up of the arches as well as a lovely view of the ruins; nearby are the **Elephant Stables,** again in Indo-Saracenic style, with 11 chambers, topped with an eclectic collection of graceful domes—octagonal, fluted, and plain among them. Near Lotus Mahal, the **Hazara Rama Temple,** probably used by the royal family, has intricately carved friezes of elephants, horses, dancers, and warriors. Directly south of this temple is **Mahanavami Dibba,** a large platform the kings used when viewing the Dussehra festivities, and again to the south is the **sacred tank** (a rather recent discovery), with gracefully graded stone-slab steps into the water. In this vicinity, the large square structure, plain on the outside, lavishly decorated inside, is the **Queen's Bath.** Its arched bays are typical of Muslim architecture. Royalty no longer splashes here; the pool is dry. Now farmers drive oxen through it taking a shortcut to the fields.

And these are only a few prize sights; there are many more. In addition, archaeologists are constantly at work at Hampi, so there may be new discoveries for you to see.

The **Archaeological Museum** (2 kilometers away) on Power House Road, in Kamalapura, houses sculpture and artifacts discovered at Hampi. Open from 10am to 6pm; closed Fridays. Entry is free.

East of the museum, the Pattabirama Temple, which bears a resemblance to the Vittala Temple, was built in the 16th century by King Achutadevaraya, who also constructed a temple at Hampi.

A Dam Excursion

Fifteen kilometers (10 miles) from Hospet is the dam built across the Tungabhadra River. The Tungabhadra Dam is about $1^1/_2$ miles long and 170 feet high, and its storage capacity is 132,559 million cubic feet spread over an area of 380 square kilometers, making it one of the largest masonry dams in India. The dam was begun in 1945 and completed in 1953 and provides electricity for irrigation in the area. Nearby, the well-manicured terrace gardens are a pretty sight. They are illuminated on Saturday and Sunday evenings and at festival times. But unless things have been severely altered, there is absolutely no reason to hike over the bridge to Munirabad to see the weed-filled, so-called Japanese gardens.

Nearby, the **Lake View Guest House** has run-down rooms under Rs 100 ($3.33). The reservation authority is Executive Engineer, no. 1 Sub-division Munirabad, Rachur District.

Guided Tours

KSTDC conducts a daily tour starting from Hospet at 9:30am to 5:30pm to Hampi and the Tungabhadra Dam. For information and booking, contact: Tourist Information Counter, Hampi Bazaar; or Tourist Office, KSTDC, Taluk Office Compound, Hospet (☎ 8537).

From Hospet, **KSRTC buses** to the dam leave regularly from the Bus Stand. KSTDC'S three-day Hampi Tour, for Rs 450 ($15), can be booked in Bangalore. There's also a special Day Tour from Bangalore for individuals. It include the overnight train from Bangalore to Hampi, breakfast, lunch, a tour, then return on the night train to Bangalore.

For information on the tours from Bangalore contact: KSTDC, 10/4 Kasturba Rd., Queen's Circle, Bangalore (☎ 2212901), or any KSTDC office.

WHERE TO STAY

Your best choice in Hospet is **Malligi Tourist Home,** 6/143 Jambunatha Rd., Hospet 583201 (☎ 48101), with 86 clean, simply but adequately furnished rooms, a few with AC, all with bathrooms attached; plus a travel counter and little shop. Single rates run from Rs 300 ($10) to Rs 550 ($18.33), doubles from Rs 400

($13.33) to Rs 650 ($21.66). The higher rate are for AC. Stays are supposedly limited to three days.

KSTDC's **Hotel Mayura Vijayanagar** (☎ 48270), on Tungabhadra Dam Road (2 kilometers from center), is spartan and has mosquito nets and a dining hall. Rates are around Rs 100 ($3.33) to Rs 200 ($.6.66).

Combining charm, dramatic location, and comfort, the **Viakunta Guest House,** Tungabhadra Dam 583225 (☎ 48254), sits above the giant reservoir like a pastel-frosted pastry set in a flower garden. Stone lions guard the entrance and generous windows offer an extensive view of the great expanse of water (sunset is especially fine). The rooms look slightly 1930-ish, with wardrobes and attached bathrooms. Rates are under Rs 300 ($10). The cook makes tasty meals to order for an additional charge. For reservations, contact: Executive Engineer, Tungabhadra Board, HLC and Head Works Division, Tungabhadra Dam (☎ 48241). One slight drawback: Occasionally overland tour buses overnight here, and their passengers sleep aboard but eat in the guest house dining room. If you'd like to avoid the crowd, the bearer will serve your meals outdoors on the upstairs terrace.

KSTDC's Tourist Complex at Kamalapura, 2 kilometers from Hampi, offers the basics for around Rs 100 ($3.33) to Rs 200 ($6.66). There are bikes for rent to pedal to the ruins and around.

WHERE TO EAT

In Hospet, **Nirmal,** the vegetarian restaurant in the Malligi Tourist Home, serves delicious dosas and other South Indian dishes. It is open from 7am to 10pm. The **Eagle Restaurant and Bar,** Malligi's nonvegetarian garden restaurant under spreading trees, is a popular place for dinner; chicken or mutton dishes cost about Rs 40 ($1.33), rice and vegetarian dishes around Rs 20 (66¢) to Rs 30 ($1). Open from 10am to 11:30pm. **Shanabhag Hotel,** Taluk Office Circle, offers Indian vegetarian thalis.

At Hampi, soft drinks and snacks are sold in the bazaar, and KSTDC runs the simple **Lotus Mahal Restaurant** in the ruins. If you plan to spend the day at the ruins, your best strategy is to take a simple sack lunch and some fruit, and picnic where you wish. Just remember to take any litter out with you.

4 Aihole, Pattadakal & Badami

In a triangle of tiny villages—Aihole, Pattadakal, and Badami—tucked in red sandstone cliffs west of Hampi lie the brilliant ruins of the Chalukyan kings who ruled much of the Deccan plateau from the 4th to the 8th centuries. In these rural enclaves are the earliest examples of Dravidian temples as well as cave shrines created before the 10th century. Here the daily tableau seems centuries old as well—the farmers' oxen still plod patiently round, pulling wooden threshers over piles of rice; and small groups of women with brass water jugs on their heads walk barefoot through rust-brown earth, bangles flashing at their wrists.

AIHOLE

Once the capital of the early Chalukyan dynasty, in the 6th to 8th centuries, Aihole is considered the birthplace of Hindu temple architecture, four examples of which are most famous today. There are also traces of an ancient fort. Even earlier civilizations lie beneath the rust-colored dust, according to archaeologists' excavation of pottery shards and structural bases predating the Chalukyan days.

Getting to Aihole

There are regular **buses** from Aminagad (10 kilometers), Badami (46 kilometers), and Pattdakal (17 kilometers)

What to See & Do

The entrance to Aihole is in a fertile valley, but the best place to begin your tour is up the rocky hill behind the village with the **Meguit Temple,** the only dated monument at Aihole. It is in the earliest Dravidian style, dated 634. It is a Jain temple, and Mahavira meditates in the inner shrine.

Down the steps from the temple are a group of early freestanding temples, with rounded corners, reminiscent of a Buddhist chaitya (prayer hall). Until the period when these temples were built, the only stone temples in India had been cut out of rocks by Buddhist monks, whose work became the inspiration for early Hindu temple architecture.

This is most clearly visible at the famous **Durga Temple,** with rounded sides and a walkway around the apse. But there is something new here as well: Artisans at this late 7th- or early 8th-century temple added purely Hindu reliefs to their Buddhist-inspired creation. The temple stands on a platform and is topped by the very first shikhara (tower), later an important feature of North Indian temples. This is the most elaborately decorated temple at Aihole. It has particularly well-executed figures of Vishnu and Shiva, Shiva Ardhanarishvara (the half-male half-female figure representing the union of Shiva and Parvati), and Chamunda Devi trampling a demon. Look around and you'll also see scenes from the *Mahabharata* and *Ramayana* and reliefs of Indra and other gods.

There are 50 temples inside the fort walls and 50 outside, showing the influences of Hoysala, Buddhist, Jain, Dravida, Nagara, and Rekhanagara styles. One has a Muslim name, **Lad Khan** (5th century), for the prince who transformed this temple into his home. South of the Durga Temple, the Lad Khan's architects experimented with a hodgepodge of styles: They built a Panchayat-style hall, with windows made of lacy latticework in the northern style; the sanctum was added later. In the main shrine are a lingam and Nandi. If you climb the stone ladder to the roof, you find a shrine with Vishnu and Surya on the walls.

At **Hucchimalli,** located to the north of the village behind the Tourist Home, the sanctum shows the northern influence. Here, the vestibule in front appears for the first time, and the shikhara is well developed.

There is much more at Aihole. It's well worth it to stroll around to discover a relief or a pillar here or a latticework window there, casting shadows like frozen lace on a temple's floors. Before you leave, look in at the **Ravanphadi cave temple** (6th century), with Shiva and his various incarnations inside and outside. Entry fee is Rs 3 (9¢); the site is open from sunrise to sunset.

A **museum** maintained by the Archeological Survey of India is located in the Durga Temple Complex, open 10am to 5pm (closed Friday). Entry is free.

Where to Stay

Most tourists base at Badami, 46 kilometers away, though I recommend none of the options in Badami with any enthusiasm. At Aihole, your choice is limited to the **Karnataka Tourist Lodge** (☎ 41, Amingad exchange), where the 11 rooms provide the basics. Some rooms share a common bath. Bring your own soap and towel. The temples are within walking distance. Be sure to call in advance if you plan to stay, so they can tidy and stock up. If you're passing through and would like to stop for a meal, just call the manager 3 hours in advance. For reservations, contact the manager at the Tourist Lodge or KSTDC tourism in Bangalore (see p. 384).

PATTADAKAL

At Pattadakal, 17 kilometers (10 miles) from Aihole, the cluster of temples sit in a lovely little park. Once upon a time, Chalukyan kings were crowned here; it was their last capital, from the 7th to the 9th centuries. The temples here develop more fully themes and styles invented at Aihole.

You will see temples with the northern-style single shikharas above their sanctuaries, and in the southern style with tall gopurams (towers) and flat-roofed sanctuaries, and buildings far more complex than those at Aihole. As the temples got more sophisticated, their increasingly elaborate sculptures became picture books to tell illiterate people about the exploits of their gods, in the same way as the old cathedrals of Europe reached out to people.

Some of the prize examples are **Galaganatha,** which, although partially in ruins, has Shiva images—inside he's killing a demon, outside he's a Natraja, dancing to keep balance in the universe. Another temple that deserves special attention is **Kashi Visheshvara** (8th century), with Nandi, Shiva's loyal mount, waiting patiently outside; inside there are detailed carvings, depicting scenes from Hindu mythology—many emphasizing Krishna's heroic exploits. Garuda, Vishnu's vehicle, waits outside. This temple, now dedicated to Shiva, earlier was a Vishnu shrine.

Two queens of Vikramaditya II built wonderful 8th-century temples to commemorate the Chalukyas victory over the Pallavas. The smaller of the two, **Mallikarjuna,** is only partially completed; the ceiling has panels with figures of Shiva and Parvati, and sculptures on the pillars inside show Krishna. The other, **Virupaksha,** was completed. Handsome pillars carved like lions and elephants support the entry porch, which is flanked by huge guardian figures. This temple has remarkable exterior and interior carvings, with all of life and legends as its subjects. Among the interior designs are 16 monolithic pillars carved with scenes from Hindu mythology. Shiva is there in many guises; scenes of the *Ramayana* and *Mahabharata* fill the walls; demons are there, too—defeated by a ferocious Durga, battled by Narasimha, Vishnu's lion incarnation. This is a Shiva temple, and a big, black, stone Nandi, glistening with sacred oil and adorned with garlands, sits before the main gateway.

All this happened before the 9th century; in years to come, Bhubaneshwar would rise in the East and Khajuraho in the North, as would Madurai and many other temples of Tamil Nadu. But there is no better place to put them into perspective than at Aihole and Pattadakal.

The entry fee at Pattadakal is Rs 3 (9¢); the temples are open daily from sunrise to sunset. Take a flashlight to see the interior decorations. Local guides can be hired at the site, and they can tell you a great deal about the temples.

WHERE TO STAY

There is nothing to recommend here. Stay at Badami or Bagalkot's **Circuit House.**

BADAMI

Half-hidden by neem and tamarind trees and nestled in rust-colored cliffs, Badami, another noted capital of the Chalukyas (540–757), has remarkable temples, both structural and rock-cut. The foundations of Badami date from Pulakesin I (535–66), but it was ruled also by the Vijayanagar kings, the Muslim rulers of the Deccan, the Marathas, Hyder Ali of Mysore, and finally the British, who made it part of the

Bombay presidency. The main attraction at Badami are four remarkable rock-cut **cave temples,** completed during the reign of Mangalesa (598–610).

ESSENTIALS

Getting to Badami

BY BUS The bus **from Bijapur** is perhaps the most reliable. It departs from the City Bus Stand at 3:30pm, takes three hours, and costs about Rs 25 (83¢) to Aihole. Here you can stay at the **Tourist Lodge** (described above under "Where to Stay"), sightsee, and then catch this same bus when you are ready to go on to Pattadakal and Badami. Ask the manager of the Tourist Home to give you directions and timings for the ongoing buses. Connecting with them requires local know-how. From Badami to Hospet, there are many buses. There are also KSRTC buses from Gadag, Hospet, Hubli, and other places.

BY TRAIN The nearest railhead is Badami, 4 kilometers from Badami town, on the Hubli-Sholapur meter-gauge line (slow), connected to Bangalore, Bagalkot, and Bijapur. From Bangalore, take the *Bangalore-Solapur-Gol Gumbaz Express.*

Getting Around

There are **tongas** and a few private **taxis. Bike** shops offer cycle rentals. Haggle for a good price.

What to See & Do

To visit the caves requires climbing about 200 stone-cut stairs to a walkway from which there's a view of **Agastyatirtha Tank,** created in the 5th century. One cave is Jain; the others are Hindu, with many motifs signifying Shaivite or Vaishnavite beliefs.

The Badami caves—like those of Ellora and Ajanta—were hewn out of solid rock by sculptors working with incredible dexterity 14 centuries ago. All the caves have a common plan: an entrance porch supported by pillars, a hall with columns, and a shrine for a deity. They have a few demons on their exterior walls and are lavishly adorned inside.

In **Cave 1,** the energetic 18-armed Shiva strikes 81 different dance poses. In **Cave 2,** there are Shaivite carvings, including notable ceiling figures. Expert opinion has it that **Cave 3** is the finest of the group. It has both Vaishnavite and Shaivite carvings; the bracket figures deserve special attention. **Cave 4,** is the Jain cave; the image of Mahavira here is unusual because the meditating figure is supported by a stone cushion.

Between caves 2 and 3, a flight of steep stone stairs goes to the southern part of Badami Fort and a gun placed there by Tipu Sultan.

There's a gentle climb up a well-worn path to **Badami fort,** which encloses the old granaries, treasury, and watchtowers, in addition to a number of temples. The oldest is **Melegitti.** Inside is a statue depicting a gentle Shiva as a garland maker. A stroll around Badami offers further discoveries of temple ruins and ancient reliefs. The entry fee for the fort is Rs 3 (9¢). Guides can be hired through the manager at the Hotel Mayura Chalukya, Ramdurg Road (☎ 46).

Archaeological Survey of India's Sculpture Gallery (open from 10am to 5pm; closed Friday; modest entry free) has images excavated from these red sandstone cliffs and fields as well as Aihole and Pattadakal. On Bhutanatha Temple Road (about 5 kilometers), en route to Pattadakal or vice versa, make a stop at **Banashankari** to see the Dravidian-style, 17th-century temple dedicated to Parvati, who is depicted in black stone, shiny with holy oils and wearing garlands. Her eight arms hold holy symbols in their golden hands as she rides a snarling lion and tramples a demon. This Parvati is a favorite of weavers. At Mahakuta is the **Mahakuteswara Temple,** dedicated to Shiva; the pond is said to be holy and, like the Ganges, a place to wash your sins away.

Where to Stay

KSTDC's **Hotel Mayura Chalukya,** Ramdurg Road, Badami 587201 (☎ 46), has 10 rooms but is too run-down to recommend. The **Inspection Bungalow** is across from the hotel. For reservations, call the Executive Engineer, Badami (☎ 82). There are some singularly unappealing hotels on Station Road. There's also the **Circuit House** at Bagalkot (35 kilometers).

Where to Eat

There also are several modest, Indian-style restaurants in Badami.

5 Bijapur—Mughal Masterpieces

Giant sunflowers spangle the fields along the roadsides to Bijapur, the walled medieval Muslim "City of Victory" and former capital of the powerful Adil Shah kings (1489–1685).

Bijapur was one of five independent states founded when the Bahmani kingdom fell in 1489. The other states were Bidar, Golconda, Ahmednagar, and Berar. It was a coalition of these states in 1565 that defeated Ramaraja at Talikota and brought an end to Vijayanagar and the largest Hindu empire in the history of India.

When they weren't fighting wars, the Adil Shahs liked nothing better than building. More than 50 mosques, 20 tombs, and probably an equal number of palaces attest to this fact, as they also trace the history of Bijapur's mighty Adil Shahs.

In Bijapur, most of the Muslim monuments don't have the airy look or rich jeweled inlays and lacelike screens that distinguish Agra's. Rather, Bijapur's have the simple grandeur associated with Turkish buildings. The founder of the Adil Shah kings, Yusuf Adil Khan, was in fact a son of the sultan of Turkey. Throughout the years, the crescent symbol of Turkey has crowned most of the town's official buildings.

ESSENTIALS

GETTING TO BIJAPUR

BY BUS There are three buses a day from Aihole, and the fare is around Rs 20 (66¢) one way. Other bus connections can be made from Badami (two daily buses); from Bellary there's an express bus, also this is the bus to take to Hospet and the Vijayanagar ruins; there are no direct buses between Bijapur and Hospet. You have to go to Bellary and change. You must take a train to Hospet, via Gadag to get the bus to the Vijayanagar ruins. There is bus service from Pattadakal (148 kilometers), Bangalore (132 kilometers), Bombay (486 kilometers), and elsewhere. From Mysore to Bijapur, the bus leaves at 1pm and stops at Sholapur, for about Rs 125 ($4.16)

BY TRAIN Bijapur is connected with Bangalore (via Sholapur), to Hospet (via Gadag), and to Vasco da Gama (via Londa and Hubli). These are passenger (slow) trains. The trip from Vasco da Gama via Londa by meter-guage train takes about 2½ hours. The trip from Bangalore, covering 250 kilometers, costs about Rs 494 ($16.47) AC First, Rs 57 ($1.90) Second. If you're heading back to Bangalore with a stop in Badami and Hospet, the journey from Bijapur via Gadag takes about 9 to 10 hours. There are trains from Secunderabad to Bijapur. Or take a train to Hubli and a taxi to Bijapur.

Visitor Information & Guides

If time or interest permit, there are many other monuments in Bijapur. A small paperback booklet, *A Visit to Bijapur,* by Shri Hanumantrao Kaujalgi, costs Rs 12 (40¢) at bookstores and can help you round up the sights efficiently. Or you can hire a guide through the **KSTDC Tourist Bureau,** Hotel Mayura Adil Shahi (☎ 20934), or through the local tourist office in the Sanman Hotel, Station Road (☎ 20359).

Getting Around

Tongas cost about Rs 40 ($1.33) to Rs 50 ($1.66) to cover the city's main attractions but will ask foreigners for Rs 60 ($2) to Rs 100 ($3.33). **Auto ricksha** drivers probably will settle for Rs 50 ($1.66) to Rs 70 ($2.33) to cover the main sightseeing attractions. Both require hardest bargaining.

What to See & Do

If you're adventurous, climbing the outside steps around the 80-foot-high **Haidar Buruj** ("watchtower")—also known as the **Upli Buruj**—built by Haidarkhan, a general under Ali I, affords the best view of the domed and turreted skyline. From here you can clearly see the crumbling 10-kilometer-long fort wall enclosing the city, and the gates that permitted entry. The two mammoth guns at the tower's summit were probably hoisted up to the top via an inclined plane; made of iron bars welded together, the longer gun is almost 40 feet long; the smaller about 20 feet.

From your perch in the tower, or from miles way, **Gol Gumbaz** is the monument that gives Bijapur's skyline great distinction. The tomb of Muhammad Adil Shah (1627–55) has a remarkable dome. It measures 124 feet in diameter, and is second only to St. Peter's in Rome when it comes to the world's domes unsupported by pillars; St. Peter's surpasses it by 15 feet. The huge square mausoleum has imposing archways on each side and octagonal multitiered turrets at each corner. Steep, narrow steps wind up the turrets to cupolas on top. At the eighth level is the famous circular "whispering gallery" under the dome, where even the drop of a pin or a rustle of paper can be heard across the vast 38-meter expanse of the gallery—but perhaps not over the din of screaming kids who use it as a playground. The gallery's remarkable echo also makes sounds reverberate 12 times (including the kids' shrieks!). Pause for the panoramic view from the outdoor platform here before going back down.

In a vault under the immense dome are the **tombs,** from east to west, of the Mohammed Adil Shah's grandson; his younger wife, Mohammed Adil Shah; his favorite mistress; his daughter; and a senior wife. The cenotaphs stand in the main hall on a platform above the crypt that contains their graves. The interior is virtually unadorned except for some inscriptions on the south door praising Muhammad Adil Shah. The Gol Gumbaz is magical when illuminated at night.

In the great front gateway, the **Nagarkhana** (former music hall), is now a small museum, displaying artifacts of the Bijapur rulers and ancient archaeological finds. There's a huge, nobly proportioned mosque to the tomb's west. Gol Gumbaz is open from 6am to 6pm. There's a modest entry fee; Fridays are free.

Several other monuments are not to be missed.

Jami Masjid, Southwest of Gol Gumbaz, is the city's main mosque, which was built between 1557 and 1686, mostly during the reign of Ali Adil Shah I but completed by Muhammad. Ali, a major player in the ransacking of wealthy Vijayanagar, used his newly acquired loot to finance many architectural treasures in Bijapur, among them this mosque, the **Gagan Mahal,** the **Anand Mahal** (not open to the public), **Chand Bauri** (a tank northwest of town), city walls, and the public water system—the latter quite advanced for its day.

Covering an area of 116,300 square feet, the mosque's most unusual feature is the floor: The invading Aurangzeb had it painted with 2,250 squares, one for each worshiper. He also added the grand entrance. Both the exterior and interior are without decoration, except for some motifs on the elegant symmetrical archways inside; a curtain hides the sacred alcove, which is said to be richly decorated with such designs as domes and minarets as well as quotes from the Koran in gold. The mosque lacks two minarets; its dome is segmented, not bulbous like the others in Bijapur.

In **Ibrahim Rauza** ("garden") are a graceful tomb and mosque built by the 6th Adil Shah sultan, Ibrahim Adil Shah II (1580–1626), when Bijapur was at its peak. The tomb is greatly admired for its perfect symmetry, delicate-looking minarets, and graceful cupolas and platforms, and is supposed to have supplied the inspiration for the Taj Mahal at Agra. (The same claim is made about the tiny Jag Mandir palace-pavilion in Udaipur.) It's one of the only monuments in Bijapur with decorative motifs—crosses, lotuses, and wheels—said to signify religious tolerance. Built for the wife of Ibrahim Adil Shah II, it also houses his remains, since he died before she did; buried here as well are his daughters and mother. When architect Malik Sandal completed this tomb, he proclaimed: "At the beauty of this structure, paradise stood amazed." This was no idle boast: It's among South India's loveliest monuments.

The Citadel, in the heart of town, is protected by a wall and moat. Here, the royalty lived, relaxed, and held court in palaces, gardens, and a durbar (audience) hall befitting the nobility of the largest Muslim empire of South India. The once-grand buildings are crumbling now but retain a romantic beauty that evoke their grandeur.

Built by Ali Adil Shah I in 1561, **Gagan Mahal** (Heavenly Palace) was both a palace and durbar hall of grandiose proportions. The immense audience hall, spanned by an archway of almost 70 feet, was open to the North to permit the visitors a full view of the proceedings on the stage inside. Originally, the upper story was hung with stone-cut screens that permitted the ladies of the seraglio to observe life below without being seen. There were apartments for royal families in the upper story as well. The crumbling structure is approached through a vibrant flower-filled garden.

Nearby is the **Sat Majli,** meaning seven-story palace, now only five stories high. Traces of colorful paintings are seen here and there in this decrepit structure. In front of Sat Majli are the remains of a dainty water pavilion that stood in the middle of a reservoir. Here the royal families must have relaxed on hot days surrounded by fragrant gardens and cooled by the breezes wafting off the waters.

There are many other tasty morsels of architecture to be seen in the Citadel—the lacy gates of **Mehtar Mahal** and the **Mecca Masjid,** built for ladies only, to name two.

To the east of the Citadel, the **Asar Mahal** overlooks the moat in which kids steal skinny dips until they are chased away. This building was constructed by Muhammad Adil Shah in 1646 as a hall of justice. It's believed to house some hairs of the prophet Muhammad. The second story is said to be richly painted with floral motifs as well as males and females in a variety of poses—I can't validate this because women are not permitted inside. My male informants tell me the figure paintings have been defaced.

Malik-e-Maidan is one of the largest bell-metal guns in the world, standing on the south wall of the city. It measures 21 feet, 7 inches long and 4 feet, 6 inches in diameter. For some unknown reason, the gun always is cool to the touch, even under the blazing sun. When gently tapped, it tinkles like a bell. The muzzle is in the shape of a roaring lion with open jaws, crushing an elephant with its fangs. Armies of laborers, elephants, and oxen dragged the gun to Bijapur from Ahmednagar, where it was cast.

WHERE TO STAY

At each of the following five hotels, you'll pay Rs 250 ($8.33) or less.

KSTDC's **Hotel Adil Shahi,** Anand Mahal Road, Bijapur 586101 (☎ 20934), has 15 slightly down-at-the heels rooms with baths attached. There are lower rates for Indians. There is a nice garden and good food. There's another **Adil Shahi** on Station Road (☎ 2041), with similar charges and accommodations. Hot water is available from 6am to 10am, and there's no electricity from 10am to 4pm.

Of the other hotels, the best seems to be the new **Sanman Hotel,** Station Road (☎ 21866), opposite the Gol Gumbaz, with 24 basic double rooms, baths attached. There is a restaurant. The tourist office is in the hotel. Similar accommodations and charges are featured at the similarly basic, clean **Hotel Samrat,** Station Road (☎ 21620), where rooms have baths attached; there is a veg restaurant. Both hotels get a lot of street noise. In the same league is **Tourist,** M. G. Road (☎ 20655).

WHERE TO EAT

The hotels above are your best dining choices. For superb South Indian dosas and coffee and other South Indian snacks, it's the **Mysore Restaurant,** a flight of stairs up above the main market. If you have trouble finding it, ask anyone in the market—it's one of the most popular places in town.

16 Bombay: India's Most "Western" City

Bombay (pop. over 12 million) is India's city nearest to Western tastes. It's Hollywood, New York, and Chicago rolled into one, and almost every visitor has a friend or contact there (or can find one). Bombay is India's biggest port, its financial and cultural center. "Bollywood," its glitzy film industry, is the second largest in the world (first is Hong Kong), churning out an estimated 300 movies a year devoted to those coy boys chasing girls around pillars, bursting into song and dance, and, more recently, Stallone-style violence. Every day dozens of films are in production in Bombay's nine studios. New releases come out every week. (Other filmmaking states are Tamil Nadu, Bengal, Andhra Pradesh, Gujarat, Karnataka, and Kerala, each working in the language of the region.)

It was Britain's East India Company that managed to link the seven islands of the Bombay area, but nobody has managed to merge the various sects and creeds—the Punjabis, Parsis, Muslims, Gujaratis, South Indians, and Maharashtrans—who give the city its rich diversity and business acumen.

Bombay is India's richest and busiest industrial center; more than 3,000 factories on immense estates ring the city for miles. They produce a full spectrum of goods, including metal and rubber products, tobacco, beverages, vegetable products, petrochemicals, paints and varnishes, textiles, and petrochemicals—just to skim the surface.

Check with the **Government of India Tourist Office** (☎ 2033144) about touring almost any enterprise. The plant owners will usually greet you warmly and show you around with pride, whether the businesses go back many years or have started up recently.

With opportunities come immigrants seeking jobs, and Bombay is full of such hopefuls. No place is the impact felt more severely than in housing; more than one million people live in the city's Dharvani, Asia's largest slum. On closer examination, this area of tin-roof shacks is not the down and out dead-end it appears, but a huge melting pot community of families from every part of India, striving to survive and to work themselves out and up the ladder to success and, eventually, the middle class.

City planners are trying to alleviate some urban congestion by developing the outlying areas into suburbs and industrial parks. A good suburban rapid transit system is already in place, carrying briefcase-toting commuters to city or suburban jobs.

Bombay has many of India's wealthiest people—and its poorest. It also has India's largest population from middle class. In the end, Bombay seems to say, "This is where it's happening now," and to point to hope for all of India.

1 Orientation

GETTING TO BOMBAY

BY PLANE A number of international airlines land at Bombay, so your visit to India can begin or end here. **Indian Airlines** has many flights connecting Bombay to such cities as Delhi ($115), Madras ($110), Aurangabad ($34), Goa (Dabolim)($46), Ahmedabad ($47), and Udaipur ($70), to name a few.

For **Indian Airlines** reservations (☎ 2876161, ext. 141). Other domestic carriers serve Bombay (their fares sometimes slightly higher than those listed above). City office phone numbers are as follows: **Sahara Airlines** (☎ 2832446); **East-West** (☎ 6441880); **Jet** (☎ 2855789); **Damania** (☎ 6102525); **Modiluft** (☎ 3635085). The **domestic airport** (Santa Cruz) is 26 kilometers (16 miles) from Nariman Point in central Bombay. Allow one hour during rush hours.

Bombay is also an international destination, so you can arrange to make your entry into India here. For information and reservations in Bombay on **Air-India** (☎ 2023747 or 204142). The **international airport** (Sahar) is 30 kilometers (18 miles) from Nariman Point. Again, you should allow one hour during rush hours.

Airport Transfers: Coach service is available to and from both airports. The fare is Rs 44 ($1.46) per person to and from Terminal 2 (international); Rs 36 ($1.20) to or from Terminal 1 (domestic). There are regular departures from the airport to the Air India building in Bombay from 4am to 1am (no service from 1 to 4am). There are regular departures from Bombay to the airports from 8am to 1am (no service from 1 to 7am). Remember, when leaving India, that there's a foreign travel tax of Rs 300 ($10).

Taxis from the international terminal can be prepaid to save a hassle over the fare when you get in. Be sure and save your prepaid taxi receipt; you will be asked to give it to the driver when you get to your destination as proof of payment. From the International Terminal, a prepaid taxi costs about Rs 93 ($3.10) to Juhu; Rs 113 ($3.76) to Dadar; Rs 138 ($4.60) to Bombay Central; Rs 187 ($6.23) to Cuffe Parade (President Hotel/Churchgate/Gateway to India); these fares are likely to have increased a bit by the time you're reading this.

Tourist cars generally charge a four-hour rate for airport transfers; it can cost about Rs 475 ($15.83) to Rs 875 ($29.16) to go to the airports from Colaba, depending on the type of car and whether or not it is air-conditioned.

BY TRAIN The best train from Delhi is the twice-weekly, completely air-conditioned *Rajdhani Express,* making the trip of 1,384 kilometers (845 miles) in 17 hours. Fares range from Rs 2,385 ($79.50) in AC First, to Rs 680 ($22.67) in AC Chair. Other trains from Delhi include: the *Frontier Mail* (1,542 kilometers, 24 hours) to Bombay Central, or the *Punjab Mail* to Victoria Terminus; fares range from Rs 1,939 ($64.63) in AC First, to Rs 207 ($6.90) in Second. Both the Bombay *Madras Mail* and *Chenna Express* leave Madras Central (1,279 kilometers, 28 hours) and go to Victoria Terminus. Fares are Rs 1,635 ($54.50) in AC First, Rs 184 ($6.13) Second.

Bombay is headquarters for Central and Western Railways. Trains link **Victoria Terminus (VT)** and **Bombay Central** to different parts of India. For trains going to the North or West, make your reservation at the Western Railway Office, Churchgate (☎ 2031952); hours are 9am to 4pm. For travel east or south (and for a few trains heading north), make your reservations at Victoria Terminus Station, Bori Bunder (☎ 2623535). There are **Railway Tourist Guides** to assist tourists at Victoria Terminus and Churchgate stations.

BY BUS Buses connect Bombay to such cities as Aurangabad, Bangalore, Baroda, Gir Forest (home of the Asian lion), Goa, Hyderabad, Udaipur, and several other popular tourist centers.

VISITOR INFORMATION

The **Government of India Tourist Office,** 123 M. Karve Rd., opposite Churchgate Station, Bombay 400020 (☎ 2033144 or 2033145), is open from 8:30am to 6pm Monday through Friday, and from 8:30am to 2pm on Saturday and holidays; closed Sunday. Bombay's tourist office, one of the best in India, has pamphlets, booklets, maps, and advice (be sure and get *Welcome to Bombay* events listings). The main office maintains a list of meet-the-people contacts should you wish to visit someone in your own line of work or one who shares mutual interests during your stay. The office also has a list of paying-guest accommodations should you be interested in staying with a family.

At the airports, **tourist office counters** are located at both the international terminal (☎ 8325331 or 8366700; ext. 3252 and 3608), open 24 hours; and the domestic terminal (☎ 6149200 or 6116466, ext. 354), open until the last flight at night. Check these counters if you come in without a hotel reservation before you traipse around town.

The **Maharashtra Tourism Development Office** is located at C.D.O. Hutments, Madame Cama Road, Opposite the LIC Building, Nariman Point (☎ 2026713, 2027762, or 2027784).

The **Foreigners Registration Office** is opposite Mahatma Phule (Crawford) Market (☎ 4150446).

2 Getting Around

Black-and-yellow **taxis** are metered, but you will probably pay around nine times above the meter rate, since meters have not been recalibrated for eons. (For instance, if the meter reads Rs 1, you pay Rs 9). You must have the meter flagged in your presence and pay only in Indian currency the fare on the revised tariff card available from the driver. **Tipping** taxi drivers is not customary, but so many foreigners do it, drivers will insist that it is. Just ignore their pleas. If you're picked up near any of the five-star hotels, taxi drivers will probably try to charge you 10 times the authorized amount. Don't give in! Ask the doorman to mediate and settle the dispute, or pick up the cab away from the hotel.

Black-and-yellow taxis are permitted to ply both city and suburbs. **Auto rickshas,** while cheaper, are confined to the suburbs and not allowed beyond Mahim into South Bombay. Their minimum fare is Rs 5.50 (18¢), but their meters are also out of date. Ask for the card.

To rent a **car and driver** you'll pay from around Rs 950 ($31.66) to Rs 1,750 ($58.33) for eight hours or 80 kilometers, depending on the make of the car and whether or not it is air-conditioned. A good source for reliable car rentals and touring the city is **Cox and Kings,** Grindlays Bank Bldg. Dr. D.N. Road (☎ 2043065).

The city's **bus service (B.E.S.T.)** operates bright red single and double decker buses throughout greater Bombay. Buses marked "CBD" are destined only for the Central Business District. All buses are jam-packed.

Bombay

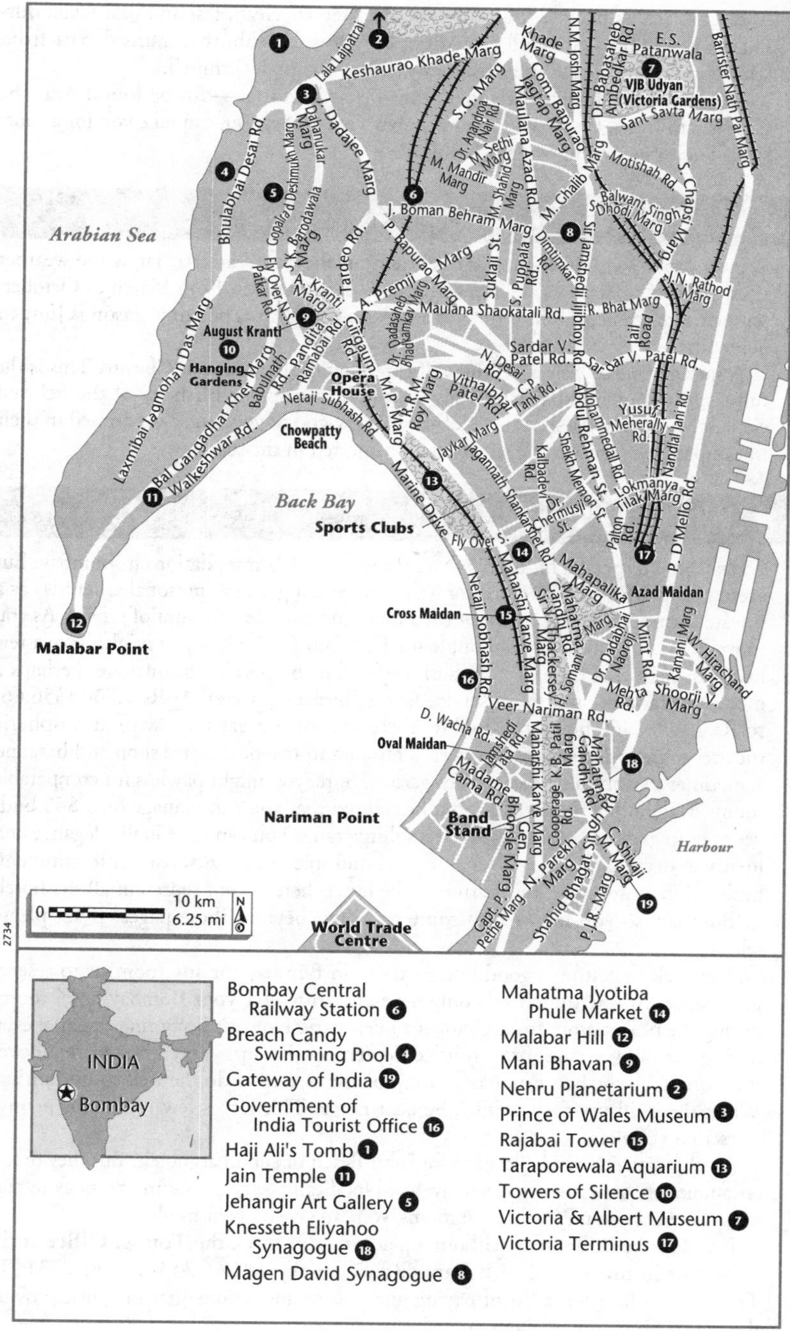

Arabian Sea
Back Bay
Harbour
Keshaurao Khade Marg
Lala Lajpatrai
J. Dadajee Marg
Dahanukar Marg
Gopalrao Deshmukh Marg
Bhulabhai Desai Rd.
Khade Marg
N.M. Joshi Marg
Dr. Babasaheb Ambedkar Rd.
E.S. Patanwala
VJB Udyan (Victoria Gardens)
Sant Savta Marg
Barrister Nath Pai Marg
S.G. Marg
Com. Bapurao Jagtap Marg
Maulana Azad Rd.
M. Ghalib Marg
Motishah Rd.
S. Chapsi Marg
M. Mandir Marg
J. Boman Behram Marg
Sir Jamshedji Jijibhoy Rd.
Balwant Singh Dhodi Marg
S.K. Barodawala Marg
Tardeo Rd.
P. Bapurao Marg
A. Premji Marg
Suklaji St.
S. Puppala Rd.
Dimtimkar Rd.
J.N. Rathod Marg
Fly Over N.S. Patkar Rd.
A. Kranti Marg
Maulana Shaokatali Rd.
R. Bhat Marg
August Kranti
Hanging Gardens
Laxmibai Jagmohan Das Marg
Bal Gangadhar Kher Marg
Babulnath Rd.
Pandita Ramabai Rd.
Girgaum Rd.
Dr. Dadasaheb Bhadkamkar Marg
Sardar V. Patel Rd.
N. Desai Rd.
Jail Road
Opera House
Netaji Subhash Rd.
M.P. Marg
R.R.M. Roy Marg
Vithalbhai Patel Rd.
C.P. Tank Rd.
Mohammedali Rd.
Abdul Rehman St.
Yusuf Meherally Rd.
Nandlal Jani Rd.
Chowpatty Beach
Walkeshwar Rd.
Jaykar Marg
Jagannath Shankarshet Rd.
Kalbadevi Rd.
Sheikh Memon St.
Dr. Chermusjid St.
Lokmanya Tilak Marg
Palton Rd.
P. D'Mello Rd.
Marine Drive
Sports Clubs
Fly Over S.
Maharshi Karve Marg
Mahapalika Marg
Azad Maidan
Cross Maidan
Mahatma Gandhi Rd.
Sir V. Thackersey Marg
H. Somani Marg
Dr. Dadabhai Naoroji Rd.
Mint Rd.
Kamani Marg
W. Hirachand Marg
Malabar Point
Netaji Sobhash Rd.
Veer Nariman Rd.
Mehta Rd.
Shoorji V. Marg
D. Wacha Rd.
Oval Maidan
Jamshedji Tata Rd.
K.B. Patil Marg
Madame Cama Rd.
Nariman Point
Band Stand
Cooperage Rd.
Gen. J. Bhonsle Marg
N. Parekh Marg
Shahid Bhagat Singh Rd.
C. Shivaji M. Marg
P.J.R. Marg
Capt. P. Pethe Marg
World Trade Centre
0
10 km
6.25 mi
N
2734
INDIA
Bombay
Bombay Central Railway Station 6
Breach Candy Swimming Pool 4
Gateway of India 19
Government of India Tourist Office 16
Haji Ali's Tomb 1
Jain Temple 11
Jehangir Art Gallery 5
Knesseth Eliyahoo Synagogue 18
Magen David Synagogue 8
Mahatma Jyotiba Phule Market 14
Malabar Hill 12
Mani Bhavan 9
Nehru Planetarium 2
Prince of Wales Museum 3
Rajabai Tower 15
Taraporewala Aquarium 13
Towers of Silence 10
Victoria & Albert Museum 7
Victoria Terminus 17

Electric **trains** operate from the suburbs; they are clean, fast and best taken during off-peak hours to avoid crowding. For Western suburbs, trains depart from Churchgate; for Eastern suburbs, they go from Victoria Terminal.

Quaint **horse-drawn carriages**—known as Victorias—can be found near the Gateway to India, Chowpatty, and Bombay Central Station, can take you for a short spin. Their rates are purely negotiable.

3 When to Go

Winter, from November through February, is the best season as far as the weather goes, when temperatures are usually in the 80s; in summer, from March to October, temperatures can climb into the 90s and keep going up. The rainy season is June to September.

A special time to visit is in August/September during **Ganesh Chatur.** This is the most spirited of Bombay's festivals, and it celebrates the birthday of the beloved elephant-headed Ganesh. Images of the chubby god of good luck are dressed in their finest, paraded through the streets, and immersed in the sea.

4 Where to Stay

Overall, you'll spend a bit more of your budget for accommodations in Bombay. But even at under Rs 500 ($16.66) for a double, you'll get such personal amenities as a private bathroom, perhaps a room telephone, and a modest amount of service. As you move higher up the scale—a double for Rs 1,000 ($33.33)—you might have a few luxuries, such as a room TV, a choice of AC or non-AC, a minifridge, perhaps a modest restaurant, and room service (sometimes a sea view). At Rs 1,700 ($56.66) to Rs 2,000 ($66.66) for a double, there are some great buys with atmospheric touches in their decor, more services, a restaurant, maybe a coffee shop and bar, and sometimes a swimming pool or roof garden. Sure, you might pay less for comparable rooms in the other major cities, but be assured that you can manage on a $45 budget even in expensive Bombay. In the splurge range you can have it all: elegance and luxury in decor, attentive personal service, multiple restaurants, bars, entertainment, health clubs, and more. Furthermore, the hotels here do not represent all the hotels in Bombay, so you might find some real buys beyond these pages. If so, please tell us.

The trick to getting a good budget room in Bombay (or any room) is to reserve in advance. At one time it was only necessary to reserve your Bombay hotel rooms during the peak season, from October to February. Now it's becoming essential even during the rainy season, from June to September. Business executives from all over the world grab the best Bombay accommodations, and so do the well-to-do tourists. When these fill up, they're into the next range. This leaves few rooms for penny-conscious travelers.

An alternative might be to head for Juhu Beach or suburban hotels. But they're not cheap, nor are taxis to town. Happily, good food can be cheap in some Bombay restaurants. So what you must spend on rooms, you can save on your meals.

If you arrive in Bombay without a place to stay, check the **Tourist Office** at the airport or in town at 123 M. Karve Rd., Churchgate (☎ 2333144 or 233145). The tourist office has a list of paying guest accommodations that may just provide the answer to your predicament.

IN FORT BOMBAY

In Fort Bombay, the city's southern tip, are many hotels, restaurants, museums, galleries, airline agents, tourist offices, and shops. Not surprisingly, it's the most convenient place to stay. Keep in mind that luxury taxes of 3% to 10%, expenditure tax of 10% (at higher priced hotels), and service charges of 5% to 10%, here and there, can add significantly to the cost of your room.

DOUBLES FOR LESS THAN RS 500 ($16.66)

In a superb location, opposite the Gateway to India, the **Gateway Hotel,** 16 P. J. Ramchandani Marg, Apollo Bunder, Bombay 400039 (☎ 2835187), once a private home, is now a 10-room hotel facing the sea. All but one room have attached bathrooms; they're clean, neat, and basic, most of them with lovely sea views. Virtually every square inch of the hotel is wallpapered, except the ceilings. The asking rate for foreigners is Rs 400 ($13.33) to Rs 500 ($16.66), but you might get it for less—a real find for the traveler who's not hung up on atmosphere and decor.

With even the most modest hotels like Gateway getting Rs 500 or more, a truly unusual find is **Fernandes Guest House,** J.N. Heredia Marg, Ballard Estate, Bombay 400038 (☎ 2610554), on the third floor of the Balmer Lawrie Building, which resembles a partitioned loft. Here singles pay Rs 200 ($6.66), doubles Rs 400 ($13.33), including breakfast. Only 16 guests can be accommodated, two to three to a room, with iron bedsteads and absolutely no frills. Everything is clean and spacious. There are two showers and three toilets. You get one sheet and a coverlet, but most guests use sleeping bags (the mattresses are not so neat). Some rooms have little balconies with a splendid harbor view. They lock up at midnight, so you must be tucked in by then.

Behind the Prince of Wales Museum is **Hotel Lawrence,** Ashok Kumar House, 28 K. Dubash Marg, Bombay 400023 (☎ 243618), in a neighborhood of bookstores. The hotel is on the third floor. There are three common bathrooms, only one with hot water. But you can always get some hot water boiled. This is a simple place. You might wish the place was a bit better maintained, but it's better than many in this under Rs 500 price range, and breakfast is included.

DOUBLES FOR LESS THAN RS 1,000 ($33.33)

On what used to be Marine Drive but is now Netaji Subhash Road (though still called Marine Drive), the **Sea Green Hotel,** 145 Netaji Subhash Rd., Bombay 400020 (☎ 222294), has 34 rooms: 30 doubles and four suites. All are simply furnished, but who's looking inside when your room has a sweeping sea view? Best rooms have AC, with minirefrigerators and TV (direct-dialing telephones soon), all for Rs 660 ($22). *For the penny-wise:* The rates include bed and full breakfast. There's a 10% service charge, and taxes run from 5% to 7%.

The **Sea Green South,** 145-A Netaji Subhash Rd., Bombay 400020 (☎ 221613), is a modest hotel with a marvelous location. If you don't expect anything lavish in the way of decor (you will have a phone, TV, and private bathroom), you'll be happy. The AC rooms also have minirefrigerators as do suites: AC doubles are Rs 850 ($28.33), a two-person suite Rs 950 ($31.66). There are 36 rooms (21 with AC), 31 with private bathrooms, five with shared facilities, but the price is not lower for sharing. There is a 10% service charge. No restaurant, but there is room service. It's a popular place.

Facing the sea at P. J. Ramachandani Marg (formerly Strand Road) is **Shelleys,** Bombay 400039 (☎ 240229). The halls are a turn-off, and the lobby won't win prizes either. The 34 rooms (all air-conditioned) are comfortable enough. The top price for a sea-facing deluxe with color TV and small refrigerator and telephone is about Rs 1,000 ($33.33). There is a 5% service charge. No restaurant, but plenty of places are nearby.

The **Strand,** Apollo Bunder, Ramachandani Marg, Bombay 400039 (☎ 241624), has a minimum of furniture and atmosphere, needs a coat of paint, and will do for those who require absolutely no frills and are not too fussy. There are 35 rooms, some non-AC. An AC double is Rs 550 ($18.33). A sea-facing AC suite is Rs 700 ($23.33). There is no restaurant.

Hotel Diplomat, 24-26 B.K. Boman Behram Marg, Apollo Bunder, Bombay 400001 (☎ 2021661), centrally air-conditioned, has 50 double rooms. Singles are priced at Rs 800 ($26.66), doubles from Rs 900 ($30) to Rs 1,100 ($36.66). Needs better maintenance. There's restaurant-cum-bar.

Looking on the sea is **Bentley Hotel,** Krishna Mahal, Third Floor, Netaji Subhash and D. Watcha roads, Bombay 400020 (☎ 2059448), with a neat reception area with carvings on the walls. The 37 rooms (22 with bath attached, a few with AC) are very basic, though clean enough. No visitors are allowed in the rooms; all company must be entertained in the reception/lounge. Tea and coffee are available on request, but no meals are served; there are many restaurants nearby. Doubles with AC are Rs 550 ($18.33); non-AC doubles are Rs 450 ($15) to Rs 500 ($16.66); 10% luxury tax.

You're paying mainly for location at the **Hotel Delamar,** 141 Sunder Mahal, Netaji Subhash Road, Bombay 400020 (☎ 2042848), which has 22 TV-equipped, AC rooms and is very overpriced for what you get: $33 for a double.

Tucked away behind the Regal Cinema is **Regency Inn,** 18 Landsdowne House, Mahakavi Bhusan Marg, Bombay 400039 (☎ 2020292; fax 2873371), run by the same family that owns A. K. Essajee, the famous curio and handicraft dealers on the ground floor. Neat and clean but in need of better maintenance, this inn has 21 snug AC rooms, 12 with private baths. Doubles are Rs 750 ($25); suites Rs 847 ($28.32); nine rooms with shared bath are Rs 525 ($17.50), including tax and service charge. A 10% discount applies March through June. There's no restaurant, but there are plenty of restaurants nearby in all price ranges.

Doubles for Less Than Rs 2,000 ($66.66)

Right off Arthur Bunder Road, Colaba, Bombay 400005, the 10-story **Fariyas** (☎ 2042911; fax 2834992), is a pleasant place with modern functional furniture in the bedrooms. The ornate chandelier in the dining room has a Hyderabadi feeling. Singles are Rs 1,200 ($40), doubles Rs 1,420 ($47.33). There's a swimming pool, health club, a well-known pub, restaurant, and roof garden.

A dandy new find in a great location is **Hotel Suba Palace,** near Gateway of India, Apollo Bunder (☎ 2020636; fax 2020812), with 49 rooms, where every Sunday one of the rooms gets a fresh coat of paint until all have been painted and they start over again. The rooms are modern, tastefully decorated, and come with the usual amenities, including AC. Singles are Rs 800 ($26.66), doubles Rs 1,000 ($33.33). There is 24-hour room service. The coffee shop should be open by now, and lots of good restaurant are steps away. The Taj is nearby.

The **West End Hotel,** 45 V. Thackersey Marg (New Marine Lines), Bombay 400020 (☎ 299121), one of the best-maintained hotels in its price range, gives its interiors a new coat of paint about once a month. The 80 well-kept rooms have a comfortable, old-fashioned feeling, with boxy 1940s-style furniture and updated tile bathrooms. All rooms are air-conditioned; doubles, including service charge and tax, are about Rs 1,700 ($56.55); a small suite for two—a good buy— is Rs 2,040 ($68).

The **Grand Hotel,** Ballard Estate, Bombay 400038 (☎ 2618211), on Ballard Pier, was receiving visitors in 1927 when Katherine Mayo's book *Mother India* described India as a mere three-week voyage from New York. Even in these jet-paced days and despite the modernization of its lobby, the hotel has lots of character. Old-fashioned touches of luxury include spacious rooms, some with separate little dressing chambers, and big, clean bathrooms. Rooms up the winding staircase to the fourth floor are best maintained—with no. 93, Rs 1,210 ($40.33) especially fine—and have balconies. Ballard Estate is not far from the Prince of Wales Museum, which is walking distance from Flora Fountain, and convenient to Victoria Terminus. But it's dead after 5pm, and taxis can be hard to get from then on.

Regent, 8 Best Rd., Colaba, Bombay 400039 (☎ 2871854; fax 2020363), in a newly built white building, is fairly well-maintained, smartly priced, and in a top location near the Taj. You'll pay Rs 1,320 ($44) for a double. This is a favorite of visiting Arabs. This new hotel replaces long-time hippie hangouts Rex and Stiffles.

Hotel Godwin, Jasmine Building, 41 Garden Rd., Colaba Reclamation, Bombay 400039 (☎ 2872050), has an attractive Krishna mural at reception. The 47 rooms are small, fairly clean, comfortable, and have AC and tile bathrooms. Best rooms are on the sixth, seventh, and eighth floors. Doubles cost Rs 1,392 ($46.40). Add 10% service charge to these rates. There's a roof garden and a restaurant with a harbor and city view. And **Shaan** restaurant has red velvet walls and crystal chandeliers.

Garden Hotel, Park View Building, 42 Garden Rd., Colaba, Bombay 400039 (☎ 2841476; fax 2044280), was once a grand mansion. The clean and cheerful rooms have modern furniture, tiled bathrooms, and all the amenities, such as TV and music. Rates range from Rs 1,000 ($33.33) to Rs 1,200 ($40). There's a 5% service charge and 7% government luxury tax. There is a roof garden restaurant.

Homelike and cheery, **Sea Palace,** Ramachandani Marg, Bombay 400039 (☎ 241828; fax 2854403), has 48 rooms, many with cool balconies allowing panoramic views of harbor activity. The rooms are comfortable, neat, and offer all amenities, including AC, phone, channel music, color TV, and complete attached bathroom. Doubles are Rs 1,045 ($34.88). There's an attractive, brick-walled restaurant. A very pleasant manager is in charge; the lobby needs work.

"Cleanliness" is the motto at **Chateau Windsor,** 86 V. Nariman Rd., Churchgate, Bombay 400020 (☎ 2043376; fax 2851415), and the friendly manager, A. K. Aggarwal, takes this seriously. There are 40 clean, neat rooms, 30 with attached bathrooms, 27 with AC, all with fans to stir the breezes. Singles are Rs 950 (($31.66); doubles with all amenities are Rs 1,125 ($37.50); there's a 10% service charge. Twenty-four-hour room service supplies breakfast—for Rs 30 ($1)—and snacks. Next door is Hotel Ambassador (with expensive restaurants) and V. Nariman Road, Bombay's "restaurant row" (with more price variations).

Worth a Splurge

At these prices and in this day and age, it will come as no surprise that the following hotels have attached bathrooms and color TV (with CNN and BBC) in the rooms, along with telephones, multichannel music, and individual minirefrigerators; services and facilities include health clubs and, of course, restaurants, bars, room service, and 24-hour coffee shops. Some quote rates in dollars for foreign travelers. They accept international credit cards.

A moderate splurge, the **Ritz Hotel,** J. Tata Road, Bombay 400020 (☎ 2039121; fax 2850494), has a quiet, old-fashioned charm. The 72 clean, spacious rooms have cream-colored walls, dark wood or white-painted furniture, solid color spreads, print drapes, and big, tiled, attached bathrooms. Singles are Rs 2,000 ($66.66), doubles from Rs 2,500 ($83.33) to Rs 2,800 ($93.33), plus a 10% service charge. There are a 24-hour coffee shop, bar, and restaurant.

At the 125-room **Ambassador Hotel,** V. Nariman Road, Bombay 400020 (☎ 2041131; fax 2040004), the revolving rooftop restaurant isn't the only thing that's high priced—there are valuable works of Indian art throughout the hotel, and the rates are high as well. (In fact, overpriced.) Singles are Rs 2,500 ($83.33), doubles Rs 3,000 ($100).

Natraj, 135 Netaji Subhash Rd., Bombay 400020 (☎ 294160), has an attractive lobby with Gujarati-style wooden chairs upholstered in earthy brocades reflected under a glittering mirrored ceiling. Pretty botanical and bird prints on silk panels decorate the hall walls. The rooms are cheerful with white cane furniture or dark woods. Corner rooms have balconies and beautiful sea views. The halls need a paint job. Singles are Rs 2,620 ($87.33), doubles Rs 3,144 ($104.80), including a service charge, 10%, luxury tax, and expenditure tax. Good kebabs in the restaurant (see "Where to Eat," below).

With 35 floors, **The Oberoi Towers,** Nariman Point, Bombay 420021 (☎ 2024343; fax 2043282), offers rooms with spectacular views. The well-appointed lobby has fountains splashing gently against marble walls and tasteful, earth-toned furniture. The 650 well-appointed guest rooms start at $190 for a single, $190 for a double, and go up to $700 for a special duplex suite. The hotel has three restaurants, two coffee shops (one of them at poolside), a discotheque and two bars, a three-level shopping center, and a swimming pool, health club, and travel desk.

Next to The Oberoi Towers and connected by an indoor walkway, is **The Oberoi,** Nariman Point, Bombay 400021 (☎ 2025757; fax 2043282), an elegant, sleek, marble-lined 11-story hotel with black and white and rust predominating in the lounge and a sophisticated international look throughout. The 375 rooms, many with fine sea views, have modern furniture with lovely woven bedspreads and draperies. Standard singles run from $235 to $270 and doubles from $260 to $300, the higher rates for sea-facing rooms. Suites start at $500 and go up to about $1,500. The hotel has two distinctive restaurants, a bar, coffee shop, swimming pool, and other amenities. Guests at The Oberoi can enjoy the restaurants, bars, and discotheque at The Oberoi Towers, then drop in here for a change of scene, and vice versa for those staying at The Oberoi Towers.

Hotel President, 90 Cuffe Parade, Bombay 400005 (☎ 4950808), in The Taj Group of hotels, is an 18-story, 300-room hotel in a residential area but a stone's throw from shops and other amusements. The pillared lobby is hung with elaborate glass-tiered chandeliers, and the rooms have modern, functional furnishings. There's a swimming pool, three restaurants, a bar, and shops. Standard singles are $160, doubles $175. A special attraction at the President is Delores Periera, a renowned card reader who divides her time between this city and Bangalore. To see what the cards say, check to see if she's in town; by appointment only.

The most famous hotel in Bombay is the more than century-old **The Taj Mahal,** Apollo Bunder, Bombay 400039 (☎ 2023366), an impressive hunk of Indo-Saracenic and Gothic architecture with elegant, old-world charm and 294 rooms and a modern wing, The **Taj Mahal Inter-Continental** with 306 rooms. All rooms have every amenity—and some suites in the Taj Mahal have truly inspired historic-themed decor. Rooms at The Taj Mahal start at around $230 for a single to $250 for double, and go up to $1,000 for the Presidential Suite. Rooms at The Taj Mahal Inter-Continental cost $190 and $205 for a single or double, respectively. The hotels share a swimming pool, shopping arcade, four restaurants, two bars (the **Harbour Bar** is the oldest in the city), a snack lounge, and a discotheque. Even if you don't stay here, you'll probably end up spending time in the lobby—a popular meeting place that bustles with activity day and night—or in the 24-hour coffee shop, where you can get snacks and light meals.

A YWCA & A Hostel—All Less Than Rs 560 ($18.66)

The well-located **YWCA International Centre,** 18 Madame Cama Rd., Fort, Bombay 400039 (☎ 2020445), has 33 cheerful rooms, at this writing restricted to single women or married couples with their children (no single men). Rates are Rs 20 ($1.15) per person as transient membership fees, which are valid for one month. Rooms are nicely furnished, and charges include linens, attached bathroom, Continental breakfast, 10% service charge, and telephone extension charge. You can take your other meals at any of the nearby cafes and restaurants.

Right behind the expensive Taj Mahal Hotel, the **Salvation Army Hostel** (also known as the **Red Shield Hostel**), 30 Mereweather Rd. (☎ 241824), is clean and simple and popular. It accommodates only 60 guests, primarily in dorms: Rs 100 ($3.33) per day in the dorm; Rs 300 ($10) for a non-AC double; and there are a few doubles with AC for Rs 400 ($13.33). Rates include bed linens and meals—bland Western-style cooking. You must reserve well in advance or show up at the crack of dawn and wait to see if you can get a room or dorm bed when a guest checks out around 9am. Visitors are not permitted in the rooms, and a sign in the entry says: "Drugs, alcohol, hashish smokers strictly prohibited."

Accommodations Elsewhere in Bombay

A YMCA—Less Than Rs 600 ($20)

Living up to the slogan on its tariff sheet, "A clean, decent, and safe accommodation for individuals and families," is the **YMCA International House and Programme Centre,** 18 YMCA Rd., Bombay Central, Bombay 400008 (☎ 891191). An AC double costs Rs 558 ($18.60); prices are lower for non-AC rooms, rooms with common baths, and singles. Tariffs include morning tea, breakfast, and dinner. In addition, there's a modest charge for transient membership. Service charge is 10% on the total bill.

Doubles for Less Than Rs 2,000 ($66.66)

Opposite the Central Station and next to the State Transport Depot, the **Hotel Sahil,** 292 J. B. Behram Marg (☎ 3081421; fax 3079244), is centrally air-conditioned and has a lavish marble lobby with a copper mural and small, cozy, clean rooms with low ceilings and tasteful decor. Doubles are priced at Rs 1,150 ($38.33). The hotel's proximity to train (three-minute walk to Bombay Central) and bus stations makes it popular with Indian business travelers. You're about a Rs 45 ($1.50) taxi ride from Hutatma Chowk (formerly Flora Fountain) or the Fort.

In a residential area and within a 15-minute walk of the famous Hanging Gardens (now S. P. Mehta Gardens), the **Regency Hotel,** 73 L. Jagmohandas Marg (formerly Nepean Sea Road), Bombay 400006 (☎ 3630002; fax 287165), opposite Petit Hall, is a pleasant, quiet place with an attractive restaurant off the reception area. Most rooms have limited sea views. A single is about Rs 1,000 ($33.33), a double around Rs 1,300 ($43.33). A taxi costs about Rs 45 ($1.50) to Rs 50 ($1.66) to Hutatma Chowk or the Fort.

Near fashionable Cumballa Hills is **Shalimar,** August Kranti Marg, Bombay 400036 (☎3631311; fax 3631317), a 68-room modern, air-conditioned hotel with pastel and gray upholstery in a mirrored lobby. Some of the 74 rooms are so tiny it's hard to believe they contain so many comforts. They're also clean. A single is about Rs 1,000 ($33.33), a double about Rs 1,400 ($46.66). There's a bar, and good North Indian, Chinese, and Continental foods in the **Gulmarg Restaurant.** The Hanging Gardens are 10 minutes away.

Hotel Midtown Pritam, Pritam Estates, Dadar, Bombay 400014 (☎ 4142033), in central Bombay, is near Bombay Central Station and the MTDC suburban tour-bus stop. The glitzy, mirrored lobby has comfortable, upholstered chairs, and large bronze figures of Nandi and a chariot. The rooms have restful earth tones and blond woods. Expect to pay $40 for a single, $45 for a double. There's a terrace garden and a nearby restaurant, **Pritham Dhaba,** well worth visiting. It's 10 kilometers to downtown from here.

AT JUHU BEACH

From here, you can count on about a Rs 200 ($6.66) to Rs 400 ($13.33) taxi fare to Colaba. For a fraction of the taxi fare, you can take Bus 231 to Santa Cruz and a local train from there to Churchgate Station, opposite the India Tourist Office. Be sure to avoid rush hours and, as you would on public transportation in many other major cities, take precautions against pickpockets. While there are hotels closer to the airports for those in transit, you can also stay at Juhu Beach and easily make your early morning plane. Some hotels have free transfer service to the airports.

Unless otherwise indicated, the following hotels have air-conditioning and attached bathrooms with hot and cold running water.

DOUBLES FOR LESS THAN RS 1,000 ($33.33)

The Krishna Consciousness Movement runs the red-and-pink sandstone, double-towered **Iskcon,** Juhu Beach, Bombay 400049 (☎ 6206860), with an adjoining temple (open from 4am to 1pm and 4:15 to 10pm) decorated with dioramas of Hindu mythology. The corridors need care. There are 43 rooms in all: 20 for members, the remaining for tourists seeking a clean, quiet, affordable place to stay. Doubles with AC are Rs 682 ($22.73). Some non-AC rooms are cheaper. Rooms have Gujarati-style lacquered furniture, print drapes, shiny marble floors, and attached bathrooms (hot water from 5 to 9am). Krishna is depicted in paintings in rooms and in wall tapestries here and there. There's no smoking or drinking on the premises. Good vegetarian thalis at the restaurant

DOUBLES FOR LESS THAN RS 2,000 ($66.66)

Golden Manor, opposite Juhu Church, Juhu, Bombay 400049 (☎ 6104271; fax 6104279), has 30 AC doubles from Rs 1,075 ($35.83) to Rs 1,250($41.66). It also has a swimming pool and a garden. While some of the rooms are small, big mirrors above the vanities make them seem larger. Rooms have white walls (some needed scraping and painting, others were in fine shape), printed bedspreads and drapes. The restaurant is open for lunch and dinner; breakfast is sent to your room.

Sands Hotel, 39/2 Juhu Beach, Bombay 400049 (☎ 6204511; fax 6205268), has 40 rooms, centrally air-conditioned. Glass chains serve as see-through window shades in the lobby, where the floors are highly polished granite shades of brown and gray; planters overflow with greenery; and there are big, brown-leather club chairs in what comes across as more a city than beach look. Some rooms have textured walls contrasted with smooth walls, distressed-wood dressing tables, and headboards. Others have marble tiles set in the walls, cafe tables and chairs, as well as the necessary furniture. Singles are Rs 1,100 ($36.66), doubles Rs 1,500 ($50). On weekends in the Rajasthani-inspired **Mehman Restaurant,** a singer performs ghazals (Urdu love songs); during the week, there's Indian classical music. The hotel has coach service to and from the airports. There's a Kashmiri shop with carpets.

An outstanding view from the **Silver Sands** restaurant at the **Citizen Hotel,** 960 Juhu Beach, Bombay 400049 (☎ 6117273; fax 6117170), is one reason to enjoy this hotel. There are also cheerful pastel rooms, the best with dramatic wraparound views, and all at not-too-high prices—singles are Rs 1,150 (($38.33), doubles Rs 1,500 ($50). A roof garden is another attraction.

Worth a Splurge

One of the oldest hotels out here, **Sun-n-Sand,** 39 Juhu Beach, Bombay 400049 (☎ 6201811), has a sleek look, from its stainless steel–accented lobby to its 118 functional modern rooms. The **Sunset Restaurant** evokes an earlier era with its lavish stained glass (beautiful at sunset). Single rates range from Rs 2,000 ($66.66) to Rs 2,500 ($83.33); doubles from Rs 2,500 ($83.33) to Rs 3,000 ($100). To this, the usual taxes on rooms and food will be added. There's a swimming pool, a nice gazebo-style coffee shop, beauty parlor, and health club.

Tailored, tasteful, **Ramada Hotel Palm Grove,** Main Point Beach, Juhu, Bombay 400049 (☎ 6112323; fax 6113682), with 114 rooms, was converting its fourth floor into executive rooms for the business traveler. Some rooms have beautiful sea views. Rates are Rs 2,400 ($80) single, Rs 2,500 ($83.33) double, Rs 2,900 ($96.66) executive. Attractive features include a glassed-in coffee shop, grill room, swimming pool health club. Conference rooms. It is affiliated with the U.S. chain.

Holiday Inn, Balraj Sahani Marg, Juhu Beach, Bombay 400049 (☎ 6204444), has 200 guest rooms overlooking the sea, four restaurants, a bar, a confectionery, and swimming pools for adults and children. The rooms are modern and well-appointed, with all the amenities expected in a five-star hotel: singles are $135; doubles are $145 to $160. There's complimentary coach service to town, Club Select lounge with business services, an in-house astrologer, and fabulous Sunday brunch (see "Where to Eat," below). It is affiliated with the U.S. chain.

The **Centaur Hotel,** Juhu Tara Road, Bombay 400049 (☎ 6143040), in the Air-India chain, blends modern architecture with 5 acres of Mughal-inspired gardens. This new/old theme continues indoors with the sleek marble reception area and contemporary lobby/lounge and a clubby, traditional, mahogany-paneled lounge bar. The 370 guest rooms and suites are functionally modern, many recently refurbished. The rates are Rs 3,000 ($100) single, Rs 3,300 ($110) double. Prompt wake-up calls (in addition to electronic wake-up) for wee hours flights are a plus. The chef knows how to make real French croissants with flaky crusts, not the Indian cakelike versions found elsewhere. Facilities include a 24-hour coffee shop, the vegetarian **Northwest Frontier,** and dinner-dance restaurants; a swimming pool, courtesy coaches to the airports, and other frills. There's a lot of traffic in and out of here and it shows—almost everything needs a bit more care.

A rooftop swimming pool with a panoramic view is an innovation at **Hotel Guestline Days,** 462 A.B. Nair Rd. (☎ 6204331; fax 55322782). The hotel has 92 delightfully beachlike, light, and airy modern rooms with seashell print drapes and spreads. Singles are Rs 1,900 ($63.33), doubles Rs 2,200 ($73.33). The Manhattan skyline decorates the coffee shop and a '30s-look predominates in the restaurant where there's jazz at night. Fine in all respects.

HOTELS NEAR THE AIRPORTS

International flights—and some domestic ones too—depart and arrive at Bombay at very early morning hours. So staying close to the airports saves you a trip from town if you're taking off for good or merely passing through to another town. It won't save you money: Rates are high at the airport area hotels. They cater not only to transiting travelers, but to well-heeled executives doing business at the nearby industrial estates. Of many hotels near the airports, here are the acceptable few with the usual amenities, plus soundproofed rooms and transfer service to and from airports.

Doubles for Less Than Rs 2,000 ($66.66)

The **Kamats Plaza,** a 70-C Nehru Rd., Vile Parle East, Santa Cruz Airport, Bombay 400099 (☎ 6123390; fax 6105974), with 68 comfortable, clean doubles—with a rate of $48—and a wealth of services and facilities make this a top airport choice. Pleasantries include an open-air restaurant, a garden restaurant, 24-hour coffee shop, bar, **Go Bananas** discotheque, swimming pool, and health club. The hotel offers transfer to and from the airports.

New and very nice **Bawa International,** Nehru Road Extn., Vile Parle (East) Bombay 400057 (☎ 6113636; fax 6107096), has 72 tasteful rooms with white furniture and solid color drapes and spreads. Rates are Rs 1,190 ($39.66) single, Rs 1,900 ($63.33) double. There is a Chinese restaurant, 24-hour coffee shop, and bar. This hotel is steps from the domestic airport and 10 minutes from the international airport. There's a couples-only disco, operating at the nondisco hours of 9:30pm to 12:30am.

Hotel Atithi, 77 A-B, Nehru Rd. (☎ 6116124; fax 6111998), is another good choice for airport stay-overs. Rates for its 48 rooms range from Rs 1,000 ($33.33) to Rs 1,300 ($43.33). There's an especially well-stocked book store in the lobby and good restaurant with Punjabi and South Indian dishes, as well as Chinese and Continental.

Airport Splurges

The **Centaur Hotel,** Bombay Airport, 400099 (☎ 6116660), is similar in its circular design to its counterpart adjacent to Juhu Beach. All the rooms are arranged around an inner courtyard that encloses a swimming pool and garden. There are courtesy coaches to and from the airports, plus twice-a-day coach service to Bombay. All rooms and public areas are soundproofed and functionally furnished. There are a host of amenities, including three restaurants and two floodlit tennis courts. Doubles start at Rs 3,000 ($100).

The luxurious **Leela Kempinski,** Sahar, Bombay 400059 (☎ 8360606; fax 8360606), near the international airport, has a splendid, spacious, lanai-inspired lobby where fountains splash amid interior gardens. The highest-quality marble and mahogany have been used everywhere, and everything is surrounded by lush gardens. Rates are $225 to $265 single, $235 to $275 double. Courtesy coaches take you to and from the airports and the city. Indeed, some people prefer to stay here away from the hubbub and commute 25 kilometers to busy Bombay for sightseeing. Large conferences are often held here, and those doing business in nearby industrial estates enjoy all manner of business amenities in the Privilege Club. A glass-walled AC squash court, swimming pool, and two floodlit tennis courts keep guests in shape.

5 Where to Eat

Bombay provides the rare chance to sample some of the delicacies of the Parsis, the Zoroastrians who fled Persia in the 7th and 8th centuries and settled in and about the city. One of these dishes is the unusual dhansak, literally meaning "wide mouth," a curry made with countless different ingredients. Other Parsi specialties include patrani machli (fish stuffed with chutney and steamed in banana leaves) and Bombay duck, which is not duck but a whitefish served curried or sautéed. Bombay also boasts

Goan specialties like vindaloos, spiced meat or chicken in a special sauce, and foogaths, vegetables made with coconut sauce.

Other local foods, of the vegetarian variety, are influenced by Maharashtra, Bombay's state, or by the neighboring state of Gujarat. What is interesting here are the subtle differences in the styles of eating. The Maharashtran takes a bit of rice to begin his meal and ends with a taste of rice. The Gujarati eats his wheat-based foods first, such as puri (also spelled *poori,* a fried bread shaped like a disc), and ends his feast with his rice. In both cases, dessert usually accompanies the main course.

A traditional Bombay meal will be served on a thali, a round plate made of brass, silver, or (more recently) stainless steel. In the center will be a little hill of rice and around the edges will be vegetables, lentils, and curds. There will also be dabs of chutney (a fruit-and-vegetable relish), pickles, your personal piece of salt, and your dessert. The idea is to eat what you want in the order you prefer.

Puris, steaming hot flat discs of wheat bread, will be served along with the meal, and the food is eaten with the fingers. Eating with the hands (please use only your right hand) is considered cleaner than with a fork or spoon because you can wash your hands seconds before you eat, whereas a regular utensil might have been washed many hours previous to the meal.

The technique is to tear off a little bit of the puri and to use the small piece to help you pick up your other foods. Rice can be used in the same way, by gathering some grains into a little ball and mixing it with a bit of curry, some dhal (the lentil preparation almost like soup), and chutney, then popping it all in your mouth. No more than the first knuckles of your fingers are ever supposed to get dirty, and this is a standard by which Bombay thali manners are judged. At the end of the meal, you wash your hands.

By the way, if you are invited to eat "trash" in Bombay, be sure to say yes immediately. This is no insult, but rather an invitation to share a great local pleasure, known as bhel-puri. This is a delicious concoction of cereals, chutneys, and sauces. Other variations are pani-puri, a puff of fried dough filled with tamarind water, and bhel-puri, which is made of raisins, puffed rice, saffron, lentils, nuts, and other spices.

Now go and enjoy the attentive service in Bombay's restaurants. Below are a handful only. Most of them are air-conditioned; if not, it's been noted. Reservations are recommended at pricey and/or popular restaurants, but not at snack bars, fast food restaurants, and some vegetarian and Chinese restaurants.

GOOD CHEAP MEALS

Modest South Indian vegetarian and Iranian nonvegetarian restaurants, located on the side streets behind The Taj Mahal Hotel, offer some of the best possibilities for good cheap meals. These places are so similar in terms of their menus and appearance that they are not described separately in the following section. Great favorites of the people who work in this part of Bombay, they all offer spicy foods to please local palates. Most are not air-conditioned; whirling fans and open windows cool their interiors.

Typical of the South Indian places is **New Laxmi Vilas,** D. Naoroji Road, where a complete vegetarian meal runs Rs 25 (83¢) with two curries, rice, and chapatis. A number of other vegetarian restaurants in this price range can be identified by the use of the word *Udipi* (meaning the cooks come from a small South Indian town famous for its chefs) in their names or on their signboards. Like New Laxmi Vilas, most of these places are open as early as 7:30am, when patrons drop in for dosas (rice-and-lentil pancakes stuffed with potato) and South Indian coffee (made with steaming milk), about Rs 10 (33¢) for both. They stay open until 10pm.

Dabbas—Lunch the Bombay Way

Bombay has an unusual food service that creates one of the great sights in the city's never-dull streets. Throughout Bombay, on workdays before noon, you will see many messengers negotiating the congested streets with large wooden platforms holding foot-high tin cylinders balanced on their heads, or pushing carts full of these receptacles. In the cylinders are hot lunches for clerks in offices, bazaar wallahs, executives, and factory hands all over Bombay. But they are not from local caterers.

The lunches, known as dabbas, were made earlier that morning in kitchens at the recipients' homes all over the outlying areas, spooned into the cylinders, which have several interlocking dishes, sealed tight, and identified with a written code standing for a person's name. With countless other identical cylinders, they then are loaded by messengers on trains to make extensive journeys from the suburbs to Victoria Terminus and Central Station, two main pickup points in Bombay. By now, I am speaking of 100,000 of these cylinders, all alike except for their codes, all lined up, ready and waiting for delivery in an hour or so to somewhere specific in the huge city of Bombay.

Picked up by the messengers, who can decipher the codes but can't read otherwise, the cylinders, remarkably, are taken to the right place to give the right person the right hot lunch at the right time. When the lunch break is over, the messengers pick up the cylinders, retrace their steps, and are themselves back home before 4pm. Another shift of messengers serves the night workers.

Aside from providing a hot meal at midday and being a lot cheaper than going out, these lunches do something else. They permit a melting pot of people working in Bombay to observe many different regional and religious customs, which are not easily abandoned anywhere in India.

The star among these is **Cafe Leopold,** 39-41 S. Bhagat Singh Rd. (☎ 2021122), a must for tourists. On the Indian/Continental menu is mutton curry with rice, vegetable cutlets, and omelets—nothing higher than about Rs 55 ($1.83)—plus a host of other main dishes, sweets, soft drinks, coffee, and tea. Figure on Rs 75 ($2.50) to Rs 80 ($2.66) for a meal. There's a separate Chinese menu; 14 fresh fruit juices are served, as well as ice-cream desserts, and much more. Open daily from 8am to 11pm.

Royal Cafe, M. Gandhi Road (☎ 2020560), opposite Regal Cinema, is another good cafe, where the price of a meal is Rs 50 ($1.66) and up. It is open from 7am to midnight.

A cross between one of the cheap Iranian cafes, a bistro pub, and an Indian snack bar is **Paradise,** Sindh Chambers, Colaba (☎ 2832874). Figure on Rs 80 ($2.66) for a meal. Dhansak (a Parsi dish made of mutton, vegetables, spices, and more) is a special. Another special is chicken vindaloo, from Goa. Always on the menu are sandwiches, samosas (turnovers), ice creams, and soft drinks. Open from 10am to 11:30pm. Cleanliness is another attraction here, but the place is not air-conditioned.

Try also **Cafe Mondegar,** near Regal Cinema, Colaba Causeway (☎202059), for a good selection of beers and snacks, and loud music.

PARSI CUISINE

Bombay is the place in India to try the delicious dishes associated with the Parsis, whose ancestors settled in this city when they fled Persia in the 7th and 8th centuries. Few restaurants serve these foods, so when I came across them, I made notes to pass on to you.

At the unpretentious, 40-seat **Piccolo Cafe,** 11-A Sir Homi Mody St., patrons pamper themselves on pastries, cakes, patrani fish (stuffed with chutney and cooked in banana leaves), and a special roti (bread) to scoop it up with, and on many other Indian and some Western items. Two can get by for Rs 200 ($6.66) for a delicious meal here. Hours are 9am to 6pm; closed Sunday. Run by Ratan Tata Institute, which donates profits to charity.

At the charming new **Indian Summer,** 80 Veer Nariman Road (☎ 2835445), there are stylized clouds, shiny green and black pillars, frosted glass, and a wonderful menu with a few Parsi dishes, among them the famous stuffed fish for Rs 130 ($4.33).

Coronation Darbar, M. Shaukatali Road, Grant Road (☎ 3075586) offers Parsi dishes as well as Indian and Continental.

Wayside Inn, K. Dubash Marg, serves Parsi dishes on Sundays.

BUFFETS

The following is a sampling of Bombay's notable buffets. The hours are usually 12:30 to 3pm, or as noted below. It's also a good idea to call in advance to double-check timings and to reserve a place. To most of the quotes below, taxes must be added.

At **The Taj Mahal,** Apollo Bunder (☎ 2023366), where the buffet originated some years back, the meal is served in the **Rooftop Rendezvous** daily from 12:30 to 3pm and costs Rs 255 ($8.50) plus tax. The meal begins with soup and is followed by a great array of main dishes, hot and cold, vegetarian and nonvegetarian, Indian and Western styles, plus salads, relishes, assorted breads and rolls, sweets, fruits, and cheeses. Coffee, tea, and other drinks are not included in the tab at "The Taj" or any of the buffets. At any of the buffets, you can taste all the dishes and return to the buffet table as often as you like. Reservations are advised here at the Taj and at all other buffets, and so is eating early for the best selection. There's a breakfast buffet in The Taj's **Shamiana** every day—Monday through Saturday, from 7 to 10am, for Rs 195 ($6.50), and Sunday brunch, from noon to 3pm for Rs 225 ($7.50).

In **The Oberoi Towers,** Nariman Point (☎ 2024343), you can have Polynesian dishes at the daily lunch buffet, for Rs 225 ($7.50), in **The Outrigger** or the same hotel; the marble and teak **Palms,** has buffets for breakfast—Rs 125 ($4.16); there is also a buffet here for lunch and dinner—each Rs 195 ($6.50).

Next door, **The Oberoi's** informal **Brasserie** offers a buffet breakfast, from Rs 75 ($2.50) continental to Rs 175 ($5.83) with eggs, etc., and a buffet Indian lunch, for Rs 178 ($5.93), inclusive of taxes, daily.

In the **President Hotel,** 90 Cuffe Parade (☎ 2150808), there's a daily lunch buffet in **Gulzar** for Rs 155 ($5.16). Italian foods are featured in the rustic-looking **Trattoria** for brunch on Sundays, for Rs 247 ($8.29), and there's a breakfast buffet, for Rs 157 ($5.23).

At the **West End Hotel,** 45 Thackersey Marg (☎ 299121), the lunch buffet in the **Gourmet** costs Rs 175 ($5.83); breakfast is Rs 110 ($3.66), including tax.

The **Ambassador,** V. Nariman Road (☎ 2041131), gives its buffet a whirl at lunch in **The Top,** the revolving rooftop restaurant, for Rs 250 ($8.33).

At the **Leela Kempinski,** Sahar (☎ 8363636), the **Waterfall**, overlooking an outdoor waterfall and garden, has three daily buffets: breakfast, from 7:30 to 10:30am, for Rs 250 ($8.33); lunch, from 12:30 to 2:30pm, and dinner, 7:30 to 9:30pm, each for Rs 413 ($13.76).

Enormously popular, the Sunday buffet, from noon to 3pm at **Bagicha,** in the **Holiday Inn,** Balraj Sahani Marg, Juhu (☎ 6204444), costs Rs 250 (8.33). It's an endless feast, including delicious bhel-puri (famous snack) and an array of dishes.

Other hotels: At **Sun-n-Sand,** 39 Juhu Beach, the buffet is in the stained-glass-accented **Sunset Room** Sunday and holidays only. The **Centaur,** Tara Road, Juhu (☎ 6126660), serves a breakfast buffet, from 7 to 11am, a lunch buffet, and a Sunday brunch buffet. There's also a Sunday brunch at both the **Centaur Bombay Airport** (☎ 6120660), and the **Ramada Inn,** Palm Grove Juhu (☎ 611323). Some restaurants outside hotels have buffets. **Rangoli,** Nariman Point, in the handsome Performing Arts Complex (☎ 2023366), has daily buffets, from 12:30 to 3:30pm, for Rs 20 (66¢). **Indian Summer,** 80 Veer Nariman Rd. (☎ 2835445), has a midnight buffet on Saturdays. **Chopsticks,** 90-A. Veer Nariman Rd. (☎ 2049284) has one at Sunday lunch. **Revival,** 39-B Chowpatty Seaface (☎ 3619206/07), a spotless, Continental vegetarian restaurant with a smashing sea view, serves a cheese and salad lunch buffet, from noon to 3pm, for Rs 70 ($2.33). Elegant **Jewel of India,** Dr. Annie Besant Road (☎ 4949204), has a buffet at lunch. At **Kamat,** opposite Electric House, Colaba (☎ 2874734), the Sunday buffet breakfast, from 8:30 to 10:30 am, costs Rs 30 ($1); it's a singularly fine opportunity to try a dozen of more South Indian dishes, luscious melt-in-the-mouth dosas among the many offerings.

FIXED-PRICE MEALS

Fixed-price meals are a good way for penny-watchers to try some of the toniest places at affordable prices.

The Taj Mahal's serene **Sea Lounge** (☎ 2023366) has a fixed-price lunch for Rs 185 ($6.16); in the same hotel, **Zodiac Grill,** has a three-course evening meal including a glass of champagne, coffee, and petit fours for Rs 995 ($33.16) veg, Rs 1,200 ($40) non-veg.

La Rotisserie, The Oberoi, Nariman Point (☎ 2043282), has a five-course fixed-price Continental meal for Rs 225 ($7.50).

Since the days of the British there's been the **Wayside Inn,** K. Dubash Marg (☎ 244324), which was about to close for paint job (needed!), and has long been known for its full lunch, presently Rs 93 ($3.10), and a different menu everyday. A typical menu features soup, fish and chips, or sauteed pomfret (a famous Bombay fish), chocolate soufflé, and coffee. On Sunday, there's a Parsi lunch, from noon to 3pm. In the days of the Raj, this was a place to be seen: Those diners who personally knew five others dining here were considered among the city's social elite.

The elegant **Thai Pavilion,** President Hotel, 90 Cuffe Parade, has a fixed-price Thai evening meal, from 7:30 to 11:30pm, for Rs 350 ($11.66) vegetarian, Rs 375 ($12.50) non-veg.

THALIS & OTHER INEXPENSIVE VEGETARIAN FEASTS

Here are places you can test your skill in eating off a thali (gleaming metal platter with little cups) and with your fingers. There are plenty of à la carte dishes if a thali doesn't appeal, and waiters or managers to explain if you need help ordering.

One of the best vegetarian restaurants is **Purohits,** V. Nariman Road (☎ 2046241), which is also one of the most modest and oldest in the city and a penny-wise choice (non-AC)—good buy, good food. If you order a complete Purohit's Deluxe, your thali will appear with rice, a variety of specially cooked vegetables, curds (to cool down your spicy foods), condiments, raita (a combination of yogurt and vegetables used to clear the palate after heavier foods), and two sweets.

About Rs 60 ($2.30) is the charge for this bountiful Bombay feast. Other thalis are Rs 45 ($1.50) to Rs 50 ($1.66). Open daily from 11am to 11pm.

Kamat Restaurant, opposite Electric House on Bhagat Singh Road (☎ 2874734), is famous for well-prepared vegetarian dishes in Bombay (as well as in Bangalore, Goa, Belgum, Hubli, and Hyderabad). There's a special thali with a variety of vegetarian dishes and rice, as well as soup, salad, and a sweet; and a less abundant thali with no soup, salad, or sweet. If you're not in a thali mood, an interesting dish is channa battura (a puffy puri crowned with spiced chickpeas) or the ravi idli (made with semolina and served with sambar on the side). Rs 30 ($1) is top price here. Open every day from 8am to 10pm with both AC and non-AC sections.

Rajasthani and Gujarati wall hangings form a colorful backdrop as well as the theme of the menu at **Chetana Vegetarian Restaurant and Bar,** 34 Rampart Row, Kala Ghoda (☎ 2844968), where thalis feature foods of these regions. Choices include thalis from lunch for Rs 35 ($1.16) to a grand Gujarati Dinner deluxe for Rs 128 ($4.26), and ranges in between. If you're feeling like something lighter, try khusta kachori, for Rs 25 ($83¢), a dal-filled pastry, delicious for a snack. Lunch is served from 12:30 to 3:30pm, snacks from 3:30 to 6:30pm, dinner from 7 to 11pm. (There's a wonderful shop attached to the store.)

Few tourists know about **Rajdhani,** opposite Mangaldas Market, near Crawford Street, 361 Sheikh Memom St. (☎ 3449014), a spotlessly clean, vest pocket-size vegetarian restaurant with shiny white tile walls. It specializes in the rich dishes of Gujarat. Try the delicious thali for Rs 55 ($1.83), an array of 16 different dishes, including a sweet. Deduct 1¢ if you're dieting and don't wish a sweet. The rush begins about 1pm, when the place is jammed with workers on lunch breaks; but tourists can come to shop at the market and eat at a nonpeak time. Open from 11am to 3:30pm and 7 to 10pm. The same management runs **Revival,** 39-B Chowpatty Seaface (☎ 3619206), with sea views, sleek decor, and a Continental vegetarian menu with such à la carte dishes as pancakes Provençale (with spinach and mushrooms, tomato sauce) or cannelloni Florentine (an Italian classic) for Rs 70 ($2.33), or any of the other dishes. Hours are noon to 3pm and 7 to 11pm (see also "Buffets," above).

For a thali with talent, try the **Tanjore Room** in The Taj Mahal Hotel, Apollo Bunder (☎ 2023366). Here, at dinner, you are graciously served on a gleaming brass platter much fancier than in the simple vegetarian restaurants, with a vast array of food, including rice, three different vegetables, condiments, puris (wheat bread discs), roti, papads, and a sweet, while being entertained by graceful, classical Indian dancers accompanied by live music. As a finale to your meal, you might try paan (an Indian digestive of spices and betel nuts, enclosed in a betel leaf), which is served from an antique silver paandaan (special chest). All this—cuisine and concert—costs Rs 350 ($11.66) veg, Rs 400 ($13.33) non-veg, and should be your thali splurge in Bombay. Classical dancer performs at 8:45pm, 9:45pm and 10:45pm. The Tanjore Room serves lunch from 12:30 to 3pm and dinner from 7:30pm to midnight daily. Reservations are advised.

CHINESE DINING AROUND TOWN

At the following, single portions are generous enough for two.

Try **Kamling,** where the Chinese sign for happiness decorates the entry and the interior is accented with tasseled lanterns. Located at 82 V. Nariman Rd. (☎ 2042618), this restaurant offers you about 200 mainly Cantonese choices, including the wonderful ye fu (stewed noodles with ham and crab) at Rs 82 ($2.73) and chicken Canton at Rs 108 ($4.10). Especially good buys are many generous noodle dishes, Rs 73 ($2.43). There are about 22 ice-cream treats also. Open from noon to 11:30pm daily.

Spicy, splurgey Hunan foods are the feature at the swanky antique-accented **Great Wall of China** in the Leela Kempinski, Sahar (☎ 6363636); figure on Rs 1,000 ($33.33) for two, without wine or beer, and a 25-kilometer drive from downtown Bombay.

Chopsticks, 90-A V. Nariman Rd., Churchgate (☎ 2049284), is cheerful with white walls contrasting with red and green linens; featured are Szechuan specialties not found all over the place, such as are taro nest (diced boneless chicken cooked in chiles, herbs, and celery leaves, served in a crispy nest built of potato sticks) for Rs 110 ($3.66). For dessert try date pancakes or toffee bananas. Figure on Rs 100 ($3.33) to Rs 250 ($8.33) per person. Open 12:00 to 3pm and 7:00pm to midnight.

Hong Kong, Dhanraj Mahal, Apollo Bunder (☎ 2022941), also has well-prepared seafood specialties. Steady customers don't look at the menu, but choose their favorites such as memorable king crab legs with soya and hot garlic sauce, for Rs 330 ($11)—one portion serves two or three—or just ask the manager to recommend something good to eat. The prices range from Rs 35 ($1.16) to Rs 330 ($11). Hours are from noon to 3pm and 6:30 to 11:30pm.

A Chinese splurge spot in Bombay is the sophisticated, white-walled **China Garden,** Om Chambers, 123 August Kranti Marg, Om's Corner (☎ 3630841). Big leather chairs and a small waterfall make the bar an inviting place to sip a drink while waiting for your table. In the restaurant, modern drawings are interspersed with semicircular mirrors that add an illusion of depth to the long, narrow room. Regal-looking white, wooden, Regency Chinese chairs and banquettes, upholstered in muted Madras plaids, complete the pleasant decor. While making up your mind about the menu—mostly Chinese, with a smattering of Thai, Korean, and Vietnamese—you can study the elegantly dressed crowd (this is no place for shabby jeans). Dishes are the Rs 65 ($2.16) to Rs 200 ($6.66) range, although some vegetarian dishes are less. Expect to pay between Rs 750 ($25) and Rs 1,000 ($33) for two for a meal, without beer, which partners well with this cuisine. Open 12:30 to 3pm and 7:00pm to midnight.

Imaginative Chinese seafood is excellent at **Kamling,** Nagin Mahal, 82 Veer Nariman Rd., Churchgate (☎ 2042618), where you cross a little stream, before settling in the elegant, bilevel room with waterfall and tree. How about a starter of stuffed crab claws? Or fried corn, crunchy on the outside, creamy inside? For an entré choose the seafood firepot. Sip the clear broth before eating the seafood. Have a barbecue for two at the table on a hibachi. On the mild side, there's steamed pomfret with mushrooms and ginger; hotter-than-hot are fiery Mongolian prawns. The tab for two can easily run Rs 650 ($21.66), without beer. Order sparingly—portions are giant—and go for dinner. There's a school behind the restaurant full of noisy kids at lunch. Open from noon to 11:30pm.

A fine place to try well-prepared, Szechuan-style dishes is the splurgey, velvet-walled **Golden Dragon,** at The Taj Mahal Hotel (☎ 2023366), where dinner for two can easily run Rs 1,000 ($33) and up if you eat modestly and stick to beer. For such a big tab, you might have kung pao prawns (hot garlic sauce flavored with young celery), then any one of several duck dishes, or a simple lemon chicken, some smoked honey noodles, sweets, and tea. Open for lunch from 12:30 to 3pm, and from 7:30pm to midnight for dinner.

BOMBAY'S INDIAN RESTAURANTS

The following restaurants are among Bombay's most popular—be sure and reserve (especially at dinner from 8pm on and weekends). The prices do not include wine, beer, or soft drinks, unless mentioned.

Khyber, 145 Mahatma Gandhi Rd., Fort (☎ 273227, 273228, or 273229), is near the chic Jehangir Art Gallery. You need to know this because the sign is so discreet you might think the old weathered door bordered by Urdu couplets is the entrance to a grand mansion. The splendid dining room is both spacious and intimate. It has a high ceiling with charred beams and charred stone walls from the old Khyber restaurant, which was destroyed by fire; fountains, great mirrors, fluted pillars, niches with graceful clay urns, and paintings by two of India's most famous modern artists, M. F. Husain and Anjolie Ela, complete the Northwest Frontier, Hindu, and Mughal decor. Chairs and banquettes, covered in earth-toned ikats and leather, are tucked in graceful alcoves or set on different levels. The copper-bound menu lists many tempting dishes; among them Northwest Frontier specialties such as rich chicken makhanwala (butter chicken) and reshmi kebab (drumsticks in yogurt sauce); there's also Khyber raan (lamb for two) and many other dishes. Each is fully explained on the menu. The highest-priced dishes are around Rs 250 ($8.33); one of the best buys is the kebab platter, at Rs 240 ($8) for two. Figure on Rs 600 ($20) and up for two.

If you've been to Khyber, you might experience a bit of déjà vu at **Palkhi** ("covered chair"), 15 Walton Road, off Colaba Causeway (☎ 2834203), because Parmeshwar Godrej designed both of them to fit cavernous spaces and used similar elements to good advantage here as well as there. Palkhi has a brick-vaulted roof, leather seats, jeweled door, murals, and dramatic lighting so that everything has a medieval look,. The cuisine is Mughali, supposedly with a nouvelle touch. Tikka Hyderabadi is a specialty. Hours are noon to 3pm, and 7pm to midnight. Figure on Rs 600 ($20) for two.

An electrified glass tree, stained glass stairs, and glass wall murals are the interesting creations of Kayur Patel, designer/artist at **Indian Summer,** Veer Nariman Road, Churchgate (☎ 2835445), a delightful restaurant focused on Indian foods primarily from the Mughlais but straying into some other areas. Enjoy veg? Try sham savera (paneer cheese with tomato, ginger, garlic) Non-veg? Try begum bahar (fish, rice, and cream sauce) or the Parsi stuffed fish, or ghost (lamb) with peppercorns. Dishes are explained in flowery prose. You can't go wrong here. Figure on Rs 200 ($6.66) per person and up for a three-course meal. Open from noon to 4, and 7pm to 12:30am.

Vintage, 4 Mandik Rd., Colaba Causeway, behind The Taj (☎ 2856316), has wonderfully evocative Raj-period decor with English Victorian and Anglo-Indian art reproductions—and genuine lithographs by Daniell (found in an antique warehouse). Skip the Continental dishes, which you can get elsewhere. This is the only restaurant in Bombay specializing in Hyderabadi cuisine. Try ghost (lamb) cooked in a stone vessel (made with crushed poppy seeds, cashew nuts, and spices) or anything else from the Hyderabadi selections. If you are in doubt, ask the manager for help. Expect to pay Rs 600 ($20) for two.

Stained glass, marble statuary, and shiny granite floors are decorative elements at the elegant **Jewel of India,** Nehru Centre, Dr. Annie Besant Road (☎ 4949435), mentioned earlier for its buffet and thali. Tiny gem-size lights twinkle on the exterior at night. The spacious main dining area is broken up by marble rails so it seems more intimate, and the tapestry-upholstered chairs pick up the colors of the glowing stained-glass skylight. On the multifaceted menu are rich Mughlai dishes, such as Kashmiri rogan josh (an elegant lamb curry); mogewala kukark (chicken chunks with tomatoes, onions, and mint on a roomali phulka—thin bread); and many other enticing selections. The highest-priced dishes are about Rs 250 ($8.33).

In a vine-covered cottage, **Mela** (meaning "fair"), Phirki Corner, Worli (☎ 4945656), re-creates the atmosphere of a fair. The bar is a replica of an old carousel with tented top and painted wooden horses for seats; the brick-walled interior is hung with colorful banners, posters, and oversize cutouts of sideshow strongmen and tour buses. At night there are fair-type amusements: a sketch artist draws portraits, another applies mehendi (henna) in intricate designs on women's palms. There's also a fortune teller. While there are dum pukht (slow-cooked casseroles) for Rs 95 ($3.16), the real headliners of this fair are the many different kebabs, and the best way to get to know them is to order the platter with eight different kinds, rice, dal, and dessert for Rs 225 ($7.50) to Rs 250 ($8.33). There's a selection of barbecue, too. A great family favorite, and often full of kids running around; tour groups, too. Hours are noon to 3pm and 6:30 to midnight.

Bombay Brasserie, 12-A Dr. Annie Besant Rd., Worli (☎ 4920505), is owned by the popular Copper Chimney (covered in the following section). The restaurant is understated and elegant, with a cool, blue-and-white color scheme, French period chairs, graceful palms, and gleaming marble floors. There are some dishes you're not apt to find often in Bombay, from the cuisines of Hyderabad, Bengal, Gujarat, Goa, and Madras. Among the highlights of the menu are a Hyderabadi-style chicken made with sesame and nut sauce, and a Hyderabadi vegetarian dish, baghare baingan (eggplants stuffed with roasted coconut). The Parsi dishes on the menu do not disappoint: Try the famous chutney-stuffed fish cooked in banana leaves, and others from various regions. Whatever you order, be sure to taste the unusual makai roti (corn bread). The average price of a main course is Rs 85 ($2.83) to Rs 110 ($3.66), so figure on Rs 500 ($16.66) for two, without beer or wine. Open from 12:30 to 4pm and 7:30pm to 12:30am. Dinner reservations are a must.

MUGHLAI, KASHMIRI, TANDOORI & GOAN MEALS

Delhi Durbar, S. Bhagat Singh Road, near the Regal Cinema, Colaba (☎ 2020235), is renowned in Bombay for its Mughlai foods and especially recommended for its mutton dishes, for which this style of cooking is world famous. The distinctive flavors of Mughlai mutton dishes come from elaborate masalas (spice mixtures) used in their preparation. Chicken dishes also are stars of Mughlai cuisine. At Delhi Durbar, there are enjoyable prices. A three-course meal for two costs Rs 200 ($6.66). Ignore the Chinese selections (better at one of the Chinese places in town). Open 11:30am to midnight; very crowded after 8pm.

Splurgey and pretty is the spacious **The Mewar** at The Oberoi Towers, Nariman Point (☎ 2024343), open from 12:30 to 3pm, and 8pm to midnight, where you can enjoy North Indian dancing and music with such delicious dishes as fish makhani and mutton begum bahar, accompanied by thin-as-paper roomali roti.

Next door, in The Oberoi (☎ 2025757), there's the elegant and hushed **Kandahar,** in a setting of muted beiges, overlooking the pool. For a well-prepared meal for two here, consisting of three to four courses of delicious foods from the Northwest Frontier, expect to pay Rs 1,000 ($33). For starters, try khatta meetha aam ras (Alphonso mango juice with subtle spices). You might follow with tandoori jhinga (tender king-size prawns marinated in yogurt and spices) or and kebab-e-chandni (deboned chicken drumsticks stuffed with minced chicken, chopped chiles, and cheese). Another good a choice is kandahar Simla mirch (crisp peppers stuffed with vegetables, raisins, and cashews). Breads include the tasty methi paratha (layered and seasoned with fenugreek leaves and butter). Desserts excel—especially the kulfis (Indian ice cream). Open from 12:30 to 3pm, and 8pm to midnight.

Goan foods are getting their own play these days in Bombay. At the amusing **O Balcao** ("Balcony") in the Hotel Metro Palace, Hill Road, Bandra (☎ 6427311), a typical Goan red-tile roof forms the ceiling, and the walls have been decorated by famous cartoonist Mario Miranda with humorous scenes of Goan life, as seen from a balcony. The menu has delectable Goan dishes, including stuffed crab, sorpatel (a spicy red curry), xacuti (chicken or mutton in masala and coconut cream), xeuto (mullet with spices), and a host of Goan desserts, including bebinia (the luscious, seven-layer cake). Figure on Rs 500 ($16.66) for a three-course meal for two. There are serenades on Saturday and Sunday evenings. Open from 11:30am to 3pm, and 7:30pm to 12:30am. Another Goan choice, **Goa Portuguesa,** T. H. Kataria Road, Mahim (☎ 4547760), has a similarly priced menu, with roast crab a notable specialty. Prices are Rs 200 ($6.66) and up.

Aside from the tasty tandooris in a rustic village setting at **Pritam da Dhaba,** Dadar (☎ 4143311), owned by Hotel Midtown Pritam and across from it, unusual entertainment gives the restaurant special appeal: A bangle-maker custom makes bright glass bangles for women diners' wrists, and a mehendi artist paints henna designs on women's hands. Main dishes fresh from the glowing tandoor run about Rs 75 ($2.50) Rs 100 ($3.33). Open from 7pm to 3am.

Copper Chimney, Dr. Annie Besant Road (☎ 4924488), near the race course, is spacious with copper-shaded lanterns, wood and bamboo accents, but terrible plastic plants. The focal point is a glassed-in kitchen with a copper chimney, where you can watch the chefs prepare the food. The menu ranges from Rs 65 ($2.16) to Rs 95 ($3.16) for veg dishes and Rs 95 ($3.16) to Rs 120 ($4) for non-veg. For a three- to four-course dinner for two, figure Rs 500 ($16.66) to Rs 600 ($20). Some good choices are murg rashida (chicken baked with mint and herbs), roomali roti (handkerchief-thin bread), Banarasi pulao (named for the holy Ganges city), assorted mixed vegetables with rice, and tandoori machi (whole fish tandoori-style). Among the higher-priced items are tiger prawns—Rs 350 ($11.66)—and a house specialty, Peshawari raan (lamb in herbs and spices). For dessert, the rasmalai (milk sweet) is wonderful, but you might try other Indian sweets as well, each Rs 50 ($1.66). Open from noon to 4pm, and 7pm to midnight.

CONTINENTAL, ITALIAN & MEXICAN CUISINE

These restaurants also feature some Indian and Chinese dishes.

An old favorite, **Gaylord's,** V. Nariman Road (☎ 2044693), sparkles with mirrors and gold. Velvet chairs and banquettes are dark against off-white walls. Big windows overlook a small outdoor cafe surrounded by well-manicured hedges—a nice place to sip a drink late in the afternoon. Some of the dishes are a trip down memory lane by Western tastes—lobster thermidor and chicken chasseur. Interesting here as budget stretchers are the assorted platters of Indian or Italian foods for about Rs 205 ($6.83). Each dish is described so you know just what you'll be eating. Hours are 12:30 to 3:30pm, and 8 to 11:30pm daily.

At the rustic **Trattoria,** in the Hotel President, Cuffe Parade (☎ 2150808), a 24-hour coffee shop with red-tile floors and ceramic plates hung on the walls, there are nicely prepared Italian dishes on the à la carte menu. Pizzas run Rs 60 ($2) to Rs 125 ($4.16); a variety of pastas are Rs 105 ($3.50) to Rs 115 ($3.83). There's a buffet at breakfast and on Sundays (see "Buffets," above).

Under the Over, Crystal, Altamount, next to Kemps Corner Flyover, is a casual cross between a restaurant and snack shop, specializing in Cajun, Creole,

Tex-Mex, and Mexican; if you miss your chimichangas, you'll find them here. Irresistible chocolate cake and cheesecake, too. For upscale Mexican, try the teak and marble **Palms** overlooking the pool at The Oberoi.

WORTH A SPLURGE

Figure on Rs 2,000 ($66.66) for two, without wine or drinks. Add about Rs 1,100 ($36.66) for a bottle of high-quality Indian wine. The best are Riviera white with a Chardonnay-like flavor, and the tasty but less remarkable Riviera red (from Bangalore) or sparkling Marquise de Pompadour, made using the traditional *methode champenoise* (from Pune), a prize-winner in wine competitions abroad. Lunch is generally served from 12:30 to 3pm, dinner from 7:30 or 8pm to midnight. Reservations are recommended.

In the supersplurge category, the elegant, understated **Cafe Royal** at The Oberoi Towers, Nariman Point (☎ 234343), offers mainly French foods.

At the stylish and sophisticated **La Rotisserie,** in The Oberoi, Nariman Point (☎ 2024343), a big crystal chandelier and gorgeous jewels on some of the well-heeled guests are the only glittering objects in this understated room. The subtle cream-and-rust color scheme, complemented by blond woods and beautiful flower arrangements, complete the low-key theme—a lovely setting for a special meal. Charcoal grills are delicious here as are spit-roasted dishes. A meal might begin with marinated prawns in two sauces, hot appetizers or Scottish smoked salmon, and end with cheese and fruits, or mousse, parfait, or pastry. Hours are 12:30 to 3pm, and 8pm to midnight.

At the rose-and-cream **Zodiac Grill** in The Taj Mahal Hotel (☎ 2023366), the handsome room has etched-glass dividers and graceful arches trimmed in the same burnished wood as the chairs and sideboard. The bar, with its black-and-white marble floor, accented by hand-knotted area rugs and comfortable leather Chesterfields, is a nice place to sip an aperitif before dining. The emphasis is on fresh, seasonal ingredients, and attractive presentation. Starters might include avocado and citrus fruits, or a rich, creamed broccoli soup. Grilled foods are cooked with care and served on a special warming platter. Among the tempting desserts, enjoy mousse or a white crème anglaise with mosaic of chocolate sauce. (See "Fixed-Price Meals," above, for best deal.) Hours are 12:30 to 3pm, and 7:30 to 11:30pm; on Sunday, dinner only is served.

If you eat in the **Rooftop Rendezvous** on top of The Taj Mahal Inter-Continental, Apollo Bunder (☎ 2023366), you get a wonderful view of Bombay, fine service, and elegant atmosphere. The room has Art Deco decor in brown and cream, with a dance band at night. The French-accented dishes are well prepared and attentively served. Some starter choices are saumon fume d'cosse or paâté de fois gras Strausbourg or a lamb-based soup. Main courses include poulet gourmandine (chicken breast, water chestnuts, coriander sauce) and tournedos, among others, as well as a number of inventive vegetarian dishes. Desserts are aptly rich; they include the rich souffle Champs-Elysées (chocolate). (See also "Buffets," above.)

Adjoining the Rendezvous is the intimate orange-and-sapphire **Apollo Bar,** where you can sip a drink and soak up the view from 11:30am to 3am. The room looks like a glamorous 1930s nightspot with boxy chairs and banquettes and soft flattering lighting. At night there's a pianist and vocalist—sometimes striking the only false note in this otherwise delightful place. Drinks are expensive—sherry, Rs 100 ($3.33); imported Scotch, Rs 600 ($20); French cognacs around the same. Indian spirits are less, and beer is about Rs 75 ($2.50). Soft drinks are available.

SEAFOOD

Oddly enough, for a city on the sea, seafood restaurants are relatively new in Bombay; here are the present leaders. They are open for lunch and dinner.

At **Trishna,** 7 Ropewalk Lane, next to Commerce House (☎ 272176), local artists' works line the walls of this earth-toned environment. There are a dozen fish dishes in many different styles. Crabs in season and lobster by weight. Try the Hyderabadi pomfret or prawns tandoori. Figure on Rs 600 ($20) for two. (Near Knesseth Eliyahoo, one of Bombay's two historic synagogues.)

At **Excellensea,** 317 Arun Chambers, Mint Road (☎ 272677), live crabs and lobsters can be hooked and cooked to order in this small, two-story restaurant. A blue and white ceiling and marine murals on mirrors set the scene in this low-ceilinged, but pleasant, restaurant. Don't feel like catching your own? Try any of the many other seafood dishes priced from Rs 85 ($2.83) to Rs 300 ($10).

Apoorva, Bombay Sanchar Marg, near Horniman Circle (☎ 2870035, serves crab specialties, Mangalore-style. Also tandoori crab, crab curry, and others; prawns also play a starring role. Hand-to-mouth, no cutlery needed. Be messy. Have fun.

Try jumbo prawns Kolhapuri at **Bharat,** 317 SBS Rd., near the Reserve Bank of India, opposite Fort Market (☎ 2618899), a simple place with a plenitude of fish: crab, tandoori pomfrets, among them.

SWEETS & LIGHT SNACKS

Here air-conditioning ceases to exist for the most part—indeed, some of the most enjoyable places are open-air or open to the street.

For Indian snacks—grains, nuts, spicy fritters, and the best panipuris (tiny puffs of dough filled with tamarind water) or bhelpuri (sweet-and-sour sauced mixture of grains, lentils, chopped vegetables, herbs, and chutney), or any number of other between-meal savories—head to **Chowpatty Beach,** the most famous snacking spot in town. Part of the fun of buying your treat is browsing for your snack among the gaily striped stalls, then downing it on the spot. A panipuri requires skill: It must be eaten in one bite to keep the luscious juices from squirting all over your shirt. The snack foods are safe to eat, with one reminder: It's more hygienic to have them served on banana leaves or in a paper cone than on crockery plates that have been washed in a bucket of dubious-looking lukewarm water. Rs 10 (33¢) will get you a couple of panipuris, and for Rs 5 (16¢) you can get a cone of some other savory snack. Fresh coconuts opened on the spot can act as the fire extinguisher if your snack is too hot. Chowpatty stalls are open from about 3pm to around midnight.

Other snack stalls around the city near the office buildings sell similar snacks for little pickups at any time of the day.

One of the nicest things about Bombay is the numerous clean, fresh fruit juice bars. Among the best is the tidy **Sukh Sagar,** opposite Chowpatty in Marina Mansion, S. V. P. Road, partly hidden by a bus stand and decorated with seasonal fruits strung up around the entrance. A long, narrow place, the electric juicers are always in action from 8am to 1am, churning out every kind of fresh juice. Prices start at Rs 20 (66¢) for orange and fresh pineapple and go up to Rs 40 ($1.33) for mango (in season). Down the lane, nearer the beach, is Sukh Sagar's snack shop serving idlis, for Rs 9 (30¢), vegetable curry, pizzas and sandwiches—all under Rs 50 ($1.66). Open from 10am to 1am and very clean.

Almost next door at Chowpatty Seaface is M. K. Tripathi's tiny, tidy **New Kulfi Center** (☎ 3612878), tucked away under the fly-over, renowned throughout Bombay for excellence in Indian ice cream (kulfi). Familiar fruit flavors—mango, orange, and pineapple, to name a few—cost about Rs 26 (87¢) a serving; and exotic flavors such as cashew, pista (pistachio), almond, fig, and such cost as high as Rs 25 (83¢) per serving. Serious browsers—those intent on buying—can have tastes before making their final decisions. Open every day from 10am to 2am.

Croissants etc., Warden Road (☎ 3643797)—and several other locations in the city, Juhu, and other suburbs—has giant croissants, salads, submarines (sandwiches), breads, and pastries, with prices ranging from Rs 12 (40¢) for a croissants to Rs 210 ($7) for a chocolate truffle cake. Nibble there, or take out for picnic.

Right in the center of everything at Flora Fountain is a Bombay institution, the **Fountain Dry Fruit Store** (est. 1922), where the owner sits cross-legged overseeing a jumbo assortment of irresistible nuts and sweets. Badami (a rich almond confection) and pedah (a milk-and-sugar sweet) are sold by the gram at prices quoted by the owner, as are all the items here. Cashews, for instance, run Rs 80 ($2.66) per 100 grams (about a quarter of a pound), and sweets are higher.

While you're sightseeing around Malabar Hill, two treats await you on Babulnath Road. At tiny, unpretentious **Dave Farsan and Sweet Mart** (open from 6:30am to 9pm) you can buy the jalebi (pretzel-shaped, syrup-dipped sweet) many Bombayites insist are the best in town—Rs 70 ($2.33) per kilo. And nearby you can see the Babulnath Temple with its 200-year-old statue of Krishna looking quite sweet in fine silks and jewels.

Most pleasant for tea or coffee is the stately, understated **Sea Lounge** at **The Taj.** Don't go for the conventional stuff which you can get anywhere. The bhel-puri is a Bombay experience; here hygienically made and pleasantly served—but authentic, just as it would be at a Chowpatty Beach stall. Portions are big enough for two. There's an picture postcard sea view with rowboats and yachts.

All the top hotels have coffee shops, most open 24 hours a day for snacks and light meals.

EATING AT JUHU BEACH

For a splurge meal, head for one of the big hotels. Outside the hotels, here are a couple of suggestions.

In a distinctive setting with silk-quilted walls, rose brocade upholstered chairs, and sparkling mirrors to add depth to the narrow room, **Sheetal Samudra,** Juhu Tara Road (☎ 61222973), has fresh seafood in a tank to be prepared to order and an excellent menu with many other seafood choices—some Indian, Chinese, and Continental. Beer is Rs 90 ($3). Open from noon to 4pm, and 7pm to midnight.

6 What to See & Do

An early stop on your exploration of Bombay should certainly be **Malabar Hill,** at the western side of town. Here there's a delightfully landscaped park clinging to the side of the hill. Needless to say, there's a wonderful view of the city curving around the bay and the best place to see this is from a table in the little **Naaz** restaurant, open from 9am to 11pm.

Across the street, on top of a covered reservoir, are the renowned **Hanging Gardens** (now called **Sir P. Mehta Gardens**), where the old English art of topiary is practiced: Here privet bushes are trained, cut, and trimmed in such shapes as cows, giraffes, monkeys, oxen, and elephants. The gardens are pleasant to stroll through in the evening, but they're not much shelter in the broiling sun of early afternoon.

Just beyond the trees, at the far end of the garden, are the **Towers of Silence,** where devout Parsis take their dead to be eaten by vultures. Grisly as this sounds, it has been a Parsi custom—the sect originally came from Persia—for centuries, and owes its origin to Parsi respect for sacred soil, which shouldn't be corrupted with rotting flesh. The only part of this procedure that can be seen, of course, is the flock of vultures hovering ominously overhead, but a scale model of the towers can be seen in the **Prince of Wales Museum** downtown.

Just down Malabar Hill, in the opposite direction from the Towers of Silence, is an interesting **Jain temple** that is worth brief inspection. Back on the promenade—Netaji Subhash Road—the famous **Chowpatty Beach** is about 1 mile down, going toward town. Here it's always liveliest in the evenings, with scores of stalls selling tasty tidbits, fortune tellers, jugglers, and even a masseur or two. The beach is renowned for its association with the fiery (verbal) struggles for Indian independence and still today is a popular spot for soapbox orators.

The **Taraporewala Aquarium**—open from 11am to 8pm, closed Monday; entry fee Rs 2 (6¢)—also on Netaji Subhash Road, is probably the best in the country, with the biggest crowds always around the fascinating tank of octopuses and striped sea snakes.

The **Prince of Wales Museum** (☎ 244484)—open from 10:15am to 6pm, closed Monday; entry fee Rs 3 (10¢)—definitely needs a few hours for full appreciation. Unlike most museums, it can't be covered in a fast runaround—at least, you won't want to rush when you see some of its treasures. The extensive collection of fascinating 18th- and 19th-century miniatures, one flight up, delays most art lovers for a while (inexpensive reproductions are for sale in the lobby), and on the same floor are elegantly carved ivory artworks as well as jade and Indian bronze images. A rich collection of Nepalese and Tibetan art occupies one whole gallery and probably has few equals anywhere. The museum was named after George V, who laid its foundation stone in 1905.

Highest among the historical landmarks is the 260-foot clock tower, the **Rajabai Tower** (1881), above the University Library on Mayo Road. Once the tower could be climbed via its spiral staircase, but that's no longer allowed. Step inside the library and ask for the deputy librarian to get permission to stroll around and see the library's wonderful gothic architecture and great stained glass windows in main reading room. It's also possible to walk through the Main Hall at the nearby Gothic High Court; visitor use the side entrance. You can walk from here to **Knesseth Eliyahoo,** a 110-year-old synagogue off Ropemaker Street (it's painted blue); knock to rouse the watchman to show you the interiors—tip Rs 10 (33¢)—with mosaic floors and

A Special Private Art Collection

A rare, beautiful, and valuable private art collection can be visited by those who have their bankers write a letter of introduction to fans of this book, **Mr. and Mrs. H. K. Swali,** 102/A Bhublabhai Desai Rd., Mehra Sadan, First Floor, Bombay, 400026. Mr. Swali, a former banker himself, and his wife, Nalini, will take true pleasure in showing you their remarkable centuries-old bronzes, miniature paintings, and stone carvings, which ordinarily you'd see only in a museum. Here, you can hold the bronzes (which warm and seem to take on life in your hands), examine everything closely, and learn the history of each piece and how it was found in a country town or city bazaar. The Swalis have written articles on Indian art, lectured on the subject, and traveled abroad focusing on art. They're acquainted with some major collections outside India and full of worthwhile information for those interested in art.

stained glass windows. It's still in use, Friday, Saturday, and High Holidays, although the congregation has dwindled.

The city's **zoo** (open 7am to 7pm) is only so-so, but far more than just so-so are the attractive **Jijabai Bhonsle Udyan** (formerly Victoria Gardens), created from 1862 to 1872 on 33 acres, with 15 acres added since then. Take bus no. 1 or 4. **The Victoria and Albert Museum** (☎ 8272731) on the grounds is open all days except Monday and eight public holidays, from 10:30am to 6pm.

Exhibits are divided into sections, covering several vast subject areas—agriculture, village life, armory, cottage industries, costumes, fine arts, fossils, coins, minerals, old Bombay, geology, religion, and mythology—each of which can command your attention endlessly.

Mani Bhavan, 19 Laburnam Rd. (☎ 3627864), was Gandhi's home in Bombay during his visits from 1917 to 1934. It is now a touching museum of his life and times and certainly should be on your itinerary. It contains a research institute, library of more than 45,000 volumes, and an auditorium. The third floor showcases Gandhi's life. On the second floor, his room has been preserved, and in an adjoining chamber are minifigures depicting his life. Slides and postcards are available. The museum is near the Gowalia Tank, a short walk up Laburnam Road from Chowpatty Beach. Admission is Rs 2 (10¢). It is open from 9am to 6pm.

Up in the northwest section of the city, the **Breach Candy Swimming Pool,** Bhulabhai Desai Road (☎ 364381), is right on the beach (no. bus 121 to Cumballa Hill) and charges a small membership fee for tourists. A little farther up the coast you'll see a famous Muslim shrine, **Haji Ali,** on a causeway that connects it with the mainland 500 yards away. You can visit only at low tide. At this point, on the other side of the coast highway, is the **Mahalaxmi Race Course** (races on Saturday and Sunday, from November to April, between 2 and 5pm), which can be visited by tourists. For more detailed information call ☎ 891220.

A bit north of Haji Ali's Tomb is the **Nehru Planetarium** on Annie Besant Road at Worli (☎ 4920510). There are shows, except Mondays, at 3 and 6:30pm in English, 4:30pm in Hindi, and 1:30pm in Marathi. Entry fee is Rs 6 (20¢) for adults, Rs 3.50 (12¢) for children under 12. Closed Sunday. Adjacent is the **Children's Science Park** (☎ 493266), with exhibits on all kinds of transportation from steam lorries to supersonic jets. Closed Mondays.

Heading back to Fort Bombay, one of Bombay's two historic synagogues, **Magen David,** is located in Byculla not far from Gloria Church on J. Juibhoy Road (look for Byculla Bridge). Once the largest in Bombay, it's Iranian-Jewish congregation has all but died out. Nearby Benai Israel school is open to boys of all denominations.

If you head south from Horniman Circle, down Old Customs House Road or Apollo Street—or, better still, from Flora Fountain (Hutatma Chowk) down Mahatma Gandhi Road—you'll eventually reach the **Wellington Fountain,** from which you can see the celebrated **Gateway of India,** a massive stone arch built on the waterfront to commemorate the visit of Britain's King George V in 1911, when the Indian Empire was but one of the many jewels in the British crown. The Gateway, built of yellow basalt quarried locally, was created by an English architect in a style recalling 16th-century Gujarat architecture. The equestrian statue nearby is of the last great Maratha emperor, Shivaji, who conducted guerrilla warfare against the British in the 18th century, until his attention was diverted by Aurangzeb, a bitterer foe. Shivaji left his legacy in the manner the local sari is still worn—looped between the legs so as not to interfere with the riding capabilities of the warrior horsewomen.

On the way from the Flora Fountain to The Taj Mahal Hotel, you will encounter the **Jehangir Art Gallery,** probably the most modern art museum in India, around which many of the city's avant-garde currents ebb and flow. There are actually several galleries (including one on the roof) rolled into one, and all have different and interesting shows.

North of Flora Fountain is the great **Victoria Terminus,** a blend of Gothic and Indian architecture. About three million passengers and 1,000 trains a day go through"VT," as it's known. See the exterior carvings on the history of India's transportation.

ELEPHANTA CAVES

Six miles across the harbor from the Gateway to India lie the celebrated Elephanta Caves, meager fare compared to Ellora and Ajanta, but certainly worth a visit if only for the pleasant one-hour boat ride where you'll see the skyline of the city as well as the modern refineries and gas rigs in the sea. For those not going to Ellora and Ajanta, Elephanta gives a good sample of early cave sculpture.

Launches leave the Gateway to India every hour from 9am to 2:15pm and return after four hours. A luxury launch with guide costs Rs 50 ($1.66) for adults, Rs 30 ($1) for children; an ordinary launch without a guide costs Rs 35 ($1.16) for adults, Rs 20 (66¢) for children. For reservations call ☎ 2026364; 2023585. Tickets are also available at India Tourist Office, 123 M. Karve Rd. Currently this tour even goes during the monsoon, unless the sea is very rough. You can find out more by telephoning the above number.

Try to avoid Sundays and public holidays—go on a weekday—when the island gets very crowded. But if you can only go when the others go, do so; it's worth it.

WHAT YOU'LL SEE

Elephanta, green and lovely, was named by the Portuguese after the huge elephant statue that stood there when they landed—pieces of which can now be seen in the Jijamata Bhonsle Udyan (formerly Victoria Gardens) in Bombay.

The six caves on the island were cut from solid rock in the 8th century during the golden age of the Guptas but were vandalized by the Portuguese, who used them as cattle sheds and artillery grounds and vandalized the images.

The caves contain many sculptures dealing with Hinduism. You can appreciate them as great art without any religious knowledge and learn something about them from the guide who picks important figures for you. Some people use a flashlight, but the chiaroscuro effect of natural light is probably what the ancient carvers had in mind.

A long flight of easy-to-climb stairs leads to the caves, lined on either side by souvenir sellers—no remarkable bargains. At the top, there's a cafe for snacks and clean toilets.

A few more stairs, flanked by carved elephants, lead to the wide-columned verandah outside the main cave. The focal point in the cave—and the highlight of the visit—is an 18-foot high sculpture of Mahesmurti: Shiva as the creator, preserver, and destroyer. (Often erroneously called the "Trimurti," which depicts the three faces of Brahma.) Notice the expressions: stern, compassionate, and loving. See how every curl and jewel has been carefully sculpted around the head. At either side of the recesses are figures of dwaraplas (guardians).

Look at the figures around the doorway and on side panels and see some of the things Shiva can do: He is Yogisvara, lord of the yogis, sitting on a lotus; as

Natraja, he strikes a graceful pose on one leg with many arms as the cosmic dancer. Look for Shiva and Parvati's marriage; elsewhere godlings (local gods) shower them with flowers. Demon Ravana's there, too, moving mount Kailasa, as well as many others.

Though many figures here have been severely damaged, they are still beautiful. Take a moment to stroll around before you leave and take a second look; each time you'll find something else to enjoy. There's a good view of Bombay from the highest point on the island.

TWO WALKING TOURS

MARINE DRIVE: BOMBAY'S BEST WALK

Marine Drive runs along Back Bay and is, officially, Netaji Subhash Drive. At night, when this long strand of road is lit by hundreds of tiny lights, it becomes its nickname, the "Queen's Necklace." The drive is protected by a seawall from the pounding waves and monsoon rains. Great old mansions, somewhat down-at-the heels recalling South Beach in Miami of a few years ago, face the drive's broad promenade.

Caught here in a traffic jam, drivers honk their way through a tangle of taxis, tongas, auto rickshaws, red double-decker buses, motorcycles carrying whole families, newspaper hawkers, and running in and out between them, beggars, vendors thrusting fresh fruits and fragrant blossoms into open car windows. "Lady, how about it?" says one dangling jasmine on a string through the taxi window.

Begin your walk at **Nariman Point,** amid the sleek modern office buildings. Follow the curving shoreline north; if it's morning, there will be a multifaceted pageant of life: joggers, yoga practitioners, fishermen, school children, kite flyers, seawall sitters engrossed in conversation, people sleeping on the benches or the beach or sprawled on the seawall. Keep going until you reach **Chowpatty Beach.** If it's evening, join the fun there strolling among the vendors selling snacks, drinks, and ice cream (see "Where to Eat," above). You're on a chunk of history: Chowpatty has been famous since before independence for political orators and rallies.

Across the way are restaurants and fine shops. You could end your walk with a bite to eat or some browsing.

BANGANGA: STEP BACK IN TIME

Bombay, modern as it is, has pockets of antiquity. One of the most unusual in the **Banganga Tank** (a man-made pool) at Walkeshwar Village (now part of the city) surrounded by temples and private homes in the center of the city, steps from the sea. Banganga, a sacred site on Malabar Point, has been the focus of Hindu pilgrimages for about 1,000 years. A few years ago, Banganga, the only remaining major tank in Bombay, was threatened by a plan to cover it and turn it into a bus depot. Today is remains but in disrepair. For how long no one knows.

A taxi can take you the narrow lane leading down to this tank, once known as Ladder Street, now **Siri Road.** There are said to be 33 temples surrounding the tank. Only most practiced eye will find all of them, some are well disguised into the urban dwellings. You can wander around the stepped basalt tank looking in at some of the many temples. The most interesting temple architecturally is a small one at the southwest dedicated to **Shiva.** Banganga was much written about by European travelers in the 17th and 18th centuries.

GUIDED TOURS

MTDC's City Tours, in semiluxury coaches, leave from Tuesday through Sunday, 9am to 1pm and 2 to 6pm, for Rs 55 ($1.83). Sites covered include the Hanging Gardens, Kamla Nehru Park, Mani Bhavan (Gandhi memorial), the Aquarium,

Council Hall (outside) Gateway to India (outside), Prince of Wales Museum, and Jehangir Gallery (outside). The afternoon route begins with the Gateway to India and covers the same ground. Departures are from MTDC's offices, C.D.O. Hutments. M. Cama Road (opposite LIC office) Nariman Point. Reservations (☎ 2026713, 2027762, or 2027784). Tickets for this tour and others run by MTDC are also available at the India Tourist Office, 123 M. Karve Road (☎ 2033144).

MTDC's Suburban Tour, guided, on semiluxury coaches depart Tuesday through Sunday, at 9:15am, returning at 6:15pm, for Rs 90 ($3); lunch is at your own expense. Sights covered include Observation Point, Kanheri Caves, National Park, Lion Safari Park, Juhu Beach (where boat rides are at your expense), and Hare Krishna Temple. The starting point is the MTDC office as above.

Should you wish to sightsee on your own with a guide, the **Government of India Tourist Office** on M. Karve Road can provide an approved guide at these rates: for one to four persons, the charge is Rs 250 ($8.33) for half day, Rs 350 ($11.66) for a full day; a lunch allowance for the guide is included in the full-day prices; additional fee for foreign-language guides (Italian, German, Spanish, Japanese, etc.).

7 Shopping

You can buy all over India, but you can shop in Bombay better than anywhere else in the country. Indeed, on first impression the city seems one gargantuan bazaar, with an endless choice of stores bursting with merchandise for every budget. There are handicraft emporiums, antique and jewelry markets, and boutiques carrying the kinds of fashions Westerners really enjoy and want to take home with them.

The following are a few of my shopping suggestions. Better yet are the shop discoveries you make on your own. Generally, shops in south Bombay are closed on Sunday; from Dadar onward, they're closed on Thursday and open on Sunday.

You bargain in all but the price-fixed stores and expect to find the most resistance in stores where many Westerners shop and merchants long ago discovered that they'll usually pay the asking price. As a general rule, merchandise is more expensive in the shops around the top hotels, but you're paying a little more for preselection of good-quality merchandise. Even so, prices are not totally out of line in the top shops and emporiums. And more good news: In Bombay, government-approved guides are not permitted to shop with tourists. When buying antiques, be sure the merchant supplies the forms you need to export them from the country.

Also, should you decide to buy a lasting memory of your trip in the form of some gold jewelry set with diamonds or other precious stones, be aware that you need a certificate to get your glittering prize out of the country. Be sure to ask for it when making your purchase.

For a good survey of handicrafts from all over India, the place to head is the **Cottage Industries Emporium,** 34C S. Maharaj Marg (formerly Apollo Pier Road) (☎ 2027537), where there is no bargaining for the interesting inventory. You'll find easy-to-pack, beautifully embroidered place mats in cotton or silk, delicate-looking rings set with semiprecious stones, and all kinds of scarves and ties in bold and subtle prints and solids in lustrous silks. Prices for silks vary greatly according to quality of the textile. You can also get ready-to-wear for everyone here. This is just a small sampling of the emporium's many wares. Open every day but Sunday from 10am to 6pm.

For everything from foods to fancy clothes, try **Akbarally's,** a department store with the atmosphere of a bazaar, at 45 V. Nariman Rd., and at Shri Sai Darshan Apartments, S. V. Road, Santa Cruz, the latter in the suburbs and open on Sunday.

At Chowpatty Seaface, the hushed marble interiors of **Amratlal Bhimj Zaveri** (open from 10:30am to 7:30pm; closed Sunday) are dotted with plants and pools in an opulent setting for extravagant jewelry, much of it made especially for this shop. It's not unusual to spend Rs 50,000 ($1,666) for a simple 22-karat necklace at this shop. There are also little 22-karat snowflakes for a cool Rs 1,000 ($33.33), among the less-expensive wares. The shop also has a branch in Jhaveri Bazaar.

Behind The Taj Hotel, there's a quarter mile of bargains in shops running from the Regal Cinema to the Temple, on the road which in a former incarnation was Colaba Causeway and is now **S. Bhagat Singh Marg.** The stores are open every day but Sunday, from around 10am to 7 or 8:30pm. Addresses are listed where I found them, but the shops can be located by name as you stroll.

A must for serious collectors of antiques—and all inveterate browsers—is **Phillips** (☎ 2020564), in the Indian Merchants Mansion on Madame Cama Road, opposite the Regal Cinema (open from 9am to 1pm, and 2:30 to 6:30pm; closed Sunday), which was established in 1860 and is a treasure trove of relics from the Raj period. There are, for example, 15,000 or more prints, sketches, and engravings documenting the 18th and 19th centuries, plus painted Staffordshire animals and Lowestoft porcelain—an 18th- and 19th-century import from China—bowls, platters, and tureens. Valuable and beautiful old glass, coins, buttons, rings, medals, jades, ivories, 19th-century vases, epergnes, and bowls abound here. Also for sale are Indian miniature paintings, which go up into the thousands for something old, detailed, and valuable, and a rare collection of old bidri ware (items elegantly inlaid with zinc, copper, lead, tin, and stones). Don't hurry when shopping at Phillips (or anywhere in India). A few minutes spent chatting with Mr. Issa, the owner, or one of his knowledgeable staff, can help you learn the history of your purchase, which will be reliably dated and documented for export formalities by the shop.

Near the Regal Cinema are a number of shops with good selections of Indian silver, which, as in Mexico, is a mixture of alloys and silver, and in India generally sold by weight. Behind the Regal Cinema, **A. K. Essajee,** Suleman Chambers, on Baltery Street, Apollo Bunder (☎ 2021071), opposite the Cottage Industries Emporium (and on the ground floor at Landsdowne House, below Regency Inn), has an excellent and huge selection of silver, bangles, necklaces, and belts. Nearby, **Framroz Sorabji Khan Co.,** in the Regal Cinema Building (open from 9:30am to 6pm; closed Sunday), specializing in old pieces, guarantees its baubles to be 90% silver and claims to have pieces about 100 years old. Also nearby, **Jehangir Khan** has old textiles, sari borders, and silver, including silver fish, which Parsis believe bring good luck, and which, luckily for you, can be bought in this shop.

More discoveries behind the Regal Cinema: **D. Popli and Sons,** Readymoney Building, Battery Street (☎ 2021694), has jewelry, silver and ivory, silk paintings, and other pretty things to buy. It's arts and jewelry again at **Curio Cottage,** 19 Landsdowne Rd. (☎ 2022607), and still more at **Mangal Arts and Crafts No. 1,** Landsdowne House, 18 Landsdowne Rd. (☎ 2873921). A few steps away, Indian perfumes and attars are the attraction at **Ajmal and Sons,** 1 Cecil Court, near Apollo Hotel (☎ 2044077), and handicrafts and objets d'art are found at **Melwani and Co.,** Florence House, Mereweather Road, right behind The Taj.

Anokkhi, Kemps Corner, opposite Cumballa Hill Hospital (☎ 3820639), is sleek and modern and known for reviving and reinterpreting Rajasthani's classic prints for today's fashion-conscious woman. Drawstring pants, shirts, blouses, and harem-style pants that look like skirts, are all available in wonderful Rajasthani textiles. There are also branches in Delhi's Santushti's Shopping Complex and at 2 Tilak Marg Jaipur.

Zewar Exports, Vasant Vihar, 8 M.L. Dahabukar Rd. (formerly Carmichael Road) (☎ 4922127), is a wonderful discovery. Located in an old bungalow, the shop features interesting costume jewelry designed by Jamini Ahluwalia and Chandu Morarji, folk art, colonial furniture, and decorative home accessories gathered from all over India. A collectors paradise and terrific resource for affordable gifts or your own memory of Bombay. Hours are 10am to 6pm; closed Sundays.

Wonderful for high-quality handicrafts is the **Chetana Crafts Centre, "Ethnic Weaves,"** K. Dubash Marg (formerly Rampart Row; ☎ 2844968). It has of all kinds of handicrafts from Gujarat, Maharashtra, Orissa, Andhra Pradesh, Tamil Nadu, Madhya Pradesh, and Rajasthan. This is an invaluable resource for unusual souvenirs at affordable prices: especially handsome attractive salwar kamiz, waistcoats, kurtas, and scarves. Open from 10:30am to 6:30pm; closed Sunday and national holidays.

To concentrate on the jewelers (at least 200 of the more than 3,000 in Bombay), zero in on the intersection of Kalbadevi and Sheikh Memon streets, beginning at the Cotton Exchange (near Mahatma Jyotiba Phule Market), which is officially known as **Jhaveri Bazaar.** This is one of Bombay's oldest, most crowded, and fascinating areas. You should walk through, browsing at the shops displaying gems, gold, and silver in such great abundance that even Shah Jahan would have been impressed. In some of the little shops that are open to the street, customers sit cross-legged on the floor bargaining over 24-karat gold bangles. **Shops 39** and **47** have antique silver jewelry, and at **Shop 62,** Siroya Champalal Uttamchand sells new silver jewelry. In front of this shop sit craftsmen winding beads by hand on silky threads, working almost too fast for the eye to follow.

If all this is too rich for your blood, you can go over to **Mangaldass Market,** nearby, which has reasonably priced saris—even more reasonably priced after you bargain.

Back in the center of things, **Khadi-Village Industries Emporium,** 286 D. Naoriji Rd. (open from 10am to 6:30pm; closed for lunch from 1:30 to 2:30pm and all day Sunday), has two floors of price-fixed merchandise, with especially good selections of hand-spun and hand-woven textiles. Other items include mirror-studded shoulder bags, greeting cards painted on Bodhi leaves, Indian toys, and jewelry.

For dedicated collectors and indefatigable bargain hunters, there's **Chor Bazaar** (Thieves Market), near Mohammed Ali Road, about a Rs 70 ($2.33) taxi from the center, and open every day but Friday and Sunday. From the riot of merchandise, you can assemble an automobile, furnish a house, stock a china closet, and find antique clocks, unstrung beads, half-strung guitars, ribbons, bangles, picture frames, china, and copper pots. The merchants heap their treasures in tiny shops, spread them on the streets, or wander among the crowds holding their wares aloft on wooden trees. Amid all this chaos, the most interesting shops are found on Mutton Street. They have woodcarvings, old coins, glass, silver, ivory, paintings, jewelry—and that's for starters only. Asking prices are very high. Haggle!

For book-lovers, second-hand book vendors spread their wares on the walks near Flora Fountain. Look carefully, you may find a valuable treasure.

Finally, opposite the Bombay Gymkhana, there's **Fashion Street,** as a long stretch of Metro Road is now called because of stall after stall selling surplus and reject garments India exports to the West—shorts, shirts, skirts, and such. But one word of warning: Here you must bargain or you will be truly ripped off. The vendor will ask about double the price the item should sell for. He knows it will appear cheap to you—if you compare it to prices in the West. Believe me, Indians pay much less, and you can and must—if you bargain.

8 Bombay After Dark

PUBS

In the pubs, expect a mostly young male clientele, and drink beer—for Rs 22 (73¢) to Rs 25 (83¢) a mug, around Rs 100 ($3.33) pitcher. Daiquiris (bananas, strawberry) are about Rs 150 ($5). Pubs usually serve inexpensive snacks such as kebabs. Pubs hours vary. The most popular times are after work and in the evenings.

Now what's hot: Starting the trend, a few years ago, **Tavern,** at Fariyas Hotel (☎ 2042911), with typical English ambience, a beamed ceiling, and wood-paneled walls is still on the hip list. The two-tiered **London Pub,** Chowpatty Seaface (☎ 3630274), gets a somewhat more sophisticated crowd because of its hefty Rs 150 ($5) cover. **Ecstacy,** August Kranti Marg (☎ 3635740), displays a mammoth neon sign. **Ghetto,** B. Desai Road, near Cadbury House (☎ 4921556), has neon graffiti wall designs and blackboard and chalk for adding comments (some chosen to endure in the wall designs); this pub has a 100-person capacity and no cover. Expect capacity crowds. In Bandra, a Western suburb, **Toto's Garage,** seems a hybrid between a garage and pub; the automotive motif carries through to car-themed drinks: How about a pink Cadillac? Wild Mercedes? These are a few pubs: for a complete listing, check *Island Magazines*'s "In and Around" section—Rs 15 (50¢) on newsstands.

BARS

Most hotels have bars—the oldest bar, **Harbour Bar,** is in The Taj; the most romantic bar, **Apollo** (see "Worth a Splurge" under "Where to Eat," above) is also in the Taj. Bars are mainly male preserves.

DISCOTHEQUES

Discos are mainly at top hotels. The most well-known are: **Cellar** at Oberoi Towers; **1990's** at The Taj; **RGs** at Natraj; **Go Bananas** at Kamats Plaza, Santa Cruz; **Raspberry Razzmatazz,** at the Juhu Hotel; **Studio,** near Sterling Cinema (not in a hotel); and **Cyclone** at Leela Kempinski. Life starts late and goes on to the wee hours; you'll find high cover and drink charges. Guests at the hotels where the discos are at usually get in for free; others play hefty membership fees. Some admit couples only.

Otherwise, top hotels dish up Western dance music in their posh restaurants.

FILMS

Several cinemas show English and American films, some pretty old and all with any sensuous parts censored. Movies are generally screened at 3, 6, and 9pm, and are listed in the daily newspapers.

DANCE PERFORMANCES & OTHER EVENTS

The India Tourist Office, 123 M. Karve, publishes *Welcome to Bombay,* a bimonthly listing of dance and other cultural events as well as useful facts for tourists. This publications lists the nightly classical dance performances at **The Taj Mahal** in the Tanjore before dinner is served—the cost is Rs 100 ($3.33); you buy tickets at the hotel. *Welcome to Bombay* also lists musical events such as sitar recitals.

For what's on at the **Prithvi Theatre** at Juhu or the **National Centre of Performing Arts** at Nariman Point, a handsome building designed by American architect Philip Johnson, the movies or other events, check the daily newspapers. You'll find these events and many others listed as you do at home. And sometimes the best entertainment is in the streets: not just the passing parade, but the growing trend toward street theater to dramatize social and political issues.

9 Excursions

JUHU BEACH

About 20.8 kilometers (33 miles) north of the city, beyond the airport, Juhu Beach is a favorite excursion. Take the Western Railway suburban line to Santa Cruz and a bus or taxi from there. The Juhu Beach waters are said to be polluted, so guests (and casual visitors) use hotel pools. A telephone call or two will tell you which hotels allow nonresidents to swim for a fee. See the Juhu Beach sections in both "Where to Stay" and "Where to Eat" if you want to spend a little more time here.

OTHER BEACHES

Lovely beaches away from Bombay serve those who wish a swim in the clean, sparkling sea. They are **Marve** and **Manori** 40 kilometers (25 miles) from the city and connected to each other by ferry. There's also **Madh Beach,** a little farther away. All three of these beaches can be reached by taking the train to Malad and taxiing from there for 3 or 4 miles.

Few tourists venture out this far—but it's a favorite getaway for city dwellers and for those on business.

STAYING AT THE BEACHES

Accommodation ranges from shacks, for Rs 125 ($4.16) to Rs 300 ($10), to elegance for a higher price.

The Retreat, Erangal Beach, Madh Island, Malad (West) Bombay 400061 (☎ 8825335; fax 8825171), 45 kilometers from South Bombay, has 144 elegant rooms surrounded by gardens, with luxe restaurants and fine service; an extraordinary 8,000-square-foot pool, with bar and waterfall; open-air Jacuzzis, billiards, and plans for a health spa; also business services. Standard doubles are Rs 2,550 ($85). This is a favorite weekend getaway for the well-to-do in Bombay. Stop off for refreshments or a meal when sight-seeing in the area, even if you don't intend to stay the night.

SANJAY GANDHI NATIONAL PARK

Sanjay Gandhi National Park is 40 kilometers from Bombay. The centerpiece of the park is the **109 Kanheri caves,** dating from the 2nd to the 9th centuries, one of the largest groups of Buddhist caves in western India. Many of them, merely holes in the ravine, were monks' cells. Caves 1, 2, and 3 have massive pillars, sculptures, and stupas well worth seeing. Wear sneakers and take a flashlight to see the interiors; also take care walking over the moss-covered rocks to some the caves. Sunday is an especially interesting time to visit as devotees go up the steep rocks to see the sadhus in two ashrams at the top. There is a modest entry; free on Friday.

About 7 kilometers from the Kahheri caves, within the national park, is **Krishnagiri Upavana,** a pretty garden with a shrine to Mahatma Gandhi on Pavilion Hill, from which there is a wonderful view. Cottages are available for picnickers, should you want to make a day of it.

Lion Safari Park, part of the national park, is where visitors in closed vehicles can observe Indian lions in their natural habitat. The lions welcome visitors every day from 9am to 5pm, except Monday when the park is closed. The entry fee is Rs 10 (33¢) per adult, less for children. Photography is permitted, but there are camera fees.

To get there, take the train to Borivli and taxi from the station to the park, or catch the lions on the suburban tour.

KARLA CAVES

Located 112 kilometers from Bombay, the renowned Buddhist rock-cut **Chaitya Hall** dates from the 2nd century A.D. and is said to be the most perfect of its type. It's a 2-kilometer walk on a rugged path to the cave; chairs with bearers are available for those unable to make it on foot. There are buses to the caves from Bombay, or you can hire a car for this excursion. You can also take the Central Railway to Lonavala and then bus or taxi to the cave. This is not a trip for anyone with limited time, but rewarding if you can manage it.

GUIDED TOURS BEYOND BOMBAY

ITDC's Aurangabad-Ellora-Ajanta Tour departs daily at 7:15pm, returning on the fourth day at 7:30am. The cost is Rs 1,100 ($36.66) double, Rs 2,900 ($96.66) single, Rs 1,100 ($36.66) child; costs include lodging and boarding at the three-star **Aurangabad Ashoka.** Departure is from the Nirmal Building, Nariman Point (☎ 20267113, 2027762, or 2027784). Tickets are available through the India Tourist Office, 123 M. Karve Rd. (☎ 2033144). ITDC also offers luxury bus service to Aurangabad (12 hours) for Rs 130 ($4.33), if you want to bus down and look around on your own. This bus also departs from Nirmal Building.

17 Contrasts: Cave Temples & Sunlit Beaches

Despite its size and considerable population, Aurangabad (pop. 592,000) is still an amiable town. Even as it has become the fastest-growing city in the area, and since the '80s a major industrial center with factories on the outskirts, it retains a pleasant air about it. The narrow streets still have oxen mingling among the many scooters and cars, whose noisy horns seem less welcome than the gentler lullaby of tinkling cow bells. Yet the shiny new shopping complexes filled with merchandise speak of new times.

But then hardly any of the thousands of tourists who come to the city come to see Aurangabad itself, or even to attend any of the apparently constant festivals that attract throngs of villagers.

The number-one tourist destination, of course, is the famous cave temples of the region—those at the easily accessible Ellora, 29½ kilometers (18 miles) away, and relatively isolated Ajanta 108 kilometers (66 miles) away, which were already being abandoned by their builders more than 600 years before the discovery of America.

1 Aurangabad

The city's history dates from 1610, when it was founded as Khirki by Malik Ambar, an Abyssinian who became prime minister to Murtaza Nizam Shah II. When the Nizam's son, Fateh, succeeded him, the city was named Fateh. The name was changed in 1635 by Aurangzeb, the last of the great Mughal emperors, who spent the last half of his 46-year reign trying to conquer the Deccan from here.

ESSENTIALS

GETTING TO AURANGABAD

BY PLANE **Indian Airlines** has regular flights to Aurangabad from Bombay ($34); from Delhi ($99); from Jaipur ($79); and from Udaipur ($70). To contact their booking office in Aurangabad call 24864; at the airport ☎ 02432.

East West flies to Aurangabad daily from Bombay ($40). For questions or reservations call 02432 or 24949.

BY TRAIN Most train travelers depart from Bombay. The best train from Bombay to Aurangabad is the *Bombay-Nanded Express,* departing Bombay at 9:20pm, arriving Aurangabad at 5:25am. The fare is Rs 700 ($23.33) AC First, Rs 110 ($3.66) Second.

Other trains from Bombay take eight hours to Jalgaon, which is about 59 kilometers (37 miles) from Ajanta. From Jalgaon station, there is frequent bus service to Ajanta and Aurangabad. The *Punjab Mail* is one of the trains that goes through Jalgaon and continues to Delhi, stopping en route in Bhopal and Gwalior, offering the traveler other possible stopovers. Alternatively, you can take the *Punjab Mail* or *Panchavati Express* from Bombay and change at Manmad to a narrow-gauge train for a snail's-pace 115-kilometer (70-mile) journey to Aurangabad. Trains also connect Hyderabad (Secunderabad) with Manmad.

BY BUS Good roads connect between Bombay and Aurangabad, and bus service is frequent. From Bombay to Aurangabad, **ITDC's** daily Luxury Bus, from Nirmal Building, departing 7:15pm, takes 10 hours, for Rs 130 ($4.33). From Aurangabad to Bombay, ITDC coach departs 9:10pm from Aurangabad Ashok. MTDC and MSRTC also operate coaches between Bombay and Aurangabad as do many private operators.

For information and reservations, check with the ITDC in the Aurangabad Ashok (☎ 31143) or in Bombay (☎ 202671).

BY CAR & DRIVER Car and driver to Bombay and back (48 hours/800 kilometers) will cost about Rs 1,000 ($33.33) to Rs 3,000 ($100). Outstation charges for driver are Rs 200 ($6.66) per day.

Visitor Information

The **Government of India Tourist Office,** Krishna Vilas, Station Road (West) (☎ 31217), is open from 8:30am to 6pm, Monday to Friday (from 8:30am to 12:30pm Saturday). There's also a counter at Chikalthana airport (☎ 82328). **MTDC,** Holiday Resort, Station Road (East) (☎ 20713), is open from 10am to 5pm. All are good and knowledgeable.

Getting Around

Auto rickshas charge Rs 2.50 (8¢) per kilometer, although they try to get more for foreigners, and it's best to make a package price. Be sure and negotiate waiting charges. They're okay for scooting around the city, but only allowed to go within 32 miles of Aurangabad. Lack of safety is the reason, although for years they've been saying this ban might be lifted. **Tongas** have no fixed rate; you bargain for a fair fare.

A car and driver for city use, four hours/50 kilometers, will cost Rs 335 ($11.16); eight hours/80 kilometers Rs 660 ($22); The intercity rate is Rs 520 ($17.33) per day, plus Rs 110 ($3.66) for the driver and Rs 120 ($4) night halt charges. These are rates from **Wheels-Rent-A-Car,** Aurangabad. Self-drive cars are also available here.

To get to the caves at Ajanta and Ellora, see the information under "Essentials" in the next section.

Festivals

The **Ellora Festival of Music and Dance,** is held annually during the third week in March. If you plan to come at this time, be sure to reserve a room well in advance.

What to See & Do

In Town

Aurangabad possesses a smaller edition of the Taj Mahal that uses the famous Agra tomb as its model. It was built about 1660 in memory of Aurangzeb's wife, sometimes known as Rabia-ud-Daurani, but there seems to be some dispute about who actually did the building. The official sign at the site attributes it to the emperor's son, but he is generally believed to have been too young for any such project at the time the building, known as the **Bibi-Ka-Maqbara,** was constructed. On the other hand, Aurangzeb was hardly the most lavish of monarchs and, in fact, imprisoned his father, Shah Jahan, original builder of the Taj. Admission is 75 paise, free on Friday. Open from sunrise to 10pm (floodlit at night).

The Bibi-Ka-Maqbara is by no means as impressive as the Taj, being more or less dominated by the four minarets around it. Although the tomb is constructed of marble from Jaipur at the base and dome, the remainder is stone covered with decorated stucco. At the left-hand side, the small mosque between two of the minarets totally destroys the balance of the vista. The grounds, although not particularly cultivated, are impressive, and the best view of all is to be obtained by climbing the 120 steps of the 72-foot minaret (only one is kept open because of numerous suicides) and gazing out over the nearby town and surrounding hills.

Another stop in Aurangabad is the beautiful **Panchakki,** or Water Mill (open from sunrise to 8pm; entry is 75 paise), which even today demonstrates the ingenuity of Mughal engineers. Underground pipes lead water from the hills five miles away to an elevated tower here, cascading it from a wide outlet as a gentle and caressing waterfall. The tower, freshly whitewashed, is still lower than the surrounding hills, so the principle of gravity is never in doubt. The water flows into an attractive pool with fountains, some of it being diverted to drive an old mill wheel used for grinding millet until recent times. The remainder flows into an adjoining river, across which can be seen some remains of the ancient clay pipe system. There is a small refreshment stand under the sheltering banyan tree, and fat gray trout fight for tidbits from numerous tourists.

At the rear is a lovely garden with more fountains, pine and cypress trees, and the red sandstone **tomb of Baba Shah Musafir,** one of Aurangzeb's favorite saints.

NEARBY

Aurangabad, too, has **caves,** only a few miles beyond Bibi-ka-Maqbara. And while they are nowhere near as awe-inspiring as those at Ellora and Ajanta, they are a must when sightseeing around town. Negotiate a taxi or auto ricksha from your hotel to the site and include waiting charges. There are no meters. Bargain. The caves are open for visitors from sunrise to sunset or 6pm.

You can drive only to the base of the cave site, then it's a healthy hike up steep stairs to inspect their interiors. There are two wings of caves, about a mile apart. With so much walking, it's best to plan this excursion early or late in the day while it's light but not too hot. A watchman will materialize to illuminate the dim interiors. Give him a rupee or two.

These caves are referred to by numbers, but they are not clearly designated. Just ask the attendant to point you in the right direction. Like their counterparts at Ellora and Ajanta, these rock-cut tabernacles were the handiwork of monks, but slightly later than those at the caves away from town. The caves here date from A.D. 700, except cave 4, which dates from the 2nd century A.D.

Of this group, **Cave 7** is most impressive, with Buddha preaching about the eight human fears (fire, sword, chains, shipwreck, lion, snake, elephant, and death).

Next to it, **Cave 6** shows Buddha with two Naga kings; **Cave 3** has a frieze telling a legend about a lioness licking the soles of a king's feet, an action that made her pregnant. She ultimately gave birth to a lion-son who gorged himself on humans and had to be annihilated for this dietary indulgence.

SHOPPING

Shop the bazaars at City Chowk, Gulmandi, Station Road, Mondha, Nawabpura, Shahganj, and Sarafa. Hours are 10am to 8pm (closed Sundays).

Look for himroo and mashru shawls; they have long been a cottage industry in Aurangabad. They combine cotton and silk and have a satin sheen. Some have designs inspired by Ajanta paintings.

The art of weaving pure silk and gold into Paithani saris, so intricate that making one can take a year, goes back 2,000 years in Maharashtra. If you see one of these treasures, consider buying it. Considering the work that goes into them, prices can be high. Be careful! Aurangabad is also known for artificial silk.

Another area specialty, Bidriware, is made from a zinc-copper base in which thread-thin is embedded or overlaid in designs on such objects as boxes, brooches, plates, vases, charms on key holders, and more.

There also are all kinds of items made from semiprecious stones, which are mined around Aurangabad.

In Shahganj, check out the **Himroo Factory Emporium,** for shawls, and **Cottage Industries Emporium,** Station Road, for all of the specialties above. Wander elsewhere and bargain.

WHERE TO STAY

Keep in mind that taxes add from 10% to 20% to your hotel bill. A good, clean, affordable room is hard to find in Aurangabad, but improving now that business people have started coming here. If you plan to attend the Ellora Festival of Music and Dance, annually the third week in March, be sure and reserve far in advance.

DOUBLES FOR LESS THAN RS 500 ($16.66)

MTDC's **Government Holiday Resort,** near the railway station (☎ 24259), needs a paint job and TLC. The price is right: Rates range from Rs 150 ($5) to Rs 450 ($15); six rooms have AC. This is a very popular place with Indian families. For reservations, you must write seven days to three months in advance to the Manager, Maharashtra Tourism Development Corporation, C.D.O. Hutments, opposite LIC Building, Madame Cama Road, Bombay 400020 (☎ 2026713).

Printavel Hotel, Dr. Ambedkar Road (☎ 24707), is a pleasant, tidy place to stay in this low-price range. The upper verandah gets the breezes from both sides and thus remains fairly cool. There are 38 clean rooms, none with AC, but with ceiling fans and mosquito nets. Good in this price range.

A pleasant **Youth Hostel,** Padampura (☎ 23801), has separate men's and women's facilities, for Rs 15 (50¢) to Rs 25 (83¢). There is a roof sit-out; breakfast and dinner are served—cheap veg thalis. Write to the Warden, Youth Hostel, Station Road, Aurangabad 431005, for reservations. Bring soap and a towel.

DOUBLES FOR LESS THAN RS 1,000 ($33.33)

Hotel Shiverni, Jalna Road, Aurangabad (☎ 84978-80; fax 83260), has 45 rooms. Corridors are run-down, but the rooms are okay, cheap and better than what one usually finds at these prices in Aurangabad: Rs 350 ($11.66) for an AC double. Next door. **Ramgiri Hotel** is under the same management.

Khemi's Inn, 11 Town Centre, behind Hotel Ramgiri, Cidco, New Aurangabad 431003 (☎ 84868), is a pension with 10 rooms where you can get home-cooked meals and a double room, bath attached, with AC, for Rs 400 ($13.33) plus 10% service charge and 10% luxury tax. With meals (the American Plan), you'll pay Rs 750 ($25) single, Rs 900 ($30) double. A good, offbeat deal.

Getting its finishing touches, **The Meadows,** Mitmita, Ellora Cave Road, near Machindranath Temple, Aurangabad 431001 (☎ 82822), consists of 36 cottages furnished in teak and cane in small gardens, for Rs 800 ($26.66) double. Some have mountains views. This is a 13-acre resort with pool, miniature golf, kids playground, jogging path, and meditation center. It's out of town.

DOUBLES FOR LESS THAN RS 2,000

The following hotels are air-conditioned and offer such amenities and services as attached baths, room telephones, color TVs, and multichannel music; they accept international credit cards.

ITDC's **Aurangabad Ashok,** Dr. Rajendra Prasad Marg, Aurangabad 431001 (☎ 31428-27; fax 31328), is an airy, attractive place, with marble backed settees in the lobby, a coffee shop and restaurant, pool, and a garden where it's pleasant to sit out with tea or a beer and look over the tree-lined grounds. The hotel has 66 rooms renting for Rs 800 ($26.66) single, a possibility for two at Rs 1,100 ($26.66) double, with AC. Furnishings are motel-modern throughout.

The stained glass dome casts interesting patterns on the shiny, granite floors in the spacious, tailored lobby of the **Quality Inn Verdant,** Station Road Aurangabad (☎ 32570; fax 24746), where plants dot the stairs. The 100 rooms are clean and modern; doubles, for Rs 1,400 ($46.66), include a complimentary buffet breakfast in the coffee lounge. There are multicuisine and vegetarian restaurants, a swimming pool, health club, shopping arcade, and business center. Affiliated with the U.S. chain.

Hotel President Park, R 7/2, Airport Road (☎ 846013; fax 84823), has adapted local fortress architecture. The all-white hotel has its reception and lobby in a colonnaded, semicircular building seemingly guarding two 30-room, semicircular wings, with stylized, glass-topped turrets at either end. The tasteful rooms, with balconies or verandahs, ranging in price from Rs 900 ($30) to Rs 1,050 ($35), face a mammoth swimming pool and gardens. It's interesting, too, because this is a vegetarian hotel. Women and men have separate health clubs; there are also tennis courts and a souvenir shop.

Taking its inspiration from local monuments, the **Taj Residency,** 8/N/SIDCO (☎ 20411; fax 31223; in Bombay ☎ 203-3366), has constructed a pink building with onion-shaped domes, crenelated terraces, graceful archways, and 40 comfortable rooms—doubles Rs 1,150 ($38.33)—off of verandahs, arranged somewhat like cells at the famous caves. There is a brilliant red and purple lobby, a color scheme that carries through to a small bar. This is both hotel and training school for Taj Group Hotels. There are lovely gardens, a pool, and restaurant-cum-bar; conference rooms.

WORTH A SPLURGE

There are two splurge hotels within a stone's throw of the airport, catering mostly to package-tour groups. One is **Welcomgroup Rama International,** R-3 Chikalthana Rd., Aurangabad 431210 (☎ 85441 or 84768), with an elaborate, mirrored lobby ceiling reflecting the peach marble floors and boldly colored furnishings. Rooms area tailored and modern. Doubles are $69 to $89. There's a garden and pool. The restaurant has an interesting mural of the *Ramayana.*

Next door, on Jalna Road, CIDCO Road, **The Ambassador Ajanta** (☎ 82211; fax 84367), has expensive works of art placed everywhere, as in its flagship Ambassador Hotel in Bombay. Even the bathroom plumbing is all dressed up—swan figures are the faucets on the sinks; some need better maintenance. Doubles are Rs 1,750 ($58.33). **Diwan-e-Aam** restaurant, a swimming pool with sunken bar, shopping arcade, and tour groups.

WHERE TO EAT

All restaurants below are air-conditioned, unless otherwise mentioned.

There's are usually buffets at in the **Welcomgroup Rama International, Ambassador Ajanta;** and **Kailasa** in Hotel Amarpreet, Pt. J. Nehru Marg (☎ 23422), has themed buffets.

For vegetarian in swank surroundings, it's **President's Park** R7/2, Airport Road (☎ 846013).

Gupty's Woodlands, Akashay Deep Plaza, near CIDCO Bus Stand, Jalna Road (☎ 82822), is a bilevel vegetarian restaurant, with a garden ice-cream parlor and juice center, decorated with Disney characters. On the main floor, walls showcase paintings by local artists and there's an open kitchen. Here it's thalis only in three styles: South Indian, Gujarati, and Punjabi, for Rs 30 ($1). Upstairs, where the decor displays handicrafts and wood carvings, there is an extensive and imaginative à la carte menu: Try South Indian pizza; fried idli, spring roll dosa; and fresh gulab jamun for dessert. The highest price is around Rs 40 ($1.33). Hours are 8am to 11pm daily.

56 Bhog, B-1, Nirala Bazar, Samarthnagar (☎ 29955), has good South Indian and Punjabi dishes. Hours are 9am to 11pm. **Mingling Chinese Restaurant,** Khushal Nagar, Jalna Road (☎ 29999), also serves Indian and Continental dishes; live ghazals (songs).

For a cheap thali, try the **Youth Hostel.**

2 Ajanta & Ellora

There are times when you have to wait to gain entry to a cave and your stay in the cave will be limited to a relatively few minutes. Walking back along the escarpments after your visits, you will feel it has all been worthwhile. At each site, I've described a few key caves.

Remember to take plenty of small change with you when sightseeing at the caves. Even after you pay the Rs 5 lighting fee, guards keep popping up out of the shadows to ask for tips. At Daulatabad Fort, the guide/guard takes you through the dark passageways and he expects a tip. Chanters and singers who demonstrate the caves' acoustics also expect tips.

Government-approved guides can be hired at set rates through the India Tourist Office in Aurangabad. It's best to book your guide in advance, especially during peak times, or you can take a guided tour.

GETTING TO AJANTA & ELLORA FROM AURANGABAD

Taxi drivers in Aurangabad like to make package deals. They'll usually settle for Rs 200 ($6.66) for four hours/40 kilometers and Rs 400 ($13.33) for eight hours/80 kilometers. They'll probably want more for driving to the caves—Ajanta is 106 kilometers (66 miles) from the city, and Ellora is 30 kilometers (18 miles).

Auto rickshas are not supposed to go beyond 32 miles of Aurangabad.

There's frequent **bus** service from Aurangabad to Ellora and to Ajanta.

Car and driver to Ellora and return (5 hours) will cost Rs 400 ($13.33) non-AC, Rs 1,000 ($33.33) with AC; to Ajanta and back Rs 800 ($26.66) non-AC; Rs 2,600 ($86.66) with AC; to Ellora and around the city, Rs 450 ($15) to Rs 1,500 ($50); to both Ellora and Ajanta and back, Rs 1,200 ($40) to Rs 1,400 ($46.66).

GUIDED TOURS TO THE CAVES (FROM AURANGABAD)

MTDC's daily conducted Ajanta coach tour departs Aurangabad at 8am, returning at 5:30pm, for Rs 120 ($4). The Ellora Tour departs Aurangabad at 9:30am, returning at about 5:30pm, for Rs 85 ($2.83)—covering Daulatabad, Ghrishneshawar Temple, Ellora, Aurangzeb's Tomb, Bibi-ka-Maqbara, Panchakki. For information or reservations, contact MTDC's Tourist Reception Centre, Holiday Resort (for reservations call ☎ 31513 or 34259). Food is extra.

ITDC's tour to Ellora departs Aurangabad at 9:30am, returning at 5:30pm, on even-numbered dates, for Rs 80 ($2.66)—it covers Daulatabad, sightseeing at the caves, Khuldabad, Bibi-ka-Makbara, and Panchakki. Their Ajanta tour departs Aurangabad at 8:30am, returning at 6pm, on odd-numbered dates, for Rs 125 ($4.16). For information or reservations, contact: Hotel Aurangabad Ashok, Dr. Rajendra Prasad Marg (☎ 31143 or 31328). All tour fees include guide charges and entrance fees.

The **ITDC** also runs an Ajanta Tour for Rs 90 ($3), which takes off only if there are sufficient bookings. Reservations can be made at the Aurangabad Ashok Hotel, Dr. Rajendra Prasad Marg (☎ 24520), where you can also check timings.

AJANTA

66 miles (106 kilometers) from Aurangabad

About the Caves

A British army officer, on the trail of a panther in desolate country some miles from the village of Ajanta, stumbled onto the overgrown entrance to a deep cave—now Cave 10, and one of the oldest—and his discovery quickly became worldwide news. The year was 1819, and the caves, a series of subterranean Buddhist temples, had lain forgotten by civilization for the better part of a thousand years. The discovery ranks among the major archaeological finds of modern times, and it's ironic that the caves' longtime neglect is responsible for their preservation. Within years of their discovery, vandals had scratched their names across paintings that had survived intact for centuries. The Indian government eventually stepped in and took over their maintenance. Today they are one of the major tourist sights of the world.

There are 30 caves in all, carved out of a horseshoe-shaped cliff, itself surrounding a deep valley, which, with its little bridges, hillside-hugging pathways, scattered rocks, river, flowers, and elevated viewing pavilion, now looks like a giant-sized Japanese garden. From the far side of the valley it's possible to obtain an excellent perspective of the whole cave area. The most dramatic (but least popular) time to visit the caves is during the summer monsoons, roughly June through September, when waterfalls pouring from the cliff above provide the caves with a natural curtain and the foliage all around is lush and green. As it is, the best times are October to March. It's hot as blazes in April and May.

The caves, and their artworks, were not the product of one particular era but were created over a period of 800 or 900 years—from about 200 B.C. to about A.D. 650—and nothing is known about the monks and/or artisans who created them beyond the obvious fact that the Ajanta site was as remote in those days as it is today. The work, in other words, was that of an isolated religious order, executed through centuries of dedication.

The frescoes were prepared by first covering the rough surface of the rock with a layer of clay mixed with cow dung and rice husks. A coating of white lime plaster was added and then the outline of the drawings, filled in later with glowing colors made mostly from locally obtained vegetable and mineral ingredients. Few of the large murals have survived intact and some, indeed, look more like examples of abstract expressionism than meaningful pictures. What can be seen, though, is a mixed grab bag of myth and legend along with real life; of the latter there are elephant fights, singing and dancing, preparing food, buying and selling, and an occasional procession or court scene.

Seeing the Caves

Get an early start to try to beat the crowds. It's 106 kilometers (66 miles), almost a two-hour drive from Aurangabad; caves open at 9am. You might have to wait in line for a ticket. Hiring an approved guide from the **India Tourist Office** in Aurangabad—Rs 250 ($8.33) to Rs 350 ($11.66)—can be helpful for in-depth explanations. Hours for the caves are 9am to 5pm; entry is 50 paise; Rs 5 (17¢) for a light pass (if you want illumination at certain caves you show it to the guards). It's a steep walk up to the entrance. There are porters with chairs for those who need assistance. Flash photography, tripods, and special lighting are not permitted in the caves without permission from the Archaeological Survey of India in Bombay; contact: Supt. Archaeologist, Sion Fort, Bombay 400002 (☎ 4071102). Video cameras can be used on the exteriors for a Rs 25 (83¢) fee.

Cave 16

The first thing to remember—and to keep constantly in mind as you investigate these extraordinary works of art—is that each temple is carved out of what was once a solid mass of rock, without scaffolding, starting at the top and chiseling downward. The difficulties must have been monumental. Yet each figure is perfectly proportioned, and in some cases the carvings are as intricate as lace.

This is particularly awesome in the case of Cave 16, a Hindu temple known as Kailasa, which was supposedly built by King Krishna I in the 8th century after Lord Shiva, the destroyer of evil, flew over the rock and claimed it for his home. Three million cubic feet of rock were chiseled away before the complex of temple buildings, life-size elephants, and realistic sculptures were completed. The focal-point sculpture shows Ravana, the evil mythological king, being subdued by Shiva, who's crushing him underfoot. The cause for this forceful confrontation involved Ravana's desire to lift this incredible temple on his head and shake it.

Ten lifetimes is what it may have taken to create this temple. Nobody can accurately tell how long this massive creation was in the making, but archaeologists estimate at least seven to eight generations.

Incomparable Kailasa cannot be likened to ancient structures such as the Pyramids, no matter how astonishing the others are. It is aptly summed up in words of a well-known British historian as "the noblest Hindu memorial of ancient India."

Cave 10

The most interesting introduction to the Buddhist series of temples, which were created between A.D. 350 and 700, is Cave 10, which is known locally as **Vishwakarma** (Carpenter's Cave). Some of the carving, indeed, is deliberately designed to simulate wood. Even the angels, with their graceful legs, on the exterior do not prepare you for the surprise when you first step inside the cave. A high-ceilinged, navelike chamber, similar in style to a Christian church, it is dominated at the far end by an enormous 15-foot-high Buddha in the preaching pose. Fluted stone beams curving across the ceiling give the impression of an upturned ship skeleton. Outside, beside the stone lions, which were damaged when part of the overhanging roof collapsed in a landslide, are steps leading to an upper gallery from which one can clearly see the rows of carved Naga queens (who were believed to have brought the monsoons) and the galaxy of dwarfs who represented court entertainers. This cave was completed in the 7th century A.D.

Caves 11 & 12

These two caves, especially the latter, are interesting examples of three-story temples, which not only contained cells for the monks in residence, but were also used as hostels for visiting pilgrims. Cave 12 is the more interesting. The facade is austere, but inside are many handsome carvings. Each of the floors contains Buddhas, the top story boasting of two fine sets of seven Buddhas all in a row. Adherents of Buddhism believe that Buddha visits the earth every 5,000 years; thus, there have been seven visits so far in history (the next one is due about 2,500 years from now). This is the final Buddhist cave at Ellora.

Openings in the cave walls allow enough sunlight for superficial inspection (reflected sun from outside was probably enough light for the original artists); to supplement this, uniformed attendants, who spend the entire day amid trailing cables, endlessly flash high-powered lamps onto the highspots. No wonder they look bored! Each cave is usually occupied by several groups of tourists listening attentively, awestruck, to commentaries by their various guides, and a cacophony of explanatory shreds floats back and forth in a variety of languages. Small children, bored by the lectures, run between the feet of bald-headed transients with determined faces. The government of India has been for years underwriting an ambitious project to copy the cave paintings exactly as they are, and a group of artists sometimes can be seen working from miniature scaffolds reproducing the fragments in surprisingly accurate hues ("Windsor and Newton watercolors," one painter explained).

Although there are 30 caves altogether, some are less interesting than others. For those with limited time, therefore, the best plan is to concentrate on Caves 1, 2, 9, 10, 16, 17, 19, and 26, which are sumptuous enough for three score.

WHERE TO STAY & EAT

At the entrance: **Foodwalla's** restaurant has snacks, drinks—tea Rs 6 (20¢), meals, and clean bathrooms.

Not far from the caves, there's the very basic, clean **Holiday Resort** in Fardapur, with rooms for Rs 100 ($3.33) to Rs 125 ($4.16) daily. There's also a dorm for Rs 40 ($1.33) per head, with a shared bathroom. The cook will make Indian and Western food with two hours' notice. You must make a reservation in advance. The manager at the Holiday Resort is very nice, giving information and advice to travelers who are backpacking through and seeing to the comforts of the guests. For reservations, contact the Senior Executive, MTDC Regional Office, Station Road, Aurangabad 431001.

The **Forest Rest House** is a gray building that has been renovated; it has two clean suites and a dining hall. It's for officials in forestry, but if there's no one staying at the house, you can move in for a few rupees. The reservation authority is Divisional Forest Officer, Osmanpura, Aurangabad 431001. It's walking distance from the caves.

EN ROUTE TO ELLORA

It's a pretty rural trip with an interesting stop en route. Fourteen kilometers (9 miles) to the northwest of Aurangabad, on the road to Ellora, is one of the most impregnable castles in India, the **Daulatabad Fort.** Constructed in the 12th century by the Yadava dynasty's Bhilama Raja, and occupied by kings from the late 13th century, it's atop an isolated rocky hill with seven outer walls and an internal moat. The sheer rock cliff on which it is perched is so smooth and steep that, legend says, even a snake would slip off it.

The steep climb to the top won't seem so strenuous if you bear in mind the monumental trek associated with this town. In the 14th century, Daulatabad was the for about as long as it takes blink the capital of India. The sultan who transferred the seat of power from Delhi also decided the entire population should join him. A great many migrants hiked the many hundreds of arduous miles; some fell in, some died. By the time the survivors straggled in, the sultan had already regretted his decision. He ordered everyone to turn around and walk back.

The only access to the top of the fort, until recent times, was via a pitch-black internal tunnel that spiraled around the inside of the hill until it culminated in a narrow opening at the top, 640 feet above. In the old days, potential intruders would see a patch of light ahead and rush forward, only to be doused with boiling hot pitch or oil poured in by the defenders above.

There is no record that any attacker reached the top, although the fort was captured—as forts inevitably are—by siege. In fact, the slender pink **Chand Minar,** an elegant minaret 100 feet high that stands not far inside the spike-studded outer gates, was built by Allaudin Ahmed Shah Bahmani (1435–57) to celebrate such a victory.

Although the impressive Mughal pavilion and upper sections remain in good condition, many of the buildings just inside the fort's outer walls are now in ruins. Among them is the palace, in which the last ruler of another fort—Golconda, near Hyderabad—was kept captive until his death in the latter part of the 16th century.

Opposite the entrance to the fort, on the main road, are several refreshment stands, which serve beer and soft drinks. There are souvenir stalls nearby.

ELLORA

18 1/4 miles (29 1/2 km) from Aurangabad

About the Caves

There are 34 cave temples at Ellora—12 Buddhist, 17 Hindu, and five Jain, built in that order, probably from the 7th to the 13th centuries A.D.—and despite what you may have heard and read, you won't be prepared for what you will actually see. The caves are only 29 1/2 kilometers (18 miles) from Aurangabad, just off the main road, and unlike those at Ajanta, they have never been "lost"—even though for many centuries they were so disregarded that local villagers actually lived in some of them, building fires for cooking and heating that have pretty well wrecked what remained of the paintings on the ceilings. It would be almost impossible, however, to remove the carvings and sculptures with anything less than a bulldozer, and it is these that will impress you most.

The caves are 30 kilometers from Aurangabad. The best time to visit is afternoon when the caves catch the light. Special events include the **Ellora Festival,** held annually during the third week in March, which features classical music and dance against the backdrop of the caves.

Caves 14, 15 & 29

All are Hindu. Among the deities to see in Cave 14 are Vishnu, Lakshmi, and Shiva. In Cave 15, the second story shows reliefs of Shiva performing various deeds. Cave 29 echoes Elephanta on Bombay's bay, with massive proportions and three entrances. It shows Shiva as the Destroyer.

Caves 30 to 34

The Jain caves, nos. 30 to 34, are a little farther away and are devoted to Buddha's contemporary, Mahavira, who died about 700 B.C. Jain followers are more ascetic than their fellow Buddhists and don't believe in killing any living creatures, including mosquitoes. One statue displays Mahavira standing on an anthill (apparently not crushing the ants) and surrounded by a scorpion, a cobra, and two deer, all of which appear to be quite compatible. This is in Cave 32, the best of the Jain temples, built in the 12th century. From the outside it appears smaller and less elaborate than the earlier caves, but inside it is really quite impressive, with traces of color still to be seen on the walls and ceiling.

Nearby: Khuldabad

Moseying around Khuldabad, about 2 miles away, can be interesting. It's the burial place of Shah Jahan's son, Aurangzeb (1658–1707). The frugal Aurangzeb's grave is set near Safed Zaimudin, his guru. The Muslim saint's tomb is marked with a plain stone slab that has no inscription. In his will, Aurangzeb stipulated that four rupees and two annas he earned during his lifetime from sewing caps be used to buy his shroud. Another Rs 305 ($10.16 at today's rates) he earned copying the Koran was to be given to holy men.

Where to Stay & Eat

People rarely overnight at Ellora, but there are some basic accommodations should you care to stop. **Khuldabad Guest House** (☎ 41026) has 10 rooms, for Rs 75 ($2.50) per room, which includes bed linen. There's a cook in attendance. Preference is given to government officials, but if there is no party booked in you can stay. Write to: Executive Engineer, B&C, P.W.D., Padampura, Aurangabad. It's within walking distance to the caves.

Travellers Bungalow (☎ 25511) at Khuldabad, again humble, charges Rs 50 ($1.66) per room. There's a cook in attendance. For reservations, write to the Executive Engineer, Zila Parishad, Aurangabad. It's within walking distance of the Ellora Caves.

Hotel Kailash is also within walking distance of the caves. The 16 simple rooms with attached bathrooms—Rs 600 ($20) to Rs 700 ($23.33) with AC—are in bungalows. Meals are served in the adjoining restaurant. Reserve rooms by writing the manager. There's absolutely nothing to rave about except that the owner's nice; there's a pretty little garden to sit out on and the restaurant's food is tasty; expect to pay Rs 30 ($1) to Rs 40 ($1.33) for entrees.

3 Goa

Goa is something like a European picture framed against an Indian background. This is because the tiny state (pop. 1,168,622)—only slightly bigger than Rhode Island—was ruled for 450 years by the Portuguese. They pulled out in 1961 and left behind their calling cards in the form of distinctive churches, convents, customs, and converts to the Catholic church.

Goa today is the place to cop out on sightseeing, apart from a token inspection of the things that made it the first important Christian colony in the East, and to head instead for its golden beaches, to bask in the sun among an abundance of coconuts, bananas, and pineapples. Even as Goa's development as a new resort goes on at a fairly rapid pace, there's still plenty of old-world charm.

Back in the 15th century, Goa was the starting point for Indian pilgrims en route to Mecca. It was a bone of contention among the English, Dutch, and Portuguese, who were vying for its possession. The Portuguese, in the person of Alfonso de Albuquerque, won out in 1510; the bearded viceroy entered Old Goa, then the capital city, after a triumphant procession up the Mandovi River with 1,200 men in 20 ships.

This was the beginning of Goa's glory as a rich trading center—spices from Malaya, coral and pearls from Persia, Chinese porcelain and silk. St. Francis of Xavier, on an evangelical mission, arrived, as did Garcia da Orta, the famed botanist who is reputed to have introduced Indian and Eastern herbs into Western pharmacology, and the epic poet Lus de Camoes, who dedicated some of his noblest lyrics to an Indian slave girl.

Then Goa's decline began. The Inquisition was set up in the late 16th century—a grim reflection of the religious fanaticism that was sweeping Europe. Hundreds of innocent victims were tortured and killed on charges of paganism during a 250-year reign of terror. Then came an even worse terror—a disastrous plague in 1635 wiped out 200,000 people. Still the city went on and the religious inquisitions continued until 1812. In 1834 the seat of power moved 6 miles downriver to Panaji, and a year later Old Goa was abandoned altogether.

But Portugal's days of glory in India were coming to a close. Time and again they found themselves in skirmishes not only with rival powers (the Dutch, Spanish, and English) but with the Goans themselves, who were becoming increasingly discontented with colonial rule. Despite the way the bazaars bulged with imported merchandise, the economy was hollow. There was no shortage of the most expensive foreign cars available—but hardly a decent road on which to drive them.

Just before the Portuguese were forced out, some drastic changes at last took place: Rich deposits of manganese and iron ore were discovered and the mining and export of these became Goa's chief industry. Since then, industrial development has blossomed, with dozens of small plants set up: rice and flour mills, cashew nut and soap factories, tile and brick plants. The main port for all this activity is Marmagoa, on a peninsula jutting into the Arabian Sea south of Dona Paula Bay. It is much more likely, however, that as a tourist you'll head for Panaji, the capital, almost at the mouth of the Mandovi River and at the northern side of Dona Paula Bay, or to a gorgeous beach away from the bustle.

ESSENTIALS

GETTING TO GOA

BY PLANE Goa is a 50-minute flight from Bombay, 2½ hours from Delhi; flights also operate from Bangalore, Madras, Cochin, Trivandrum, Pune, and Ahmedabad.

Airlines serving Goa are **Indian Airlines** (☎ Panaji 223826; airport, 0834-512781); **Damania Airways** (☎ 222791); **East West Airlines** (☎ 226291); **Modiluft** (☎ 224424).

From the Airport: Going or coming, the **KTC Bus** from Dabolim, an 80-minute drive to or from Panaji, costs Rs 25 (83¢). Starred hotels pick up guests. **Yellow-top taxis** are available through Traffic Police, who make sure you get the right rate—around Rs 5.50 (18¢) per kilometers each way. **Tourist taxis** also available at the hotels and main cities to the airport.

BY TRAIN Trains connect from Bangalore, Rs 487 ($16.23) First, Rs 159 ($5.30) Second; Bombay, Rs 541 ($18.03), Rs 165 ($5.50); Delhi, Rs 1,104 ($36.80), Rs 308 ($10.26); Mysore, Rs 487 ($16.23), Rs 159 ($5.30); Pune, Rs 430 ($14.33), Rs 143 ($4.76); Secunderabad, Rs 553 ($18.43), Rs 188 ($6.26); and Tirupati, Rs 553 ($18.43), Rs 188 ($6.26).

Vasco da Gama, 35 kilometers from Panjai, is the major rail terminal; another station is **Margao,** about 40 kilometers from Panjai. From October 1996, the new Konkan Railways Corporation from Mangalore will operate through Goa opening new areas.

Booking/inquiry offices: Panjai KTC Terminal (☎ 225620); Margao Railway Station (☎ 222252); Vasco Railway Station (☎ 512620). Hours are 9:30am to 1pm, 2:30 to 5pm.

BY BUS Goa Government's Kadamba Transport Corporation operates bus services on interstate roads to and from: Bangalore, Rs 170 ($5.66) luxury; Bombay, Rs 270 ($9) AC coach, Rs 221 ($7.36) luxury; Mangalore, Rs 105 ($3.50) luxury; Pune, Rs 178 ($5.93) luxury. The **Maharashtra and Karnataka State Road Transport Corporations** also operate buses on these routes in their respective states to Goa, and so do private lines. Bookings can be made seven days in advance.

BY SHIP Steamer service has been discontinued; Catamaran service (similar to a Hovercraft), departs Bombay at 5:30am, arrives Panaji at 1pm; departs 3pm, arrives Bombay 10:30pm. The fare is Rs 900 ($30) to Rs 1,100 ($36.66). For information, contact the Damania Shipping Service, Fisheries Bldg., Panaji (☎ 228711).

Visitor Information

The **Government of India Tourist Office** is located in the Communidade Building, Church Square, Panaji (☎ 223412). Also try the **Government of Goa, Directorate of Tourism,** Tourist Home, Pato Bridge, Panaji (☎ 225583).

You'll also find tourist information counters at the Interstate Bus Terminus, Panaji (☎ 225620); Britona Tourist Complex Britona (Betim); Tourist Hotel Margao (☎ 222620); Tourist Hotel, Vasco (☎ (☎ 512673); and Dabolim Airport, 512644.

Each of these offices are extremely helpful and fine resources. *The Goa Guide,* a local publication—Rs 30 ($1)—has a wealth of information for the tourist. Particularly appealing are such off-beat essays on "The Goan Fish Fantasy."

Getting Around

The most enjoyable way to get from place to place is on ferries which cross the rivers of Goa. Ferries for passengers only operate **between Dona Paula and Mormugao,** at regular intervals, from September to May (fair weather only). There are crossings all day long; there can be long between ferries at certain hours. Take along a snack, some bottled water, and hat for protection from the sun and something to read during the delay. The trip takes 30 to 45 minutes and costs Rs 5 (17¢) to Rs 7 (23¢).

The following ferries carry both passengers and vehicles and operate about every 10 minutes from 7am to 11pm, but double-check the timings and frequency. Buses also meet these ferries:

- Aldona-Corjuem
- Amona-Khandola
- Aronda-Kiranpani
- Assolna-Cavelossim
- Carona-Calvin
- Cortalim-Marcaim
- Keri-Therehol (Tirakol)
- Naroa-Diver
- Old Goa–Divar/Piedade
- Panaji-Betim (24 hours)
- Panaji (Pato)-Malim
- Pomburpa-Chorao
- Raia-Shiroda
- Ribandar-Chorao
- Sarmanos-Tonca
- Savoi–Verem Tishem Kothambi
- Siolam-Chopdem
- Vanixm-Itagam (Divar)
- Vanixam-Old Goa
- Volvoi-Surla-Maina

Yellow-top taxi should charge about Rs 5.50 (18¢) for the first kilometer and Rs 5 (16¢) per kilometer thereafter. Bargain to set a fare rate. These taxis do not cross state lines.

Auto rickshas, near the Azad Maidan and elsewhere, charge Rs 6 (20¢) for the first kilometer and Rs 3.20 (11¢) for each kilometer thereafter, plus package and luggage fees.

Both yellow-top and auto rickshas have these additional charges: Return journey for trips beyond the municipal limit is 50% of normal fare; luggage is Rs 1 per package; detention: taxis, Rs 12 (40¢) per hour, rickshas, Rs 6 (20¢) per hour or Rs 2 (7¢) per 10 minutes, respectively.

Tourist taxis will be found near the major hotels. Agree to a price before getting in. You should be able to negotiate the use of a tourist taxi for eight hours for Rs 500 (16.66) and an additional Rs 5 (16¢) for every kilometer over 100; after eight hours, waiting time is Rs 20 (33¢) per hour. To phone a tourist taxi call the **Tourist Hotel** (☎ 227103).

Ambassador **cars with drivers,** non-AC, cost Rs 5 (16¢) per kilometer for eight hours, with a detention charge of Rs 15 (50¢) within Goa; for night halts at outstations, add Rs 80 ($2.66) per night. A Datsun with AC should cost Rs 10 (33¢) per kilometer for eight hours, with a dentation charge of Rs 15 (50¢); night halt charges of Rs 80 ($2.66). These rates are from the **GTDC's Travel Division,** Trionara Apartments, Panaji (☎ 226515).

Motorcycle taxis (means hopping a ride with a cycler, and very dangerous; helmets are not generally worn) cost about Rs 3 (9¢) for the first kilometer and Rs 1 (3¢) per additional kilometer or part thereof. You can tell motorcycle taxis from the others by their yellow mudguards. It's illegal to rent a motorcycle, even if you have a valid license, but lots of people do it—if the price is right. Just ask at any cafe, and someone will probably help you locate a cycle-renter. Expect to pay Rs 75 ($2.50) to Rs 200 ($6.66) per day. You get it with a full tank of gas and must bring it back with a full tank. Your passport is your security deposit.

In **Share taxis** (get them near ferry wharves, bus stands, marketplaces), you pay per seat, five passengers to a car. For example, from Panaji it's Rs 10 (33¢) to Mapusa and vice versa; from Colva to Margao, Rs 10 (33¢) to Rs 15 (50¢).

Bicycles can be rented in town and at the popular beaches for Rs 25 (83¢) to Rs 50 ($1.66) per day.

There is frequent **bus** service from Panaji to every place in Goa. Here are some routes that are important to tourists:

- From Panaji to Old Goa, the service is every 10 minutes; the trip takes about 30 minutes. The Ponda bus also goes to Old Goa.
- To Miramar Beach take the Dona Paula bus from Panaji.
- To get a bus going anywhere in North Goa, take the ferry from Panaji to Betim, where you'll make connections.
- The bus to Calangute/Baga takes about 45 minutes; the first stop is Calangute.
- From Panaji to Mapusa is about a 30-minute trip. Some buses to Chapora Village (near Vagator Beach) also go through Mapusa. Remember that locally it's "Mapsa"—that's what to ask for and what the driver will announce.
- Buses also go to Margao, Vasco da Gama, and throughout Goa.

Bus drivers announce their destinations. They pull out when full and, as elsewhere in India, are usually very crowded. You can get buses at the Kadamba bus terminal in Panaji to all Goan towns.

When to Visit

December to mid-January is very popular and most expensive. This period coincides with three major festivals: the **Feast of St. Francis Xavier** (December 3), **Christmas,** and **Reis Magos** (Feast of the Three Kings) on January 6. Unless you've booked in advance, it's almost impossible to find accommodations in Panaji. In February/March, the uninhibited antics at the four-day, pre-Lenten **carnival** also draw crowds. Festivals are plentiful, so whenever you arrive you're apt to find some celebration. Many budget travelers celebrate the monsoon season, when the rain falls and so do tariffs.

Every 10 years Goa's most important festival is celebrated when the remains of St. Francis are displayed and huge numbers of pious the world over come to bear witness. A grand procession opens and closes the exposition. It will be held next in late November 2004 to mid-January 2005. Reservations must be booked far in advance. If you arrive without them, well, there's always a beach to stretch out on.

FINDING ACCOMMODATIONS

Things have gotten pretty touristy over the past few years in some parts of Goa, what with the publicity given the beaches and the promotion of package tours. Happily, however, this beach-studded seacoast state remains relatively unspoiled.

The good life also comes fairly cheap in Goa. Some of the more extravagant resorts aside, you can still get by well within this book's budget, especially if there are two of you. You also will find a number of Goa's hoteliers willing to bargain, particularly in the off-season.

Most hotels require one day's tariff as a deposit when you book your room, and a number levy cancellation charges up to 50%. You'll want to make sure of the policy when making reservations. Then there are luxury taxes: 5% on rates up to Rs 500 ($16.66); 10% on per day on rates from Rs 501 to Rs 800 ($26.66); and 15% on rates above Rs 801; expenditure tax adds another 10% in high-priced hotels.

WHAT TO EAT

Goa's distinctive dishes are quite tasty, often using superb seafood in complicated preparations. You'll want to try such local specialties as vindaloos (sharply spiced prawns, meat, or chicken and vegetables marinated in a vinaigrette before cooking); sanna (rice cakes steeped in toddy); foogaths (vegetables simmered with coconut and spices); buffads (stewed meat and vegetables); and bebinca (seven-layer cake). Goans also make some delicious sausages similar to those in the West. If you crave something with a kick, try sip feni, made from cashews and coconut—powerful stuff. The local wine is a bit on the sweet side with meals, even when dry, but goes nicely with a sweet. Beer is good with spicy Goan dishes. Whisky prices are somewhat less than in other tourist centers in India—provided you stick to domestic brands.

PANAJI (PANJIM)

WHAT TO SEE & DO

In Panaji, the capital, the most historic building is the **Secretariat,** once a Muslim Palace, then a Portuguese fort. Nearby, look for the strange **statue of Abbe Faria,** a priest, hypnotizing a woman. Climb the steps of the marble church, **Our Lady of Pilar,** for a panoramic view of the surrounding countryside. And be sure to see the sunset from **Dona Paula,** at the tip of the peninsula; you'll get a fine view of Vasco da Gama across the Marmagoa Harbor.

The **Handicrafts Emporium** in the Tourist Hotel will give you an overall knowledge of local prices that will serve you well when you pay a visit (Friday) to the renowned weekly **market at Mapusa** and the various shops in town and at the beaches.

Near Indian Airlines is the 160-year-old **Medical College Hospital,** said to be the oldest medical institute in Asia. And next to police headquarters is **Menzes Braganza Hall,** with an entryway done in tiles and paintings depicting scenes from a Portuguese poet's epic about Vasco da Gama's stormy voyage from Portugal to India.

The nearest beaches to Panaji are **Gaspar Dias** (also called Miramar and said to be polluted) and **Dona Paula,** both southwest of the city (See "Resorts Near Panaji," below). As near as they are, they're rarely overcrowded. They're only five to 10 minutes away, so another thing to do is go to a nearby beach. (Farther afield are the splendid beaches of **Calangute,** to the north, and **Colva,** to the south, described later in this chapter.)

You might also want to visit the **Archives Museum,** Ashirvad Building, First Floor, Santa Inez, Panaji, which is open from 9:30am to 1pm, 2pm to 5:30pm, Monday to Friday.

Tours from Panaji

GTDC's conducted tours offer a good way to see the main sights in Goa. They can be booked at the Tourist Hotels in Panaji and other cities throughout Goa. Advance booking is necessary in season. Tours depart from the Tourist Hotel in Panaji.

- **North Goa Tour** Altinho Hillock, Mayem Lake, Shri Datta Temple, Shri Vithal Temple, Mapusa, the Vagator, Anjuna, Calangute beaches, and Aguada Fort. Departs 9:30am; returns 6:30pm. Cost: Rs 40 ($1.33), Rs 60 ($2) with AC.
- **South Goa Tour** Old Goa, Shri Manguesh, Shri Shantadurga, Margao, Colva Beach, Mormugao Harbor, Pilar Monetary, and Dona Paula and Miramar beaches. Departs 9:30am; returns 6pm. Cost: Rs 60 ($2), Rs 80 ($2.66) AC.
- **Pilgrim Special** Old Goa churches; Shri Manguesh, Shri Ramnathi, and Shri Shantadurga Temples. Departs 9:30am; returns 1pm. Cost: Rs 50 ($1.66).
- **Beach Special** Calangute, Anjuna, and Vagator beaches. Departs 3pm; returns 7pm. Cost: Rs 50 (1.66¢).
- **Holiday Special** Bondla Sanctuary and Tambidi Surla, a famous temple not far from Molem Wildlife Sanctuary. Departs 9:30am, returns 6pm. Cost Rs 60 ($2).
- **Island Special** Old Goa churches, Divar Island, Sri Saptakoteshwar Temple, Mayem Lake, bird sanctuary at Chorao. Departs 9:30am; returns 6pm. Cost Rs 70 ($2.33).
- **Dudhsagar Special** The awesome Dudhsagar Waterfalls, with sightseeing along the way. Departs 10am; returns 6pm next day. Cost Rs 300 ($10). You take the train back to Panaji.
- **River Cruises** One-hour Sunset Cruise at 4pm; cost Rs 55 ($1.83); one-hour Sundown Cruise at 7:15pm; cost Rs 55 ($1.83); two-hour Full Moon Cruise, Rs 100 ($3.33). Sometimes live entertainment accompanies the boats. GTDC also operates a couple of two- to three-hour day cruises for Rs 100 ($3.33). All cruises depart from the jetty opposite the passport office.

Emerald Waters, a private company, 5th Floor, Nizari Bhavan, Menezes Braganza Road, Panaji (☎ 46960 or 46967), or The Boat Center, opposite Hotel Mandovi (☎ 42739), conducts river cruises every day from 5:30 onwards: **Sunset, Sundown, Goa by Night, Late Night Show.** Each cruise costs Rs 60 ($2), with folk dancers and band. Emerald also cruises to **Old Goa** on Monday, Wednesday, Thursday, and Saturday. The cost is Rs 150 ($5). A **Scenic Backwaters** cruise leaves on Tuesday; departs 10am, returns 4pm; lunch and beer served. Cost: Rs 500 ($16.66) with lunch. An **Exotic Grande Island Adventure** departs Sunday at 10am, returns 4pm; lunch and beer served. Cost Rs 600 ($20).

Trekking

There are some beautiful trails through forest areas, and treks through them are organized frequently in December and January. For more information, contact the **Hiking Association of Goa,** Daman Dui, c/o Capt. A. Rebello (president), Captain of Ports Office, Government of Goa, Panaji (☎ 45070).

Shopping

You'll find **Goa Handicrafts Rural and Small Scale Industries Development Corporation Ltd.** emporia in the Tourist Hotels at Panaji, Margao, Vasco, and Mapusa, and the Interstate Bus Terminus in Panaji. Some other states have emporiums in Panaji, and there are many boutiques—trendy and traditional, such as **Kashmir Fair** outside the Taj Holiday Village, or **Sinquerim-Bardez,** specializing in high-quality Kashmiri merchandise. Prices tend to be high since much of the merchandise on sale is imported from Bombay. Cashews are an excellent buy.

For markets of note see Anjuna and Mapusa.

Where To Stay

Some people head for a beach as soon as they get to Goa. Others prefer to stay in Panaji (Panjim) a few days at least, before getting away from the madding crowd. So, first, a few hotel choices in Panaji. Unless otherwise indicated, they are air-conditioned, with all amenities: attached bathrooms, color TV, telephones, etc. To a Goan, balconies are as much a part of life as sun and sea, so quite pleasantly, hoteliers share this with visitors by putting balconies on all kinds of hotel rooms.

Generally, rates are highest from December 15 to January 15; they are the lowest from July to September, but this can vary somewhat. Some hotels have peak, high, and regular monsoon rates.

Doubles for Less Than Rs 100 ($3.33)

Lowest-budget accommodations in Panaji are too grungy for my minimal standards. Typical is **Safari Lodge,** opposite the Municipal Gardens (☎ 6475), a dreary, unkempt place, where rooms cost Rs 40 ($1.33) to Rs 95 ($3.16), without attached bathrooms. You'll have no trouble finding others of this type on the streets around the General Post Office.

Some families take in paying guests, presenting perhaps more attractive possibilities. The best way to shop for a low-budget room or any price category is with the Directorate of Tourism's *Accommodation* booklet in hand. Pick up a copy at the India Tourist Office or Government of Goa Tourist Information (see "Visitor Information," above).

Doubles for Less Than Rs 500 ($16.66)

On Dr. Dada Vaidya Road, the **Mayfair** and **Mayfair Deluxe (Rohma) Hotels,** near Mahalaxmi Temple, Panaji 403001 (☎ 225772), have an old Portuguese look with their wrought-iron balconies and tiled roofs. In the lobby a cheerful tile mural in coloring-box colors shows women with baskets on their heads. This is a simple place with concrete floors, small rooms, and several different rates depending on the season and whether you stay in the Mayfair or Rohma building. In the high season AC doubles cost from Rs 310 ($10.33) to Rs 390 ($13), deluxe doubles Rs 460 ($15.33); off-season rates are lower. There's a 10% service charge. Bar and restaurant.

At the **Hotel Neptune,** Malaca Road, Panaji 403001 (☎ 2247747), the warmth and enthusiasm of the management makes up for the lack of decor. True, some rooms need a little tender loving care, and a paint job would do no harm, but for the money this is a good deal. Rates range from Rs 175 ($5.83) non-AC to Rs 275 ($9.16) double-deluxe AC. Hot water is available from 7 to 9am. There's a small restaurant. One day's tariff must be paid in advance; there's a 50% charge if you cancel with less than three days notice.

Vistar Hotel, Dr. Shirgaokar Road, Panaji 403001 (☎ 45411), is almost always booked to overflowing, and the wear and tear shows throughout. The low rates are the main reason it's busy and why I'm recommending it. A double, non-AC is Rs 210 ($7); deluxe AC Rs 350 ($11.66). All rooms have bathrooms attached.

A block from the riverfront on Campal is the appropriately named **Hotel Campal,** Panaji 403001 (☎ 224532), a big old mansion set in a spacious garden and topped by a roof garden, which is promoted by the hotel as "the longest in Panjim." AC doubles are about Rs 450 ($15).

Doubles for Less Than Rs 1,000 ($33.33)

Hotel Nova Goa (formerly Golden and Nova Hotels), Dr. Atmaram Borkar Road, Panaji (☎ 226231/29) is possibly the best buy in town. This hotel's 85 rooms are clean and cheerfully decorated, with cream walls, cane-backed furniture, and printed spreads and drapes. Doubles range from Rs 750 ($25) to Rs 1,000 ($33.33), depending on the season. Swimming pool. The hotel's restaurant get high marks, too.

Hotel Park Plaza, Azad Maidan, Panjim, Goa 403001 (☎ 222601; fax 225635), has 37 rooms (some non-AC), fairly clean, with modern furniture and everything you need for a comfortable stay. Rates range from Rs 750 ($25) to Rs 1000 ($33.33), twin AC, with a 20% discount from June 15 to September 15. Higher rates January 1–15.

Keni's Hotel, 18th June Road, Panaji 403001 (☎ 224581), has a lobby bar overlooking a garden. The 38 rooms (some non-AC) are neat, containing spartan but adequate furnishings, and each has a pretty, patterned-tile bathroom. Non-AC rates are Rs 250 ($8.33) single, Rs 300 ($10) double; Rs 500 ($16.66) AC double; Rs 550 ($18.33) deluxe. Special rates from July 1 to September 15.

Doubles for Less Than Rs 2,000 ($66.66)

An old favorite in Panaji (and a good buy) is the **Hotel Mandovi,** P.O. Box 164, Panaji 403001 (☎ 224405; fax 225451), a white 1930s structure, with balconies on rooms overlooking the river. Room rates range from Rs 1,500 ($50) for a double with a river view; Rs 1,000 ($33.33) for a double with a city view. There's a 10% service charge. Though renovated, the hotel retains its gracious, Old World charm. A pleasant outdoor bar is a good place to stop for refreshment even if you don't stay here. The **Riorico** restaurant is popular for dinner (see "Where to Eat," below) Two epicurean landmarks have branches in this hotel: **A Pastelaria,** a famous bakery, and **Goenchin,** the well-known Chinese restaurant. Off-season discounts, February to September.

Though pleasantly decorated with antique reproductions and spacious, the rooms at **Hotel Fidalgo,** 18th June Road, Panaji 403001 (☎ 226291/9), are not well maintained. Doubles are about Rs 1,000 ($33.33). There's a pool. **Machila** restaurant re-creates old Goa in decor, but its menu is Continental, Chinese, and Indian, with only few Goan dishes.

Government Accommodations

There's only one thing wrong with the GTDC's **Tourist Hotel** in the center of Panaji (☎ 227103 or 223396): It's almost always fully booked. But if you write two or three months in advance, you might get into this pleasant, low-priced place. All 40 rooms are simply furnished with private bathrooms and balconies to catch the refreshing breezes. Some rooms have triple refreshment with river views, breezes, and AC (the restaurant. too, has AC). Rates in season (October 4 to June 15) are Rs 250 ($8.33) to Rs 370 ($12.33) with AC.

In Panaji, the GTDC also runs the **Patto Tourist Home** (☎ 45715), where you can get a double for Rs 200 ($6.66) non-AC. For reservations, write two to three months in advance to the Travel Division, Goa Tourism Development Corporation Ltd., Trionora Apartments, Panaji 403001, Goa (☎ 226515; fax 223926).

Other GTDC hotels are in **Margao** (☎ 221966); **Vasco da Gama** (☎ 513119); and **Mapusa** (☎ 262794). There are GTDC cottages at **Colva** (☎ 22287), Farmagudi (Hill Resort) (☎ 312922); and resorts at **Mayem Lake** (☎ 2144) and **Molem** (☎ 5238)—all with similar rates. GTDC's has a Tourist Resort at **Calangute** (☎ 276024) and a Rest House at **Terekhol** (☎ 5238). Some of these are covered in detail later.

Where to Eat

Gracious service, good food, and wonderful deco atmosphere are a winning combination at **Riorico** restaurant in the Mandovi. Enjoy a drink on the terrace while waiting for your food. Expect to spend about Rs 500 ($16.66) for two, including wine, beer and tip. Also in the hotel, are **Goenchin,** pastry shops, and **High Tidebar,** a great gathering place for Goans.

For Indian Food, try one of the following three places. **Delhi Darbar,** M. G. Road (☎ 222544), a branch of the Bombay restaurant, concentrates on Mughali styles, among them lamb and chicken dishes, in the Rs 55 ($1.83) to Rs 60 ($2) range, and makes terrific tandooris in the Rs 35 ($1.16) to Rs 55 ($1.83) range. Try veg tandooris for a change. Skip the Chinese, which you can have elsewhere. Hours are 11am to 3pm, 6:30 to 11pm.

Sher-e-Punjabi, 18th June Road, features Punjabi and Mughali dishes. For inexpensive Indian veg, try **Kamat,** at the top of Municipal Gardens.

For Chinese, here are a few choices: **Goenkar,** near police headquarters, is bileveled and immensely popular. It's dressier downstairs, where the decor relies heavily on mirrors. There are tasty Goan fish specialties as well as a wide range of Indian dishes for Rs 25 (83¢) and up. There are fish and vegetarian thalis. Upstairs, in the simpler **Small Goenkar,** everything's a bit cheaper. Open from 12:30 to 10:30pm every day (also try the Mandovi's **Goenchin**).

A good cafe is **Hospedaria Venite,** Rua 31 de Janeiro, near the Tourist Hotel, one flight up off the street. A cozy place with a thrift-shop-chic decor combining old cane-backed chairs, wooden tables, antique spoons, and shell collages, it's a refuge for many tourists. They'll drop in regularly to sip coffee, write postcards, and check out the crowd. The menu changes daily and features Portuguese and Goan specialties, as well as Indian and Continental fare in the Rs 25 (83¢) to Rs 30 ($1) range. Two rooms upstairs are for rent.

A Pastelaria, Dr. Dada Vaidya Road, has delicious pastries and snacks; it also has a take-out counter at the Mandovi; try **Eurasia,** Dr. Dada Vaidya, for pizzas.

Choices out of town: Worth the 4-kilometer (2½-mile) trip from Panaji (or combined with a visit to Mapusa) is **O Coqueiro,** Alto Porvorim (☎ 2177221 or 217344), one of Goa's most popular and famous restaurants, for good Goan cooking. The decor is heavily into coconuts. Try the chicken carfrail (ginger, chiles, garlic) for around Rs 70 ($2.33), a restaurant specialty. The restaurant also has Goan sausages and a large seafood selection in the Rs 35 ($1.16) to Rs 50 ($1.66) price range. Open every day from 11am to 3pm and 6 to 11pm. The owner is often on hand to assist and make suggestions. Another choice in Porvorim is **Village Nook,** a simple outdoor eatery.

Panaji After Dark

Bars

Bars are lively and less forbidding than in some other parts of India. You might feel transported to some coastal Mediterranean town.

Cultural Shows

Many festivals showcase the Goan culture are sponsored by the **Kala Academy,** Campal, Panjim. The academy holds a Pop, Beat, and Jazz Music Festival in May and other local events. The Teatro Festival in November, promotes folk dances and drama of Goa.

Excursions from Panaji

Old Goa

If you make only one sightseeing trip during your stay, go to Old Goa, 10 kilometers from Panaji. You can bus from Panaji or take a **yellow-top taxi**—supposedly Rs 5.50 (18¢) per kilometer, but you can probably negotiate with the driver for a flat, round-trip rate. You can also take a guided tour (see that section under "What to See and Do," above). During some of the major Goan festivals, boats cruise from Panaji to Old Goa, where you'll dock and enter, as did the viceroys of old, through the grand **Viceregal Arch.** The arch is only one of the highlights of Old Goa.

The **Bom Jesus Basilica,** dating from the 16th century, is where the remains of St. Francis are interred—less the two toes that were reputedly stolen by fanatics and an arm that was sent to an early pope on special request. The upper portion of the shrine depicts scenes from the saint's life in varicolored marble, and more scenes are carved on the bronze covering of the elaborate three-tiered marble and silver monument and casket. Adjoining is a small museum containing sacred relics. The last exposition of the relics was November 21 to January 7, 1995.

Across the square from the basilica is the huge **Cathedral of St. Catherine** (also called the *Se,* which is Portuguese for "cathedral") with its high-vaulted ceiling, spanning and covering numerous small chapels; in one of the chapels stands a cross that carries local fame because a vision of Christ is said to have been seen on it in 1919. There are 14 magnificent altars dedicated to the saint. The cathedral was built on a battlefield.

Also of interest are the **St. Francis of Assisi Church and Convent,** its porch retained from the original Muslim structure; an adjoining museum with archaeological artifacts and portraits of former governors; and **St. Cajetan Church,** where the Portuguese archbishops and viceroys were entombed. The area in front, calm and lovely now, was once the site of ugly inquisition trials. Also **St. Monica's Convent,** with enough of the original structure and murals intact to show how the nuns lived. On a small hill above the basilica, **Monte Sante,** are the ruins of **St. Paul's College** and two other churches.

Nearby Temples

About 12 miles from Panaji are eight Hindu temples, constructed here after the Portuguese destroyed the ones in the coastal region. Finest is the **Manguesh Temple,** with a lovely tower, tank, and residential quarters for pilgrims, and lots of kids to pester tourists.

Resort Towns near Panaji

Miramar

Closest to Panaji, Miramar has a few resort hotels, which have become down at the heels. **Hotel Goa International,** Jonca Miramar (☎ 223716), more a business-style hotel than a resort, has 27 clean, simple rooms with balconies, baths attached. There are restaurants, and it is within walking distance from the beach. Expect to pay around Rs 300 ($10) for a double.

Dona Paula

Dona Paula, 7 kilometers (4 miles) south of Panaji, is a peaceful place and a favorite with picnicking families. It has a view of the Zuari Estuary and Marmugoa Harbor, which can be admired from the broad promenade while you shop the souvenir sellers' stalls. Here are some hotels at Dona Paula for your consideration:

The charming **Prainha Cottages,** Dona Paula (☎ 224126), has AC doubles for Rs 750 ($25) to Rs 850 ($28.33); non-AC rooms go for as low as Rs 600 ($20). Simply furnished, the rooms contain all the essentials for a comfortable beach stay. Candlelight dinners of home-cooked Goan foods and serenades by singers in the Portuguese fado style keep guests well-fed and entertained.

The imaginative **Cidade de Goa,** Curta, Vainguinim Beach, Dona Paula, Goa 403111 (☎ 3301), takes its inspiration from a medieval Portuguese city and is built on levels to blend with the terrain. There are 201 rooms. The older wing, furnished simply and tastefully in a way that recalls old Goan styles, is where you want to be. The characterless rooms in the new wing (built to handle charters) recall U.S. motel modern. Rates range from Rs 120 ($4) to Rs 275 ($9.16), depending on the season. The hotel's shops jut in and out of little streets within the hotel, as in an old Latin town. There are two swimming pools—one fresh, one salt water—a private beach, tennis court, putting greens, and many open patios and plazas.

Eating in Dona Paula & Miramar

Cidade de Goa, Dona Paula, offers several amusing possibilities: **Saturday Night Buffet Barbecue** features hot food and entertainment: belly dancers, limbo, and a live band. Figure on Rs 600 ($20), the **poolside buffet** costs Rs 325 ($10.83) per person; at splurgey **Alfama,** serving high-class Indian, Portuguese, and French cuisines, figure on Rs 500 ($16.66) to Rs 600 ($20); and **Dekhni,** with authentic Goan cuisine, also has folk music, Rs 250 ($8.33) per person; there is a live band every evening. Reservations for all are a must (☎ 221133). The resort attracts groups.

For cheap fast foods try **Foodland** in Miramar.

Bambolim

Located 8 kilometers from Panaji and tucked in a palm grove, **Bambolim Resort,** Nunes Beach (☎ 464947; fax 46499), has 52 neat, double rooms, in six blocks spread over palm-studded grounds, with lovely sea views. The rate is Rs 1,500 ($50), including breakfast. Tranquility is a plus here: no cafes or guest houses, shops nearby. Taxis go to town. The **Green Valley Retreat** restaurant is set around an elegant old banyan tree; there's also a beach restaurant. Efficient and pleasant service. Swimming pool.

THE FAMOUS GOAN BEACHES

BEACH BACKGROUND In the 1960s, and well into the '70s, Goa's beaches were the number-one circus in the East. Hippies freaking out all over the place were a sightseeing attraction on the package tours, and the press frequently wrote about their antics.

The maddest part of this carnival took place at Christmas, when hordes of hippies turned Calangute into a discotheque, head shop, and skin show with revelries to rival India's most revealing temple friezes. As conventional holiday-goers moved in, Calangute's hippies tripped on to popularize the more remote beaches. There are still many hard-core hippie dropouts in Goa, but they're not as highly visible now.

They've shifted their base to Anjuna, where they crash in the fishermen's' huts for a few rupees a day.

CHOOSING A BEACH Each Goan beach has a distinct personality, so check them out first to see which suits you before settling down: Of the beaches north of Panaji, **Calangute** is the most touristy, with a number of little hotels and restaurants. Also north, **Baga, Anjuna, Vagator,** and **Chapora** have less development. The southeast coast beach, **Benaulim,** near Margao, attracts a young German crowd, and beautiful **Colva** sports a number of large beach resorts, aimed at charters and tour groups.

RENTING A BUNGALOW Tourists planning to stay awhile often rent beach bungalows. Bungalow rentals are generally advertised only by word of mouth. To find out what's available, just ask around at the local cafes and someone will steer you to a landlord. You can also check to see if anyone has left word about a rental at the tourist office in Panaji.

WHAT YOU WILL PAY You must bargain for your rental. Prices have risen steadily over the years. While you can get something cheaper, for the most part expect to pay anywhere from Rs 5,000 ($166.66) to Rs 7,000 ($233.33) for a well-maintained bungalow with indoor flush toilet. The entire fee is usually payable in advance and nonrefundable, so select with care. Check a few houses before deciding on yours. But don't expect a palace, or even a beach house in the Fire Island, Hamptons, or Malibu sense of the word. With few exceptions, these modest cottages are located not on the beaches, but in little lanes and groves a stroll away from the beaches.

WHAT YOU WILL GET The cottages are usually simple, single-story affairs with pillared verandahs, painted as brightly as pictures in a children's coloring book. One or two bedrooms and a rudimentary kitchen sum up their interior space and decor. Some landlords have been adding indoor toilets to please the tourists.

There's well water for cooking and cleaning up **(be sure and boil or buy bottled water for drinking).** If you'd rather not keep house, your landlord will probably know someone to do the chores for you. You might have to supply bed linens and towels, which you can buy in Mapusa on market day rather than dragging them from home. Being a householder in Goa for a month or more can be so enjoyable you may find it hard to tear yourself away.

PAYING-GUEST ACCOMMODATIONS If you don't want to rattle around in a house, you can be a paying guest in a Goan's home. *Accommodation in Goa,* published by the Directorate of Tourism, lists paying guest accommodations throughout Goa. You can find a copy at the India Tourist Office or Government of Goa Tourist Information Bureaus.

When people today speak of Goa's beaches, they generally have in mind Calangute to the north of Panaji, and Colva to the south. The following is a run-down of Calangute, Colva, and neighboring beaches. *Penny-wise tip:* Avoid peak season, December 15 to January 15, when rates soar, sometimes double.

NORTH BEACHES

Calangute/Baga—10 miles (17 kilometers) north of Panaji

Calangute, the most developed beach, offers a remarkable expanse of sand, but not much in the way of palms. And here the spirit of the 1960s lives on each May when Youth Fete showcases young musicians and dancers and makes this beach look a little like Spring Break in Florida. (It all calms down again.)

Less than a mile away, **Baga,** at the top of Calangute, seems far more remote. Goans lovingly describe neighboring Baga as "nature's spoiled daughter" because its beach and palms both seem to do exactly as they please—a perfect description for the relaxed ambience at Baga as well.

WHERE TO STAY

Doubles for Less Than Rs 750 ($25)

An 800 year-old Ganeseha sits atop the entrance at **Falcon Resorts,** Calangute (☎ 277327, 277328, or 277329; fax 277330), where the owner decorates with his personal antique collection. Stained-glass windows bear the falcon's portrait. Fifty rooms—some lofts, some cottages—each with an individual look add distinction to this resort. Highest price around Rs 690 ($23), due for an increase. Restaurant, barbecue, bar, pool. Interesting, different.

At **Varma's Beach Resort,** Calangute (☎ 276077), all rooms have balconies and a blend of modern and new period reproductions. Doubles are Rs 550 ($18.33). Feels like a private club for grown-ups only; no children. Breakfast, snacks, and light refreshments. Meals taken out in the restaurants. Well maintained. Closed June through September.

Annette Beach Resort, Calangute-Baga Road (☎ Panaji 224485), offers neatly furnished flats with living room, dining room, bedroom, kitchen with refrigerator (no cooking allowed), balcony. Doubles Rs 700 ($23.33).

At the 18-room **Hotel Linda Goa,** Baga Road (☎ 276066), AC doubles are about Rs 500 ($16.66) to Rs 595 ($19.83). Some rooms are non-AC.

For simplicity, cleanliness, and friendliness, it would be hard to beat Michael Mascarenhas' **Hotel Golden Eye,** Gauravaddo Calangute (☎ 6117; fax 0091), with 15 small, spartan rooms both upstairs and at beach level. Each has a bathroom attached with hot and cold running water and a verandah with a sea view. Doubles are Rs 250 ($8.33) to Rs 600 ($20). The golden sands are at your doorstep, and so is **Golden Eye** restaurant, with some of the tastiest food around (see "Where to Eat," below).

Cheerful and friendly in Calangute, **Villa Bomfim,** Baga Road (☎ 276105), has 16 rooms, a few with AC. They're not imaginative, but adequate and clean. Doubles with AC (in season) are around Rs 500 ($16.66); in peak season Rs 750 ($25).

Cavala, Baga, Sauntavaddo, Calangute (☎ 276090), is a rustic, white-washed brick building with tile roof and the look of an old Goan house. There are 21 clean rooms with balconies, some looking out on paddy fields. Doubles are Rs 300 ($10) to Rs 400 ($13.33). According to a couple of English people who stayed there, it is "jolly good."

Similarly priced, **Chalson,** Cobravaddo (☎ 276088), has had problems opening and is operating at half mast. Rooms are simple and spare, but wonderful sea views make up for lack of opulence. Natural sun-heated water. Doubles Rs 350 ($11.66).

Doubles for Less Than Rs 1,500 ($50)

On Baga Beach, Calangute, the cozy **Baia do Sol** (☎ 276084) has 23 rooms (five AC), some in the cream-colored main building and others in little cream bungalows right on the beach. Clean and comfortable, every room has a patio or verandah. The restaurant offers Goan, Italian, and Indian dishes. Highest-priced AC doubles are Rs 975 ($32.50).

With the walls at reception displaying pictures of ships he sailed during a long stint at sea, a retired sea captain has started a new career with **Capt. Lobos,**

Baga-Calangute (☎ 276103). His concept is 20 ship-shape furnished apartments (six AC), each with a balcony, sitting room, bedroom, fully stocked refrigerator, and room service. Rates are Rs 1,000 ($33.33). An open-air restaurant and lovely, palm-shaded swimming pool make add to this snug hideaway.

Concha Beach Resort, Umta Waddo, Calangute Beach, Bardez (☎ 276056; fax 2662481), has 15 non-AC rooms and pleasant ambience, for Rs 1,080 ($36). The rates include Continental breakfast.

The Ronil Royale, Baga, P.O. Calangute, Bardez (☎ 276183; fax 27600), in neat white buildings with red tile roofs and blue trim, has 20 rooms (one AC), furnished with an old Goa feeling, each with a balcony or sit-out. Best views are from upstairs rooms. Rates are Rs 800 ($26.66) to Rs 850 ($28.33).

The nicest feature of the **Hotel Goan Heritage,** Gaurovaddo, Calangute, Bardez (☎ 276120), is the garden with lounge chairs and thatch-covered tables, and the restaurant. The rooms (all non-AC) are not inspired but okay, although they and could use better maintenance. Rates range from Rs 600 ($20) to Rs 800 ($26.66). Rooms have fans to stir the breezes. Restaurant and lawn service.

The budget traveler's standby on Calangute is the GTDC's **Calangute Tourist Resort** (☎ 276024), right on the beach. It consists of a cream-and-rust main building with a nice terrace, cottages, and dorm accommodations, all overlooking the sea. Nothing very fancy, you understand. Four cottages, with rosewood furniture and some antique pieces, are a cut above the rooms. Six rooms have private balconies overlooking the sea. Season rates for doubles range from Rs 220 ($7.33) for a regular room to Rs 450 ($15) for an AC suite. Rear side rooms are slightly lower. Write two to three months in advance for reservations if you hope to get in: Goa Tourism Development Corporation, Ltd., Trionora Apartments, Panaji 403001, Goa (☎ 226515). Be specific about which accommodation you are interested in since the GTDC runs many around the region (see "Government Accommodations" in the Panaji section above).

Where to Eat

Infantana, The Pastry Shop, Calangute (☎ 277421), is spotless and has an irresistible assortment of puff pastries, cinnamon buns, pies, and donuts. Black forest cake, a local favorite, is Rs 20 (66¢) a slice. Everything is made fresh. Open from 8am to 7:30pm.

Hotel Souza Lobo (☎ 276463) is not known primarily as a "hotel," but for being one of the oldest and most popular restaurants on the beach, serving breakfast, lunch, and dinner. The prices peak at around Rs 100 ($3.33) for king prawns. One look at the dreary, cell-like rooms, priced at Rs 200 ($6.66), will demonstrate why most people would prefer to eat, not sleep, here.

Famous, popular, and located right on Baga, thatch-covered **Tito's** (☎ 276154) serves both snacks and meals and changes it menu frequently. From a large selection of fresh juices, the watermelon is especially tasty. After 7pm, local specialties are a feature: try kingfish in garlic butter. A meal here isn't complete without chocolate cake or chocolate roll. Figure on Rs 100 ($3.33) per person, but some portions are big enough for two. Hours are 10am to 11pm.

St. Anthony's Cafe and Bar, Baga Beach (near Baia do Sol), is another old-timer, well-known for good Goan foods, especially prawns baldrao, made with vinegar, chiles, and other seasonings. Open from 8am to 11pm.

Crave delicious French toast or brownies? You'll find them at **Golden Eye,** Calangute, which locals like to keep secret so it won't be overrun by tourists. It's a tiny place where extra tables are put outside at night, and the specialties also include seafood and fish dishes, in the Rs 35 ($1.16) range. The French toast and brownies cost about Rs 6 (20¢). Open from 8am to 11pm. Nice music and sea view, too!

Planter's Restaurant, Candolim Junction, Calangute, has a funky combination of snooker, pub, and Continental fare; it is famous for steaks. An average meal for two costs around Rs 300 ($10).

Casa Portuguesa, Baga, in an old Goan home, with antiques and verandah or indoor dining, serving Portuguese and Goan cuisines. Goan seafood dishes are excellent. Folk singer. A meal for two will cost about Rs 500 ($16.66). Dinner only, 6:30to 11pm nightly.

What to See & Do

At **Kerkar Art Complex,** Calangute, Gaurawado (☎ 276017), Subodh Kerkar, former M.D. and currently an artist, turns his attention full time here at the center to exhibits of contemporary paintings, sculptures, developing handicrafts, and cultural events, such as classical Indian music and dance performances under one roof. Aside from exhibits, there are sitar and tabla concerts, Tuesdays and Saturdays from 6:30 to 8:30pm, Rs 150 ($5) per person. Definitely worth visiting. Kerkar's beautiful silk screen postcards for sale.

Candolim

Where to Stay

Nestled among the dunes are a few places to stay.

Aguada Holiday Resort, Candolim (☎ 276071; fax 276068), has 11 functional, modern rooms (two with AC), priced from Rs 500 ($16.66) to Rs 600 ($20), plus apartments equipped with refrigerators and hot plates, priced from Rs 650 ($21.66) to Rs 750 ($25).

Sea Shell Inn, opposite Canara Bank, Candolim (☎ 276131), has 10 simple rooms (non-AC) for Rs 200 ($6.66) to Rs 350 ($11.66).

Whispering Palms Beach Resort, Candolim, Bardez, Goa (☎ 276140; fax 276140), has 54 doubles, priced from Rs 1,800 ($60) to Rs 2,000 ($66.66). It is comfortable and upscale.

Where to Eat

Teama, near the Car Park, is a cheerful, clean cantina-like place for breakfast, lunch, and dinner. It serves Indian and Goan foods, in the Rs 30 ($1) to Rs 50 ($1.66) range.

At **Coconut Inn,** Candolim Beach, the evocative atmosphere of an old Goan home, combined with well-prepared food, makes for a satisfying experience. You can eat on the terrace or in the garden. Try the specialty, king prawns and garlic toast for Rs 135 ($4.50). The restaurant is on the main road between Condolim and Calangute beaches. Open from 9am to 11pm.

Sinquerim

Where to Stay (All Splurges)

Poshness is administered by The Taj Group of Hotels in three distinctive places surrounded by a singularly beautiful garden. The dramatic backdrop is an old coastal fort.

The **Fort Aguada Beach Resort,** Sinquerim, Bardez, Goa 403515 (☎ 276201; fax 276044), is built into the ruins of a fort more than 300 years old, where galleons used to call for fresh water from natural springs. The resort is situated on a finger of topaz-colored sand and designed to harmonize with the landscape. There's a swimming pool, bar, and two restaurants, including the **Sea Shell,** where the focal point is a chandelier made of local transparent seashells. Standard doubles are priced from $120 to $185, depending on the season. The hotel offers a wide range of sports activities.

Adjacent to the Fort Aguada is the **Aguada Hermitage** (☎ 287501; fax 276044), with 15 rooms in luxurious villas built into a hillside overlooking the sea. Spacious and tastefully furnished in elegant old-Goan style, each villa has a porch and is surrounded by lovely gardens. Expect to pay $300 to $500, depending on the location of the villa, its size (one or two bedrooms), and the season. Leisure center with card tables, chess. Shares pool and restaurants with Fort Aguada Beach Resort.

The Taj Holiday Village, Sinquerim, Bardez, Goa (☎ 287514), is a cluster of rustic cottage re-creating the ambience of a Goan village. Prices for the 142 doubles range from $125 to $175; some non-AC rooms are less expensive. There's a separate restaurant cottage and poolside barbecue; bar, swimming pool, minigolf, fitness trail, yoga, and many sports.

Where to Eat

Try the pricey Thai food in the **Banyan Tree** in Fort Aguada Resort complex, and their very good **barbecues** at both Aguada Resort and Taj Village. Grilled fresh fish with delicious Indian bread, vegetables, and dessert will cost about Rs 500 ($16.66) to Rs 600 ($20) per person for either Thai or barbecue. For reservations call 276201.

What to See & Do

Hike up to see sunset from the Portuguese-built Aguada Fort and lighthouse, open from 4 to 5:30pm.

ANJUNA

Because of its unusual red cliffs, Anjuna is a great scenic favorite of many travelers. When your tire of surf and sun, take a look at the handsome 1920s-style Albuquerque mansion, built by a Goan doctor who practiced in Zanzibar but moved back home.

When to Go

Anjuna is where hippies still live, and every full moon the beach becomes what the late Yogi Berra would call "déjà vu all over again" as over-the-hill flower children and new age imitators gather on the beach, dance to music from 5,000-watt speakers, and smoke grass. Now, however, one has a feeling it's more tourist spectacle than spontaneous rite. Every Wednesday, a mammoth flea market turns Anjuna into fabulous mart of merchandise from all over India. Take special note of the colorful Karnataka gypsies and their bold, beautiful appliquéd jackets. Fake and semi-precious stone jewelry. Bargains everywhere.

Where to Stay & Eat

Near Anjuna Beach, **Bougainvillea/Granpa's Inn Hotel,** Gaunwadi, Anjuna, Goa (☎ 273271), in a renovated ancestral mansion, has unusual oyster-shell windows. Clean and simply furnished, with 10 rooms—eight doubles, two suites—peak rates range from Rs 1,000 ($33.33) to Rs 1,500 ($50); otherwise, Rs 600 ($20) to Rs 1,000 ($33.33). Hefty off-season discounts. Anjuna Beach is a 10-minute stroll. Breakfast, lunch, snacks at poolside.

TEREKHOL/ARAMBOL

Off a splendid, deserted beach in the northern part of Goa, 52 kilometers from Panaji, you can catch the ferry to historic Terekhol Fort, the only old Portuguese fort converted into a **Tourist Rest House,** 48 via Redi. Now a Heritage Resort. Rates are Rs 120 ($4) to Rs 280 ($9.33) in season.

At Arambol, the northern most beach—and virtually untouristed at the moment—there are modest, spare accommodations in one- to three-room guest houses in a tiny village, a three-hour bus trip from Mapusa. Rates are Rs 40 ($1.33) to Rs 50 ($1.66). The nearest town, Pernem, is 13 kilometers away.

SOUTH BEACHES

Lovely southern beaches are rapidly being built up by developers for charters and package tour groups. For many years Westerners have made a beeline to Colva and neighboring Benaulim. Yet with all this development, the beaches are not swarming with vacationing tourists, and the area is not grossly commercialized (although this may change as the new hotels fill up with package tourists). What little scene there is consists of cruising the modest cafes and bargaining with the gypsies who come to Goa to sell a variety of embroidered wares.

COLVA

Doubles for Less Than Rs 750 ($25)

Silver Sands Beach Resort, Colva Beach (☎ 221645), resembles a two-story motel. Inside, its decor emphasizes cheerful prints. The 50 functionally furnished rooms (some non-AC) have balconies. Rates for doubles range from Rs 550 ($18.33) to Rs 600 ($20). There is a lovely, kidney-shaped swimming pool and adjoining outdoor cafe, bar, and restaurant. The hotel provides transportation in a van to the airport. A very good buy.

Many visitors head for the GTDC's **Tourist Cottages** (☎ 222287), also a main building and dorm. All rooms are simple, neat, and clean, with attached bathrooms with running cold water. Hot water is supplied in buckets upon request. Rates run Rs 110 ($3.66) to Rs 250 ($8.33). Restaurant, garden.

Modest, clean **Sukhsagar Beach Resort,** Colva Beach (☎ 221888 or 731888) has 19 rooms (five AC) in what might be a large home with an annex. AC doubles are Rs 380 ($12.66); during peak season, November 21 to January 20, doubles are Rs 480 ($16). There is a non-AC restaurant and a small garden.

Ma Mickey House, 24/1 Novo Vaddo, Salcete, Colva (telephone probably installed by now), is a new guest house and was in top condition. There are eight simple, clean rooms: three upstairs are priced from Rs 120 ($4) to Rs 200 ($6.66); five on main floor are Rs 100 ($3.33). Clean common bathroom; TV lounge upstairs. There's a garden with cafe under thatch.

Vincy's, the most well-known cafe in Colva, also has a small hotel attached. Rooms go for Rs 150 ($5), are non-AC, and fairly clean, but could use better maintenance.

Doubles for Less Than Rs 1,500 ($50)

Penthouse Beach Resort, Colva, Salcette, Goa (☎731030 or 221221; fax 223737), is as different from a penthouse as night from day. There are 62 rooms (17 AC), priced at Rs 1,300 ($43.33) in quaint, two-story bungalows in a landscaped garden with pool. They have vaguely old Goan decor and are a bit dark, but clean. Pleasant. Restaurant and bar.

William's Resort, Colva (☎ 732964; fax 732852), has 36 rooms, some non-AC, with brown-and-white color schemes, balconies, and tiled bathrooms. Doubles with AC are Rs 770 ($25.66). Swimming pool and garden. The menu at **William's** restaurant has some English specialties (see "Where to Eat," below).

…Beach Resort (☎ 221975) has 24 small rooms (seven AC), with doubles …or Rs 850 ($28.33), some with smashing sea views and all with attached bathrooms. The decor is nothing to rave about, but it's always good to find a neat and clean place. Restaurant, bar, and 100 meters from the sea.

Trying for a village look with blocks of two-story buildings with peaked roofs and balconies, the **Sea Queen** (☎ 220499; fax 6922861), looks instead like an upscale motel; 50-plus suites and deluxe are fairly clean, but unimaginative and a bit dark. Doubles begin at Rs 975 ($32.50), peaking at Rs 2,000 ($66.66); pool.

Where to Eat

Cafes are plentiful, popular, and open for breakfast, lunch, and dinner. Here are some of the perennial favorite hangouts for Westerners.

Vincy's, Colva, probably the south beaches' most well-known and oldest cafe, has expanded into a modest hotel (see above), with rooms above the street-level cafe. Many people feel Vincy's is now living on its past reputation. See for yourself. Seafood, chicken, and steak dishes go for around Rs 50 ($1.66) to Rs 75 ($2.50). Open for breakfast, lunch, and dinner.

There's a young crowd at **Lactancia Bar and Restaurant,** where a palmist keeps them fascinated.

William's Resort (see its listing under "Where to Stay," above) is the place to head for such English dishes as braised beef and beef roast are in the Rs 40 ($1.33) to Rs 60 ($2) range.

BENAULIM

Penny-wise tip: Along the Colva Benaulim Road in the sun-spangled palm groves are many small accommodations—ranging from a room in a private home to a home-style resort—perfectly adequate for a simple beach holiday; I've listed only a few below. They offer only snacks or meals, but you'll find little seafood cafes on this route. Here are some examples of cheap accommodations.

Carina Beach Resort, Tamdi, Mati, Benaulim (☎ in Vaswado 224050), has 14 spotless rooms. Prices are in the Rs 450 ($15) to Rs 550 ($18.33) range; two rooms with outside toilet and shower are priced at Rs 200 ($6.66) to Rs 250 ($8.33); swimming pool.

Palm Grove Cottages, Tamdi, Mati (☎ 222533), has four rooms with hot showers for Rs 400 ($13.33), and two cheapies with cold showers (six more in the planning stages). Pleasant, clean.

Litleo Cottages, Colva Benaulim Road (look for sign), has simple, clean rooms, with baths attached. Doubles are Rs 150 ($5) to Rs 200 ($6.66). Tea and snacks only are served.

One more place in this price range is south of the Colva/Benaulim area. **Nanu Resort,** Betalbatim Beach (☎ 223029; fax 223870), has 72 four-room cottages. Doubles with AC go for Rs 800 ($26.66); some cheaper rooms are non-AC. All have large balconies and verandahs. The resort has a pool, restaurant, bar, travel counter, book shop.

BEACHES SOUTH OF COLVA—ALL SPLURGES

While some resorts below cater to charters, they also offer accommodations for independent travelers.

Mediterranean-style villas at **Dona Sylvia,** Cavelossim Beach (☎ 246321; fax 287876), have generous verandahs; the 240 AC rooms (all doubles) are comfortable and tastefully furnished. There are five rates from Rs 1,500 ($50) to Rs 4,100

($136.66), depending on season. It's really a cross between moderately priced and a splurge. Swimming pool, water sports, live entertainment, and dancing at night.

The Old Anchor, Cavelossim Beach (☎ 246337), between the sea and River Sal, a combination hotel and time-share apartments, has 183 large rooms in small bungalows, comfortably furnished in blond modern with cheerful prints. Doubles range from Rs 2,100 ($70) to Rs 3,500 ($116.66). Myriad activities keep guests going day and night: pool, health club, water sports, billiards, disco. Snack bar, restaurant, coffee shop along the river, where there's a sugar-fine beach. But scuttle that reception in a dumb, cartoonish boat.

At **Goa Renaissance Resort,** Survey No. 132, Varca Village, Salcette, Goa 400713 (☎ 23611), the lobby with a waterfall and greenery is a blend of lanai and Goan styles; imaginative lighting fixtures are clay pots upside down. Rooms have the right mixture of white stucco and cane and offer balconies with sea views. The bathrooms have some of the best lighting in India. There are all the restaurants and bars and activities anyone needs for a colorful complete beach stay. Doubles are around $134 to $145.

Majorda Beach Resort, Majorda, Salcette, Goa 400713 (☎ 20751), has 10 cottages and 98 rooms surrounded by 20 landscaped acres. Designed to resemble an old Portuguese or Spanish town, the hotel has an inner courtyard. The rooms are spacious and pleasant, but they depart from the old-world theme. Well, they offer old-world comforts but modern decor: wicker chairs and headboards, flowered spreads and draperies, balconies, and tiled bathrooms. The hotel boasts of one of Goa's largest outdoor pools, and there's also an indoor pool. Doubles are Rs 2,295 ($76.50). A buffet breakfast is Rs 175 ($5.83), lunch Rs 250 ($8.33), dinner Rs 325 ($10.83).

A lobby with a vaulted ceiling, splashing fountains, rock gardens, and a bridge over a moat figure into the lobby at **The Regency,** Utorda, P.O. Majorda, Salcete Goa 403713 (☎ 223978; fax 254186). Rooms are quietly elegant, with queen- or king-sized poster beds, light woods, settees with bolsters, and spotless marble floors (easy to keep clean). The usual menu of resort activities, restaurants, bar, and coffee shop round it all out nicely. New owners had taken over, who promised to fax new rates; they never came.

Pavilions with little, rose-red stucco villas, set around a lagoon linked by graceful bridges, give the **Leela Beach Goa,** Mobor, Goa (☎ 246373; fax 246352), the ambience of an earlier era. There are old-fashioned shutters on the tall windows, and rooms in the older wing have excellent copies of period furniture, complemented by marble countertops. The newer wing is less evocative with modern furniture. Rates for deluxe rooms are variable, starting at $125 in the low season and going up to Rs 275 (and higher) in the high season. There are all kinds of sports facilities, restaurants, and bars.

Holiday Inn, Mobor Beach, Cavelossim, Salcete (☎ 246303; fax 246333), evokes the Raj with archways opening onto a wide verandah and an uncluttered lobby that catches sea breezes. The 139 rooms are tailored contemporary, in dark woods with restful earth tone drapes and spreads. A variety of rates peak around Rs 2500 ($83.33). **Whispers of the East** restaurant, featuring Eastern cuisine from China, Japan, Thailand, and Indonesia, is a change of pace. Large, gracefully shaped swimming pool, health club, tennis court, table tennis, and beach volley ball.

Vasco da Gama

About 30 kilometers south of Panaji, near the airport and Marmagoa Harbor—and the railway terminus for Goa—Vasco da Gama is aptly described as "The Gateway to Goa." There is nothing here to detain you. But in case you have to spend the night or have a meal on your way to more interesting sites in or out of Goa, you'll want to know about accommodations.

Where to Stay

The best place is **Hotel La Paz Gardens,** Swatantra Path, Vasco da Gama 403802 (☎ 512121), with little gardens dotted everywhere inside—off the corridors, in the courtyards and halls. The rooms are attractive with earth-tone quilted bedspreads and coordinating curtains. Doubles go for Rs 650 ($21.66). The hotel has three restaurants—**Goodyland** for fast food (10am to 10pm); **Sweet and Sour** for Chinese food (11:30am to 3pm, 7:30 to 11pm); and **Regency** for Indian and Continental dishes (9am to 11pm). The prices for main courses range from Rs 25 (83¢) in Goodyland, to Rs 35 ($1.16) to Rs 65 ($2.16) in the other restaurants.

GTDC's **Tourist Hotel** (☎ 513119), near the State Transport Office, is a convenient place to stay, and pleasant too. The doubles are Rs 120 ($4) and Rs 220 ($7.33), higher for AC.

Where to Eat

Your best bets are the restaurants in the **Hotel La Paz Gardens,** Swatantra Path (☎ 512121), where there are three restaurants serving snacks as well as Chinese, Indian, and Continental food.

Little Chef Bar and Restaurant, Francesco L., Gomes Road (☎ 512121), is a popular local hangout for snacks and espresso. They also serve Goan and North Indian dishes. The highest-priced dishes on the menu are about Rs 55 ($1.83); snacks are less. It's air-conditioned and cheerful. Open from 11:30am to 2:30pm, 5 to 10pm.

What to Do

Aside from the ordinary such as shopping or eating, the next best thing is to go to Bogmolo Beach, 8 kilometers.

Guided Tours **GTDC's** Traditional Tour—departing Vasco da Gama Tourist Hotel at 10am, returning at 6pm, Rs 70 ($2.33)—goes to Pilar Monastery, key temples, Mayem Lake, several beaches, and Fort Aguada. Check with the Tourist Hotel for details.

MARGAO

This town, about 34 kilometers (21 miles) from Panaji, is the industrial heart of Goa. It's most important to travelers as being en route to beautiful Colva Beach. Intrepid shoppers and browsers will appreciate Margao's wonderful covered market. The **Kadamba Bus Terminal** is about five minutes from town. Take the bus in Margao city market stand to reach South Goa.

Where to Stay

Business travelers stay at Margao; most tourists stay at Colva Beach, 6 kilometers away, coming in to shop and take a beach break. There are few hotels well maintained enough to recommend; here are the best.

Goa Woodlands Hotel, Mingual Loyala Furtado Road, opposite the city bus stand, Margao 403601 (☎ 221121), has a cut-stone base with brown-and-white balconies trimming the exterior. Plants accent the exterior and interiors. This is a friendly place and considerably upgraded over the years. The 46 rooms are spacious and clean, with balconies from which you can admire the view. Doubles run Rs 310 ($10.33) with AC and TV, Rs 150 ($5) sans AC and TV. Two restaurants and bars to serve you. This is a very popular hotel and almost always booked.

About the same rates prevail at the **Metropole,** Avenida Conceicao (☎ 221582), which is a bit ritzier, with central AC, pool, and roof garden. **Hill View,** Aquem Alto (☎ 221121), with 22 rooms, partially AC, is a cut below.

Clean, low-budget hotels are rare. The best is **Mabai,** opposite the Municipal Garden (☎ 221653), with 30 rooms, some AC, which are clean and have private bathrooms. There is a roof garden, restaurants, and a bar. A cut above many low-budget hotels in Margao, the GTDC's **Tourist Hotel,** Margao (☎ 22715), could use better maintenance, Rates are Rs 130 ($4.33) to Rs 270 ($9) in season.

If you need to pay under Rs 100 ($3.33), try **Rurkrish,** Station Road, opposite Bank of India.

Where to Eat

From the time it opens at 8am until closing at 11pm, **Longuinhos,** opposite the Tourist Hotel and the Municipality, is bursting with life, and the music blares as it would from a cantina in a small Portuguese town. The restaurant is famous for its prawns, prepared in a variety of ways—grilled, fried, or in a vindaloo—and there are other seafood dishes. You won't go hungry here if you've got the Rs 35 ($1.16) for a generous entrée, although stuffed pomfret is sold according to size and can run much higher. At this restaurant you can get everything from breakfast to snacks, sweets, and whisky.

You'll find good vegetarian food in Margao at the clean, simple, and partially air-conditioned **Milan Kamat Hotel,** Station Road (☎ 221235). Enjoy well-prepared North and South Indian dishes—idli, dosas, puris, a host of curries—all no more than Rs 12 (40¢) to Rs 15 (50¢)—which is almost enough to buy a hearty meal. Open 6:30am to 9:30pm.

Get more vegetarian dishes at **Kamat Cafe,** Karpe House, Gold Star Building, Isidoro Baptista Road. Prices and hours similar to Milan Kamat.

Also near the Municipal Garden is **Maria Luiza Bakers and Confectioners,** George Baretto Square, with cakes to satisfy your sweet tooth and delicious breads as well—a nice place to stop if you want to pack a picnic for a day at the beach. Open 7am to 1pm and 4 to 8:30pm. Closed Sunday.

What to See & Do

The dominant structure near the market square is the **Church of the Holy Spirit,** an example of baroque Goan architecture. Built in 1564 atop the ruins of a Hindu temple, the Muslims tore it down in 1589, and the structure today dates from the rebuilding in 1675. Stately old mansions that welcome visitors are **da Silva** (in the 17th century known as "7 Shoulders") and **de Figueriredo House,** with old Goan furniture.

Guided Tours **GTDC's** North Goa Darshan Tour—departs Margao Tourist Hotel at 10am, returns 6pm, Rs 70 ($2.33)—goes to Pilar Monastery via Neura Rivandar, Chorao Island, Saptakoteswhar Temple, Temple at Narva, Mayem Lake, Mapusam, several beaches, and Fort Aguada. For details, contact the Tourist Hotel.

Excursions from Margao

Rachol Seminary

Two kilometers from Margao, Rachol Seminary is built on the site of a Muslim fortress that was overbuilt by the Portuguese with a church and then a prison. Between 1574 and 1610 it was converted to a seminary and now houses both a beautiful church and, since l994, the **Museum of Christian Art**—open from 9:30am to 5pm, entry Rs 5 (16¢)—with beautiful sacred articles such as crosses, sculptures, textiles, and paintings.

Chandor

In Chandor you'll find **Casa Braganca,** a vast home built in the 1600s, now shared as two homes by Aida de Menezes Braganca and Alvaro de Braganca Pereira, who grew up here. They invite you to see the usually unseen India—through personally guided tours of silk-lined halls, a golden chapel, ancestral paintings, china, crystal, and personal mementos and memories. Aida de Menezes Braganca recalls when it was a vast colonial plantation with seamstresses, furniture designers, and a goldsmith for making personal baubles. Tours are by appointment only (☎ 284227). Leave a generous donation in the boxes in both homes provided for these tips.

MAPUSA

If you're staying for a while at Anjuna or Vagator Beach, then Mapusa (pronounced "Mapsa") will be your **shopping** center. Friday is market day at Mapusa. You can also use Mapusa for shopping if you're at Calangute or Baga, but from either of them it's a fairly easy trip to Panaji.

Mapusa Friday Market

Mapusa market, in a modern, streamlined, building, is lots of fun whether you need supplies for your rented beach house or for the enjoyment of wandering around amid piles of exotic fruits and fragrant spices, masses of bangle-sellers (very pretty too), and row after row of saris and salwar kamiz. Your sure to find some irresistible bargain. It's crowded.

18

Gujarat: Gandhi's Home State

Until May 1, 1960, Gujarat was a territory within the state of Maharashtra, from which it differed linguistically. When the official partition took place, it was on these linguistic grounds.

1 Ahmedabad

Ahmedabad (pop. 3.5 million) is Gujarat's biggest city. Known as a city of mosques and minarets, it is equally well known today for a rather different sort of tower—the numerous factory chimneys of the 70 textile mills that make it, after Bombay, the major textile center in India.

The city is also renowned for other seemingly incompatible things—as the headquarters for 16 years of Mahatma Gandhi and his **Sabarmati Ashram** and as a place blessed by Lakshmi, the goddess of wealth. Both seem to have their shrines: The original site of Gandhi's ashram is now a lovely complex of buildings popular with sightseers, and this area's wealth is symbolized by the architecturally unique headquarters of the **Mill Owners' Association,** designed by Le Corbusier. Both are on the western bank of the sometimes dry Sabarmati River. And, recently, for a skyline that's made Ahmedabad look like a mini-Bombay.

When moving on from Ahmedabad, don't forget **Sansangir** Wildlife Sanctuary, the only place in the world where Asian lions can be seen in their natural habitat. It is described under "Excursions," below.

ESSENTIALS

GETTING TO AHMEDABAD

BY PLANE There are frequent flights from Bombay ($47); Delhi ($79); Madras ($143); and from a number of other cities. Airlines serving Ahmedabad are: **Indian Airlines** from Bombay, Bangalore, and Madras (airport ☎ 869234); **Jetair** (airport ☎ 868307) from Delhi and Bombay; **ModiLuft** (airport ☎ 866689) from Bangalore and Calcutta with a halt in Delhi. **Air India** connects Ahmedbad to London and New York twice weekly.

BY TRAIN From Bombay (484 kilometers), the best train for tourists is the speedy *Shatabdi Express,* departing Bombay at 2:30pm, arriving Ahmedabad at 6:15pm, via Vadodara and Surat, for Rs 390 ($13) AC Chair; other good trains from Bombay are the *Gujarat*

Express (nine hours), or the *Saurashtra Express* (about 11 hours), both departing in the morning and arriving in the afternoon, for Rs 865 ($28.83) AC First, Rs 101 ($3.36) Second. From Delhi, try to get the *Sarvodaya Express,* which takes 17 hours to cover the 960 kilometers, or you'll be stuck with a 24-hour train ride: Rs 1,370 ($45.66) First, Rs 162 ($5.00) Second.

Special Train: The *Royal Orient,* elegant and air-conditioned, journeys from Delhi for seven days to the historic cities of Gujarat, making a sight-seeing stop in Ahmedabad on the sixth day before going on to Jaipur and Delhi. (For more information, see Chapter 2, "Planning a Trip to India.")

BY BUS The **State Road Transport Corporation** (☎ 344764) connects Ahmedabad to all major towns, cities, and pilgrim centers in Gujarat, as well as to Jodhpur, Mount Abu, Jaipur, and Ajmer in Rajasthan; Ujain and Indore in Madhya Pradesh; and Bombay and Nasik in Maharashtra.

Visitor Information

For information on tours, tourist attractions, and special events for tourists, it's the **Tourist Information Bureau,** Gujarat Tourism, opposite Bata Showroom (purportedly the largest in India), Ashram Road, Ahmedabad (☎ 449683), which is open from 10:30am to 6:30pm.

Getting Around

City **bus** fares run from Rs 1.20 (4¢) to a maximum of Rs 13 (43¢). They usually increase 10% annually. Board buses at the main bus station, Lal Darwaza Railway Station, and all major places in the city.

Yellow top taxis are rare; when you find one, the minimum fare is Rs 10 (33¢). Bargain for the best deal before you get in. **Auto rickshas** are plentiful. Ricksha meters are said to be updated, but always ask for the card. They are supposed to charge Rs 3.75 (13¢) per kilometer. After 11pm, auto ricksha fares go up about 150% until morning.

Cars and drivers are available through Gujarat Tourism, Tourist Office, travel agencies, and hotels. An air-conditioned Datsun, for four hours/75 kilometers, costs Rs 500 ($16.66); for eight hours/130 kilometers, you'll pay Rs 900 ($30). These rates are from the Gujarat Tourism (TCGL), H.K. House, opposite Bata Showroom, Ashram Road (☎ 449683).

Prohibition

Prohibition, once widely enforced in India, is now enforced only in Gujarat. This means you will need a liquor permit to buy alcoholic beverages. Permits can be obtained by foreign nationals at Government of India Tourist Offices before departure or while in India. They aren't fond of issuing them here. See Chapter 2, "Planning a Trip to India," for more information.

When to Go

October to March is best; April to June is hot. The monsoon is roughly mid-June to mid-September. For Sansangir (see "Excursions from Ahmedabad," below), the lion sanctuary, the best time is March to May.

What to See & Do

The Gandhi Ashram

The Gandhi Ashram dates from 1917 (it was actually disbanded in 1933) and was the starting point for the celebrated 24-day, 241-mile march to Dandi in March 1930, when Bapu and 81 followers—by the march's end, the active supporters numbered 90,000—protested the British administration's unjust Salt Tax laws. (The manufacture of salt was then a government monopoly.)

Although Gandhi himself maintained good relations with the British, having been educated in London, he was a firm advocate of Indian independence and never missed a chance to further that cause in some nonviolent way. By March 1930, he thought he had found the issue. "Salt," writes Vincent Sheenan, "was the commonest of necessities and it had been monopolized by the foreign government. Salt was something every peasant could understand. Salt was God's gift and the wicked foreign government had stolen it from the people."

On March 2, Gandhi wrote to the British viceroy and announced his plans for the march. It began 10 days later, with 78 followers, and ended at Dandi Beach on April 6, when Gandhi went down to the sea and picked up a pinch of salt. He had broken the law, for which he was arrested one month later. But during that month his example was joyously followed by hundreds of thousands. The fledgling Congress Party, many of whose leaders were to become officials in India's first independent government 17 years later, organized the public—and illegal—sale of salt all over India. More than 60,000 people were arrested by the British, who, by doing so, underwrote their own demise.

A picture gallery containing large painted panels, a library, and photo gallery depicts Gandhi's life in pictures; and a five-minute film devoted to his life is shown periodically between 8am and 7pm. Gandhi's original room—simple mats, small desk, and spinning wheel—remains undisturbed, overlooking the central prayer corner and the river where the local women still gather to wash their clothes. An adjoining room displays some of Gandhi's own meager possessions: his dhoti (loin cloth), bedsheet, some beautifully inscribed bamboo tributes to him, and photostats of letters and cards from all over the world.

The entire inspiring struggle for freedom is the subject of an hour-long **son-et-lumière** show at the ashram: in English, Sunday, Wednesday, and Friday at 8:30pm; in Hindi, Monday, Tuesday, and Thursday, 8:30pm; in Gujarati daily, 7pm. Entry for all performances is Rs 3 (10¢).

From April 1 to September 30, the ashram is open from 8:30am to noon, and 2:30 to 7pm (last entry at 6pm); from October 1 to March 31, from 8:30am to noon, and 2 to 6:30pm (last entry at 6pm). Admission is free.

Other Sights in Ahmedabad

The various mosques around town are pretty much like mosques anywhere. Two, however, have special features: the delicately carved stone windows, in the pattern of a tree with spreading branches, of the **Sidi Sayed** mosque, near the Tourist Information Center; and the celebrated "Shaking Towers" of the **Jhulta Minara** (part of Siddi Bashir mosque), not far from the Ahmedabad Railway Station outside the Sarangpur Gate. A sign at the latter describes the 75-foot twin minarets as "a challenge to modern architecture," and the structure certainly does seem unique. Visitors used to pay a modest fee to climb the 68 steps of the narrow staircase to the top of one tower, and while they were huffing and puffing, a youth started up the other tower—and shook it! The vibrations, transmitted by the stone bridge connecting the towers 40 feet below, can clearly and somewhat frighteningly be felt in the other tower. This was, believe it or not, fun for the adventurous, but is no longer permitted. The skillful builder of this architectural phenomenon, in 1450, was Malik Shahnang Sahib, who lived at the time of Sultan Ahmed, founder of this city which now bears his name. The minarets, still in use to call the faithful at sunset (via microphone and loudspeaker), are closed between 12:30 and 2:30pm.

In Bhadra, you'll find **Ahmad Shah's Mosque,** built in 1411, for his personal use and among the oldest in the city. Vestiges of what are believed to be an earlier Hindu temple are seen in the gallery, 152 pillars, and five domes. The 80-plus year-old caretaker will tell you more details.

The other not-to-be missed mosque is **Jama Masjid,** Mahatma Gandhi Road, designed by Ahmad Shah (1424) is a nice peaceful stop, either going to or from the hectic City Market. It has a spacious courtyard and a tank. The impressive architecture is Indo-Saracenic style: There are 250 pillars set close together surmounted by 15 domes. British traveler Sir John Marshal swooned when he saw this mosque, calling it, "the most superb and imposing monument of its class in the world."

The 800-seat **Tagore Memorial Hall,** Sanskar Kendra, is an impressive piece of architecture too—soaring concrete beams, colored panels suspended from the ceiling, and a mural in the lobby ingeniously constructed from mirrors, beads, and beaten copper panels. Adjoining the theater—and both are situated just at the western end of the Sardar Bridge across the river—is a square, squat **museum** (open from 8 to 11am, and 4 to 8pm; closed Monday) containing some lovely miniatures, some suspended from the ceiling and others displayed in glass cases.

The five-story **Dada Hari,** located in the southern part of Ahmedabad, is but one of the Gujarati step wells you can see. (Others, outside of Ahmedabad, are described in the second section of this chapter.) It more or less blends in with the neighborhood. Built in 1501, it has retained traces of its former glory in the carved walls and pillars, best seen if you walk down the stairs. As with other step wells, it once offered a cool drink and respite from the heat to travelers.

At the southeast side of town is **Kankaria Lake,** a circular tank built in 1451, at the center of which is a small island housing the **Nagira Wadi** temple. Connected to the mainland by a causeway, it's also accessible by little boats and at night is illuminated with orange lights. There's a small restaurant overlooking the lake, a pleasant spot in the evening.

Adjoining the lake, which is ringed with busy little stalls, are a **children's garden, zoo, swimming pool, and open-air theater**. A scooter ricksha will cost about Rs 50 ($1.66) out from the town center.

Or perhaps you might be interested in one of the city's unusual museums. A most fascinating choice is the unique **Calico Textile Museum,** Shahibagh, in a lovely old haveli in the beautiful botanical flower- and peacock-filled botanical gardens that are part of the Sarabhai Foundation, an appropriate museum for this city in which prosperity is interwoven in three threads—cotton, silk, and gold. "Calico" is a real understatement when it comes to describing the displays in this museum. They are anything but humble cotton: lavish heavy brocades, delicate fine embroideries, carpets, turbans, saris, and costumes of maharajas and other royalty. This is one of the finest museums of its type in the world, and deserves time for peaceful quiet investigation. Hours are 10:15am to 12:30pm, and 2:30 to 5pm; closed Wednesday. Hour-long tours are given at 10:15am and 2:30pm. There is a well-stocked shop with books, postcards, souvenirs.

In this area also is a 15th-century **Jain temple,** under renovation for the past 200 years.

Another interesting museum is the **Shreyas Folk Museum,** Shreyas Foundation, housing a comprehensive collection of folk arts and crafts of Gujarat. It is open from 9 to 11am, and 4 to 7pm; closed Wednesday.

The **N.C. Mehta Collection** in Sanskar Kendra, Paldi, houses Gujarati and Rajput artworks in a building designed by Le Corbusier; it is open from 9 to 11am and 4 to 7pm; closed Monday.

Perhaps the most unusual museum in town is the **Kite Museum,** in Sanskar Kendra, Paldi, a collection of about 100 kites from all over India, documented with the history of kites from ancient times. Expansion plans include adding a permanent display of foreign kites. The museum is open from 11am to noon, and 3 to 5pm; closed Mondays.

Also worth a visit are the **Tribal Research and Training Institute Museum,** Gujarat Vidyapith, Ashram Road, open from 11:30am to 7:30pm (to 2:30pm on Saturday; closed Sunday and holidays); and the **Institute of Indology,** University Campus, Vidyapith (☎ 446148), open from 11:30am to 7:30pm (11:20am to 2:30pm on Saturday; closed Sunday). Entry to both is free.

Guided Tours

Low-priced tours twice daily (including Sunday and holidays) take in the major sights in and about Ahmedabad; they are conducted by the **Ahmedabad Municipal Corporation** (☎ 352739). The cost for each is Rs 30 ($1); times are from 9:30am to 1:30pm, and 2 to 6pm; they leave from the AMTS Terminus, Lal Darwaja. A number of hotels have information on these tours.

The **National Tourism Consortium** also runs tour. A half-day Ahmedabad tour—daily, from 8:10am to 12:30pm, Rs 50 ($1.66)—covers Bhavnizar Temple, Sarkej, Vechaar Utensils Museum, Kankaria Lake, Hathessingh Temple, Gandhi Ashram, and other city sights. A tour to Kankaria Lake—daily, from 1:15 to 8pm, for Rs 180 ($6) adults, Rs 150 ($5) children three to 10—includes water rides and time for swimming. The Consortium is located at G/3 "Hemkoot" Complex, opposite Capital Commercial Centre, Ashram Road, Ahmedabad (☎ 462866).

The **Tourism Corporation of Gujarat** has tours throughout the state and to other states, commencing from Ahmedabad.

Shopping

One look at all the fine carvings and textiles and you have no doubt; there's plenty of good stuff to buy. Among the most attractive places to shop, and very interesting too, is **Gujari,** National Chambers, near Dipalee Cinema on Ashram Road—three floors of beautifully displayed and carefully selected handicrafts from all over the area. Textiles, of course, and rugs are both outstanding, and very impressive as well is the local lacquered and inlaid furniture, as bright as a summer's day. The rosewood beads here make lovely gifts, which are easy to pack and easy on the pocketbook too. Wool shawls are good buys for rough quality or merino. Open every day but Sunday, from 10:30am to 7pm; closed for lunch between 2 and 3pm.

For embroideries, beadwork, antiques, wood carvings, spice trays, silver, and traditional textiles, target **Rani no Haziro,** Dani Linda and Manek Chowk areas. More contemporary textiles are found at **Sindhi Market,** and adjoining **Revid Bazaar,** Ratanpole, **New Cloth Market,** and **Teen Darwaja.** Ratanpole is also headquarters for jewelry and silverware.

C.G. Road has been called the "Oxford Street of Ahmedabad," but that's selling it short. It's block after block of stalls and lots of fun, with places to snack, sip a drink, and bargain until you drop.

For more bargaining, head to the shops on **Tilak Road,** in Bhadra; to haggle, try the **Junk Bazaar** on Sunday on the banks of the Sabarmati, near B.K. Municipal Garden under Ellis Bridge. There are also a dozen department stores in Ahmedabad, and a wide range of classy boutiques. There's the wonderful **City Market** where you find everything you need to live life anywhere in the world; most especially attractive are the displays of fruit in this market. If you admire some jewel-like fruit, the merchant is apt to take one, slice it, and offer you a nibble.

WHERE TO STAY

Gujarat is very expensive—taxes can add 50% to your room and food bills. So when a room rate looks low (and there are precious few of these), remember the added taxes when calculating your actual costs. In addition, most accommodations—even modest ones—are high-priced in comparison to many other cities of India.

IN AHMEDABAD

Doubles for Less Than Rs 350 ($11.66)

The accommodations in this category are non–air-conditioned, basic, and have baths attached.

In these simple, low-budget places ask to see a room or two before checking in: **Prime,** Vishal Commercial Centre, Pattharkuva, Relief Road (☎ 352582), doubles Rs 250 ($8.33); **Shakunt,** opposite Railway Station, Reid Road (☎ 345614), doubles Rs 200 ($6.66); **Raamville,** O/S Raipur Gate (☎ 312615), doubles Rs 325 ($10.83)—basic; **Good Night,** opposite Sidi Syed Masjid, Laldarwaja (☎ 351997), doubles Rs 275 ($9.16) to Rs 325 ($10.83).

Doubles for Less Than Rs 600 ($20)

About a kilometer (half a mile) from town, the 27-room **Hotel Meghdoot,** Gupta Chambers, outside Sarangpur Gate, near New Cloth Market, Ahmedabad 380002 (☎ 313054 or 313066), has fairly clean rooms, nine AC doubles Rs 475 ($15.83), non-AC Rs 375 ($12.50). Restaurants and Delhi chat (snacks); good in this price range.

Ambassador Hotel, Khanpur Road, Ahmedabad 380001 (☎ 3532444 or 3532445; fax 302327), has 30 rooms, 10 with AC, rates of Rs 375 ($12.50); it has declined badly. In its present state, it is not recommended unless everywhere else is full. There's 24-hour room service, but no restaurant; many places to eat are nearby.

Alif International, Khanpur Road, opposite B.M.C. Bank, Khanpur (☎ 359440, 359441, 359442, or 359443), has a good location, near the Holiday Inn, and good food, but maintenance is not so good (exposed wiring in bathrooms, peeling paint). Simply for the unfussy, AC doubles are Rs 310 ($10.33) to Rs 525 ($17.50). A price-fixed veg meal—two vegetables, dal, rice, pappar, paratha, and chach (buttermilk)—is Rs 22 (73¢), a bargain.

Stay Inn, near Khanpur Gate, opposite UUshakiran Flats (☎ 300727; fax 442243), is hard to beat in this price range, with a terrace garden and pleasant service. The 14 rooms (seven AC) are clean, cheerful, and adequately furnished. AC doubles range in price from Rs 410 ($13.66) to Rs 550 ($18.33). Room service; no restaurant.

Doubles for Less Than Rs 1,500 ($50)

Recently, the city has undergone an expansion of hotels in this price range.

Inder Residency, opposite Gujarat College (☎ 425050), sets the scene in the lobby with a waterfall and teak furniture with woven upholstery; there are 79 snug, adequately furnished rooms, with prices for doubles from Rs 1,400 ($46.66) to Rs 1,490 ($49.66). Village murals perk up the restaurant. Nearby is the similarly priced, but less well maintained, **Hotel Kanak,** opposite Gujarat College (☎ 467291).

Glass elevators and a waterfall are decorative accents at **West End,** near Gujarat College (☎ 462627), where maintenance is a problem. Still you could do worse; doubles from Rs 900 ($30) to Rs 1,000 ($33.33). Multicuisine restaurant.

At **Nalanda,** Mithakali 6 Roads (☎ 426262; fax 426090), the overall ambience is sleek and modern, and, more importantly, spotlessly clean. Each of the 37 tailored rooms, has a bold, colorful patchwork spread on its bed. Doubles range in price from Rs 950 ($31.66) to Rs 1,200 ($40). The hotel's **Tulips** restaurant is pink accented and lined with mirrored walls.

Rock Regency, Law Garden Road (☎ 40933, fax 46558), is tailored and acceptably neat. For a pleasant change, it offers two veg restaurants—one multicuisine, the other dedicated to delicious Gujarati thalis.

Hotel Mascot, Khanpur (☎ 303848; fax 303221), is a cheerful place with a colorful village mural at reception and pink walls in the lobby contrasting with red and gray settees and chairs. There are 44 rooms, some with river and skyline views. Standard singles are Rs 700 ($23.33), doubles are Rs 900 ($30); to these rates add 15% for taxes. Apparently, the management thinks no one will look down and notice the condition of the carpet in the restaurant—maybe they changed it.

Spare lobby decor and compact, modern rooms are yours at **Rivera** in Khampur, on the riverbank (☎ 304201). Maintenance needs improvement, but it's still an okay place. Doubles are Rs 750 ($15) to Rs 850 ($28.33). Restaurant; liquor store.

Acceptable in this price range are other fairly new hotels: **Klassic Gold,** B/H Telephone Exchange, Navrangapura (☎ 445508, 445578, or 445581; fax 429195); **Hotel Nest,** B/H Telephone Exchange (☎ 402211; fax 426259). Both have all amenities.

Doubles for Less Than Rs 2,000

Holiday Inn, Khanpur, near Nehru Bridge (☎ 305505; fax 305501), is well situated and near both old and new areas of Ahmedabad. The hotel is well run, pleasant with a sleek modern ambience enhanced by lots of white marble, functional rooms, and a hospitable staff. Standard doubles are Rs 2,000 ($66.66)—perhaps a tad above this now. The restaurant is a popular meeting spot for the city's power elite. Also a pastry shop, coffee shop, pool, and health club. From the back rooms, there's a view of a squatters' settlement that offers a fascinating pageant of Gujarati life. Affiliated with the U.S. chain.

The 55-room **Cama Hotel,** Khanpur Road, Ahmedabad 380001 (☎ 305281; fax 305285), on the riverbank. The front of the hotel faces the road, and in back there's a terrace and garden with a swimming pool and view of the river and shanty town. Big, leather club chairs give the lounge a clubby feel, and each floor has a minilounge, some with antique furniture and accessories. Doubles are Rs 1,400 ($46.66).

Light filters through stained-glass window panes into the lobby at **Shalin Suites,** Gujarat College Cross Road, Ellis Bridge (☎ 426967; fax 46002), a hotel with a lot of personality. Crewel patterned settees and club chairs add to the lobby's ambience. The 72 tailored lounge-and-bedroom suites—doubles start at Rs 1600 ($53.33) could have a tad more pizzazz. There's a lunch buffet in **Petals,** where floral fixtures bloom with soft light. Swimming pool.

A Guest House Away from Town

Away from the bustle of town is the serene **Gandhi Ashram Guest House** (☎ 407742), opposite the Gandhi Ashram. A contemporary, redbrick building with natural cement accents, the guest house is managed by the Tourism Corporation of Gujarat. It has simple furniture accented by modern paintings and photographs. The bulletin board has listings of everything travelers need to know for a pleasant visit to Ahmedabad—movie times, phone numbers, buses, **son-et-lumière** shows, tours, taxi hire services, etc. There are 10 double bedrooms, all with attached bathrooms with hot and cold running water. Two rooms are air-conditioned, and rent for Rs 250 ($8.33) double. Non–air-conditioned rooms are Rs 125 ($4.16). Vegetarian food is modestly priced. Buses and auto rickshas are readily available to town. Readers write that the ashram is often fully booked by government officials.

Resorts Away from Town

Greenwoods Lake Resort, Sarkhej-Gandhinagar Highway, Chanodi Farm Complex, North West Safaris and Travel Services, 91/92 Kamdhenu Complex, Ambawadi (☎ 441511; fax 23729), and **Visa Travels,** above Wardrobe, Swastik, Char Rasta. This resort is on a private lake, with boating and all manner of resort activities, from badminton to tennis. Temporary membership in country club. Non-AC doubles are Rs 500 ($16.66); with AC they are Rs 700 ($23.33). Business center, conference rooms.

Silver Oak, Heritage Club, Sarkhej-Gandhinagar Highway (apply for tariff), offers doll houses, tree houses, and all kinds of sports from archery and horseback riding to swimming and squash; there is a private lake and a fast-food counter.

Balaram Palace Resorts (174 kilometers from Ahmedabad), Chitrasani Village, Abu-Palanpur Highway—now 14 (B.K.)—(☎ 02742-84636; in Ahmedabad ☎ 76388).

None of these make much sense for the tourist, unless you plan to stay for a while.

WHERE TO EAT

A large percentage of the population here is vegetarian, and Gujarati meatless dishes are some of the most distinctive in all of India. Local cooking is less spicy and a little sweeter than some other Indian styles, which makes it easier for many Westerners to enjoy. There's prohibition in the entire state, so you'll need your liquor permit to purchase even a bottle of beer.

A good place to try typical Gujarati food is the simple, clean, air-conditioned **Gopi Dining Hall,** Ashram Road, opposite Town Hall (☎ 76388). Have the thali: Rs 22 (73¢) with limited (meaning no) refills at lunch, Rs 28 (93¢) at dinner. A sweet is extra; coffee or black tea are on the house. This is a good deal in terms of price, and it permits you to taste a whole lot of good things you might not otherwise order. Foods are to be eaten in a certain order, but there's nothing too rigid about this pattern except for the rice. In Gujarat, ghee-topped rice is traditionally served after your wheat breads and farsan (a kind of snack) to mop up your wet foods, rather than with the meal as elsewhere. Nor is rice always brought to the table without notifying the waiters. They will continue to bring you puris and rotis like the "Sorcerer's Apprentice" until halted. Unless you know the local etiquette, it's very easy to overeat on puris and not have room for a grain of rice, let alone the mountain that's inevitably heaped on your tray. Hours are 10am to 2:30pm, 6 to 10pm daily.

Also on Ashram Road, offering similar thalis, are **Torana,** Saurashtra, and **Gaurav Dining Hall,** near the Shiv Cinema Compound (there is no English sign, so look for the restaurant, near the movie theater).

For South Indian vegetarian fare, try **Old Madras Brahmin Hotel,** opposite the City Civil Court, Woodlands, C.G. Road, Kalpi. **Chetna Dining Hall,** Tilak Relief Road, does good, unlimited Gujarati vegetarian thalis: Rs 35 ($1.16) plus Rs 10 (33¢) for a sweet. Open from 10:30am to 3pm, 6:30 to 10pm. Another good Gujurati vegetarian thali is served at Vishala, discussed under "Excursions from Ahmedabad," below.

Smart, stylish **Gallops,** GF/2 Samrat, Smruti Kunj Society, Navrangpura (☎ 408569), has distressed beams, beautiful antiques, and spotless whitewashed walls, and concentrates on Indian cuisine (no Continental, no Chinese). The well-edited menu is mainly vegetarian, with prices from Rs 32 ($1.06) to Rs 70 ($2.33), but there are five chicken dishes for Rs 125 ($4.16). Rice is served at the end of the meal, Gujarati-style. Dum biryani (a veg rice dish), murg ka hawa (chicken), and bhindi (okra), with Indian bread, made a satisfying meal for three for about Rs 200 ($6.66), plus sweets for Rs 100 ($3.33). There are number of unusual veg dishes on the menu; ask the manager to help you if you don't know what to order. Hours are 11:30am to 3pm, 7:30 to 11pm. This place is dressy, dignified.

Mirch Masala ("Black Pepper"), Chandan Complex, C.G. Road, Swastik Char Rasta (☎ 4033340), is a casual, rustic, funky restaurant with movie posters, hanging footwear, vehicles, and a dhaba mural, and it focuses on dhaba (truckstop) cuisine. Start with jal jeera (lime juice, salt, sugar, black pepper, and chiles) to wake up your taste buds, and order any two or three of the dishes on the menu—you will not have tasted anything like this unless, of course, you're from Gujarat. Prices range from Rs 35 ($1.16) to Rs 150 ($5). Like its name, Mirch Masala, is hot. Reservations recommended. Hours are 12:30 to 3pm; 7 to 11pm.

Elegant, upscale **"10"** ("perfection"), Urja House, Swastik Char Rasta (☎ 445070), does a good job with Indian and Continental cuisines. A new recipe introduced recently is tomato cheese soup; a veg shashlik (mixed veg with paneer) on a bed of rice makes a fine meal. There several chicken dishes, including escalope of chicken with a brown sauce. Figure on Rs 200 ($6.66) veg and Rs 300 ($10) non-veg for a meal for two. Hours are 11am to 11pm.

If you'd like some Punjabi food, the AC Russian-named **Volga,** on Ashram Road (☎ 78533), is the place to go. Hours are 11:30am to 3:30pm, and 7 to 11pm every day. Specialties are butter chicken, chicken tikka masala, and other familiar northern fare. The prices for main dishes are Rs 50 ($1.66) to Rs 75 ($2.50).

Kwality, 9 Tilak Rd., is another good bet if you're not interested in vegetarian foods. There are about 75 Chinese specialties, about 75 Continental dishes, a dozen or so tandoori specialties, plus snacks and sweets galore on the menu. The highest prices are around Rs 125 ($4.16). Hours are noon to 4pm, 7 to 11pm.

For snacks and light meals, try the following: **Havmor,** Stadium Complex behind Navrangpura Bus Stand (☎ 4081100), hours noon to 3pm and 6 to 10:45pm, strictly veg; a three-course evening meal runs Rs 80 ($2.66) per person. You might also try **Havmor Panchvati Ice Cream Parlor,** C.Z. Road (☎ 463946), open from 11am to 11pm; or **Havmor** (main branch), opposite Krishna Cinema (☎ 357373), open from 11am to 9pm.

If you are looking for a buffet, Cama Hotel has two: from 12:30 to 3pm, and from 7:30 to 11pm—Rs 125 for each ($4.16); **Petals** at Sholin Suites has a lunch buffet, Rs 130 ($4.33), plus 32% tax and service charges; **Holiday Inn** also should have a buffet by now.

EXCURSIONS FROM AHMEDABAD

VAISHALA

For a sight-seeing and eating experience, there's charming Vaishala (open daily from 11am to 11pm). About four miles from town, it is a re-creation of a traditional village, which is designed and owned by Surinder Patel, an architect/contractor. A focal point of this excursion is the well-designed **Vechaar Utensil Museum,** where displays of cooking utensils and various household implements, hookahs, and other objects are used tell a cultural history. Well-trained guides explain the highlights.

There's a shop where handicrafts are on sale, and you can see some craftspeople at work with pottery, embroidery, and other crafts.

Getting to Vaishala

From town to Vaishala, a scooter ricksha cost about Rs 70 ($2.33) round-trip. There's a tariff chart, but settle the price before you get in, and keep it for the trip home. Or you can take the bus headed for Sarkhej and ask the conductor to let you off at Hagi Bawakvai, then walk a short distance to the site. Busing it is risky for a couple of reasons: Few people speak English for directions, and you may not get a bus going back when you want it.

Eating at Vaishala

You sit outdoors on charpoys (cots) under the trees as you snack or sip fresh coconut milk; or have a thali meal served by bearers wearing snappy turbans who welcome guests the traditional way, by placing a tilak (dot) on their foreheads. And what thalis these are: They have about 23 different kinds of dishes. In the evening, dinner is accompanied by music, puppet shows, and other entertainment, including the occasional snake charmer. Lunch is Rs 25 (83¢), dinner Rs 55 ($1.83).

SANSANGIR

When moving on from Ahmedabad, keep in mind **Sansangir,** the only place in the world where the Asian lions can be seen in their natural habitat. There's a good road to the sanctuary, 395 kilometers from Ahmedabad. There are rail connections as well.

Sansangir is miles from anywhere, and it's best to have all your plans in place before you take off. If you haven't firmed them up before leaving home, consult with the Government of India Tourist Office, 123 M. Karve Rd., Bombay (☎ 293144), or the State Government Tourism Offices, Tourist Information Bureau in Ahmedabad before taking off. They can advise you of conditions and give you a list of government-approved travel agents who might help you arrange this trip.

The sanctuary is open from mid-October to mid-June and closed during the monsoon months. The **Lion Safari Lodge** has been taken over by The Taj Group, who was renovating it, and should be open by now. However, the **Saurashtra Safari Gir Jungle Camp** is open and offers deluxe cottages for Rs 1,200 ($40) each.

2 Step Wells, Sarkhej Roza, Lothal & Modhera

Unique to Gujarat are **step wells.** Easiest to see, but by no means the most outstanding, is the five-story **Dada Hari** in the southern part of Ahmedabad itself (described under "What to See & Do," above).

AROUND GUJARAT

ADALAJ VIEW

A more handsome step well is Adalaj Vav, 11½ miles north of Ahmedabad in the village of Adalaj. This is superior to the other step wells in town: its carved pillars and walls are covered with birds and flowers, leaves and fishes, and designs that unify the whole.

SARKHEJ ROZA

About five miles southwest of the city is **Sarkhej Roza,** architecturally of interest because it lacks archways commonly associated with this kind of structure. Here is the renowned domed tomb of Ahmed Khattu Ganji Bakhsh (1445), spiritual adviser to Sultan Ahmed Shah. Inside the octagonal shrine, sunlight forms graceful patterns through some of the loveliest brass latticework to be seen today. Handsome marble inlay flooring embellishes the courtyard. The adjoining mosque from the 16th century is simple architecturally, noted for its rows of supporting pillars and, like the other structures, its absence of arches. Also to be seen in the courtyard near the entrance is the tomb of Mehmud Shah Begada and his wife, Queen Rajabai, through a portico on the tank bank. In proximity are palace ruins and pavilions and the tombs of brothers' Azam and Mu'azzam, believed to be the architects of Sarkhej.

Getting There

You can get to Sarkhej by bus from Ahmedabad's Lal Darwaja Terminus; take Bus 36/1 or 31/1, both of which run about every 45 minutes to an hour. At the site, a self-designated expert sells booklets for Rs 10 (33¢)—the asking price—but he will part with them for less, and the added information is good to have.

LOTHAL

Fifty-three miles southwest of Ahmedabad is **Lothal,** an important archaeological find made only 20 years ago. This site dates from the Harappan era, 1,000 years before Christ. This finding is of great significance, as it extends the borders of the Harappan civilization as far south as the Gulf of Cambay.

Remains of a dockyard and an inlet channel connecting to the River Bhogavo bear witness of Lothal's importance as an ancient port. An excavated Persian seal is evidence that there had been gulf trade. Also excavated was a planned city with houses having such amenities as baths and fireplaces. On view at the small museum are jewelry, bowls, and other early artifacts.

Getting There

Lothal is a day's excursion from Ahmedabad by rail to Bhurkhi on the Ahmedabad-Bhavnagar line of the Western Railway. Buses are available at Bhurkhi. It's a nice walk from there as well. There are buses from Ahmedabad to Uthelia, 2½ hours, Rs 50 ($1.66); it is 7 kilometers from Lothal.

Staying the Night

Should you want to spend the night, there's a Heritage Hotel, **Palace-Utelia,** with 14 rooms. Doubles are Rs 650 ($21.66). Book through North West Safaris, 91/92 Kamdhenu Complex, Ahmedabad 380001 (☎ 079-441411; fax 02712-23729).

MODHERA

Sixty miles northwest of Ahmedabad, Modhera boasts a Sun Temple from 1026, two centuries older than the Sun Temple at Konarak and, like it, dedicated to Surya the Sun. Against a barren landscape, the temple is an outstanding sight, set off like a work of art in an outdoor museum. Built on a platform above a deep tank, the temple was attacked and nearly destroyed by Mehmud of Gazni, but remarkably still has beautiful carvings of goddesses, birds, blossoms, and beasts inside and outside. Surya's image is missing from the sanctum now, but originally it was strategically placed to be illuminated by the first rays of the rising sun. Archaeologists have been restoring the temple and replacing some of the damaged stones with plain sandstone so you can tell which are new additions to the temple.

Getting There

There are state transport buses from Ahmedabad to Modhera or you can get a direct bus (meaning few stops) to Mehsana and then get a bus for the remaining 24 miles to the temple. There are two direct buses a day from Ahmedabad to Mehsana, and a bus from there every hour to the Sun Temple. By train, you go via Mehsana and then transfer to a bus.

Appendix

A Glossary of Terms

aarti (or arti) a type of prayer
atcha okay
ahimsa nonviolence
ashram holy retreat
ayurveda Indian herbal medicine
avatar commonly an incarnation, but in a religious sense applied to manifestations of Vishnu
bagh garden
baksheesh alms, tips
bearer personal servant, waiter
betel nut from the betel tree
Bhagavadgita short bible of Hinduism, part of the epic *Mahabharata*
bhavan (or bhawan) grand mansion
bhikhu Buddhist monk
chaitya Buddhist hall of worship
chapati pancakelike bread
chappals sandals
chhattri cenotaph, tomb
chota small
chowk square, courtyard
coolie porter, hall porter
dargah Muslim shrine
darshan audience with important/admired person, often a guru
dharma Hindu sacred law of the universe that determines both cosmic and human order; moral and religious law
dharmashala pilgrims' inn near a shrine
dhobi laundry man
dhoti floor-length skirt/drape worn by men
ghat steps down to river; mountain ranges parallel to east and west coasts of India
gompa Buddhist monastery
gopuram tall, pyramid-shaped tower on a South Indian temple
gurdwara Sikh temple
guru spiritual teacher
haveli fancy carved or painted home

leela (lila) play, performance, sport
lingam phallic symbol and symbol of Shiva
mahal palace, queen
maidan open square, plain
Mahabbharata epic poem
maharaja Hindu king, prince
mandir Hindu temple
mantra chants, incantations
masjid mosque
monsoon rainy season in India
mughals Muslim dynasty ruling from the 16th to the 18th century
nawab Muslim nobleman/landowner
nizam title of the rulers of Hyderabad
pan leaf wrapped around betel nuts, spices, and tobacco; chewed as a digestive
pandit teacher, wise man
puja prayer
purdah custom of hiding Muslim women behind veils
rath holy chariot
rishi a wise man, sage
Sadhu wandering ascetic
samadhi memorial
sanyasi an ascetic
sari women's draped dress
Shaivites followers of Shiva
shikara cushioned, curtained rowboats used in Kashmir
sikhara Hindu temple or spire
swami holy man, teacher
tanka painted scroll in Buddhist monasteries
tank artificial lake, reservoir
thali brass or stainless-steel platter with foods on it
Thirthankara Jain prophet, teacher
Thimurti three-faced Hindu trinity image (Brahma, Vishnu, Shiva)
Vaishnavites followers of Lord Vishnu
Vedas ancient Hindu scriptures
Vihar monastery
yoga one of six ancient schools of Indian philosophy involving a system of meditation

B Hindu and Tamil Phrases

Hindi has been the official language of India for years, but in reality it still isn't. English came with the British, and despite the fact that they pulled out decades ago, there is still no indigenous language that is universally used in the country, which is why English is still spoken everywhere. Hindi is the most widely used Indian language, but it is largely used in the north. Tamil is the most important South Indian language.

While the British brought the English language to India, they returned with phrases and words of Indian origin that have become part of the English language. Among these are *bungalow, curry, chutney, dungarees, jungle, khaki, pajamas, shampoo, shawl,* and *veranda,* to name a few.

Although almost everyone the tourist meets will speak some English, it's always nice to know a few phrases of the country, if only to bring smiles. I only wish I had the resources and room to be truly polite and include all 16 major languages in the following phrase vocabulary.

Useful Terms and Expressions: Hindi

English	Hindi	Pronounced
Greetings	**Namaste/Namaskar**	Nah-*maas*-tay
Thanks	**Shukriya**	Shook-*ree*-yah
Please	**Kripya**	Kreep-yah
Yes	**Ha (nasal *n*)**	Haa (nasal *n*)
No	**Nahin (silent *n*)**	Naa-hee
What is the price for this?	**Iska kya dam hai?**	Ees-ka ke-yah daam ha-ay
I want this	**Mujhe yeh chahiye**	Mooj-hey yea cha-ee-eh
I do not want this	**Mujhe yeh nahin chahiye**	Mooj-hey yea na-hee cha-ee-eh
How are you?	**Aap Kaise hai**	Aap kaa-eh-se ha-eh
Where	**Kahan (silent *n*)**	Kaa-ha
Why	**Kyon (nasal *n*)**	Key-ohn (nasal *n* but not emphatic)
What	**Kya**	Kay-ah
Water	**Pani**	Pa-nee
Where is the post office?	**Dak ghar kahan hai**	Daak ghar ka-ha ha-ay
Today	**Aaj**	Aaj
Tomorrow	**Kal**	Kaal
The day after tomorrow	**Purso**	Perso
Here	**Idhar**	Id-haar
There	**Udhar**	Ud-haar
I liked this	**Mujhe achchha laga**	Mooj-hey aachaa laaga
I did not like this	**Mujhe achchha nahin laga**	Mooj-hey aachaa na-hee laaga
Expensive	**Mehenga**	Mung-ha
I want more	**Mujhe aur chahiye**	Mooj-hey ah-ur cha-ee-eh
I did not want more	**Mujhe aur nahin chahiye**	Mooj-hey ah-ur na-hee cha-ee-eh
Help me	**Meri madad kijiye**	Mary maadaad kee-jee-eh
Call doctor	**Doctor bulaiye**	Doctor boo-la-ee-eh
Take me to a hospital	**Mujhe haspatal le jaiye**	Mooj-hey haspaataal lee-ja-ee- eh
Cal the police	**Police bulaiye**	Police boo-la-ee-eh

Numbers: Hindi

English	Hindi	Pronounced
One	**ek**	ack
Two	**do**	doe
Three	**tin**	teen
Four	**char**	chaar
Five	**panch**	paanch (nasal *n*)
Six	**chhe**	chay (hard *h*)
Seven	**Sat**	saat

Eight	**ath**	aath
Nine	**nau**	now
Ten	**das**	dus

Useful Terms and Expressions: Tamil

I/me	**Naan/en**
You	**Nee/neegal (plural)**
My/mine	**Ennudaiya**
We	**Naangal**
They	**Avargal**
All right	**Seri**
Yes	**Aam**
No	**Illai**
Good	**Nallathu**
Bad	**Kettathu**
Stop	**Niruthu**
Sorry	**Varunthukiren**
Excuse me	**Manniyungal**
More	**Innum**
How much?	**Ennavillai**
Too expensive	**Athikavilai**
Reduce	**Kuraikkavum**
Male	**Aann**
Female	**Penn**
This	**Ithu**
That	**Aathu**
There	**Angu**
Here	**Ingu**
Why	**Ean**
What	**Yenna**
Who	**Yaar**
When	**Yeppothu**
Where	**Yengey**

Numbers: Tamil

One	**Onru**
Two	**Irandu**
Three	**Moonru**
Four	**Naangu**
Five	**Ainthu**
Six	**Aaru**
Seven	**Eezhu**
Eight	**Ettu**
Nine	**Onpathu**
Ten	**Pathu**

Index

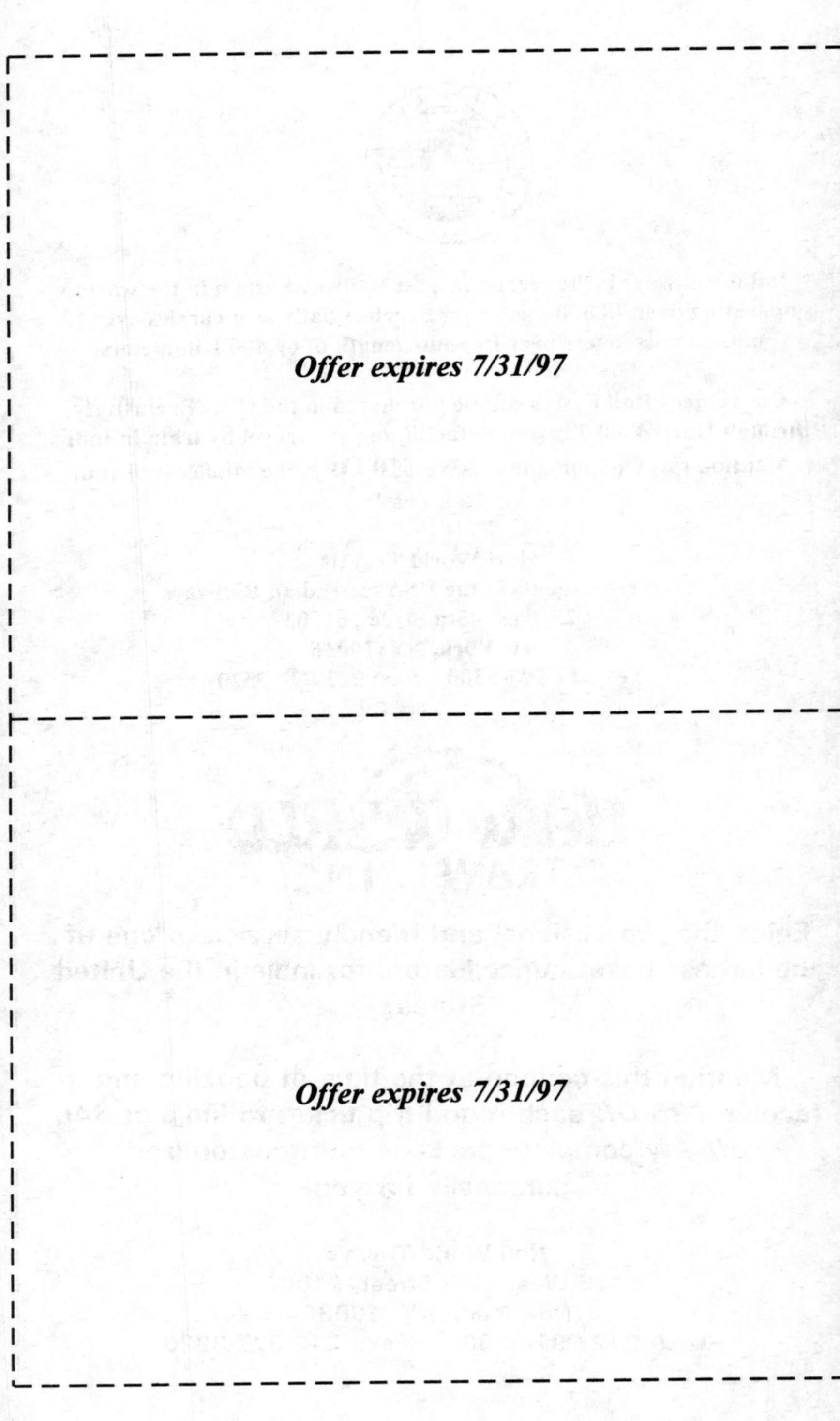

Offer expires 7/31/97

Offer expires 7/31/97

Offer expires 7/31/97